Toyota Conquest / Tazz
Service and Repair Manual

T. H. Robert Jones

(4879-288)

Models covered

All South African Toyota Conquest and Tazz models (including Carri) with 1295 cc and 1587 cc engines (engine codes 2E, 4AF and 4AGE).

The engine code is at the beginning of the engine number. The engine number can be found on your car's licence disc.

Does not cover Conquest 180i Sport or RSi models

ABCDE
FGHIJ
KL

© Haynes Publishing 2009

A book in the **Haynes Service and Repair Manual Series**

ISBN 978 1 84425 879 6

Printed in the UK

Haynes Publishing
Sparkford, Yeovil, Somerset BA22 7JJ, England

Haynes North America, Inc
859 Lawrence Drive, Newbury Park, California 91320, USA

Contents

Contents

Introduction to the Toyota Conquest / Tazz

Toyota Tazz

Toyota Carri

Toyota Conquest

The Toyota Conquest first appeared in South Africa as the Hatchback for the Toyota sixth-generation Corolla. Toyota had a suitable model but it was only available as a three-door, so it was asked to develop a five-door version model for the South African market. This uniquely South African Corolla hatch was first introduced in 1986, with the Tazz derivative launched 10 years later as a model within the now self standing Conquest range.

The Tazz was introduced in August 1996 as a "budget" Conquest hatchback. There was also a van version known as the Carri.

The Tazz brand became so successful that Toyota SA dropped the Conquest name in 2001 in favour of Tazz for the whole hatchback range, along with a styling update and a number of engineering changes.

The Tazz models are listed below:

TAZZ 130: A basic entry-level five-door hatch continuing the theme that entrenched the Tazz with SA buyers. It has the 1300cc motor that develops 55kW @ 6200rpm and has a maximum torque of 103Nm @ 4200rpm. Drive is through a five-speed transmission. Steel wheels are fitted with 155 SR13 tyres. A full size spare wheel is provided on this model and all others in the Tazz range. Brakes are disc at the front and drum at the rear. Seat facings are cloth and the rear seat folds down in a 60/40 split.Security features include a gear lock, VIN parts numbering and Toyota's secret-code identification system.

TAZZ 130 SPORT: Like the Tazz 130 but with a slightly more sporty specification. It has the same engine and transmission as the Tazz 130 but includes 5.5JJX14 alloy wheels and 175/65 TR14 tyres, front mudflaps, window

frame blackouts, a tailgate-mounted rear spoiler, courtesy lamp with delay feature and remote control alarm/immobiliser.

TAZZ 160i: This model is powered by Toyota's 4A-FE 1600 quad-valve and electronically fuel-injected engine capable of 79kW @ 6000rpm and 140Nm of torque @ 4400rpm. As with the 1300 Tazz, a five-speed transmission is fitted but with a revised first gear ratio. Steel 5.5JJX14 wheels are fitted with 175/65 TR14 tyres. Front disc brakes are ventilated with drums at the rear.

Power-assisted steering is standard on the Tazz 160i. Front and rear wipers, with intermittent on the front, are fitted along with a rev counter and a clock. Security features include a gear lock, remote alarm/immobiliser and Toyota's parts VIN marking and secret-code marking The courtesy light delay feature is integrated with the security system.

TAZZ 160i XE: The top-of-the-range Tazz has much the same features as the popular Corolla GLE and to the Tazz 160i spec adds air-conditioning, radio/CD and a rear-window demister.

The last unit came off the assembly line at Toyota South Africa's facility at Prospecton, near Durban, on the 5th July 2006. The last Tazz was registered in 2007. This ended a 21 year production line in South Africa, with a total of 245 750 units being sold.

Acknowledgements

Certain illustrations are the copyright of Toyota (GB) Ltd., and are used with their permission. Thanks are also due to Draper Tools Limited, who provided some of the workshop tools, and to all those people at Sparkford who helped in the production of this Manual.

Working on your car can be dangerous. This page shows just some of the potential risks and hazards, with the aim of creating a safety-conscious attitude.

General hazards

Scalding

• Don't remove the radiator or expansion tank cap while the engine is hot.
• Engine oil, automatic transmission fluid or power steering fluid may also be dangerously hot if the engine has recently been running.

Burning

• Beware of burns from the exhaust system and from any part of the engine. Brake discs and drums can also be extremely hot immediately after use.

Crushing

• When working under or near a raised vehicle, always supplement the jack with axle stands, or use drive-on ramps. *Never venture under a car which is only supported by a jack.*
• Take care if loosening or tightening high-torque nuts when the vehicle is on stands. Initial loosening and final tightening should be done with the wheels on the ground.

Fire

• Fuel is highly flammable; fuel vapour is explosive.
• Don't let fuel spill onto a hot engine.
• Do not smoke or allow naked lights (including pilot lights) anywhere near a vehicle being worked on. Also beware of creating sparks (electrically or by use of tools).
• Fuel vapour is heavier than air, so don't work on the fuel system with the vehicle over an inspection pit.
• Another cause of fire is an electrical overload or short-circuit. Take care when repairing or modifying the vehicle wiring.
• Keep a fire extinguisher handy, of a type suitable for use on fuel and electrical fires.

Electric shock

• Ignition HT voltage can be dangerous, especially to people with heart problems or a pacemaker. Don't work on or near the ignition system with the engine running or the ignition switched on.

• Mains voltage is also dangerous. Make sure that any mains-operated equipment is correctly earthed. Mains power points should be protected by a residual current device (RCD) circuit breaker.

Fume or gas intoxication

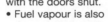

• Exhaust fumes are poisonous; they often contain carbon monoxide, which is rapidly fatal if inhaled. Never run the engine in a confined space such as a garage with the doors shut.
• Fuel vapour is also poisonous, as are the vapours from some cleaning solvents and paint thinners.

Poisonous or irritant substances

• Avoid skin contact with battery acid and with any fuel, fluid or lubricant, especially antifreeze, brake hydraulic fluid and Diesel fuel. Don't syphon them by mouth. If such a substance is swallowed or gets into the eyes, seek medical advice.
• Prolonged contact with used engine oil can cause skin cancer. Wear gloves or use a barrier cream if necessary. Change out of oil-soaked clothes and do not keep oily rags in your pocket.
• Air conditioning refrigerant forms a poisonous gas if exposed to a naked flame (including a cigarette). It can also cause skin burns on contact.

Asbestos

• Asbestos dust can cause cancer if inhaled or swallowed. Asbestos may be found in gaskets and in brake and clutch linings. When dealing with such components it is safest to assume that they contain asbestos.

Special hazards

Hydrofluoric acid

• This extremely corrosive acid is formed when certain types of synthetic rubber, found in some O-rings, oil seals, fuel hoses etc, are exposed to temperatures above 400°C. The rubber changes into a charred or sticky substance containing the acid. *Once formed, the acid remains dangerous for years. If it gets onto the skin, it may be necessary to amputate the limb concerned.*
• When dealing with a vehicle which has suffered a fire, or with components salvaged from such a vehicle, wear protective gloves and discard them after use.

The battery

• Batteries contain sulphuric acid, which attacks clothing, eyes and skin. Take care when topping-up or carrying the battery.
• The hydrogen gas given off by the battery is highly explosive. Never cause a spark or allow a naked light nearby. Be careful when connecting and disconnecting battery chargers or jump leads.

Air bags

• Air bags can cause injury if they go off accidentally. Take care when removing the steering wheel and/or facia. Special storage instructions may apply.

Diesel injection equipment

• Diesel injection pumps supply fuel at very high pressure. Take care when working on the fuel injectors and fuel pipes.

⚠ *Warning: Never expose the hands, face or any other part of the body to injector spray; the fuel can penetrate the skin with potentially fatal results.*

Remember...

DO

• Do use eye protection when using power tools, and when working under the vehicle.

• Do wear gloves or use barrier cream to protect your hands when necessary.

• Do get someone to check periodically that all is well when working alone on the vehicle.

• Do keep loose clothing and long hair well out of the way of moving mechanical parts.

• Do remove rings, wristwatch etc, before working on the vehicle – especially the electrical system.

• Do ensure that any lifting or jacking equipment has a safe working load rating adequate for the job.

DON'T

• Don't attempt to lift a heavy component which may be beyond your capability – get assistance.

• Don't rush to finish a job, or take unverified short cuts.

• Don't use ill-fitting tools which may slip and cause injury.

• Don't leave tools or parts lying around where someone can trip over them. Mop up oil and fuel spills at once.

• Don't allow children or pets to play in or near a vehicle being worked on.

Dimensions

Overall length:
  5-door Hatchback and Van .... 3995 mm
  4-door Saloon .... 4195 mm
  5-door Liftback .... 4215 mm
  5-door Estate .... 4205 mm
Overall width (all models) .... 1655 mm
Overall height:
  GTi 16 model .... 1160 mm
  Estate model .... 1425 mm
  All other models .... 1365 mm
Wheelbase (all models) .... 2430 mm
Front track:
  GTi 16 model .... 1445 mm
  All other models .... 1430 mm
Rear track:
  GTi 16 model .... 1425 mm
  All other models .... 1410 mm
Ground clearance:
  GTi 16 model .... 150 mm
  Estate model .... N/A
  All other models .... 155 mm
Turning circle:
  1.3 models .... 9.6 m
  1.6 models .... 9.8 m

Weights

Kerb weight:
  1.3 Hatchback models:
    With manual gearbox .... 980 kg
    With automatic transmission .... 1000 kg
  1.3 Saloon models .... 990 kg
  1.3 Liftback models:
    With manual gearbox .... 1015 kg
    With automatic transmission .... 1035 kg
  1.3 Estate .... 1005 kg
  1.3 Van .... 950 kg
  1.6 GL Executive models:
    With manual gearbox .... 1055 kg
    With automatic transmission .... 1075 kg
  GTi 16 model .... 1075 kg
Maximum gross vehicle weight:
  1.3 models:
    With manual gearbox .... 1450 kg
    With automatic transmission .... N/A
  1.6 GL Executive models:
    With manual gearbox .... 1490 kg
    With automatic transmission .... N/A
  GTi 16 models .... 1525 kg
Maximum towing weight:
  Braked trailer:
    1.3 models .... 1000 kg
    1.6 models .... 1200 kg
  Unbraked trailer (all models) .... 450 kg

Jump starting

HAYNES HiNT *Jump starting will get you out of trouble, but you must correct whatever made the battery go flat in the first place. There are three possibilities:*

1 *The battery has been drained by repeated attempts to start, or by leaving the lights on.*

2 *The charging system is not working properly (alternator drivebelt slack or broken, alternator wiring fault or alternator itself faulty).*

3 *The battery itself is at fault (electrolyte low, or battery worn out).*

When jump-starting a car using a booster battery, observe the following precautions:

✔ Before connecting the booster battery, make sure that the ignition is switched off.

✔ Ensure that all electrical equipment (lights, heater, wipers, etc) is switched off.

✔ Take note of any special precautions printed on the battery case.

✔ Make sure that the booster battery is the same voltage as the discharged one in the vehicle.

✔ If the battery is being jump-started from the battery in another vehicle, the two vehicles MUST NOT TOUCH each other.

✔ Make sure that the transmission is in neutral (or PARK, in the case of automatic transmission).

1 Connect one end of the red jump lead to the positive (+) terminal of the flat battery

2 Connect the other end of the red lead to the positive (+) terminal of the booster battery.

3 Connect one end of the black jump lead to the negative (-) terminal of the booster battery

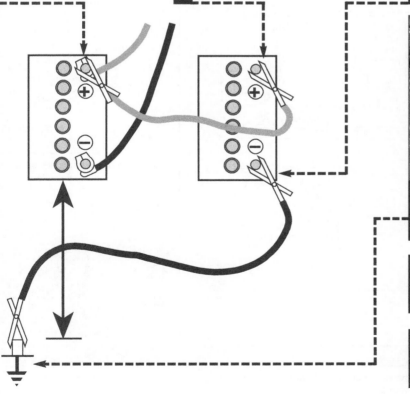

4 Connect the other end of the black jump lead to a bolt or bracket on the engine block, well away from the battery, on the vehicle to be started.

5 Make sure that the jump leads will not come into contact with the fan, drive-belts or other moving parts of the engine.

6 Start the engine using the booster battery and run it at idle speed. Switch on the lights, rear window demister and heater blower motor, then disconnect the jump leads in the reverse order of connection. Turn off the lights etc.

Jacking, towing and wheel changing

To change a wheel, remove the spare wheel and jack, apply the handbrake and chock the wheel diagonally opposite the one to be changed. On automatic transmission models, place the selector lever in 'P'. Make sure that the car is located on firm level ground then remove the wheel trim (where applicable) and slightly loosen the wheel nuts with the brace provided. Locate the jack head in the jacking point nearest to the wheel to be changed and raise the jack using the other end of the brace. When the wheel is clear of the ground remove the nuts and lift off the wheel. Fit the spare wheel and moderately tighten the nuts. Lower the car and then tighten the nuts fully. Refit the trim where applicable. With the spare wheel in position, remove the chock and stow the jack and tools.

When jacking up the car to carry out repair or maintenance tasks position the jack as follows.

If the front of the car is to be raised, position the jack beneath the engine crossmember then firmly apply the handbrake and jack up the car. Support the car by placing axle stands under the front sill jacking positions.

To raise the rear of the car, chock the front wheels then position the jack beneath the rear subframe. Jack up the rear of the car and support it by positioning axle stands beneath the rear sill jacking points.

Never work under, around or near a raised car unless it is adequately supported in at least two places with axle stands or suitable sturdy blocks.

The car may be towed for breakdown recovery purposes only using the towing eyes positioned at the front and rear of the vehicle (photo). These eyes are intended for towing loads only and must not be used for lifting the car either directly or indirectly.

On models equipped with manual gearbox,

the vehicle can be towed from either the front or the rear. Preferably a front end suspended tow should be used. If the vehicle is to be towed using a rear end suspended tow, the front wheels should be positioned on a towing dolly. **Note:** *On no account should the car be towed with the front wheels on the ground if the transmission is faulty or the transmission oil level is low.*

The above information also applies to models equipped with automatic transmission noting the following. To prevent extensive damage to the transmission components, the vehicle must **never** be towed from the rear with its front wheels on the ground. If the car is to be towed from the front with its four wheels on the ground, first ensure that the transmission fluid level is in the HOT range (Chapter 1). **Note:** *With the front wheels on the ground the car must not be towed at speeds in excess of 30 mph (50kmh) or for a distance in excess of 50 miles (80 km).*

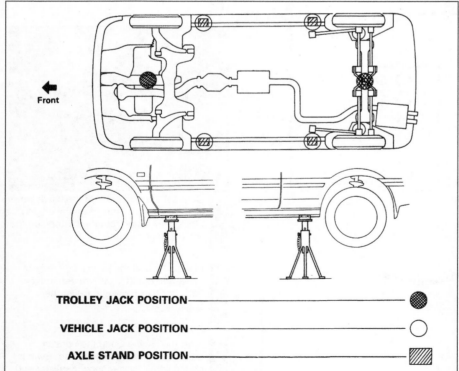

TROLLEY JACK POSITION ⬤

VEHICLE JACK POSITION ◯

AXLE STAND POSITION ▨

An underside view of the vehicle, showing the designated jacking points and axle stand support positions

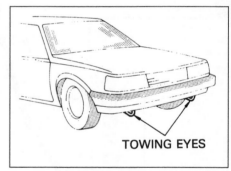

TOWING EYES

Location of towing eyes on the front of the vehicle

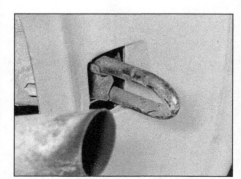

Rear towing eye

Identifying leaks

Puddles on the garage floor or drive, or obvious wetness under the bonnet or underneath the car, suggest a leak that needs investigating. It can sometimes be difficult to decide where the leak is coming from, especially if the engine bay is very dirty already. Leaking oil or fluid can also be blown rearwards by the passage of air under the car, giving a false impression of where the problem lies.

 Warning: Most automotive oils and fluids are poisonous. Wash them off skin, and change out of contaminated clothing, without delay.

 HAYNES HiNT *The smell of a fluid leaking from the car may provide a clue to what's leaking. Some fluids are distinctively coloured. It may help to clean the car carefully and to park it over some clean paper overnight as an aid to locating the source of the leak.*
Remember that some leaks may only occur while the engine is running.

Sump oil

Engine oil may leak from the drain plug...

Oil from filter

...or from the base of the oil filter.

Gearbox oil

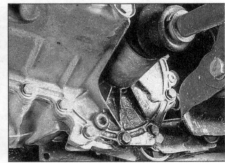

Gearbox oil can leak from the seals at the inboard ends of the driveshafts.

Antifreeze

Leaking antifreeze often leaves a crystalline deposit like this.

Brake fluid

A leak occurring at a wheel is almost certainly brake fluid.

Power steering fluid

Power steering fluid may leak from the pipe connectors on the steering rack.

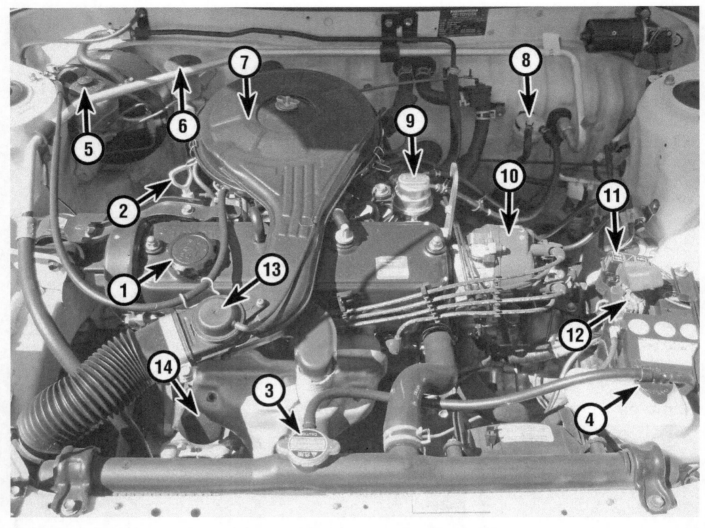

A view of the engine compartment - Tazz with 2E engine

1	Engine oil filler cap
2	Engine oil dipstick
3	Radiator pressure cap
4	Expansion tank filler cap
5	Brake hydraulic fluid reservoir
6	Clutch hydraulic fluid reservoir
7	Air filter housing
8	Fuel filter
9	Fuel pump
10	Distributor
11	Fuse / relay box
12	Battery positive terminal
13	Hot air intake diaphragm

Chapter 1 Routine maintenance and servicing

Contents

Degrees of difficulty

Easy, suitable for novice with little experience	**Fairly easy,** suitable for beginner with some experience	**Fairly difficult,** suitable for competent DIY mechanic	**Difficult,** suitable for experienced DIY mechanic	**Very difficult,** suitable for expert DIY or professional

Specifications

Engine

Valve clearances:
   1.3 models (engine at normal operating temperature) . . . .   0.20 mm
   1.6 models (engine cold):
      Inlet . . . .   0.20 ± 0.05 mm
      Exhaust . . . .   0.25 ± 0.05 mm

Cooling system

Radiator tank pressure cap release pressure . . . .   0.74 to 1.03 bar

Antifreeze mixtures:	**Anti-freeze**	**Water**
Protection to –23°C (–9°F)	35%	65%
Protection to –40°C (–40°F)	50%	50%

Fuel and exhaust system

Idle speed (cooling fan off):
   1.3 models:
      Models equipped with a manual gearbox . . . .   800 rpm
      Models equipped with automatic transmission . . . .   850 rpm
   1.6 carburettor models:
      Models equipped with automatic transmission and power
      steering . . . .   900 rpm
      All other models . . . .   800 rpm
   1.6 fuel-injection models . . . .   800 rpm
Idle mixture CO content . . . .   1.5 ± 0 5%
Fuel octane requirement
   1.3 models . . . .   Unleaded 91 RON (minimum) or leaded 97 RON
   1.6 models . . . .   Unleaded 95 RON (minimum) or leaded 97 RON

Specifications

Ignition system

Firing order	1-3-4-2	
Location of No 1 cylinder	Timing cover end of engine	

Ignition timing:
Stroboscopic at idle speed:

1.3 models (vacuum hose disconnected and plugged – see text)	5° BTDC at a maximum of 950 rpm	
1.6 carburettor models (vacuum hose disconnected and plugged – see text)	10° BTDC at a maximum of 900 rpm	
1.6 fuel-injection models (with check connector terminals connected – see text)	10° BTDC at 800 rpm	

Spark plugs:

	Type	Electrode gap
1.3 models	Bosch WR 8 D+X	1.1 mm
1.6 carburettor models	Bosch FR 8 HC	0.8 mm
1.6 fuel-injection models	Bosch FR 78 X	Not adjustable

HT lead resistance (maximum)	25 k ohms

Braking system

Minimum front brake pad lining thickness	1.0 mm
Minimum rear brake pad lining thickness – GTi 16 models	1.0 mm
Minimum rear brake shoe lining thickness – all models except GTi 16	1.0 mm

Suspension and steering

Power steering pump drivebelt deflection under a force of 10 kg (22 lb):
New drivebelt (see text):

1.3 models	5 to 6 mm
1.6 carburettor models	5 to 6 mm
1.6 fuel-injection models	6 to 8 mm

Used drivebelt (see text):

1.3 models	11 to 13 mm
1.6 carburettor models	6 to 8 mm
1.6 fuel-injection models	8 to 10 mm

Tyre pressures (cold):

	Front	Rear
155 SR 13, 155 R 13 78S and 155/80 R 13 78S tyres	1.9 bar (27 lbf/in^2)	2.3 bar (33 lbf/in^2)
165 SR 13, 165 R 13 82S and 165/80 R 13 82S	1.8 bar (26 lbf/in^2)	1.9 bar (27 lbf/in^2)
175/70 SR 13,175/70 R 13 82S, 175/70 HR 13, 175/70 R 13 82H and 185/60 R14 82 H	1.8 bar (26 lbf/in^2)	2.1 bar (30 lbf/in^2)

Note: *Pressures apply only to original equipment tyres at speeds of up to 100 mph and may vary if any other make or type is fitted; check with the tyre manufacturer or supplier for correct pressures if necessary. For optional pressures at reduced loads and/or higher speeds, consult the vehicle's handbook or your Toyota dealer.*

Electrical system

Alternator/water pump drivebelt deflection under a force of 10 kg (22 lb):
New drivebelt (see text):

1.3 models	3.5 to 4.5 mm
1.6 carburettor models	8.5 to 10.5 mm
1.6 fuel-injection models	4 to 5 mm

Used drivebelt (see text):

1.3 models	5.0 to 6.5 mm
1.6 carburettor models	10 to 12 mm
1.6 fuel-injection models	6 to 7 mm

Torque wrench settings

	Nm	lbf ft
Sump drain plug:		
1.3 models	25	18
1.6 models	34	25
Spark plugs	18	13
Manual gearbox filler/level and drain plugs	39	29
Automatic transmission drain plug	49	36

Introduction

This Chapter is designed to help the D.I.Y. owner maintain the Toyota Corolla with the goals of maximum economy, safety, reliability and performance in mind.

On the following pages is a master maintenance schedule, listing the servicing requirements, and the intervals at which they should be carried out as recommended by the manufacturers. Alongside each operation in the schedule is a reference which directs the user to the Sections in this Chapter covering maintenance procedures or to other Chapters in the Manual, where the operations are described and illustrated in greater detail. Specifications for all the maintenance operations, together with a list of lubricants, fluids and capacities are provided at the beginning of this Chapter. Refer to the accompanying photographs of the engine compartment and the underbody of the vehicle for the locations of the various components.

Servicing your vehicle in accordance with the mileage/time maintenance schedule and step-by-step procedures will result in a planned maintenance programme that should produce a long and reliable service life. Bear in mind that it is a comprehensive plan, so maintaining some items but not others at the specified intervals will not produce the same results.

The first step in this maintenance programme is to prepare yourself before the actual work begins. Read through all the procedures to be undertaken then obtain all the parts, lubricants and any additional tools needed.

Note: *The following maintenance schedule is for vehicles operating under normal conditions. If the vehicle is used for extensive towing, is operated in adverse conditions, is subjected to repeated short trips of under 5 miles (8 km) and/or extensive periods of idling and/or extensive low speed operation, certain operations on the schedule should be carried out at double the normal rate (at equally spaced intervals); consult your owners information pack literature, or your Toyota dealer, for further details if necessary.*

Every 250 miles (400 km) or weekly

- ☐ Check the engine oil level (Section 1)
- ☐ Check the engine coolant level (Section 1)
- ☐ Check the clutch fluid level (Section 1)
- ☐ Check the brake fluid level (Section 1)
- ☐ Check the power steering fluid level (Section 1)
- ☐ Visually examine the tyres for wear or damage (Section 2)
- ☐ Check and if necessary adjust the tyre pressures (Section 2)
- ☐ Check the battery electrolyte and terminals (Section 3)
- ☐ Check all electrical systems for correct operation(Section 4)
- ☐ Check the screen washer fluid level (Section 5)

Every 6000 miles (10 000 km) or 6 months – whichever comes first

- ☐ Renew the engine oil and filter (Section 6)
- ☐ Inspect all components for security and leakage (Section 7)
- ☐ Inspect the cooling system hoses (including the heater hoses) for security and signs of leakage (Section 8)
- ☐ Check the fuel system pipes, hoses and connections for security and signs of leakage (Section 9)
- ☐ Inspect the exhaust system for security (Section 10)
- ☐ Check the condition of the spark plugs (Section 11)
- ☐ Check the clutch system connections (Section 12)
- ☐ Check the clutch pedal adjustment (Chapter 6)
- ☐ Check the brake pads, and renew if necessary (Section13)
- ☐ Check the brake system connections (Section 14)
- ☐ Check the brake vacuum servo unit for operation (Section 15)
- ☐ Check the handbrake adjustment (Chapter 9)
- ☐ Check the brake pedal adjustment (Chapter 9)
- ☐ Check the steering for oil/fluid leakage
- ☐ Check the power steering pump drivebelt (Section 16)
- ☐ Check the tightness of the roadwheel nuts
- ☐ Check the seatbelts and the anchorage points (Section 17)
- ☐ Check the alternator/water pump drivebelt (Section 18)
- ☐ Check the exterior lights (Chapter 12)

Every 12 000 miles (20 000 km) or 12 months – whichever comes first

In addition to all the items listed above, carry out the following:

- ☐ Check the valve clearances (Section 19)
- ☐ Clean the air filter element (Section 20)
- ☐ Check the idle speed and exhaust CO content (Section 21)
- ☐ Check the operation of the choke (Chapter 4)
- ☐ Renew the evaporative emission control check valve (Chapter 4)
- ☐ Check the fast idle speed, throttle positioner/dash pot setting speed – carburettor models (Chapter 4)
- ☐ Renew the spark plugs (Section 11)
- ☐ Check the ignition timing (Section 22)
- ☐ Inspect the HT leads and distributor (Section 23)
- ☐ Check the ignition timing advance mechanism (Chapter 5)
- ☐ Check the automatic transmission fluid level and condition, and check for leakage (Section 25)
- ☐ Check the gearbox oil and inspect for leaks (Section 24)
- ☐ Check the differential (final drive) fluid level and inspect for leakage (automatic transmission) (Section 26)
- ☐ Inspect the driveshaft CV joint gaiters (Section 27)
- ☐ Check the brake shoes (as applicable) (Section 28)
- ☐ Inspect the front and rear suspension (Section 29)
- ☐ Check all the steering linkages for wear and security; grease the relevant joints and linkages (Section 29)
- ☐ Check the front roadwheel alignment (tracking) (Chapter 10)

Every 24 000 miles (40 000 km) or 2 years – whichever comes first

In addition to all the items listed above, carry out the following:

- ☐ Renew engine coolant (Section 30)
- ☐ Renew the air filter element (Section 20)
- ☐ Renew the fuel filter (Section 31)
- ☐ Renew the gearbox/transmission oil/ fluid (Section 32)
- ☐ Renew the differential (final drive) fluid (Section 33)
- ☐ Renew the brake fluid (Section 34)
- ☐ Check the security of all nuts and bolts (Section 35)

Every 48 000 miles (80 000 km)

- ☐ Renew the timing belt on 2E and 4A-GE engines (Chapter 2)

Every 60 000 miles (100 000 km)

- ☐ Renew the timing belt on 4A-F engines (Chapter 2)

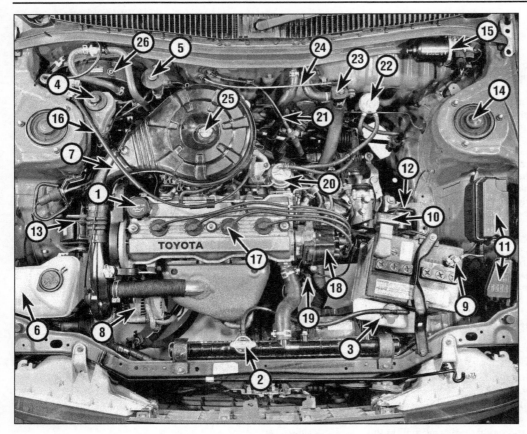

A view of the engine compartment – 4A-F engine

1 Engine oil filler cap
2 Radiator pressure cap
3 Cooling system expansion tank
4 Brake hydraulic fluid reservoir
5 Clutch hydraulic fluid reservoir
6 Windscreen/tailgate washer fluid reservoir
7 Engine oil dipstick (under housing)
8 Alternator
9 Battery earth (negative) terminal
10 Main (battery) fusible links
11 Fuse and relay boxes
12 Left-hand engine mounting
13 Right-hand engine mounting
14 Front suspension strut
15 Windscreen wiper motor
16 Accelerator cable
17 HT lead spark plug cap
18 Distributor
19 Tachometer terminal/service connector
20 Fuel pump
21 Speedometer drive cable
22 Fuel filter
23 Heater valve
24 Heater valve control cable
25 Air filter housing
26 Brake vacuum servo unit

A view of the front underside – GTi 16 model shown (undershields removed for clarity)

1 Front suspension lower arm
2 Front suspension lower arm rear mounting bracket
3 Anti-roll bar
4 Balljoint to front suspension lower arm fixings
5 Brake caliper assembly
6 Front suspension crossmember
7 Engine/transmission crossmember
8 Rear engine/transmission mounting to front suspension crossmember fixings
9 Exhaust main section forward mounting retaining nut
10 Plastic blanking plates covering the forward and centre engine/transmission mounting to crossmember fixings
11 Radiator cooling fan motor wiring connector
12 Radiator mounting grommets
13 Exhaust downpipe section
14 Exhaust main section
15 Engine oil cooler sump union
16 Engine oil sump
17 Engine oil drain plug
18 Driveshaft
19 Alternator/water pump drivebelt
20 Power steering pump drivebelt
21 Adjusting bolt for power steering pump drivebelt

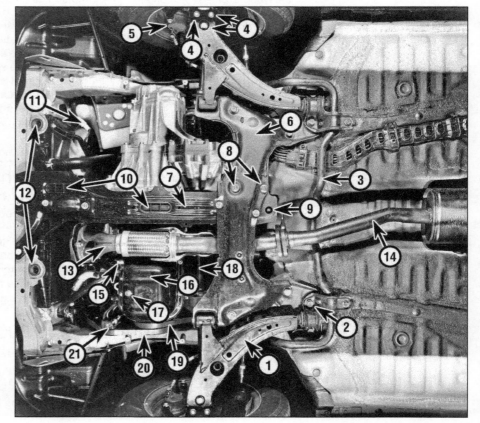

A view of the engine compartment – 4A-GE engine

1 Engine oil filler cap
2 Engine oil dipstick
3 Radiator pressure cap
4 Cooling system expansion tank
5 Brake hydraulic fluid reservoir
6 Clutch hydraulic fluid reservoir
7 Power steering fluid reservoir
8 Windscreen/tailgate washer fluid reservoir
9 Air filter housing
10 Distributor
11 Battery earth (negative) terminal
12 Main (battery) fusible links
13 Fuse and relay boxes
14 Front suspension strut
15 Brake vacuum servo unit
16 Ignition coil
17 Windscreen wiper motor
18 Igniter module
19 Fuel filter
20 Heater valve
21 Throttle position sensor
22 Fuel inlet connection
23 Cold start injector
24 Fuel pressure regulator
25 Fuel injector
26 Fuel rail

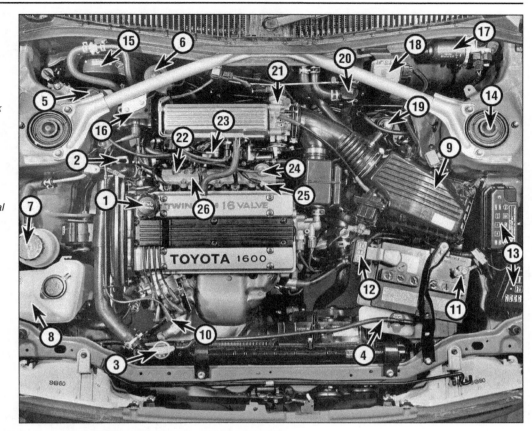

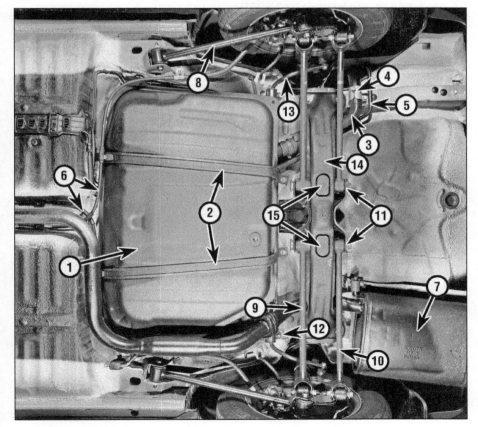

A view of the rear underside (GTi 16 model shown)

1 Fuel tank
2 Fuel tank securing straps
3 fuel filler pipe
4 Fuel filler pipe support clamp
5 Fuel filler vent pipe
6 Handbrake secondary cables
7 Exhaust rear silencer
8 Rear suspension radius rod
9 Rear suspension forward arm
10 Rear suspension rearward arm
11 Rear suspension toe-setting adjustment cams
12 Anti-roll bar to body mounting bracket
13 Anti-roll bar
14 Rear suspension crossmember
15 Rear suspension crossmember access hole covers

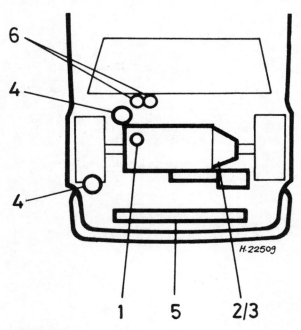

H.22509

Lubricants and fluids

Component or system	Lubricant type/specification
1 Engine	Multigrade engine oil, SAE 10W/30 to 20W/50, to API SG/CC or SG/CD
2 Manual gearbox	Hypoid gear oil, viscosity SAE 75W/90S, to APL GL-4 or GL-5
3 Automatic transmission	Dexron II automatic transmission fluid (ATF)
4 Power steering reservoir	Dexron II automatic transmission fluid (ATF)
5 Cooling system	Ethylene-glycol based antifreeze
6 Brake/clutch fluid reservoir	Universal brake and clutch fluid to SAE J1703 DOT 4

Capacities

Engine oil
Capacity (including filter):
2E and 4A-F engines	3.2 litres
4A-GE engine	3.7 litres

Cooling system
2E engine with manual gearbox	5.0 litres
2E engine with automatic transmission	4.9 litres
4A-F engine with manual gearbox	5.2 litres
4A-F engine with automatic transmission	5.5 litres
4A-GE engine	6.0 litres

Fuel tank
Fuel tank	50 litres

Manual gearbox
2E engines	2.4 litres
4A-F and 4A-GE engines	2.6 litres

Automatic transmission
Total capacity	5.5 litres
Drain and refill	Up to 2.5 litres
Final drive capacity	1.4 litres

Weekly checks

1 Fluid level checks

Engine oil

1 The engine oil level is checked with a dipstick that is located towards the rear right-hand side of the engine.

2 The oil level should be checked with the vehicle standing on level ground and before it is driven, or at least 5 minutes after the engine has been switched off.

> **HAYNES HiNT** *If the oil is checked immediately after running the engine, some of the oil will remain in the upper engine components and oil galleries, resulting in an inaccurate reading on the dipstick.*

3 Withdraw the dipstick from the tube and wipe it clean with a clean rag or paper towel. Insert the clean dipstick back into the tube as far as it will go, then withdraw it once more. Note the oil level on the end of the dipstick. If the level is towards the lower (MIN or L) mark/notch, unscrew the oil filler cap on the camshaft cover and add fresh oil of the specified type (a little bit at a time, allowing for it to run down into the sump) until the level is on the upper (MAX or F) mark/notch. Refit the dipstick and the oil filler cap upon completion (photos).

4 Always maintain the level between the two dipstick marks. If the level is allowed to fall below the lower mark, oil starvation may result which could lead to severe engine damage. If the engine is overfilled by adding too much oil, this may result in oil fouled spark plugs, oil leaks or oil seal failures.

5 An oil can spout or funnel may help to reduce spillage when adding oil to the engine. Always use the correct grade and type of oil as shown in 'Lubricants fluids and capacities.'

Coolant

> ⚠️ **Warning: DO NOT attempt to remove the radiator pressure cap when the engine is hot, as there is a very great risk of scalding.**

6 All vehicles covered by this Manual are equipped with a pressurised cooling system. An expansion tank is located on the left-hand side of the engine compartment, by the battery. As the engine temperature increases, the coolant expands and travels through the hose to the expansion tank. As the engine cools, the coolant is automatically drawn back into the system to maintain the correct level.

7 The coolant level in the expansion tank should be checked regularly. The level in the tank varies with the temperature of the engine. When the engine is cold, the coolant level should be up to the maximum (MAX or FULL) level mark on the side of the tank. When the engine is hot the level will be slightly above the mark.

8 If the coolant level in the expansion tank is low, add a mixture of water and antifreeze (see below) through the expansion tank filler neck until the coolant is up to the maximum (MAX or FULL) level mark. Refit the expansion tank cap upon completion.

9 With a sealed type cooling system, the addition of coolant should only be necessary at very infrequent intervals. If frequent topping up is required, it is likely that there is a leak in the system. Check the radiator, all hoses, drain plugs and joint faces for any sign of staining or actual wetness, and rectify as necessary. If no leaks can be found it is advisable to have the pressure cap and the entire system pressure tested by a dealer, or a suitably equipped garage, as this will often show up a small leak not previously visible.

Clutch hydraulic fluid

> ⚠️ **Warning: Hydraulic fluid can harm your eyes and damage painted surfaces, so use extreme caution when handling and pouring it. Do not use fluid that has been standing open for some time as it absorbs moisture from the air, this will be detrimental to the operation of the clutch system.**

10 The clutch fluid level is readily visible through the translucent material of the master cylinder reservoir. With the vehicle parked on

level ground, the fluid level should be maintained within 5 mm of the maximum fluid level line on the side of the reservoir. Note that wear of the clutch friction plate lining causes the clutch fluid level to drop gradually over a long period of time; any sudden drop in the level is indicative of a leak within the hydraulic system which should be investigated immediately.

11 If topping up is necessary, first wipe any accumulated grime from the reservoir cap then remove the cap. See the 'Lubricants, fluids and capacities' information at the beginning of this Chapter and use only the hydraulic fluid specified; adding different types of fluid can cause system damage, and ultimately failure. Prior to adding fresh fluid, inspect the remaining fluid in the reservoir and the reservoir sides for signs that there is contamination within the system; if evident, the system should be drained and refilled. When adding fluid, pour it carefully into the reservoir and avoid spilling it onto surrounding painted surfaces; if spillage does occur, wash the affected area immediately with plenty of cold water (photo). Once the fluid level is correct, securely refit the cap.

Brake hydraulic fluid

> ⚠️ **Warning: Hydraulic fluid can harm your eyes and damage painted surfaces, so use extreme caution when handling and pouring it. Do not use fluid that has been standing open for some time as it absorbs moisture from the air, this will be detrimental to the operation of the braking system.**

12 The brake fluid level is readily visible through the translucent material of the master cylinder reservoir. With the vehicle parked on level ground, the fluid level should be maintained within 10 mm of the maximum (MAX) fluid level line on the side of the reservoir; it must not, however, be allowed to drop below the minimum (MIN) fluid level line.

13 If topping up is necessary, first wipe the area around the filler cap with a clean rag, then disconnect the wiring connector and

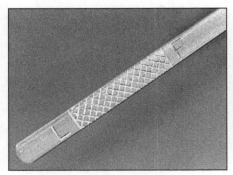
1.3A Engine oil dipstick markings

1.3B Engine oil topping up/refilling

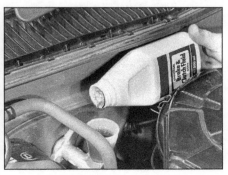
1.11 Topping up the clutch fluid level

1.14 Topping up the brake master cylinder reservoir

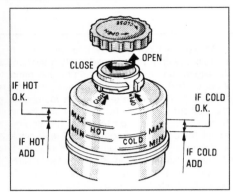

Fig. 1.1 Power steering fluid reservoir markings, and level checking, topping up information – 1.3 and GTi 16 models (Sec 1)

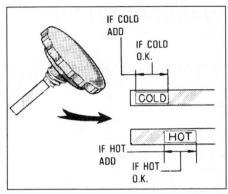

Fig. 1.2 Power steering fluid reservoir cap dipstick markings, and level checking, topping up information – 1.6 carburettor models (Sec 1)

remove the cap. When adding fluid, pour it carefully into the reservoir to avoid spilling it on surrounding painted surfaces. Be sure to use only the specified brake hydraulic fluid since mixing different types of fluid can cause damage to the system. See 'Lubricants fluids and capacities' at the beginning of this Chapter.

14 Prior to adding fluid it is a good idea to inspect the reservoir for contamination. The system should be drained and refilled if deposits, dirt particles or contamination are seen in the fluid. When adding fluid, pour it carefully into the reservoir up to the dotted line (where applicable); this brings the fluid to the correct level after the cap has been refitted (photo).

15 After filling the reservoir to the proper level, make sure that the cap is refitted securely, then reconnect the wiring connector.

16 The fluid level in the master cylinder reservoir will drop slightly as the brake pads and shoes wear down during normal operation. If the reservoir requires repeated topping up to maintain the proper level, this is an indication of a hydraulic leak somewhere in the system which should be investigated immediately.

Power steering fluid

17 Two types of power steering fluid reservoir are used on the Corolla range; the type fitted to 1.6 carburettor models is integral with the pump, whilst that fitted to all other models is a remote type (and is clipped onto the right-hand front inner wing in the engine compartment).

18 The fluid level may be checked when the fluid is hot (after the vehicle has been driven at approximately 50 mph (80km/h) for at least 20 minutes (a little longer in really cold weather), or when it is cold (if the vehicle has not been driven for at least five hours). Note that the vehicle should be on level ground, with the front wheels pointing in the straight-ahead position.

19 On all vehicles except the 1.6 carburettor model, the fluid level can be seen through the translucent material of the reservoir (after any necessary wiping of the reservoir), and it should be within the COLD range (if the fluid is cold) or within the HOT range (if the fluid is hot).

20 On 1.6 carburettor models (after cleaning the cap and its surrounding area), the method of checking the fluid level is to remove the reservoir cap with its attached dipstick, wipe the dipstick clean then refit the cap. Remove the cap again, and check the fluid level on the dipstick: it should be within the COLD range (if the fluid is cold) or within the HOT range (if the fluid is hot).

21 If the fluid level is outside its range (either HOT or COLD) for either type of reservoir, top up with fresh fluid of the specified type, referring to the 'Lubricants, fluids and capacities' information at the beginning of this Chapter for the fluid type required. Wipe the area around the reservoir cap clean, if not already having done so, then remove the cap and carefully add the fluid until it reaches the correct level (Figs. 1.1 or 1.2); do not overfill the reservoir as this can cause damage within the power steering system. Recheck the fluid level then, once it is correct, refit the cap securely.

22 Check the power steering system for signs of leakage upon completion.

2 Wheel and tyre maintenance and tyre pressure checks

1 The original tyres on this car are equipped with tread wear safety bands which will appear when the tread depth reaches approximately 1.6 mm. Tread wear can be monitored with a simple, inexpensive device known as a tread depth indicator gauge (photo).

2 Wheels and tyres should give no real problems in use provided that a close eye is

2.1 Checking the tyre tread depth using a depth indicator gauge

2.3 Checking the tyre pressures using a tyre pressure gauge

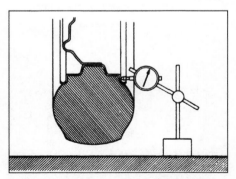

Fig. 1.3 Checking wheel run-out using a dial gauge and stand (Sec 2)

kept on them with regard to excessive wear or damage. To this end, the following points should be noted.

3 Ensure that tyre pressures are checked regularly and maintained correctly. Checking should be carried out with the tyres cold and not immediately after the vehicle has been in use (photo). If the pressures are checked with the tyres hot, an apparently high reading will be obtained owing to heat expansion. Under no circumstances should an attempt be made to reduce the pressures to the quoted cold reading in this instance, or underinflation will result.

4 Note any abnormal tread wear with reference to the illustration. Tread pattern irregularities such as feathering, flat spots and more wear on one side than the other are indications of front wheel alignment and/or balance problems. If any of these conditions are noted, they should be rectified as soon as possible.

5 Underinflation will cause overheating of the tyre owing to excessive flexing of the casing, and the tread will not sit correctly on the road surface. This will cause a consequent loss of adhesion and excessive wear, not to mention the danger of sudden tyre failure due to heat build up.

6 Overinflation will cause rapid wear of the centre part of the tyre tread coupled with reduced adhesion, harsher ride, and the danger of shock damage occurring in the tyre casing.

7 Regularly check the tyres for damage in the form of cuts or bulges, especially in the sidewalls. Remove any nails or stones embedded in the tread before they penetrate the tyre to cause deflation. If removal of a nail does reveal that the tyre has been punctured, refit the nail so that its point of penetration is marked. Then immediately change the wheel and have the tyre repaired by a tyre dealer. Do not drive on a tyre in such a condition. In many cases a puncture can be simply repaired by the use of an inner tube of the correct size and type. If in any doubt as to the possible consequences of any damage found, consult your local tyre dealer for advice.

8 Periodically remove the wheels and clean any dirt or mud from the inside and outside surfaces. Examine the wheel rims for signs of rusting, corrosion or other damage. Light alloy wheels are easily damaged by 'kerbing' whilst parking, and similarly steel wheels may become dented or buckled. Renewal of the wheel is very often the only course of remedial action possible.

9 The balance of each wheel and tyre assembly should be maintained to avoid excessive wear, not only to the tyres but also to the steering and suspension components. Wheel imbalance is normally signified by vibration through the vehicle's bodyshell, although in many cases it is particularly noticeable through the steering wheel. Conversely, it should be noted that wear or damage in suspension or steering components may cause excessive tyre wear. Out-of-round or out-of-true tyres, damaged wheels and wheel bearing wear/maladjustment also fall into this category. Balancing will not usually cure vibration caused by such wear.

10 Wheel balancing may be carried out with the wheel either on or off the vehicle. If balanced on the vehicle, ensure that the wheel-to-hub relationship is marked in some way prior to subsequent wheel removal so that it may be refitted in its original position.

11 General tyre wear is influenced to a large degree by driving style – harsh braking and acceleration or fast cornering will all produce more rapid tyre wear. Interchanging of tyres may result in more even wear, however it is worth bearing in mind that if this is completely effective, the added expense is incurred of replacing simultaneously a complete set of tyres, which may prove financially restrictive for many owners.

12 Front tyres may wear unevenly as a result of wheel misalignment. The front wheels should always be correctly aligned according to the settings specified by the vehicle manufacturer.

13 Legal restrictions apply to many aspects of tyre fitting and usage and in the UK this information is contained in the Motor Vehicle Construction and Use Regulations. It is suggested that a copy of these regulations is obtained from your local police if in doubt as to current legal requirements with regard to tyre type and condition, minimum tread depth, etc.

Tyre tread wear patterns

Shoulder Wear

Underinflation (wear on both sides)
Under-inflation will cause overheating of the tyre, because the tyre will flex too much, and the tread will not sit correctly on the road surface. This will cause a loss of grip and excessive wear, not to mention the danger of sudden tyre failure due to heat build-up.
Check and adjust pressures
Incorrect wheel camber (wear on one side)
Repair or renew suspension parts
Hard cornering
Reduce speed!

Centre Wear

Overinflation
Over-inflation will cause rapid wear of the centre part of the tyre tread, coupled with reduced grip, harsher ride, and the danger of shock damage occurring in the tyre casing.
Check and adjust pressures

If you sometimes have to inflate your car's tyres to the higher pressures specified for maximum load or sustained high speed, don't forget to reduce the pressures to normal afterwards.

Uneven Wear

Front tyres may wear unevenly as a result of wheel misalignment. Most tyre dealers and garages can check and adjust the wheel alignment (or "tracking") for a modest charge.
Incorrect camber or castor
Repair or renew suspension parts
Malfunctioning suspension
Repair or renew suspension parts
Unbalanced wheel
Balance tyres
Incorrect toe setting
Adjust front wheel alignment
Note: *The feathered edge of the tread which typifies toe wear is best checked by feel.*

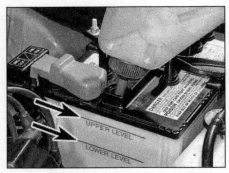

3.5 Topping up the battery electrolyte level. Note the upper and lower level marks shown (arrowed)

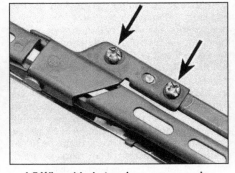

4.5 Wiper blade to wiper arm securing screws (arrowed)

4.10 Remove the windscreen wiper arm

3 Battery check and maintenance

 Caution: Before carrying out any work on the vehicle battery, read through the precautions given in Safety First! at the beginning of this Manual.

1 The battery is located on the left-hand side of the engine compartment.

2 The electrolyte level in the battery should be checked (and if necessary topped up) at the interval given at the beginning of this Chapter; the check should be made more often if the car is operated in high ambient temperature conditions.

3 On some batteries, the case is translucent and incorporates minimum (or lower) and maximum (or upper) level marks; with the vehicle parked on level ground, the electrolyte level in each cell must be maintained between these marks. On batteries without a translucent case and suitable level marks, the general rule is that the electrolyte level must be maintained just above the top of the cell plates.

4 If topping up is necessary, proceed as described in the following paragraph.

5 Remove the cell covers from the top of the battery then carefully add distilled or de-ionized water to raise the electrolyte level in each cell but do not overfill (photo). With the electrolyte level replenished, refit the cell covers.

6 The exterior of the battery should be inspected periodically for damage such as a cracked case or cover.

7 Check the tightness of the battery cable terminal clamps to ensure good electrical connections, and check the entire length of each cable for cracks and frayed conductors.

8 If corrosion (visible as white, fluffy deposits) is evident, remove the cable terminal clamps from the battery terminals, clean them with a small wire brush then refit them. Corrosion can be kept to a minimum by applying a layer of petroleum jelly to the clamps and terminals after they are reconnected.

9 Make sure that the battery tray is in good condition and the retaining clamp is tight.

10 Corrosion or deposits on the tray, retaining clamp and the battery itself can be removed with a solution of water and baking soda. Thoroughly rinse all cleaned areas with cold water.

11 Any metal parts of the vehicle damaged by such corrosion should be covered with a zinc-based primer then painted (Chapter 11).

12 Further information on the battery, charging and jump starting can be found in Chapter 12 and in the preliminary sections of this Manual.

4 Windscreen/tailgate wiper blade check and renewal

1 Check the operation of the windscreen and tailgate wipers, and rectify any defects found, noting the following information.

Wiper blades

2 The wiper blades should be renewed when they are deteriorated, cracked, or no longer clean the windscreen or tailgate glass effectively.

3 Although it is possible to renew the wiper blade rubbers on their own, this can often lead to smearing and juddering problems caused by the blade section being distorted. It is therefore recommended that the complete blade assembly is renewed as follows.

4 Lift the wiper arm away from the glass.

5 Detach the blade from the arm by undoing its retaining screws, or releasing its clip, as applicable (photo).

6 Fit a new blade by reversing the method of removal.

Wiper arms

7 Check the wiper arms for worn hinges and weak springs, and renew if evident.

8 Covers are fitted over each wiper arm retaining nut, and these must be raised for access to the nut if the arm is being removed.

9 Make sure that the wiper is at its rest (parked) position, if necessary, switch the wipers on and off in order to allow them to return to the rest position. Mark this position by laying a strip of masking tape alongside the wiper blade.

10 Unscrew the retaining nut and pull the arm from the spindle; note the order of any collars, washers or spacers fitted (photo). If necessary, use a screwdriver to prise off the arm, being careful not to damage the paintwork. On the tailgate wiper it will help if the arm is moved to its fully raised position before removing it from the spindle.

11 Fit the new arm using a reversal of the removal procedure, aligning the blade edge with the masking tape. On completion remove the masking tape from the screen.

5 Windscreen/headlamp washer system check and adjustment

1 The windscreen/tailgate washer fluid reservoir is located in the righ-hand front corner of the engine compartment. Check that the fluid level in the reservoir is at least up to the bottom of the filler neck, and top up if necessary. When topping up the reservoir, a screen wash should be added in the recommended quantities.

2 Check that the washer jets direct the fluid onto the middle of the windscreen/tailgate and, if applicable, adjust the small sphere on the jet with a pin.

Every 6000 miles (10 000 km) or 6 months - whichever comes first

6 Engine oil and filter renewal

> **HAYNES HINT**
> *Frequent oil and filter changes are the most important preventative maintenance procedures that can be undertaken by the D.I.Y. owner. As engine oil ages, it becomes diluted and contaminated, which leads to premature engine wear.*

1 Before starting this procedure, gather together all the necessary tools and materials. Also make sure that you have plenty of clean rags and newspapers handy to mop up any spills. Ideally, the engine oil should be warm as it will drain better and more built-up sludge will be removed with it. Take care however, not to touch the exhaust or any other hot parts of the engine when working under the vehicle. To avoid any possibility of scalding and to protect yourself from possible skin irritants and other harmful contaminants in used engine oils, it is advisable to wear gloves when carrying out this work. Access to the underside of the vehicle will be greatly improved if it can be raised on a lift, driven onto ramps or jacked up and supported on axle stands. Whichever method is chosen, make sure that the car remains level, or if it is at an angle, that the sump drain plug is at the lowest point.

2 Remove the undershield(s) (where necessary), to gain access to the drain plug, and position a suitable container beneath the sump drain plug. Clean the drain plug and the area around it, then slacken it using a spanner or preferably a suitable socket and bar (photo). If possible, try to keep the plug pressed into the sump while unscrewing it by hand the last couple of turns. As the plug releases from the threads, move it away sharply so the stream of oil issuing from the sump runs into the container, not up your sleeve!

3 Allow some time for the old oil to drain noting that it may be necessary to reposition the container as the oil flow slows to a trickle.

4 After all the oil has drained, wipe off the drain plug with a clean rag and renew the sealing washer. Clean the area around the drain plug opening and refit the plug. Tighten the plug securely, preferably to the specified torque using a torque wrench.

5 Move the container into position under the oil filter which is located on the front face of the engine.

6 Using an oil filter removal tool, slacken the filter initially then unscrew it by hand the rest of the way (photo). Empty the oil in the old filter into the container.

7 Use a clean rag to remove all oil, dirt and sludge from the filter sealing area on the engine. Check the old filter to make sure that the rubber sealing ring hasn't stuck to the engine. If it has, carefully remove it.

8 Apply a light coating of clean engine oil to the sealing ring on the new filter then screw it into position on the engine. Tighten the filter firmly by hand only, do not use any tools.

9 Remove the old oil and all tools from under the car then if applicable, lower the car to the ground.

10 Unscrew the oil filler cap on the camshaft cover and fill the engine, using the specified grade and type of oil. Pour in half the specified quantity of oil first, then wait a few minutes for the oil to fall to the sump. Continue adding oil a small quantity at a time until the level is up to the MAX or F mark on the dipstick.

11 Start the engine and run it for a few minutes while checking for leaks around the oil filter seal and the sump drain plug.

12 Switch off the engine and wait a few minutes for the oil to settle in the sump once more. With the new oil circulated and the filter now completely full, recheck the level on the dipstick and add more oil as necessary.

13 Dispose of the used engine oil safely with reference to *General repair procedures* in the reference section of this Manual.

7 Engine checks

1 Visually inspect the engine joint faces, gaskets and seals for any signs of water or oil leaks. Pay particular attention to the areas around the cylinder head gasket joint, the camshaft cover gasket joint, the oil pump and sump joint faces. Bear in mind that over a period of time some very slight seepage from these areas is to be expected but what you are really looking for is any indication of a serious leak. Should a leak be found, renew the offending gasket or oil seal by referring to the appropriate Chapters in this Manual.

2 Also check the security and condition of all the engine related pipes and hoses (including the oil cooler hoses, where fitted). Ensure that all cable ties or securing clips are in place and in good condition. Clips which are broken or missing can lead to chafing of the hoses pipes or wiring which could cause more serious problems in the future.

8 Cooling system checks

1 The engine should be cold for the cooling system checks, so perform the following procedure before driving the vehicle or after the engine has been switched off for at least three hours.

2 Remove the radiator pressure cap carefully and clean it thoroughly inside and out with a rag. Clean the filler neck on the radiator; the presence of rust, corrosion or oil in the filler neck indicates that the coolant should be changed (the presence of oil in the coolant may also indicate a cylinder head gasket leak). The coolant inside the radiator and the expansion tank should be relatively clean and transparent. If it is rust coloured or oily, drain and flush the system and refill with a fresh coolant mixture.

3 Carefully check the radiator hoses and heater hoses along their entire length. Renew any hose which is cracked, swollen or deteriorated. Cracks will show up better if the hose is squeezed. Pay close attention to the hose clips that secure the hoses to the cooling system components.

> **HAYNES HINT**
> *Hose clips can pinch and puncture hoses, resulting in cooling system leaks. If wire type hose clips are used, it may be a good idea to replace them with screw-type clips.*

6.2 Slackening off the sump drain plug

6.6 Using an oil filter removal tool to slacken the oil filter

4 Inspect all the cooling system components (hoses, joint faces, etc.) for leaks. A leak in the cooling system will usually show up as white or rust coloured deposits on the area adjoining the leak. Where any problems of this nature are found on system components, renew the component or gasket with reference to Chapter 3.

5 Clean the front of the radiator with a soft brush to remove all insects, leaves, etc, imbedded in the radiator fins. Be extremely careful not to damage the radiator fins or cut your fingers on them.

6 Testing procedures for the electric cooling fan operation, and the thermostat operation, are covered in Chapter 3.

Heating/air conditioning system

7 Check that the heating system operates correctly, by running through its full range of functions, and take appropriate action to cure any defects found.

9 Fuel system checks

Warning: Certain procedures require the removal of fuel lines and connections which may result in some fuel spillage. Before carrying out any operation on the fuel system refer to the precautions given in Safety First! at the beginning of this Manual and follow them implicitly. Petrol is a highly dangerous and volatile liquid and the precautions necessary when handling it cannot be overstressed On fuel injection equipped vehicles the fuel system is highly pressurised, therefore reference must be made to Section 25 in Chapter 4 when disconnecting fuel unions.

1 The fuel system is most easily checked with the vehicle raised on a hoist or suitably supported on axle stands so the components underneath are readily visible and accessible.

2 If the smell of petrol is noticed while driving or after the vehicle has been parked in the sun, the system should be thoroughly inspected immediately.

3 Remove the petrol tank filler cap and check for damage, corrosion and an unbroken sealing imprint on the gasket. Renew the cap if necessary.

4 With the vehicle raised, inspect the petrol tank and filler neck for punctures, cracks and other damage. The connection between the filler neck and tank is especially critical.

5 Carefully check all rubber hoses and metal fuel lines leading away from the petrol tank. Check for loose connections, deteriorated hoses, crimped lines and other damage. Pay particular attention to the vent pipes and hoses which often loop up around the filler neck and can become blocked or crimped. Follow the lines to the front of the vehicle carefully inspecting them all the way. Renew damaged sections as necessary.

6 From within the engine compartment, check the security of all fuel hose attachments and inspect the fuel hoses and vacuum hoses for kinks, chafing and deterioration.

7 Check the operation of the throttle linkage and lubricate the linkage components with a few drops of light oil.

10 Exhaust system check

1 With the engine cold (at least an hour after the vehicle has been driven), check the complete exhaust system from the engine to the end of the tailpipe. Ideally the inspection should be carried out with the vehicle on a hoist to permit unrestricted access. If a hoist is not available, raise and support the vehicle on axle stands.

2 Check the exhaust pipes and connections for evidence of leaks, severe corrosion and damage. Make sure that all brackets and mountings are in good condition and tight. Leakage at any of the joints or in other parts of the system will usually show up as a black sooty stain in the vicinity of the leak.

3 Rattles and other noises can often be traced to the exhaust system, especially the brackets and mountings. Try to move the pipes and silencers. If the components can come into contact with the body or suspension parts, secure the system with new mountings or if possible, separate the joints and twist the pipes as necessary to provide additional clearance.

11 Spark plug check and renewal

1 The correct functioning of the spark plugs is vital for the correct running and efficiency of the engine. It is essential that the plugs fitted are appropriate for the engine, and the suitable type is specified at the beginning of this Chapter. If this type is used and the engine is in good condition, the spark plugs should not need attention between scheduled replacement intervals. Spark plug cleaning is rarely necessary and should not be attempted unless specialised equipment is available as

damage can easily be caused to the firing ends.

2 To remove the plugs, first open the bonnet. On fuel-injected models the spark plug lead cover must first be removed after undoing the securing bolts (photo). Mark the HT leads one to four to correspond to the cylinder the lead serves (number one cylinder is at the timing cover end of the engine). Pull the HT leads from the plugs by gripping the cap, not the lead otherwise the lead connection may be fractured.

3 It is advisable to remove the dirt from the spark plug recesses using a clean brush, vacuum cleaner or compressed air before removing the plugs, to prevent the dirt dropping into the cylinders.

4 Unscrew the plugs using a spark plug spanner, suitable box spanner or a deep socket and extension bar (photo). Keep the socket in alignment with the spark plugs, otherwise the porcelain top of the spark plug may be broken off.

5 Examination of the spark plugs will give a good indication of the condition of the engine. If the insulator nose of the spark plug is clean and white, with no deposits, this is indicative of a weak mixture or too hot a plug (a hot plug transfers heat away from the electrode slowly, a cold plug transfers heat away quickly).

6 If the tip and insulator nose are covered with hard black-looking deposits, then this is indicative that the mixture is too rich. Should the plug be black and oily, then it is likely that the engine is fairly worn, as well as the mixture being too rich.

7 If the insulator nose is covered with light tan to greyish brown deposits, then the mixture is correct and it is likely that the engine is in good condition.

8 If the spark plugs have only completed 6000 miles (10 000 km), in accordance with the routine maintenance schedule they should still be serviceable until the 12 000 mile (20 000 km) service when renewal is due. However, it is recommended that they are gapped in order to maintain peak engine efficiency. If, due to engine condition, the spark plugs are not serviceable, they should be renewed.

9 The spark plug gap is of considerable

11.2 Remove the spark plug lead cover to reach the HT leads

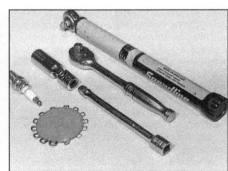
11.4 Tools required for the removal, gap adjustment and refitting of the spark plugs

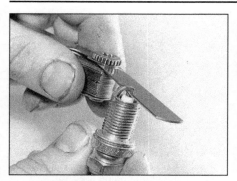

11.10 Measuring the spark plug gap using a feeler blade

11.11A Measuring the spark plug gap using a wire blade

11.11B Adjusting the spark plug gap using a special adjusting tool

importance as, if it is too large or too small, the size of the spark and its efficiency will be seriously impaired. For the best results the spark plug gap should be set in accordance with the Specifications at the beginning of this Chapter.

10 To set it, measure the gap with a feeler gauge, and then bend open, or close, the outer plug electrode until the correct gap is achieved (photo). The centre electrode should never be bent, as this may crack the insulation and cause plug failure, if nothing worse.

11 Special spark plug electrode gap adjusting tools are available from most motor accessory shops (photos).

12 Before fitting the spark plugs check that the threaded connector sleeves are tight and that the plug exterior surfaces and threads are clean.

13 Refit the spark plugs.

HAYNES HINT

It is very often difficult to insert spark plugs into their holes without cross-threading them. To avoid this possibility, fit a short length of rubber hose over the end of the spark plug. The flexible hose acts as a universal joint to help align the plug with the hole. Should the plug begin to cross-thread, the hose will slip on the spark plug, preventing thread damage to the aluminium cylinder head. Once the thread has 'taken' properly, remove the rubber hose and tighten the plug to the specified torque using the spark plug socket and a torque wrench.

14 Reconnect the HT leads in their correct order. On fuel-injected models refit the spark plug lead cover (where fitted) and tighten its retaining screws securely.

12 Clutch system pipe and connections check

1 Examine the pipe for signs of corrosion or damage, and the connections for signs of leakage; also check that the pipe support brackets are secure. Take appropriate action to rectify any faults found.

13 Brake pad wear check

Front brakes

1 The brake pads are fitted with pad wear indicator plates. These emit a squeaking noise when the brake pad friction material wears down to 2.5 mm and they rub against the brake disc. The brake pads are checked as follows.

2 Slacken the front roadwheel nuts, then raise the front of the vehicle and support it securely using axle stands.

3 Remove the front roadwheels.

4 The front brake pads can be viewed through the inspection holes in the calipers but, if in any doubt as to the amount of friction material remaining, the pads should be

13.4 Brake pad inspection hole (front brake caliper)

removed (Chapter 9) and the friction material measured (photo). Compare the thickness of the remaining friction material on each of the brake pads with the minimum thickness specified and, if any brake pad is approaching, or less than the specified minimum thickness, all four front brake pads must be renewed as an axle set as described in Chapter 9. Renewal will also be required if evidence of friction material contamination is found.

5 Whilst the brake discs are accessible, inspect them as described in Chapter 9.

6 Clean away any dust accumulation using a damp cloth before refitting (taking care not to inhale any), and dispose of the cloth safely.

7 Fully tighten the roadwheel nuts (to their specified torque) with the vehicle resting on its roadwheels.

Rear brakes

8 The procedure is similar to that described for front brake pads, noting that the front roadwheels must be chocked, and first gear must be selected before raising the rear of the vehicle.

14 Braking system hydraulic pipes, hoses and connections check

1 Examine all braking system hydraulic pipes, hoses and connections for signs of damage, deterioration and fluid leakage; further inspection details are given in Chapter 9. Renew any items found to be defective, with reference to the appropriate text.

15 Vacuum servo unit operation test

1 To test the operation of the servo unit depress the footbrake four or five times to exhaust the vacuum, then start the engine. As the engine starts there should be a noticeable 'give' in the brake pedal as vacuum builds up. Allow the engine to run for at least two minutes and then switch it off. If the brake pedal is now depressed again, it should be

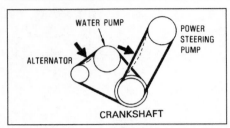

Fig. 1.4 Power steering pump (where fitted) and alternator/water pump drivebelt tension checking points (arrowed) – 1.3 litre engine (Sec 16)

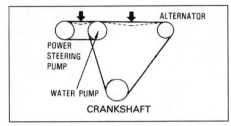

Fig. 1.5 Power steering pump and alternator/water pump drivebelt tension checking points (arrowed) – 1.6 litre carburettor engine (Sec 16)

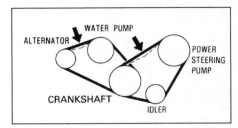

Fig. 1.6 Power steering pump and alternator/water pump drivebelt tension checking points (arrowed) – 1.6 litre fuel injection engine (Sec 16)

possible to detect a hiss from the servo when the pedal is depressed. After about four or five applications no further hissing will be heard and the pedal will feel considerably stronger.

Vacuum servo unit check valve test

2 To test the check valve, remove it from the vehicle as described in Chapter 9, and blow through it from the servo side; air should pass through easily. Turn the check valve around and attempt to blow through it from the inlet manifold (engine) side; there should be no air leakage. If it allows air to flow in both directions, or does not allow air to flow in either direction, it is faulty and must be renewed. Refit the check valve as described in Chapter 9.

16 Power steering drivebelt check, adjustment and renewal

1 The power steering pump drivebelt is located at the timing cover end of the engine. Due to its function and material make-up, the drivebelt is prone to failure after a period of time and should therefore be inspected and adjusted periodically.
2 The power steering pump drivebelt is independent of the alternator/water pump drivebelt, and requires separate adjustment. On 1.6 carburettor models, the drivebelt is driven by the water pump pulley, itself belt driven from the crankshaft pulley. On other

models, it is driven directly by the crankshaft pulley; the drivebelt fitted to the GTi 16 runs around an idler pulley (at which point tensioning adjustments are performed).
3 Since the drivebelt is located very close to the right-hand side of the engine compartment, probably the best course of action to enable thorough checking is to remove the drivebelt from the vehicle (as described below); another possible method of checking (if access permits), without removing the drivebelt, is described in the following paragraph.
4 With the engine switched off, and neutral (or 'N' on automatic transmission) selected, inspect the accessible section of drivebelt between the pulleys, then mark the section inspected (with a light chalk mark or similar). Turn the engine using a spanner on the crankshaft pulley bolt in order to inspect the remainder of the drivebelt, marking it as each section is inspected, until the whole belt has been checked. If the drivebelt is being inspected in this manner, twist the section between the pulleys so that both sides can be viewed. Inspect the drivebelt contact faces of the pulleys using a similar marking technique.
5 Inspect the drivebelt for cracks, missing sections and separation of the plies; also check for fraying, and for glazing which gives the belt a shiny appearance. Check the pulleys for nicks, cracks, distortion and corrosion. If any of these faults are found, the drivebelt (and any defective pulley) must be renewed.

6 The tension of the power steering pump drivebelt is checked at the point indicated in Figs. 1.4, 1.5 or 1.6 (as applicable), by applying pressure at that point and measuring the resultant drivebelt deflection; Toyota technicians use a special spring tensioned tool which applies a force of 10 kg (22 lb) to the drivebelt and then measures the deflection. An alternative arrangement can be made by using a straight-edge, steel ruler and spring balance. Hold the straight-edge across the two relevant pulleys, and position the steel ruler against the drivebelt: apply the force with the spring balance, then measure the drivebelt deflection. Compare the deflection observed against that specified.
7 If adjustment is necessary, on all vehicles except the GTi 16, it can be achieved by loosening the power steering pump pivot and adjustment bolts (as applicable) and moving the pump accordingly; tighten the relevant bolts after adjustment. On the GTi 16, adjustment is made from underneath the vehicle by turning the idler pulley adjusting bolt until the correct tension is achieved. Run the engine for about five minutes, then recheck the drivebelt tension; note that after this period of time, a new drivebelt is classified as a used drivebelt for the purpose of tension checking (photos).
8 To renew the power steering pump drivebelt, first fully slacken the drivebelt tension, at the adjustment points (given above, according to type). Slip the drivebelt off the pulleys then fit the new one ensuring

16.7A Slackening the power steering pump pivot bolt (undershield removed)

16.7B Slackening the power steering pump adjustment bolt

16.7C Power steering pump drivebelt idler pulley adjustment bolt (arrowed)

that it is routed correctly. With the drivebelt in position, adjust the tension as described above. In most applications, the power steering pump drivebelt can be removed without removing the alternator/water pump drivebelt; where this is not possible, refer to Section 18.

17 Seat belt check

1 arefully examine the seat belt webbing for cuts or any signs of serious fraying or deterioration. If the seat belt is of the retractable type, pull the belt all the way out and examine the full extent of the webbing.
2 The seat belts are designed to lock up during a sudden stop or impact, yet allow free movement during normal driving. Fasten and unfasten the belt ensuring that the locking mechanism holds securely and releases properly when intended. Check also that the retracting mechanism operates correctly when the belt is released.

18 Alternator drivebelt check, adjustment and renewal

1 The alternator/water pump drivebelt is located at the timing cover end of the engine. Due to its function and material make-up, the drivebelt is prone to failure after a period of time and should therefore be inspected and adjusted periodically.
2 The alternator/water pump drivebelt is independent of the power steering pump drivebelt, and requires separate adjustment. It is driven by the crankshaft pulley (Figs. 1.4, 1.5 or 1.6).
3 Inspection of the drivebelt, and tension checking, may be carried out in the same manner as that described for power steering pump drivebelts (Section 16).
4 If adjustment of the drivebelt tension is necessary, it can be achieved by loosening the alternator pivot and adjustment bolts and moving the alternator (using a suitable lever) to obtain tension; tighten the relevant bolts after adjustment. Run the engine for about five minutes, then recheck the drivebelt tension; note that after this period of time, a new drivebelt is classified as a used drivebelt for the purpose of tension checking.
5 To renew the alternator/water pump drivebelt, it will first be necessary to remove the power steering pump drivebelt (where fitted) (Section 16, then slacken the alternator/water pump drivebelt tension by slackening the alternator pivot and adjustment bolts. Slip the drivebelt off the pulleys then fit the new one ensuring that it is routed correctly. With the drivebelt in position, adjust the tension as previously described.

Every 12 000 miles (20 000 km) or 12 months - whichever comes first

19 Valve clearance adjustment

1 On 1.3 litre engines, the valve clearances must be checked and adjusted after the engine has reached its normal operating temperature (perform the operation as soon as possible after switching the engine off); on 1.6 litre engines, the valve clearances must be checked and adjusted with the engine cold.
2 With number one piston set to TDC and the camshaft cover removed (Chapter 2), measure the clearances of those valves shown in Fig. 1.7 or Fig. 1.8 (as applicable); the feeler gauge should slide with slight drag (photo). On 1.3 litre engines, any clearance that is outside specification may be adjusted by slackening the individual rocker arm adjusting screw locknut and turning the adjusting screw (Fig. 1.9). When the appropriate clearance is obtained, hold the adjusting screw then tighten the locknut securely and recheck the clearance upon completion. On 1.6 litre engines, record the clearance measurement for each valve that is outside specification, as it will be used later in determining the required shim size to bring the clearance back to normal.

19.2 Measuring the valve clearances (4A-F engine shown)

3 Turn the crankshaft pulley a full 360° then repeat the measuring procedure on the valves shown in Fig. 1.10 or Fig. 1.11 (as applicable). On 1.3 litre engines, adjustment may be made in the same manner as previously described, whilst on 1.6 litre engines again record the

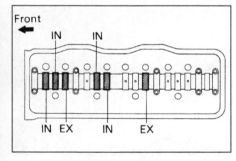

Fig. 1.7 On 1.3 litre engines, measure the clearance of the valves shown with number one piston set to TDC (Sec 19)

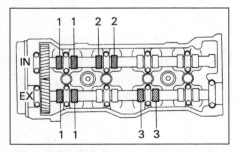

Fig. 1.8 On 1.6 litre engines, measure the clearance of the valves shown with number one piston set to TDC (4A-F engine shown) (Sec 19)

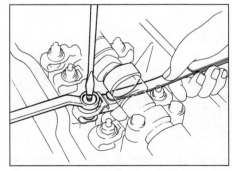

Fig. 1.9 Adjusting the valve clearance on a 1.3 litre engine (Sec 19)

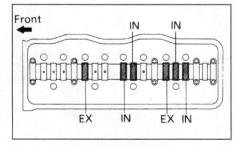

Fig. 1.10 Rotate the crankshaft by 360° (number four piston at TDC) and measure the clearance of the valves shown on 1.3 litre engines (Sec 19)

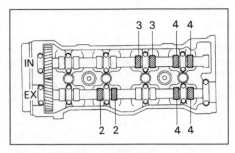

Fig. 1.11 On 1.6 litre engines rotate the crankshaft by 360° (number four piston at TDC) then measure the clearance of the valves shown (4A-F engine shown) (Sec 19)

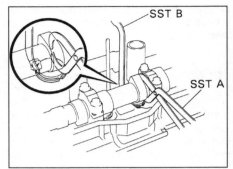

Fig. 1.12 Special Toyota shim removal tools in use (Sec 19)

19.6 Removing a shim (4A-F engine shown)

clearance measurement of those valves that are outside their specification.

4 The remaining procedure is concerned with the corrective measures necessary for any clearance measurement that was outside specification on 1.6 litre engines.

5 Tackling each shim that has to be renewed as a separate operation, turn the crankshaft pulley so that the camshaft lobe above the shim being attended to points upwards.

6 A special shim removal tool kit is available (SST 09248-55010) (Fig. 1.12), but it should be possible to use a suitable alternative tool to depress and hold the camshaft followers down. With the camshaft follower held depressed, remove the shim using a suitable screwdriver and a magnetic probe (possibly another magnetised screwdriver) (photo).

20.1 Remove the air filter element from the housing

7 Measure the thickness of the removed shim using a micrometer (photo), then calculate the thickness of the required shim using the following formulae where the variables are T (the thickness of the removed shim), A (the valve clearance measured) and N (the thickness of the new shim required):

Inlet valves: $N = T + (A - 0.20 \text{ mm})$
Exhaust valves: $N = T + (A - 0.25 \text{ mm})$

Shims are available in a variety of sizes, and the shim selected (from your Toyota dealer's parts department) should be as close as possible to the calculated value.

8 Install the new shim, then remove the tool(s) used to depress the camshaft follower.

9 Repeat the process for all the remaining shims that require renewal, then repeat the valve clearance measuring procedure upon completion.

10 On completion refit the camshaft cover(s) as described in Chapter 2.

20 Air filter element cleaning and renewal

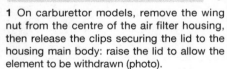

1 On carburettor models, remove the wing nut from the centre of the air filter housing, then release the clips securing the lid to the housing main body: raise the lid to allow the element to be withdrawn (photo).

2 On fuel-injected models, first disconnect the battery earth terminal, then disconnect the

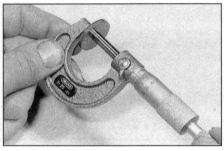

19.7 Measuring a shim using a micrometer

wiring connectors from the air control valve (or the vacuum switching valve, if applicable) and the intake air temperature sensor; the valve and sensor are located on the air filter housing lid. Disconnect the VSV hose (between the throttle housing and the air filter housing) at the filter housing end, and release the clip securing the trunking to the filter housing lid. Release the securing clips then remove the lid to allow the element to be withdrawn; the task can be performed with the lid raised, but this is fiddly (photos).

3 At the specified intervals, element cleaning or renewal will be required; to clean the air filter element (having first ensured that it is not damaged, oily or excessively dirty), blow from its underside using compressed air then blow off its upper surfaces.

4 To refit an element, reverse the method of removal.

20.2A Disconnect the wiring connector from the intake air temperature sensor. . .

20.2B . . .then release the air filter housing lid securing clips (two arrowed). . .

20.2C . . .and withdraw the air filter element. Note that the position of the idle up VSV (arrowed)

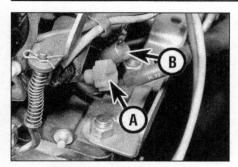

21.10 Idle speed adjusting screw (A), and mixture adjusting screw (B) – 1.6 carburettor model

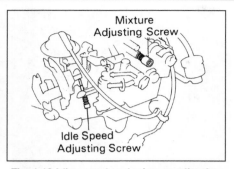

Fig. 1.13 Idle speed and mixture adjusting screw locations – variable venturi (V type) carburettor (early 1.3 models) (Sec 21)

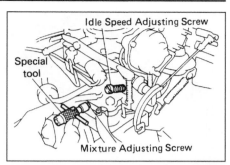

Fig. 1.14 Idle speed and mixture adjusting screw locations. Note special tool necessary to adjust mixture screw – twin fixed-venturi (K type) carburettor (later 1.3 models) (Sec 21)

21 Idle speed and mixture adjustment

1 A suitable tachometer will be required for this procedure, along with an exhaust gas analyser (CO meter); refer to Chapter 5 where further information regarding tachometer connection is given for each ignition system type. With the equipment checked for compatibility, follow the manufacturer's instructions. Also note that, should adjustments to the fuel mixture be necessary, a special tool is required to turn the mixture adjusting screw: consult your Toyota dealer for availability.

2 Prior to carrying out this procedure, ensure that the ignition system components are in good condition and that the ignition timing is correctly set (Section 22). Also ensure that the air filter element is correctly fitted and all vacuum hoses are connected. On models equipped with automatic transmission ensure the gear selector is in the N position, and on models equipped with power steering ensure the front wheels are positioned in the straight-ahead position.

Note: *The following adjustments must be carried out whilst the cooling fan is off. If at any time the cooling fan cuts in, stop and wait for the fan to switch off before continuing with the adjustment procedure.*

Early 1.3 models with variable-venturi (V type) carburettor

3 Warm the engine up to normal operating temperature then run it for approximately 30 to 60 seconds, at approximately 2000 rpm, before allowing it to idle. Wait for the meters to stabilise (approximately 3 minutes) then record the idle speed and CO content readings.

4 If either reading is outside specification, disconnect the vacuum supply (inlet manifold) hose from the hot idle compensation (HIC) control valve, situated on the underside of the air filter housing, and plug the end.

5 Allow the meters to stabilise, then turn the idle speed adjusting screw to obtain the specified idle speed (Fig. 1.13).

6 Repeat the operation described in para-

graph 3 then adjust the CO content, as necessary, by turning the mixture adjusting screw.

7 Repeat the procedure as necessary until the idle speed and CO content are within specification. If the CO content is high and cannot be adjusted to within its specification, it is likely that the air filter or crankcase ventilation system is defective or blocked or that there is an internal fault in the carburettor. If it is low and cannot be adjusted to within its specification, a vacuum leak is the likely source. If when the CO content is adjusted to within its specification the engine idles roughly, this points to incorrect ignition timing, incorrect valve clearances or general engine wear.

8 Stop the engine, then reconnect the vacuum supply hose to the HAI and HIC control valve and disconnect the test equipment.

Later 1.3 models with twin fixed-venturi (K type) carburettor

9 Follow the above procedure, but note that the engine should be allowed to run at 2500 rpm for approximately 2 minutes before allowing it to idle as described in paragraph 3; the idle speed adjusting screw and mixture adjusting screw are as shown in Fig. 1.14.

1.6 model with twin fixed-venturi (K type) carburettor

10 Follow the procedure described in paragraphs 3 to 8 inclusive, but ignore the instruction to disconnect the hot idle

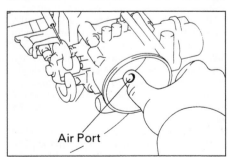

Fig. 1.15 Block off the air port in the throttle housing, to check the operation of the auxiliary air valve (Sec 21)

compensation (HIC) control valve vacuum supply hose. The idle speed adjusting screw and the mixture adjusting screw are grouped together on the rearward facing side of the carburettor (photo).

Fuel-injected model

11 Prior to checking and adjusting the idle speed and fuel mixture, but after connecting the test equipment, disconnect the air filter trunking from the throttle housing to enable the auxiliary air valve operation to be checked.

12 Start the engine then check that with the engine cool (coolant temperature below 80°C), the engine idle speed drops significantly when the auxiliary air valve port is blocked off (Fig. 1.15). Repeat the check when the engine has reached normal operating temperature noting that the idle speed should not drop by more than 100 rpm. If this is not the case, the auxiliary air valve is suspect and it should be renewed as described in Chapter 4.

13 After the auxiliary air valve has been checked and its correct operation confirmed, reconnect the air filter trunking and check the idle speed and mixture settings as follows.

14 Run the engine until it reaches normal operating temperature then disconnect the wiring connector from the idle up vacuum switching valve (VSV). Run the engine at approximately 2500 rpm for a few seconds then allow it to idle. If the engine does not idle at the specified speed adjust it by turning the idle speed adjusting screw (Fig. 1.16). Once

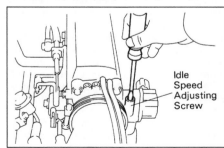

Fig. 1.16 Adjusting the idle speed fuel-injected models (Sec 21)

21.15 Fuel mixture control variable resistor mixture – adjusting screw arrowed

22.7 Disconnect and plug the sub-diaphragm vacuum hose (arrowed)

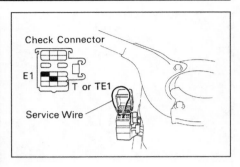

Fig. 1.17 Connect terminals E1 and T (or TE1) using a suitable service wire before checking the ignition timing (Sec 22)

the engine is idling at the correct speed reconnect the VSV wiring connector.

15 Run the engine at approximately 2500 rpm for 90 seconds then allow the engine to idle. If the mixture CO content is not within the specified range adjust it by rotating the mixture adjusting screw. The adjusting screw is part of the fuel mixture control variable resistor which is mounted on the left-hand front suspension turret and can be reached once its cap has been removed (photo). **Note:** *The adjusting screw can only be rotated within a span of 130° each way from its central position. Do not try to rotate the screw beyond this range*. If the adjusting screw is forced beyond its limits, the variable resistor will become damaged and must be renewed as described in Chapter 4. If the CO content is high and cannot be adjusted to within its specification, it is likely that a fault exists within the fuel-injection system (Chapter 4).

22 Ignition timing check and adjustment

Warning: Voltages produced by an electronic ignition system are considerably higher than those produced by conventional systems. Extreme care must be taken when working on the system with the ignition switched on. Persons with surgically-implanted cardiac pacemaker devices should keep well clear of the ignition circuits, components and test equipment.

1 In order that the engine can run efficiently, it is necessary for a spark to occur at the spark plug and ignite the fuel/air mixture at the instant just before the piston reaches the top of its travel on the compression stroke. The precise instant at which the spark occurs is determined by the ignition timing; this is quoted in degrees before top dead centre (BTDC) and is measured for number one piston.

2 Refer to the Specifications at the beginning of this Chapter and note the specified setting for stroboscopic ignition timing. To make subsequent operations easier it is advisable to highlight the mark on the crankshaft pulley

and the appropriate mark on the timing belt cover scale with white paint.

3 Connect the timing light in accordance with the manufacturer's instructions (usually interposed between the end of No 1 spark plug HT lead and No 1 spark plug terminal).

4 Making reference to the relevant information given in Chapter 5, connect up a suitable tachometer; certain tachometers may not be compatible with the ignition systems used.

5 Start the engine and warm it up to normal operating temperature.

6 Prior to carrying out this procedure, on models equipped with automatic transmission ensure the gear selector is in the N position, and on models equipped with power steering ensure the front wheels are positioned in the straight-ahead position.

Note: *The following adjustments must be carried out whilst the cooling fan is off. If at any time the cooling fan cuts in, stop and wait for the fan to switch off before continuing with the adjustment procedure.*

Carburettor models

7 Disconnect the vacuum advance pipe from the distributor sub-diaphragm and plug the end (photo).

8 Leave the engine to run at the specified idling speed.

9 Point the timing light at the timing marks and they should appear to be stationary, with the mark on the crankshaft pulley aligned with the appropriate mark on the timing belt cover scale.

10 If adjustment is necessary (ie the crankshaft pulley mark does not line up with the appropriate mark on the timing cover scale), slacken the distributor retaining bolt(s) and turn the distributor body until they do align. Once the setting is correct and the marks align, tighten the distributor bolt(s) securely then recheck the alignment of the marks.

11 Gradually increase the engine speed while still pointing the timing light at the marks. The mark on the crankshaft pulley should appear to advance further, indicating that the distributor centrifugal advance mechanism is functioning; if the mark remains stationary or

moves in a jerky, erratic fashion, the advance mechanism must be suspect (Chapter 5).

12 Reconnect the vacuum hose to the sub-diaphragm and check that the advance alters when the hose is connected. If not, the diaphragm unit may be faulty, or the hose may be defective (Chapter 5).

13 After completing the checks and adjustments, switch off the engine and disconnect the timing light and tachometer.

Fuel-injected models

14 The procedure for fuel-injected models is significantly different in that no physical advance functions are featured, these being incorporated into the ECU circuitry.

15 Connect the terminals in the check connector as shown in Fig. 1.17, using a suitable service wire.

16 With the engine idling, point the timing light at the timing marks and they should appear to be stationary, with the mark on the crankshaft pulley aligned with the appropriate mark on the timing belt cover scale.

17 If adjustment is necessary (ie the crankshaft pulley mark does not line up with the appropriate mark on the timing cover scale), slacken the distributor retaining bolt(s) and turn the distributor body until they do align. Once the marks align, tighten the bolt(s) securely then recheck the alignment of the marks.

18 Remove the service wire from the check connector and, with the timing light still pointed at the timing marks, observing the advance increase; if no increase in advance is observed, it is likely that there is a fault within the engine management system.

19 After completing the checks and adjustments, switch off the engine and disconnect the timing light and tachometer.

23 HT leads, distributor cap and rotor arm check and renewal

1 The spark plug HT leads should be checked whenever new spark plugs are installed in the engine.

2 Pull the HT leads from the plugs by gripping the cap, not the lead, otherwise the lead connection may be fractured.

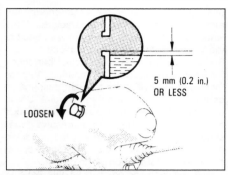

Fig. 1.18 Manual gearbox oil level checking (Sec 24)

24.4 Topping up/refilling a manual gearbox with the specified oil

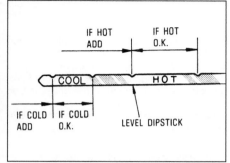

Fig. 1.19 Automatic transmission fluid dipstick markings (Sec 25)

HAYNES HiNT *Ensure that the HT leads are numbered before removing them to avoid confusion when refitting.*

3 Check inside the cap for signs of corrosion, which will look like a white crusty powder. Push the cap back onto the spark plug ensuring that it is a tight fit on the plug. If it isn't, remove the lead again and use pliers to carefully crimp the metal connector inside the cap until it fits securely on the end of the spark plug.

4 Using a clean rag, wipe the entire length of the lead to remove any built-up dirt and grease. Once the lead is clean, check for burns, cracks and other damage. Do not bend the lead excessively or pull the lead lengthwise – the conductor inside might break.

5 Disconnect the other end of the lead from the distributor cap. Again, pull only on the end fitting. Check for corrosion and a tight fit in the same manner as the spark plug end. If an ohmmeter is available, check the resistance of the HT lead by connecting the meter between the spark plug end of the lead and the segment inside the distributor cap. Refit the lead securely on completion.

6 Check the remaining HT leads one at a time, in the same way.

7 If new HT leads are required, purchase a set for your specific vehicle and engine.

8 Remove the distributor cap and gasket, wipe it clean and carefully inspect it inside and out for signs of cracks, carbon tracks (tracking) and worn, burned or loose contacts. Similarly inspect the rotor arm. Renew these components if any defects are found. It is common practice to renew the cap and rotor arm whenever new HT leads are fitted. When fitting a new cap, remove the HT leads from the old cap one at a time and fit them to the new cap in the same location – do not simultaneously remove all the leads from the old cap, or firing order confusion may occur. Note that a new gasket should also be used when refitting the cap.

9 Even with the ignition system in first class condition, some engines may still occasionally experience poor starting attributable to damp ignition components.

24 Manual gearbox oil level check

1 Position the car over an inspection pit, on car ramps, or jack it up (and support it securely using axle stands) but make sure that it is level. Where necessary, remove the undershield(s).

2 Unscrew the filler/level plug from the front face of the gearbox.

3 Feel inside the hole with your finger (or make up a gauge using a piece of wire, or welding rod, bent at 90° and suitably marked) and check that the oil level is not more than 5 mm below the bottom of the hole (Fig. 1.18).

4 If the level is low, add the specified oil through the filler/level hole until it begins to trickle out of the hole (photo).

5 Allow time for the oil level to settle then refit the filler/level plug and tighten it securely.

6 If the gearbox requires frequent topping up, check it for leakage (paying special attention to the driveshaft oil seals) and rectify any defects found.

7 Where necessary, refit the undershield(s) and lower the vehicle to the ground.

25 Automatic transmission fluid level check

1 The automatic transmission fluid level should be checked after the vehicle has been driven in a normal manner over 10 miles (16 km) in normal temperatures, or over 15 miles (24 km) in cold temperatures. This will ensure that the transmission fluid is up to its normal operating temperature.

2 With the vehicle parked on a level surface (in a well ventilated area), and the handbrake applied, start the engine and depress the brake pedal. Move the transmission selector lever through its range, from 'P' to 'L' and back to 'P'.

3 With the engine still idling, pull the transmission fluid dipstick out from its guide tube (near the battery) and wipe it clean. Reinsert the dipstick as far as it will go then withdraw it and observe the fluid level; the level should be within the HOT range

(Fig. 1.19). If the fluid is black or smells burnt, fluid renewal is required.

4 If topping up is required, add the specified fluid slowly through the transmission fluid dipstick tube, with the aid of a suitable funnel; take care not to overfill the transmission or damage may occur (check the fluid level frequently after adding small amounts and allowing it time to run down into the transmission sump).

5 Refit the dipstick upon completion.

6 If the transmission requires frequent topping up, this is an indication that leakage is occurring; inspect the transmission and carry out/arrange for any rectification work necessary immediately.

26 Differential (final drive) fluid level check – automatic transmission models

1 Position the car over an inspection pit, on car ramps, or jack it up (and support it securely using axle stands) but make sure that it is level. Where applicable remove the undershield(s).

2 Unscrew the filler/level plug (Fig. 1.20).

3 Feel inside the hole with your finger (or make up a gauge using a piece of wire, or welding rod, bent at 90°and suitably marked) and check that the fluid level is not more than 5 mm below the bottom of the filler/level hole.

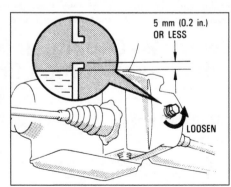

Fig. 1.20 Differential (final drive) fluid level checking – (automatic transmission models) (Sec 26)

4 If the level is low, add the specified fluid through the filler/level hole until it begins to trickle out of the hole.

5 Allow time for the oil level to settle then refit the filler/level plug and tighten it securely.

6 If the differential (final drive) requires frequent topping up, check it for leakage (paying special attention to the driveshaft oil seals) and rectify any defects found.

7 Where applicable, refit the undershield(s) and lower the vehicle to the ground.

27 Driveshaft rubber gaiter and CV joint check

1 With the vehicle raised and securely supported on stands, turn the steering onto full lock then slowly rotate the roadwheel. Inspect the condition of the outer constant velocity (CV) joint rubber gaiters while squeezing the gaiters to open out the folds. Check for signs of cracking, splits or deterioration of the rubber which may allow the grease to escape and lead to water and grit entry into the joint. Also check the security and condition of the retaining clips. Repeat these checks on the inner CV joints. If any damage or deterioration is found, the gaiters should be renewed as described in Chapter 8.

2 At the same time check the general condition of the CV joints themselves by first holding the driveshaft and attempting to rotate the wheel. Repeat this check by holding the inner joint and attempting to rotate the driveshaft. Any appreciable movement indicates wear in the joints, wear in the driveshaft splines or loose driveshaft retaining nut.

28 Brake shoe wear check

1 Remove the rear brake drums as described in Chapter 9 and clean away any dust accumulation using a clean damp cloth (taking care not to inhale any).

2 Compare the thickness of the remaining friction material on each of the brake shoes with the minimum thickness specified. If any brake shoe is close to or less than the specified minimum thickness, all four brake

shoes must be renewed as an axle set as described in Chapter 9. Renewal will also be required if evidence of friction material contamination is found.

3 Inspect the rear brake drums as described in Chapter 9 before refitting them.

4 Fully tighten the rear roadwheel nuts (to their specified torque) with the vehicle resting on its roadwheels.

5 Dispose of the cloth safely.

29 Suspension and steering check

Front suspension and steering

1 Raise the front of the vehicle and securely support it on axle stands.

2 Visually inspect the balljoint dust covers and the steering rack and pinion gaiters for splits, chafing or deterioration. Any wear of these components will cause loss of lubricant together with dirt and water entry, resulting in rapid deterioration of the balljoints or steering gear.

3 On vehicles equipped with power steering, check the fluid hoses for chafing or deterioration and the pipe and hose unions for fluid leaks. Also check for signs of fluid leakage under pressure from the steering gear rubber gaiters which would indicate failed fluid seals within the steering gear.

4 Grasp the roadwheel at the 12 o'clock and 6 o'clock positions and try to rock it. Very slight free play may be felt, but if the movement is appreciable further investigation is necessary to determine the source. Continue rocking the wheel while an assistant depresses the footbrake. If the movement is now eliminated or significantly reduced, it is likely that the hub bearings are at fault. If the free play is still evident with the footbrake depressed, then there is wear in the suspension joints or mountings.

5 Now grasp the wheel at the 9 o'clock and 3 o'clock positions and try to rock it as before. Any movement felt now may again be caused by wear in the hub bearings or the steering track rod balljoints. If the outer balljoint is worn the visual movement will be obvious. If the inner joint is suspect it can be felt by

placing a hand over the rack and pinion rubber gaiter and gripping the track rod. If the wheel is now rocked, movement will be felt at the inner joint if wear has taken place.

6 Using a large screwdriver or flat bar check for wear in the suspension mounting bushes by levering between the relevant suspension component and its attachment point. Some movement is to be expected as the mountings are made of rubber, but excessive wear should be obvious. Also check the condition of any visible rubber bushes, looking for splits, cracks or contamination of the rubber.

7 With the car standing on its wheels, have an assistant turn the steering wheel back and forth about an eighth of a turn each way. There should be very little, if any, lost movement between the steering wheel and roadwheels. If this is not the case, closely observe the joints and mountings previously described, but in addition check the steering column universal joints for wear and check the rack and pinion steering gear itself.

Rear suspension

8 Chock the front wheels then jack up the rear of the vehicle and support it on axle stands. Referring to the information given for the front suspension, check all the rear suspension components in a similar manner.

Suspension strut/shock absorber check

9 Check for any signs of fluid leakage around the suspension strut/shock absorber body or from the rubber gaiter around the piston rod. Should any fluid be noticed, the suspension strut/shock absorber is defective internally and should be renewed. **Note:** *Suspension struts/shock absorbers should always be renewed in pairs on the same axle.*

10 The efficiency of the suspension strut/shock absorber may be checked by bouncing the vehicle at each corner. Generally speaking the body will return to its normal position and stop after being depressed. If it rises and returns on a rebound, the suspension strut/shock absorber is probably suspect. Examine the suspension strut/shock absorber upper and lower mountings for any signs of wear.

Every 24 000 miles (40 000 km) or 2 years - whichever comes first

30 Coolant renewal

 Warning: Wait until the engine is cold before starting this procedure. Do not allow antifreeze to come in contact with your skin or painted surfaces of the vehicle. Rinse off spills immediately with plenty of water.

Draining

1 If the engine is cold, unscrew and remove the pressure cap from the radiator. If it is not possible to wait until the engine is cold, place a cloth over the pressure cap and slowly unscrew it. Wait until all pressure has escaped, then remove the cap.

2 Drain plugs are provided on the radiator and the engine, and suitable containers should be placed beneath these to catch the

flow of escaping coolant prior to opening them; disconnecting the bottom hose from the radiator is another alternative (but less thorough) method (photos).

3 With all the coolant drained into the containers, tighten the drain plugs and reconnect the bottom hose to the radiator (if applicable); if the system needs to be flushed after draining refer to the following sub-section.

4 When draining the cooling system, do not

30.2A Slackening off the coolant drain plug (arrowed) on the engine

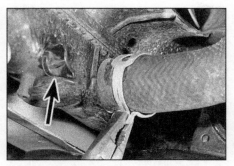

30.2B Releasing the radiator bottom hose securing clip. Note the radiator drain plug (arrowed)

30.10 Refilling the cooling system after draining

forget about the coolant in the expansion tank: refer to Chapter 3 regarding expansion tank removal and refitting. The heater hoses and matrix also contain engine coolant, although no recommendations are made to attend to this as the relatively small amount of coolant will circulate back into the main volume of coolant in the engine during heater usage.

System flushing

5 With time the cooling system may gradually lose its efficiency if the radiator matrix becomes choked with rust and scale deposits. If this is the case, the system must be flushed as follows. First drain the coolant as described above.

6 Loosen the clip and disconnect the top hose from the radiator. Insert a garden hose in the radiator top hose connection stub and allow the water to circulate through the radiator until it runs clear from the bottom outlet.

7 To flush the engine and the remainder of the system, first remove the thermostat as described in Chapter 3 (temporarily refitting its housing to enable the water to run out through the disconnected bottom coolant hose and not all over the gearbox/transmission housing) then insert a garden hose into the top coolant hose and allow the water to circulate through the engine until it runs clear from the bottom hose. Refit the thermostat (Chapter 3).

8 In severe cases of contamination the radiator should be reverse flushed. To do this, first remove it from the car, as described in Chapter 3, invert it and insert a hose into its bottom hose connection. Continue flushing until clear water runs from its top hose connection.

9 If, after a reasonable period, the water still does not run clear, the radiator should be flushed with a good proprietary cleaning system. The regular renewal of corrosion inhibiting antifreeze should prevent severe contamination of the system. Note that the radiator should **not** be cleaned using caustic soda or alkaline compounds.

Refilling

10 With all drain plugs secured, and all hoses reconnected and secured (where applicable), pour the specified mixture of water and antifreeze into the system through the

pressure cap opening in the radiator until the level of coolant in the system can be seen in the radiator (photo). Start the engine then top up the radiator and also half fill the expansion tank, refitting the pressure cap and the expansion tank cap as soon as this is done.

11 Run the engine up to normal operating temperature and check for signs of leakage, then switch off. Check the coolant level in the expansion tank once the system has cooled down, topping up as necessary.

Antifreeze mixture

12 The antifreeze should always be renewed at the specified intervals. This is necessary not only to maintain the antifreeze properties, but also to prevent corrosion which would otherwise occur as the corrosion inhibitors become progressively less effective.

13 Always use an ethylene-glycol based antifreeze which is suitable for use in mixed metal cooling systems. The quantity of antifreeze and levels of protection are indicated in the Specifications.

14 Before adding antifreeze the cooling system should be completely drained, preferably flushed, and all hoses checked for condition and security.

15 After filling with antifreeze, a label should be attached to the radiator or expansion tank stating the type and concentration of antifreeze used and the date installed. Any subsequent topping up should be made with

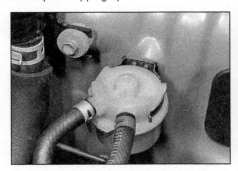

31.2 Fuel filter fitted to carburettor engined vehicles

the same type and concentration of antifreeze.

16 Do not use engine antifreeze in the screen washer system, as it will cause damage to the vehicle paintwork. A screen wash should be added to the washer system in the recommended quantities.

31 Fuel filter renewal

> ⚠ **Warning: Refer to Section 9 for fuel system precautions**

1 Disconnect the battery earth terminal.

2 On carburettor equipped models, the fuel filter is clipped to a bracket on the engine compartment bulkhead. To renew the filter, note the correct fitted positions of the fuel hoses, disconnect them and plug the ends to minimise fuel loss. Unclip the filter from its retaining bracket and remove it from the car (photo).

3 On fuel-injected models, the fuel filter is located in the left-hand rear corner of the engine compartment. To remove the filter, slacken and remove the filter union bolts, referring to the warning given at the start of this Section, then disconnect the hoses from the filter and remove the sealing washers. Plug the hose ends to minimise fuel loss then undo the two retaining bolts and remove the fuel filter from the vehicle (photo).

31.3 Fuel filter fined to fuel injection engined vehicles. Note the filter retaining bolts (arrowed)

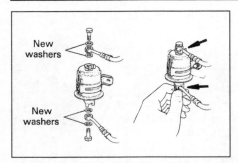

Fig. 1.21 fit new sealing washers each side of the hose unions – ensure hose unions are correctly positioned between locating pins (arrowed) (Sec 31)

4 Refitting is a reversal of the removal procedure. On fuel-injected models, position a new sealing washer on each side of the hose unions and ensure that the hose union is positioned between the locating pins on the filter (Fig. 1.21).

32 Transmission lubricant renewal

Manual gearbox

1 Position the car over an inspection pit, on car ramps, or jack it up (and support it securely using axle stands) but make sure that it is level. Where necessary remove the undershield(s).
2 Remove the filler/level plug (Fig. 1.18).
3 Position a suitable container beneath the oil drain plug, then remove the drain plug; try to hold it in as it is unscrewed the last few turns, then move it away sharply so that the oil flows into the container and not up your sleeve! (photo).
4 Once the oil has fully drained (it may be necessary to reposition the container as the flow slows down) refit the drain plug, using a new sealing washer (where fitted), and tighten it securely.
5 Fill the gearbox with the specified type and amount of oil through the filler/level hole. Add the oil slowly until it begins to trickle out of the hole.
6 Allow the oil level to settle then refit and tighten the filler/level plug.
7 Check for signs of leakage (paying special attention to the driveshaft oil seals), and rectify any defects found.
8 Where necessary, refit the undershield(s) and lower the vehicle to the ground.

Automatic transmission

9 Open the bonnet and remove the transmission fluid dipstick (near the battery).
10 Position the car over an inspection pit, on

32.3 Draining the oil from a manual gearbox

car ramps, or jack it up (and support it securely using axle stands) but make sure that it is level. Where necessary remove the undershield(s).
11 Position a suitable container beneath the transmission fluid drain plug, then unscrew it.
12 Once the fluid has fully drained, refit the drain plug using a new sealing washer (where fitted), and tighten it securely.
13 Add the specified fluid slowly through the transmission fluid dipstick tube, with the aid of a suitable funnel; take care not to overfill the transmission or damage may occur (check the fluid level frequently after adding small amounts and allowing it time to run down into the transmission sump). The 'drain and refill operation' fluid quantity is given in the *'Lubricants, fluids and capacities'* information at the beginning of this Chapter.
14 Start the engine and move the transmission selector lever through its range, from 'P' to 'L' and back to 'P' (with the handbrake on and the brake pedal depressed).
15 With the engine idling, check the fluid level and add fluid (if necessary) to bring it up to the COOL level on the dipstick (Fig. 1.19).
16 Refit the dipstick upon completion, and check the transmission to ensure that there is no fluid leakage.
17 Refit the engine undershield(s), if applicable, and lower the vehicle to the ground.
18 Take the vehicle on a short run and check the transmission fluid level.

33 Differential (final drive) fluid renewal – automatic transmission models

1 Position the car over an inspection pit, on car ramps, or jack it up (and support it securely using axle stands) but make sure that it is level. Where applicable remove the undershield(s).

2 Unscrew the filler/level plug (Fig. 1.20).
3 Position a suitable container beneath the transmission fluid drain plug, then unscrew it.
4 Once the fluid has fully drained, refit the drain plug using a new sealing washer (where fitted), and tighten it securely.
5 If the level is low, add the specified type and quantity of fluid through the filler/level hole. Add the oil slowly until it begins to trickle out of the hole.
6 Allow time for the oil level to settle then refit the filler/level plug and tighten it securely.
7 Where necessary, refit the undershield(s) and lower the vehicle to the ground.
8 Take the vehicle on a short run then check the oil level.

34 Brake fluid renewal

1 The procedure is similar to that for the bleeding of the hydraulic system as described in Chapter 9, except that the brake fluid reservoir should be emptied by syphoning, using a clean poultry baster or similar before starting, and allowance should be made for the old fluid to be removed from the circuit when bleeding a section of the circuit.

35 Underbody and general body check

1 With the car raised and supported on axle stands, or over an inspection pit, thoroughly inspect the underbody and wheel arches for signs of damage and corrosion. In particular examine concealed areas where mud can collect. Where corrosion and rust is evident, press firmly on the panel by hand and check for possible repairs. If the panel is not seriously corroded, first clean away the rust, treat it (where possible) and apply a new coating of underseal. Refer to Chapter 11 for more details of body repairs.
2 Check all external body panels for damage and rectify where necessary.
3 Check the security of all nuts and bolts on the chassis and body, and tighten as necessary; make reference to the Specifications at the beginning of the appropriate Chapters for tightening torque details, where applicable.
4 Whilst attending to the security of the body and chassis nuts and bolts, note that the hinges and locks should be examined for correct operation and any defects rectified; lubricating hinges and locks on a regular basis ensures longer trouble free life, and assists smooth operation.k

Chapter 2 Engine

Contents

Degrees of difficulty

| **Easy,** suitable for novice with little experience | **Fairly easy,** suitable for beginner with some experience | **Fairly difficult,** suitable for competent DIY mechanic 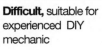 | **Difficult,** suitable for experienced DIY mechanic | **Very difficult,** suitable for expert DIY or professional |

Specifications

Part A: 1296 cc 2E engine

Engine (general)

Type	Four-cylinder, in-line, single overhead camshaft
Bore	73.0 mm
Stroke	77.4 mm
Capacity	1296 cc
Firing order	1-3-4-2 (No 1 cylinder at timing cover end)
Direction of crankshaft rotation	Clockwise
Compression ratio	9.5 : 1
Compression pressure – @ 250 rpm:	
Standard	12.75 bars
Minimum	9.81 bars
Maximum compression pressure difference between cylinders	0.98 bar
Maximum torque – ECE 15-04	103 Nm @ 4200 rpm
Maximum power – ECE 15-04	74 bhp @ 6200 rpm

Crankshaft

Number of main bearings	5
Main bearing journal diameter:	
Standard	46.985 to 47.000 mm
Undersize (0.25 mm)	46.735 to 46.750 mm
Main bearing journal running clearance:	
Standard	0.016 to 0.049 mm
Maximum	0.080 mm
Crankpin (big-end) journal diameter:	
Standard	39.985 to 40.000 mm
Undersize (0.25 mm)	39.735 to 39.750 mm
Crankpin (big-end) journal running clearance:	
Standard	0.016 to 0.048 mm
Maximum	0.080 mm
Crankshaft endfloat:	
Standard	0.02 to 0.22 mm
Maximum	0.30 mm
Thrustwasher thickness:	
Standard	2.440 to 2.490 mm
Oversize	2.503 to 2.553 mm
Maximum run-out – at centre main bearing journal	0.06 mm
Connecting rod big-end cap-to-crankshaft web thrust clearance (endfloat):	
Standard	0.15 to 0.35 mm
Maximum	0.45 mm

Pistons and piston rings

Piston diameter – at right angles to gudgeon pin, 23 mm below piston crown:	
Standard	72.91 to 72.94 mm
Oversize (0.25 mm)	73.16 to 73.19 mm
Piston-to-bore clearance:	
Standard	0.08 to 0.10 mm
Maximum	0.20 mm
Piston ring installed end gaps – 100 mm from top of bore:	
Top compression ring:	
Standard	0.26 to 0.49 mm
Maximum	1.09 mm
Second compression ring:	
Standard	0.15 to 0.43 mm
Maximum	1.03 mm
Oil control ring:	
Standard	0.20 to 0.83 mm
Maximum	1.43 mm
Piston ring-to-groove clearance:	
Top compression ring	0.04 to 0.08 mm
Second compression ring	0.03 to 0.07 mm

Gudgeon pins

Matched individually to piston. Fully-floating fit in piston, interference fit in connecting rod

Cylinder block

Material	Cast iron
Bore diameter:	
Standard	73.00 to 73.03 mm
Oversize (0.25 mm)	73.25 to 73.28 mm
Maximum bore wear	0.20 mm
Maximum gasket face warpage	0.05 mm

Cylinder head

Material	Cast aluminium alloy
Maximum gasket face warpage	0.05 mm
Valve seat angle	45°
Valve seat width	1.2 to 1.6 mm
Seat cutter correction angle:	
Upper – inlet	75°
Upper – exhaust	60°
Lower	30°

Camshaft

Drive	Toothed belt
Number of bearings	4
Bearing journal diameter	26.979 to 26.995 mm
Bearing journal running clearance:	
Standard	0.037 to 0.073 mm
Maximum	0.100 mm
Camshaft endfloat (thrust clearance):	
Standard	0.08 to 0.18 mm
Maximum	0.25 mm
Maximum run-out – at centre bearing journal	0.04 mm
Cam lobe height:	
Inlet – main:	
Standard	35.87 to 35.97 mm
Minimum	35.67 mm
Inlet – sub:	
Standard	35.38 to 35.48 mm
Minimum	35.18 mm
Exhaust:	
Standard	35.83 to 35.93 mm
Minimum	35.63 mm

Valves

Operation	Via rocker arms, from overhead camshaft
Face angle	44.5°
Length:	
Inlet – main:	
Standard	92.26 mm
Minimum	91.76 mm
Inlet – sub:	
Standard	98.50 mm
Minimum	98.00 mm
Exhaust:	
Standard	92.26 mm
Minimum	91.76 mm
Head margin (edge) thickness:	
Standard	1.0 mm
Minimum	0.8 mm
Stem diameter:	
Inlet	5.970 to 5.985 mm
Exhaust	5.965 to 5.980 mm
Stem-to-guide clearance:	
Inlet:	
Standard	0.025 to 0.060 mm
Maximum	0.080 mm
Exhaust:	
Standard	0.030 to 0.065 mm
Maximum	0.100 mm
Spring free length	41.52 mm
Guide internal diameter	6.01 to 6.03 mm

Lubrication system

System pressure – at normal operating temperature:
  At idle speed .... At least 0.29 bar
  At 3000 rpm .... 4.9 bars
Oil pump type .... Eccentric rotor, driven by timing belt
Oil pump clearances:
  Outer rotor-to-pump body clearance:
    Standard .... 0.10 to 0.16 mm
    Maximum .... 0.20 mm
Oil pump clearances:
  Rotor side clearance (endfloat):
    Standard .... 0.03 to 0.09 mm
    Maximum .... 0.10 mm
  Inner rotor-to-outer rotor tip clearance:
    Standard .... 0.06 to 0.16 mm
    Maximum .... 0.20 mm

Torque wrench settings

	Nm	lbf ft
Main bearing cap bolts	57	42
Connecting rod big-end cap nuts	39	29
Cylinder head bolts – see text:		
Stage 1	29	22
Stage 2	49	36
Stage 3	Tighten through 90°	
Sump drain plug	25	18
Sump nuts and bolts	8.3	6.1
Oil pick-up pipe/strainer bolts	7.4	5
Oil pressure regulator valve	29	22
Oil pump bolts	7.4	5
Oil pump toothed pulley nut	26	20
Camshaft bearing cap bolts	14	10
Camshaft toothed pulley bolt	50	37
Timing belt tensioner pulley bolt	18	13
Timing belt idler pulley bolt	20	14
Crankshaft pulley bolt	98 to 147	72 to 108
Crankshaft left-hand oil seal housing bolts	7.4	5
Flywheel/driveplate-to-crankshaft bolts	83	61
Engine lifting eye fasteners:		
Forward side of cylinder head	21	15
Gearbox/transmission end of cylinder head	43	32
Engine mountings:		
Insulator bolt	78	58
Left-hand end plate:		
10 mm bolt	24	17
8 mm bolt	11	8
Central mountings-to-crossmember assembly	61	45

Part B: 1587 cc 4A-F engine

Engine (general)

Type .... Four-cylinder, in-line, twin overhead camshaft
Bore .... 81.0 mm
Stroke .... 77.0 mm
Capacity .... 1587 cc
Firing order .... 1-3-4-2 (No 1 cylinder at timing cover end)
Direction of crankshaft rotation .... Clockwise
Compression ratio .... 9.5 : 1
Compression pressure – @ 250 rpm:
  Standard .... 13.24 bars
  Minimum .... 9.81 bars
  Maximum compression pressure difference between cylinders ..... 0.98 bar
Maximum torque – ECE 15-04 .... 136 Nm @ 3600 rpm
Maximum power – ECE 15-04 .... 94 bhp @ 6000 rpm

Cylinder block

Material .... Cast iron
Bore diameter:
  Standard .... 81.00 to 81.03 mm
  Oversize (0.5 mm) .... 81.50 to 81.53 mm
Maximum bore wear .... 0.20 mm
Maximum gasket face warpage .... 0.05 mm

Crankshaft

Number of main bearings	5
Main bearing journal diameter:	
Standard	47.982 to 48.000 mm
Undersize (0.25 mm)	47.745 to 47.755 mm
Main bearing journal running clearance:	
Standard	0.015 to 0.033 mm
Undersize (0.25 mm)	0.013 to 0.053 mm
Maximum	0.100 mm
Crankpin (big-end) journal diameter:	
Standard	39.985 to 40.000 mm
Undersize (0.25 mm)	39.745 to 39.755 mm
Crankpin (big-end) journal running clearance:	
Standard	0.020 to 0.051 mm
Undersize (0.25 mm)	0.019 to 0.073 mm
Maximum	0.080 mm
Main bearing and crankpin (big-end) journals maximum taper and ovality	0.02 mm
Crankshaft endfloat:	
Standard	0.02 to 0.22 mm
Maximum	0.30 mm
Thrustwasher thickness	2.440 to 2.490 mm
Maximum run-out – at centre main bearing journal	0.06 mm
Connecting rod big-end cap-to-crankshaft web thrust clearance (endfloat):	
Standard	0.15 to 0.25 mm
Maximum	0.30 mm

Valves

Operation	Direct from camshaft lobes, via inverted camshaft followers (buckets), clearance adjusted by shims
Face angle	45.5°
Length:	
Inlet:	
Standard	91.45 mm
Minimum	90.95 mm
Exhaust:	
Standard	91.90 mm
Minimum	91.40 mm
Head margin (edge) thickness:	
Standard	0.8 to 1.2 mm
Minimum	0.5 mm
Stem diameter	
Inlet	5.970 to 5.985 mm
Exhaust	5.965 to 5.980 mm
Stem-to-guide clearance:	
Inlet:	
Standard	0.025 to 0.060 mm
Maximum	0.080 mm
Exhaust:	
Standard	0.030 to 0.065 mm
Maximum	0.100 mm
Spring free length	43.8 mm
Guide internal diameter	6.01 to 6.03 mm
Guide fitted height	12.7 to 13.1 mm

Cylinder head

Material	Cast aluminium alloy
Thickness	95.3 mm
Maximum gasket face warpage:	
Exhaust manifold face	0.10 mm
All other faces	0.05 mm
Valve seat angle	45°
Valve seat width	1.0 to 1.4 mm
Seat cutter correction angle:	
Upper	60°
Lower	30°
Camshaft follower bore diameter	28.00 to 28.021 mm
Spark plug tube fitted height	46.6 to 47.4 mm

Camshaft

Drive . . . . Toothed belt to exhaust camshaft, anti-backlash gears from exhaust to inlet camshafts

Number of bearings . . . . 5 per camshaft

Bearing journal diameter:
   Exhaust camshaft right-hand bearing . . . . 24.949 to 24.965 mm
   All others . . . . 22.949 to 22.965 mm

Bearing journal running clearance:
   Standard . . . . 0.035 to 0.072 mm
   Maximum . . . . 0.100 mm

Camshaft endfloat (thrust clearance):
   Standard – inlet . . . . 0.030 to 0.085 mm
   Standard – exhaust . . . . 0.035 to 0.090 mm
   Maximum . . . . 0.110 mm

Maximum run-out – at centre bearing journal . . . . 0.04 mm

Gear backlash:
   Standard . . . . 0.020 to 0.200 mm
   Maximum . . . . 0.300 mm

Distance between free ends of inlet camshaft sub-gear spring . . . . . . 17.1 to 17.5 mm

Cam lobe height:
   Inlet:
      Standard . . . . 35.21 to 35.31 mm
      Minimum . . . . 34.81 mm
   Exhaust:
      Standard . . . . 34.91 to 35.01 mm
      Minimum . . . . 34.51 mm

Camshaft follower diameter . . . . 27.975 to 27.985 mm

Follower-to-cylinder head bore clearance:
   Standard . . . . 0.015 to 0.046 mm
   Maximum . . . . 0.100 mm

Pistons and piston rings

Piston diameter – at right angles to gudgeon pin, 38.5 mm above skirt base:
   Standard . . . . 80.93 to 80.96 mm
   Oversize (0.50 mm) . . . . 81.43 to 81.46 mm

Piston-to-bore clearance . . . . 0.06 to 0.08 mm

Piston ring installed end gaps – 87 mm from top of bore:
   Top compression ring:
      Standard . . . . 0.25 to 0.35 mm
      Maximum . . . . 1.07 mm
   Second compression ring:
      Standard . . . . 0.15 to 0.30 mm
      Maximum . . . . 1.02 mm
   Oil control ring:
      Standard . . . . 0.10 to 0.60 mm
      Maximum . . . . 1.62 mm

Piston ring-to-groove clearance:
   Top compression ring . . . . 0.04 to 0.08 mm
   Second compression ring . . . . 0.03 to 0.07 mm

Gudgeon pins . . . . Matched individually to piston. Fully-floating fit in piston, interference fit In connecting rod

Lubrication system

System pressure – at normal operating temperature:
   At idle speed . . . . At least 0.29 bar
   At 3000 rpm . . . . 4.9 bars

Oil pump type . . . . Trochoidal rotor, driven from crankshaft

Oil pump clearances:
   Outer rotor-to-pump body clearance:
      Standard . . . . 0.080 to 0.135 mm
      Maximum . . . . 0.200 mm
   Rotor side clearance (endfloat):
      Standard . . . . 0.025 to 0.065 mm
      Maximum . . . . 0.100 mm
   Inner rotor-to-outer rotor tip clearance:
      Standard . . . . 0.116 to 0.156 mm
      Maximum . . . . 0.350 mm

Torque wrench settings

	Nm	lbf ft
Main bearing cap bolts	60	44
Connecting rod big-end cap nuts	49	36
Cylinder head bolts	60	44
Sump drain plug	34	25
Sump nuts and bolts	4.9	3.6
Oil pick-up pipe/strainer nuts and bolts	9.3	6.9
Oil pressure regulator valve hexagon-headed plug	37	27
Oil filter bracket/oil pressure regulator valve housing double-threaded stud	44	33
Oil pump bolts	21	16
Oil pump body cover screws	10	8
Camshaft bearing cap bolts	13	9
Camshaft toothed pulley bolt	47	34
Timing belt tensioner pulley bolt	37	27
Crankshaft pulley bolt	118	87
Oil cooler pipe union bolt (on the combined bracket/housing)	29	22
Crankshaft left-hand oil seal housing bolts	9.3	6.9
Flywheel-to-crankshaft bolts – manual gearbox	78	58
Driveplate-to-crankshaft bolts – automatic transmission	64	47
Alternator bracket bolts	49	36
Engine lifting eye fasteners	27	20
Engine mountings:		
Right-hand bracket-to-cylinder block	49	36
Insulator bolt	78	58
Left-hand end plate:		
10 mm bolt	24	17
8 mm bolt	11	8
Central mountings-to-crossmember assembly	61	45

Part C: 1587 cc 4A-GE engine

Note: *Information is given ONLY where different from that given above for the 4A-F engine.*

Engine (general)

Compression ratio	10.0: 1
Compression pressure – @ 250 rpm:	
Standard – early models	12.36 bars
Standard – later models	13.14 bars
Maximum torque – ECE 15-04	145 Nm @ 5000 rpm
Maximum power – ECE 15-04	123 bhp @ 6600 rpm

Crankshaft

Crankpin (big-end) journal diameter:	
Standard	41.985 to 42.000 mm
Undersize (0.25 mm)	41.745 to 41.755 mm

Pistons and piston rings

Piston diameter – at right angles to gudgeon pin, 42 mm above skirt base:	
Standard	80.89 to 80.92 mm
Oversize (0.50 mm)	81.39 to 81.42 mm
Piston-to-bore clearance	0.10 to 0.12 mm
Piston ring installed end gaps – 87 mm from top of bore:	
Top compression ring:	
Standard	0.25 to 0.47 mm
Maximum	1.07 mm
Second compression ring:	
Standard	0.20 to 0.42 mm
Maximum	1.02 mm
Oil control ring:	
Standard	0.15 to 0.52 mm
Maximum	1.12 mm

Gudgeon pins

Diameter	20.006 to 20.016 mm (matched for clearance fit in the connecting rod small-end bush)
Small-end bush inside diameter	20.012 to 20.022 mm
Gudgeon pin-to-bush clearance:	
Standard	0.004 to 0.008 mm
Maximum	0.05 mm
Fit to piston	Push (at piston temperature of 80° C)

Camshaft

Drive	Toothed belt
Bearing journal diameter	26.949 to 26.965 mm

Camshaft endfloat (thrust clearance):
Standard	0.08 to 0.19 mm
Maximum	0.30 mm

Cam lobe height:
Standard.	35.41 to 35.51 mm
Minimum	35.11 mm

Follower-to-cylinder head bore clearance:
Standard	0.015 to 0.046 mm
Maximum	0.070 mm

Valves

	Standard	Minimum
Face angle . . . . 44.5°		
Length:	**Standard**	**Minimum**
Inlet:	99.60 mm	99.10 mm
Exhaust	99.75 mm	99.25 mm
Spring free length	41.09 mm	

Lubrication system

Oil pump type:
Up to September 1989	Trochoidal gear and crescent
September 1989 on	As 4A-F

Gear-type pump clearances:

Outer gear-to-pump body clearance:
Standard	0.100 to 0.191 mm
Maximum	0.200 mm

Gear side clearance (endfloat):
Standard	0.025 to 0.075 mm
Maximum	0.100 mm

Gear tip-to-crescent clearance:
Inner gear – standard	0.107 to 0.248 mm
Outer gear – standard	0.058 to 0.310 mm
Both gears – maximum	0.350 mm

Rotor-type pump clearances:

Outer rotor-to-pump body clearance:
Standard	0.100 to 0.191 mm
Maximum	0.200 mm

Rotor side clearance (endfloat):
Standard	0.025 to 0.075 mm
Maximum	0.100 mm

Inner rotor-to-outer rotor tip clearance:
Standard	0.060 to 0.180 mm
Maximum	0.350 mm

Torque wrench settings

	Nm	lbf ft
Connecting rod big-end cap nuts:		
Hexagonal nuts	49	36
12-sided nuts – see text	39	29
Cylinder head bolts – see text:		
Stage 1	29	22
Stage 2	Tighten through 90	
Stage 3	Tighten through a further 90°	
Union-to-cylinder head	29	22
Combined oil filter bracket/oil pressure regulator valve housing double-threaded stud	54	40
Timing end cover bolts	9.3	6.9
Camshaft toothed pulley bolts	59	43
Crankshaft pulley bolt	137	101
Flywheel-to-crankshaft bolts	74	54
Oil nozzles-to-cylinder block	25	18
Oil cooler pipe union bolts:		
To combined bracket/housing	29	22
To sump	25	18
Camshaft cover nuts	13	9
Right-hand mounting-to-cylinder block (main bracket only type)	25	18
Right-hand mounting main section-to-cylinder block (main and upper section type)	39	29
Right-hand mounting upper section-to-cylinder block (main and upper section type)	21	15

Part A: 1296 cc 2E engine – in-car engine repair procedures

1 General information

How to use this Chapter

This Part describes those repair procedures for the 1296 cc 2E engine that can reasonably be carried out on the engine while it remains in the car. Similar information covering the 1587 cc 4A-F and 4A-GE engines will be found in Parts B and C respectively. If the engine has been removed from the car and is being dismantled as described in Part D, any preliminary dismantling procedures can be ignored.

Note that while it may be possible physically to overhaul items such as the piston/connecting rod assemblies while the engine is in the car, such tasks are not usually carried out as separate operations and usually require the execution of several additional procedures (not to mention the cleaning of components and of oilways), for this reason all such tasks are classed as major overhaul procedures and are described in Part D.

Part D describes the removal of the engine/transmission unit from the car and the full overhaul procedures that can then be carried out.

For ease of reference, all specifications are given in the one Specifications Section at the beginning of the Chapter.

Engine description

The liquid-cooled, 4-stroke engine has four cylinders in-line, uses a cast iron cylinder block and an aluminium alloy cylinder head and is mounted transversely. It is of single overhead camshaft design, with two inlet valves and one exhaust valve per cylinder; the valves being controlled by end-pivoting rocker arms. The camshaft is belt-driven from the crankshaft toothed pulley and is supported in four bearings; the fuel pump and distributor are driven from the camshaft whilst the oil pump is driven by the timing belt. The cast iron crankshaft runs in five main bearings, endfloat being controlled by thrustwashers at the central main bearing.

Repair operations possible with the engine in the car

The following work can be carried out with the engine in the car.
(a) Compression pressure – testing.
(b) Camshaft cover – removal and refitting.
(c) Crankshaft pulley – removal and refitting.
(d) Timing belt covers – removal and refitting.
(e) Timing belt – removal, refitting and adjustment.
(f) Timing belt tensioner – removal and refitting.
(g) Camshaft oil seal – renewal.
(h) Camshaft and rocker arms – removal, inspection and refitting.
(i) Cylinder head – removal and refitting.
(j) Cylinder head and pistons – decarbonising.
(k) Sump – removal and refitting.
(l) Oil pump – removal, overhaul and refitting.
(m) Crankshaft oil seals – renewal.
(n) Engine/transmission mountings – inspection and renewal.
(o) Flywheel/driveplate – removal, inspection and refitting.

2 Compression test – description and interpretation

1 A compression test will tell you what mechanical condition the upper end (pistons, rings, valves, head gasket) of the engine is in. Specifically, it can tell you if the compression is down due to leakage caused by worn piston rings, defective valves and seats or a blown head gasket. For the test to be accurate the engine must be at normal operating temperature and the battery must be fully charged.

2 Remove the spark plugs (Chapter 1).

3 Disconnect the coil HT lead from the centre of the distributor cap, and earth it on the cylinder block. Use a jumper lead or similar wire to make a good connection.

4 Fit the compression gauge into the No 1 spark plug hole.

5 Have your assistant hold the accelerator pedal fully depressed to the floor while at the same time cranking the engine over several times on the starter motor. Observe the compression gauge noting that the compression should build up quickly in a healthy engine. Low compression on the first stroke, followed by gradually increasing pressure on successive strokes, indicates worn piston rings. A low compression reading on the first stroke, which does not build up during successive strokes, indicates leaking valves or a blown head gasket (a cracked head could also be the cause). Deposits on the underside of the valve heads can also cause low compression. Record the highest gauge reading obtained, then repeat the procedure for the remaining cylinders.

6 Add some engine oil (about three squirts from a plunger-type oil can) to each cylinder through the spark plug hole, then repeat the test.

7 If the compression increases after the oil is added, the piston rings are definitely worn. If the compression does not increase significantly, the leakage is occurring at the valves or head gasket. Leakage past the valves may be caused by burned valve seats

and/or valve faces, or warped, cracked or bent valves.

8 If two adjacent cylinders have equally low compression, there is a strong possibility that the head gasket between them is blown. The appearance of coolant in the combustion chambers or the crankcase would verify this condition.

9 If the compression is unusually high, the combustion chambers are probably coated with carbon deposits. If this is the case, the cylinder head should be removed and decarbonised.

3 Top Dead Centre (TDC) for number one piston – locating

1 Remove the spark plugs (Chapter 1).

2 Remove the camshaft cover (Section 4).

3 Using a socket or spanner on the crankshaft pulley bolt, turn the crankshaft pulley clockwise (viewed from the right-hand side of the vehicle) until the pulley groove and the timing belt lower cover '0' mark align; it may be helpful to use white paint or similar carefully to highlight the pulley groove and the cover '0' mark.

4 Numbers one and four cylinders are now both at TDC, one of them being on the compression stroke.

5 Check that the rocker arms of number one cylinder (closest to the timing cover end of the engine) are loose (ie, the valves are closed) and that those of number four cylinder are tight (ie, these valves are partially open). If so, it is number one piston that is on the compression stroke and the crankshaft is now correctly positioned for work to begin; if number four is on the compression stroke, turn the crankshaft pulley one full turn further (again in a clockwise direction) to bring number one piston to TDC on the compression stroke.

6 Refit all disturbed components when finished.

4 Camshaft cover – removal and refitting
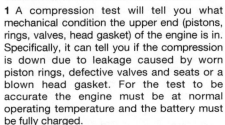

Removal

1 Remove the air filter housing/trunking (Chapter 4).

2 Disconnect the hoses from the camshaft cover.

3 Disconnect the HT leads from their locating clips, and release any other relevant wiring/hose clips.

4 Undo and remove the two dome nuts securing the camshaft cover (along with their insulators/seals), then release the mounting brace (where fitted), and carefully remove the cover and gasket.

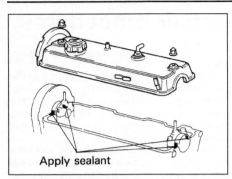

Apply sealant

Fig. 2.1 Apply suitable sealant to shaded areas on refitting camshaft cover (Sec 4)

Refitting

5 Ensure that the gasket is in good condition.
6 Refitting is a reversal of the removal procedure, but apply a little sealant to the cylinder head (Fig. 2.1) and ensure that the gasket seats correctly in the cover before the cover is fitted.

5 Crankshaft pulley – removal and refitting

Removal

1 Disconnect the battery earth terminal.
2 Slacken the right-hand roadwheel nuts, raise the front of the vehicle and support it securely on axle stands, then remove the roadwheel.
3 Remove the right-hand engine undershield (if fitted).
4 Slacken the crankshaft pulley bolt; if the bolt is tight the crankshaft can be locked by having an assistant select first gear and firmly applying the brakes.

5 Release the power steering pump and alternator/water pump drivebelts from the crankshaft pulley, as applicable (Chapter 1).
6 Remove the crankshaft pulley bolt and washer, then carefully lever the pulley off the end of the crankshaft. Note that to gain the necessary clearance to remove the pulley, it may be necessary to move the engine/transmission unit slightly. If so, support the engine using an engine support bar or a hoist, then disconnect the engine/transmission mounting(s) and move the engine slightly whilst taking great care not to strain or crush any wiring, hoses, pipes, linkages, etc. If the pulley is a tight fit on the crankshaft end it can be drawn off using a legged bearing puller.

Refitting

7 Refitting is a reversal of the removal procedure, noting the following points.
(a) Ensure the groove in the centre of the crankshaft pulley is aligned with the crankshaft Woodruff key.
(b) Lightly oil the threads and under the head of the pulley bolt before refitting it.
(c) Tighten the pulley bolt to its specified torque setting, holding the crankshaft by the method employed on removal.
(d) Refit the power steering pump and/or alternator/water pump drivebelt(s) (Chapter 7).

6 Timing belt covers – removal and refitting

Removal

Upper cover

1 Disconnect the battery earth terminal and remove the camshaft cover (Section 4).
2 On vehicles equipped with power steering,

disconnect the small hoses from the pump air control valve. Note the correct fitted positions of the hoses as a guide on refitting.
3 Unbolt and remove the upper cover.

Lower cover

4 Remove the upper cover, as described above.
5 Remove the crankshaft pulley (Section 5).
6 Unbolt and remove the lower cover.

Refitting

7 Refitting is a reversal of the removal procedure.

7 Timing belt – removal and refitting

Removal

1 Disconnect the battery earth terminal.
2 Set number one piston to TDC (Section 3) then remove the crankshaft pulley (Section 5); take care not to rotate the crankshaft.
3 Remove the timing belt upper and lower covers (Section 6).
4 Remove the timing belt guide from the crankshaft toothed pulley, noting which side faces the timing belt (photo).
5 If the timing belt is to be re-used, mark the alignment of the belt to the toothed pulleys and the direction of travel (ie, normal engine rotation) on the belt (Fig. 2.3).

7.4 Removing timing belt guide from crankshaft toothed pulley

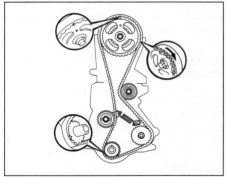

Fig. 2.3 Timing belt and toothed pulley alignment marks (Sec 7)

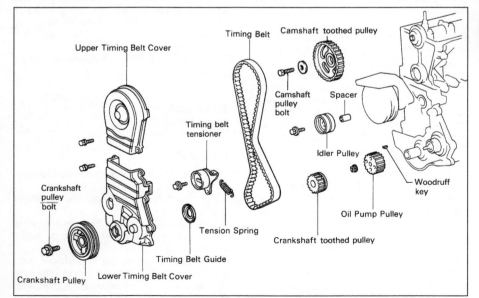

Upper Timing Belt Cover

Timing Belt

Camshaft toothed pulley

Camshaft pulley bolt

Spacer

Timing belt tensioner

Idler Pulley

Woodruff key

Crankshaft pulley bolt

Oil Pump Pulley

Tension Spring

Crankshaft toothed pulley

Timing Belt Guide

Crankshaft Pulley

Lower Timing Belt Cover

Fig. 2.2 Timing belt covers and toothed pulleys (Sec 7)

7.6 Slackening timing belt tensioner bolt to allow tensioner pulley to be moved

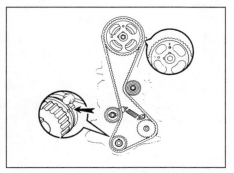

Fig. 2.4 Crankshaft toothed pulley and oil pump body TDC marks (Sec 7)

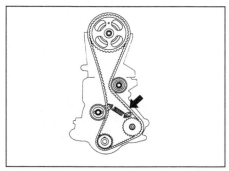

Fig. 2.5 Checking point for timing belt tension (Sec 7)

6 Slacken the timing belt tensioner bolt, then push the tensioner pulley away from the timing belt and temporarily retighten the bolt (photo).

7 Remove the timing belt. Do **not** alter the position of the camshaft or crankshaft toothed pulleys with the timing belt removed.

Refitting

8 In addition to the regular renewal called for as part of the normal service schedule (Chapter 1), the timing belt should be renewed, regardless of age or mileage, if it appears to be defective in any manner or if it has been in contact with water, oil or steam; if the belt has evidence of any damage, examine the condition and alignment of all pulleys before fitting a replacement.

9 Before refitting the timing belt, check that the hole on the camshaft toothed pulley (designated '2' or '2E') is centrally aligned with the dot on the camshaft right-hand bearing cap; also check that the TDC marks on the crankshaft toothed pulley and the oil pump body are aligned (Fig. 2.4).

10 Check that the camshaft and crankshaft toothed pulleys have not moved, then fit the timing belt so that it is taut on the run around the oil pump toothed pulley and idler pulley. If the original belt is being refitted, ensure that the directional arrow marked on the belt during removal faces the correct way and that the belt-to-toothed pulley alignment marks line up.

11 Slacken the timing belt tensioner bolt, and allow the tensioner to return against its spring pressure so that the pulley bears on the timing belt; do not tighten the bolt at this stage.

12 Temporarily install the crankshaft pulley bolt.

13 Use a spanner or socket on the crankshaft pulley bolt to turn the crankshaft through two full turns clockwise (when viewed from the right-hand side of the vehicle), then check that the camshaft and crankshaft toothed pulley alignment marks remain as described in paragraph 9. If the marks are not correctly aligned, re-adjust the toothed pulley position, turn the crankshaft through two further turns and recheck.

14 Tighten the timing belt tensioner pulley

bolt to the specified torque, then check that there is belt tension at the position indicated in Fig. 2.5.

15 Remove the temporarily-installed crankshaft pulley bolt.

16 Refit the timing belt guide to the crankshaft toothed pulley, ensuring that it faces the correct way.

17 Refit the timing belt covers, crankshaft pulley (Sections 6 and 5).

18 Refit the power steering pump and/or alternator/water pump drivebelt(s) (Chapter 1).

8 Timing belt tensioner – removal and refitting

Removal

1 Work as described in paragraphs 1 to 5 of Section 7.

2 Unhook the spring from the timing belt tensioner.

3 Undo the timing belt tensioner pulley bolt, then remove the timing belt tensioner assembly.

Refitting

4 Check that the tension spring is in good condition and that the timing belt tensioner pulley freely rotates. The tension spring should have a free length of 38.4 mm, and should extend to 51.5 mm when subjected to a load of 50 N (5.11 kg).

5 Refit the timing belt tensioner with its bolt, but do not fully tighten the bolt yet.

6 Reconnect the tension spring, and allow the timing belt tensioner pulley to bear against the timing belt; the timing belt should be taut on the run around the oil pump toothed pulley and idler pulley.

7 Proceed as described in paragraph 12 onwards of Section 7.

9 Camshaft oil seal – renewal

1 Disconnect the battery earth terminal.

2 Remove the timing belt (Section 7).

3 Prevent the camshaft from rotating with an open-ended spanner applied to its hexagonal

section, then slacken the camshaft pulley bolt. Remove the bolt and withdraw the toothed pulley; the camshaft must **not** be rotated with the timing belt removed.

4 Punch or drill two small holes opposite each other in the seal. Screw a self-tapping screw into each hole and pull on the screws with pliers to extract the seal.

5 Clean the seal housing and polish off any burrs or raised edges which may have caused the seal to fail in the first place.

6 Lubricate the lips of the new seal with clean engine oil and apply a smear of gasket sealant to the outer edge of the seal. Ease the seal over the end of the camshaft and drive it squarely into position using a suitable tubular drift, such as a socket, which bears only on the hard outer edge of the seal until it seats on its locating shoulder. Once the seal is correctly positioned wipe off any excess gasket sealant.

7 Install the camshaft toothed pulley, having first ensured that the locating pin on the camshaft is still positioned in the 12 o'clock position and aligns with the dimple on the right-hand camshaft bearing cap. Refit the pulley bolt and tighten it to the specified torque whilst holding the camshaft with an open-ended spanner.

8 Refit the timing belt (Section 7, paragraph 9 onwards) and reconnect the battery negative terminal.

10 Camshaft and rocker arms – removal, inspection and refitting

Removal

1 Disconnect the battery earth terminal.

2 Remove the distributor (Chapter 5).

3 Remove the fuel pump (Chapter 4).

4 Remove the timing belt (Section 7).

5 Remove the camshaft toothed pulley (Section 9, paragraph 3).

6 Use a dial gauge to measure the camshaft thrust clearance. This must be within specification; if it is greater than the maximum specified, either the camshaft and/or the cylinder head must be renewed.

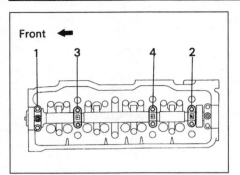

Fig. 2.6 Camshaft bearing cap slackening sequence (Sec 10)

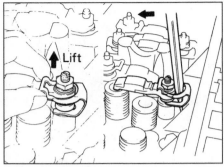

Fig. 2.7 Releasing rocker arm spring clip (Sec 10)

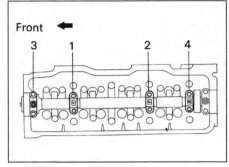

Fig. 2.8 Camshaft bearing cap tightening sequence (Sec 10)

7 Slacken all the camshaft bearing cap retaining bolts by half a turn at a time, in the sequence shown in Fig. 2.6, until all valve spring pressure is relieved from the bearing caps.

8 Remove the camshaft bearing caps, having noted the markings on their tops which identify the fitted position and orientation of each one.

9 Remove the camshaft and seal.

10 Starting at the right-hand (timing belt end) of the engine, remove the rocker arms and their spring clips; keep the components in order of removal so that they may be refitted to their original positions. To remove a rocker arm, lift the top of its spring clip then prise the main body of the spring clip away from the rocker arm (Fig. 2.7).

Inspection

11 Examine the camshaft bearing surfaces, cam lobes and fuel pump eccentric for wear ridges and scoring, and the distributor drive for wear. Renew the camshaft if worn or if either the minimum cam lobe height and/or journal diameter is outside specification; also check that the maximum circle runout of the camshaft (at its central journals) is within the specified limits (using V-blocks and a dial gauge) and renew if necessary. If the cylinder head bearing surfaces are worn excessively, the cylinder head must be renewed. The camshaft seal should be renewed as a matter of course.

12 Clean the bearing caps and the camshaft journals, then check the camshaft running clearances using Plastigage as follows. Place the camshaft in the cylinder head (with the locating pin on the right-hand of the camshaft in its uppermost position) then lay a strip of Plastigage across each camshaft journal. Refit and fully tighten the bearing caps (see paragraph 17 below); do **not** rotate the camshaft. Remove the bearing caps (see paragraphs 7 and 8 above), then compare the width of each compressed strip with the scale printed on the Plastigage pack. If any journal's clearance is worn to the specified service limit or more, the camshaft and/or cylinder head must be renewed.

13 Inspect each rocker arm's bearing surfaces for signs of scuffing, scoring or other wear; renew any that are excessively worn.

Refitting

14 Refit the rocker arms and spring clips to their original locations. Ensure that the adjusting screw of each rocker arm fits correctly in its pivot, and press down on the bottom part of the spring clip to locate it on its pivot groove: lever the spring clip fully into position until its upper edge clips into the ridge on the rocker arm (photos).

15 Oil the camshaft bearing journals and refit the camshaft, noting that the locating pin on its right-hand end must be uppermost.

16 Grease the lip of the new camshaft oil seal, then apply sealant to its outer

circumference and slide the seal into position on the camshaft.

17 Refit the camshaft bearing caps, ensuring that their markings are positioned as noted on removal, then tighten the bearing cap bolts evenly and progressively to their specified torque in the sequence shown in Fig. 2.8.

18 Refit the camshaft toothed pulley (Section 9, paragraph 7).

19 Refit the timing belt (Section 7, paragraph 9 onwards).

20 Refit the distributor and fuel pump (Chapters 5 and 4), then reconnect the battery negative terminal.

11 Cylinder head – removal and refitting

Removal

1 Drain the cooling system and remove the spark plugs (Chapter 1).

2 Remove the fuel pump and the distributor (Chapters 4 and 5).

3 Remove the camshaft cover and timing belt (Sections 4 and 7).

4 Slacken their retaining clips and disconnect the hoses and wiring from the water outlet housing.

5 On models equipped with power steering, remove the power steering pump (Chapter 10).

10.14A Fitting a rocker arm

10.14B Rocker arms and spring clips correctly refitted

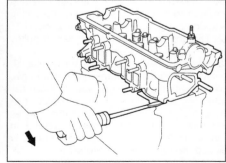

Fig. 2.9 Use leverage only at point shown to release cylinder head (Sec 11)

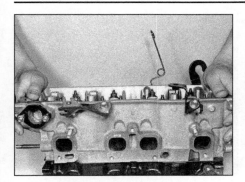

11.15 Refitting cylinder head

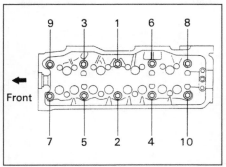

Fig. 2.10 Cylinder head bolt tightening sequence (Sec 11)

11.16 Using angular torque gauge to tighten cylinder head bolts

6 Remove the inlet and exhaust manifolds (Chapter 4).

7 Progressively slacken the cylinder head bolts by half a turn at a time using the **reverse** of the sequence shown in Fig. 2. 10. Remove each bolt in turn along with any washers and store it in its correct fitted position by pushing it through a clearly marked cardboard template. **Note:***Cylinder head warpage or cracking may occur if the bolts are not removed as instructed*

8 Lift the cylinder head off its dowels, then remove it from the vehicle: if it is difficult to lift the cylinder head off, use a suitable screwdriver or bar to lever it up in the position shown in Fig. 2.9, taking great care not to damage the block and head mating surfaces. Place the cylinder head on wooden blocks. If the locating dowels are loose remove them and store them with the cylinder head for safe keeping. Remove the gasket.

9 If the cylinder head is to be dismantled, remove the camshaft and rocker arms (Section 10), then refer to the relevant Sections of Part D.

Refitting

10 Check the condition of the cylinder head bolts, particularly their threads, whenever they are removed. Keeping all the bolts in their correct fitted order, wash them and wipe dry, then check each for any sign of visible wear or damage, renewing any bolt if necessary.

11 The mating faces of the cylinder head and cylinder block/crankcase must be perfectly clean before refitting the head. Use a hard plastic or wood scraper to remove all traces of gasket and carbon; also clean the piston crowns. Take particular care as the soft aluminium alloy is damaged easily. Also, make sure that the carbon is not allowed to enter the oil and water passages; this is particularly important for the lubrication system, as carbon could block the oil supply to any of the engine's components. Using adhesive tape and paper, seal the water, oil and bolt holes in the cylinder block/crankcase. To prevent carbon entering the gap between the pistons and bores, smear a little grease in the gap. After cleaning each piston, use a small brush to remove all traces of grease and carbon

from the gap, then wipe away the remainder with a clean rag. Clean all the pistons in the same way.

12 Check the mating surfaces of the cylinder block crankcase and the cylinder head for nicks, deep scratches and other damage. If slight, they may be removed carefully with a file, but if excessive, machining may be the only alternative to renewal.

13 If warpage is suspected of the cylinder head gasket surface, use a straight-edge to check it for distortion. Refer to Part D if necessary.

14 Ensure the locating dowels are correctly positioned then place a new cylinder head gasket in position on the engine block; ensure that the passages in the engine block align with those of the gasket.

15 Place the cylinder head squarely in position on the cylinder block then, having applied a light smear of oil to their threads and under their heads, insert the cylinder head bolts and washers in their original positions

(photo). Tighten all the bolts by hand then torque them as follows.

16 Always tighten the bolts evenly and progressively in the sequence shown in Fig. 2.10. Tighten the bolts, first to the Stage 1 torque setting, then Stage 2. Stage 3 involves tightening each bolt, still in the sequence shown, through a further 90° (one quarter of a turn). This is best achieved using an angular torque gauge for accuracy, although it is possible to mark the bolt heads and cylinder head surface using a felt tip pen and to then rotate the bolt until the marks align (photo).

17 The remainder of refitting is a reversal of the removal sequence, noting the following points.

(a) *Before refitting the camshaft cover, check and adjust the valve clearances (Chapter 1).*

(b) *On completion, refill the cooling system, then start the engine and check the ignition timing, idle speed and fuel mixture settings (Chapter 1).*

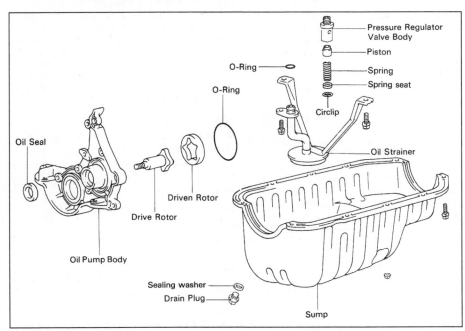

Fig. 2.11 Sump, oil pump and oil pressure regulator valve (Sec 12)

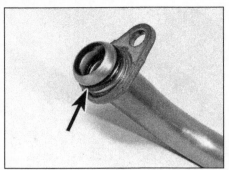

12.11 New dipstick guide tube O-ring (arrowed)

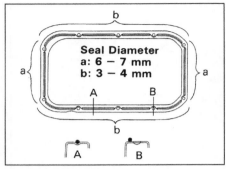

Fig. 2.12 Sump gasket surface sealant application (Sec 12)

13.6 Oil pressure regulator valve

12 Sump – removal and refitting

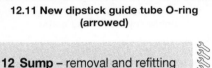

Removal

1 Disconnect the battery earth terminal.
2 Raise the front of the vehicle and support it securely on axle stands.
3 Remove the engine undershields (where fitted).
4 Drain the engine oil (Chapter 1). Once the oil has drained fully, refit the sump drain plug and tighten it to the specified torque.
5 Remove the dipstick and guide tube.
6 For increased working clearance, remove the exhaust downpipe (Chapter 4). If necessary, disconnect the engine/transmission mountings then raise the engine/transmission unit, using an engine support bar or a hoist, to be able to remove the centre mounting from the engine/transmission mounting crossmember (Section 17).
7 Unscrew the eight nuts and two bolts which secure the sump to the engine block, then break the seal by tapping the sump with a soft-faced mallet and remove the sump.

Refitting

8 Thoroughly clean the engine block, oil pump and sump mating faces.
9 Apply sealant sparingly to the sump mating surface (Fig. 2.12). Offer the sump into position (ensuring that no oil contaminates the mating surfaces) and tighten the retaining nuts and bolts to the specified torque.
10 Where necessary, refit the disturbed engine/transmission components (Section 17), ensuring that all mounting bolts are tightened to the specified torque settings.
11 Fit a new O-ring to the dipstick guide tube then refit the tube and tighten its retaining bolt securely (photo).
12 Reconnect the exhaust downpipe (Chapter 4).
13 Refit the undershields (where fitted) then lower the vehicle to the ground and reconnect the battery.
14 Refill the engine with oil (Chapter 1), then start up the engine and check for oil leaks.

13 Oil pump and pressure regulator valve – removal and refitting

Removal

1 Remove the timing belt (Section 7), noting that if the oil pump is to be dismantled the toothed pulley retaining nut should be slackened before the belt is removed.
2 Remove the sump (Section 12).
3 Withdraw the crankshaft toothed pulley; if it is a tight fit, carefully lever it off using two screwdrivers. Remove the Woodruff key from the crankshaft and store it with the pulley for safe keeping.
4 Remove the timing belt tensioner (Section 8), then slacken the retaining bolt and remove the idler pulley and its spacer.
5 Unbolt and remove the oil pick up pipe/strainer assembly.
6 Unbolt and remove the oil pressure regulator valve assembly (photo).
7 Unbolt and remove the oil pump (noting the locations of the longer bolts, and the fitted position of the tensioner spring anchor); it will probably need to be tapped off using a soft-faced hammer (photo). Retrieve the O-ring.
8 Oil pump dismantling, inspection and reassembly is covered in Section 14, the oil pressure switch in Chapter 12.

Refitting

9 Clean the sump and ensure that the oil pick up pipe/strainer is clear.

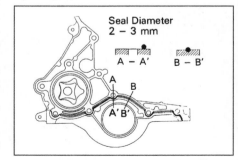

Fig. 2.13 Sealant application on oil pump body (Sec 13)

10 Renew the crankshaft right-hand oil seal whilst the oil pump is removed (Section 15).
11 Thoroughly clean the pump and engine block mating faces.
12 Apply sealant to the pump body (Fig. 2.13), then fit the new O-ring and offer up the pump. Insert the pump bolts, ensuring that the longer bolts are refitted to their original locations and that the tensioner spring anchor is fitted correctly, and tighten them to the specified torque.
13 Install the oil pressure regulator valve assembly and tighten it to the specified torque.
14 Lubricate the new O-ring with clean engine oil and fit it to the oil pick up pipe/strainer. Refit the assembly to the engine and tighten its retaining bolts to the specified torque setting.
15 Refit the Woodruff key to the crankshaft then align the crankshaft toothed pulley slot with the Woodruff key and slide the pulley onto the crankshaft.
16 Refit the timing belt and tensioner (Sections 7 and 8), remembering to retighten the oil pump toothed pulley nut (if slackened).
17 Refit the sump (Section 12).

14 Oil pump and pressure regulator valve – inspection, dismantling and reassembly

Inspection

1 Measure the oil pump clearances (photos). If the outer rotor-to-body clearance or side

13.7 Timing belt tensioner spring anchor (arrowed) on oil pump

14.1A Measuring oil pump outer rotor-to-body clearance

14.1B Measuring oil pump rotor side clearance

14.1C Measuring oil pump inner-to-outer rotor tip clearance

clearance is incorrect, the rotors and/or pump body must be renewed; if the rotor tip clearance is incorrect only the rotors need be renewed. If severe wear is evident, the oil pump assembly must be renewed complete.

2 The oil pressure regulator valve assembly can be checked once it has been dismantled (paragraph 4). Coat the valve piston with clean engine oil then check that it falls slowly into its bore under its own weight; if this is not the case, renew the complete valve assembly.

Dismantling

3 Pull the rotors out of the main pump body.

4 Dismantle the oil pressure regulator valve assembly after removing the spring retaining circlip; take care not to allow the spring to fly out and cause injury or damage, and note the order and orientation of the components as they are removed.

Reassembly

5 Before reassembling the oil pump, the drive rotor shaft seal must be renewed. Remove the old seal using a screwdriver, being careful not to raise any burrs on the pump body which could prevent the new seal from seating correctly. Install the new seal squarely, using a suitably-sized section of tubing as a drift, until it is 1 mm below the pump body edge.

6 Refit the rotors to the pump body, having lubricated the seal lip with clean oil.

7 The oil pressure regulator valve is reassembled by reversing the order of dismantling; ensure that the circlip locates securely.

15 Crankshaft oil seals – renewal

Right-hand seal

1 To renew the seal with the oil pump removed from the vehicle, carefully prise out the old seal using a flat-bladed screwdriver. Clean the seal housing and polish off any burrs or raised edges which may have caused the seal to fail in the first place. Apply multi-purpose grease to the new seal, then drive it squarely into position using a suitably-sized tubular drift, such as a socket, which bears only on the hard outer edge of the seal; the outer face of the seal should be 1 mm below the pump face.

2 To renew the seal with the oil pump in place on the vehicle, first remove the timing belt (Section 7), then remove the crankshaft toothed pulley (Section 13, paragraph 3).

3 Punch or drill two small holes opposite each other in the seal. Screw a self-tapping screw into each hole and pull on the screws with pliers to extract the seal. Clean the seal housing and polish off any burrs or raised edges which may have caused the seal to fail in the first place. Lubricate the lips of the new seal with clean engine oil and apply a smear of grease to the outer edge of the seal. Ease the seal over the end of the crankshaft and drive it squarely into position as described above (photo).

4 Wipe off any excess grease then refit the

crankshaft toothed pulley (Section 13, paragraph 15) and install the timing belt (Section 7).

Left-hand seal

5 To renew the seal with its housing removed from the vehicle, work as described in paragraph 1 above.

6 To renew the seal with its housing in place in the vehicle, first remove the flywheel/driveplate (Section 16); the seal can then be renewed as described in paragraph 3 (photo).

7 Wipe off any excess grease, then refit the flywheel/driveplate (Section 7).

16 Flywheel/driveplate – removal, inspection and refitting

Removal

1 Remove the gearbox/transmission (Chapter 7).

2 Remove the clutch, where appropriate (Chapter 6).

3 Mark the relationship of the flywheel/driveplate to its crankshaft flange.

4 Prevent the flywheel from turning by locking the ring gear teeth then progressively slacken the flywheel/driveplate retaining bolts, using a **reversal** of the tightening sequence (Fig. 2.14). Remove the bolts and lift off the flywheel/driveplate.

15.3 Fitting new crankshaft right-hand oil seal

15.6 Removing crankshaft left-hand oil seal

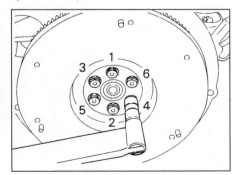

Fig. 2.14 Flywheel/driveplate bolt tightening sequence (Sec 16)

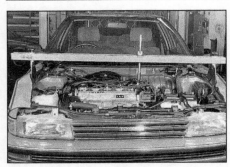

17.5 Engine support bar in use

17.7A Right-hand (upper) mounting throughbolt (arrowed)

17.7B Left-hand (upper) mounting throughbolt (arrowed)

Inspection

5 Examine the flywheel for scoring on its clutch driven plate face; if evident it may be possible for a competent engineering works to machine the surface, but renewal is the preferable option. Check the flywheel/driveplate carefully for signs of distortion, or any hairline cracks around the bolt holes or cracks radiating outwards from the centre; renewal will be required if evident.

6 If the ring gear is worn or damaged it may be possible to renew it separately, but this job should be entrusted to a Toyota dealer or engineering works.

Refitting

7 Clean the flywheel/driveplate and crankshaft flange faces, and remove all traces of

17.8A Forward of three central mountings on engine/transmission crossmember (arrowed)

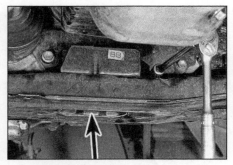

17.8B Plastic blanking plate (arrowed) is removed to expose crossmember mounting nuts

thread locking compound from the retaining bolts.

8 Locate the flywheel/driveplate on its crankshaft flange, aligning the marks made on removal. Apply a little thread locking compound to the threads of the retaining bolts, then fit the bolts and progressively tighten them to the specified torque setting, in the sequence shown in Fig. 2.14.

9 Refit the clutch (where appropriate) and remove the ring gear locking tool.

10 Refit the gearbox/transmission (Chapter 7).

17 Engine/transmission mountings – inspection and renewal

Inspection

1 If improved access is required, raise the front of the car and support it securely on axle stands.

2 Check the mounting rubber to see if it is cracked, hardened or separated from the metal at any point: renew the mounting if any such damage or deterioration is evident.

3 Check that all mounting fasteners are securely tightened; use a torque wrench to check if possible.

4 Using a large screwdriver or a pry bar, check for wear in the mounting by carefully levering against it to check for free play; where this is not possible, enlist the aid of an assistant to move the engine/transmission

17.8C Withdrawing mounting directly beneath engine/transmission with engine raised up

unit back and forth, or from side to side while you watch the mounting. While some free play is to be expected even from new components, excessive wear should be obvious. If excessive free play is found, check first that the fasteners are correctly secured, then renew any worn components as described below.

Renewal

5 The engine/transmission mountings can be unbolted and removed once the weight of the engine/transmission unit is taken off them using either a suitable hoist, an engine support bar or a jack with an interposed block of wood (photo). Lifting eye attachment facility is provided on the engine.

6 The mountings are located in the following positions:

(a) Right-hand (upper) mounting by the timing belt cover.

(b) Left-hand (upper) mounting to the rear of the battery tray.

(c) Three central mountings along the length of the engine/ transmission mounting crossmember; forward of, centre of and rearward of the underside of the engine/transmission unit.

7 The left- and right-hand mountings are each secured by throughbolts to the body. The brackets may be removed after unbolting them, having noted the fitted position of their components (photos). Refer to the Specifications for tightening torque details during refitting.

8 The central mountings are secured by nuts and bolts to the engine/transmission crossmember, suspension crossmember and the engine/transmission, and are accessible from underneath the vehicle; plastic blanking plates are fitted over the crossmember access holes for the forward and centre mountings (photos). All mountings may be renewed separately, as required. Refer to the Specifications for tightening torque details during refitting.

9 There are a number of different versions of the mountings used, so, when ordering replacement parts, ensure that full vehicle details are provided to enable the correct component(s) to be obtained. If possible, take the old component(s) along to your Toyota dealer for positive identification.

Part B: 1587cc 4A-F engine – in-car engine repair procedures

18 General information

How to use this Chapter

This Part covers in-vehicle repair procedures for the 1587cc 4A-F carburettor engine. The Chapter's structure is explained in Section 1.

Engine description

The engine is of in-line 4-cylinder design and is mounted transversely. A cast iron cylinder block and cast aluminium cylinder head are fitted.

The engine has twin overhead camshafts, with two inlet valves and two exhaust valves per cylinder. Valve clearance adjustment is by means of shims located directly between the bucket-type camshaft followers and the camshaft lobes; thus permitting the replacement of shims without camshaft removal. The exhaust camshaft is belt-driven from the crankshaft toothed pulley, while the inlet camshaft is driven from the exhaust camshaft via a pair of gears; each camshaft is supported by five bearings.

The pistons are attached to their connecting rods by semi-floating gudgeon pins.

The fuel pump and distributor are driven directly from the camshafts, whilst the oil pump is driven by the crankshaft.

The cast iron crankshaft runs in five main bearings; endfloat is controlled by semi-circular thrustwashers at the central main bearing.

Repair operations possible with the engine in the car

The following work can be carried out with the engine in the car.

(a) Compression pressure – testing.
(b) Camshaft cover – removal and refitting.
(c) Crankshaft pulley – removal and refitting.
(d) Timing belt covers – removal and refitting.
(e) Timing belt – removal, refitting and adjustment.

(f) Timing belt tensioner – removal and refitting.
(g) Camshaft oil seal – renewal.
(h) Camshaft and followers – removal, inspection and refitting.
(i) Cylinder head – removal and refitting.
(j) Cylinder head and pistons decarbonising.
(k) Sump – removal and refitting.
(l) Oil pump – removal, overhaul and refitting.
(m) Crankshaft oil seals – renewal.
(n) Engine/transmission mountings – inspection and renewal.
(o) Flywheel/driveplate – removal, inspection and refitting.

19 Compression test – description and interpretation

Refer to Section 2.

20 Top Dead Centre (TDC) for number one piston – locating

Apart from the need to refer to Section 21 for details of camshaft cover removal and the fact that the cam followers must be rotated to determine whether or not the valves are closed, this procedure is as described in Section 3 (photo).

20.1 Crankshaft pulley groove aligned with timing belt lower cover 'O' mark – numbers one and four cylinders at TDC

21 Camshaft cover – removal and refitting

Removal

1 Remove the air filter housing/trunking (Chapter 4).
2 Disconnect the hoses from the camshaft cover (photo).
3 Disconnect the HT leads from their locating clips and from their spark plugs; release the alternator wiring harness 'bridge' from the right-hand side of the camshaft cover (it may also be necessary to disconnect the wiring from the alternator and the oil pressure switch), and release any other relevant wiring/cable clips (photo).
4 Unscrew the three dome nuts (with their seals) and the cable support bracket bolt, then carefully remove the cover and gasket (photo).

Refitting

5 Examine the condition of the cover gasket and renew the spark plug tube seals, drifting out the defective seals and installing new ones using a suitably-sized socket or section of tube (photos).
6 Refitting is a reversal of the removal procedure, but apply a little sealant to the

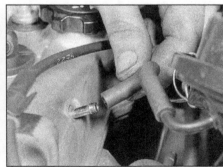

21.2 Disconnecting a hose from camshaft cover

21.3 Releasing alternator wiring harness 'bridge' securing clip at rear end

21.4 Removing a camshaft cover seal

21.5A Drifting out spark plug tube seal from camshaft cover

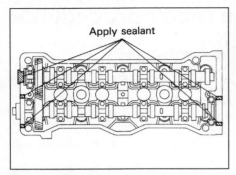

Fig. 2.15 Apply suitable sealant to shaded areas on refitting camshaft cover (Sec 21)

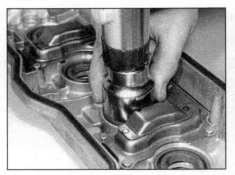

21.5B Installing new spark plug tube seal

23.3 Withdrawing timing belt upper cover; note retaining bolt locations (arrowed)

cylinder head (Fig. 2.15) and ensure that the gasket seats correctly in the cover before the cover is fitted; as the cover is being fitted, ensure that the spark plug tube seals seat correctly.

22 Crankshaft pulley – removal and refitting

Refer to Section 5.

23.6 Withdrawing timing belt centre cover

23 .9 Removing timing belt lower cover

23 Timing belt covers – removal and refitting

Removal

Upper cover

1 Disconnect the battery earth terminal.
2 Remove the camshaft cover (Section 21).
3 Remove the retaining bolts, noting that it may be necessary to release the alternator/water pump and power steering pump drivebelts to allow the water pump pulley to be withdrawn to gain access to the lower rear bolt (Chapters 1 and 3, as necessary) (photo).
4 Remove the upper cover.

Centre cover

5 Remove the upper cover as described above, removing the drivebelts and the water pump pulley.
6 Unbolt and remove the centre cover (photo).

Lower cover

7 Remove the upper and centre covers as described above.
8 Remove the crankshaft pulley (Section 22).
9 Unbolt and remove the lower cover (photo).

Refitting

10 Refitting is a reversal of the removal procedure.

24 Timing belt – removal and refitting

Removal

1 Disconnect the battery earth terminal.
2 Remove the alternator/water pump and power steering pump drivebelts (Chapter 1).
3 Set number one piston to TDC (Section 20) then remove the crankshaft pulley (Section 22); take care not to rotate the crankshaft.
4 Remove the timing belt covers (Section 23).
5 Remove the timing belt guide from the crankshaft toothed pulley, noting which side faces the timing belt (see photo 7.4).

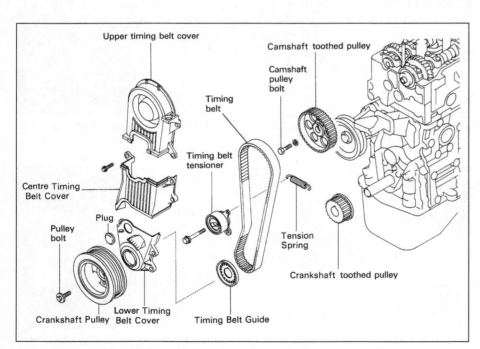

Fig. 2.16 Timing belt covers and toothed pulleys (Sec 23)

Upper timing belt cover
Camshaft toothed pulley
Camshaft pulley bolt
Timing belt
Timing belt tensioner
Centre Timing Belt Cover
Plug
Pulley bolt
Tension Spring
Crankshaft toothed pulley
Crankshaft Pulley
Lower Timing Belt Cover
Timing Belt Guide

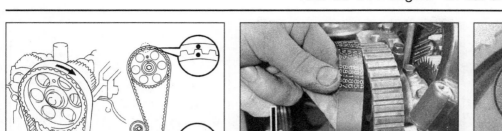

Fig. 2.17 Timing belt and toothed pulley alignment marks (Sec 24)

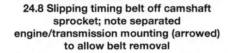

24.8 Slipping timing belt off camshaft sprocket; note separated engine/transmission mounting (arrowed) to allow belt removal

24.10A Camshaft sprocket hole (arrowed) aligned with mark on exhaust camshaft right-hand bearing cap

6 If the timing belt is to be re-used, mark the alignment of the belt to the pulleys and the direction of normal engine rotation on the belt (Fig. 2.17). Note the camshaft and crankshaft toothed pulley alignment marks described in paragraph 10.

7 Slacken the timing belt tensioner bolt, then push the tensioner pulley away from the belt and temporarily retighten the bolt.

8 Slip the timing belt from the pulleys. Do **not** alter the position of the camshaft or crankshaft toothed pulleys with the timing belt removed. To enable the timing belt to be fully removed from the vehicle, the weight of the engine must be taken off the right-hand engine/transmission mounting and the mounting separated (if not already done) (photo).

Refitting

9 In addition to the regular renewal called for as part of the service schedule (Chapter 1), the timing belt should be renewed, regardless of age or mileage, if it appears to be defective in any manner or if it has been in contact with water, oil or steam; if the belt has evidence of any damage, examine the condition and alignment of all pulleys before fitting a replacement.

10 Before refitting the timing belt, check that the small hole in the camshaft toothed pulley is in the 12 o'clock position and is centrally aligned with the mark on the camshaft right-hand bearing cap; also check that the TDC

marks on the crankshaft toothed pulley and the oil pump body are aligned (photos).

11 Check that the camshaft and crankshaft toothed pulleys have not moved, then fit the timing belt so that it is taut on the run around the oil pump toothed pulley and idler pulley. If the original belt is being refitted, ensure that the arrow marked on the belt during removal faces the correct way and that the belt-to-toothed pulley alignment marks made line up. Reconnect the right-hand engine/transmission mounting, but do not fully tighten the bolts at this stage.

12 Slacken the tensioner bolt and allow the tensioner to return against spring pressure so that the pulley bears on the timing belt; do not tighten the bolt at this stage.

13 Temporarily install the crankshaft pulley bolt.

14 Use a spanner or socket on the crankshaft pulley bolt to turn the crankshaft clockwise (viewed from the vehicle's right-hand side) through two full turns, then check that the camshaft and crankshaft toothed pulley alignment marks remain as described in paragraph 10. If the marks are not correctly aligned, adjust the toothed pulley position until the setting is correct, rotate the crankshaft through two further turns and recheck.

15 Tighten the tensioner pulley bolt to the specified torque, then use a spring balance or similar to ensure there is 5 to 6 mm of belt

deflection at the position indicated in Fig. 2.18 when a load of 2 kg is applied (photo). If adjustment is required, move the tensioner pulley slightly.

16 Remove the temporarily-installed crankshaft pulley bolt.

17 Refit the timing belt guide to the crankshaft toothed pulley, ensuring that its concave side is outermost.

18 Refit the timing belt covers and crankshaft pulley (Sections 23 and 22).

19 Refit the power steering pump and alternator/water pump drivebelts (Chapter 1).

25 Timing belt tensioner – removal and refitting

Removal

1 Work as described in Section 24, paragraphs 1 to 6.

2 Unhook the spring from the tensioner.

3 Unbolt the tensioner pulley and remove the tensioner assembly.

Refitting

4 Check that the tension spring is in good condition and that the tensioner pulley freely rotates. The tension spring should have a free length of 43.3 mm, extending to 50.2 mm when subjected to a load of 69 N (7.0 kg).

5 Refit the tensioner and tighten its bolt by hand only at this stage.

6 Reconnect the spring and allow the

24.10B TDC mark on crankshaft sprocket (A) aligned with mark on oil pump body (B)

24.15 Checking timing belt deflection

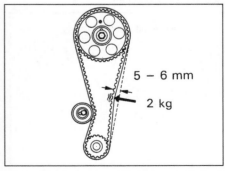

Fig. 2.18 Timing belt deflection measuring point (Sec 24)

26.4 Holding exhaust camshaft to prevent rotation as toothed pulley bolt is undone

26.7 Installing new camshaft oil seal

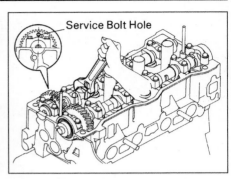

Fig. 2.19 Positioning inlet camshaft for removal (Sec 27)

tensioner pulley to bear against the timing belt; the belt front run should be taut.

7 Proceed as described in Section 24, paragraph 13 onwards.

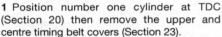

26 Camshaft oil seal – renewal

1 Position number one cylinder at TDC (Section 20) then remove the upper and centre timing belt covers (Section 23).

2 With number one cylinder at TDC the small hole in the camshaft toothed pulley should be in the 12 o'clock position and should align with the dot on the camshaft right-hand bearing cap. Also the dot on the outer edge of the pulley (also in the 12 o'clock position) should align with a corresponding dot on the timing belt. If these marks are not visible, make your own using a marker pen or white paint.

3 Once the marks have been checked, remove the plug from the lower timing belt cover to reach the timing belt tensioner bolt. Slacken the bolt, push the tensioner pulley away from the belt and temporarily retighten the bolt. Slip the belt off the camshaft pulley and position it clear of the working area. Do not alter the position of the camshaft or crankshaft whilst the belt is removed from the pulleys.

4 Using an open-ended spanner, hold the exhaust camshaft by its hexagonal section to prevent it from rotating, then unscrew the camshaft toothed pulley bolt (photo). Withdraw the pulley, noting the locating pin fitted to the camshaft end.

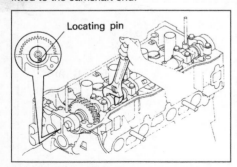

Fig. 2.20 Positioning exhaust camshaft for removal (Sec 27)

5 Punch or drill two small holes opposite each other in the seal. Screw a self-tapping screw into each hole and pull on the screws with pliers to extract the seal.

6 Clean the seal housing and polish off any burrs or raised edges which may have caused the seal to fail in the first place.

7 Lubricate the lips of the new seal with a little multi-purpose grease and ease the seal over the end of the camshaft. Using a socket as a drift which bears only on the seal's hard outer edge, drive the seal squarely into position until it seats on its locating shoulder, then wipe off any surplus grease (photo).

8 Align the slot in the centre of the camshaft toothed pulley with the exhaust camshaft locating pin, then refit the pulley bolt. Tighten the bolt to its specified torque whilst holding the exhaust camshaft (paragraph 4).

9 Work as described in Section 24, paragraphs 11, 12, 14 and 15.

10 Refit the plug to the lower timing belt cover, then install the camshaft and timing belt covers (Sections 21 and 23).

27 Camshaft and followers – removal, inspection and refitting

Removal

1 Disconnect the battery earth terminal.

2 Remove the distributor (Chapter 5), and the spark plugs (Chapter 1).

3 Remove the fuel pump (Chapter 4).

4 Remove the camshaft toothed pulley (Section 26, paragraphs 1 to 4).

5 Using a dial gauge, measure the thrust clearance of each camshaft. This must be

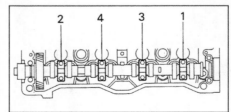

Fig. 2.21 Exhaust camshaft bearing cap slackening sequence (right-hand bearing cap removed) (Sec 27)

within specification; if it exceeds its maximum permissible limit, the camshaft(s) and/or cylinder head must be renewed.

6 Using an open-ended spanner on its hexagonal section, set the inlet camshaft drive gear service bolt hole to the 12 o'clock position (Fig. 2.19), the lobes of numbers one and number three cylinders should now be pushing evenly on their followers.

7 Progressively slacken the inlet and exhaust camshaft right-hand bearing cap retaining bolts, a little at a time, then remove both bearing caps.

8 To release the pressure of the sub-gear spring, secure the inlet camshaft sub-gear to its main gear using a 6 mm bolt (16 to 20 mm long) (photo).

9 Progressively slacken the inlet camshaft bearing cap bolts, a little at a time, in the **reverse** of the sequence shown in Fig. 2.23 until all valve spring pressure has been relieved. Remove the bearing caps, noting their correct fitted positions, then lift out the camshaft. Do **not** attempt to prise it out or it will be damaged; if the camshaft cannot be lifted out, re-tighten number three bearing cap then loosen each of its bolts alternately whilst pulling upwards the camshaft gear.

10 Rotate the exhaust camshaft until its toothed pulley locating pin is positioned as shown in Fig. 2.20; the lobes of numbers one and three cylinders should be pushing evenly on their followers.

11 Remove the exhaust camshaft, working as described in paragraph 9 above but referring to Fig. 2.21 (photo).

27.8 Inlet camshaft sub-gear secured to main gear by bolt (arrowed)

27.11 Camshaft bearing cap markings identify cap (number three exhaust shown) – arrow points to timing cover end

27.12 Removing camshaft follower and shim

27.13 Dismantling inlet camshaft gear – bolt (A) securing sub-gear to main gear, bolts (B) act as leverage points

12 Lift out the shims and camshaft followers, keeping all components in order for refitting to their original locations (photo).

13 The inlet camshaft sub-gear can be removed as follows. Mount the camshaft by its hexagonal section in a soft-jawed vice and screw in two further bolts to act as leverage points. Using a screwdriver between these bolts, apply pressure in a clockwise direction to hold the sub-gear against the torsional spring pressure, then remove the first bolt (inserted to secure the sub-gear to the main gear) and carefully allow the sub-gear to rotate anti-clockwise until all spring pressure is released (photo). Remove the sub-gear securing circlip then remove the washer, sub-gear and spring.

Inspection

14 Examine the camshaft bearing surfaces, cam lobes and fuel pump eccentric for wear ridges and scoring, and the distributor drive for wear. Renew the camshaft(s) if any of these conditions are apparent, or if any cam lobe height is worn to less than the minimum specified. Supporting the ends of each camshaft on V-blocks and using a dial gauge at its centre journal, measure the camshaft runout.

15 Clean the bearing caps and the camshaft journals, then check the running clearances of each camshaft using Plastigage, as follows. Place the camshaft in the cylinder head, then lay a strip of Plastigage across each journal and refit the bearing caps (paragraphs 24 to 30 below); do **not** rotate the camshaft. Remove the bearing caps (paragraphs 7 to 11 above), then compare the width of the compressed strips with the scale on the Plastigage pack. If the running clearance on any journal is worn to the specified maximum or beyond, the camshaft and/or cylinder head must be renewed. Measure the camshaft journal diameters; if any is excessively worn the camshaft must be renewed. If the cylinder head bearing surfaces are worn excessively, the cylinder head must be renewed. Remove all traces of Plastigage.

16 if the inlet camshaft sub-gear has been removed, install the camshafts and check the

gear backlash using a dial gauge (Fig. 2.24). If the backlash is outside specification, the camshafts must be renewed. Remove the camshafts (as described above) upon completion of the check. Using vernier calipers, measure the distance between the ends of the sub-gear spring. The gap should be 17.1 to 17.5 mm; if not, the spring must be renewed.

17 Using calipers, check that the distance between the ends of the sub-gear torsional spring is as specified (with the spring in a 'free' state); renew the spring if not.

18 Before reassembling the inlet camshaft gear, check that there are no signs of chipping or cracking on any of the teeth (check also the exhaust camshaft gear): the camshaft must be renewed if any such fault is evident.

19 Inspect the shims and camshaft followers for wear ridges or scoring. Renew any worn

followers, but note that any shims required can be selected only when the cylinder head is reassembled and the valve clearances can be checked (Chapter 1).

20 Check the camshaft follower clearances as follows, taking great care not to mix them up; check each separately, noting the measurement. Measure the follower diameter, then measure its bore in the cylinder head; subtract the follower diameter from its bore diameter to obtain the clearance. If this is excessive, the follower(s) or the cylinder head (whichever is excessively worn) must be renewed.

Refitting

21 If it was dismantled, reassemble the inlet camshaft sub-gear, reversing the method of dismantling; remove the two bolts used as leverage points once the single bolt is in place securing the sub-gear to the main gear.

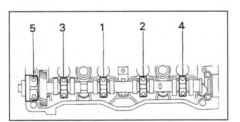

Fig. 2.22 Exhaust camshaft bearing cap tightening sequence (Sec 27)

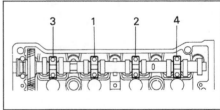

Fig. 2.23 Inlet camshaft bearing cap tightening sequence (Sec 27)

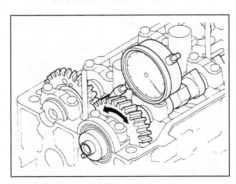

Fig. 2.24 Checking camshaft gear backlash (Sec 27)

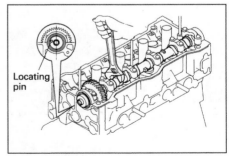

Fig. 2.25 Exhaust camshaft must be set as shown before refitting inlet camshaft (Sec 27)

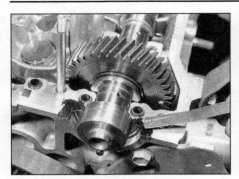

27.24 Applying sealant to exhaust camshaft right-hand bearing cap location on cylinder head

27.30 Fitting inlet camshaft right-hand bearing cap

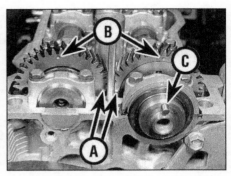

27.31 Camshaft installation – (A) TDC markings, (B) installation marks, (C) exhaust camshaft locating pin in uppermost position

22 Install the camshaft followers and shims to their original bores, where applicable, having lightly oiled the bores; check that the followers can be rotated smoothly in the bores by hand.

23 Lightly oil the exhaust camshaft journals and cam lobes, then place the exhaust camshaft on the cylinder head so that the camshaft toothed pulley locating pin is positioned as shown in Fig. 2.20; the cam lobes of number one and number three cylinders should push evenly on their followers.

24 Apply sealant to the camshaft right-hand bearing cap location on the cylinder head, then refit the camshaft bearing caps in their original fitted positions. Insert the bolts then

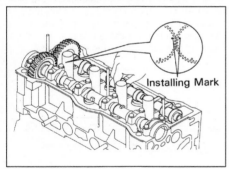

Fig. 2.26 Camshaft gear installing marks must be aligned as shown when inlet camshaft is refitted (Sec 27)

tighten them evenly and progressively to their specified torque setting in the sequence shown in Fig. 2.22 (photo).

25 Install a new camshaft oil seal (Section 26, paragraph 7).

26 Lightly oil the inlet camshaft journals and cam lobes.

27 Set the exhaust camshaft locating pin to the position shown in Fig. 2.25, then engage the inlet camshaft gear with that of the exhaust camshaft so that their installation marks are aligned (Fig. 2.26). Once the camshaft gears are correctly engaged, roll the inlet gear down the exhaust gear until the inlet camshaft is seated in the cylinder head.

28 Refit the inlet camshaft bearing caps (with the exception of the right-hand cap), and their bolts, in their original fitted positions. Evenly and progressively, in the sequence shown in Fig. 2.23, tighten the bolts to their specified torque setting.

29 Unscrew the bolt securing the sub-gear to the main gear.

30 Refit the inlet camshaft right-hand bearing cap so that its arrow faces to the right, and tighten its retaining bolts alternately to their specified torque; if difficulty is experienced, push the camshaft towards the cylinder head left-hand end (photo).

31 Using an open-ended spanner, rotate the exhaust camshaft through one complete revolution, then return to the TDC position so that its locating pin is in the 12 o'clock position. Check that the TDC marks align on

the right-hand face of the camshaft gears and that the installation marks are both in the 12 o'clock position (photo).

32 If all is well proceed as described in Section 26, paragraph 8 onwards, noting that the valve clearances should be checked (Chapter 1) before the camshaft cover is refitted.

28 Cylinder head – removal and refitting

Removal

1 Drain the cooling system (Chapter 1).

2 Slacken the retaining clips then disconnect the hoses and wiring from the water inlet housing on the cylinder head left-hand end; unbolt the housing if required (photo).

3 Remove the power steering pump, where fitted (Chapter 10).

4 Remove the fuel pump (Chapter 4).

5 Remove the alternator adjusting clamp bolt.

6 Remove the carburettor and inlet manifold (Chapter 4) (photo).

7 Remove the exhaust heat shields and stay, disconnect the exhaust downpipe from the manifold and remove the exhaust manifold (Chapter 4).

8 Remove the camshaft and followers (Section 27).

9 Evenly and progressively slacken the cylinder head bolts in the sequence shown in Fig. 2.27. Remove each bolt in turn, with any washers, and store it in its correct fitted position by pushing it through a clearly-

28.2 Removing water inlet housing from cylinder head

28.6 Removing inlet manifold and carburettor

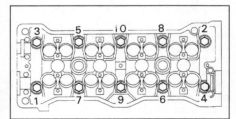

Fig. 2.27 Cylinder head bolt slackening sequence (Sec 28)

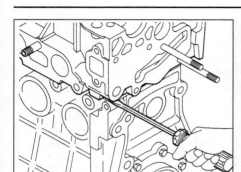

Fig. 2.28 Use leverage only at point shown to release cylinder head (Sec 28)

28.9 Withdrawing cylinder head bolt and washer

28.12 New cylinder head gasket fitted to cylinder block

marked cardboard template. Note that cylinder head warpage or cracking may occur if the bolts are not removed as instructed (photo).

10 Lift the cylinder head off its dowels and remove it; if it is difficult to release, use a suitable screwdriver or bar to prise it up at the point shown in Fig. 2.28, but be careful not to damage the mating surfaces. Place the cylinder head on wooden blocks on the workbench. If the locating dowels are loose, remove them and store them with the cylinder head for safe keeping. Remove the gasket.

11 Cylinder head overhaul procedures are in Part D.

Refitting

12 Check the condition of the cylinder head bolts and the mating surfaces, clean the surfaces, then fit a new gasket and refit the cylinder head, bolts and washers as described in Section 11, paragraphs 10 to 15 (photo).

13 Progressively tighten the cylinder head bolts to the specified torque setting in several stages, in the sequence shown in Fig. 2.29.

14 The remainder of reassembly is a reversal of the removal sequence, noting the following points:

(a) *Before refitting the camshaft cover, check and adjust the valve clearances (Chapter 1).*

(b) *On completion refill the cooling system*

then start the engine and check the ignition timing, idle speed and fuel mixture settings (Chapter 1).

29 Sump – removal and refitting

Removal

1 Disconnect the battery earth terminal.

2 Raise the front of the vehicle and support it securely on axle stands.

3 Remove the engine undershields (where fitted).

4 Drain the engine oil (Chapter 1). Once the oil has drained, refit the sump drain plug and tighten it to the specified torque.

5 For increased working clearance, remove the exhaust downpipe section (Chapter 4). If necessary, disconnect the mountings then raise the engine/transmission. using an engine support bar or a hoist, to be able to remove the centre mounting from the engine/transmission mounting crossmember (Section 17).

6 Unscrew the nineteen bolts and two nuts

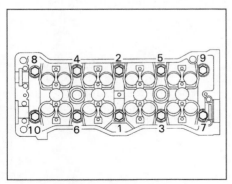

Fig. 2.29 Cylinder head bolt tightening sequence (Sec 28)

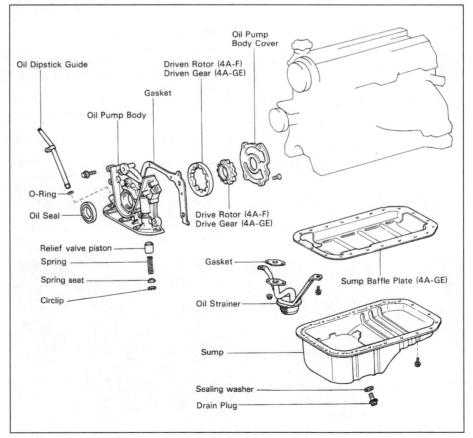

Fig. 2.30 Sump, oil pump and relief valve assembly (Sec 29)

29.6 Disconnecting oil cooler pipe union from sump

29.7 Removing sump

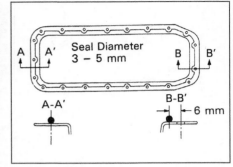

Fig. 2.31 Sump mating surface sealant application (Sec 29)

which secure the sump to the engine block, having first disconnected the relevant oil cooler pipe union (photo).

7 Break the seal by tapping the sump with a soft-faced mallet, then remove the sump (photo).

Refitting

8 Thoroughly clean the engine block, oil pump and sump mating faces.

9 Apply sealant sparingly to the sump mating surface (Fig. 2.31). Offer the sump into position, ensuring that no oil contaminates the mating faces, and tighten its retaining nuts and bolts to the specified torque setting. Reconnect the oil cooler pipe union, using new seals, and tighten it to the specified torque.

30.2 Removing oil pick-up pipe/strainer

10 Where necessary, refit the disturbed engine/transmission components (Section 17), ensuring that all mounting bolts are tightened to the specified torque settings.

11 Reconnect the exhaust downpipe (Chapter 4).

12 Refit the undershields (where fitted), then lower the vehicle to the ground and reconnect the battery.

13 Refill the engine with oil (Chapter 1) then start the engine and check for oil leaks.

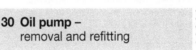

30 Oil pump – removal and refitting

Removal

1 Remove the sump (Section 29).

2 Undo the nuts and bolts securing the oil pick-up pipe/strainer, then remove it with its gasket (photo).

3 Remove the timing belt from its toothed pulleys (Section 24); there is no need to fully remove it.

4 Remove the timing belt tensioner (Section 25).

5 Remove the crankshaft toothed pulley (photo). If it is a tight fit, lever the pulley off using two screwdrivers. Remove the Woodruff key from the crankshaft and store it with the pulley for safe keeping.

6 Withdraw the engine oil dipstick, then unbolt and withdraw the guide tube (photo);

where applicable, release the power steering pump and remove the water pump pulley for access (there will be no need to disturb the power steering hydraulic circuit).

7 Unscrew the pump retaining bolts, noting their correct fitted positions, then remove the pump; if necessary carefully tap the pump with a soft-faced hammer to release it.

8 The oil pump relief valve assembly is covered in Section 31, the oil pressure regulator valve in Section 32.

9 Oil pump inspection, dismantling and reassembly is covered in Section 31, the oil pressure switch in Chapter 12.

Refitting

10 Clean the sump and ensure that the oil pick-up pipe/strainer is clear.

11 Renew the crankshaft right-hand oil seal whilst the oil pump is removed (Section 15).

12 Thoroughly clean the pump's sump mating face and ensure that the engine block-to-pump mating faces are clean.

13 Lightly oil the crankshaft oil pump drive and oil seal contact surfaces.

14 Position a new pump gasket on the cylinder block, then refit the pump, ensuring that its drive rotor engages with the crankshaft drive. Refit the pump bolts and tighten them to their specified torque.

15 Fit a new O-ring to the base of the engine oil dipstick guide tube lubricating it with oil, then install the guide tube: refit the dipstick (photo). Where necessary, refit the power

30.5 Removing crankshaft toothed pulley

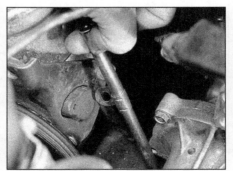

30.6 Withdrawing engine oil dipstick guide tube

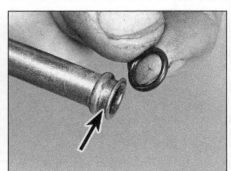

30.15 Fit a new O-ring to groove (arrowed) on base of engine oil dipstick guide tube

32.1 Oil cooler securing bolt locations (arrowed) seen from underneath with radiator removed

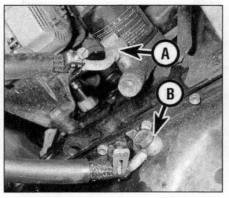

32.2 Oil cooler unions – feed (A), return (B)

32.5A Removing filter mounting stud (arrowed) which also secures combined oil filter bracket/oil pressure regulator valve housing to cylinder block

steering pump and the water pump pulley.

16 Refit the Woodruff key to the crankshaft, then align the crankshaft toothed pulley slot with the Woodruff key and slide the pulley onto the crankshaft.

17 Refit the timing belt tensioner and timing belt (Sections 25 and 24).

18 Using a new gasket, refit the oil pick-up pipe/strainer and tighten its nuts and bolts to their specified torque.

19 Refit the sump (Section 29).

---

31 Oil pump and relief valve – inspection, dismantling and reassembly

Inspection

1 With the pump removed and the body cover removed as described in paragraph 3, measure the oil pump clearances with reference to Section 14, paragraph 1.

2 Once it has been dismantled (paragraph 4 below), the relief valve assembly can be checked as described in Section 14, paragraph 2.

Dismantling

3 Remove the five screws securing the body

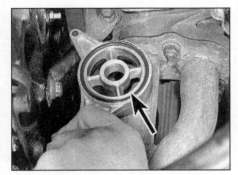

32.5B O-ring (arrowed) on cylinder block mating face of bracket/housing

cover to its reverse side then lift off the cover. Withdraw the drive and driven rotors.

4 Dismantle the relief valve assembly after removing the spring retaining circlip; take care not to allow the spring to fly out and cause injury or damage, and note the order and orientation of the components as they are removed.

Reassembly

5 Renew the crankshaft right-hand oil seal (Section 15).

6 Reassemble the oil pump by inserting the rotors to the pump body, then locate the body cover and tighten the screws to the specified torque.

7 The relief valve is reassembled by reversing the order of dismantling, ensuring that the valve piston is fitted the correct way around and that the circlip is securely located in its groove.

---

32 Oil cooler and pressure regulating valve – general information

Oil cooler

1 The oil cooler is mounted between the radiator and the radiator grille, its bracket being secured by three bolts (photo).

2 The oil cooler hose connections are secured by clips. If the sump unions themselves are to be removed, new gaskets (behind the union and behind its bolt) will be required on refitting; tighten the union bolts to the specified torque (photo).

Oil pressure regulating valve

3 The valve is located in the combined oil filter bracket/oil pressure regulator valve housing on the forward-facing side of the engine block.

4 To remove the valve, unscrew and remove the hexagon-headed plug on its base (with the gasket) then withdraw the spring and valve

piston noting their orientation; catch oil spillage in a suitable container. Refitting is a reversal of the removal procedure, but fit a new gasket and tighten the hexagon-headed plug to its specified torque.

5 To remove the combined oil filter bracket/oil pressure regulator valve housing or the valve itself, remove the oil filter (Chapter 1), then disconnect the union from the combined bracket/housing and remove the gaskets; catch oil spillage in a suitable container. Remove the filter mounting stud that also secures the combined bracket/housing to the cylinder block, with its gasket; remove the combined bracket/housing and its O-ring (photos). The valve assembly can now be removed (paragraph 4), if required.

6 Test the pressure regulator by coating the valve piston with clean engine oil and checking that it falls into its housing bore under its own weight; if not, renew the complete assembly.

7 Refitting is a reversal of the removal procedure, but use a new O-ring and gaskets, and tighten all fastenings to the specified torques.

---

33 Crankshaft oil seals – renewal

Refer to Section 15.

---

34 Flywheel/driveplate – removal, inspection and refitting

Refer to Section 16.

---

35 Engine/transmission mountings – inspection and renewal

Refer to Section 17.

Part C: 1587cc 4A-GE engine – in-car engine repair procedures

36 General information

How to use this Chapter

This Part covers in-vehicle repair procedures for the 1587 cc 4A-GE engine (fitted to the GTi 16 model).

The Chapter's structure is explained in Section 1.

Engine description

The engine is similar to the 4A-F unit described in Part B (Section 18), except that a single (crankshaft-driven) timing belt drives both the inlet and the exhaust camshafts and the pistons are attached to their connecting rods by fully-floating gudgeon pins, circlips being used to retain the gudgeon pins.

Repair operations possible with the engine in the car

The following work can be carried out with the engine in the car.

(a) Compression pressure – testing.
(b) Camshaft covers – removal and refitting.
(c) Crankshaft pulley – removal and refitting.
(d) Timing belt covers – removal and refitting.

Fig. 2.32 The inlet camshaft cavity is visible when number one piston (nearest the timing end of the engine) is at TDC on compression stroke (Sec 38)

(e) Timing belt – removal, refitting and adjustment
(f) Timing belt tensioner – removal and refitting.
(g) Camshaft oil seal – renewal.
(h) Camshaft and followers – removal, inspection and refitting.
(i) Cylinder head – removal and refitting.
(j) Cylinder head and pistons – decarbonising.
(k) Sump – removal and refitting.
(l) Oil pump – removal, overhaul and refitting.
(m) Crankshaft oil seals – renewal.
(n) Engine/transmission mountings – inspection and renewal.
(o) Flywheel – removal, inspection and refitting.

37 Compression test – description and interpretation

Refer to Section 2.

38 Top Dead Centre (TDC) for number one piston – locating

1 It may be necessary to release the windscreen/tailgate washer fluid reservoir and move it out of the working area (Chapter 12).
2 Drain sufficient coolant from the cooling system to allow the radiator top hose to be disconnected and removed without coolant spillage (Chapter 1).
3 Remove the spark plugs and the power steering pump and alternator/water pump drivebelts (Chapter 1).
4 Using a socket or spanner on the crankshaft pulley bolt, turn the crankshaft pulley clockwise (viewed from the right-hand side of the vehicle) until the pulley groove and the timing belt lower cover '0' mark align; it may be helpful to use white paint or similar carefully to highlight the pulley

groove and the cover '0' mark (photo 20.1).
5 Numbers one and four cylinders are now both at TDC, one of them being on the compression stroke.
6 Remove the engine oil filler cap and check that the camshaft cavity is visible through the oil filler hole (Fig. 2.32). If so, it is number one piston that is on the compression stroke and the crankshaft is now correctly positioned for work to begin; if number four is on the compression stroke, turn the crankshaft pulley one full turn further (again in a clockwise direction) to bring number one piston to TDC on the compression stroke.
7 Refit all disturbed components when finished.

39 Camshaft covers – removal and refitting

Removal

1 Disconnect the battery earth terminal.
2 If applicable, unbolt and remove the HT lead cover (Chapter 1).
3 Unclip the leads from their guides, then disconnect the leads from the spark plugs (having noted their fitment).
4 Disconnect the distributor and the oil pressure gauge sender wiring, then release the wiring 'bridge' from the top of the timing belt upper cover (photo).
5 Disconnect the hose(s) from the rear camshaft cover (photo).
6 Unscrew the retaining nuts and bolts, then remove the plate/cover and the camshaft covers with their gaskets.

Refitting

7 Refitting is a reversal of the removal procedure, noting the following points.
(a) On refitting the camshaft covers, apply sealant to the cylinder head mating surface (Fig. 2.33).
(b) Tighten the camshaft cover retaining nuts to the specified torque setting.

39.4 Releasing wiring 'bridge' from top of timing belt upper cover

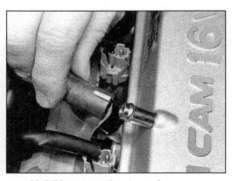

39.5 Disconnecting hose from rear camshaft cover

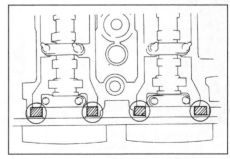

Fig. 2.33 Apply sealant to shaded areas of cylinder head before installing camshaft covers (Sec 39)

40.1A Slackening crankshaft pulley bolt using fabricated tool to prevent crankshaft rotation

40.1B Removing crankshaft pulley – note timing scale on lower timing belt cover in background

41.6 Removing timing belt upper cover

40 Crankshaft pulley – removal **and refitting**

Refer to Section 5 (photos).

41 Timing belt covers – removal and refitting

Removal

Upper cover

1 Disconnect the battery earth terminal.
2 Release the windscreen/tailgate washer fluid reservoir and move it out of the working area (Chapter 12).
3 Drain sufficient coolant from the cooling system to allow the radiator top hose to be disconnected and removed without coolant spillage (Chapter 1).

4 Unclip and move aside the coil-to-distributor HT lead.
5 Disconnect the distributor and the oil pressure gauge sender wiring, then release the wiring 'bridge' from the top of the timing belt upper cover.
6 Unbolt the upper cover, noting the correct locations of the different length bolts, then remove the cover and gasket (where fitted), note the HT lead clip plate fitted under the two top bolts (photo). It may be necessary to release the power steering fluid pipe support bracket to allow the upper cover to be withdrawn.

Centre cover

7 Remove the upper cover, as described above, then remove the power steering pump and alternator/water pump drivebelts and the water pump pulley (Chapters 1, 3 and 10).
8 Remove the crankshaft pulley (Section 40).
9 Unbolt the centre cover, noting the correct

locations of the different length bolts, then remove the cover and gasket (where fitted) (photo).

Lower cover

10 Remove the upper and centre covers as described above.
11 Unbolt the lower cover, noting the correct locations of the different length bolts, then remove the cover and gasket (where fitted) (photo).

Refitting

12 Refitting is the reverse of the removal procedure.

41.9 Removing timing belt centre cover

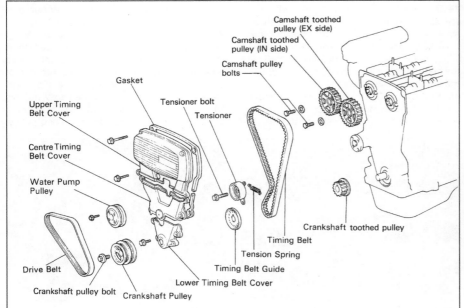

Fig. 2.34 Timing belt, covers and toothed pulleys (Sec 41)

41.11 Removing timing belt lower cover

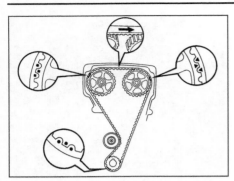

Fig. 2.35 Timing belt-to-toothed pulley alignment marks (Sec 42)

42 Timing belt – removal and refitting

Removal

1 Disconnect the battery earth terminal.
2 Set number one piston to TDC (Section 38) then remove the crankshaft pulley (Section 40); take care not to rotate the crankshaft.
3 Remove the timing belt covers (Section 41).
4 Remove the timing belt guide from the crankshaft toothed pulley, noting which side faces the timing belt (photo).
5 If the timing belt is to be re-used, mark the alignment of the belt to the pulleys and the direction of normal engine rotation. Note the camshaft and crankshaft toothed pulley alignment marks described in paragraph 9 (Fig. 2.35).
6 Slacken the timing belt tensioner bolt, then push the tensioner pulley away from the timing belt and temporarily retighten the bolt.
7 Slip the timing belt from the pulleys. Do **not** alter the position of the camshaft or crankshaft toothed pulleys with the timing belt removed. To enable the timing belt to be fully removed from the vehicle, the weight of the engine must be taken off the right-hand engine/transmission mounting and the mounting separated (if not already done).

Refitting

8 In addition to the regular renewal called for

as part of the normal service schedule (Chapter 1), the timing belt should be renewed, regardless of age or mileage, if it appears to be defective in any manner or if it has been in contact with water, oil or steam; if the belt has evidence of any damage, examine the condition and alignment of all pulleys before fitting a replacement.
9 Before refitting the timing belt, check that the timing marks on the camshaft toothed pulleys are aligned with the marks on the timing end cover; also check that the TDC marks on the crankshaft toothed pulley and the oil pump body are aligned (photos).
10 Fit the timing belt, ensuring that the toothed pulley positions do not alter, so that it is taut on the top and front runs; if the original belt is being refitted, ensure that the arrow marked on the belt during removal faces the correct way and that the belt-to-toothed pulley alignment marks made line up. Reconnect the right-hand engine/transmission mounting, but do not fully tighten the bolts at this stage.
11 Slacken the tensioner bolt and allow the tensioner to return against spring pressure so that the pulley bears on the timing belt; do not tighten the bolt at this stage.
12 Temporarily install the crankshaft pulley bolt.
13 Use a spanner or socket on the crankshaft pulley bolt to turn the crankshaft clockwise (viewed from the vehicle's right-hand side) through two full turns, then check that the camshaft and crankshaft toothed pulley alignment marks remain as described in paragraph 9. If the marks are not correctly aligned, adjust the toothed pulley position until the setting is correct, rotate the crankshaft through two further turns and recheck.
14 Tighten the tensioner pulley bolt to the specified torque, then use a spring balance or similar to ensure there is 4 mm of belt deflection midway between the camshaft toothed pulleys when a downwards force of 2 kgf is applied to the belt top run. If adjustment is required, move the tensioner pulley slightly.
15 Remove the temporarily-installed crankshaft pulley bolt.
16 Refit the timing belt guide to the

crankshaft toothed pulley, ensuring that its concave side is outermost.
17 Refit the timing belt covers and crankshaft pulley (Sections 40 and 41).
18 Refit the power steering pump and alternator/water pump drivebelts and refill the cooling system (Chapter 1).

43 Timing belt tensioner – removal and refitting

Removal

1 Work as described in Section 42, paragraphs 1 to 6.
2 Unhook the spring from the tensioner.
3 Unbolt the tensioner pulley and remove the tensioner assembly.

Refitting

4 Check that the tension spring is in good condition and that the tensioner pulley freely rotates. The tension spring should have a free length of 43. 5 mm, extending to 50.2 mm when subjected to a load of 98 ± 5 N (9.97 ± 0.50 kg).
5 Refit the tensioner and tighten the bolt by hand only at this stage.
6 Reconnect the spring and allow the tensioner pulley to bear against the timing belt; the belt top and front runs should be taut and the belt-to-toothed pulley markings should align.
7 Proceed as described in Section 42, paragraph 12 onwards.

44 Camshaft oil seal – renewal

1 Position number one cylinder at TDC (Section 38) then remove the upper and centre timing belt covers (Section 41).
2 With number one cylinder at TDC the timing marks on the outer edges of the camshaft toothed pulleys should be aligned with marks on the timing end cover (paragraph 9 of Section 42). Also there should be alignment marks between the timing belt and pulleys which should be visible at the 10 o'clock position on the inlet camshaft toothed pulley,

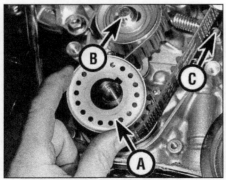

42.4 Removing timing belt guide (A) from crankshaft – note tensioner bolt (B) and tensioner spring anchor (C)

42.9A Timing marks aligned on camshaft sprockets and timing end cover (arrowed)

42.9B TDC marks aligned on crankshaft sprocket and oil pump body (arrowed)

44.6 Removing timing end cover

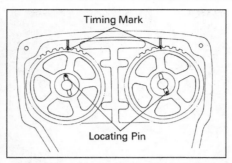

Timing Mark

Locating Pin

Fig. 2.36 Position inlet and exhaust camshaft locating pin and timing marks as shown (Sec 44)

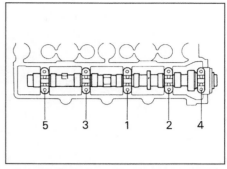

5 3 1 2 4

Fig. 2.37 Camshaft bearing cap tightening sequence (Sec 45)

and the 2 o'clock position on the exhaust camshaft toothed pulley. If these marks are not visible make your own using a marker pen or white paint.

3 Once all the marks have been checked remove the plug from the lower timing belt cover to reach the timing belt tensioner bolt. Slacken the bolt, push the tensioner pulley away from the belt and temporarily retighten the bolt. Slip the belt off the camshaft pulleys and position it clear of the working area. Do not alter the position of the camshaft or crankshaft whilst the belt is removed from the pulleys.

4 Using an open-ended spanner, hold the exhaust camshaft by its hexagonal section to prevent it from rotating, then unscrew the camshaft toothed pulley bolt. Withdraw the pulley, noting the position of the locating pin fitted to the camshaft end. Repeat for the inlet camshaft.

5 Unbolt and remove the right-hand engine/transmission mounting bracket section(s) from the engine, noting the bolt locations; two bracket sections are fitted to later models (Section 53).

6 Unbolt and remove the timing end cover (photo).

7 Punch or drill two small holes opposite each other in the seal. Screw a self-tapping screw into each hole and pull on the screws with pliers to extract the seal.

8 Clean the seal housing and polish off any burrs or raised edges which may have caused the seal to fail in the first place.

9 Lubricate the lips of the new seal with a little multi-purpose grease and ease the seal over the end of the camshaft. Using as a drift a socket which bears only on the seal's hard outer edge, drive the seal squarely into position until it seats on its locating shoulder, then wipe off any surplus grease.

10 Refit the timing end cover, tightening the bolts to the specified torque setting.

11 Fit the right-hand engine/transmission mounting bracket section(s) to the cylinder block, and tighten the bolts to their specified torque.

12 Align the camshaft toothed pulleys with their locating pins as shown in Fig. 2.36, then refit the toothed pulley bolts and washers.

Tighten the bolts to their specified torque whilst holding the camshafts to prevent them rotating.

13 Work as described in Section 42, paragraphs 10, 11, 13 and 14.

14 Refit the plug to the timing belt lower cover, then refit the centre and upper timing belt covers and camshaft covers (Sections 41 and 39).

45 Camshaft and followers – removal, inspection and refitting

Removal

1 Disconnect the battery earth terminal.

2 Remove the distributor (Chapter 5) and the spark plugs (Chapter 1).

3 Remove the camshaft toothed pulleys and timing end cover (Section 44, paragraphs 1 to 6).

4 Using a dial gauge, measure the thrust clearance of each camshaft. This must be within specification; if it exceeds its maximum permissible limit, the camshaft(s) and/or cylinder head must be renewed.

5 Working in several stages, **in the reverse** of the sequence shown in Fig. 2.37, progressively slacken the camshaft bearing cap bolts. Remove the bearing caps, having noted their markings and their correct fitted positions, then lift out the camshafts and remove the oil seals.

45.11 Tightening inlet camshaft bearing cap bolt

6 Lift out the shims and camshaft followers, keeping all components in order for refitting to their original locations.

Inspection

7 Work as described in Section 27, paragraphs 14, 15, 19 and 20.

Refitting

8 Install the camshaft followers and shims to their original bores, where applicable, having lightly oiled the bores, check that the followers can be rotated smoothly in their bores by hand.

9 Lightly oil the camshaft journals and cam lobes, then place the camshafts on the cylinder head with their locating pins positioned as shown in Fig. 2.36. Ensure that the inlet and exhaust camshafts are correctly fitted; the exhaust camshaft has a distributor drive gear.

10 Apply sealant to the cylinder head (Fig. 2.38), then place all the camshaft bearing caps in their original fitted positions.

11 Lightly oil the threads and under the heads of the bearing cap bolts, refit the bolts and tighten them evenly and progressively to the specified torque setting in the sequence shown in Fig. 2.37 (photo).

12 Fit new camshaft oil seals (Section 44).

13 Proceed as described in paragraph 10 onwards of Section 42, noting the valve clearances should be checked (Chapter 1) before the camshaft covers are installed.

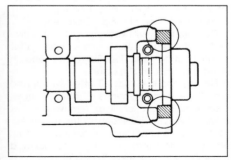

Fig. 2.38 Apply sealant to shaded areas of cylinder head before refitting camshaft bearing caps (Sec 45)

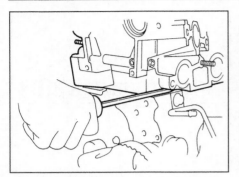

Fig. 2.39 Use leverage only at point shown to release cylinder head (Sec 46)

46.13 Refitting cylinder head

46.14 Tightening cylinder head bolt

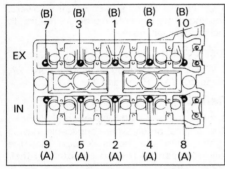

Fig. 2.40 Cylinder head bolt tightening sequence – 4A-GE engine (Sec 46)

A 90 mm bolts   *B 108 mm bolts*

46 Cylinder head – removal and refitting

Removal

1 Drain the cooling system (Chapter 1).
2 Remove the camshafts and followers (Section 45).
3 Remove the exhaust manifold upper heat shield, manifold and stays (Chapter 4).
4 Disconnect and remove the cold start injector fuel pipe, the main fuel delivery pipe and the injectors (Chapter 4). Label all pipe/hose and wiring connections as they are removed, to aid refitting.
5 Disconnect and remove the water inlet housing on the cylinder head left-hand end, labelling the connections for refitting.
6 Remove the throttle body (Chapter 4).
7 Remove the T-VIS vacuum switching valve and vacuum tank assembly after disconnecting (and labelling) the vacuum hoses and undoing the bolts.
8 Having ensured that all other wiring and pipe/hose connections have been disconnected (and labelled), remove the inlet manifold stay and disconnect the crankcase ventilation hose before unscrewing the nuts and bolts and removing the inlet manifold assembly and gasket(s) (Chapter 4).
9 Unbolt and remove the small-bore cooling pipe and water outlet housing and gasket.
10 Working **in the reverse** of the sequence

shown in Fig. 2.40, evenly and progressively slacken the cylinder head bolts. Remove each bolt in turn, with any washers, and store it in its correct fitted position by pushing it through a clearly-marked cardboard template. Note that cylinder head warpage or cracking may occur if the bolts are not removed as instructed.
11 Lift the cylinder head off its dowels and remove it; if it is difficult to release, use a suitable screwdriver or bar to prise it up at the point shown in Fig. 2.39, but be careful not to damage the mating surfaces. Place the cylinder head on wooden blocks on the workbench. If the locating dowels are loose, remove them and store them with the cylinder head for safe keeping. Remove the gasket.
12 Cylinder head overhaul procedures are in Part D.

Refitting

13 Check the condition of the cylinder head bolts and the mating surfaces, clean the surfaces, then fit a new gasket and refit the cylinder head bolts (longer bolts are fitted on the exhaust side of the cylinder head) and washers as described in Section 11, paragraphs 10 to 15 (photo).
14 Working progressively and in several stages, tighten the cylinder head bolts to their Stage one torque setting in the sequence shown in Fig. 2.40 (photo).
15 Mark each bolt head with a spot of paint on the side closest to the cylinder head timing cover end and tighten them, again in the sequence shown, through 90° (Stage 2 of the tightening procedure).
16 Tighten the bolts through a further 90°, again in the sequence shown (Stage 3); each bolt's paint mark should now be facing the cylinder head left-hand end.
17 The remainder of reassembly is a reversal of the removal sequence, noting the following points.
(a) Before refitting the camshaft cover, check and adjust the valve clearances (Chapter 1).
(b) On completion refill the cooling system then start the engine and check the ignition timing, idle speed and fuel mixture settings (Chapter 1).

47 Sump – removal and refitting

Refer to Section 29.

48 Oil pump – removal and refitting

Removal

1 Remove the sump (Section 29).
2 Undo the nuts and bolts securing the oil pick up pipe/strainer, then remove it with its gasket. Remove the sump baffle plate from the base of the cylinder block.
3 Remove the timing belt from the toothed pulleys (Section 42); there is no need to fully remove it.
4 Remove the timing belt tensioner (Section 43).
5 Remove the crankshaft toothed pulley. If it is a tight fit, lever it off using two screwdrivers. Remove the Woodruff key from the crankshaft and store it with the pulley for safe keeping.
6 Withdraw the engine oil dipstick, then unbolt and withdraw its guide tube.
7 Unbolt and remove the oil pump: if necessary carefully tap the pump with a soft-faced hammer to release it.
8 The oil pump relief valve assembly is covered in Section 49, the oil pressure regulator valve in Section 50.
9 Oil pump inspection, dismantling and reassembly is covered in Section 49, the oil pressure gauge sender and gauge in Chapter 12.

Refitting

10 Clean the sump and ensure that the oil pick-up pipe/strainer is clear.
11 Renew the crankshaft right-hand oil seal whilst the oil pump is removed (Section 15).
12 Thoroughly clean the pump's mating faces and ensure that the engine block mating face is clean.
13 Lightly oil the crankshaft oil pump drive and oil seal contact surfaces.
14 Position a new pump gasket on the cylinder block, then refit the pump, ensuring

that its drive rotor engages with the crankshaft drive. Refit the pump bolts and tighten them to the specified torque.

15 Fit a new O-ring to the base of the engine oil dipstick guide tube, lubricating it with oil, then install and secure the guide tube; refit the dipstick.

16 Refit the Woodruff key to the crankshaft then align the crankshaft toothed pulley slot with the Woodruff key and slide the pulley onto the crankshaft.

17 Refit the timing belt tensioner and timing belt (Sections 42 and 43).

18 Apply sealant sparingly to the sump mating surface (Fig.2.31). Offer the baffle plate into position, ensuring that no oil contaminates the mating faces.

19 Using a new gasket, refit the oil pick-up pipe/strainer and tighten the nuts and bolts to the specified torque.

20 Refit the sump (Section 47).

49 Oil pump and relief valve – inspection, dismantling and reassembly

Rotor-type oil pump

1 Refer to Section 31.

Gear-type oil pump

2 Working methods are similar to those given for the rotor type except for the gears and the crescent in between; refer therefore to Section 31, noting the following.

3 Body clearance and side clearance are measured as described for the rotor type, as is relief valve inspection. Tip clearance measurement is made as shown in Fig. 2.41 (between each gear tip and the crescent).

50 Oil cooler and pressure regulator valve – general information

Refer to Section 32; note the exhaust manifold stay must be removed for access to the oil pressure regulator valve or the combined bracket/housing.

51 Crankshaft oil seals – renewal

Refer to Section 15.

52 Flywheel – removal, inspection and refitting

Refer to Section 16 and Fig. 2.42.

53 Engine/transmission mountings – inspection and renewal

Refer to Section 17, noting that the later right-hand mounting has two sections (one main and one upper) which bolt to the engine; earlier mountings had a single section.

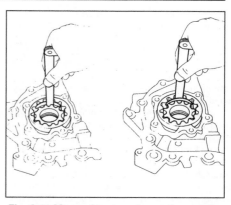

Fig. 2.41 Measuring gear-type oil pump tip clearances (Sec 49)

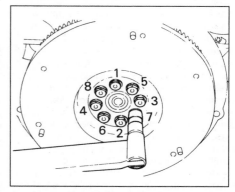

Fig. 2.42 Flywheel retaining bolt tightening sequence – 4A-GE engines (Sec 52)

Part D: Engine removal and general overhaul procedures

54 General information

Included in this Part of Chapter 2 are details of removing the engine/ transmission unit from the car and general overhaul procedures for the cylinder head, cylinder block/ crankcase and all other engine internal components.

The information given ranges from advice concerning preparation for an overhaul and the purchase of replacement parts, to detailed step-by-step procedures covering removal, inspection, renovation and refitting of engine internal components.

After Section 58, all instructions are based on the assumption that the engine has been removed from the car. For information concerning in-car engine repair, as well as the removal and refitting of those external components necessary for full overhaul, refer to the relevant Section of Part A, B or C of this Chapter (as appropriate) and to Section 58. Ignore any preliminary dismantling operations described in Part A, B or C that are no longer

relevant once the engine has been removed from the car.

All specifications relating to engine overhaul are at the beginning of this Chapter.

55 Engine overhaul – general information

It is not always easy to determine when, or if, an engine should be completely overhauled, as a number of factors must be considered.

High mileage is not necessarily an indication that an overhaul is needed, while low mileage does not preclude the need for an overhaul. Frequency of servicing is probably the most important consideration; an engine which has had regular and frequent oil and filter changes, as well as other required maintenance, should give many thousands of miles of reliable service. Conversely, a neglected engine may require an overhaul very early in its life.

Excessive oil consumption is an indication that piston rings, valve seals and/or valve

guides are in need of attention. Make sure that oil leaks are not responsible before deciding that the rings and/or guides are worn. Perform a compression test (Section 2), to determine the likely cause of the problem.

Check the oil pressure with a gauge fitted in place of the oil pressure switch and compare it with that specified (photo). If it is extremely low, the main and big-end bearings and/or the oil pump are probably worn out.

55.1 Oil pressure switch (arrowed)

Loss of power, rough running, knocking or metallic engine noises, excessive valve gear noise and high fuel consumption may also point to the need for an overhaul, especially if they are all present at the same time. If a complete service does not remedy the situation, major mechanical work is the only solution.

An engine overhaul involves restoring all internal parts to the specification of a new engine. During an overhaul, the cylinder liners, the pistons and the piston rings are renewed. New main and big-end bearings are generally fitted and if necessary, the crankshaft may be renewed to restore the journals. The valves are also serviced as well, since they are usually in less than perfect condition at this point. While the engine is being overhauled, other components, such as the distributor, starter and alternator, can be overhauled as well. The end result should be an as-new engine that will give many trouble-free miles. **Note:** *Critical cooling system components such as the hoses, thermostat and water pump should be renewed when an engine is overhauled The radiator should be checked carefully to ensure that it is not clogged or leaking. Also it is a good idea to renew the oil pump whenever the engine is overhauled*

Before beginning the engine overhaul, read through the entire procedure to familiarize yourself with the scope and requirements of the job. Overhauling an engine is not difficult if you follow carefully all of the instructions, have the necessary tools and equipment and pay close attention to all specifications; however, it can be time-consuming. Plan on the car being off the road for a minimum of two weeks, especially if parts must be taken to an engineering works for repair or reconditioning. Check on the availability of parts and make sure that any necessary special tools and equipment are obtained in advance. Most work can be done with typical hand tools, although a number of precision measuring tools are required for inspecting parts to determine if they must be renewed. Often the engineering works will handle the inspection of parts and offer advice concerning reconditioning and renewal. **Note:** *Always wait until the engine has been completely dismantled and all components, especially the cylinder block/crankcase and the crankshaft have been inspected before deciding what service and repair operations must be performed by an engineering works. Since the condition of these components will be the major factor to consider when determining whether to overhaul the original engine or buy a reconditioned unit, do not purchase parts or have overhaul work done on other components until they have been thoroughly inspected . As a general rule, time is the primary cost of an overhaul, so it does not pay to fit worn or substandard parts.*

As a final note, to ensure maximum life and minimum trouble from a reconditioned engine, everything must be assembled with care in a spotlessly clean environment.

56 Engine/transmission removal – methods and precautions

If you have decided that the engine must be removed for overhaul or major repair work, several preliminary steps should be taken.

Locating a suitable place to work is extremely important. Adequate work space, along with storage space for the car, will be needed. If a shop or garage is not available, at the very least a flat, level, clean work surface is required.

Cleaning the engine compartment and engine/transmission before beginning the removal procedure will help keep tools clean and organized.

An engine hoist or A-frame will also be necessary. Make sure the equipment is rated in excess of the combined weight of the engine and transmission (290 lb/130 kg approximately). Safety is of primary importance, considering the potential hazards involved in lifting the engine/transmission out of the car.

If the engine/transmission is being removed by a novice, a helper should be available. Advice and aid from someone more experienced would also be helpful. There are many instances when one person cannot simultaneously perform all of the operations required when lifting the engine out of the car.

Plan the operation ahead of time. Before starting work, arrange for the hire of, or obtain all of the tools and equipment you will need. Some of the equipment necessary to perform engine/transmission removal and installation safely and with relative ease are (in addition to an engine hoist) a heavy duty trolley jack, a complete set of spanners and sockets as described in the front of this Manual, wooden blocks and plenty of rags and cleaning solvent for mopping up spilled oil, coolant and fuel. If the hoist must be hired, make sure that you arrange for it in advance and perform all of the operations possible without it beforehand. This will save you money and time.

Plan for the car to be out of use for quite a while. An engineering works will be required to perform some of the work which the do-it-yourselfer cannot accomplish without special equipment. These places often have a busy schedule, so it would be a good idea to consult them before removing the engine to accurately estimate the amount of time required to rebuild or repair components that may need work.

Always be extremely careful when removing and refitting the engine/transmission. Serious injury can result from careless actions. Plan ahead, take your time and a job of this nature, although major, can be accomplished successfully.

57 Engine/transmission – removal and refitting

Note: *The recommended method of removal is to raise the front of the vehicle and to support it (securely) high enough that the engine/ transmission can be unbolted, lowered to the ground and removed from underneath. To do this, an engine hoist or similar will be required to take the weight of the unit as it is raised or lowered; a strong trolley jack (obtainable from a local tool-hire shop) could be used provided that a wooden spacer is available to spread the load and to prevent damage to the sump/transmission casing. Also, a pair of axle stands will be required and an engine dolly (a wheeled platform) would be very useful to save strain and prevent the risk of damage when moving the unit out of the vehicle.*

Removal

1 Disconnect the battery earth terminal.
2 Remove the bonnet (Chapter 11).
3 Remove the air filter housing/trunking (Chapter 4), and the windscreen/tailgate washer fluid reservoir (Chapter 12).
4 Disconnect the speedometer cable in the engine compartment and secure it clear of the engine (Chapter 12).
5 On models with manual gearboxes, disconnect the reversing lamp switch multi-plug and the gearchange control cables (Chapter 7).
6 Disconnect the clutch slave cylinder (where applicable). It will also be necessary to release its pipe/hose support bracket(s) and remove the pipe/hose (Chapter 6).
7 Disconnect the accelerator cable and secure it clear of the engine (Chapter 4).
8 Disconnect the brake servo vacuum hose from the inlet manifold (Chapter 9) (photo).
9 Disconnect the fuel hoses (Chapter 4).
10 Disconnect all remaining hoses, having labelled and noted them for refitting.
11 Except for the starter motor wiring and, (automatic transmission-equipped vehicles only) the neutral start switch wiring, disconnect the wiring from all electrical components, having labelled and noted the

57.8 Disconnecting brake servo vacuum hose from inlet manifold

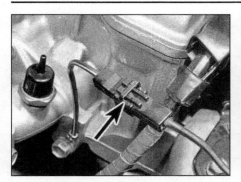

57.11A Inlet manifold earth connection multiplug (arrowed)

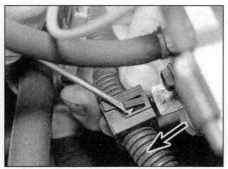

57.11B Releasing loom (with clip) from loom support bracket

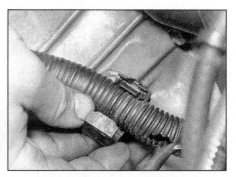

57.11C Releasing loom from fixed clip on gearbox

connections for refitting, then secure them clear of the engine. Note the routes taken and the clips used to secure the loom sections (photos). Where applicable, the wiring 'bridge' over the timing end of the engine must be released and withdrawn after disconnecting its connections.

12 Disconnect and remove the power steering pump, if necessary, (Chapter 10). Also release the pipes from their support brackets where necessary, so that they can be moved out of the way if they are likely to impede engine removal.

13 Slacken the front roadwheel nuts, then raise the front of the vehicle and support it securely on axle stands; ensure that there will be sufficient clearance to allow the engine and gearbox/transmission to be withdrawn from underneath. Remove the front roadwheels.

14 Working underneath the vehicle, remove the undershields.

15 Drain the cooling system, engine oil and gearbox/transmission oil/fluid (Chapter 1).

16 Disconnect and remove all coolant and heater hoses, having noted their connections and labelled them for refitting (photos).

17 On vehicles equipped with automatic transmission, disconnect the selector cable and the neutral start switch wiring (Chapter 7).

18 Disconnect the starter motor wiring (and the alternator and oil pressure switch/sender wiring if it was not disconnected from above) (Chapter 12). Also check to ensure that all earth leads have been disconnected.

19 Disconnect and remove the exhaust downpipe, release the forward mounting of the main exhaust section from the engine/transmission mounting crossmember, and support (or suspend) it to avoid straining its mountings (Chapter 4).

20 Where applicable, disconnect the oil cooler hose unions (Sections 32 and 50). Catch spillage in a suitable container, then tuck the hoses out of the way.

21 On automatic transmission-equipped vehicles, disconnect the transmission fluid cooler hoses.

22 Working as described in Chapter 8, Section 2, disconnect the driveshafts from the gearbox and suspend them out of the way using lengths of strong wire; note that (unless they are to be removed anyway) the driveshafts need not be disconnected from the hub carriers, therefore the instructions can be ignored in paragraphs 6, 7, 10, 11 and 13 of that procedure.

23 Remove both front suspension lower arm rear mounting brackets and, if applicable, move the anti-roll bar towards the rear of the vehicle or remove it (Chapter 10).

24 Take the weight of the engine and gearbox/transmission. Disconnect the rearmost engine/transmission mounting from the front suspension crossmember by undoing its securing nuts, then disconnect the forward and centre engine/transmission mountings from the mounting crossmember (Section 17); remove the centre engine/

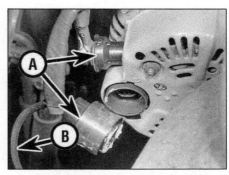

57.11D Alternator wiring connections (A) oil pressure switch wire (B)

transmission mounting (this may need to be done as the crossmember assembly is removed).

25 With the aid of an assistant, unbolt and remove the suspension and engine/transmission crossmember assembly; note the bolt locations as they are removed (Chapter 10) (photo).

26 Disconnect the engine and transmission right- and left-hand (upper) mountings, noting that it may also be necessary to remove the bracket sections from the engine/transmission, then make a final check that all components have been removed or

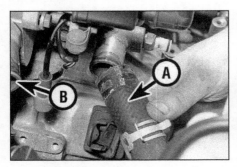

57.16A Disconnecting radiator bottom hose (A) from water inlet housing – note radiator top hose connection (B)

57.16B Heater hose being disconnected from water inlet/thermostat housing

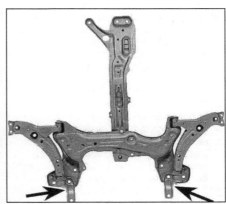

57.25 Suspension and engine/transmission crossmember – front suspension lower arm rear mounting brackets (arrowed)

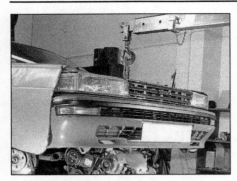

57.27 Lowering engine and gearbox/ transmission assembly from vehicle

disconnected that will prevent the removal of the engine/transmission from the car.

27 Carefully and slowly lower the engine and gearbox/transmission unit; take care to ensure that no damage is caused or that nothing becomes snagged (photo).

28 Separate the engine from the gearbox/transmission (Chapter 7), noting the following.

(a) The starter motor must be removed (Chapter 12).

(b) It may be necessary to remove the water housing on the gearbox/ transmission end of the engine for access to the flange bolts.

(c) On manual gearbox-equipped vehicles it may be necessary to remove the clutch slave cylinder (Chapter 6).

(d) On automatic transmission-equipped vehicles, the kickdown cable must be disconnected from the throttle linkage (Chapter 7).

Refitting

29 Refitting is a reversal of the removal procedure, noting the following points.

(a) Ensure that any engine adaptor plates removed are refitted.

(b) On manual gearbox-equipped vehicles, if the clutch has been disturbed, centralise the driven plate before offering the gearbox to the engine (Chapter 6).

(c) On automatic transmission-equipped vehicles, if the torque converter has been disturbed ensure that it has been refilled and installed correctly before mating the engine and transmission (Chapter 7).

(d) Do **not** draw the gearbox/transmission onto the engine using the flange bolts.

(e) Where the water housing has been removed for access to remove/refit the flange bolts, suitable sealant should be used during refitting.

(f) Use new split pins, gaskets and snap rings, during refitting, also new anti-roll bar link nuts, if applicable.

(g) Tighten the roadwheel nuts and the front suspens/on lower arm rear mounting bracket fixings to their specified torques with the weight of the vehicle resting on its roadwheels.

(h) On automatic transmission-equipped vehicles, the kickdown cable and selector cables must be adjusted (Chapter 7).

(i) Check/adjust the accelerator cable (Chapter 4).

(j) Refill the clutch hydraulic system on manual gearbox equipped vehicles, then bleed it (Chapter 6).

(k) The power steering system must be topped up/refilled (where applicable), and the engine, gearbox/transmission and cooling system must be refilled (Chapter 1).

(l) The power steering pump drivebelt (and the alternator drivebelt, if disturbed) must be tensioned (Chapter 1).

(m) Reconnect the battery earth terminal, then start the engine (Section 71).

(n) Where applicable, bleed the power steering system (Chapter 10).

58 Engine overhaul – dismantling sequence

1 It is much easier to dismantle and work on the engine if it is mounted on a portable engine stand. These stands can often be hired from a tool hire shop. Before the engine is mounted on a stand, the flywheel/driveplate should be removed (Section 16), so that the stand bolts can be tightened into the end of the cylinder block/crankcase.

2 If a stand is not available, it is possible to dismantle the engine with it blocked up on a sturdy workbench or on the floor. Be extra careful not to tip or drop the engine when working without a stand.

3 If you are going to obtain a reconditioned engine, all external components must be removed first to be transferred to the replacement engine (just as they will if you are doing a complete engine overhaul yourself). These components include the following:

(a) Alternator and brackets.

(b) Distributor, HT leads and spark plugs.

(c) Thermostat and cover.

(d) Carburettor.

(e) Inlet and exhaust manifolds

(f) Oil filter (use a new one when reassembling the engine).

(g) Fuel pump.

(h) Engine mountings.

(i) Flywheel/driveplate and left-hand end plate.

(j) Starter motor.

(k) Power steering pump and brackets (where applicable).

(l) All other components not fitted on the reconditioned engine.

Note: When removing the external components from the engine, pay close attention to details that may be helpful or important during refitting. Note the fitted position of gaskets, seals, spacers, pins, washers, bolts and other small items.

4 If you are obtaining a short motor (which consists of the engine cylinder block/

crankcase and main bearing ladder, crankshaft, pistons and connecting rods all assembled), then the cylinder head, sump, oil pump, and timing belt will have to be removed also.

5 If you are planning a complete overhaul, the engine can be dismantled and the internal components removed in the following order:

(a) Inlet and exhaust manifolds.

(b) Timing belt, toothed pulleys and associated components.

(c) Water pump and associated components.

(d) Cylinder head.

(e) Flywheel.

(f) Sump.

(g) Oil pump.

(h) Pistons.

(i) Crankshaft.

6 Before beginning the dismantling and overhaul procedures, make sure that you have all of the correct tools necessary. Refer to the introductory pages at the beginning of this Manual for further information.

59 Cylinder head – dismantling

Note: New and reconditioned cylinder heads are available from the manufacturer and from engine overhaul specialists. Due to the fact that some specialist tools are required for the dismantling and inspection procedures, and new components may not be readily available, it may be more practical and economical for the home mechanic to purchase a reconditioned head rather than dismantle, inspect and recondition the original head.

1 Remove the camshaft(s) and the rocker arms/followers, then remove the cylinder head as described in the relevant Sections of Part A, B or C (as applicable).

2 It is essential that the valves (and associated components) are kept in their exact original fitted sequence unless they are so badly worn that they are to be renewed. If they are going to be kept and used again, place them in a labelled polythene bag or alternatively use a suitable sub-divided box, labelled so that it corresponds to the fitted positions of the valves (photo).

59.2 Store valves and their associated components individually in labelled polythene bags

59.3A After removing split collets, remove valve spring retainer . . .

59.3B . . . followed by valve spring. . .

59.3C . . . and spring seat

3 Using a suitable valve spring compressor, compress each valve spring in turn until the split collets can be removed. Release the compressor and lift off the valve spring retainer, spring and spring seat (photos). If, when the valve spring compressor is screwed down, the valve spring retainer refuses to free and expose the split collets, gently tap the top of the tool (directly over the retainer) with a light hammer; this will free the retainer.

4 Withdraw the valves and remove the oil seal from each valve guide (photos).

5 On 4A-F engines, do not remove the spark plug tubes; if renewal of a spark plug tube is necessary the task should be entrusted to a suitable engineering workshop or a Toyota dealer.

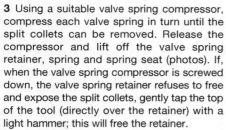

60 Cylinder head and valves – cleaning and inspection

1 Thorough cleaning of the cylinder head and valve components, followed by a detailed inspection, will enable you to decide how much valve service work must be carried out during the engine overhaul. **Note:** *If the engine has been severely overheated, it is best to assume that the cylinder head is warped and to check carefully for signs of this.*

Cleaning

2 Scrape away all traces of old gasket

material and sealing compound from the cylinder head (Section 11).

3 Scrape away the carbon from the combustion chambers and ports, then wash the cylinder head thoroughly with paraffin or a suitable solvent.

4 Clean the valve guides using a brush and suitable solvent.

5 Scrape off any heavy carbon deposits that may have formed on the valves, then use a power-operated wire brush to remove deposits from the valve heads and stems.

Inspection

Note: *Be sure to perform all the following inspection procedures before concluding that the services of a machine shop or engine overhaul specialist are required. Make a list of all items that require attention.*

Cylinder head

6 Inspect the head very carefully for cracks, evidence of coolant leakage and other damage. If cracks are found a new cylinder head should be obtained.

7 Use a known straight-edge and feeler blades to check that the cylinder head mating surfaces are not excessively distorted (Fig. 2.43). If they are, the cylinder head must be renewed.

8 Examine the valve seats in each of the combustion chambers. If they are severely pitted, cracked or burned then they will need to be renewed or recut by an engine overhaul

specialist. If they are only slightly pitted, this can be removed by grinding the valve heads and seats together (with fine grinding paste) as described below.

9 If the valve guides are worn, indicated by a side-to-side motion of the valve in its guide, new guides and valves must be fitted. This work should be entrusted to an engine overhaul specialist as, in addition to the facilities required to install the guides, the guides must be accurately reamed after installation to ensure that the clearance between them and the new valves is as specified.

Valves

10 Examine the heads of each valve for pitting, burning, cracks and general wear; look for severe pitting and excessive wear on the end of each valve stem. Should any of these

59.4A Withdraw valves through combustion chambers

59.4B Removing seal from a valve guide

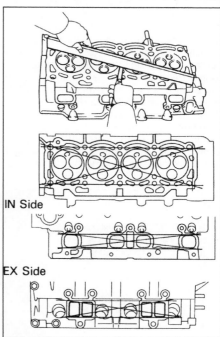

IN Side

EX Side

Fig. 2.43 Using straight-edge and feeler blades to check cylinder head mating surfaces for distortion (Sec 60)

60.12 Measuring valve stem diameter

60.15 Measuring valve spring free length

conditions be apparent, the valve(s) must be renewed. If minor pitting is present on the end of any valve stem, it can be resurfaced on a grinding wheel, ensuring that the overall valve length is not reduced to below its specified minimum. However this is a very specialised task and should be entrusted to an engine repair specialist.

11 Check each valve stem for scoring and wear ridges, then rotate the valves and check for any obvious indication that they are bent. If any of the conditions outlined are present, the affected valves and their respective valve guides should be renewed by an engine overhaul specialist.

12 Measure each valves stem diameter (at several points) using a micrometer (photo), then measure the internal diameter of its valve guide (again at several points in the bore) using suitable internal calipers; if any measurement stands out as being significantly difference to that expected, it is a likely indication of wear. Subtract the valve stem diameter from the valve guide bore diameter to obtain the oil clearance; if the oil clearance is outside the maximum specified figure, the valve and its guide must be renewed by an engine overhaul specialist. Repeat the operation for the remaining valves.

13 If the valves are in a satisfactory condition, or replacements obtained, they should be ground (lapped) into their respective seats to ensure a smooth gas-tight seal. Valve grinding is carried out as follows,

with the cylinder head placed upside down on a bench and a block of wood placed under each end to give clearance for the valve stems (and the spark plug tubes on 4A-F engines).

14 Smear a trace of fine carborundum paste (on a modern engine, if the seats are so bad as to require coarse compound, they should be re-cut) on the seat face and press a suction grinding tool onto the valve head. With a semi-rotary action, grind the valve head to its seat, lifting the valve occasionally to redistribute the grinding paste. A light spring placed under the valve head will greatly ease this operation. When a smooth unbroken 'ring' of light grey matt finish is produced on both the valve and seat, the grinding operation is complete (the 'ring' produced should be centrally located on the valve's contact face; if it is not, the valve seat in the cylinder head will require recutting by your Toyota dealer or engine overhaul specialist). Be sure to remove **all** traces of grinding paste using paraffin or a suitable solvent before reassembly of the cylinder head.

Valve components

15 Examine the valve springs for signs of damage and discoloration, and measure their free length (photo) or compare the original spring with a new component.

16 Stand each spring on a flat surface and check it for squareness. If any of the springs are damaged, distorted or have lost their tension, obtain a complete new set of springs.

1 Lubricate the stem of the first valve to be installed (using clean engine oil), then insert it into its original location in the cylinder head. If new valves are being fitted, they must be inserted in the locations into which they have been ground.

2 Dip the new oil seal in clean engine oil then carefully locate it over the protruding valve stem and onto the guide; on 4A-F engines, the top surface of intake seals is painted brown, that of exhaust seals is black. Take care not to damage the seal as it is passed over the valve stem, and use a suitable socket or metal tube to press it firmly onto the guide (photo).

3 Locate the spring seat followed by the spring and retainer; where applicable the spring should be fitted with its closest coils towards the head.

4 Compress the valve spring and locate the split collets in the recess in the valve stem; use a little grease to hold the collets in place (photo). Release the compressor, then repeat the procedure on the remaining valves.

5 With all the valves installed, place the cylinder head flat on the bench and lightly tap the end of each valve stem (using a soft-faced hammer) to settle the components.

6 Refit the brackets and housings removed from the cylinder head on dismantling, using new gaskets where necessary; refer to the Specifications for tightening torque details and note that the engine lifting eyes on 2E engines have thread-locking compound applied to their bolt threads before insertion.

7 On 4A-F engines, if the semi-circular plug has been removed from the cylinder head, clean it then apply suitable sealant to its cylinder head mating face before installing it; it should ideally be installed during the cylinder head refitting procedure, so that it is firmly held in place by the camshaft cover.

1 Remove the cylinder head, sump, the oil pick up pipe/strainer and, on 4A-GE engines, the sump baffle plate as described in the relevant Sections of Part A, B or C (as applicable). Note that if extra clearance is required, it may also be necessary to remove the oil pump.

2 Rotate the crankshaft so that number 1 big-end cap (nearest the timing belt) is at the lowest point of its travel. If the cap and rod are not already numbered, mark them with a centre punch in relation to the cylinder they operate in; also note which side of the engine block the rod and cap marks face (photo).

3 Use feeler gauges, measuring between the side of each big-end cap and the crankshaft web, or a dial gauge to check the connecting

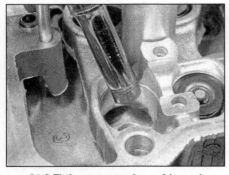

61.2 Fitting a new valve guide seal

61.4 Use grease to hold collets in place on refitting

62.2 Punch marks (arrowed) made to identify connecting rod and cap cylinder numbers

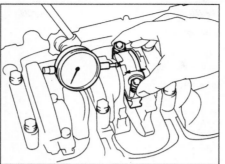

Fig. 2.44 Checking connecting rod thrust clearance (Sec 62)

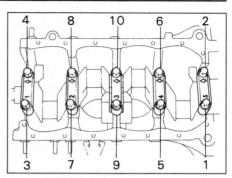

Fig. 2.45 Main bearing cap bolt slackening sequence – note cap markings – 1.6 models shown (Sec 63)

rod thrust clearance (Fig. 2.44); if the clearance is excessive, the connecting rods or the crankshaft must be renewed. Big-end bearing running clearance checking is covered in Section 70.

4 Unscrew and remove the big-end bearing cap nuts and withdraw the cap from the connecting rod, complete with bearing shell. The cap may need a light tap with a soft-faced mallet to free it. If only the bearing shells are being attended to, push the connecting rod up and off the crankpin and remove its bearing shell (noting its fitted orientation). Keep the bearing shells and caps together in their correct sequence if they are to be refitted.

5 Push the connecting rod up and remove the piston and rod from the bore; remove the wear ridge at the top of the cylinder bore (measure and note the diameter at the top of each cylinder) (Section 64) before the piston and rod assembly is removed. Ensure that any debris is contained and thoroughly cleaned away. Refit the bearing shell (correctly orientated) to the connecting rod, then refit the cap and bearing shell to the connecting rod to avoid any possible mix-up of components.

6 Repeat the appropriate steps for the remaining piston/connecting rod assemblies, as required.

7 It is strongly recommended that the original cap nuts and bolts are discarded and new ones obtained for reassembly.

63 Crankshaft – removal

1 With the oil pump, flywheel, left-hand end plate and left-hand oil seal housing removed, and the piston/connecting rod assemblies withdrawn, proceed as follows.

2 Before the crankshaft is removed, check the endfloat using a dial gauge applied to the crankshaft end. Push the crankshaft fully one way and zero the gauge. Push the crankshaft fully the other way and check the endfloat. The result can be compared with that specified and will show whether new thrustwashers are required; if a dial gauge is not available, feeler gauges can be used (photos).

3 Identification numbers should be cast onto the base of each main bearing cap, but if not, number the caps and crankcase using a centre punch.

4 Uniformly unscrew the main bearing cap retaining bolts, in the sequence shown in Fig. 2.45, making several passes, then withdraw the caps complete with bearing shells; note the original fitted positions of the caps. Also remove the semi-circular thrustwashers from either side of the centre main bearing cap, noting that the oil grooves face outwards.

5 Carefully lift the crankshaft from the crankcase.

6 Remove the thrustwashers and the bearing

shell upper halves from their crankcase locations, noting how each is installed (photos). Place each shell with its respective bearing cap.

64 Cylinder block/crankcase – cleaning and inspection

Cleaning

1 For complete cleaning, the core plugs should be removed (where fitted). Drill a small hole in them, then insert a self-tapping screw and pull out the plugs using a pair of grips or a slide hammer; use new core plugs when the engine is reassembled. Also remove all

63.2A Checking crankshaft endfloat using a dial gauge

63.2B Checking crankshaft endfloat using feeler gauges

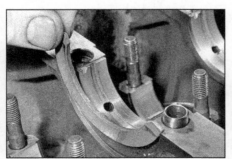

63.6A Removing thrustwasher from crankcase centre main bearing — note thrustwasher oil grooves face outwards

63.6B Removing main bearing shell upper half from crankcase

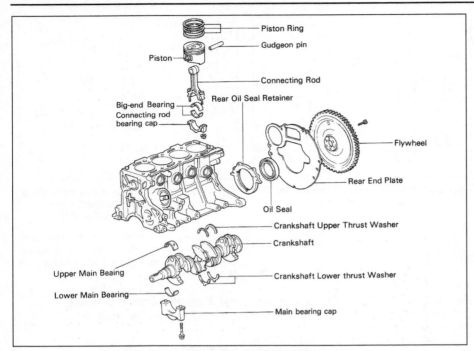

Fig. 2.46 Cylinder block components – 1.3 models (Sec 64)

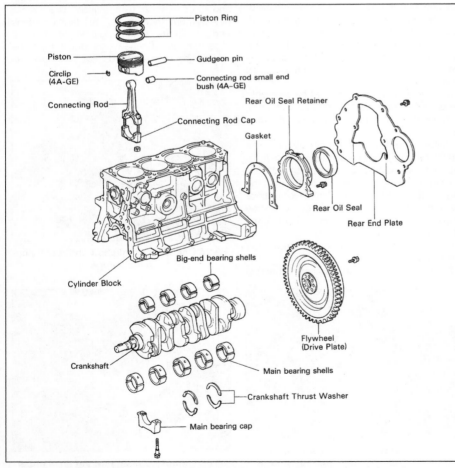

Fig. 2.47 Cylinder block components – 1.6 models (Sec 64)

external components and senders, noting their fitted positions.

2 Scrape all traces of gasket from the cylinder block, taking care not to damage the head and sump mating faces.

3 Remove all oil gallery plugs, where fitted. The plugs are usually very tight; they may have to be drilled out and the holes re-tapped – this task is best entrusted to your Toyota dealer, or engine overhaul specialist, if you have any doubt as to your ability to ensure effective removal and correct sealing during refitting. Use new plugs when the engine is reassembled. The oil nozzles and check valves should also be removed on 4A-GE engines.

4 If the block is extremely dirty, it should be steam-cleaned.

5 After the block is returned, clean all oil holes and oil galleries one more time. Flush all internal passages with warm water until the water runs clear, dry the block thoroughly and wipe all machined surfaces with a light rust-preventive oil. If you have access to compressed air, use it to speed the drying process and to blow out all the oil holes and galleries.

> ⚠ **Warning: Wear eye protection when using compressed air!**

6 If the block is not very dirty, you can do an adequate cleaning job with hot soapy water and a stiff brush. Take plenty of time and do a thorough job. Regardless of the cleaning method used, be sure to clean all oil holes and galleries very thoroughly, dry the block completely and coat all machined surfaces with light oil.

7 The threaded holes in the block must be clean to ensure accurate torque readings during reassembly. Run the proper size tap into each of the holes to remove rust, corrosion, thread sealant or sludge and restore damaged threads. If possible, use compressed air to clear the holes of debris produced by this operation. Now is a good time to clean the threads on the head bolts and the main bearing cap bolts as well.

> ⚠ **Warning: Wear eye protection when using compressed air!**

8 Refit the main bearing caps and tighten the bolts finger tight.

9 After coating the mating surfaces of the new core plugs with suitable sealant refit them in the cylinder block. Make sure that they are driven in straight and seated properly or leakage could result. Special tools are available for this purpose, but a large socket, with an outside diameter that will just slip into the core plug will work just as well.

10 Apply suitable sealant to the new oil gallery plugs and insert them into the holes in the block; tighten them securely. On 4A-GE engines, refit the oil nozzles and check valves and tighten them to their specified torque.

11 Refit the senders and external

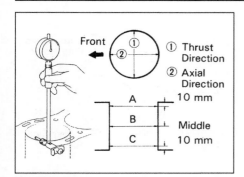

Fig. 2.48 Measuring cylinder bore (Sec 64)

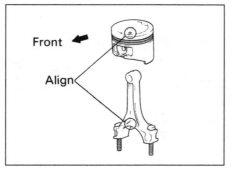
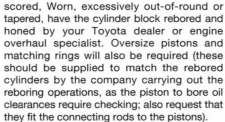

Fig. 2.49 Connecting rod mark and piston cavity must face same way – 1.3 models (Sec 65)

65.1 Measuring a piston

components after checking the cylinder block in accordance with the text below. If the engine is not going to be reassembled right away, cover it with a large plastic bag to keep it clean and prevent it rusting.

Inspection

12 Visually check the block for cracks, rust and corrosion. Look for stripped threads in the threaded holes. If there has been any history of internal water leakage, it may be worthwhile having an engine overhaul specialist check the block with special equipment. If defects are found, have the block repaired (if possible) or renewed.
13 Using a straight-edge and feeler blades, check the cylinder head mating face of the cylinder block to ensure that it is not warped; if warpage is greater than specified, the cylinder block must be renewed.
14 Check the cylinder bores for scuffing and scoring.
15 Measure and note the diameter of each cylinder bore (Fig. 2.48).
16 If there is a significant difference between any of the measurements taken, the cylinder is excessively out-of-round or tapered it must be rebored. Additionally, the cylinder bore must not be worn more than the specified maximum allowable amount from its standard or oversize diameter; the wear can be determined by measuring right at the top of the cylinder (on the wear ridge) to obtain the (standard or oversize) cylinder bore diameter, then subtracting it from the largest reading obtained.
17 Another method of determining the standard cylinder bore diameter (on applicable engines), assuming that the engine has not been rebored, is to look for the marks 1, 2 or 3 adjacent to the cylinders on the top surface of the cylinder block; the marks represent a 0.01 mm increase in diameter from the lower standard cylinder bore diameter figure (eg. the number 2 indicates that the bore diameter is 0.02 mm larger than the lowest standard bore size specified). If the original pistons are fitted, similar marks will be on the piston crowns.
18 If the cylinder walls are badly scuffed,

scored, worn, excessively out-of-round or tapered, have the cylinder block rebored and honed by your Toyota dealer or engine overhaul specialist. Oversize pistons and matching rings will also be required (these should be supplied to match the rebored cylinders by the company carrying out the reboring operations, as the piston to bore oil clearances require checking; also request that they fit the connecting rods to the pistons).
19 If the cylinder bores are in reasonably good condition then it may only be necessary to renew the piston rings and, using a suitable reamer, to remove the wear ridges at the top of each cylinder bore, if not already done during piston removal.
20 If the wear ridges have been removed and new piston rings fitted, the bores should be honed to allow the new rings to bed in correctly and provide the best possible seal. If the necessary equipment is not available, or if you are not sure whether you are competent to undertake the task yourself, an engine overhaul specialist will carry out the work at moderate cost.

65 Piston/connecting rod assembly – inspection

1 Clean the pistons, then examine them for ovality, scoring and scratches. Use a micrometer to measure the pistons and renew them (Section 64) if any faults are apparent (photo).
2 Check the clearance of the pistons as follows. Measure and note the diameter of the piston at the point specified. Measure and note the cylinder bore diameter in the thrust direction (Fig. 2.48), then subtract the piston diameter from the cylinder bore diameter, the result is the clearance which should be checked against that specified. If the clearance is excessive, renew the piston(s) and/or renew/rebore the cylinder block (Section 64).
3 On 2E and 4A-F engines, numerous special tools and a hydraulic press are required to remove/refit the gudgeon pin; therefore if either the piston or connecting rod is to be renewed the task should be entrusted to your

Toyota dealer or engine overhaul specialist. On 4A-GE engines the gudgeon pins are retained by circlips; to remove, withdraw one circlip, then gently tap out the gudgeon pin, using a soft metal drift, whilst supporting the piston. If the pin is a tight fit, gently warm the piston. On refitting; position the piston and connecting rod marks as described below, then tap the gudgeon pin back into position, again warming the piston if necessary. Secure the pin in position with two new circlips, ensuring that they are correctly located in their grooves.
4 Always check that the pistons have been correctly installed; the small cavity on the piston crown (which is on the side of the piston closest to the timing cover end of the engine when installed) and the connecting rod mark must be facing the same way. The connecting rod mark is a dimple on 4A-F and 4A-GE engines; on 2E engines it is as shown in Fig. 2.49.
5 Prior to removing the piston rings, check the piston ring groove clearance, using feeler gauges; if the clearance is greater than specified, the piston must be renewed (photo).
6 If new rings are to be fitted to the original pistons, first expand the old rings off over the top of the pistons. The use of two or three old feeler blades will be helpful in preventing the rings dropping into empty grooves (photo).
7 Before fitting the new rings, ensure that the ring grooves in the piston are free of carbon

65.5 Checking piston ring-to-groove clearance

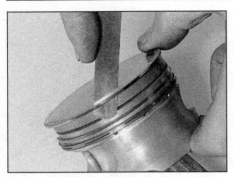

65.6 Using feeler blade to remove piston rings

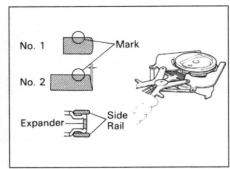

Fig. 2.50 Piston ring fitting details (Sec 65)

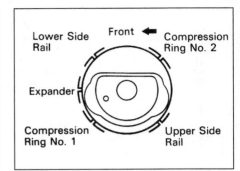

Fig. 2.51 Piston ring end gap spacing – 1.3 models (Sec 65)

by cleaning them using an old ring; break the old ring in half to do this, but be careful of the sharp edges.

8 Check the end gap of the new rings after pushing them squarely down into the cylinder bores, to the point specified. If the end gap is greater than specified, try measuring with another piston ring; if the end gap is still excessive, the cylinder will require reboring and oversize pistons and rings must be used (Section 64).

9 Install the new rings by fitting them over the top of the piston, starting with the oil control scraper ring (expander and two side rails) which should be fitted by hand. Note that the second compression ring is tapered and that the compression rings must be fitted with their markings upwards (Fig. 2.50).

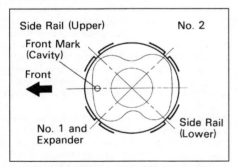

Fig. 2.52 Piston ring end gap spacing – 1.6 models (Sec 65)

10 With the rings in position, space their end gaps as shown in Figs. 2.51 or 2.52, as applicable.

66 Crankshaft – inspection

1 Clean the crankshaft and dry it with compressed air (if available). Be sure to clean the oil holes with a pipe cleaner or similar probe.

> ⚠ *Warning: Wear eye protection when using compressed air!*

2 Check the main and big-end bearing journals for signs of uneven wear, scoring, pitting and cracking.

3 Rub a penny across each journal several times (photo). If a journal picks up copper from the penny, it is too rough and must be reground.

4 Remove all burrs from the crankshaft oil holes with a stone, file or scraper.

5 Using a micrometer, measure and note the diameters of the main and connecting rod big-end journals then compare the results with those specified; if any measurement is not as given, the running clearance(s) must be checked (Sections 69 and 70) (photo). Take measurements at either end of each journal (near the webs) to determine if taper is present, and, by measuring the diameter at a number of points around each journal's circumference, you will also be able to

determine whether or not the journal is out-of-round; if the maximum permissible taper or out-of-round is exceeded, the crankshaft must be reground and have undersize bearings fitted, or it must be renewed. Use V-blocks and a dial gauge to check the runout at the centre journal (Fig. 2.53); if it is outside the maximum specified, the crankshaft must be renewed.

6 Check the oil seal journals at each end of the crankshaft for wear and damage. If a seal has worn an excessive groove in its journal, consult an engine overhaul specialist who will be able to advise whether a repair is possible or whether a new crankshaft is necessary.

67 Main and big-end bearings – inspection

1 Even though the main and big-end bearing shells should be renewed during the engine overhaul, the old bearing shells should be retained for close examination as they may reveal valuable information about the condition of the engine; also, the bearing shell size is stamped on the back metal. Where the crankshaft has been reground, matched new bearing shells will normally be supplied. Information on bearing shell selection and fitting is given in Sections 69 and 70.

2 Bearing failure occurs because of lack of lubrication, the presence of dirt or other foreign particles, overloading the engine, and corrosion.

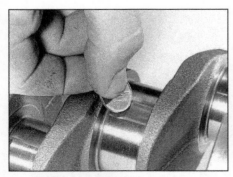

66.3 Using a penny to check crankshaft journal

66.5 Measuring crankshaft journal

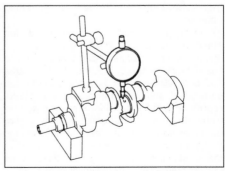

Fig. 2.53 Checking crankshaft runout (Sec 66)

Regardless of the cause of bearing failure, it must be corrected before the engine is reassembled to prevent it from happening again.

3 When examining the bearings, remove them from the engine block, the main bearing caps, the connecting rods and the rod big-end caps and lay them out on a clean surface in the same general position as their location in the engine. This will enable you to match any bearing problems with the corresponding crankshaft journal.

4 Dirt and other foreign particles get into the engine in a variety of ways. It may be left in the engine during assembly, or it may pass through filters or the crankcase ventilation system. It may get into the oil, and from there into the bearings. Metal chips from machining operations and normal engine wear are often present. Abrasives are sometimes left in engine components after reconditioning, especially when parts are not thoroughly cleaned using the proper cleaning methods. Whatever the source, these foreign objects often end up embedded in the soft bearing material and are easily recognized. Large particles will not embed in the bearing and will score or gouge the bearing and journal. The best prevention for this cause of bearing failure is to clean all parts thoroughly and keep everything spotlessly clean during engine assembly. Frequent and regular engine oil and filter changes are also recommended.

5 Lack of lubrication (or lubrication breakdown) has a number of interrelated causes. Excessive heat (which thins the oil), overloading (which squeezes the oil from the bearing face) and oil leakage (from excessive bearing clearances, worn oil pump or high engine speeds) all contribute to lubrication breakdown. Blocked oil passages, which usually are the result of misaligned oil holes in a bearing shell, will also oil starve a bearing and destroy it. When lack of lubrication is the cause of bearing failure, the bearing material is wiped or extruded from the steel backing of the bearing. Temperatures may increase to the point where the steel backing turns blue from overheating.

6 Driving habits can have a definite effect on bearing life. Full throttle, low speed operation (labouring the engine) puts very high loads on

bearings, which tends to squeeze out the oil film. These loads cause the bearings to flex, which produces fine cracks in the bearing face (fatigue failure). Eventually the bearing material will loosen in pieces and tear away from the steel backing. Short trip driving leads to corrosion of bearings because insufficient engine heat is produced to drive off the condensed water and corrosive gases. These products collect in the engine oil, forming acid and sludge. As the oil is carried to the engine bearings, the acid attacks and corrodes the bearing material.

7 Incorrect bearing installation during engine assembly will lead to bearing failure as well; tight fitting bearings leave insufficient bearing oil clearance and will result in oil starvation. Oil starvation may also be attributed to misaligned oilways. Dirt or foreign particles trapped behind a bearing shell result in high spots on the bearing which lead to failure.

68 Engine overhaul – reassembly sequence

1 Before reassembly begins, ensure that all new parts have been obtained and that all necessary tools are available. Read through the entire procedure to familiarise yourself with the work involved, and to ensure that all items necessary for reassembly of the engine are at hand. In addition to all normal tools and materials, a thread locking compound will be needed. Suitable sealants will be required during reassembly; consult your Toyota dealer regarding supply, and the applicability of proprietary products, where necessary.

2 To save time and avoid problems, engine reassembly can be carried out in the following order:

(a) *Crankshaft.*
(b) *Pistons.*
(c) *Oil pump.*
(d) *Sump.*
(e) *Flywheel.*
(f) *Cylinder head.*
(g) *Water pump and associated components.*
(h) *Timing belt, toothed pulleys and associated components.*
(I) *Engine external components.*

3 At this stage, all engine components should be absolutely clean and dry, with all faults repaired and should be laid out (or in individual containers) on a completely clean work surface.

69 Crankshaft – refitting and main bearing running clearance check

1 Clean the backs of the bearing shells and the bearing recesses in both the cylinder block and main bearing caps.

2 Press the bearing shells into their correct locations in the cylinder block and caps, ensuring that the shells with oil holes align with the oil holes in the cylinder block; the tags on the bearing shells must engage in their respective notches (photo). Note that if the original main bearing shells are being re-used these must be refitted to their original locations in the block and caps.

Main bearing running clearance chock

3 Before the crankshaft can be permanently installed, the main bearing running clearance should be checked; this can be done in either of two ways. One method is to fit the main bearing caps to the cylinder block, with bearing shells in place. With the cap bolts tightened to the specified torque, measure the internal diameter of each assembled pair of bearing shells using a vernier dial indicator or internal micrometer. If the diameter of each corresponding crankshaft journal is measured and then subtracted from the bearing internal diameter, the result will be the main bearing running clearance. The second (and more accurate) method is to use an American product known as Plastigage. This consists of a fine thread of perfectly round plastic which is compressed by the action of tightening down the main bearing caps with the crankshaft in position. When the cap is removed, the plastic is deformed and the running clearance can be measured with a special card gauge supplied with the kit.

4 With the upper main bearing shells in position on the cylinder block, ensure that the crankshaft journals and bearing shells are perfectly clean and dry, then carefully lower the crankshaft into position.

5 Cut several lengths of Plastigage and place one on each crankshaft journal (photo).

6 With the bearing shells in position, refit the caps to their original locations; take care not to disturb the Plastigage.

7 Tighten the cap bolts to their specified torque setting (see below); do **not** rotate the crankshaft at any time during this operation.

8 Unscrew the bolts and carefully lift off the bearing caps whilst taking great care not to disturb the Plastigage or rotate the crankshaft.

9 Compare the width of the crushed

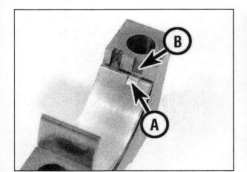

69.2 Bearing shell tag (A) must engage notch (B)

69.5 Plastigage thread in position on crankshaft journal

69.9 Measuring width of crushed Plastigage, using scale printed on pack

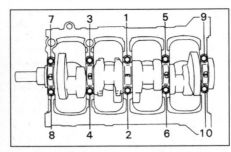

Fig. 2.54 Main bearing cap bolt tightening sequence – note cap markings – 1.3 models shown (Sec 69)

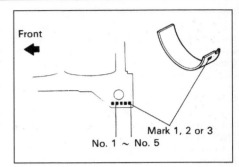

Fig. 2.55 Main bearing shell selection – 1.3 models (Sec 69)

Plastigage on each journal to the scale printed on the Plastigage envelope to obtain the main bearing running clearance (photo).

10 If the clearance is not as specified, the bearing shells may be the wrong size (or excessively worn if the original shells are being re-used). Before deciding that different size shells are needed, make sure that no dirt or oil was trapped between the bearing shells and the caps or block when the clearance was measured. If the Plastigage was wider at one end than at the other, the journal may be tapered.

11 Carefully scrape away all traces of the Plastigage material from the crankshaft and bearing shells using your fingernail or other object which is unlikely to score the shells.

Final crankshaft refitting

12 On 4A-F and 4A-GE engines, if necessary, obtain new bearing shells which carry the same number as that stamped on the reverse side of the defective ones (unless the crankshaft has been reground); if the number is not visible, select a bearing from the table below, according to the numbers imprinted on the crankshaft and cylinder block (Fig. 2.55}.

Cylinder block number	Crankshaft number	Correct shell
1	0	1
2	0	2
3	0	3
1	1	2
2	1	3
3	1	4
1	2	3
2	2	4
3	2	5

13 On 2E engines, if necessary, obtain new bearing shells which carry the same number as that stamped on the reverse side of the defective ones (unless the crankshaft has been reground); if the number is not visible, select a bearing which carries the same number as that stamped on the cylinder block (refer to Fig. 2.56).

14 With any protective grease removed from the new bearing shells and the bearing shells correctly positioned (paragraph 2), the running clearance should be checked (as described above) whenever the bearings shells have been renewed. If the running clearance is

outside specification with the new bearings fitted, consult your Toyota dealer or engine overhaul specialist regarding crankshaft regrinding/renewal.

15 Check that the bearing shells are correctly installed to their cylinder block and cap locations as described in paragraph 2.

16 Install the upper thrustwashers on either side of the centre (number 3) main bearing in the cylinder block so that their oil grooves are facing outwards. If necessary they can be held in position using a smear of grease.

17 Lubricate the main bearing journals, the upper bearing shell-to-journal contact faces and the upper thrustwashers with clean engine oil.

18 Carefully lay the crankshaft in position on the cylinder block, being careful not to dislodge the upper thrustwashers.

19 Lubricate the lower bearing shell faces and the lower thrustwashers, then install the bearing caps to their original locations; ensure that the arrows on the caps face the timing end of the engine, and that the lower thrustwashers are fitted to the centre (number 3) main bearing cap with their oil grooves facing outwards.

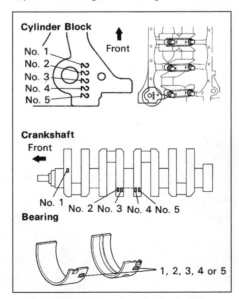

Fig. 2.56 Main bearing shell selection – 1.6 models (Sec 69)

20 Fit the main bearing cap bolts, having applied a light coating of clean engine oil to their threads and under their heads, then progressively tighten them to the specified torque in the sequence shown in Fig. 2.54. Check that the crankshaft is free to turn, then recheck the endfloat (Section 63).

70 Piston/connecting rod assembly – refitting and big-end bearing running clearance check

1 Clean the backs of the bearing shells and the recesses in the connecting rods and big-end caps. Wipe dry the shells and connecting rods, using a clean, lint-free cloth.

2 Press the bearing shells into the connecting rods and caps in their correct positions; make sure that the location tags are engaged with their notches, and that the oil holes align. Note that if the original bearing shells are being re-used, these must be refitted to their original locations in the connecting rod(s) and cap(s).

Big-end bearing running clearance check

3 Having ensured that the piston ring end gaps are correctly positioned, oil the rings of number 1 piston then clamp them using a suitable piston ring compressor. Oil number 1 cylinder bore, then insert the piston/connecting rod assembly (from the top surface of the cylinder block) by tapping the piston crown using the handle of a hammer (photo); ensure that the small cavity (front

70.3 Inserting a piston into its bore

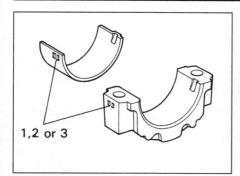

Fig. 2.57 Connecting rod (big-end) bearing shell and cap markings (Sec 70)

mark) on the piston crown is facing the timing belt end of the engine.

4 Ensure that the crankpin and bearing shells are perfectly clean and dry then engage number 1 piston/connecting rod assembly with its crankpin. Lay a strip of Plastigage across the crankpin. Fit the number 1 big-end cap and bearing shell to its piston/connecting rod assembly, aligning the marks on the connecting rod and the cap, then tighten the cap retaining nuts (see below). Do **not** rotate the crankshaft.

5 Remove the big-end cap, then measure the width of the Plastigage at its widest point to obtain the running clearance (Section 69). Check the figure obtained against that specified.

6 Clean away all traces of Plastigage after measuring.

7 Repeat the procedure for the remaining piston/connecting rod assemblies.

Final connecting rod refitting

8 Note that if new bearing shells are being fitted, all traces of protective grease must be first be removed. Standard shells must carry the same number as that marked on the big-end caps (Fig. 2.57), and the bearing shells must be correctly positioned (paragraph 2). Whenever new bearing shells are fitted the running clearances should be checked as described above. If these are outside specification, consult your Toyota dealer or engine overhaul specialist regarding crankshaft regrinding/renewal.

9 Particularly on 4A-GE engines manufactured since August 1987, use new connecting rod nuts and bolts on refitting.

70.11 Refitting a connecting rod big-end cap and bearing

10 Having checked the running clearance of all crankpin journals and taken any corrective action necessary, insert the piston/connecting rod assemblies as described in paragraph 3 and engage the piston/connecting rod assemblies with their crankpins, having liberally lubricated the crankpin journals with clean engine oil.

11 Refit the bearing caps once more, ensuring they are correctly positioned as previously described (photo). Lightly oil the bolt threads and under the nut heads.

12 On all except 4A-GE engines manufactured since August 1987 (hexagonal bearing cap nuts), progressively tighten the nuts alternately to their specified torque. Once both nuts are tightened to the specified torque rotate the crankshaft to ensure that it moves freely before moving on to the next piston/connecting rod assembly. Repeat the procedure, as necessary, until all piston/connecting rod assemblies are refitted.

13 On 4A-GE engines manufactured since August 1987 (12-sided bearing cap nuts), first tighten the nuts alternately to their specified torque setting, then turn the crankshaft to ensure that it moves freely. Mark each nut with a spot of quick-drying paint (on the side closest to the timing cover), then alternately tighten the nuts through a further 90°, using the paint spots as reference. The paint spots should both be 90° from their original positions upon completion. Once both nuts are fully tightened, rotate the crankshaft to ensure that it moves freely before moving on to the next piston/connecting rod assembly. Repeat the procedure, as necessary, until all

piston/connecting rod assemblies are refitted.

14 On all engines, check the thrust clearance (side play) between the connecting rods and the crankshaft webs (Section 62, paragraph 3) and take remedial action if necessary.

71 Engine – initial start-up after overhaul

1 With the engine refitted in the vehicle, double-check the engine oil and coolant levels, and check to ensure that all necessary connections have been made (with the exception of those covered in paragraph 3). Also check that the gearbox/transmission has been refilled, if applicable.

2 Make sure that all rags, tools, etc., have been removed from the engine compartment.

3 With the spark plugs removed and the ignition system disabled, crank the engine over on the starter until the oil pressure light goes out.

4 Refit the spark plugs and connect all the HT leads.

5 Start the engine, noting that this may take a little longer than usual due to the fuel pump and carburettor/fuel rail being empty.

6 While the engine is idling, check for fuel, water and oil leaks. Don't be alarmed if there are some odd smells and smoke from parts getting hot and burning off oil deposits.

7 Keep the engine idling until hot water is felt circulating through the top hose, then switch it off.

8 After a few minutes, recheck the oil and water levels and top up as necessary.

9 Check and adjust the valve clearances when the engine is warmed up to normal operating temperature (Chapter 1).

10 Check the ignition timing, the idle speed and fuel mixture settings (Chapter 1).

11 If new internal components have been fitted (ie., pistons, rings, crankshaft, bearings), the engine must be treated as new and run in for the first 600 miles (1000 km). Do not operate the engine at full throttle or allow it to labour in any gear during this period. It is recommended that the engine oil and filter be changed at the end of this period, and the tension of the drivebelts adjusted (Chapter 1); also recheck the idle speed and fuel mixture settings.

Notes

Chapter 3
Cooling, heating and ventilation systems

Contents

Degrees of difficulty

Easy, suitable for novice with little experience	**Fairly easy,** suitable for beginner with some experience	**Fairly difficult,** suitable for competent DIY mechanic	**Difficult,** suitable for experienced DIY mechanic	**Very difficult,** suitable for expert DIY or professional

Specifications

System type .... Pressurised, pump-assisted. Front-mounted radiator with electric cooling fan and expansion tank

Thermostat
Type .... Wax
Start-to-open temperature .... 80 to 84°C
Fully-open temperature .... 95°C
Minimum lift height .... 8 mm

Radiator cap pressure .... 0.74 to 1.03 bar

Cooling fan operating temperature
Early 1.3 models .... 88°C
Later 1.3 models .... 94°C
1.6 GL Executive and early GTi 16 models .... 90°C
Later GTi 16 model .... 93°C

Torque wrench settings	**Nm**	**lbf ft**
Water pump:		
1.3 models	17	13
1.6 models	15	11
Water inlet pipe-to-water pump – 1.6 models	20	15
Water inlet pipe support bracket	13	10
Thermostat cover/water inlet – 1.6 GL Executive model	20	15
Water outlet pipe – 1.6 GL Executive model	20	15
Water outlet and bypass pipe-to-cylinder head – GTi 16 model	27	20
Water outlet and bypass pipe-to-cylinder block – GTi 16 model	13	10
Cylinder block coolant drain plug:		
1.3 models	25	18
1.6 GL Executive and early GTi 16 models	13	10
Later GTi 16 model	34	25

1 Cooling system – general information

The cooling system is pressurised and incorporates a radiator and expansion tank, a belt-driven water pump, a thermostat and an electric cooling fan.

The radiator is of conventional design, with an upper and lower tank connected by the radiator core; automatic transmission-equipped models have a fluid cooler built into the lower tank.

The system functions as follows. The coolant is heated as it passes through the cylinder block and head passages. After cooling the cylinder bores, combustion surfaces and valve seats, the coolant flows into the top of the radiator and down through the radiator core where it is cooled by the inrush of air when the car is in forward motion. Airflow is supplemented by the action of the electric cooling fan when necessary. Upon reaching the bottom of the radiator, the coolant passes back into the engine {through the action of the water pump) to repeat the cycle.

When the vehicle is started from cold, the thermostat restricts coolant flow (thus promoting a more rapid engine warm up); as the coolant temperature rises, the thermostat opens to allow the coolant to circulate. When the engine is at normal operating temperature the coolant expands and some of it is displaced into the expansion tank. This coolant is returned to the radiator when the system cools.

The electric cooling fan mounted behind the radiator is controlled by a thermostatic switch located in the thermostat cover/water inlet so that the fan operates when a predetermined coolant temperature is exceeded.

2 Electric cooling fan – testing, removal and refitting

Testing

1 To test the operation of the electric cooling fan motor circuit, switch on the ignition and first check that the fan blades are not rotating. With the ignition still switched on, disconnect the multi-plug from the electric cooling fan thermostatic switch on the thermostat cover/water inlet and check that the fan blades now rotate, if the fan blades do not rotate, the fuse, relay, wiring or the fan motor itself may be defective.

2 The fan motor may be directly checked (assuming that the wiring between the fan motor and its multi-plug connector is not defective), by disconnecting its multi-plug and connecting up the circuit shown in Fig. 3.2; the fan motor should rotate smoothly and the ammeter reading should be between 3.2 and 4.4 amps. If the ammeter reading is not as specified, the motor must be renewed.

Removal

3 Disconnect the battery negative terminal.
4 Raise the front of the vehicle and support it securely on axle stands. Remove any applicable engine compartment undershields.
5 Drain sufficient coolant from the radiator (Chapter 1) to allow the radiator top hose to be disconnected without coolant spillage.
6 Withdraw the radiator expansion tank from its bracket and secure it clear of the working area; there is no need to disconnect it.
7 Disconnect the electric cooling fan motor multi-plug. Unbolt the cooling fan shroud from the radiator, then withdraw it upwards (photo).
8 The fan blade may be removed by undoing the securing nut; the fan motor is secured to the shroud by three screws – accessible after removing the fan blade (photo).

Refitting

9 Refitting is the reverse of the removal procedure, noting the following points.
(a) Ensure that the drain plugs are securely tightened.
(b) Top up the coolant level (Chapter 1).

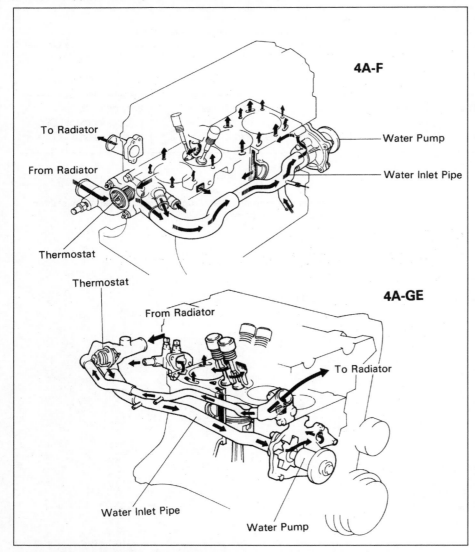

Fig. 3.1 Cutaway view of cooling system operation – 1.6 models (Sec 1)

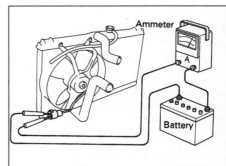

Fig. 3.2 Testing electric cooling fan motor operation (Sec 2)

2.7 Electric cooling fan motor multi-plug (A), shroud bolts (B), radiator drain plug (C)

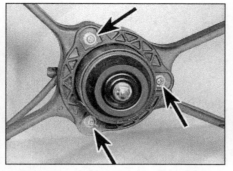

2.8 Electric cooling fan motor-to-shroud screws (arrowed)

3.4 Releasing radiator top hose clip

3 Radiator and expansion tank – removal, inspection and refitting

Removal

1 Disconnect the battery negative terminal.
2 Raise the front of the vehicle and support it securely on axle stands. Remove any applicable engine compartment undershields.
3 Drain the coolant (Chapter 1).
4 Release the hose clips and disconnect the radiator hoses; tuck the hoses out of the way or remove them, as necessary (photo). On automatic transmission-equipped vehicles, the transmission fluid cooler pipes must also be disconnected from the radiator lower tank; label the pipes to ensure correct reconnection and plug the ends of both pipes and unions to minimise fluid loss and prevent the entry of dirt.
5 Disconnect the expansion tank hose from the radiator, then withdraw the expansion tank upwards; take care not to spill any coolant (photo).
6 Disconnect the electric cooling fan motor multi-plug.
7 Unbolt each of the two radiator top mounting brackets, then lift the radiator and the cooling fan upwards to disengage the radiator bottom mounting grommets and withdraw the assembly (photos).

8 The electric cooling fan shroud can be unbolted from the radiator, as required (see photo 2.7).

Inspection

9 If the radiator fins are clogged with flies or dirt, clean using a soft brush or direct a hosepipe from the rear face of the radiator.
10 Inspect the radiator for signs of damage, leakage and corrosion. Extensive damage should be repaired by a specialist or the unit exchanged for a new or reconditioned radiator. If the radiator from a vehicle with automatic transmission is to be exchanged, repaired or renewed, empty as much fluid as possible from the fluid cooler section and flush it clean.
11 Inspect the expansion tank for cracks or splits and check that there are no traces of oil in it – traces of oil may indicate a leaking cylinder head gasket.

Refitting

12 Refitting is the reverse of the removal procedure, noting the following points.
(a) *Ensure that the radiator mounting grommets engage correctly in their body locations.*
(b) *Ensure that the drain plugs are securely tightened.*
(c) *Refill the system with coolant (Chapter 1) then start the engine and check all*

disturbed joints for leaks as soon as the engine is fully warmed up.
(d) *Where applicable check the automatic transmission fluid level and top up if necessary (Chapter 1).*

4 Thermostat – removal, testing and refitting

Note: *The thermostat gasket must be renewed on refitting.*

Removal

1 Disconnect the battery negative terminal.
2 Raise the front of the vehicle and support it securely on axle stands. Remove any applicable engine compartment undershields.
3 Drain the coolant (Chapter 1).
4 Remove the air filter housing/trunking if required for increased working access (Chapter 4).
5 Disconnect the electric cooling fan thermostatic switch multi-plug on the thermostat cover/water inlet, also the coolant hose, as necessary.
6 Undo the two nuts or bolts securing the thermostat cover/water inlet (noting any brackets), then remove the thermostat cover/water inlet and withdraw the thermostat and its gasket (photos).

Testing

7 To test the thermostat operation, first check that its valve is closed when cold. Suspend

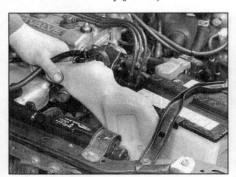

3.5 Withdraw expansion tank upwards from its bracket

3.7A Removing radiator top mounting bracket

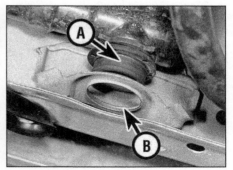

3.7B Mounting grommet on radiator base (A), body location (B)

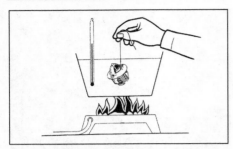

Fig. 3.3 Testing the thermostat (Sec 4)

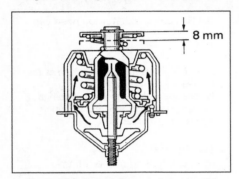

Fig. 3.4 Checking thermostat valve lift (Sec 4)

the thermostat in a pan of water with a thermometer; neither should be allowed to touch the sides of the pan.

8 Heat the water gradually and check that the thermostat valve starts to open at the specified temperature (also marked on the thermostat itself). When the valve is fully open check that the valve lift (Fig. 3.4) is at least that specified.

9 If the thermostat does not start to open at the specified temperature, or does not fully open in boiling water or fully close when removed from the water, then it must be discarded and a new one fitted.

Refitting

10 Refitting is the reverse of the removal procedure, noting the following points.
(a) The thermostat gasket must be renewed.
(b) The jiggle pin must be positioned as shown in photo 4.6A for 7.6 models while on 1.3 models it must be aligned with the protrusion on the thermostat cover/water inlet.
(c) Top up the coolant level (Chapter 1).

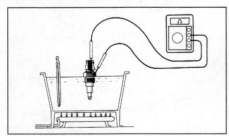

Fig. 3.6 Testing electric cooling fan thermostatic switch (Sec 5)

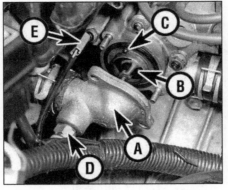

4.6A Removing the thermostat (1.6 GL Executive model shown)

A Thermostat cover/water inlet
B Thermostat
C Correct jiggle pin position – all 1.6 models
D Electric cooling fan thermostatic switch
E Temperature gauge sender unit

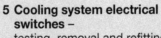

5 Cooling system electrical switches –
testing, removal and refitting

Testing

Electric cooling fan thermostatic switch

⚠️ *Warning: Take particular care when working under the bonnet (unless the battery is disconnected) as the electric cooling fan may suddenly operate without warning. Remember that the coolant temperature will continue to rise for a short time after the engine is switched off. Ensure that clothing hair and hands are kept away from the fan.*

1 The switch is screwed into the thermostat cover/water inlet (photo).

2 Testing may be carried out (after the switch has been removed with the engine cold) by immersing its temperature-sensing end, with a thermometer, in a pan of cold water and testing for continuity (Chapter 12, Section 2) as the water is heated (Fig. 3.6).

3 While the water remains below 78°C (early

5.1 Electric cooling fan thermostatic switch (arrowed) on thermostat cover/water inlet – GTi 16

4.6B Removing thermostat gasket

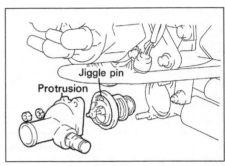

Fig. 3.5 Correct positioning of thermostat jiggle pin – 1.3 models (Sec 4)

1.3 models) or 83°C (all other models), there should be continuity; when the water temperature rises above the appropriate specified cooling fan operating temperature, there should be no continuity. If the performance of the tested switch differs significantly, the switch must be renewed.

Temperature gauge sender unit

4 The unit is located on the rearward-facing side of the engine's timing cover end on GTi 16 models, on the engine's gearbox end on all other models (photo).

5 The unit must be tested by the substitution of a known good component. Any problems with persistent high or low gauge readings is usually a symptom of a further fault, or faults, in the system.

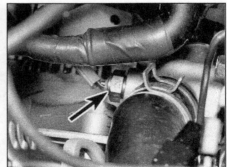

5.4 Temperature gauge sender unit (arrowed) – GTi 16

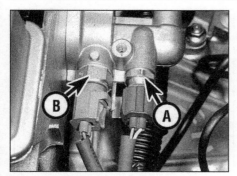

5.6 ECU water temperature sensor (A) cold start injector time switch (B) – GTi 16

ECU water temperature sensor – GTi 16

6 The sensor is located in the heater outlet housing on the engine's gearbox end, next to the cold start injector time switch (photo).

7 Testing may be carried out (after the switch has been removed with the engine cold) by immersing its temperature-sensing end, with a thermometer, in a pan of cold water and measuring the resistance between its terminal pins whilst the water is gradually heated; if the resistance does not fall within the band indicated in Fig. 3.7 the sensor is defective and must be renewed.

Cold start injector time switch – GTi 16

8 The switch is located in the heater outlet housing on the engine's gearbox end, next to the ECU water temperature sensor.

9 Testing may be carried out (after disconnecting the switch multi-plug) by measuring the resistance at the switch terminal pins (Fig. 3.8). First measure the resistance between switch terminal pins STA and STJ, this should be between 20 and 40 ohms at coolant temperatures below 30°C, between 40 and 60 ohms at coolant temperatures above 40°C. A measurement between switch terminal pin STA and a good earth point should provide a reading of between 20 and 80 ohms. If any measurement obtained differs significantly from those specified, the switch must be renewed.

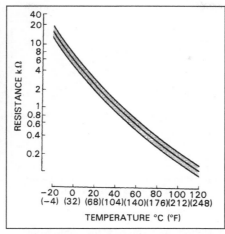

Fig. 3.7 ECU water temperature sensor resistance response to temperature change – GTi 16 (Sec 5)

Removal

10 The component is removed (with the engine cold) by first disconnecting, then unscrewing it; plug its location to prevent excessive coolant loss. Note whether an O-ring is fitted, or if sealant is evident on the threads.

Refitting

11 Refitting is the reverse of the removal procedure, noting the following points.
(a) If an O-ring was originally fitted this should be renewed.
(b) If sealant was noted on the component's threads on removal the threads must be cleaned and a suitable sealant applied on refitting.
(c) Top up the coolant level (Chapter 1).

6 Water pump – removal and refitting

Note: *The water pump and engine oil dipstick O-rings must be renewed on refitting. On 1.3 models 'formed-in-place gasket' sealant is required (refer to your Toyota dealer).*

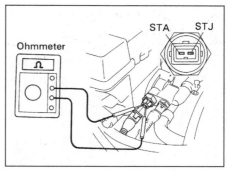

Fig. 3.8 Testing cold dart injector time switch – GTi 16 (Sec 5)

Removal

1.6 models

1 Disconnect the battery negative terminal.

2 Where applicable, remove the air filter housing/trunking for increased working access (Chapter 4).

3 Drain the coolant (Chapter 1).

4 Slacken the water pump pulley securing bolts, then remove the alternator/water pump and power steering pump drivebelts, as applicable (Chapter 1).

5 Remove the pulley bolts and withdraw the water pump pulley; it may be necessary to support the engine using an engine support bar or a hoist, then to disconnect the engine mounting(s) (Chapter 2) and to move the engine slightly (taking great care not to strain or crush any wiring, hoses, pipes, linkages, etc, or to damage components) to allow the pulley to be withdrawn.

6 On 1.6 GL Executive models, unbolt the power-assisted steering pump adjuster bracket (photo).

7 Disconnect the hoses from the water inlet pipe (on the engine's rearfacing side) then undo the two securing nuts and the clamp bolt; remove the inlet pipe, noting its O-ring (photos).

8 Unbolt the engine oil dipstick tube and withdraw it, noting the O-ring; plug the dipstick tube aperture.

9 Remove the upper and centre timing belt cover sections (Chapter 2).

6.6 Removing power-assisted steering pump adjuster bracket (arrowed) – 1.6 GL Executive model

6.7A Removing water inlet pipe (inlet manifold removed for clarity) . . .

6.7B . . . noting O-ring (arrowed) on rear of water pump . . .

6.10 . . . withdrawing water pump –
1.6 GL Executive model shown

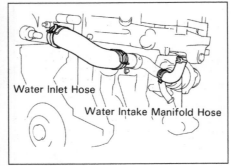

Fig. 3.9 Disconnecting hoses from water
inlet pipe – 1.3 models (Sec 6)

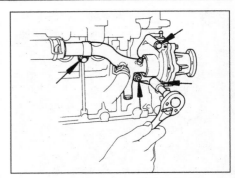

Fig. 3.10 Undoing water inlet pipe and
water pump securing nuts and bolts
(arrowed) – 1.3 models (See 6)

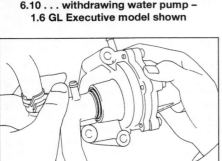

Fig. 3.11 Separating water pump from inlet
pipe – 1.3 models (Sec 6)

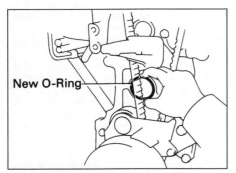

Fig. 3.12 Fitting new water pump O-ring to
cylinder block on refitting pump –
1.6 models (Sec 6)

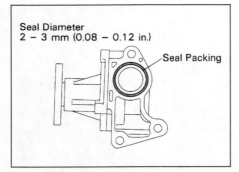

Fig. 3.13 Apply specified sealant as shown
to water pump mating face – 1.3 models
(Sec 6)

10 Unbolt and remove the water pump, noting its O-ring; take care not to spill coolant on the timing belt as the water pump is withdrawn (photo). If the water pump is defective, it must be renewed.

1.3 models

11 Proceed as described in paragraphs 1 to 5 inclusive.

12 Unbolt the engine oil dipstick tube and withdraw it, noting the O-ring; plug the dipstick tube aperture.

13 Disconnect all relevant coolant hoses from the water inlet pipe and the carburettor.

14 Unbolt and remove, as an assembly, the water pump and water inlet pipe.

15 Pull the water inlet pipe away from the water pump; remove the water inlet pipe O-ring. If the water pump is defective, it must be renewed.

Refitting

16 Refitting is the reverse of the removal procedure, noting the following points.

(a) Renew all disturbed sealing O-rings; use soap to lubricate all coolant hoses and O-rings as they are refitted engine oil to lubricate the dipstick tube O-ring.

(b) On 1.3 models thoroughly clean the pump-to-cylinder block mating faces and apply 'formed-in-place gasket' sealant to the pump face as shown in Fig. 3.13.

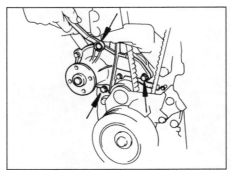

Fig. 3.14 Water pump bolts (arrowed) –
1.6 models

(c) Tighten all disturbed fastenings to their specified torque wrench settings (where given).

(d) Refit and tension the drivebelts as described in Chapter 1.

(e) Refill the system with coolant (Chapter 1) then start the engine and check all disturbed joints for leaks as soon as the engine is fully warmed up.

7 Heating and ventilation systems – general information

The heater has a multi-speed blower housed in the passenger compartment, face level vents in the centre and at each end of the facia and air ducts to the front footwells. Illuminated sliding controls for air temperature and distribution are housed, with the heater blower/fan motor switch, in the heater control panel and operate flap valves to deflect the air flowing through the heater.

Cold air enters through the grille at the rear of the bonnet, and boosted when required by the blower's radial fan then flows through the ducts, according to the control setting; stale air is exhausted through ducts at the rear of the vehicle. If warm air is required, the cold air is passed over the heater matrix which is heated by the engine's coolant; the flow of coolant through the matrix being controlled by the heater temperature slide control via the heater valve in the engine compartment. The other cable attached to the heater temperature slide control operates a flap valve in the heater casing either to deflect air over the matrix or to bypass it.

If rapid heating is desired, the air in the vehicle can be recirculated (instead of drawing in fresh air to be heated) by an intake air slide control which allows the full recirculation of air, the intake of fresh air from outside the vehicle, or the blending of recirculated and fresh air.

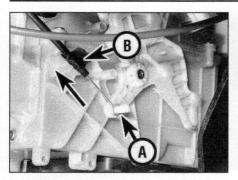

8.6A Air distribution cable flap valve connection (A), clip (B), on heater casing. Arrow indicates valve setting direction on adjustment

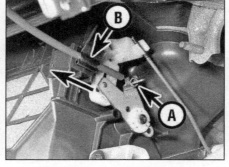

8.6B Intake air cable flap valve connection (A), clip (B), on heater blower/fan motor casing. Arrow indicates valve setting direction on adjustment

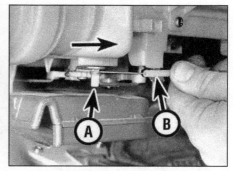

8.6C Temperature cable flap valve connection (A), clip (B), on heater casing. Arrow indicates valve setting direction on adjustment

8 Heater controls – removal, refitting and adjustment

Removal

1 Disconnect the battery negative terminal.
2 Prise up and remove the steering lock/ignition switch lock barrel trim.
3 Remove the facia switches from the centre stack finish panel (Chapter 1 2).
4 Remove the centre stack finish panel (Chapter 12, Section 17).
5 Remove the facia lower finish panels from the front footwells, and unclip the footwell trim panels from in front of the centre console (Chapter 11).
6 Disconnect the heater control cables from the heater casing, heater blower/fan motor casing and the heater valve in the engine compartment; label the control cables to aid refitting and note their routing (photos). If access to the control cable connection on the base of the heater casing is too restricted, it may be necessary to remove the stowage bin or radio/cassette player from the centre stack, or the centre console (Chapters 11 and 12).
7 Undo the screws securing the heater control panel to the facia, then withdraw the panel; disconnect the wiring from the heater control panel as it is withdrawn and guide the control cables out (photos).

Refitting

8 Refitting is the reverse of the removal procedure, noting the following points.
(a) Guide the heater valve control cable through its bulkhead grommet as the heater control panel is refitted.
(b) Ensure that none of the control cables become twisted or excessively bent.
(c) Adjust the cables as described below.

Adjustment

9 The control cables will require adjustment only after they have been disturbed.
10 Secure the control cable outer with its clip once the slide control and the valve have been set, take care not to move the set positions when securing the cable. Set the slide control and the valve as follows.
(a) The air distribution slide control and its valve should be set to the face level ventilation position (see photo 8.6A).
(b) The intake air slide control and its valve should be set to the fresh air position (see photo 8.6B).
(c) The temperature slide control and its valves (on the base of the heater casing and in the engine compartment) should be set to the cool position; each cable may be adjusted separately if required (see photos 8.6C and 9.2).

9 Heater components – removal and refitting

Removal

Heater valve

1 Disconnect the battery negative terminal.
2 Partially drain the coolant from the system (Chapter 1), then disconnect the hoses from the valve; catch any spillage in a suitable container and plug the hose ends as they are disconnected (photo).
3 Disconnect the control cable.
4 Unbolt the heater valve and remove it.

Heater blower/fan motor

5 Disconnect the battery negative terminal.
6 Remove the facia lower finish panel/glovebox assembly from the passenger footwell (Chapter 11).
7 Disconnect the multi-plugs from the heater

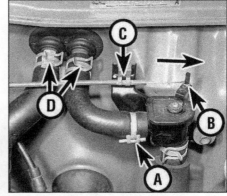

9.2 Heater valve in engine compartment. Arrow indicates valve setting direction on adjustment

A Heater valve hose connections
B Temperature cable connection
C Cable clip
D Heater matrix connector pipe hose connections

8.7A Removing heater control panel screws (arrowed)

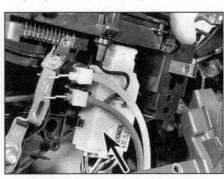

8.7B Disconnect multi-plug (arrowed) as control panel is withdrawn

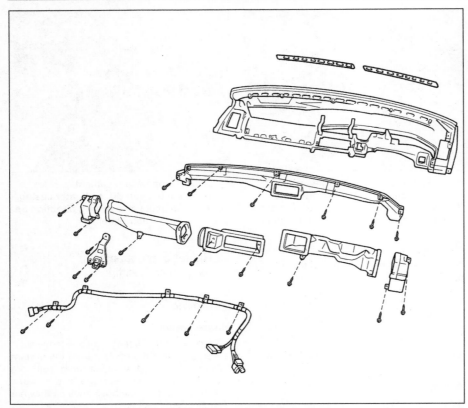

Fig. 3.15 Heater ducts and vents (and wiring loom section) on facia reverse side – typical – left-hand drive shown (Sec 9)

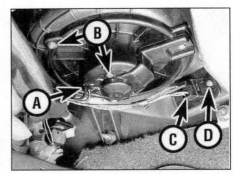

9.7 Heater blower/fan motor assembly (passenger footwell facia lower finish panel removed)

A Heater blower/fan motor multi-plug
B Heater blower/fan motor securing bolts
C Resistor assembly multi-plug
D Resistor assembly securing screw

9.8 Removing heater blower/fan motor and fan assembly

blower/fan motor and its resistor assembly (photo).

8 Support beneath the heater blower/fan unit then remove the securing bolts; lower the heater blower/fan motor and fan assembly from its casing and remove it (photo).

9 The resistor assembly may be withdrawn (if required) after its single securing screw has been removed.

Heater casing

10 Disconnect the battery negative terminal.
11 Drain the cooling system (Chapter 1).
12 Working in the engine compartment, disconnect the hoses from the heater matrix connector pipes (see photo 9.2); plug the

pipes to prevent coolant from the heater matrix spilling into the passenger compartment as the heater casing is removed.

13 Remove both front seats and the centre console (Chapter 11).
14 Prise up and remove the steering lock/ignition switch lock barrel trim.
15 Remove the facia lower finish panels from the front footwells (Chapter 11) and the centre stack finish panel (Chapter 12, Section 17).
16 On GTi 16 models, remove the radio/cassette player (Chapter 12).
17 On all other models, remove the stowage bin from the centre stack (Chapter 11).
18 Disconnect the heater control cables from the heater casing, heater blower/fan motor casing and the heater valve in the engine compartment, then remove the heater control panel (Section 8).
19 Remove the screws securing the remaining centre stack trim and remove it (Chapter 11).
20 Remove both of the centre stack support brackets, noting the earth connections on their upper ends (photo).
21 Unbolt and remove the main duct between the heater blower/fan motor and the heater casing (photo).

9.20 Earth lead connection (arrowed) on centre stack left-hand support bracket

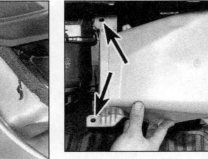

9.21 Remove bolts (arrowed) to withdraw main heater blower/fan motor-to-heater casing duct

9.22 Removing black plastic duct from heater casing right-hand side

9.23 Removing heater casing – left-hand securing nuts arrowed

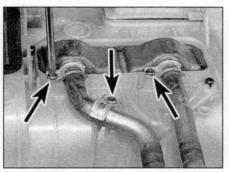

9.25A Remove screws (arrowed) to release heater matrix connector pipe brackets

9.25B Withdrawing matrix from heater casing

22 Remove the screw(s) securing the black plastic duct to the heater casing right-hand side, then remove the duct (photo).

23 Undo the heater casing securing nuts and/or bolts, then draw the heater casing rearwards to free the heater matrix connector pipes from their bulkhead grommets; manoeuvre the heater casing and matrix assembly from the vehicle (photo).

Heater matrix

24 Remove the heater casing and matrix assembly as described above.

25 Slacken the screws securing the heater matrix connector pipe brackets, then move aside or remove (as necessary) the brackets so that the matrix can be withdrawn (photos).

Heater ducts and vents

26 With the exception of the demister vent grilles – which may be prised up at their rear edge to remove – and the central adjustable vents in the centre stack finish panel, the majority of the heater distribution ducts and vents are secured to the reverse side of the facia (Fig. 3.15); refer to Chapter 11, Section 29 for details of facia removal and refitting.

27 Removal of the main duct between the heater blower/fan motor and the heater casing is described in paragraphs 10 to 21 above.

Refitting

Heater valve

28 Refitting is the reverse of the removal procedure, noting the following points.
(a) Adjust the heater valve control cable (Section 8).
(b) Refill the system with coolant (Chapter 1), then start the engine and check all disturbed joints for leaks as soon as the engine is fully warmed up.

Heater blower/fan motor

29 Refitting is the reverse of the removal procedure.

Heater casing

30 Refitting is the reverse of the removal procedure, noting the following points.
(a) Ensure that the heater matrix connector pipes are correctly inserted through the bulkhead and that the grommet seats correctly.
(b) Refit the heater control panel and adjust the cables (Section 8).
(c) Refill the system with coolant (Chapter 1), then start the engine and check all disturbed joints for leaks as soon as the engine is fully warmed up.

Heater matrix

31 Refitting is the reverse of the removal procedure.

Heater ducts and vents

32 Refitting is the reverse of the removal procedure.

Notes

Chapter 4
Fuel, exhaust and emission control systems

Contents

Degrees of difficulty

Easy, suitable for novice with little experience	**Fairly easy,** suitable for beginner with some experience	**Fairly difficult,** suitable for competent DIY mechanic	**Difficult,** suitable for experienced DIY mechanic	**Very difficult,** suitable for expert DIY or professional

Specifications

Part A: Carburettor engines

Fuel pump type . . . . Mechanical, operated by eccentric on camshaft

Carburettor (general)

Type . . . . Aisan variable-venturi (V type) or twin fixed-venturi (K type)
Application:
  Aisan V type . . . . 1.3 models (up to August 1989)
  Aisan K type . . . . 1.3 models (from August 1989)
  Aisan K type . . . . 1.6 carburettor models
Choke type . . . . Automatic

V type carburettor data

Idle speed – cooling fan off:	
Manual gearbox	800 rpm
Automatic transmission	850 rpm
Idle mixture CO content	1 to 2 %
Fast idle speed – cooling fan off	3600 ± 200 rpm
Dashpot system setting speed – cooling fan off	2000 ± 200 rpm
Float-to-carburettor body clearance	5.4 mm
Needle valve plunger-to-float lip clearance	0.9 to 1.1 mm
Accelerator pump stroke	4.5 mm
Throttle valve fully-open angle	87 to 93° from horizontal

K type carburettor data – 1.3 models

Idle speed – cooling fan off:	
Manual gearbox	800 rpm
Automatic transmission	850 rpm
Idle mixture CO content	1 to 2%
Fast idle speed – cooling fan off	1600 rpm
Power-assisted steering idle-up setting speed – cooling fan off	1200 rpm
Dashpot system setting speed – cooling fan off:	
With power-assisted steering	1800 to 2200 rpm
Without power-assisted steering	2000 rpm
Throttle position switch setting speed – cooling fan off	1400 rpm
Float-to-carburettor body clearance	8.0 mm
Needle valve plunger-to-float lip clearance	1.5 to 1.7 mm
Accelerator pump stroke	4.75 to 5.25 mm
Choke coil resistance @ 20°C	17 to 19 ohms
PTC heater resistance @ 20°C	2 to 6 ohms
Throttle valve fully-open angle:	
Primary	90° from horizontal
Secondary	80° from horizontal

K type carburettor data – 1.6 model

Idle speed – cooling fan off:	
With automatic transmission and power-assisted steering	900 rpm
All others	800 rpm
Idle mixture CO content	1 to 2%
Fast idle speed – cooling fan off	3000 ± 200 rpm
Throttle positioner system setting speed – cooling fan off	1400 rpm
Float-to-carburettor body clearance	7.2 mm
Needle valve plunger-to-float lip clearance	1.67 to 1.99 mm
Accelerator pump stroke	4.0 mm
Choke coil resistance @ 20°C	19 to 24 ohms
Throttle valve fully-open angle:	
Primary	90° from horizontal
Secondary	80° from horizontal

Part B: Fuel-injected engine

General

System type	Electronic Fuel Injection (EFI), controlled by Toyota Computer Control System (TCCS)

System data

Fuel pump type	In-tank electric fuel pump
Regulated fuel pressure – under test conditions	2.6 to 3.0 bars
Normal regulated fuel pressure @ idle speed, vacuum hose connected	2.1 to 2.6 bars
Cold start injector:	
Leakage – under normal fuel pressure	Less than one drop per minute
Resistance	2 to 5 ohms
Injectors:	
Leakage – under normal fuel pressure	Less than one drop per minute
Injection volume	46 to 53 cc per 15 seconds
Maximum volume difference between injectors	5 cc
Idle speed – cooling fan off	800 rpm
Idle mixture CO content	1 to 2%

Part C: All models

Fuel octane requirement

1.3 models	Unleaded 91 RON (minimum) or leaded 97 RON (four-star)
1.6 models	Unleaded 95 RON (minimum) or leaded 97 RON (four-star)

Torque wrench settings

	Nm	lbf ft
Fuel line unions:		
Banjo bolts	29	21
Flare nuts	30	22
Cold start injector pipe	15	11
Cold start injector-to-manifold	7.4	5.5
Fuel pressure regulator-to-fuel rail	7.4	5.5
Main fuel supply pipe connection-to-fuel rail	29	21
Fuel rail bolts	17	13
Throttle housing-to-inlet manifold	22	16
Fuel tank strap bolts	39	29
Inlet manifold-to-cylinder head:		
Carburettor engines	19	14
Fuel-injected engine	27	20
Inlet manifold stay:		
Upper end 1.6 GL Executive model	19	14
Upper end – GTi 16 model	22	16
Lower end – all 1.6 models	39	29
Exhaust manifold-to-cylinder head:		
1.3 models	42 to 47	31 to 35
1.6 GL Executive model	25	18
GTi 16 model	39	29
Exhaust manifold stay:		
1.6 GL Executive model	25	18
GTi 16 model	39	29
Exhaust manifold-to-downpipe	62	46
Exhaust pipe clamp bolt	19	14

Part A: Carburettor engines

1 General information and precautions

The fuel system consists of a fuel tank mounted under the rear of the car, a mechanical fuel pump and a carburettor.

The mechanical fuel pump is operated by a camshaft eccentric and is mounted on the rearward facing side of the cylinder head, whilst a disposable in-line fuel filter is located on the engine compartment bulkhead. A conventional fuel gauge sender unit, mounted from the upper surface of the fuel tank, conveys information regarding the amount of fuel remaining in the tank to the gauge in the instrument cluster.

The air filter housing contains a disposable filter element, and incorporates an automatic Hot Air Intake system (HAI). This system allows cold air from the outside of the car and warm air from around the exhaust manifold to enter the air cleaner in the correct proportions, according to ambient air temperatures and engine operating conditions.

The inlet manifold is coolant heated to improve initial engine warm-up.

The exhaust system consists of three sections secured by flanged joints, and a cast iron exhaust manifold. The system is suspended throughout its length on rubber mountings.

⚠️ **Warning: Many of the procedures in this Chapter require the removal of fuel lines and connections which may result in some fuel spillage. Before carrying out any operation on the fuel system refer to the precautions given in Safety First! at the beginning of this Manual and follow them implicitly. Petrol is a highly dangerous and volatile liquid and the precautions necessary when handling it cannot be overstressed.**

2.1 Undo the wing nut securing the forward section of the air filter housing – 1.6 model

2 Air filter housing/trunking – removal and refitting

Removal

1 Remove the wing nut from the centre of the air filter housing. On later 1.3 models, the air filter housing is further secured by means of a bolt to an external support bracket: on 1.6 models, another wing nut by the timing cover must be undone (photo).

2 Release the trunking securing clips and clamps, as necessary (photo).

2.2 Release the air filter housing/trunking securing clip

3 Disconnect all relevant hoses from the air filter housing, having noted their locations and labelled them to aid subsequent refitting, then remove the air filter housing.

4 The trunking may be removed separately, after releasing its securing arrangements, as required.

Refitting

5 Refitting is a reversal of the removal procedure, ensuring that all hoses are correctly connected.

3 Air filter housing hot air intake (HAI) system – general information and component renewal

General information

1 The system is controlled by the hot idle compensation (HIC) valve (Section 15) which is mounted in the air filter housing; when the engine is started from cold, the valve is closed and allows inlet manifold depression to act on the hot air intake (HAI) diaphragm in the intake duct. This creates a vacuum in the diaphragm and draws a flap valve across the cold air intake, thus allowing only (warmed) air from the exhaust manifold to enter the air filter.

2 As the temperature rises of the exhaust-warmed air in the air filter, a wax capsule in the HIC valve deforms and gradually opens the valves atmospheric port. This allows the atmospheric pressure to return to the HAI diaphragm which then causes the flap to slowly close across the hot air intake so that only cold air from the intake duct is entering the air filter.

3 To check the system, allow the engine to cool down completely, then disconnect the trunking from the air filter housing; the flap valve in the duct should be securely seated across the hot air intake. Start the engine; the flap should immediately rise to close off the cold air intake and should then lower steadily as the engine warms up until it is eventually seated across the hot air intake again.

4 To check the HIC valve, disconnect the vacuum pipe from the HAI valve when the engine is running and place a finger over the pipe end. When the engine is cold, full inlet manifold vacuum should be present in the pipe, and when the engine is at normal operating temperature there should be no vacuum in the pipe. If this is not the case it is likely that the HIC valve is faulty. Refer to Section 15 for further information on testing the valve.

5 To check the HAI diaphragm, disconnect the trunking from the air filter housing and check that the flap valve is securely seated across the hot air intake. Disconnect the vacuum pipe and suck hard at the HAI diaphragm stub; the flap should rise to shut off the cold air intake. If not the diaphragm is faulty.

6 If either component is faulty, it must be renewed.

HIC valve – renewal

7 Refer to Section 15.

HAI diaphragm – renewal

8 Disconnect the trunking from the air filter housing then undo the HAI valve retaining bolt.

9 Unhook the HAI diaphragm rod from the flap valve then remove the assembly from the air filter housing.

10 Refitting is a reverse of the removal procedure ensuring that the diaphragm rod is correctly engaged with the flap valve.

4 Fuel pump – testing, removal and refitting

Note: *Refer to the warning note in Section 1 before carrying out the following operation.*

Testing

1 To test the output of the fuel pump, first disconnect the hose from the carburettor and place its open end in a small clear container.

2 Disconnect the distributor LT wiring connector.

3 Have an assistant operate the ignition key to turn the engine over using the starter motor, whilst you observe the fuel flowing into the container; well defined, regular spurts of fuel should be seen to be ejected from the open fuel hose end.

Removal

4 Disconnect the battery earth terminal.

5 Having labelled them to aid subsequent refitting, disconnect the fuel hoses from the fuel pump; insert plugs to avoid dirt ingress and avoid excessive spillage.

6 Undo and remove the pump mounting bolts, then withdraw the fuel pump; note the spacer and gaskets fitment.

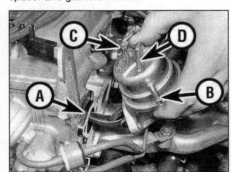

4.8 Refitting the fuel pump – 1.6 model

A Spacer and gaskets
B Supply hose connection (from the filter)
C Hose connection to carburettor
D Return hose connection

7 The fuel pump is a completely sealed unit, no cleaning or repairs being possible. Note that two types of pump may be fitted on 1.3 models; if a new pump is to be fitted ensure that it is of the same type as that removed.

Refitting

8 Refitting is a reversal of the removal procedure, but note that new gaskets must be fitted and that the mating faces must be perfectly clean (photo).

5 Fuel gauge sender unit – removal and refitting

Note: *Refer to the warning note in Section 1 before carrying out the following operation.*

Removal

1 Disconnect the battery earth terminal.

2 Remove the rear seat cushion (Chapter 11).

3 If applicable, raise the protective sheeting from the exposed seat base.

4 Disconnect the sender unit wiring connector, and release the wiring from any tapes or clips.

5 Undo and remove the two bolts retaining the access hole cover, then raise it to expose the sender unit; if necessary, release the wiring grommet from the cover to allow the cover to be removed separately (photo).

6 The sender unit may be removed from the top of the fuel tank after undoing its retaining bolts/screws, but be careful not to damage or bend the float arm as the unit is withdrawn. Remove the old gasket.

Refitting

7 Refitting is a reversal of the removal procedure using a new gasket.

6 Fuel tank and filler pipe – removal and refitting

Note: *Refer to the warning note in Section 1 before carrying out the following operation.*

Removal

1 Before removing the tank run the fuel level down as low as possible.

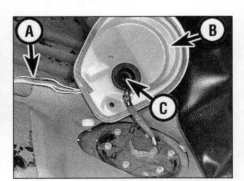

5.5 Fuel gauge sender unit wiring (A), access hole cover (B) and grommet (C)

6.10 Undo and remove the fuel tank support strap bolts

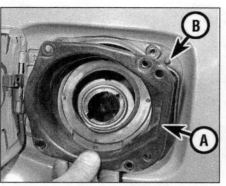

6.11 Removing the fuel filler surround (A), and gasket (B)

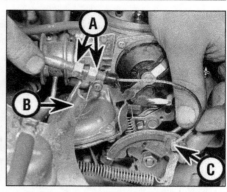

7.3 Disconnect the accelerator cable (1.6 model)

A *Cable bracket nuts* C *Inner cable end*
B *Abutment bracket*

2 Disconnect the battery earth terminal.
3 Syphon out the remaining fuel in the tank (not by mouth), and transfer it to a suitable container; take all normal safety precautions.
4 Disconnect and release the fuel gauge sender unit wiring and release the grommet from the access hole cover (after removing the cover retaining bolts) (Section 2). Push the disconnected sender unit wiring through the access hole, onto the top of the fuel tank.
5 Raise the rear of the vehicle, and support it securely using axle stands.
6 Disconnect the handbrake secondary cable securing clips, then tie the cables out of the working area.
7 If necessary, disconnect the exhaust main section from its rear silencer section flange for increased clearance (Section 18).
8 Make a note of the correct fitted positions, then disconnect the rubber fuel and breather hoses (at the front end of the fuel tank) from the rigid pipes; insert plugs to avoid dirt ingress and avoid excessive spillage.
9 Release the relevant filler and vent pipe hose clips to allow the pipes to be separated from the fuel tank as the tank is withdrawn.
10 With the fuel tank supported, undo the bolt securing each tank strap at its rear end (photo); lower the straps, then carefully lower the fuel tank ensuring that the filler pipe and vent pipe become detached. Note that new gaskets must be fitted, where applicable, if any of the tank fitments are removed.
11 The filler pipe assembly may be removed in sections, as required, noting the following. The fuel filler flap remote release catch must be withdrawn into the luggage compartment (Chapter 11) to allow the filler cap surround components to be removed, and the filler pipe support bracket(s) must be released (photo).

Refitting

12 Refitting is a reversal of the removal procedure, ensuring that all fuel and breather hoses are securely retained and do not become trapped as the tank is lifted into position.

7 Accelerator cable – removal, refitting and adjustment

Removal

1 Disconnect the battery earth terminal.
2 For increased working access, remove the air filter housing (Section 2).
3 Slacken the cable bracket retaining nuts and lift the outer cable out of the bracket, then release the inner cable from the throttle lever quadrant (photo).
4 Release the accelerator cable from its support clip(s) in the engine compartment.
5 Remove the facia lower finish panel in the driver's side footwell.
6 Release the inner cable from the top of the accelerator pedal, then undo the two bolts securing the outer cable abutment at the accelerator pedal end and withdraw the cable.

Refitting and adjustment

7 Refitting is a reversal of the removal procedure. On completion adjust the cable as follows.
8 Turn the cable bracket nuts by the carburettor until all but the slightest free movement (cable slack) has been eliminated. Once adjustment is correct, tighten the nuts securely then check that the throttle valve opens fully when the accelerator pedal is fully depressed. On vehicles with automatic transmission, check the adjustment of the kickdown cable after the accelerator cable has been adjusted (Chapter 7).

8 Accelerator pedal – removal and refitting

Removal

1 Remove the facia lower finish panel in the driver's side footwell.
2 Release the inner cable from the top of the accelerator pedal, then unbolt the accelerator pedal assembly from the bulkhead.

Refitting

3 Refitting is a reversal of the removal procedure. On completion check the accelerator cable adjustment as described in Section 7.

9 Unleaded petrol – general information and usage

All the engines covered by this Manual (United Kingdom specification) can run on either 4-star leaded fuel or unleaded fuel, refer to the Specifications at the start of this Chapter for octane rating details. No adjustments to the ignition timing are necessary.

10 Carburettor – general information

The variable-venturi type carburettor fitted to early (pre-August 1989) 1.3 models is often referred to as a V type carburettor, whilst that fitted to later (August 1989 onwards) 1.3 models is broadly similar in principle to the carburettor used on the 1.6. The 1.6 has a twin fixed-venturi type carburettor (often referred to as a K type carburettor).

A brief description of the operation of each carburettor type is given below.

Variable-venturi (V type) carburettor

The variable-venturi carburettor principal features are a suction chamber, a piston with a tapered fuel metering needle attached, a jet arrangement (within the carburettor body), a float chamber and the remaining body and ancillary systems.

As air is drawn into the carburettor body, it creates a slight vacuum over the jet which causes fuel to be drawn into the airstream thus forming the fuel/air mixture. The amount of fuel drawn into the airstream depends on the position of the metering needle in the jet, as, when the needle is moved, its taper profile effectively alters the size of the jet orifice.

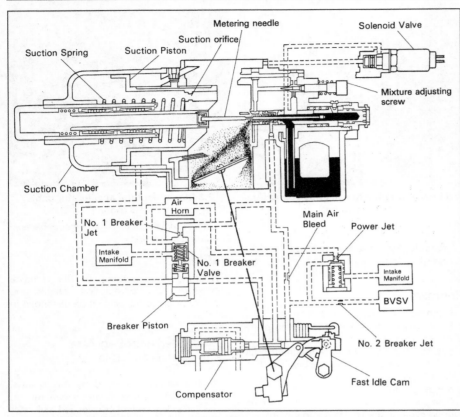

Fig. 4.1 A general schematic view of the variable-venturi (V type) carburettor fitted to early 1.3 models (Sec 10)

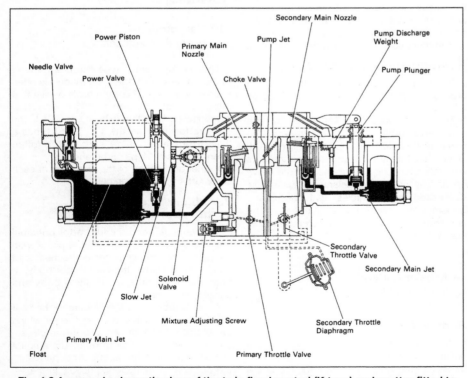

Fig. 4.2 A general schematic view of the twin fixed-venturi (K type) carburettor fitted to later 1.3 models (Sec 10)

The position of the piston and thus that of the metering needle is determined by engine vacuum controlled by the throttle valve. The piston has an orifice linking the venturi and the inside of the suction chamber; when there is vacuum in the venturi, the air inside the suction chamber is drawn out and this causes the piston to rise into the chamber. The piston keeps the depression over the jet almost constant, so that fuel will continue to be drawn into the venturi; at low engine speeds, the piston restricts the air entering the carburettor and this speeds up the passage of air to allow the formation of a suitable vacuum, whilst at higher speeds the piston rises into the suction chamber.

An accelerator pump arrangement is featured, to supply additional fuel when the accelerator pedal is depressed.

A dashpot system serves to reduce exhaust emissions during deceleration (Section 13).

Mixture enrichment for cold starting is performed by a coolant heated automatic choke control (known as the compensator).

An electrically-operated fuel cut-off solenoid valve cuts the supply of fuel when the ignition is turned off to reduce the possibility of run-on.

Twin fixed-venturi (K type) type carburettor

The twin-fixed venturi carburettor described below is that fitted to 1.6 models; the carburettor fitted to later 1.3 models is broadly similar in principle, but certain features differ.

The carburettor uses its primary venturi to provide the optimum fuelling under normal conditions, with the secondary venturi supplementing it when the engine is operating under high speed or load conditions; the primary throttle valve is mechanically operated through the linkage, accelerator cable and pedal, whilst the secondary throttle valve is controlled by a vacuum diaphragm.

Each venturi has two fuel supply circuits, a slow, and a high speed system, to match the engine fuel requirements; the fuel is metered by fixed jets. The power and acceleration systems both utilise vacuum for their operation, whilst the acceleration system also features a mechanical linkage to enable it to respond instantly.

The throttle positioner on 1.6 models or dashpot system on 1.3 models, is fitted to reduce CO and HC exhaust emissions during deceleration (Section 13).

During cold starting, the choke valve plate at the top of the primary venturi is closed to supply a rich fuel/air mixture. The choke coils are heated electrically. A vacuum controlled choke breaker system determines the positioning of the choke valve plate to prevent too rich a

mixture during starting and forcibly opens it further when the engine is running (Section 14)

An electrically-operated fuel cut-off

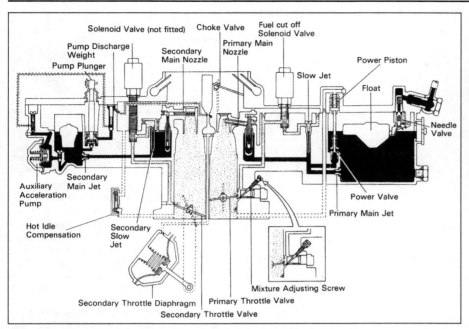

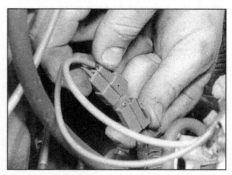

11.4 Disconnecting carburettor wiring connector (1.6 model)

Fig. 4.3 A general schematic view of the twin fixed-venturi (K type) carburettor fitted to 1.6 models (Sec 10)

solenoid valve cuts the supply of fuel when the ignition is turned off to reduce the possibility of run-on.

11 Carburettor – removal and refitting

Note: *Refer to the warning note in Section 1 before carrying out the following operation.*

Removal

1 Disconnect the battery earth terminal.
2 Remove the air filter housing/trunking as described in Section 2.
3 Disconnect the accelerator cable (Section 7); on vehicles with automatic transmission it will be necessary to disconnect the kickdown cable (Chapter 7).
4 Disconnect the carburettor wiring connector(s) (photo).
5 Disconnect the fuel inlet hose.
6 Where applicable, partially drain the cooling

system (Chapter 1), then disconnect the coolant hoses from the carburettor (having labelled them to aid subsequent refitting).
7 Make a note of the correct fitted positions of all relevant vacuum hoses then disconnect them from the carburettor (note that the rigid vacuum pipework will be removed with the carburettor assembly, where applicable) (photo).
8 Release the accelerator cable bracket from the inlet manifold, where necessary.
9 Undo the nuts and bolts securing the carburettor and its rigid vacuum pipework assembly (where applicable), then remove it from the vehicle (photo).
10 Remove the carburettor spacer/insulator and gaskets.
11 The rigid vacuum pipework may be removed from the carburettor, as necessary.

Refitting

12 Refitting is a reversal of the removal procedure noting the following points (photo).

(a) Ensure that all traces of old gasket are removed.
(b) Position a new gasket on either side of the spacer/insulator on refitting.
(c) Use the notes made on removal to ensure all hoses are reconnected to their original positions.
(d) Adjust the accelerator cable as described in Section 7.
(e) Top up the cooling system (where applicable) and adjust the idle speed and mixture settings as described in Chapter 1.

12 Carburettor – fault finding, overhaul and adjustments

Note: *Refer to the warning note in Section 1 before carrying out the following operation.*

Fault finding

1 Faults with the carburettor are usually associated with dirt entering the float chamber and blocking the jets, causing a weak mixture or power failure within a certain engine speed range. If this is the case, then a thorough clean will normally cure the problem, but note that a disconnected or split vacuum hose may also cause similar problems, so check this out first. Carry out the checks described in Section 14 as these may also help to pinpoint a fault. If the carburettor is well worn, uneven running may be caused by

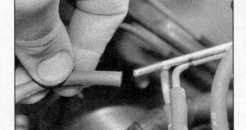

11.7 Disconnecting a vacuum hose from a rigid pipework connection

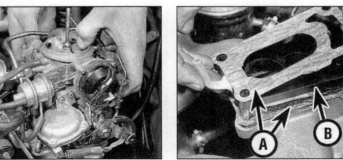

11.9 Remove the carburettor and pipework assembly from the inlet manifold (1.6 model)

11.12 On refitting position new gaskets (A) on either side of the spacer/insulator (B) (1.6 model)

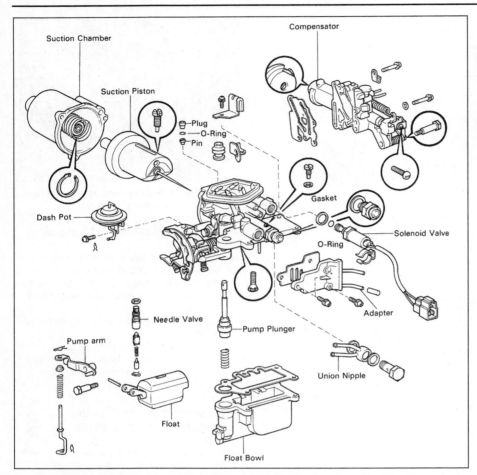

Fig. 4.4 An exploded view of the variable-venturi (V type) carburettor fitted to early 1.3 models (Sec 12)

12.8 Removing the suction chamber adjusting (guide) pin cover plug

air entering through the throttle valve spindle bearings.

Overhaul and adjustments

2 The following paragraphs describe certain cleaning, inspection and adjustment procedures which can be carried out by the home mechanic after the carburettor has been removed; certain other operations (not covered) require the use of special measuring gauges, and these must be left to your dealer

(or other suitable specialist) in the event of the carburettor still malfunctioning after overhaul. If the carburettor is worn or damaged, it should either be renewed or be overhauled by a specialist.

Variable-venturi (V type) type carburettor

3 With this type of carburettor, overhaul will usually mean cleaning sediment from the float bowl and checking for worn components, as

there are no fixed jets to become clogged.
4 Remove the air filter housing support bracket from the top of the carburettor.
5 Unscrew the fuel cut-off solenoid valve; note the O-ring and gasket fitment.
6 Remove the fuel pipe banjo union, noting its gasket fitment.
7 The compensator should not be removed unless absolutely necessary, as its operational settings will require checking by a Toyota dealer (or a suitable specialist) upon refitting.
8 To remove the suction chamber piston adjusting (guide) pin, screw a 4 mm bolt into the plug then prise out the plug using the flat blade of a screwdriver underneath the bolt head (photo). Remove the O-ring, then shake out the pin.
9 Remove the screws, then remove the suction chamber, spring and piston from the carburettor (photo). Note that the fuel metering needle must not be removed from the piston, and ensure that it does not get damaged whilst it is exposed.
10 Extract the spring clip, then remove the accelerator pump arm pivot screw and the pump arm.
11 Remove the clamps and undo the four float bowl securing screws, then remove the float bowl and its gasket (photo). Remove the pump plunger, damping spring and the gaiter.
12 Noting how the clip arrangement locates, remove the float pivot pin, float and needle

12.9 Removing the suction chamber, spring and piston assembly

12.11 Removing the float bowl

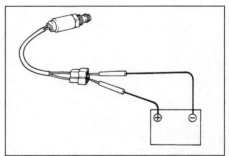

Fig. 4.5 Testing the operation of the fuel cut-off solenoid – V type carburettor (Sec 12)

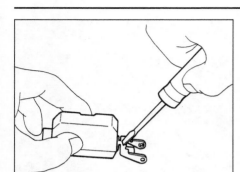

Fig. 4.6 Bend the float arm, as shown, if the float to carburettor body clearance is not as specified (Sec 12)

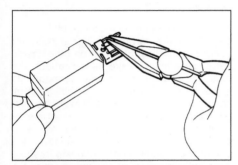

Fig. 4.7 Bending the lip on the float to correct the needle valve plunger to float lip clearance (Sec 12)

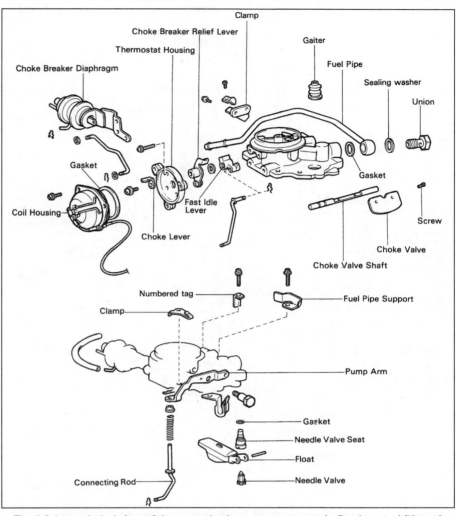

Fig. 4.8 An exploded view of the upper body components – twin fixed-venturi (K type) carburettor fitted to 1.6 models (Sec 12)

valve sub-assembly, followed by the needle valve seat and gasket.

13 Clean all components using carburettor cleaning solution, then examine them for signs of wear, damage, scoring, corrosion and deformation, and check that the fuel cut-off solenoid operates by applying battery voltage to its terminals as shown in Fig. 4.5; the solenoid should be heard to click. Renew any defective components as necessary.

14 Substitute new gaskets and O-rings for the ones removed, then begin reassembling, in a reversal of the removal sequence, with the following considerations.

15 Make sure that the needle valve seat is screwed in tightly, with a new gasket; a leak here is the main cause of flooding.

16 Adjust the float level in the following manner: note that the needle valve clip is installed after adjustment. Install the needle valve, spring and plunger onto the seat arrangement, then install the float and its pivot pin. With the float hanging down by its own weight, measure the float to carburettor body clearance (without the gasket fitted); if it is not as specified, adjust it by bending the portion of the float arm shown in Fig. 4.6. With the clearance correct, raise the float and check that the clearance between the needle valve plunger and the float lip is as specified. If adjustment is necessary, bend the lip, then recheck the clearance. After the float level adjustment procedure has been completed,

remove the components and assemble the needle valve and float arrangement with the clip.

17 If the compensator has been removed, or a new compensator has been fitted, its operational settings must be checked by a Toyota dealer (or other suitable specialist).

18 Ensure that the adjusting (guide) pin locates to the groove in the suction chamber piston, and remember to fit a new O-ring before the plug is inserted.

19 If the mixture adjusting screw has been disturbed or removed, return it to its initial setting by screwing it right in then backing it off three complete turns; take care not to damage its tip by screwing it in too tightly. Note that a special tool will be required to turn the mixture adjusting screw.

Twin fixed-venturi (K type) type carburettor

20 The procedure given below refers specifically to the carburettor fitted to the 1.6 model, but the procedure is broadly

similar for the version fitted to the later 1.3 models.

21 Remove the rigid vacuum pipework, if applicable, after labelling its hose connections to the carburettor.

22 Remove the fuel inlet pipe clamp and union bolt, then remove the pipe and its gaskets (photo).

12.22 Fuel inlet pipe union connection and gaskets

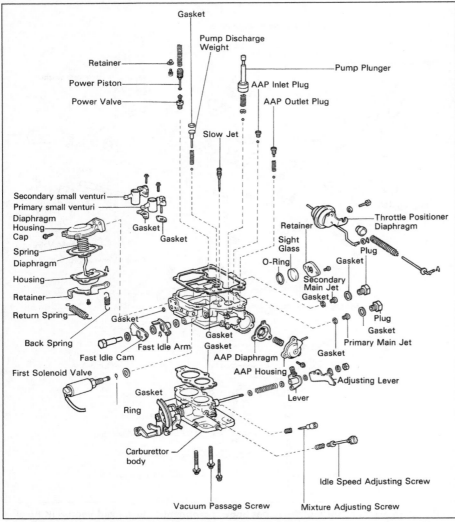

Gasket
Pump Discharge Weight
Retainer
Power Piston
Power Valve
Pump Plunger
AAP Inlet Plug
AAP Outlet Plug
Slow Jet
Secondary small venturi
Primary small venturi
Diaphragm Housing Cap
Spring
Diaphragm
Housing
Retainer
Return Spring
Back Spring
First Solenoid Valve
Gasket
Gasket
Fast Idle Arm
Fast Idle Cam
Gasket
Ring
Carburettor body
Gasket
Gasket
AAP Diaphragm
AAP Housing
Throttle Positioner Diaphragm
Retainer
Sight Glass
O-Ring
Plug
Gasket
Secondary Main Jet
Gasket
Gasket
Plug
Gasket
Primary Main Jet
Gasket
Adjusting Lever
Lever
Idle Speed Adjusting Screw
Vacuum Passage Screw
Mixture Adjusting Screw

Fig. 4.9 An exploded view of the carburettor main body components – twin fixed-venturi (K type) carburettor fitted to 1.6 models (Sec 12)

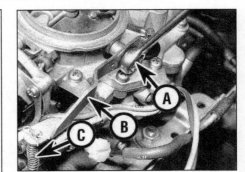

12.24 Removing the accelerator pump arm

A *Accelerator pump arm pivot bolt*
B *Accelerator pump arm*
C *Connecting link*

lug inside the wiring connector (photo).

28 Lift off the carburettor upper body for access to the float chamber and the needle valve assembly. Make notes about the location and order of any components removed, to aid correct reassembly (photo). Noting the clip arrangement, remove the float pivot pin, the float and the needle valve sub-assembly followed by the needle valve seat and gasket. Note that apart from removing the choke coil assembly (after undoing its three collar retaining screws), the remainder of the choke mechanism should not be removed unless the choke breaker requires renewal: make a note of the position of the line on the coil housing, in relation to the scale marking, if the coil assembly is to be removed.

29 The primary and secondary main jets can be exposed by first releasing the throttle positioner reaction arm and spring and moving it out of the way, then removing the hexagonal headed cover plugs in the main carburettor body; note the plug gasket fitment (photos).

30 The solenoid valve can be unscrewed from the main carburettor body; note the O-ring and gasket fitment.

31 Dismantle the auxiliary accelerator pump diaphragm arrangement (after removing its three housing retaining screws) and remove the secondary throttle valve vacuum diaphragm unit (after disconnecting the

23 Label and disconnect all the relevant vacuum hoses still attached.

24 Undo the accelerator pump arm pivot bolt then disconnect and remove the arm (photo).

25 Disconnect the choke operating link (photo).

26 Remove the eight carburettor upper body securing screws and the numbered tag(s), the fuel pipe support and the choke and solenoid wiring clamps.

27 Disconnect the solenoid wiring, using a screwdriver to release the locking

12.25 Disconnecting the choke operating link

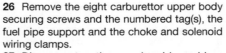

12.27 Release the wire from the wiring connector, using a screwdriver

12.28 Removing the accelerator pump plunger from the carburettor upper body

operating link and undoing the two securing screws, noting its gasket fitment), so that compressed air may be used to blow through the jets and passages within the carburettor without danger of splitting any internally actuated diaphragms.

32 Clean all removed components using carburettor cleaning solution. Examine the components for signs of wear, damage, scoring, corrosion and deformation. Check that the power piston moves smoothly in its bore, and check the operation of the power valve as shown in Fig.4.12. Renew any defective components, as necessary. Check that the fuel cut-off solenoid operates by applying battery voltage to its terminals; the solenoid should be heard to click. Measure the resistance between the choke coil wire terminal and the coil housing; if it is not within specification, renew the coil housing assembly. On later 1.3 models; a similar operation must be performed on the positive temperature coefficient (PTC) heater (where fitted), if the measurement is outside that specified, renewal of the carburettor upper body will be required. On 1.3 models equipped with a throttle switch, connect an ohmmeter between the switch wire and switch body (Fig. 4.15) and test the operation of the switch. When the switch plunger is pushed in there should be continuity between the switch terminals, when the rod is released there should be an open circuit. If not the throttle switch must be renewed.

33 Blow through the jets and passages within the carburettor using compressed air, to remove dirt particles and other possible sources of blockage.

34 Substitute new gaskets and O-rings for the ones removed, then begin reassembling, in a reversal of the removal sequence, with the following considerations.

35 If the choke coil housing has been removed, ensure that the bi-metal spring and the choke actuating lever align as it is refitted (Fig. 4.16). The coil housing position may be adjusted with the carburettor fitted to the vehicle, if necessary; turn it clockwise if the starting mixture is too rich, and anti-clockwise if it is too lean (note that the choke valve will be fully withdrawn, or non-operational, at an

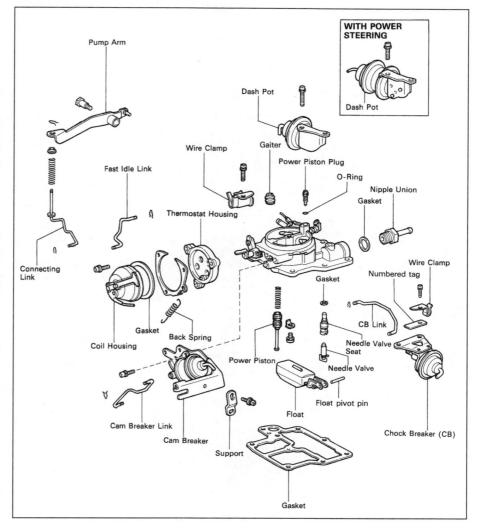

Fig. 4.10 An exploded view of the carburettor upper body components – twin fixed-venturi (K type) carburettor fitted to later 1.3 models (Sec 12)

ambient temperature of 30° C or 86° F).

36 Make sure that the needle valve is screwed in tightly, with a new gasket; a leak here is the main cause of flooding (photo).

37 Adjust the float level in the following manner; note that the needle valve clip is installed after adjustment. Install the float and its pivot pin. With the float hanging down by its own weight, measure the float to carburettor body clearance (without the gasket fitted); if it is not as specified, adjust it by bending the portion of the float arm shown

12.29A Releasing the throttle positioner reaction arm

12.29B Unscrewing the secondary main jet. Primary main jet cover plug (arrowed) also shown

12.36 Refitting the fuel inlet (needle valve) seat

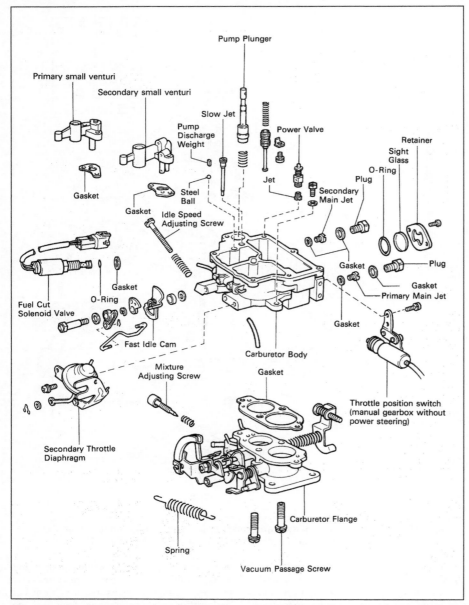

Fig. 4.11 An exploded view of the carburettor main body components – twin fixed-venturi (K type) carburettor fitted to later 1.3 models (Sec 12)

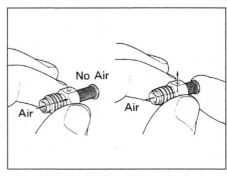

Fig. 4.12 Checking the operation of the power valve (Sec 12)

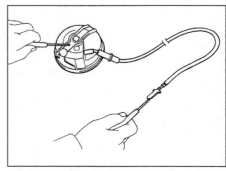

Fig. 4.13 Measuring the resistance between the choke coil wire terminal and the coil housing (Sec 12)

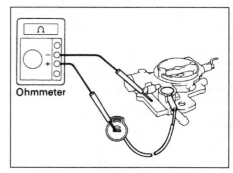

Fig. 4.14 Checking the PTC heater resistance – later 1.3 models (Sec 12)

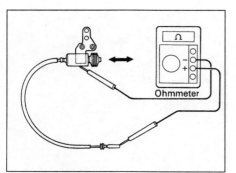

Fig. 4.15 Testing the operation of the throttle switch – later 1.3 models (Sec 12)

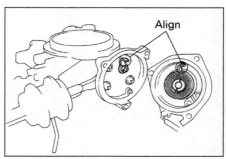

Fig. 4.16 When refitting the choke coil housing, ensure that the spring and actuating lever align (Sec 12)

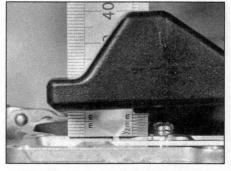

12.37A Measuring the float to carburettor body clearance

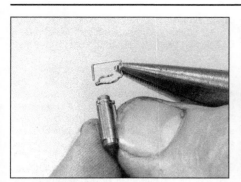

12.37B Refitting the needle valve clip to the needle valve

12.37C Installing tile needle valve and float assembly

12.37D Inserting the float retaining (pivot) pin

in Fig. 4.6. With the float to carburettor body clearance correct, raise the float and check that the clearance between the needle valve plunger and the float lip is as specified; bend the lip if it is incorrect then recheck the clearances (Fig. 4.7). After the float level adjustment procedure has been completed, remove the components and assemble the needle valve and float arrangement with the clip (photos).

38 With all relevant internal components refitted, refit the carburettor upper body using a new gasket (photos).

39 If the mixture adjusting screw has been disturbed or removed, return it to its initial setting by screwing it right in then backing it off three complete turns (three and a half turns on later 1.3 models) take care not to damage its tip by screwing it in too tightly. A special tool will be required to turn the mixture adjusting screw.

13 Carburettor – on-car adjustments

Note: *All carburettor adjustments must be carried out whilst the cooling fan is off. If at any time the cooling fan operates wait for it to stop before continuing with the adjustment procedure.*

1 Prior to carrying out any of the following adjustments ensure that the idle speed and fuel mixture are correctly adjusted as

described in Chapter 1, noting that the tachometer should be left connected until all the relevant adjustments have been completed.

Variable-venturi (V type) carburettor

Fast idle speed

2 Warm the engine up to normal operating temperature then, whilst holding the throttle valve slightly open. set the fast idle adjusting cam and release the throttle valve. The engine should now be idling at the specified fast idle speed. If not adjust it by rotating the fast idle adjusting screw as necessary.

3 Once the fast idle speed is set, release the fast idle cam and check that the engine returns to its specified idle speed (Chapter 1).

Dashpot system

4 Warm the engine up to normal operating temperature, then disconnect the vacuum hose from the carburettor dashpot and plug the end of the hose.

5 Increase the engine speed to 3000 rpm and hold it there for a few seconds then release the accelerator pedal and allow the engine to idle. The engine should now be idling at the specified dashpot system setting speed. If not, adjust it by rotating the dashpot adjusting screw as necessary.

6 If adjustment proves difficult, check the dashpot system components as follows. With the engine idling, disconnect the vacuum

hose from the dashpot and check that there is a vacuum at the hose end. Reconnect the hose to the dashpot, then disconnect it whilst observing the dashpot rod movement. As the hose is connected the rod should be pulled into the dashpot and when the hose is disconnected the rod should move out under spring pressure. If this is not the case the dashpot must be renewed.

7 To check the vacuum transmitting valve (VTV) trace the vacuum hose back from the dashpot to the VTV then disconnect both hoses noting the correct fitted direction of the valve, and remove the valve. Check the operation of the VTV by blowing air into it either end of the valve. If the VTV is functioning correctly, air should flow freely through the valve from B to A, and the flow of air should be severely restricted from A to B (Fig.4.17). If the vacuum transmitting valve does not perform as specified it must be renewed.

8 Once the dashpot idling speed is correctly set reconnect the vacuum hose to the dashpot and check that the engine returns to the specified idle speed (Chapter 1).

Twin fixed-venturi (K type) carburettor – 1.3 models

Fast idle speed

9 Warm up the engine to normal operating temperature then stop it.

10 Remove the air filter housing cover (Section 2), then disconnect the vacuum

12.38A Use a new gasket on refitting the upper body section

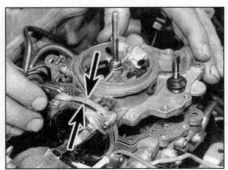

12.38B Alignment mark on the choke coil housing and the scale markings on the thermostat housing (arrowed)

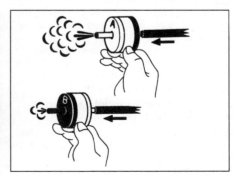

Fig. 4.17 Checking the operation of the vacuum transmitting valve (VTV) (Sec 13)

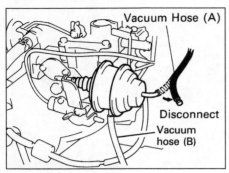

Fig. 4.18 Disconnect and plug vacuum hose A before adjusting idle up setting – later 1.3 models equipped with power steering (Sec 13)

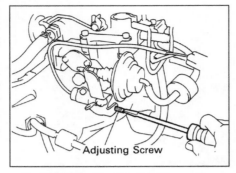

Fig. 4.19 Adjusting the throttle position switch – later 1.3 models equipped with manual gearbox without power steering (Sec 13)

hoses from the cam breaker diaphragm and plug the hose ends.

11 Whilst holding the throttle valve slightly open. pull up the fast idle cam then release the throttle valve so that the throttle lever rests on the third step of the fast idle cam.

12 Refit the air filter housing cover then start the engine. **Note:** *Do not touch the accelerator pedal or throttle lever because the fast idle cam position will have to be reset.* The engine should now be idling at the specified fast idle speed. If not, adjust it by rotating the fast idle adjusting screw as necessary.

13 Once the fast idle speed is correctly set, operate the throttle lever or accelerator pedal a few times and check that the engine returns to its specified idle speed (Chapter 1). Reconnect the vacuum hoses to their original positions on the cam breaker diaphragm.

Dashpot system – models without power steering

14 Warm the engine up to normal operating temperature then disconnect the vacuum hose from the dashpot and plug the end of the hose.

15 Increase the engine speed to 3000 rpm and hold it there for a few seconds, then release the accelerator pedal and allow the engine to idle. The engine should now be idling at the specified dashpot setting speed. If not, adjust it by rotating the dashpot adjusting screw as necessary.

16 If adjustment proves difficult inspect the dashpot system components as described above in paragraphs 6 and 7.

17 Once the dashpot idling speed is correctly set, reconnect the vacuum hose to the dashpot and check that the engine returns to its specified idle speed (Chapter 1).

Dashpot system – models equipped with power steering

18 Warm the engine up to normal operating temperature then disconnect the vacuum hose 'A' from the dashpot and plug the end of the hose (Fig. 4.18).

19 Increase the engine speed to 3000 rpm and hold it there for a few seconds then

release the accelerator pedal and allow the engine to idle. The engine should now be idling at the specified power steering idle up setting. If not, adjust it by rotating the dashpot adjusting screw as necessary.

20 Once the idle up speed is correctly set, disconnect the second vacuum hose 'B' from the diaphragm and plug the end of hose. The engine should now be idling at the specified dashpot setting speed. If this is not the case, the dashpot is faulty and must be renewed.

21 Reconnect the vacuum hose to their correct locations on the dashpot and check that the engine returns to its specified idle speed (Chapter 1).

Throttle position switch adjustment – manual gearbox models without power steering

22 Warm the engine up to normal operating temperature then stop it.

23 Disconnect the throttle position switch wire from the carburettor wiring connector then connect one probe of an ohmmeter to the wire and the other to the throttle switch body.

24 Start the engine and allow it to idle at the specified speed, there should be an open circuit between the switch body and wire. Slowly increase the engine speed whilst observing the ohmmeter reading. Continuity between the switch body and wire should be present when the engine speed reaches the specified throttle position switch setting speed. If not adjust the switch setting using the throttle position switch adjusting screw (Fig. 4.19).

25 Once the throttle switch is correctly adjusted reconnect the switch wire to the carburettor wiring connector.

Twin fixed-venturi (K type) carburettor – 1.6 model

Fast idle speed

26 Warm the engine up to normal operating temperature then stop it.

27 Remove the air filter housing cover (Section 2).

28 While holding the throttle valve slightly

open, pull up the fast idle cam and hold it closed whilst you release the throttle valve. Check that the fast ide cam is set on the first step.

29 Refit the air filter housing cover then start the engine. **Note:** *Do not touch the accelerator pedal or throttle lever because the fast idle cam position will have to be reset.* The engine should now be idling at the specified fast idle speed. If not, adjust it by rotating the fast idle adjusting screw as necessary.

30 Once the fast idle speed is correctly set operate the throttle lever or accelerator pedal a few times then check that the engine returns to its specified idle speed (Chapter 1),

Throttle positioner system

31 Warm the engine up to normal operating temperature then stop it.

32 Remove the air filter housing as described in Section 2 and plug the end of the HAI vacuum hose to prevent the engine from idling roughly during the adjustment procedure.

33 Disconnect the vacuum hose from the throttle positioner diaphragm and plug the end of the hose.

34 Start the engine then increase the engine speed to 3000 rpm, hold it there for a few seconds. then release the accelerator pedal and allow the engine to idle. The engine should now be idling at the specified throttle positioner setting speed. If not, adjust it by rotating the throttle positioner adjusting screw as necessary.

35 Once the throttle positioner speed is correctly set, remove the plug from the vacuum hose and reconnect the hose to the throttle positioner diaphragm, noting the effect this has on the idle speed. If the system is functioning correctly the engine should return to its normal specified idle speed within 2 to 6 seconds of the hose being connected. If this is not the case, or adjustment proves difficult inspect the throttle positioner system diaphragm and vacuum transmitting valve using the information given in paragraphs 6 and 7.

36 Once the system is correctly adjusted refit the air filter housing and check the engine idle speed (Chapter 1).

14 Carburettor –
  on-car inspection

Note: *Refer to the warning note in Section 1 before carrying out the following operations.*

1 This Section describes checks which should be made whenever a carburettor fault is suspected.

Variable-venturi (V type) carburettor

Cold enrichment breaker system check

2 The cold enrichment breaker system uses a vacuum control valve (VCV), which is situated

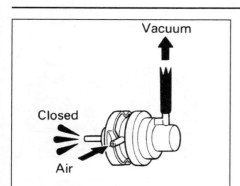
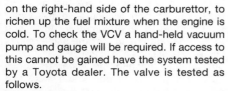

Fig. 4.20 Cold enrichment breaker vacuum control (VCV) operation when cold – early 1.3 models (Sec 14)

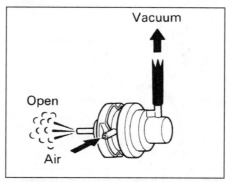

Fig. 4.21 Cold enrichment breaker vacuum control (VCV) operation when hot – early 1.3 models (Sec 14)

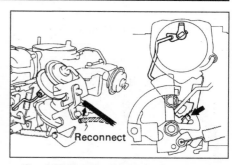

Fig. 4.22 Reconnect the lower vacuum hose to the cam breaker diaphragm and check that the cam breaker link is released onto the third step (arrowed) – later 1.3 models (Sec 14)

on the right-hand side of the carburettor, to richen up the fuel mixture when the engine is cold. To check the VCV a hand-held vacuum pump and gauge will be required. If access to this cannot be gained have the system tested by a Toyota dealer. The valve is tested as follows.

3 Disconnect the three vacuum hoses, making a note of their correct fitted positions, and remove the valve from the carburettor.

4 Referring to Fig. 4.20, ensure that the valve is below 9°C then connect the vacuum pump and apply a vacuum of 200 mm Hg to the valve. Blow down the stub on the side of the valve and check that no air passes through the valve. Warm the valve to above 23°C then repeat the test, noting that air should now flow freely through the valve and come out of the lower stub (Fig. 4.32). If this is not the case, the vacuum control valve must be renewed.

5 On refitting ensure the vacuum hoses are connected to their original positions on the vacuum control valve.

Accelerator pump check

6 Remove the air filter housing (Section 2) and operate the throttle valve whilst looking down the carburettor. Every time the throttle valve is opened, a spurt of fuel should be ejected from the acceleration nozzle. If not, it is likely that the accelerator pump is faulty. Refer to Section 12 for information on carburettor overhaul.

Twin fixed-venturi (K type) carburettor – 1.3 models

7 Before carrying out the following checks remove the air filter housing (Section 2) and plug the HAI diaphragm vacuum hose to prevent the engine idling roughly.

Carburettor electrical component checks

8 Check the operation of the fuel cut-off solenoid and the resistances of the choke coil wire terminal and PTC heater as described in paragraph 32 of Section 12.

Carburettor float level check

9 Start the engine, allow it to idle for a few minutes then switch it off. Check that the fuel level is visible between the marks on the sightglass situated on the side of the carburettor body. If not, it is likely that the carburettor float height is incorrect. Refer to Section 12 for information on float height adjustment.

Cam breaker system check

10 Ensure that the engine is cold (coolant temperature below 9°C), then disconnect the lower vacuum hose from the cam breaker diaphragm.

11 Fully depress the accelerator pedal once and start the engine. **Note:** *The accelerator pedal must not be touched again until the test is complete.*

12 With the engine running, reconnect the vacuum hose to the cam breaker diaphragm whilst observing the diaphragm pushrod. The pushrod should not move at all.

13 Warm the engine up to normal operating temperature then stop it and disconnect both hoses from the cam breaker diaphragm. Whilst holding the throttle valve slightly open, push the choke valve fully closed then hold it closed and release the throttle valve. Check that the choke valve is held in the fully closed position then start the engine, again without touching the accelerator pedal.

14 Whilst observing the movement of the cam breaker link, reconnect the lower vacuum hose to the diaphragm. As the hose is connected the cam breaker link should be released onto the third step (Fig.4.22). Reconnect the upper vacuum hose to the diaphragm and check that the cam breaker link is fully released.

15 If the cam breaker system does not perform as described above it is faulty and the car should be taken to a Toyota dealer who will have the necessary equipment to locate the fault by testing the individual system components.

Choke breaker system check

16 Ensure that the engine is cold (coolant temperature below 9°C) then start the engine. Disconnect the vacuum hose from the choke breaker diaphragm whilst observing the movement of the diaphragm pushrod. The pushrod should not move at all.

17 Reconnect the hose and warm the engine up to normal operating temperature. With the engine running, disconnect the vacuum hose noting that this time the pushrod should extend out of the diaphragm.

18 If the system does not perform as described above it is faulty and the car should be taken to a Toyota dealer who will have the necessary equipment to locate the fault by testing the individual system components.

Accelerator pump check

19 Operate the throttle valve whilst looking down the carburettor. Every time the throttle valve is opened, a spurt of fuel should be ejected from the acceleration nozzle. If not, it is likely that the accelerator pump is faulty. Refer to Section 12 for information on carburettor overhaul.

Twin fixed-venturi (K type) carburettor – 1.6 model

20 Before carrying out the following checks remove the air filter housing (Section 2) and plug the HAI diaphragm vacuum hose to prevent the engine idling roughly. Once all the relevant tests have been completed refit the air filter housing.

Carburettor electrical component checks

21 Check the operation of the fuel cut-off solenoid and the resistance of the choke coil wire terminal as described in paragraph 32 of Section 12.

Carburettor float level check

22 Refer to paragraph 9.

Choke breaker system check

23 The choke breaker system consists of a thermostatic vacuum switching valve which is

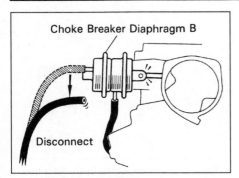

Fig. 4.23 With the engine cold, disconnect the vacuum hose from diaphragm B and check that choke breaker diaphragm pushrod does not move – 1.6 models (Sec 14)

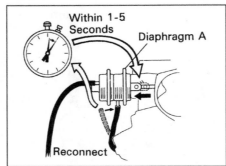

Fig. 4.24 With the engine cold, reconnect the vacuum hose to diaphragm A and check that choke breaker diaphragm pushrod retracts within 1 to 5 seconds – 1.6 models (Sec 14)

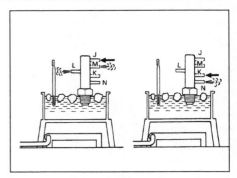

Fig. 4.25 TVSV operation below 7°C – 1.6 models (Sec 14)

screwed into the right-hand end of the inlet manifold, and the choke breaker diaphragm. When the choke valve is closed and the engine is cold (below 7°C), the choke breaker system opens the choke valve slightly, by applying inlet manifold vacuum to diaphragm A, to prevent an over-rich mixture being supplied. As the engine starts to warm up (above 17°C) the system increases the choke valve opening slightly, by applying inlet manifold vacuum to diaphragm B, and so weakens the mixture further. The system is tested as follows.

24 Ensure the engine is cold (coolant temperature below 7°C) then start the engine. Disconnect the vacuum hose from diaphragm B of the choke breaker diaphragm and check that the pushrod does not move (Fig. 4.23). Reconnect the vacuum hose to diaphragm B, then disconnect the hose from diaphragm A and check the pushrod extends slightly. Reconnect the hose to diaphragm A and check that the pushrod is pulled back into the diaphragm within one to five seconds of the hose being connected (Fig. 4.24).

25 Warm the engine up to normal operating temperature then disconnect the hose from diaphragm B and check that the pushrod extends out of the diaphragm. Reconnect the hose and check that the pullrod is pulled fully in. If the system does not perform as described, the thermostatic vacuum switching

valve and choke breaker diaphragm should be tested as follows.

26 To test the choke breaker diaphragm, warm the engine up to normal operating temperature and disconnect both hoses from the diaphragm. Check that there is a vacuum present in vacuum hose B then connect the hose first to diaphragm A and then to diaphragm B whilst checking that the pushrod is pulled into the diaphragm as the hose is connected. If the pushrod does not move when the hose is connected to either or both diaphragms the diaphragm assembly is faulty and must be renewed.

27 To test the thermostatic vacuum switching valve (TVSV), make a note of the correct fitted positions of the vacuum hoses then disconnect them all from the TVSV. Unscrew the TVSV from the inlet manifold and insert a suitable plug into the manifold hole to minimise the loss of coolant (photo). Mop up any spilt coolant before proceeding further.

28 Suspend the TVSV in a pan of cold water and measure the temperature of the water with a thermometer. Do not let either the switch or the thermometer touch the pan itself. Cool the water to below 7°C, by adding ice if necessary, then blow down valve port J and check that air flows freely out of ports L and M, and down port K and check that air flows freely out of port N (Fig. 4.25).

29 Gently heat the water to approximately

20°C then blow down port K and check that air is expelled through ports L and N, and blow down port J and check that air flows freely out of port M. Increase the water temperature to approximately 45°C and repeat the test noting that the same results should be obtained (Fig. 4.26).

30 Continue heating the water to above 68°C, then blow down port K and check that air is expelled through ports L and M, then blow down port J and check that no air flows through the valve (Fig. 4.27).

31 If the TVSV does not perform as described above, the valve is faulty and must be renewed. On refitting apply a suitable sealant to the threads of the TVSV and tighten it securely. Use the notes made on removal to ensure that the vacuum hoses are reconnected to their original positions.

Auxiliary acceleration pump system check

32 The auxiliary acceleration pump (AAP) is fitted to assist the main acceleration pump in situations where the capacity of the main pump is insufficient, ie. hard acceleration with a cold engine. The system consists of the vacuum controlled AAP diaphragm and the thermostatic vacuum switching valve.

33 To test the system, ensure that the engine is cool (coolant temperature below 50°C), then start the engine. Pinch the AAP vacuum hose then release the hose whilst looking down the carburettor venturi. As the hose is released a

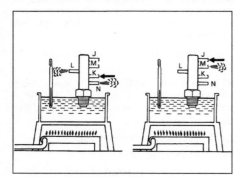

Fig. 4.26 TVSV operation between 17 and 50°C – 1.6 models (Sec 14)

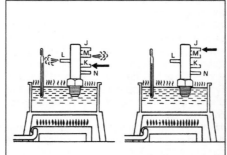

Fig. 4.27 TVSV operation above 68°C – 1.6 models (Sec 14)

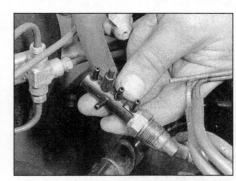

14.27 Removing the thermostatic vacuum switching valve

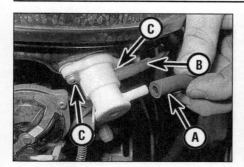

15.3 HIC valve inlet manifold vacuum hose (A), HAI diaphragm hose (B) and valve retaining screws (C)

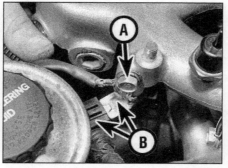

16.4 Earth connection (A) and wiring loom support clip (B)

16.8 Refit the inlet manifold using a new gasket

spurt of fuel should be ejected from the acceleration nozzle. Warm the engine up to normal operating temperature and repeat the check noting that no spurt of fuel should be ejected from the acceleration nozzle. If the AAP does not perform as expected test the pump diaphragm as follows.

34 Start the engine and disconnect the vacuum hose from the AAP. With the engine idling, disconnect and reconnect the hose to the AAP, noting that the idle speed should change as the hose is disconnected and connected. If this is not the case the pump diaphragm is faulty and must be renewed.

35 If the diaphragm is okay it is likely that the TVSV is at fault. The TVSV is tested as described in paragraphs 27 to 31.

15 Hot idle compensation system – general information and testing

General information

1 The hot idle compensation (HIC) system is fitted to ensure that the fuel mixture remains correct when the engine is idling at high temperatures. It does this by means of the hot idle compensation valve, sometimes known as the intake air temperature compensating valve, which is fitted to the underside of the air filter housing. The valve is connected to the inlet manifold and the hot air intake (HAI) diaphragm and has a vent to atmosphere. At low temperatures (below 26°C) the HIC valve supplies the inlet manifold vacuum to the HAI diaphragm, as the temperature rises the valves wax capsule deforms and the valve gradually opens its vent port until, at between 34°C and 47°C, no vacuum is being supplied to the HAI diaphragm and the valve is shut (see Section 3 for further information). At around 54°C the HIC valve starts to allow air from the vent port through the valve and into the inlet manifold and so slightly weakens the idle mixture. The valve continues to open gradually until it reaches 84°C at which point it is fully open.

2 If at any time the HIC valve is thought not to be functioning correctly, it should be tested as described below.

Testing

3 Disconnect the vacuum hoses from the HIC valve, noting their correct fitted positions, then undo the retaining screws and withdraw the valve from the underside of the air filter housing (photo).

4 With the valve removed, place a finger over the vent port then blow down the valve stub which is connected to the HAI diaphragm and check that air flows freely out of the valve inlet manifold stub. Then remove your finger from the vent port and blow down the valve stub which is connected to the inlet manifold and check that no air flows through the valve.

5 Ensure the valve is below 26°C, place a finger over the inlet manifold valve stub then blow down the HAI diaphragm stub and check that no air flows out of the valve vent port. Gently warm the valve to above 34°C then repeat the test noting that the air should now flow out of the vent port.

6 If the HIC valve does not perform as described it must be renewed.

7 On refitting ensure that the vacuum hoses are correctly connected and tighten the valve retaining screws securely.

16 Inlet manifold – removal and refitting

Note: Refer to the warning note in Section 1 before carrying out the following operation.

Removal

1 Remove the carburettor, as described in Section 11.

2 Drain the cooling system as described in Chapter 1 then disconnect the inlet manifold coolant hose(s). Mop up any spilt coolant immediately.

3 Make a note of the fitted positions of the relevant inlet manifold vacuum hose connections then disconnect them from the manifold.

4 Where applicable, disconnect the earth lead(s) from the inlet manifold and release the wiring loom retaining clip(s) (photo).

5 Release the accelerator cable bracket from the inlet manifold.

6 Undo the inlet manifold stay retaining bolts, and remove the stay.

7 Undo the nuts and bolts securing the inlet manifold to the cylinder head, then withdraw the manifold off its studs and remove it along with the gasket.

Refitting

8 Refitting is a reversal of the removal procedure noting the following points (photo).

(a) Remove all traces of old gasket and fit a new gasket over the studs.

(b) Tighten all retaining bolts to the specified torque setting.

(c) Ensure all hoses are reconnected to their original positions and held securely by retaining clips.

(d) Refit the carburettor (Section 11).

(e) Refill the cooling system as described in Chapter 1.

17 Exhaust manifold – removal and refitting

Removal

1 Disconnect the battery earth terminal.

2 On 1.6 carburettor models, disconnect and remove the warm air intake tube from the exhaust manifold heatshield.

3 On 1.3 models, remove the air filter housing/trunking (including the warm air intake tube).

4 Undo the securing bolts and remove the heatshield located above the manifold (photo).

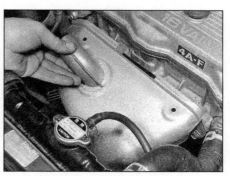

17.4 Removing the upper exhaust manifold heatshield

17.7 Separating the exhaust downpipe from the manifold

17.8 The exhaust manifold stay and heatshield

17.9A Ensure that the 'E' marking on the exhaust manifold gaskets face the front of the vehicle

5 Raise the front of the vehicle and support it securely using axle stands; remove the undershield(s), where applicable.

6 Where fitted, remove the lower heatshield (beneath the manifold) and the exhaust manifold stay; if the clearance is too tight it may be easier to remove these once the manifold has been removed from the vehicle.

7 Undo the manifold to exhaust downpipe section securing nuts, then disconnect the downpipe section from the manifold. Remove the gaskets (photo).

8 Undo the nuts and bolts securing the exhaust manifold to the cylinder head, then draw the manifold off its securing studs and remove the gasket(s). On 1.3 models, a further insulating block is fitted between the manifold and the cylinder head; this can be drawn off in the same manner as the manifold. Remove the stay and lower heatshield, if required (photo).

Refitting

9 Refitting is a reversal of the removal procedure; ensure that the mating faces are clean and use new gaskets. Where applicable, the 'E' marking on the gaskets must face towards the front of the vehicle. Tighten the manifold nuts and bolts evenly and progressively to the specified torque (photos).

18 Exhaust system – general information and component renewal

1 The exhaust system is of a conventional design, and uses gaskets at all flange joints: the system is suspended throughout its entire length by rubber mountings.

2 To remove the exhaust system (or a section of it) it will first be necessary to raise and support the vehicle securely using axle stands or, alternatively, over an inspection pit for unhindered access; remove the undershield(s) as necessary. Refer to Fig. 4.28 for information regarding the separation of system components and the types of mounting fitted.

3 Note that new gaskets must be fitted if the exhaust section joint flanges are separated, to maintain a gas-tight seal (photo).

4 The rubber exhaust mountings should be examined for signs of splits or perishing, and renewed if necessary. Note that if a mounting is broken, or missing, this puts unnecessary strain on the remaining mountings and may ultimately result in damage to the exhaust system itself.

5 Where applicable, a heatshield is fitted to the exhaust downpipe section where it passes beneath the sump, to avoid the exhaust heat affecting the temperature and therefore the viscosity of the engine oil. If this is removed for whatever reason, ensure that it is refitted afterwards.

17.9B Fit new gaskets to the exhaust front pipe

18.3 Always fit new gaskets before reconnecting exhaust section joints

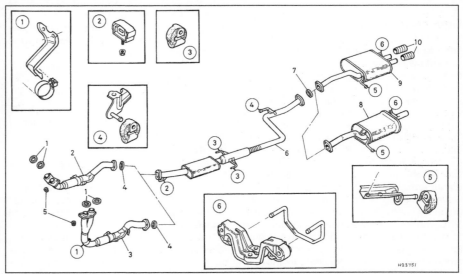

Fig. 4.28 An exploded view of the exhaust system components, and mountings. Circled numbers shown locations of mountings in boxes (Sec 18)

1 Gaskets – manifold to downpipe
2 Downpipe section – 1.6 models
3 Downpipe section – 1.3 models
4 Gasket – downpipe to centre section
5 Nut – downpipe to manifold
6 Centre section
7 Gasket – centre section to tailpipe
8 Tailpipe – 1.3 and 1.6 GL Executive models
9 Tailpipe – GTi 16 models
10 Tailpipe trims – GTi 16 models

Part B: Fuel-injected engine

19 General information and precautions

The fuel system consists of a fuel tank mounted under the rear of the car, an electric fuel pump and the various fuel injection components.

Fuel is supplied from the tank by an electric fuel pump, located inside the tank, via a pressure regulator, to the fuel rail. The fuel rail acts as a reservoir for the four fuel injectors, which inject fuel into the cylinder inlet tracts.

A fuel filter is incorporated in the fuel supply line to ensure that the fuel supplied to the injectors is clean.

The fuel system is controlled by a function of the overall Toyota Computer Control System (TCCS) which is known as Electronic Fuel Injection (EFI), and is integral with the engine management function; further information regarding the TCCS ignition function may be found in Chapter 5, while further information regarding its EFI function is given in Section 24.

Warning: Many of the procedures in this Chapter require the removal of fuel lines and connections which may result in some fuel spillage. Before carrying out any operation on the fuel system refer to the precautions given in Safety first! at the beginning of this Manual and follow them implicitly. Petrol is a highly dangerous and volatile liquid and the precautions necessary when handling it cannot be overstressed.

Note: *Residual pressure will remain in the fuel lines long after the vehicle was last used, before disconnecting any fuel line depressurise the fuel system as described in Section 25.*

20 Air filter housing/trunking – removal and refitting

Removal

1 Disconnect the battery earth terminal.
2 Disconnect the wiring connectors from the idle up vacuum switching valve (VSV) and the intake air temperature sensor.
3 Disconnect the vacuum hose from the idle up VSV and the throttle housing.
4 Release the relevant trunking securing clips (photo).
5 Release the air filter housing lid securing clips, then remove the lid; the trunking between the air filter housing lid and the throttle housing can be withdrawn, as required.
6 Withdraw the air filter to expose the three air filter housing body securing bolts; undo the bolts and withdraw the air filter housing body, disconnecting any hoses or wiring support clips as necessary (photos). The remaining trunking can be removed, as necessary.

Refitting

7 Refitting is a reversal of the removal procedure.

21 Accelerator cable – removal, refitting and adjustment

Refer to Part A, Section 7 of this Chapter, but note that there is no need to remove the air filter housing. Note also that all references to the carburettor should be substituted by references to the throttle housing.

22 Accelerator pedal – removal and refitting

Refer to Part A, Section 8

23 Unleaded petrol – general information and usage

Refer to Part A: Section 9

24 Fuel injection system – general information

The Electronic Control Unit (ECU), which controls both the Electronic Spark Advance (ESA) and Electronic Fuel Injection (EFI) functions of the Toyota Computer Control System (TCCS), is located inside the vehicle, behind the facia, along with its circuit opening relay. In the case of its EFI function, it is pre-programmed with data for optimum fuelling under all possible operating conditions; the system works as follows.

The ECU is fed with data from a variety of sensors which monitor the engine operating conditions, then compares the data received with its own pre-programmed values to determine the appropriate electrical signals to send out to the injectors; the injectors are supplied with fuel at a constant pressure (by means of an electric fuel pump and a pressure regulator), and it is the period of time that the injectors remain open or 'on' (in response to the electrical signals from the ECU) that determines the volume of fuel injected for an optimum fuel/air mixture.

The prime information used to compute the injection duration signal (at any given time) is the engine speed, inlet manifold absolute pressure (vacuum), intake air temperature, coolant temperature, and whether the engine is accelerating or decelerating. The engine speed information is gathered from the pick up coil (signal generator) circuitry in the distributor (Chapter 5), the inlet manifold vacuum is sensed by the Manifold Absolute Pressure (MAP) sensor, and the acceleration/deceleration state is determined

20.4 Release the air filter trunking clip and disconnect the VSV hose (arrowed)

20.6A Release the air filter housing lid clips (two arrowed) to remove the lid, withdraw the air filter element. . .

20.6B . . .to expose the housing body securing bolts (arrowed)

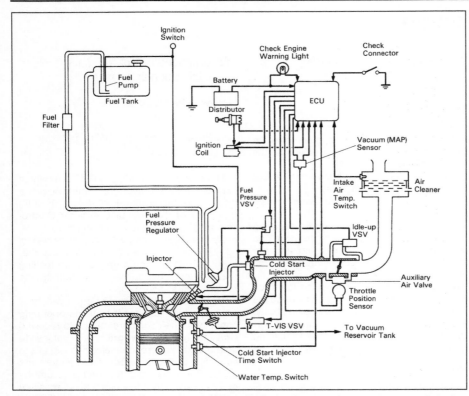

Fig. 4.29 A schematic view of the electronic fuel injection system on pre-August 1989 models (Sec 24)

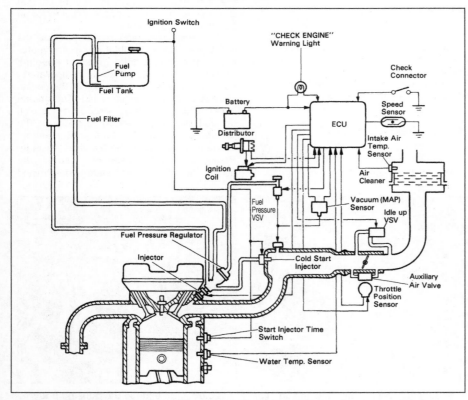

Fig. 4.30 A schematic view of the electronic fuel injection system on models from August 1989 on (Sec 24)

by the throttle position sensor. There is no airflow meter in the system.

The ECU also controls other system actuators according to the particular engine operating conditions and requirements. A cold start enrichment function is incorporated into the ECU circuitry, to enrich the fuel/air mixture entering the cylinders during the initial start up. This is done via a separate cold start injector which is mounted in the plenum chamber. The operation of the injector being controlled by the cold start injector time switch.

Certain features of the EFI system have been changed during its production lifetime; early models (pre-August 1989) are equipped with a variable induction system (T-VIS) (Section 33). Another feature on early models is an injector solenoid resistor mounted on the engine compartment bulkhead. On later models (August 1989 on) the provision of road speed information input to the ECU, from the speedometer gauge, has been incorporated; in addition, a modified air filter housing/trunking assembly is also fitted.

A 'fail-safe' function is incorporated so that if one of the sensors fails, a back up circuit will take over to allow the vehicle to be driven albeit at reduced power and efficiency; the instrument panel 'Engine System/Check Engine' warning lamp will light to indicate that this condition is present, and a fault code will be stored in the ECU relating to the circuit affected. These fault codes are accessed by your Toyota dealer, or other suitable specialist, as an aid to fault diagnosis.

Due to the sophisticated nature of the EFI system, the following precautions must be observed to prevent damage to the components and reduce risk of personal injury.

(a) *Before working on the fuel system or associated wiring, disconnect the battery earth (negative) terminal. Note that when the battery is disconnected, all diagnostic fault codes stored in the ECU will be erased (Section 31).*

(b) *Do not disconnect the battery earth terminal whilst the engine is running, or reverse the terminal connections.*

(c) *Ensure that the ignition is switched off before connecting or disconnecting any electrical test equipment. If connecting a tachometer to the system, for the purpose of checking and adjustment, refer to Section 5 in Part B of Chapter 5 for further details.*

(d) *Do not leave the ignition switched on for more than 10 minutes with the engine not running.*

(e) *Do not attempt to improvise test procedures, expensive component damage may be caused.*

(f) *Do not drop the ECU or allow it to receive any impact; this also applies to all the other associated system components.*

(g) *Do not open the ECU cover.*

(h) *Prevent water getting into system wiring connectors and components when inspecting inside the engine compartment in wet weather, or when washing the engine bay.*

(i) Ensure that the system wiring connectors are released and reconnected correctly; the connectors have locking mechanisms moulded in.

(j) Always check the fuel system to ensure that there are no leaks present after work has been completed.

25 Fuel system – depressurisation

Note: *Refer to the warning note in Section 19 before carrying out the following operation.*
Warning: The following procedure will merely relieve the pressure in the fuel system – remember that fuel will still be present in the system components and take precautions accordingly before disconnecting any of them.

1 The fuel system will contain fuel which will be under pressure while the engine is running and/or while the ignition is switched on. The pressure will remain for some time after the ignition has been switched off and must be relieved before any component is disturbed.

2 Disconnect the battery earth terminal.

3 Place a suitable container beneath the relevant connection/union to be disconnected, and have a large rag ready to soak up any escaping fuel not being caught by the container.

4 Slowly loosen the connection/union to avoid a sudden release of pressure and position the rag around the connection to catch any fuel spray which may be expelled. Once the pressure is released, disconnect the fuel line and insert plugs to minimise fuel loss and prevent the entry of dirt into the fuel system.

5 When reconnecting union nuts, note that new sealing washers (where fitted) must be used and, where possible, the unions should be tightened to their specified torque setting. When reconnecting flexible hoses ensure they are securely held in position by their retaining clips. Always check the fuel system to ensure that there no leaks present after work has been completed (Section 26).

26 Fuel system – pressure and leak testing

Note: *Refer to the warning note in Section 19 before carrying out the following operations.*

Pressure checking

1 The following procedure is based on the use of the Toyota pressure gauge (Service Tool Number 092668 - 45012).

2 To check the fuel pump output first turn the ignition on (but do not start the engine), then using a suitable jumper wire, connect the terminals in the check connector (located by the left-hand front suspension turret) as shown in Fig. 4.46. As the terminals are connected there should be pressure in the fuel filter feed hose and the noise of fuel returning from the pressure regulator should be heard. If there is no fuel pressure evident up to the fuel pressure regulator, check the relevant fuses, relays and wiring; if these prove to be satisfactory, the fuel pump or ECU may be defective.

3 With the above check completed, remove the wire from the check connector and turn the ignition off. Disconnect the battery earth terminal, then disconnect the wiring connector from the cold start injector. Making reference to Section 25, slacken and remove the cold start injector supply pipe union bolts and remove the pipe. Fit the fuel pressure gauge to the fuel rail, positioning a sealing washer on either side of its adaptor, and secure it in position with the supply pipe union bolt. Tighten the union bolt to its specified torque. Mop up any spilt fuel, then reconnect the battery earth terminal and carry out the following tests.

4 Reconnect the terminals in the check connector as before, then turn the ignition switch on (but do not start the engine) and observe the fuel pressure gauge reading. If the observed fuel pressure is high in relation to its specified pressure, renew the fuel pressure regulator (Section 32); if it is low, there is likely to be a problem with the fuel hoses and/or unions, the fuel pump, fuel filter and/or the fuel pressure regulator system.

5 Remove the jumper wire from the check connector, then start the engine; disconnect the fuel pressure regulator vacuum hose and plug the hose end. Observe the fuel pressure at engine idle speed, and check it against that specified. Remove the plug from the hose end, then reconnect the hose to the fuel pressure regulator and again observe the fuel pressure at idle speed; if it is not within its specified range, it is likely that the fuel pressure regulator is defective or its vacuum hose is incorrectly connected or split.

6 Stop the engine and check that the fuel pressure gauge retains a pressure of 1.47 bar or more for a period of five minutes after the engine has been switched off; if this is not the case, the fuel pump, pressure regulator and/or injector(s) may be defective, or a leak may be present in the high pressure supply line.

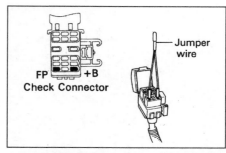

Fig. 4.31 Check connector terminals utilised during fuel pressure checking and leak testing procedures (Sec 26)

7 With the checks completed. disconnect the battery earth terminal. Disconnect the fuel pressure gauge from the fuel rail and discard the gaskets. Refit the cold start injector supply pipe, positioning a new sealing washer on each side of its unions, and tighten the union bolts to the specified torque. Reconnect the cold start injector wiring connector and the battery earth terminal then test the fuel system for leaks as follows.

Leak testing

8 Turn the ignition switch on, but do not start the engine, then connect the terminals in the check connector (located by the left-hand front suspension turret) as shown in Fig. 4.31 using a suitable service wire.

9 Pinch the fuel return hose to raise the fuel pressure in the system above normal, then check for any fuel leaks in the system. Do not bend the hose, or this may cause it to crack.

10 Upon completion, remove the service wire and switch the ignition off. Refit the check connector cover.

27 Fuel pump – removal and refitting

Note: *Refer to the warning note in Section 19 before carrying out the following operation*

Removal

1 Disconnect the battery earth terminal.
2 Remove the fuel tank (Section 29).

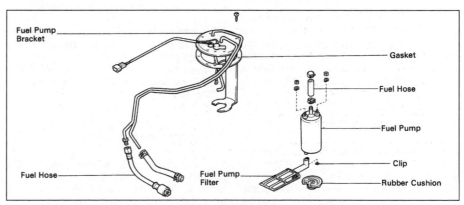

Fig. 4.32 An exploded view of the fuel pump (Sec 27)

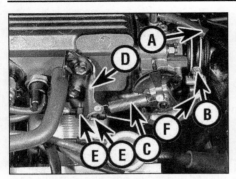

30.3 A general side view of the throttle housing

A VSV hose
B Air filter trunking retaining clip
C Throttle valve return spring
D Accelerator cable abutment bracket
E Accelerator cable bracket nuts
F Accelerator inner cable end

3 Remove the pump bracket retaining screws, then withdraw the bracket assembly with the pump. Remove the pump seal.
4 Label and note the fitment then disconnect the wires from the fuel pump.
5 Release the fuel pump from its bracket, disconnecting the hose as it is withdrawn.
6 If required, the fuel pick up filter on the base of the pump assembly can be removed after releasing the rubber cushion and removing the securing clip. Inspect the filter for signs of clogging or splitting and renew it if necessary.

Refitting

7 Refitting is a reversal of the removal procedure, noting the following points.
(a) Renew the pump seal if there is any doubt as to its condition.
(b) Clean the fuel pick up filter with a suitable solvent and secure it in position with a new retaining clip.
(c) Tighten all the retaining nuts to their specified torque settings.

28 Fuel gauge sender unit – removal and refitting

Refer to Part A, Section 5, noting that from the information available, it is not known whether access to the sender unit can be gained once the seat has been removed. If not it will be necessary to remove the fuel tank to gain access to the fuel gauge sender unit.

29 Fuel tank – removal and refitting

Refer to Part A: Section 6, noting that the fuel system must be depressurised as described in Section 25 when the first fuel hose is disconnected and the fuel pump wiring connector must be disconnected as the tank is lowered out of position.

30.6 Throttle housing retaining nuts (A), and bolts (B)

30 Throttle housing – removal and refitting

Note: Refer to the warning note in Section 19 before carrying out the following operation.

Removal

1 Disconnect the battery negative terminal then drain the cooling system as described in Chapter 1.
2 Disconnect the air filter trunking and the VSV hose from the throttle housing.
3 Disconnect the throttle valve return spring from the accelerator cable abutment bracket and the lever, and release the accelerator cable from its quadrant (photo).
4 Disconnect the throttle position sensor wiring connector.
5 Make a note of the correct fitted positions of all the relevant vacuum and coolant hoses then disconnect them from the throttle housing.
6 Undo the retaining nuts and bolts, then remove the throttle housing along with its gasket (photo). Do not disturb the throttle position sensor unless absolutely necessary.

Refitting

7 Refitting is a reverse of the removal sequence, noting the following points.
(a) Clean the mating surfaces and fit a new gasket to the throttle housing.
(b) Tighten the retaining nuts and bolts to their specified torque settings.
(c) Adjust the accelerator cable (Section 21).
(d) Adjust the throttle position sensor (Section 32) if disturbed.
(e) Refill the cooling system and check the idle speed and mixture settings (Chapter 1).

31 Fuel injection system components – testing

1 Do not immediately assume that a fault is caused by a defective ECU, sensor or actuator. First check that all relevant wiring is in good condition and that the wiring connectors are securely connected. Similarly

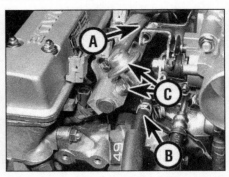

32.4 Disconnect vacuum hose (A) and fuel return hose (B) before removing bolts (C)

check all vacuum hose connections for leakage/blockage.
2 Due to the complexity of the system, it is generally beyond the scope of the home mechanic to accurately pinpoint a component problem without the specialised knowledge or equipment necessary to understand the results of the checks and tests which follow an ECU fault code 'reading'; your Toyota dealer should be entrusted with the diagnosis, giving you the choice of having the dealership carry out any work or using the information to carry out any component renewal work yourself.
3 If you carry out component renewal work yourself, note that the fault code stored in the ECU memory will be cancelled by the action of disconnecting the battery; if the vehicle is not operating correctly after repair, return to your Toyota dealer who can again 'read' the fault code (which will have been regenerated if the problem has not been completely cured) and take any necessary action.

32 Fuel injection system components – removal and refitting

Note: Refer to the warning note in Section 19 before carrying out the following operations.
1 Disconnect the battery earth terminal before carrying out any of the following operations.

Fuel filter

2 Refer to Chapter 1.

Fuel pressure regulator

Removal

3 Depressurise the fuel system by unscrewing the union bolt which secures the cold start injector supply pipe on the fuel rail (Section 25). Position a new sealing washer on each side of the pipe union, then refit the union bolt and tighten it to the specified torque.
4 Disconnect the vacuum hose from the top of the fuel pressure regulator (photo).
5 Disconnect the fuel return hose from the

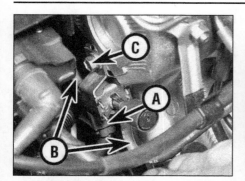

32.9 Disconnect wiring connector (A) and vacuum hoses (B) before removing bolt (C)

base of the fuel pressure regulator, and plug the hose.

6 Undo the two retaining bolts, then withdraw the fuel pressure regulator. Remove the O-ring from around the connecting flange.

Refitting

7 Refitting is a reversal of the removal procedure, using a new O-ring and tightening the regulator retaining bolts to the specified torque. On completion check the fuel system for leaks as described in Section 26.

Fuel pressure regulator vacuum switching valve

Removal

8 Make a note of the correct fitted positions of the vacuum hoses then disconnect them from the valve. Disconnect the valve wiring connector.

9 Slacken and remove the bolt securing the valve bracket to the right-hand side of the inlet manifold body and remove the valve (photo).

Refitting

10 Refitting is a reversal of the removal procedure.

Fuel rail and injectors

Removal

11 Disconnect the crankcase ventilation hose (between the rearmost camshaft cover and the inlet manifold) and remove it.

12 Depressurise the fuel system by unscrewing the union bolt which secures the cold start injector supply pipe to the fuel rail (Section 25). Remove the union bolt along with its sealing washers.

13 Undo the union bolt which secures the supply pipe to the cold start injector and remove the pipe and sealing washers.

14 Slacken and remove the union bolt and washers which secures the main fuel supply hose to the fuel rail (photo).

15 Disconnect the fuel return and vacuum hoses from the fuel pressure regulator: plug the hose end to minimise the loss of fuel.

16 Note their correct fitted positions then disconnect the wiring connectors from the injectors.

17 Undo the three retaining bolts then

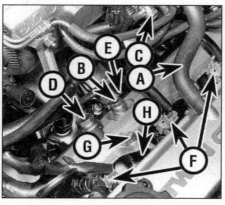

32.14 A general view of some of the connections and components affected by the fuel rail and injectors removal and refitting procedure

A Crankcase ventilation hose
B Cold start injector supply pipe fuel rail union
C Cold start injector supply pipe injector union
D Main fuel supply hose union
E Fuel pressure regulator vacuum supply hose
F Injector wiring connectors
G Fuel rail retaining bolt
H Fuel rail spacer

carefully withdraw the fuel rail and the four injectors as an assembly, taking great care not to drop any of the injectors. Remove the four insulators and three spacers from the cylinder head, noting their original fitted positions.

18 Pull the injectors out of the fuel rail, then remove the O-rings and grommets.

Refitting

19 Carefully fit a new grommet to each injector then apply a light coat of petrol to the new O-rings and install them on the injectors.

20 Carefully refit the injectors to the fuel rail, using a light twisting motion. Once each injector is fully home, check that it is free to rotate smoothly in the fuel rail. If not, it is likely that the O-ring has been damaged. If this is the case the injector must be removed and a new O-ring fitted.

21 Refit the four insulators and three spacers to their original positions on the cylinder head (Fig. 4.33), then manoeuvre the fuel rail and

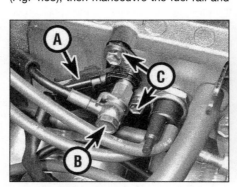

32.23 Disconnect wiring connector (A), pipe union (B) before removing bolts (C)

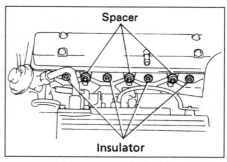

Fig. 4.33 Ensure spacers and insulators are positioned as shown before installing fuel rail assembly (Sec 32)

injector assembly into position. Ensure that all the injector wiring connectors face upwards then refit the fuel rail retaining bolts and tighten them to the specified torque.

22 The remainder of the refitting procedure is a reversal of the removal procedure, noting the following points.

(a) Fit new sealing washers on each side of all fuel pipe unions and tighten the union bolts to the specified torque.

(b) Check the fuel system for leaks (Section 26).

Cold start injector
Removal

23 Disconnect the wiring connector from the cold start injector (photo).

24 Depressurise the fuel system by unscrewing the union bolt which secures the cold start injector supply pipe to the fuel rail (Section 25). Remove the union bolt and sealing washers.

25 Undo the union bolt which secures the supply pipe to the cold start injector and remove the pipe along with the sealing washers.

26 Undo the two retaining bolts, then withdraw the cold start injector along with its gasket.

Refitting

27 Refitting is a reversal of the removal procedure noting the following.

(a) Fit a new gasket to the cold start injector and tighten the retaining bolts to the specified torque.

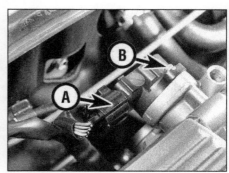

32.28 Throttle position sensor wiring connector (A), and one of two retaining screws (B)

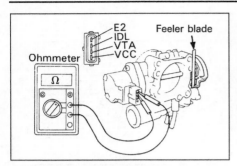

Fig. 4.34 Checking the positional adjustment of the throttle position sensor with feeler blade inserted between throttle stop and lever (arrowed) (Sec 32)

(b) *Fit new sealing washers on each side of all fuel pipe unions and tighten the union bolts to the specified torque.*
(c) *Check the fuel system for leaks (Section 26).*

Throttle position sensor

Removal

28 Disconnect the throttle position sensor wiring connector (photo).
29 Using a dab of white paint or a suitable marker pen, make alignment marks between the throttle position sensor body and the throttle housing.
30 Undo the two retaining screws then remove the throttle position sensor along with its gasket (where fitted).

Refitting

31 Fit a new gasket (where necessary) to the throttle position sensor and refit the sensor to the throttle housing. Align the marks made on removal and tighten the retaining screws securely. Before reconnecting the wiring connector check the sensor adjustment as follows.
32 Using an ohmmeter, measure between the terminals given in the following table and check that the resistance is within the specified range for each particular clearance. The small throttle lever to stop screw clearances are set by inserting a feeler blade of the required thickness (0.35 mm or 0.59 mm) between the stop and lever as shown in Fig. 4.34.

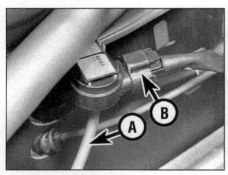

32.43 Disconnect sensor vacuum hose (A), and wiring connector (B)

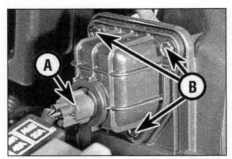

32.39 Disconnect wiring connector (A) and housing assembly retaining bolts (B)

Terminals	Clearance between lever and stop screw (mm)	Resistance (Ω)
VTA to E2	0	200 to 800
IDL to E2	0.35	2300 or less
IDL to E2	0.59	Open circuit
VTA to E2	Throttle valve fully open	3300 to 10 000
VCC to E2	–	3000 to 7000

33 If the resistances are not as specified, connect the ohmmeter between the terminals IDL and E2 then adjust the position of the throttle position sensor as follows. Slacken the retaining screws then, insert a 0.47 mm feeler gauge between the stop screw and the throttle lever. Turn the sensor body fully anti-clockwise then turn it slowly clockwise until continuity is just present between the terminals. Hold the switch in this position then tighten the retaining screws securely and recheck the switch terminal resistances. If the resistances are still outside those given in the above table, renewal of the throttle position sensor will be required.
34 Once the throttle position sensor is correctly adjusted, reconnect the throttle position sensor wiring connector and check the idle speed and mixture settings as described in Chapter 1.

Auxiliary air valve

Removal

35 Remove the throttle housing as described in Section 30.
36 Undo the five screws securing the valve to the base of the throttle housing then remove the valve, noting the correct fitted position of its gasket and O-ring.

32.45 Withdraw the sensor from the air filter housing lid

Refitting

37 Ensure the mating surfaces are clean then fit a new gasket to the valve and install a new O-ring on the valve stub.
38 Refit the auxiliary air valve to the throttle housing and tighten its retaining screws securely then refit the throttle housing as described in Section 30.

Idle up vacuum switching valve

Removal

39 The idle up vacuum switching valve is located on the air filter housing lid. Disconnect the wiring connector, remove the retaining bolts, then separate the housing assembly; note the order and fitment of components (photo).

Refitting

40 Refitting is a reversal of the removal procedure, using a new housing gasket (where fitted).

Fuel pressure vacuum switching valve

Removal

41 The fuel pressure vacuum switching valve is mounted on the right-hand end of the inlet manifold assembly. Note the correct fitted positions of the vacuum hoses, then disconnect the hoses and wiring connector. Undo the retaining bolt and remove the valve.

Refitting

42 Refitting is a reverse of the removal procedure ensuring the vacuum hoses are correctly connected.

Manifold absolute pressure (MAP) sensor

Removal

43 The MAP sensor is mounted on the engine compartment bulkhead. Disconnect the vacuum hose and wiring plug and remove the mounting bracket retaining bolt (photo).

Refitting

44 Refitting is a reversal of the removal procedure.

Intake air temperature sensor

Removal

45 Disconnect the wiring connector and withdraw the sensor from the air filter housing grommet (photo).

Refitting

46 Refitting is a reverse of the removal procedure.

ECU water temperature sensor

47 Refer to Chapter 3.

Cold start injector time switch

48 Refer to Chapter 3.

Injector solenoid resistor (pre-August 1989 models)

Removal

49 The injector solenoid resistor is mounted on the engine compartment bulkhead. Disconnect the wiring connector and undo the retaining screws.

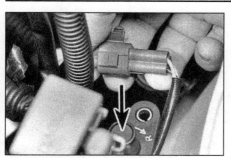

32.51 Disconnect the wiring connector. Note the plug (arrowed) fitted over the resistor adjusting screw location

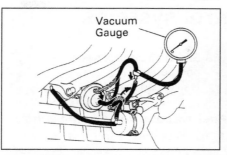

Fig. 4.35 Connect a vacuum gauge into the system between the vacuum switching valve and actuating diaphragm – pre-August 1989 models (Sec 33)

36.1 The exhaust tailpipe trims are retained by bolts

Refitting

50 Refitting is a reversal of the removal procedure.

Fuel mixture control variable resistor

Removal

51 Disconnect the wiring connector then undo the bolt securing the resistor to the left-hand front suspension turret and remove the resistor from the car (photo).

Refitting

52 Refitting is a reverse of the removal procedure.

Electronic control unit (ECU) and circuit opening relay

Removal

53 Remove the facia as described in Chapter 11.
54 Disconnect the wiring connectors then undo the mounting bracket retaining nuts and remove the ECU.
55 To remove the circuit opening relay, disconnect the wiring connector and free it from the mounting bracket.

Refitting

56 Refitting is a reversal of the removal procedure ensuring that the wiring connectors are securely connected.

33 Toyota variable induction system – general information and component removal and refitting

General information

1 The Toyota variable induction system (T-VIS) regulates the airflow through one of two inlet manifold tracts per cylinder. The system consists of a vacuum reservoir (connected to the inlet manifold), a vacuum switching valve (VSV) and the T-VIS valve assembly. The T-VIS valve assembly consists of a plate containing four disc valves and an actuating diaphragm and is situated between the cylinder head and the inlet manifold.
2 At low engine speeds the VSV is open and the inlet manifold depression, which is present in the vacuum reservoir, is supplied to

the actuating diaphragm which then causes the T-VIS disc valves to open. At high engine speeds the VSV receives a signal from the ECU which causes the valve to close. The VSV then isolates the inlet manifold depression from the actuating diaphragm and so the T-VIS valves close.
3 To test the system, using a T-piece and suitable lengths of tubing, connect a vacuum gauge into the hose between the VSV and the actuating diaphragm (Fig. 4.35). Warm the engine up to normal operating temperature, then allow the engine to idle whilst noting the gauge reading. If all is well there should be full inlet manifold depression present in the hose. Increase the engine speed to approximately 5000 rpm whilst observing the gauge reading, noting that atmospheric pressure should now be present in the hose. If the T-VIS system does not perform as described it is likely that the VSV is faulty or the vacuum reservoir or one of the hoses is split.

T-VIS valve assembly

4 Remove the valve assembly as described in Section 34.
5 To test the valve operation, apply a vacuum to the actuating diaphragm and check that the disc valves move freely, then release the vacuum and check that they return smoothly. If not the assembly is faulty and must be renewed.
6 Refitting is described in Section 34.

Vacuum switching valve and reservoir assembly

7 Make a note of the correct fitted positions of the vacuum hoses, then disconnect them from the vacuum reservoir and VSV. Disconnect the VSV wiring connector then undo the two mounting bracket retaining bolts and remove the assembly from the engine.
8 Refitting is a reversal of the removal sequence ensuring the vacuum hoses are correctly connected.

34 Inlet manifold – removal and refitting

Note: *Refer to the warning note in Section 19 before carrying out the following operation.*

Removal

1 Remove the throttle housing as described in Section 30.
2 Remove the vacuum switching valve and reservoir as described in Section 33.
3 Make a note of the correct fitted positions of all relevant hoses and disconnect them from the manifold.
4 Remove the two manifold support stay retaining bolts and remove the stay.
5 Slacken the manifold retaining nuts and bolts evenly and progressively then withdraw the manifold assembly and remove the gasket.
6 On pre-August 1989 models the T-VIS disc valve assembly can then be withdrawn along with its gasket.

Refitting

7 Remove all traces of old gasket from the mating surfaces.
8 On pre-August 1989 models fit a new gasket over the studs and refit the T-VIS valve assembly.
9 Fit a new inlet manifold gasket and install the inlet manifold. Refit the manifold retaining nuts and bolts and tighten them evenly and progressively to the specified torque setting.
10 Using the notes made on removal, reconnect the vacuum hoses and coolant hoses to their original positions on the inlet manifold. Ensure that all hoses are securely fastened by their retaining clips.
11 Refit the T-VIS vacuum switching valve and reservoir as described in Section 33, then refit the throttle housing as described in Section 30.

35 Exhaust manifold – removal and refitting

Refer to Part A, Section 17, noting that it may also be necessary to remove the distributor (Chapter 5), to gain access to the exhaust manifold retaining bolt at the timing cover end of the engine.

36 Exhaust system – general information, removal and refitting

Refer to Part A, Section 18, noting that the tailpipe trims may be removed from an old system and transferred to the replacement; they are secured by bolts on their underside (photo).

Part C: Emission control systems

37 General information

Fuel evaporative emission control

The function of this system is to reduce the amount of fuel vapour released into the atmosphere. The system is controlled by a check valve which is linked to the fuel tank.

Crankcase emission control

The function of the Positive Crankcase Ventilation (PCV) system is to draw blow-by gases from the crankcase and camshaft cover chamber and direct them into the inlet tract. From there the gases are drawn into the combustion chambers with the fuel/air mixture and burnt in the combustion process.

38 Emission control system components – testing and renewal

Fuel evaporative emission control

1 The check valve is mounted on the left-hand front inner wing in the engine compartment. To remove the valve, disconnect both vacuum
hoses and release it from the mounting bracket noting the direction of flow cast on the surface of the valve. To test the valve, check that air flows freely through the valve in one direction but not in the other. If this is not the case the valve must be renewed.
2 Refitting is a reversal of removal ensuring that the arrow on the valve is pointing downwards (photo).

Crankcase emission control
Carburettor models

3 Check all the positive crankcase ventilation hoses for signs of cracking or deterioration, and renew them if necessary. The PCV valve is fitted to the camshaft cover and is held in position by a grommet.
4 To ensure that a PCV valve is functioning correctly, blow through it in the direction of normal gas travel and check that air passes freely; repeat the check by blowing from the other end of the valve and note that air should pass with difficulty.

> ⚠ Warning: Do not suck through the valve, as the petrol residues within it are harmful to health. If a PCV valve is defective, it must be renewed.

Fuel-injected models

5 On early models there is no PCV valve in the system, the engine being linked to the inlet tract via a hose on the rear of the camshaft cover. Maintenance is therefore limited to checking the PCV hose for signs of cracking or deterioration and renewing if necessary.
6 On later models there are two valves in the PCV system; one fitted into the left-hand rear face of the cylinder block/crankcase, and one screwed into the left-hand corner of the rear camshaft cover. Both valves are linked by a hose. The crankcase gases are drawn up the hose into the camshaft cover where they are drawn into the inlet tract via the hose on the rear of the camshaft cover.
7 Check all the PCV hoses for signs of cracking or deterioration, and renew them if necessary. Remove the valves and test them as described in paragraph 4 noting that the normal direction of gas travel is from the cylinder block/crankcase to the camshaft cover.

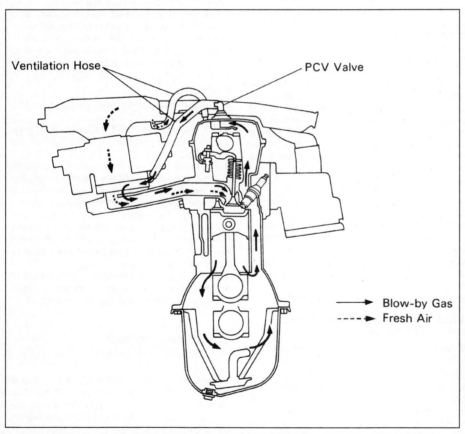

Ventilation Hose

PCV Valve

→ Blow-by Gas
---→ Fresh Air

Fig. 4.36 A cross-sectional view of the positive crankcase ventilation (PCV) emission control system (1.3 engine shown) (Sec 37)

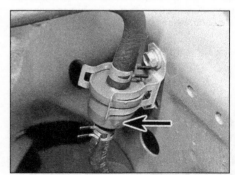

38.2 Location of fuel evaporative emission control check valve, note arrow showing direction of flow (arrowed)

Chapter 5 Ignition system

Contents

Degrees of difficulty

Easy, suitable for novice with little experience	**Fairly easy,** suitable for beginner with some experience	**Fairly difficult,** suitable for competent DIY mechanic	**Difficult,** suitable for experienced DIY mechanic	**Very difficult,** suitable for expert DIY or professional

Specifications

General

System type:
   Carburettor engines .... Toyota Integrated Ignition Assembly (IIA) – ignition coil and igniter module mounted in distributor
   Fuel-injected engine .... Toyota Electronic Spark Advance (ESA), under control of TCCS ECU – ignition coil, igniter module and distributor
Firing order 1-3-4-2
Location of No 1 cylinder .... Timing cover end

Distributor

Type:
   Carburettor engines .... Breakerless, signal-generating rotor and pick-up coil, mechanical and vacuum spark advance
   Fuel-injected engine .... Breakerless, signal-generating rotor and pick-up coil, ECU-controlled spark advance
Direction of rotor arm rotation:
   Carburettor engines .... Anti-clockwise
   Fuel-injected engine .... Clockwise
Signal rotor-to-pick-up coil air gap .... 0.2 to 0.4 mm
Pick-up coil resistance .... 140 to 180 ohms

Ignition coil resistances – cold

Primary windings:
   Carburettor engines .... 1.2 to 1.5 ohms
   Fuel-injected engine .... 0.41 to 0.50 ohms
Secondary windings .... 10.2 to 13.8 k ohms

Part A: Carburettor engines

1 General information and precautions

The transistorised ignition system combines the ignition coil and igniter module inside the distributor housing, this being called the Integrated Ignition Assembly (IIA). The distributor is driven from the end of the (exhaust) camshaft.

The system consists of two circuits; low tension/LT (or primary) circuit and high tension/HT (or secondary).

The low tension circuit consists of the battery, ignition switch, ignition coil low tension or primary windings, the distributor pick-up coil and the igniter module.

The high tension circuit consists of the ignition coil high tension or secondary windings, the distributor cap, the rotor arm, the spark plugs and their leads.

Low tension voltage from the battery is changed within the ignition coil to high tension voltage by the distributor signal rotor moving past the pick-up coil and the igniter module momentarily cutting off the LT circuit current in response to the signal thus generated. High tension voltage from the ignition coil is then fed, via the distributor rotor arm and cap and the spark plug HT leads, to the spark plugs where it finally jumps the gap between each plug's two electrodes.

So that the engine may run correctly, the spark must ignite the fuel/ air mixture in the combustion chamber at exactly the right moment in relation to engine speed and load. The ignition timing is advanced and retarded automatically, by both a mechanical and a vacuum-operated system.

The mechanical system consists of two weights which move out under centrifugal force to cause the signal rotor shaft to move relative to the pick-up coil and so advance the spark. The weights are held in position by two springs which are responsible for correct spark advance.

The vacuum control consists of a twin-diaphragm assembly, two chambers of which are connected (via small-bore hoses) to different induction vacuum sources while the diaphragms are connected to the pick-up coil assembly. Inlet manifold depression, which varies with engine speed and throttle opening, causes the diaphragms to move so rotating the coil and advancing or retarding the spark.

Refer to Chapter 10 for details of removal and refitting of the steering lock/ignition switch lock barrel and to Chapter 12, Section 12, for details of removal and refitting of the switch loom plate.

The following precautions must be observed to prevent damage to system components and to reduce any risk of personal injury.

(a) Do NOT leave the ignition switched on for more than 70 minutes when the engine is not running.

(b) Ensure that the ignition is switched OFF before disconnecting any of the system wiring or connecting or disconnecting any test equipment (even a timing light or tachometer).

(c) Do NOT disconnect the battery earth terminal while the engine is running, or reverse the terminal connections at any time.

(d) If connecting a tachometer to the system, ensure that it is compatible; some are not.

Always use the tachometer terminal/service connector to connect up a tachometer, but NEVER allow the terminal/service connector to be earthed: this could damage the igniter and/or ignition coil.

(e) Do NOT attempt to improvise test procedures, take care when carrying out the tests given that accidental contact is NOT made between the tester probe(s) and adjacent components or terminals.

(f) Do NOT allow an HT lead to short out or spark against the distributor housing.

(g) ALWAYS ensure that the igniter is correctly earthed to the distributor housing.

(h) Do NOT earth the coil primary or secondary circuits.

 Warning: The voltages produced by the electronic ignition system are considerably higher than those produced by conventional systems. Extreme care must be taken when working on the system with the ignition switched on. Persons with surgically-implanted cardiac pacemaker devices should keep well clear of the ignition circuits, components and test equipment.

2 Ignition system – testing

Note: Refer to the warning and precautions in Section 1 before proceeding.

1 The components of electronic ignition systems are normally very reliable; most faults are far more likely to be due to loose or dirty connections or to 'tracking' of high tension voltage due to dirt dampness or damaged insulation than to the failure of any of the system's components. **Always** check thoroughly all wiring before condemning an electrical component and work methodically to eliminate all other possibilities before deciding that a particular component is faulty.

2 There are two main symptoms indicating faults in the ignition system. Either the engine will not start or fire, or the engine is difficult to start and misfires. If it is a regular misfire (ie the engine is running on only two or three cylinders), the fault is almost sure to be in the high tension circuit. If the misfiring is intermittent, the fault could be in either the high or low tension circuits. If the car stops suddenly, or will not start at all, it is likely that the fault is in the low tension circuit. Power loss and/or overheating problems, apart from the possibility of incorrect fuel system settings, are normally due to faults in the distributor or to incorrect ignition timing.

3 The old practice of checking for a spark by holding the live end of a spark plug lead a short distance away from the engine is not

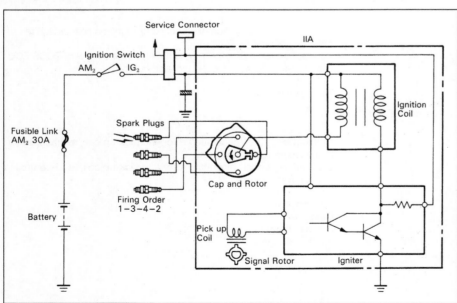

Fig. 5.1 Ignition system schematic diagram – carburettor engines (Sec 1)

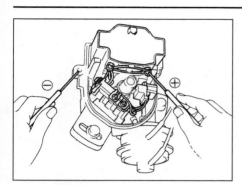

Fig. 5.2 Checking ignition coil feed from battery (See 2)

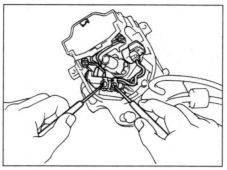

Fig. 5.3 Checking operation of igniter power transistor (Sec 2)

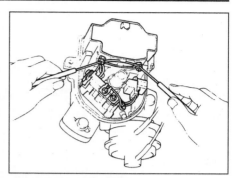

Fig. 5.4 Checking resistance of ignition coil primary windings (Sec 2)

recommended; not only is there a high risk of a powerful electric shock but the ignition coil or igniter module will be damaged. Similarly, **never** try to 'diagnose' misfires by pulling off one HT lead at a time.

Engine fails to start

4 If the engine fails to start, yet was running normally when the vehicle was last used, first check that there is fuel in the tank. If the engine turns over normally on the starter motor, the battery is evidently well charged then the fault may be in either the high or low tension circuits; check the HT circuit first. If the battery is known to be fully charged, the ignition warning lamps light, but the starter motor fails to turn the engine, check the security of the leads on the battery terminals and of the earth lead to its body connection. Remember, however, that it is possible for a poor connection to exist even if the leads look and feel secure; if one of the battery terminal posts gets very hot when trying to work the starter motor, this is a sure indication of a faulty connection to that terminal.

5 One of the most common reasons for bad starting is damp on the spark plug leads and in the distributor cap. Remove the cap, dry it with a rag and wipe the leads clean, then refit the cap.

6 If the engine still fails to start, check that voltage is reaching the spark plugs by connecting a timing light to each spark plug lead in turn and turning the engine over on the starter motor: if the light flashes, voltage is

reaching the spark plugs, so these should be checked first. If the light does not flash, check the leads themselves followed by the distributor cap, carbon brushes and rotor arm (Chapter 1, but note also the checks given in Section 3 below). The timing light can be connected to quickly check that there is output from the ignition coil itself.

7 If there is a spark, check the fuel system for faults (Chapter 4).

8 If there is no spark check the ignition system, starting with the low tension circuit.

9 Check the low tension wiring connector at the distributor; if it is clean, dry and securely connected, ensure that there is battery voltage reaching the ignition coil (Fig. 5.2); if not, check the wiring back to the ignition switch.

10 Next check the operation of the igniter module power transistor by using a dry cell battery to apply a voltage of 1.5V for **no more than 5 seconds** (or the power transistor will be destroyed) across the terminals as shown in Fig. 5.3, with a voltmeter connected to observe the resultant output. The voltmeter should display a reading of 12V initially, dropping to between 0 and 3 volts during the connection of the 1.5V supply; if it does not the igniter module must be renewed (Section 3).

11 With the ignition switched off, check the resistances of the ignition coil primary and secondary windings (Figs. 5.4 and 5.5): if either reading obtained differs significantly from that specified, the coil must be renewed (Section 3).

12 Using an ohmmeter, check the resistance of the pick-up coil as shown in Fig. 5.6; if the reading obtained differs significantly from that specified, the coil assembly must be renewed (Section 3).

Engine misfires

13 An irregular misfire suggests either a loose connection or intermittent fault on the low tension circuit, or a high tension circuit fault on the coil side of the rotor arm.

14 With the ignition switched off, check carefully through the system ensuring that all connections are clean and securely fastened. If the equipment is available, check the low tension circuit as described in paragraphs 9 to 12 above.

15 Check that the ignition coil, the distributor cap and the spark plug leads are clean and dry. Check the cap carefully for tracking (sometimes known as arcing). This can be recognised as a very thin black line running between two or more segments, or between a segment and some other part of the distributor; these lines are paths which conduct electricity across the cap, thus letting it run to earth. The only answer is to renew the cap. Check the leads themselves and the spark plugs (by substitution, if necessary), then check the distributor cap, carbon brushes and rotor arm (Chapter 1).

16 Regular misfiring is almost certainly due to a fault in the distributor cap, spark plug leads or spark plugs. Use a timing light (paragraph 6

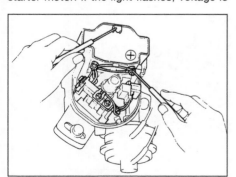

Fig. 5.5 Checking resistance of ignition coil secondary windings (Sec 2)

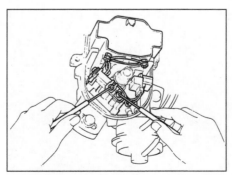

Fig. 5.6 Checking resistance of pick-up coil (Sec 2)

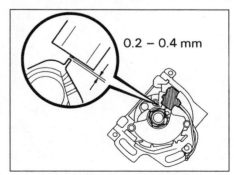

Fig. 5.7 Signal rotor-to-pick-up coil air gap – carburettor engines (Sec 2)

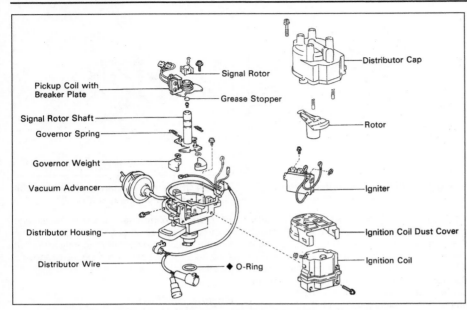

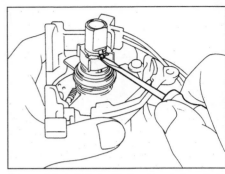

Fig. 5.9 Releasing signal rotor and spring (Sec 3)

Fig. 5.8 Exploded view of Integrated Ignition Assembly distributor (Sec 3)

above) to check whether HT voltage is present at all leads.

17 If HT voltage is not present on any particular lead, the fault will be in that lead or in the distributor cap. If voltage is present on all leads, the fault will be in the spark plugs; check them and renew them if there is any doubt about their condition.

18 If no voltage is present, check the ignition coil (paragraph 11 above); its secondary windings may be breaking down under load.

19 Check the signal rotor-to-pick-up coil air gap using feeler gauges (Fig. 5.7); if the gap is not as specified, renew the coil assembly (Section 3).

20 If the misfire still exists, remember that it is possible for the ignition timing to be so far out that it is causing the engine to misfire, or for a fault to exist in one or both of the distributor advance systems; check the ignition timing and adjust it (Chapter 1) or overhaul the distributor (Section 3) as necessary.

3 Distributor –
removal, overhaul and refitting

Note: *Refer to the warning and precautions in Section 1 before proceeding.*

Removal

1 Disconnect the battery earth terminal.
2 Disconnect the distributor wiring.
3 Labelling them to ensure correct refitting, disconnect and plug the vacuum hoses.
4 Position the engine so that number 1 cylinder is at TDC on the compression stroke (Chapter 2, Section 3).
5 Remove the distributor cap and rotor arm (Chapter 1).
6 Mark the relationship of the distributor housing to the camshaft cover, using a scribe or similar (photo). On 1.3 models, note that the distributor flange projection aligns with the camshaft cover securing nut.
7 Unbolt and withdraw the distributor. Do not disturb the crankshaft setting while the

distributor is removed, or rotate the distributor shaft (unless the unit is to be overhauled).
8 Remove the distributor housing O-ring, this must be renewed whenever it is disturbed.

Overhaul

Note: *High melting-point grease, a new signal rotor spring, suitable adhesives and sealants (refer to your Toyota dealer), a new cap gasket and a new O-ring will be required.*

9 Check the advance mechanism by turning the rotor arm anti-clockwise, then releasing it; it should return quickly clockwise to its previous position and should not be excessively loose.
10 Check the vacuum advance by sucking on the advancer hose stubs and checking that the pick-up coil moves in response; if the advancer is thought to be faulty, check first that there are no splits in the hoses and that they are securely connected.
11 Remove the ignition coil dust cover (photo).
12 Unscrew the ignition coil terminal nuts, label the wires to ensure correct refitting and disconnect them. Undo the securing screws and remove the ignition coil.
13 Disconnect and remove the distributor wiring, with (where fitted) the suppression capacitor; label the wires to ensure correct refitting.
14 Remove the terminal screws, label the wires to ensure correct refitting and disconnect the igniter module wiring. Undo the securing screws and remove the module (photo).

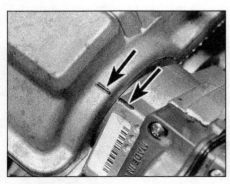

3.6 Distributor body-to-camshaft cover alignment marks (arrowed) made before distributor removal – 1.6 model shown

3.11 Removing ignition coil dust cover . . .

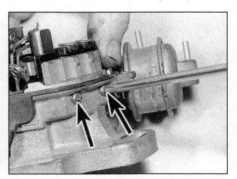

3.14 . . . undoing igniter securing screws (arrowed) . . .

3.25A . . . applying sealant to distributor housing before refitting ignition coil . . .

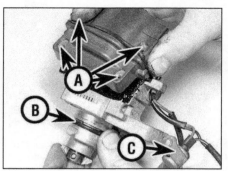

3.25B . . . and tighten screws (locations 'A' arrowed) – always renew O-ring (B) and note condenser (C) – 1.6 model shown

15 Remove the retaining screw and withdraw the vacuum advancer, disconnecting its pick-up coil link.

16 Remove the signal rotor and spring, using a screwdriver to release it as shown in Fig. 5.9.

17 Remove its two securing screws, noting their washers, and withdraw the pick-up coil and breaker plate assembly.

18 Remove the governor springs.

19 Remove the grease stopper from the top of the signal rotor shaft, then undo its securing screw from inside the shaft and pull the signal rotor shaft off the main distributor shaft.

20 Use a screwdriver to release their securing E-rings, then remove the governor weights; note their fitted positions.

21 Check that the pick-up coil can be rotated easily and smoothly, with a slight drag present, on the breaker plate; if it is sticking, excessively loose or requires significant effort to move it, renew the assembly.

22 Turn the main distributor shaft and check that it rotates smoothly; if the bearing is rough or worn, the distributor housing must be renewed. Check the fit of the signal rotor shaft on the main distributor shaft and renew either as necessary if excessive wear or free play is found.

23 Renew the components of the mechanical advance mechanism if they are worn or damaged; if it is thought to be faulty, the vacuum advancer must be renewed as a single unit.

24 Check the distributor cap, rotor arm and spark plug leads (Chapter 1); renew any defective items.

25 Reassembly is the reverse of the dismantling procedure, noting the following points (photos).

(a) *Apply a smear of high melting-point grease to the mating surfaces of the main distributor and signal rotor shafts, once it is refitted and secured by its screw pack with grease the signal rotor shaft and refit the grease stopper.*

(b) *When refitting the pick-up coil and breaker plate assembly, align the cut-out with the distributor housing.*

(c) *Use a new spring when refitting the signal rotor.*

(d) *Using feeler gauges, check the signal rotor-to-pick-up coil air gap (Fig. 5.7); if major adjustment is required the pick-up coil and breaker plate assembly must be removed (paragraphs 16 and 17 above) and a new one selected that produces the correct air gap when installed. Note, however, that if the pick-up coil-to-breaker plate Torx screws are disturbed to make minor adjustments, the screw and*

hole threads must be thoroughly degreased and a few drops of anaerobic adhesive/sealant (such as Three Bond 1324) must be applied to 3 to 5 mm of each screw's tip on refitting. The engine must not be run for at least half an after installing, or at high speeds for at least two hours, to allow the adhesive to cure properly.

(e) *Reconnect the igniter module wiring using the notes made on dismantling.*

(f) *Secure the pick-up coil wiring as shown in Fig. 5.10; ensure the wires cannot touch the distributor housing or the signal rotor.*

(g) *Reconnect the distributor wiring using the notes made on dismantling.*

(h) *When refitting the ignition coil, apply sealant to its distributor housing mating face; when reconnecting the coil wiring, use the notes made on dismantling and secure the wires (into their grooves, where applicable) so they cannot touch the signal rotor or distributor housing.*

Refitting

26 First check that number 1 cylinder is at TDC (Chapter 2, Section 3), then rotate the rotor arm to align with the distributor cap's number 1 terminal; the groove on the shaft coupling should align with the housing protrusion (Fig. 5.11). Fit a new O-ring to the distributor housing and lubricate it with a smear of engine oil.

27 Aligning the marks made on removal, refit the distributor. If necessary, rotate the rotor arm very slightly to help the distributor drive coupling locate in the camshaft slots. Refit the clamp bolt(s).

28 Refit the distributor cap, fitting a new gasket and ensuring that both the cap, the gasket and the suppression capacitor bracket are correctly located, then reconnect the HT leads (Chapter 1).

29 Reconnect the vacuum hoses, using the notes made on removal, and the distributor wiring.

30 Check, and adjust if necessary, the ignition timing (Chapter 1).

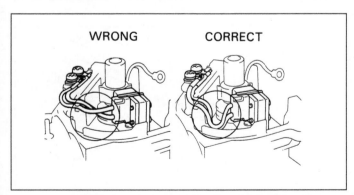

Fig. 5.10 Correct routing of pick-up coil wires (Sec 3)

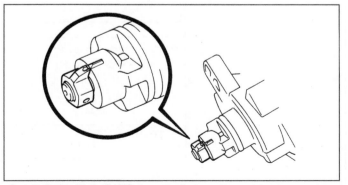

Fig. 5.11 With rotor arm aligned with cap number 1 cylinder terminal, shaft coupling groove should align with housing protrusion (Sec 3)

Part B: Fuel-injected engine

4 General information and precautions

The ignition system is fully electronic in operation, incorporating the Electronic Control Unit (ECU) mounted inside the vehicle behind the facia, the igniter mounted on the engine compartment bulkhead, a distributor (driven off the exhaust camshaft right-hand end), the spark plugs and their leads, the ignition coil and associated wiring.

The system consists of two circuits; low tension/LT (or primary) and high tension/HT (or secondary). The low tension circuit is as described in Section 1 of this Chapter, but includes the ECU and wiring. The high tension circuit is exactly as described in Section 1.

Apart from the fact that the ignition timing is entirely controlled by the ECU, the system operates as described in Section 1 of this Chapter.

The ECU controls both the ignition system, known as Electronic Spark Advance (ESA), and the fuel injection system, integrating the two in a complete engine management system known as Toyota Computer Control System (TCCS); refer to Part B of Chapter 4 for information on any part of the system not given here.

As far as the ignition system is concerned, the ECU receives information in the form of electrical impulses or signals from the pick-up coil (which gives it the engine speed and crankshaft position), from the water temperature sensor (which gives it the engine temperature) and from the Manifold Absolute Pressure sensor (which gives it the load on the engine). All these signals are compared by the ECU, using digital techniques, with set values pre-programmed (mapped) into its memory, based on this information the ECU selects the ignition timing appropriate to those values and controls the igniter accordingly.

A 'fail-safe' function is incorporated so that if one of the system's sensors fails, a back-up circuit will take over to allow the vehicle to be driven, albeit at reduced power and efficiency; the instrument panel 'Engine System/Check Engine' warning lamp will light to indicate that this is happening and a fault code will be stored in the ECU relating to the circuit affected; refer to Chapter 4.

Refer to Section 1 of this Chapter for details of the ignition switch.

In addition to the warning and precautions given in Section 1, note the following.

(a) *When a tachometer is to be connected, always use the check connector 'IG –' terminal but NEVER allow the terminal to contact earth as this could damage the igniter and/or ignition coil.*

(b) *Do NOT allow an HT lead to short out or spark against the distributor housing, the igniter or the ignition coil.*

(c) *Do NOT drop the ECU or allow it to receive any impact.*

(d) *Do NOT open the ECU cover.*

(e) *Prevent the entry of water if the distributor is inspected in wet weather or when washing the car.*

(f) *Although non-damaging and not dangerous, note that if the battery earth terminal is disconnected, all diagnostic fault codes stored in the ECU will be erased; refer to Chapter 4 for further information.*

5 Ignition system – testing

Note: *Refer to the warnings and precautions given in Sections 1 and 4 of this Chapter before proceeding.*

General

1 The general comments made in Section 2 apply equally to this system, but note that in this case the ECU is also at risk if the system is triggered with an open (ie, not properly earthed) HT circuit: ECUs are much more expensive to replace, so take care!

2 If you are in any doubt as to your skill and ability to test an ignition system's components and to understand what is happening, or if you do not have the required equipment, take the car immediately to a Toyota dealer; it is better to pay the labour charges involved in having the car checked by an expert than to risk damage to the system or to yourself.

3 Note that a fault within the system may allow the engine to continue running on the system's 'fail-safe' function: this may mask the symptoms, making accurate diagnosis very difficult.

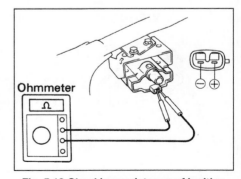

Fig. 5.13 Checking resistance of ignition coil primary windings (Sec 5)

Fig. 5.12 Ignition system schematic diagram – fuel-injected engine (Sec 4)

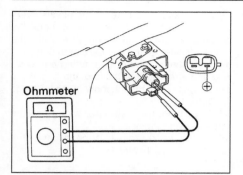

Fig. 5.14 Checking resistance of ignition coil secondary windings (Sec 5)

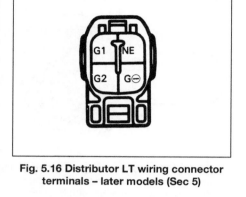

Fig. 5.15 Distributor LT wiring connector terminals – early models (Sec 5)

Fig. 5.16 Distributor LT wiring connector terminals – later models (Sec 5)

Engine fails to start

4 Check whether the fault is in the ignition system or not (Section 2, paragraphs 4 to 6) and check the high tension circuit as described.

5 If the high tension circuit appears to be in good condition, the feed to the ignition coil can be checked as described in paragraph 9, while the coil itself can be checked as described in paragraph 11 and Figs. 5.13 and 5.14.

6 Check the pick-up coil resistance using an ohmmeter connected between the distributor LT wiring connector 'G –' terminal and each of the remaining connector terminals (Fig. 5.15 or 5.16, as applicable). If the reading obtained on any test is significantly outside the specified range the distributor housing must be renewed.

7 When checking the low tension circuit wiring, DO NOT attempt to 'test' the ECU with anything other than the correct test equipment, which will be available only at a Toyota dealer. If any of the wires are to be checked which lead to the ECU, always first unplug the relevant connector from the ECU so that there is no risk of its being damaged by the application of incorrect voltages from test equipment. If the wiring between the ECU and the distributor is sound, the ECU and igniter must be tested by a Toyota dealer (or other competent specialist), unless a known good ECU and igniter are available for testing by substitution.

8 If all components have been checked for signs of obvious faults such as dirty or poorly-fastened connections, damp, or 'tracking' and have been tested as far as is possible but the system is still thought to be faulty, the car must be taken to a Toyota dealer for testing on the correct equipment.

Engine misfires

9 Refer to Section 2, paragraphs 13 to 20 (and to Figs. 5.17 and 5.18), but note that the possible causes of partial failures which might result in a misfire are far too numerous to be eliminated without the correct test equipment. Once the ignition system components have been checked for signs of obvious faults such

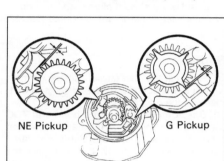
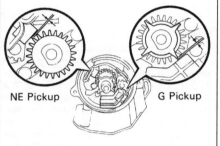
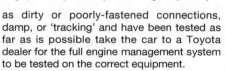
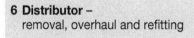
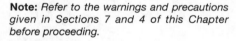

Fig. 5.17 Signal rotor-to-pick-up coil air gap – early fuel-injected engine (Sec 5)

as dirty or poorly-fastened connections, damp, or 'tracking' and have been tested as far as is possible take the car to a Toyota dealer for the full engine management system to be tested on the correct equipment.

6 Distributor –
removal, overhaul and refitting

Note: *Refer to the warnings and precautions given in Sections 7 and 4 of this Chapter before proceeding.*

Removal

1 Disconnect the battery earth terminal.
2 Disconnect the distributor wiring (photo).
3 Position the engine so that number 1

6.2 Disconnecting distributor low tension wiring

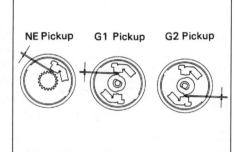

Fig. 5.18 Signal rotor-to-pick-up coil air gap – later fuel-injected engine (Sec 5)

cylinder is at TDC on the compression stroke (Chapter 2, Section 38).

4 Remove the distributor cap and rotor arm (Chapter 1); discard the cap O-ring, which must be renewed on reassembly. Remove the dust shield from behind the rotor arm, noting (where applicable) the mark showing the relationship of the dust shield to the wiring grommet (photo).

5 Mark the relationship of the distributor housing to the cylinder head, using a scribe or similar.

6 Unbolt and withdraw the distributor. Do not disturb the crankshaft setting while the distributor is removed, or rotate the distributor shaft (unless the unit is to be overhauled).

7 Remove the distributor housing O-ring; this must be renewed whenever it is disturbed.

6.4 Dust shield arrow mark (A) aligns with wiring grommet (B)

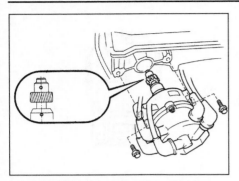

Fig. 5.19 With rotor arm aligned with cap number 1 cylinder terminal, driven gear drilled mark should align with housing groove – early fuel-injected engine (Sec 6)

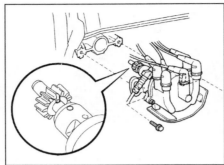

Fig. 5.20 With rotor arm aligned with cap number 1 cylinder terminal, driven gear drilled mark should align with housing groove – later fuel-injected engine (Sec 6)

Overhaul

8 Unbolt and withdraw the heat shield. Do not attempt further dismantling.
9 Check the distributor cap, rotor arm and spark plug leads (Chapter 1); renew any defective items.
10 Check the pick-up coil resistance and the signal rotor-to-pick-up coil air gap (Section 5 and relevant Figs); renew the distributor housing if any of these is incorrect or if any other signs are found of damage or of excessive wear.

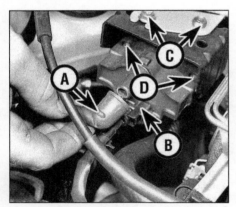

7.2 Ignition coil HT lead (A), low tension wiring connector (B), mounting bracket bolts (C) and coil-to-mounting bracket screws (D) (two arrowed)

Refitting

11 First refit the dust shield, aligning its mark (where applicable) with the wiring grommet, then refit the rotor arm.
12 Check that number 1 cylinder is at TDC (Chapter 2, Section 38), then rotate the rotor arm to align with the distributor cap's number 1 terminal; the drilled mark (not the securing pin hole) on the driven gear should align with the housing groove (Fig. 5.19 or 5.20, as appropriate). Fit a new O-ring to the distributor housing and lubricate it with a smear of engine oil.
13 Refit the distributor, aligning the marks made on removal: if no marks were made, align the centre of the flange slot with the

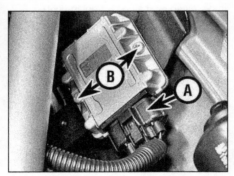

8.2 Igniter multi-plug (A) and securing screws (B)

cylinder head bolt hole. If necessary, very slightly rotate the rotor arm to help the distributor driven gear engage with the camshaft drive gear. Refit the clamp bolts.
14 Refit the distributor cap, fitting a new O-ring and ensuring that the cap and O-ring are correctly located, then reconnect the HT leads (Chapter 1).
15 Reconnect the distributor wiring and the battery earth terminal.
16 Check, and adjust if necessary, the ignition timing (Chapter 1).

7 Ignition coil – removal and refitting

Note: *Refer to the warnings and precautions given in Sections 1 and 4 of this Chapter before proceeding.*

Removal

1 Disconnect the battery earth terminal.
2 Disconnect the HT lead and the low tension wiring connector from the ignition coil (photo).
3 To remove the coil with its mounting bracket, undo and remove the two bolts securing the bracket to the front suspension strut brace; to remove the coil from its mounting bracket, undo the four securing screws and withdraw it.

Refitting

4 Refitting is the reverse of the removal procedure.

8 Igniter – removal and refitting

Note: *Refer to the warnings and precautions given in Sections 1 and 4 of this Chapter before proceeding.*

Removal

1 Disconnect the battery earth terminal.
2 The igniter is located on the engine compartment bulkhead. Disconnect the multi-plug then undo the screws securing it to the bulkhead mounting plate and remove it; note any washers or insulators fitted (photo).

Refitting

3 Refitting is the reverse of the removal procedure.

Chapter 6 Clutch

Contents

Degrees of difficulty

Easy, suitable for novice with little experience	Fairly easy, suitable for beginner with some experience	Fairly difficult, suitable for competent DIY mechanic	Difficult, suitable for experienced DIY mechanic	Very difficult, suitable for expert DIY or professional

Specifications

Type . . . .   Dry, single plate, diaphragm spring, with hydraulic actuation

Driven plate
Minimum distance from friction material surface to rivet heads . . . . . .   0.3 mm
Maximum run-out . . . .   0.8 mm

Clutch cover
Maximum wear of diaphragm spring fingers:
  Depth . . . .   0.6 mm
  Width . . . .   5.0 mm

Clutch pedal
Height from asphalt sheet . . . .   139.0 to 149.0 mm
Free play . . . .   5.0 to 15.0 mm

Clutch master cylinder pushrod play – at pedal top . .   1.0 to 5.0 mm

Torque wrench settings	Nm	lbf ft
Clutch hydraulic unions	15	11
Fluid reservoir to master cylinder	25	18
Clutch master cylinder securing nuts	13	10
Clutch pedal setting nut	25	18
Clutch slave cylinder securing bolts	12	9
Clutch slave cylinder bleed nipple	11	8
Clutch cover to flywheel	19	14
Clutch release fork pivot	37	27

1 General information

A dry, single plate, diaphragm spring clutch is fitted to models with manual gearbox to provide the driver with a means of smoothly taking up the drive on starting off and of interrupting the drive when changing gear.

The clutch consists of a driven (friction) plate, a cover assembly, a release bearing and the release mechanism; all of these components are contained in the large cast aluminium alloy bellhousing sandwiched between the engine and the gearbox. The release mechanism is hydraulic, being operated by a master cylinder connected to the pedal and a slave cylinder mounted on the gearbox housing.

The driven plate is fitted between the engine flywheel and the clutch pressure plate and is allowed to slide on the gearbox input shaft splines. It consists of two circular facings of friction material riveted in position to provide the clutch bearing surface and a spring-cushioned hub to damp out transmission shocks.

The clutch cover assembly is bolted to the engine flywheel and is located by dowel pins; it comprises the cover, the diaphragm spring and the pressure plate. When the engine is running drive is transmitted from the crankshaft via the flywheel and clutch cover to the driven plate (these last three components being clamped securely together by the pressure plate and diaphragm spring) and from the driven plate to the gearbox input shaft.

To interrupt the drive the spring pressure must be relaxed. This is achieved by a sealed release bearing which is fitted concentrically around the gearbox input shaft; when the driver depresses the clutch pedal the release bearing is pressed against the fingers at the centre of the diaphragm spring. Since the spring is held by rivets between two annular fulcrum rings the pressure at its centre causes it to deform so that it flattens and thus releases the clamping force it exerts, at its periphery, on the pressure plate.

2.2 Clutch cover to flywheel alignment mark (A), clutch cover securing bolt (B), locating dowel (C)

2.4 Removing clutch cover and driven plate – note locating dowels (arrowed) on flywheel

2.15 Using alignment tool to centralise clutch driven plate

2 Clutch assembly – removal, inspection and refitting

⚠️ **Warning: Dust created by clutch wear and deposited on the clutch components may contain asbestos which is a health hazard. DO NOT blow it out with compressed air or inhale any of it. DO NOT use petrol or petroleum based solvents to clean off the dust. Brake system cleaner or methylated spirit should be used to flush the dust into a suitable receptacle. After the clutch components are wiped clean with rags, dispose of the contaminated rags and cleaner safely.**

Removal

1 The clutch can be reached only by first removing the gearbox (Chapter 7). If the engine and/or gearbox are removed for overhaul, check the clutch for wear and renew any necessary components – the relatively low cost of clutch components, in relation to the time and trouble spent overhauling them, warrants their renewal unless they are new or in near-perfect condition.

2 With the gearbox removed, mark the relative position of the clutch cover to the flywheel (photo).

3 Unscrew each of the clutch cover bolts one turn at a time, in a diagonal sequence, until the diaphragm spring tension is released. It may be necessary to prevent the flywheel from turning by jamming the flywheel ring gear teeth using a stout screwdriver or similar tool.

4 Remove the clutch cover slowly; be prepared to catch the driven plate which may just drop out (photo).

Inspection

5 When cleaning clutch components, first read the warning at the beginning of this Section; remove dust using a clean, dry cloth and working in a well-ventilated atmosphere, then dispose safely of the cloth; asbestos dust is harmful and must not be inhaled (see 'Safety First!'). Although some friction materials may no longer contain asbestos it is safest to assume that they do and to take precautions accordingly.

6 Check the driven plate friction material for

wear. If the distance from the friction material surface to any of the rivets is worn to the minimum specified or less, the friction plate must be renewed; as it must if the friction material is oil-contaminated, or if the plate itself exhibits signs of cracking or distortion. If oil-contamination is evident on the friction material, the source of the oil should be located and any necessary repairs made before renewing the driven plate. Also check the driven plate for worn central splines and broken hub springs.

7 Check the machined faces of the clutch cover pressure plate and the flywheel. If either is grooved, light machining may save the component if the grooves are deep, renewal will be necessary.

8 Any cracks or splits in the clutch cover pressure plate will necessitate renewal of the clutch cover assembly, as will worn, weak, broken or otherwise damaged spring fingers.

9 Check the condition of the clutch release bearing (Section 3).

10 It is always advisable to renew clutch components as a set (and include the clutch release bearing unless it is nearly new), as components from the same reputable manufacturer should be perfectly matched.

Refitting

11 During refitting it is extremely important that no oil or grease is allowed to come into contact with the friction material or with the clutch cover pressure plate and flywheel faces. To this end, wash your hands and wipe all traces of grease from the tools to be used, then wipe the flywheel and pressure plate surfaces using a clean, dry rag.

12 Having ensured that any protective coatings have been removed from new components, offer the driven plate up to the flywheel; the greater projection of the driven plate faces towards the gearbox and the flywheel side of the driven plate may carry a marking to that effect. The driven plate must be fitted the correct way round.

13 Offer the clutch cover onto its locating dowels, aligning the marks made on removal. Use a screwdriver or similar tool to roughly centralise the driven plate and tighten finger-tight the cover bolts.

14 The driven plate must now be correctly

aligned. The tool required for this task may be obtained in your local tool-hire shop, or alternatively purchased from most good motor accessory shops; a further alternative is to use an old input shaft.

15 Insert the alignment tool through the centre of the driven plate hub and engage it in the centre of the flywheel (photo). This will centralise the driven plate so that the gearbox input shaft will pass smoothly through it when the gearbox is connected to the engine.

16 Working evenly and progressively, making several passes, tighten the clutch cover bolts to the specified torque wrench setting. Start with the topmost bolt of the three near the locating dowels, followed by the other two near the dowels before tightening the remaining bolts; repeat the sequence at each pass.

17 Lubricate sparingly the clutch components as described in Section 3.

18 Refit the gearbox (Chapter 7).

3 Clutch release bearing and release arm – removal and refitting

Note: *Before starting work, refer to the warning in Section 2 concerning the dangers of asbestos dust.*

Removal

1 Remove the gearbox (Chapter 7).

2 Unclip the release bearing from the release arm and slide it off its guide sleeve (photo).

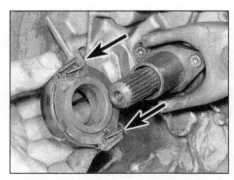

3.2 Release clips (arrowed) to remove clutch release bearing

Check the release bearing for smoothness of operation; there should be no harshness or slackness in it and it should spin reasonably freely. If this is not the case, it must be renewed.

3 The clutch release arm may be removed from its pivot, after the release bearing and the release arm rubber boot have been withdrawn, by releasing the retaining clips (photos). The pivot may be unscrewed if required.

Refitting

4 Refitting is the reverse of the removal procedure, noting the following points.

(a) Tighten the pivot to its specified torque wrench setting, if applicable.

(b) Lubricate the gearbox input shaft splines, the release bearing guide sleeve, the inside of the release bearing, the release arm pivot and retaining clips, the release arm forked ends and the slave cylinder actuating rod contact face with a smear of lithium based grease incorporating molybdenum disulphide. DO NOT apply excessive amounts of grease or contamination of the driven plate friction material is likely.

4 Clutch hydraulic system – bleeding

Note: Hydraulic fluid is poisonous, wash off immediately and thoroughly in case of skin contact and seek immediate medical advice if any fluid is swallowed or gets into the eyes. Certain types of hydraulic fluid are inflammable and may ignite when allowed into contact with hot components; when servicing any hydraulic system it is safest to assume that the fluid is inflammable and to take precautions against the risk of fire as though it is petrol that is being handled. Finally it is hygroscopic (it absorbs moisture from the air)

3.3A Removing clutch release arm rubber boot

– old fluid may be contaminated and unfit for further use. When topping-up or renewing the fluid, always use a good quality fluid of the specified type and ensure that it comes from a freshly-opened sealed container.

> **HAYNES HiNT** *Hydraulic fluid is an effective paint stripper and will attack plastics if any is spilt, it should be washed off immediately using copious quantities of fresh water.*

1 The bleeding procedure is exactly the same as that described in Chapter 9.

2 The clutch hydraulic system is bled via the bleed nipple on the clutch slave cylinder.

5 Clutch master cylinder – removal, overhaul and refitting

Note: Before starting work, refer to the note in Section 4 concerning the dangers of hydraulic fluid.

Removal

1 Disconnect the battery negative terminal.

2 Remove the air filter housing (Chapter 4), or

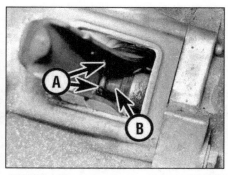

3.3B Clutch release arm retaining clips (A) pivot (B)

the suspension strut brace (Chapter 10) for increased working clearance, according to model.

3 Syphon the hydraulic fluid from the clutch master cylinder reservoir (**not** by mouth).

4 On GTi 16 models, remove the vacuum servo unit (Chapter 9).

5 Disconnect the hydraulic pipe from the master cylinder and catch any spillage in a suitable container.

6 Working inside the vehicle, remove the facia lower finish panel from the driver's footwell (Chapter 11), disconnect the clutch pedal return spring and remove the clip and clevis pin to separate the pushrod from the clutch pedal arm.

7 Unscrew the two master cylinder securing nuts (on the passenger compartment side of the bulkhead) and carefully withdraw the master cylinder from the vehicle.

Overhaul

Note: Before attempting to overhaul the unit check the price and availability of individual components and the price of a new or reconditioned unit, as overhaul may not be viable on economic grounds alone. Also, read through the procedure and check that the lubricants required are available.

8 Remove the master cylinder from the vehicle and clean it thoroughly.

9 Unscrew the reservoir securing bolt and remove the reservoir.

10 Pull back the cylinder dust-excluding boot and extract the circlip. Withdraw the pushrod and plate, noting their fitment.

11 Tap the end of the cylinder on a block of wood, or apply air from a tyre pump, to eject the piston.

12 Thoroughly clean all components using as a cleaning medium only methylated spirit, isopropyl alcohol or clean hydraulic fluid. Never use mineral-based solvents such as petrol or paraffin which will attack the hydraulic system's rubber components. Dry the components immediately using compressed air or a clean, lint-free cloth.

13 Check all components and renew any that are worn or damaged. Check particularly the cylinder bore and piston; the complete assembly should be renewed if these are scratched, worn or corroded. If there is any

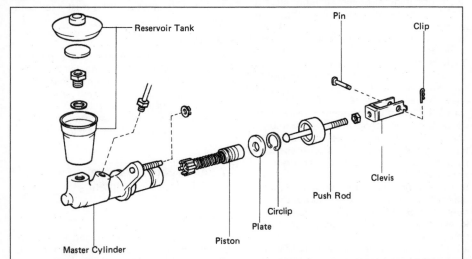

Fig. 6.1 Exploded view of tine clutch master cylinder components (See 5)

Reservoir Tank

Pin

Clip

Clevis

Push Rod

Circlip

Plate

Piston

Master Cylinder

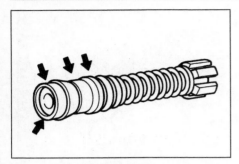

Fig. 6.2 Apply the specified grease to the master cylinder piston components, where arrowed (Sec 5)

doubt about the condition of the assembly or of any of its components, renew it. Check that the body's passages are clear. Inspect the pushrod for wear or damage and renew if necessary.

14 If the components are in good condition, discard the seals (having noted their lip orientation on the piston) and obtain a repair kit which contains all the necessary renewable items.

15 Manipulate the new seals into position on the piston using fingers only, and ensure that the lips of the seals are correctly orientated.

16 Apply lithium soap base glycol grease where indicated in Fig. 6.2 and insert the piston assembly carefully into the cylinder bore.

17 Fit the pushrod, plate and circlip, then reposition the dust-excluding boot.

18 Fit the reservoir and its new sealing washer, then tighten the securing bolt to the specified torque.

Refitting

19 Refitting is the reverse of the removal procedure, noting the following points.
(a) Tighten securely the disturbed fasteners and unions, to their specified torque wrench settings (where given).
(b) Refill the reservoir with new fluid and bleed the system (Section 4).

6 Clutch slave cylinder – removal, overhaul and refitting

Note: Before starting work, refer to the note in Section 4 concerning the dangers of hydraulic fluid.

Removal

1 Disconnect the battery negative terminal.
2 Disconnect the hydraulic pipe from the slave cylinder, located on the forward side of the gearbox housing, then either quickly plug the end of the pipe to prevent excessive fluid loss or allow the fluid to drain into a suitable container.
3 Undo the slave cylinder securing bolts, then withdraw the slave cylinder. Note the hydraulic pipe support bracket arrangement.

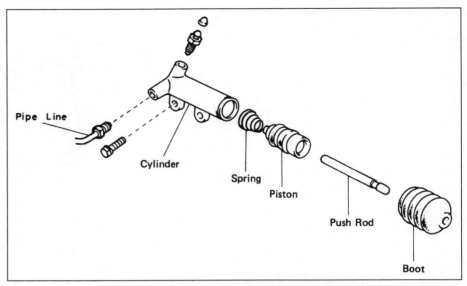

Fig. 6.3 Exploded view of the clutch slave cylinder components (Sec 6)

Overhaul

Note: Before attempting to overhaul the unit, check the price and availability of individual components and the price of a new or reconditioned unit, as overhaul may not be viable on economic grounds alone. Also, read through the procedure and check that the lubricants required are available.

4 Remove the slave cylinder from the vehicle and clean it thoroughly.
5 Withdraw the pushrod and the cylinder dust-excluding boot.
6 Tap the end of the cylinder on a block of wood, or apply air from a tyre pump, to eject the piston; the spring behind the piston is also withdrawn.
7 Thoroughly clean all components using as a cleaning medium only methylated spirit, isopropyl alcohol or clean hydraulic fluid. Never use mineral-based solvents such as petrol or paraffin which will attack the hydraulic system's rubber components. Dry the components immediately using compressed air or a clean, lint-free cloth.
8 Check all components and renew any that are worn or damaged. Check particularly the cylinder bore and piston; the complete assembly should be renewed if these are scratched, worn or corroded. If there is any doubt about the condition of the assembly or of any of its components, renew it. Check that the body's passages are clear. Inspect the pushrod for wear or damage and renew if necessary.
9 If the components are in good condition, discard the seals (having noted their lip orientation on the piston) and obtain a repair kit which contains all the necessary renewable items.
10 Manipulate the new seals into position on the piston using fingers only; ensure that the seal lips are correctly orientated.

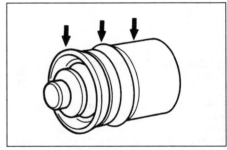

Fig. 6.4 Apply the specified grease to the slave cylinder piston components, where arrowed (Sec 6)

11 Apply lithium soap base glycol grease where indicated in Fig. 6.4 and insert the spring and piston carefully into the cylinder bore.
12 Fit the pushrod and the dust-excluding boot.

Refitting

13 Refitting is the reverse of the removal procedure, noting the following points.
(a) Tighten securely the disturbed fasteners and unions, to their specified torque wrench settings (where given).
(b) Refill the master cylinder reservoir with new fluid and bleed the system (Section 4).

7 Clutch pedal – removal, refitting and adjustment

Removal

1 Disconnect the battery negative terminal. Working inside the vehicle, remove the facia lower finish panel from the driver's footwell (Chapter 11).

2 Unhook the return spring from the upper end of the pedal arm.

3 Disconnect the pushrod from the pedal arm by removing the clevis pin securing clip and the clevis pin (photo).

4 Unscrew the nut from the end of the pedal pivot bolt and remove the washer, remove the bolt, then withdraw the pedal arm. The pivot cross -shaft and bushes can be withdrawn as required.

Refitting

5 Refitting is the reverse of the removal procedure, noting the following points.

(a) *Tighten securely the disturbed fasteners, to their specified torque wrench settings (where given).*

(b) *Apply a smear of general-purpose grease to the pivot cross-shaft.*

(c) *Check the pedal height setting as described below.*

Adjustment

Pedal height

6 With the battery negative terminal disconnected and the facia lower finish panel removed, peel back the carpet and measure the pedal height; see Fig. 6.5. Note that the measurement should be taken to the asphalt sheet; if it is not within specification, slacken the pedal height adjusting bolt locknut and turn the adjusting bolt until the correct pedal height is achieved. Tighten the locknut upon completion.

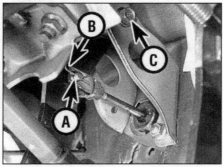

7.3 Master cylinder pushrod to pedal clevis pin (A), securing clip (B) pedal pivot bolt (C)

7 Once the pedal height is correct, check the free play as described below.

Pedal free play and pushrod play

8 The pedal free play and pushrod play must now be checked. Depress the pedal with the fingers until the beginnings of resistance can be felt, then measure the distance through which the pedal travels from the fully-released position to the point where the resistance starts; this gives the pedal free play. Measure the distance from the point at which the resistance begins to where it increases significantly (using light finger pressure); this gives the pushrod play. Compare the measurements obtained with those specified. If adjustment is required, slacken the clevis locknut and turn the pushrod until the settings

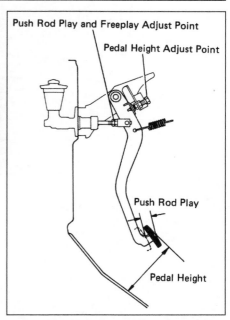

Fig. 6.5 Clutch pedal adjustment (Sec 7)

are correct; recheck the pedal height on completion and repeat the procedure if necessary. Tighten the clevis locknut.

9 Reconnect the facia lower finish panel components and refit the panel, then reconnect the battery negative terminal.

Notes

Chapter 7 Transmission

Contents

Degrees of difficulty

Easy, suitable for novice with little experience	Fairly easy, suitable for beginner with some experience	Fairly difficult, suitable for competent DIY mechanic	Difficult, suitable for experienced DIY mechanic	Very difficult, suitable for expert DIY or professional

Specifications

Part A: Manual gearbox

Type . . . . Five forward speeds and reverse, synchromesh on all forward gears, final drive integral with gearbox

Identification

1.3 models . . . . C 150
1.6 models . . . . C 52

Gear ratios

	1.3 models	1.6 models
1st	3.545 : 1	3.166 : 1
2nd	1.904 : 1	1.904 : 1
3rd	1.310 : 1	1.310 : 1
4th	0.969 : 1	0.969 : 1
5th	0.815 : 10	0.815 : 1
Reverse	3.250 : 1	3.250 : 1
Final drive:		
GTi 16 model	4.312 : 1	
All other models	4.058 : 1	

Part B: Automatic transmission

Type . . . . Torque converter, three forward speeds and reverse, final drive integral with transmission

Identification

1.3 models . . . . A 131 L
1.6 models . . . . A 132 L

Gear ratios

1st . . . . 2.810 : 1
2nd . . . . 1.549 : 1
3rd . . . . 1.000 : 1
Reverse . . . . 2.296 : 1
Final drive:
   1.3 models . . . . 3.526 : 1
   1.6 models . . . . 3.722 : 1

Part C: All models

Torque wrench settings	Nm	lbf ft
Manual gearbox only		
Oil filler and drain plugs	39	39
Shift and select lever shaft cover retaining bolts	20	15
Shift and select lever shaft assembly lock bolt	29	22
Bearing retainer securing bolts – 1.6 models	11	8
Selecting bellcrank-to-gearbox – 1.3 models	25	18
Automatic transmission only		
Neutral start switch bolts	5.4	4
Fluid cooler pipe union nut	34	25
Bellhousing cover plate	23	17
Torque converter-to-driveplate	27	20
Sump drain plug	49	36
All models		
Speedometer driven gear retaining plate bolt	11	8
Engine-to-gearbox/transmission bolts:		
10 mm	46	34
12 mm	64	47
Engine/transmission mountings-to-engine/transmission mounting crossmember	61	45
Engine/transmission mounting crossmember-to-body	61	45

Part A: Manual gearbox

1 General information

The gearbox is mounted transversely on the engine's left-hand end and incorporates the final drive/differential; both gearbox and final drive use the same oil supply.

Engine torque is transmitted via the clutch to the gearbox input shaft and from the input shaft to the output shaft according to the gear selected. Drive passes from the gear on the end of the output shaft to the final drive/differential crownwheel; the differential transmits the drive to the roadwheels via the driveshafts.

Gear selection is made via a floor-mounted lever mechanism, which acts through control cables.

2 Gearchange control cables – removal and refitting

Removal

1 Disconnect the battery negative terminal.
2 Remove the clips and washers and the cable-to-abutment bracket retainers, then disconnect the control cables at the gearbox end (photo).
3 Remove the centre console (Chapter 11).
4 Disconnect the select control cable (on the side of the gearchange lever mechanism) by removing its clip and washer, then removing its abutment bracket retainer (photo).
5 Unbolt the gearchange lever mechanism and disconnect the shift control cable by releasing its clip to allow the cable end to be separated from the base of the gearchange

lever, then removing its abutment bracket retainer (photo).
6 On some models the bulkhead grommet plate will be secured by bolts accessible from underneath the vehicle, while on others the centre stack trim must be removed (Chapter 11, Section 29) and a cranked screwdriver will be required to remove the plate securing

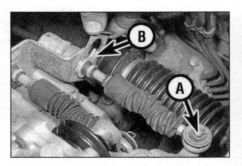

2.2 Remove clip (A) and washer, then retainer (B) to disconnect gearchange (select) control cable at gearbox

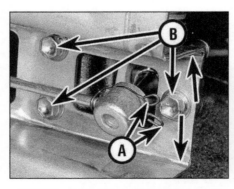

2.5 Spread ears (A) of shift control cable securing clip as shown to release cable – note gearchange lever retainer bolts (B)

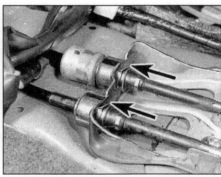

2.4 Gearchange control cable-to-lever mechanism abutment bracket retainers (arrowed)

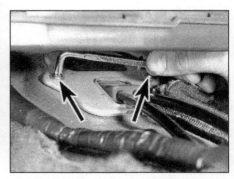

2.6 Unscrewing bulkhead grommet plate screws (arrowed)

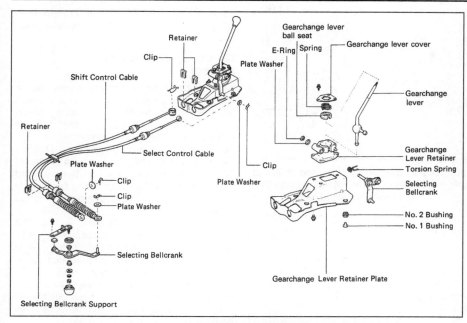

Fig. 7.1 Gearchange lever mechanism and control cables (Sec 3)

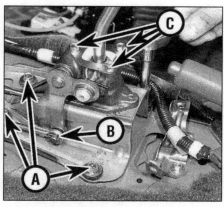

3.4 Gearchange lever mechanism-to-floor bolts (A), select control cable (B), gearchange lever cover bolts (C)

screws under the heater casing (photo). Undo the bolts or screws and withdraw the plate, grommet and control cables.

Refitting

7 Refitting is the reverse of the removal procedure; ensure that the shift control cable securing clip locates correctly in its cable end slot.

3 Gearchange lever mechanism – removal, overhaul and refitting

Removal

1 Disconnect the battery negative terminal.
2 Remove the centre console (Chapter 11).
3 Disconnect the gearchange control cables from the mechanism (Section 2, paragraphs 4 and 5).
4 Unbolt the mechanism from the floor and remove it, noting the insulator washers fitted (photo).

Overhaul

5 Before dismantling the mechanism, ensure that the lever vertical play does not exceed 0.15 mm; if the play is excessive, the ball seat must be renewed. Dismantle the mechanism, check all components for wear or damage and renew if necessary.
6 On reassembly, ensure that the gearchange lever retainer and cover bolts are securely tightened, then check that the lever vertical play is within limits.

Refitting

7 Refitting is the reverse of the removal procedure, noting the following points.

(a) Ensure that the insulator washers are correctly refitted to the mounting bolts and that the bolts are securely tightened.
(b) Ensure that the shift control cable securing clip locates correctly in its cable end slot.

4 Speedometer driven gear – removal and refitting

Removal

1 Disconnect the battery negative terminal and, where applicable, remove the air filter housing/trunking for access (Chapter 4).
2 Disconnect the speedometer drive cable from the transmission (Chapter 12).
3 Unbolt and remove the speedometer driven gear retaining plate.
4 Using a suitable flat-bladed screwdriver, prise the speedometer driven gear assembly out of the transmission.

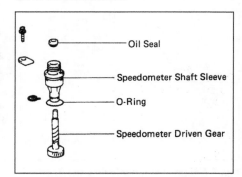

Fig. 7.2 Speedometer driven gear components (Sec 4)

5 Remove the securing clip, then dismantle the assembly, noting the sealing O-ring.

Refitting

6 Refitting is the reverse of the removal procedure, noting the following points.
(a) Renew the oil seal if it is worn or damaged (Section 5).
(b) Renew, as a matter of course, the sealing O-ring and securing clip.
(c) Ensure that the gear teeth mesh correctly as the driven gear is refitted.
(d) Tighten the retaining plate bolt to the specified torque wrench setting.

5 Oil seals – renewal

Driveshaft oil seals

1 Remove the driveshaft. On GTi 16 models, also remove the differential sideshaft (Chapter 8).
2 Prise out the seal, taking care not to scratch the seal housing.
3 Dip the new seal in clean gearbox oil or transmission fluid (as appropriate) and press it as far as possible, by hand only, into its housing. Then use, as a drift, the appropriate special service tool, if available, or a section of suitably-sized tube to carefully tap the seal fully into place. Do not allow the seal to tilt as it is being installed and take great care to avoid damaging the seal lip.
4 Refit the (sideshaft and) driveshaft (Chapter 8).

Input shaft oil seal
1.3 models

5 Seal renewal requires the gearbox to be dismantled, which is beyond most D.I.Y. mechanics (see Section 8). For those with experience, the procedure is as follows.
6 Prise the seal out of the casing from the reverse side, taking care not to scratch the seal housing.

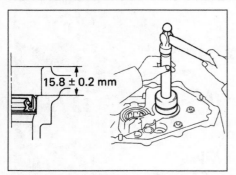

Fig. 7.3 Input shaft oil seal renewal – 1.3 models (Sec 5)

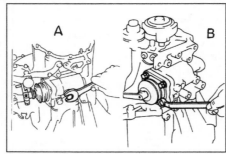

Fig. 7.4 Remove lock bolt (A) and shift and select lever shaft cover retaining bolts (B) – 1.6 models shown (Sec 5)

13 Refit the clutch release components (Chapter 6), then refit the gearbox (Section 7).

Gearchange selector oil seal

14 Note that a new E-ring and circlip may be required on reassembling the shift and select lever shaft components, suitable thread sealant and a new cover gasket will be required on refitting the assembly.

15 Remove the gearbox (Section 7), then remove (as applicable) the selecting bellcrank.

16 Remove the lock bolt and the shift and select lever shaft cover retaining bolts, then withdraw the shift and select lever shaft assembly.

17 Dismantle the assembly, noting the orientation and order of components as they are removed. Drive out the spring pins using a suitable punch; a pair of screwdrivers may be used to remove the E-ring and circlip.

18 With the shift and select lever shaft cover separated from the shaft, prise out the oil seal; take care not to scratch the seal housing.

19 Support the cover and drive in a new oil seal using a suitably-sized section of tubing as a drift; ensure that the seal does not twist as it is installed and ensure that it fully locates.

20 Refitting is the reverse of the removal procedure, noting the following points.

(a) Apply a smear of multi-purpose grease to the shaft before reassembling.

(b) Ensure the gaiter drain/bleed points downwards.

(c) Align and install the shift inner levers and the interlock plate as shown in Fig. 7.7.

(d) Apply suitable thread sealant to the cover retaining bolts.

(e) Fit a new gasket, install the shaft assembly and tighten the cover retaining bolts to their specified torque.

(f) Install the selecting bellcrank (as applicable) and the lock bolt tightening the lock bolt to its specified torque wrench setting.

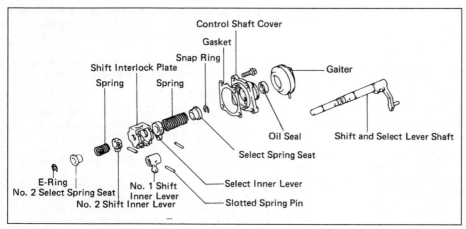

Fig. 7.5 Shift and select lever shaft components (Sec 5)

7 Dip the new seal in clean gearbox oil and use a suitably-sized section of tubing as a drift to drive it squarely into position, to a depth of 15.6 to 16.0 mm (Fig. 7.3). Do not allow the seal to tilt as it is installed.

8 Reassemble and refit the gearbox.

1.6 models

9 Remove the gearbox (Section 7) and dismantle the clutch release bearing and arm (Chapter 6).

10 Unbolt the bearing retainer, then prise out the seal taking care not to scratch the seal

housing. Wipe the seal housing clean using a lint-free cloth.

11 Wrap insulating tape around the input shaft splines to protect the lips of the new seal as it is installed. Dip the new seal in clean gearbox oil and use a suitably-sized section of tubing as a drift to drive it squarely into position, ensuring that it fully locates. Do not allow the seal to tilt as it is installed.

12 Remove the tape from the shaft splines, then refit the bearing retainer; tighten the retainer securing bolts to their specified torque wrench setting.

Speedometer driven gear oil seal

21 Remove the speedometer driven gear (Section 4).

22 Prise out the seal taking care not to scratch the seal housing.

23 Apply a light smear of multi-purpose grease to the lip of the new seal, then drive it fully and squarely into position using a suitable tool to a depth of 25 mm.

24 Reassemble and refit the speedometer driven gear (Section 4).

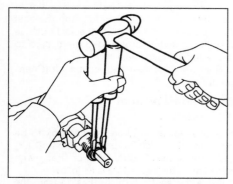

Fig. 7.6 Removing shift and select lever shaft E-ring (Sec 5)

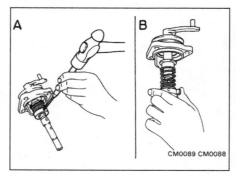

Fig. 7.7 Align shift inner levers and interlock plate as shown (A) . Use a punch to drive spring pins into position (B) (Sec 5)

6 Reversing lamp switch – removal and refitting

Refer to Chapter 12, Section 12.

7 Manual gearbox –
removal and refitting

Note: *The method of removal is to raise the front of the vehicle and to support it (securely) high enough that the gearbox can be unbolted from the engine lowered to the ground and removed from underneath. To do this, an engine hoist or similar will be required to lower the gearbox and a second, similar, piece of equipment (such as an engine support bar) must be available to take the weight of the engine as it is raised or lowered; a strong trolley jack could be used in either case provided that a wooden spacer is available to spread the load and prevent the risk of damage to the sump/gearbox casing. These should be obtainable from a local tool-hire shop. Also a pair of suitable axle stands will be required and an engine dolly (a wheeled platform) would be very useful to save strain and prevent the risk of damage when moving the gearbox out of the vehicle.*

Removal

1 Remove the bonnet (Chapter 11).
2 Disconnect the battery negative terminal.
3 On GTi 16 models, remove the air filter housing and trunking (Chapter 4).
4 Disconnect the speedometer drive cable and the reversing lamp switch multi-plug (Chapter 12).
5 Disconnect the gearchange control cables from the gearbox Section 2).
6 Disconnecting the hydraulic pipe/hose only if necessary, unbolt the clutch slave cylinder and hydraulic pipe/hose support bracket (Chapter 6), then move them clear of the working area; take care not to bend, twist or kink the pipe or hose (photo).
7 Slacken the front roadwheel nuts. Raise the front of the vehicle (see note above) and support it securely on axle stands, then remove the roadwheels.
8 Working as described in Chapter 8, Section 2, disconnect the driveshafts from the gearbox and suspend them out of the way using lengths of strong wire; note that (unless they are to be removed anyway) the

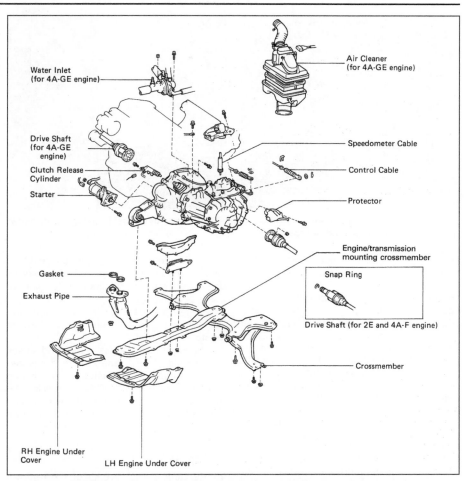

Fig. 7.8 Components to be removed or disconnected on removing manual gearbox (Sec 7)

driveshafts need not be disconnected from the hub carriers, therefore the instructions can be ignored in paragraphs 6, 7, 10, 11 and 13 of the procedure in Chapter 8.
9 Remove the starter motor (Chapter 12).
10 Drain the coolant (Chapter 1).
11 Disconnecting the coolant hoses and unbolting, releasing or disconnecting any support brackets and wiring as necessary, remove the thermostat cover/water inlet, noting the gasket (Chapter 3).

12 Disconnect the exhaust downpipe from the manifold, or remove the downpipe if required (Chapter 4). Disconnect the exhaust main section forward mounting from the engine/gearbox mounting crossmember; support the exhaust system to prevent it from being damaged or strained (photo).
13 Disconnect all earth leads, wiring and wiring/pipework support brackets from the gearbox, having labelled them to aid refitting (photo).

7.6 Unbolting clutch hydraulic pipe support bracket from gearbox – note reversing lamp switch (arrowed) . . .

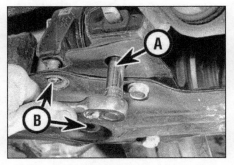

7.12 . . . unbolting exhaust main section forward mounting (A) – note rearmost engine/transmission mounting nuts (B) . . .

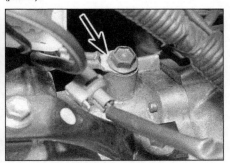

7.13 . . . earth connection (arrowed) on left-hand side of gearbox . . .

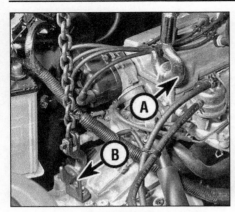

7.16 . . . supporting weight of engine/
gearbox at engine (A) and gearbox (B) . . .

7.20 . . . removing bellhousing cover plate
securing bolt . . .

7.23 . . . lowering gearbox from vehicle –
1.6 GL Liftback model shown

14 Where fitted, disconnect the anti-roll bar from the front suspension lower arms (Chapter 10).

15 Attach the lifting equipment (see note above) to the lifting eye on the engine's gearbox end, then take the weight of the engine and gearbox.

16 Unbolt the engine/gearbox left-hand mounting (Chapter 2) and bolt a lifting hook to the gearbox as shown (photo). Attach the lifting equipment to the hook, then take the weight of the engine and gearbox.

17 Working beneath the vehicle, remove both front suspension lower arm rear mounting brackets and move the anti-roll bar, where fitted, towards the rear of the vehicle or remove it (Chapter 10).

18 Undo their securing nuts to disconnect the engine/transmission mountings from the suspension and engine/transmission mounting crossmembers; remove completely the centre mounting (Chapter 2).

19 With the aid of an assistant, unbolt and remove the suspension and engine/transmission crossmember assembly.

20 Remove the bolt(s) securing the bellhousing cover plate to the gearbox (photo).

21 Make a final check that all wires, hoses, pipes, etc, have been removed or disconnected which might impede removal.

22 Unbolt the gearbox from the engine and gently prise the gearbox off the locating dowels. Move the gearbox squarely away from the engine, ensuring that the clutch components are not damaged; do not allow the gearbox input shaft to bear any weight and remove the bellhousing cover plate when possible. Lower the engine slightly (in unison

with the gearbox) to allow separation, but take care to avoid crushing, straining or otherwise damaging adjacent components, wiring, hoses or pipes.

23 Lower the gearbox to the floor and withdraw it from under the vehicle (photo).

24 Whenever the gearbox is removed, check the mountings and renew them if necessary (Chapter 2). Overhaul the clutch components (Chapter 6); if the gearbox is to be overhauled or renewed, unbolt any mounting brackets and remove the clutch release mechanism and speedometer drive assembly.

Refitting

25 Refitting is the reverse of the removal procedure, noting the following points.

(a) Ensure that any engine adaptor plates removed are refitted.

(b) If the clutch was disturbed centralise the driven plate before offering the gearbox to the engine (Chapter 6).

(c) Do NOT draw the gearbox onto the engine using the bolts.

(d) Fit new split pins gaskets snap rings, etc, as required.

(e) Tighten to their specified torque wrench settings the roadwheel nuts the front suspension lower arm rear mounting bracket fasteners and the anti-roll bar (if fitted) fasteners with the weight of the vehicle resting on its roadwheels.

(f) If it was disconnected refill and bleed the clutch hydraulic system (Chapter 6).

(g) Refill the gearbox and cooling system (Chapter 1).

8 Manual gearbox overhaul – general information

1 Overhauling a manual gearbox is a difficult and involved job for the DIY home mechanic. In addition to dismantling and reassembling many small parts, clearances must be precisely measured and, if necessary, changed by selecting shims and spacers. Gearbox internal components are also often difficult to obtain and in many instances, extremely expensive. Because of this, if the gearbox develops a fault or becomes noisy, the best course of action is to have the unit overhauled by a specialist repairer or to obtain an exchange reconditioned unit.

2 Nevertheless, it is not impossible for the more experienced mechanic to overhaul a gearbox if the special tools are available and the job is done in a deliberate step-by-step manner so that nothing is overlooked.

3 The tools necessary for an overhaul include internal and external circlip pliers, bearing pullers, a slide hammer, a set of pin punches, a dial test indicator and possibly a hydraulic press. In addition, a large, sturdy workbench and a vice will be required.

4 During dismantling of the gearbox, make careful notes of how each component is fitted to make reassembly easier and accurate.

5 Before dismantling the gearbox, it will help if you have some idea of what area is malfunctioning. Certain problems can be closely related to specific areas in the gearbox which can make component examination and replacement easier. Refer to the Fault finding Section at the beginning of this Manual for more information.

Part B: Automatic transmission

9 General information

Note: *Due to the complexity of the transmission and the need for special tools and gauges it is recommended that any DIY work is restricted to the operations covered in the following Sections. Any internal fault diagnosis or major overhaul work should be entrusted to your Toyota dealer.*

The transmission is mounted transversely on the engine's left-hand end and incorporates a torque converter (mounted between the engine and transmission) and the final drive/differential. The final drive/differential lubricant is separate from the transmission fluid.

Three manually-selectable forward speeds and reverse gear are provided. A 'lock-up' on top gear improves fuel economy when cruising by transmitting drive mechanically (when operating conditions are suitable), thus eliminating hydraulic slip within the torque converter. The different ratios are selected automatically, by means of epicyclic gearsets controlled hydraulically by internal brake and clutch mechanisms; hydraulic pressure being generated by an internal pump.

10 Kickdown cable – removal, refitting and adjustment

Removal

1 Where necessary, disconnect and remove the air filter housing/trunking (Chapter 4).
2 Slacken the cable adjusting nuts and disconnect the cable inner wire from the carburettor throttle linkage.
3 Disconnect the cable from the transmission and withdraw it.

Refitting

4 Refitting is the reverse of the removal procedure; adjust the cable as described below.

Adjustment

5 Remove the air filter housing/trunking (Chapter 4).

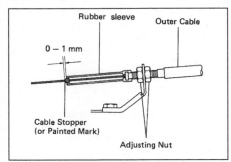

Fig. 7.10 Kickdown cable adjustment (Sec 10)

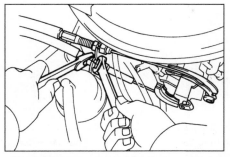

Fig. 7.9 Disconnecting kickdown cable at carburettor throttle linkage (Sec 10)

6 Check the accelerator cable adjustment is correct (Chapter 4).
7 Holding the accelerator pedal fully depressed, slacken the cable adjusting nuts (Fig. 7.10) and adjust them so that the cable stopper (or painted mark) projects between 0 and 1.0 mm from the end of the rubber sleeve, then tighten the adjusting nuts.
8 Re-check the adjustment and refit the air filter housing/trunking.

11 Selector cable – removal, refitting and adjustment

Removal

1 Raise the front of the vehicle and support it securely on axle stands.
2 Unscrew its securing nut and disconnect the cable from the transmission control shaft lever. Working backwards along the cable until it enters the passenger compartment, release it from its securing clips.
3 Lower the vehicle to the ground.
4 Remove the centre console (Chapter 11).
5 Remove its spring clip to disconnect the cable from the selector lower end, then remove the securing clip.
6 On some models the bulkhead grommet plate will be secured by bolts accessible from underneath the vehicle, while on others the centre stack trim must be removed (Chapter 11, Section 29) and a cranked screwdriver will be required to remove the plate securing

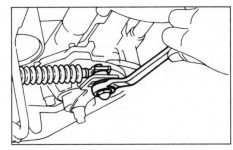

Fig. 7.11 Undoing nut securing selector cable to transmission control shaft lever (Sec 11)

screws under the heater casing. Undo the bolts or screws and withdraw the plate, grommet and cable.

Refitting

7 Refitting is the reverse of the removal procedure; adjust the cable as described below.

Adjustment

8 Raise the front of the vehicle and support it securely on axle stands.
9 Slacken (or unscrew if necessary) the nut securing the selector cable to the transmission control shaft lever, then push the lever fully towards the right-hand side of the vehicle and pull it back two notches to the 'Neutral' position.
10 Set the selector to position 'N'.
11 Apply light pressure, in the direction of 'Reverse' position, to the transmission control shaft lever whilst tightening the cable-to-lever securing nut.
12 Lower the vehicle to the ground.
13 Check that all transmission positions can be selected and re-adjust if necessary.

12 Selector – removal and refitting

Removal

1 Remove the centre console (Chapter 11).
2 Disconnect the selector cable from the selector lower end (Section 11) and disconnect the selector illumination wiring where necessary.

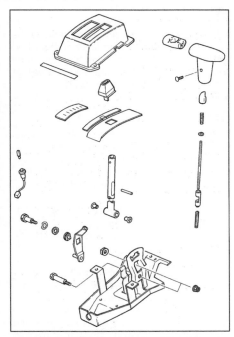

Fig. 7.12 Gear selector (Sec 12)

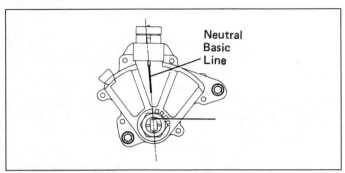

Fig. 7.13 Setting neutral start switch (Sec 13)

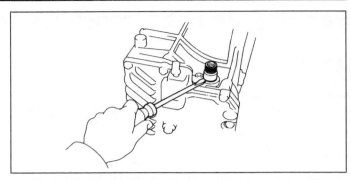

Fig. 7.14 Prising out speedometer driven gear – automatic transmission (Sec 14)

3 Unbolt and withdraw the selector, noting the insulator bushes fitted, if applicable.

Refitting

4 Refitting is the reverse of the removal procedure, noting the following points.
(a) *Ensure that the selector bolts are securely tightened.*
(b) *Ensure that the selector cable is correctly located and that the wiring is secured clear of the selector components.*
(c) *Adjust the selector cable (Section 11).*

13 Neutral start switch – removal, refitting and setting

Removal

1 Disconnect the battery negative terminal.
2 Raise the front of the vehicle and support it securely on axle stands.
3 Disconnect the selector cable from the transmission (Section 11).
4 Disconnect the switch wiring.
5 Unscrew the retaining nut and remove the transmission control shaft lever and washer. Flatten back the lockwasher tabs, then unscrew and remove the nut and lockwasher behind the lever; note any seals fitted.
6 Unbolt and remove the switch.

Refitting

7 Refitting is the reverse of the removal procedure, noting the following points.
(a) *Set the switch as described below.*
(b) *Before refitting the lever, securely tighten the nut behind it and secure it with the lockwasher tabs.*
(c) *Tighten the switch bolts to their specified torque wrench setting.*
(d) *Adjust the selector cable (Section 11).*

Setting

8 If the engine will start with the selector indicating any position other than 'N' or 'P', the neutral start switch must be reset.
9 To set the switch, set the selector to position 'N', raise the front of the vehicle and support securely on axle stands, then slacken the switch bolts.

10 Align the groove and the neutral basic line, as shown in Fig. 7.13, then hold the switch whilst tightening the bolts to their specified torque wrench setting.
11 Lower the vehicle to the ground and recheck the switch setting: repeat if necessary.

14 Speedometer driven gear – removal and refitting

Refer to Section 4 and Fig. 7.14.

15 Oil seals – renewal

Driveshaft oil seals

1 Refer to Section 5.

Input shaft (torque converter) oil seal

2 Remove the transmission (Section 17), and withdraw the torque converter.
3 Examine the torque converter boss for signs of burrs, scratches or other damage which may have caused the seal to fail; if such damage is present, it may be possible to rectify faults of this nature by light polishing with fine abrasive paper but, if this is not successful, the torque converter must be renewed.
4 Prise out the seal, taking care not to scratch the seal housing. Wipe the seal housing clean using a lint-free cloth.
5 Apply a smear of multi-purpose grease to the new seal lip and wrap insulating tape around the shaft splines to protect the seal as it is installed. Using a suitably-sized section of tubing as a drift, drive the seal squarely into position; ensure that it does not twist and ensure that it fully locates.
6 Remove the tape from the shaft splines and refit the torque converter.
7 Refit the transmission (Section 17).

Speedometer driven gear oil seal

8 Refer to Section 5; note that on refitting the seal should be installed to a depth of 19 mm.

16 Fluid cooler – general information

1 A transmission fluid cooler is incorporated into the radiator lower tank. It is an integral part of the radiator and cannot be renewed or repaired separately; see Chapter 3 for details of radiator removal, repair and refitting.
2 If the transmission fluid and/or coolant become emulsified, indicating contamination, usually – but not necessarily – accompanied by the need for more frequent topping-up of one and a rise in level of the other, or if a fluid cooler leak is suspected for any other reason, consult your Toyota dealer or other competent specialist for an accurate diagnosis as soon as possible. If either the engine or the transmission is allowed to overheat repeatedly due to a faulty radiator/cooler, the consequences could prove extremely expensive. Note, however, that emulsified coolant could also be due to contamination by engine oil: this usually caused by a leaking cylinder head gasket or a cracked cylinder head or block.

17 Automatic transmission – removal and refitting

Removal

1 Work as described in Section 7, but ignore all non-applicable references and note the following changes.
2 Disconnect the selector cable from the transmission (Section 11).
3 Disconnect the neutral start switch wiring (Section 13).
4 Disconnect the fluid cooler pipes; plug the ends of the pipes and unions to minimise fluid loss and prevent the entry of dirt.
5 Drain the final drive/differential fluid and transmission fluid (Chapter 1).
6 Disconnect the kickdown cable at its throttle linkage (Section 10).
7 It may be necessary to remove the centre and the rearmost engine/transmission mountings.

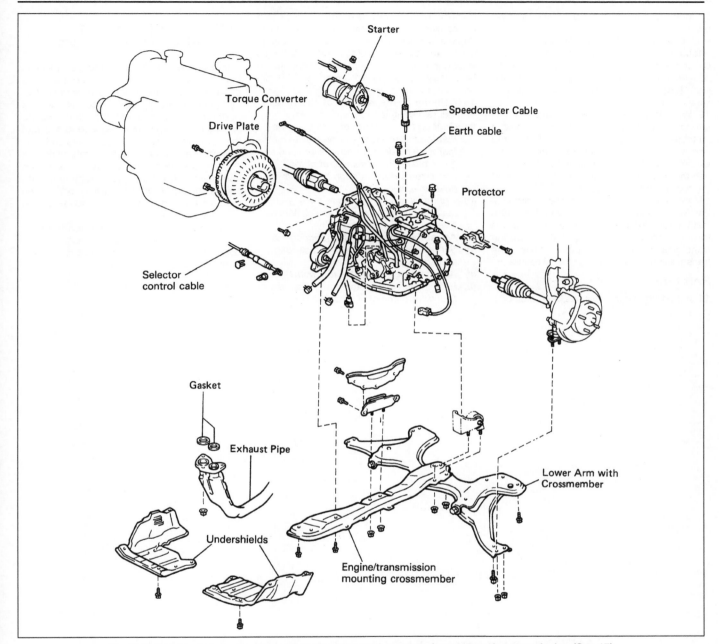

Fig. 7.15 Components to be removed or disconnected on removing automatic transmission (Sec 17)

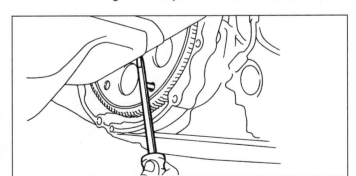

Fig. 7.16 Levering transmission assay from engine (Sec 17)

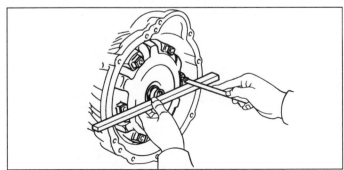

Fig. 7.17 Checking torque converter installed depth (Sec 17)

8 Unbolt and remove the bellhousing cover plate.

9 Use white paint or similar to mark the relationship of the torque converter to the driveplate, then turn the engine (by means of a spanner on the crankshaft pulley bolt) to bring each torque converter-to-driveplate bolt into view for unscrewing.

10 With the bolts removed, make up a temporary guide pin by cutting the head off a suitable bolt, then screw this guide pin into one of the torque converter bolt holes. Unscrew the engine/transmission bolts and use the guide pin as a fulcrum to lever apart the engine and transmission.

11 As soon as possible bolt a short section of bar (which has been bent to give it a slight 'set') across the bellhousing face to keep the torque converter in position during transmission removal (and while the transmission is out of the vehicle, if required).

Refitting

12 If the torque converter has been drained it must be refilled with fresh fluid. Check that the converter is fully installed by measuring its depth in the bellhousing; place a straight edge across the bellhousing face and measure as shown in Fig. 7.17. The measurement should be at least 13.5 mm on 1.3 models, 23.0 mm on 1.6 models.

13 Refitting is the reverse of the removal procedure, noting the following points.

(a) Offer up the transmission to the engine so that the torque converter/driveplate marks that were made on removal align, and the guide pin (at the lowest point of the converter) passes through its original driveplate hole.

(b) Tighten all nuts and bolts to their specified torque wrench settings (where given).

(c) Adjust the kickdown cable (Section 10).

(d) Set the neutral start switch if disturbed (Section 73).

(e) Adjust the selector cable (Section 11).

(f) Refill the cooling system transmission and final drive/differential (Chapter 1).

18 Automatic transmission overhaul – general information

1 In the event of an automatic transmission fault occurring, it is first necessary to determine whether it is of a mechanical or hydraulic nature; to accurately diagnose a problem within an automatic transmission, special test equipment is required, along with the ability to assess the results obtained. It is therefore essential to entrust this task to a Toyota dealer or other automatic transmission specialist who has the equipment and knowledge quickly and accurately to diagnose the problem and who can then advise on the best course of action.

2 Do not remove the transmission from the vehicle before professional fault diagnosis has been carried out, since most tests require the transmission to be in the vehicle.

Chapter 8 Driveshafts

Contents

Degrees of difficulty

Easy, suitable for novice with little experience	Fairly easy, suitable for beginner with some experience	Fairly difficult, suitable for competent DIY mechanic	Difficult, suitable for experienced DIY mechanic	Very difficult, suitable for expert DIY or professional

Specifications

Type . . . . Unequal-length, constant velocity joint at each end. Dynamic damper on (longer) right-hand driveshaft

Lubrication
CV joint gaiter renewal – see text
Lubricant type/specification . . . . Use only special grease supplied in sachets with gaiter kits – joints are otherwise pre-packed with grease and sealed

Quantity:
Outer joint . . . . 120 to 130 g
Inner joint:
    GTi 16 model . . . . 212 to 222 g
    All other models . . . . 180 to 190 g

Driveshaft standard length
GTi 16 model:
    Left-hand . . . . 424.0 ± 5.0 mm
    Right-hand . . . . 704.0 ± 5.0 mm
All other models:
    Left-hand . . . . 528.0 ± 5.0 mm
    Right-hand . . . . 843.0 ± 5.0 mm

Torque wrench settings	Nm	lbf ft
Driveshaft retaining nut	186	137
Main driveshaft section to differential sideshaft nuts – GTi 16	36	27
Left-hand driveshaft inner CV joint protector:		
Manual gearbox	13	10
Automatic transmission	18	13

1 General information

The driveshafts are of unequal length, with a constant velocity (CV) joint at either end. The solid right-hand (longer) driveshaft incorporates a dynamic vibration damper.

The inner CV joints are of the sliding tripod type, to allow for differences in driveshaft effective length at extremes of suspension travel, whilst the outer CV joints are of the Birfield ball-and-cage type.

On all models except the GTi 16 the inner CV joints take drive directly from the differential; on GTi 16 models the inner CV joints are secured by nuts and studs to differential sideshafts.

2 Driveshafts – removal and refitting

Note: *Do not subject the hub bearing to the full weight of the vehicle, such as when moving the vehicle with a driveshaft removed, or hub bearing damage may occur. A new snap ring must be fitted to each driveshaft during refitting.*

Removal
1 Slacken the relevant roadwheel nuts with the vehicle resting on its wheels.
2 Raise the front of the vehicle and support it securely on axle stands.
3 Remove the relevant roadwheel.
4 Remove the engine undershields.
5 Drain the gearbox oil/transmission fluid (Chapter 1).
6 Extract the split pin, then remove the driveshaft nut cap (photo).
7 Unscrew the driveshaft retaining nut (photo). This will be particularly tight, so have an assistant depress the brake pedal to prevent the driveshaft from rotating. Note the

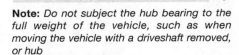

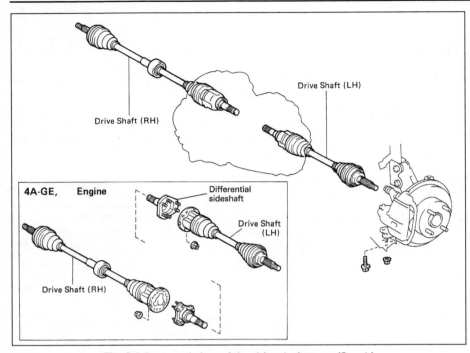

Fig. 8.1 A general view of the driveshaft types (Sec 1)

Fig. 8.2 Driving right-hand (longer) driveshaft from automatic or manual transmission – except GTi 16 (Sec 2)

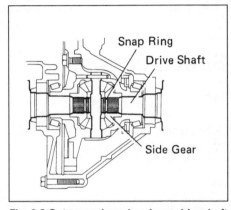

Fig. 8.3 Cutaway view showing a driveshaft inner CV joint/differential sideshaft correctly located, with its end contacting the pinion shaft (Sec 2)

washer fitment. If the effort required to slacken the nut threatens the stability of the vehicle on the axle stands, refit the roadwheel and lower the vehicle to the ground to safely slacken the nut; prise out the roadwheel centre-cap to reach the nut.

8 Separate the track rod end from the hub carrier steering arm (Chapter 10).

9 On GTi 16 models, have an assistant depress the brake pedal while you slacken the six nuts securing the main driveshaft section to the differential sideshaft; where fitted, unbolt the driveshaft inner CV joint shield.

10 On all models, remove the brake caliper complete with torque plate and suspend it clear of the working area (Chapter 9).

11 Make alignment marks on the hub and brake disc, then remove the disc (Chapter 9).

12 Undo the two nuts and the single bolt securing the suspension arm to the balljoint, then separate the two (Chapter 10).

13 Drive the driveshaft out of the hub, using a soft-faced hammer; cover the driveshaft CV joint gaiter with a thick cloth to reduce the risk of damage.

14 On GTi 16 models, remove the six nuts securing the main driveshaft section to the differential sideshaft and withdraw the driveshaft.

15 On all other models, unbolt (if fitted) the driveshaft inner CV joint shield, then prise or drive out the driveshaft before removing it (photo). If levering, use the handle of a hammer placed to gain extra leverage. In all cases, take care to avoid damaging adjacent components.

Refitting

16 Before refitting, check the driveshaft oil seal and renew it if it is worn or damaged (Chapter 7).

17 On all models except the GTi 16, a new snap ring must be fitted to the groove of the driveshaft inner CV joint splined shaft. With the seal lip greased and the snap ring opening facing downwards, insert the driveshaft inner CV joint into the transmission and drive it in using a hammer and a soft metal drift until it contacts the pinion shaft; take care to avoid damaging adjacent components. Refit the inner CV joint shield, as applicable. Fit the outer CV joint to the hub. Check that there is 2 to 3 mm of axial play at the inner CV joint and

2.6 Driveshaft nut cap and split pin arrangement

2.7 Removing driveshaft retaining nut and washer

2.15 Removing left-hand driveshaft inner CV joint shield

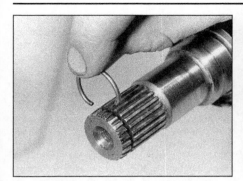

2.17A Fit a new snap ring to the groove on inner CV joint splined shaft

2.17B Installing outer CV joint to hub

2.23 Driveshaft retaining nut can be tightened after removing roadwheel centre-cap

attempt to pull the joint out by hand to check that it is securely fitted (photos).

18 On GTi 16 models, install the outer CV joint to the hub, then align the differential sideshaft dowels and studs with their holes on the main driveshaft section. Tighten the six securing nuts finger-tight only at this stage.

19 Reconnect the balljoint to the suspension arm, tightening the nuts and bolt to the specified torque wrench setting (Chapter 10).

20 Reconnect the track rod end to the hub carrier steering arm (Chapter 10).

21 Refit the brake disc to the hub, aligning the marks made on removal (Chapter 9).

22 Refit the brake caliper assembly (Chapter 9).

23 Refit the driveshaft retaining nut and washer and tighten to the specified torque wrench setting. Have an assistant depress the brake pedal to prevent the driveshaft from rotating during tightening, then refit the hub driveshaft nut cap and secure using a new split pin. If the effort required to tighten correctly the nut threatens the stability of the vehicle on the axle stands, refit the roadwheel and lower the vehicle to the ground to fully tighten the nut: prise out the roadwheel centre-cap to reach the nut. Note that the roadwheel will have to be removed again after the nut has been tightened to enable the nut cap and split pin to be fitted (photo).

24 On GTi 16 models, again engage an assistant to depress the brake pedal whilst

the six nuts securing the driveshaft main section to the differential sideshaft are tightened to their specified torque. Refit the inner CV joint shield.

25 Refill the gearbox/transmission with fresh fluid or oil of the specified type (Chapter 1).

26 Refit the engine undershields.

27 Refit the roadwheel, remove the axle stands, then lower the vehicle to the ground. Tighten the roadwheel nuts to the specified torque. Refit the centre-cap if applicable.

28 Check the front roadwheel alignment (Chapter 10).

3 Differential sideshaft (GTi 16) – removal and refitting

Note: *A new snap ring must be fitted to each differential sideshaft during refitting.*

Removal

1 Remove the relevant driveshaft (Section 2).

2 Push the differential sideshaft inwards towards the differential, then measure and note the distance between the transmission casing and the sideshaft itself. This dimension will be required when refitting.

3 Using a slide hammer, pull out the differential sideshaft until its snap ring releases from the differential and it can be withdrawn. Be careful not to damage adjacent components.

Refitting

4 Before refitting, check the driveshaft oil seal and renew it if it is worn or damaged (Chapter 7).

5 With the seal lip greased and a new snap ring fitted to the groove on the sideshaft splined section, drive the differential sideshaft into position (using the slide hammer as an impact tool – a hammer and a suitable piece of wood may suffice) until it contacts the pinion shaft.

6 Check that there is 2 to 3 mm of axial play, then further check that the differential sideshaft is securely fitted by attempting to pull it out by hand.

7 Push the differential sideshaft inwards towards the differential, then check that the distance between the transmission casing and the sideshaft is as noted on removal.

4 Driveshaft CV joint gaiters – renewal

Note: *Obtain a gaiter repair kit which contains all the required components.*

1 Remove the relevant driveshaft (Section 2).

2 Undo the inner CV joint gaiter clamps, then slide the inner CV joint gaiter towards the outer CV joint (photo). Wipe away the old lubricant.

3 Using quick-drying paint make alignment marks on the inner CV joint tulip and tripod. Do **not** punch the marks on.

Fig. 8.4 Using a slide hammer (A) to remove/install a differential sideshaft – GTi 16 (Sec 3)

Fig. 8.5 Alignment marks on inner CV joint tulip and tripod (Sec 4)

4.2 Sliding inner CV joint gaiter up driveshaft

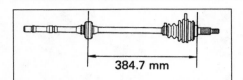

Fig. 8.6 Dynamic vibration damper fitting dimension (Sec 4)

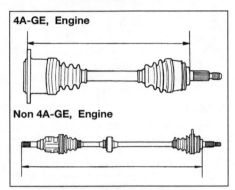

Fig. 8.7 Driveshaft standard length measurement reference points (Sec 4)

4 Remove the inner CV joint tulip from the driveshaft.

5 Extract the tripod circlip (photo).

6 Using a hammer and a suitable punch, make dot alignment marks on the driveshaft and the tripod so as to ensure that their original fitted relationship is maintained during subsequent refitting (photo).

7 Drive the tripod off the end of the driveshaft.

8 Slide the inner CV joint gaiter off the driveshaft.

9 If renewing the outer CV joint gaiter on the right-hand (longer) driveshaft, first use quick-drying paint to mark the position of the dynamic vibration damper, then use a screwdriver to release its clamp before sliding the damper off the driveshaft (photo). Note which way the damper faces for refitting.

10 Use a screwdriver to undo the outer CV joint gaiter clamps, then slide the gaiter off the driveshaft. Do not attempt to dismantle the outer CV joint.

11 Prior to fitting a CV joint gaiter, wrap some insulating tape around the driveshaft splines to prevent damage to the gaiter. Note that the gaiter and large clamp of the outer CV joint are smaller than those of the inner CV joint.

12 Slide the outer CV joint gaiter onto the driveshaft along with its new clamps, the dynamic vibration damper (if applicable) and the inner CV joint gaiter and its new clamps (photo). Do not secure at this stage.

13 Drive the tripod onto the driveshaft so that the chamfered or bevelled side of the splines goes onto the shaft first and the marks made before its removal are in alignment.

14 Fit a new tripod circlip.

15 Pack the outer CV joint using the grease supplied with the gaiter kit, then fit the gaiter and its large clamp. Ensure that the gaiter is seated correctly, then bend the tongue of the clamp back and lock it with the retaining tags.

16 Pack the inner CV joint tulip using the grease supplied with the gaiter kit, then fit the tulip to the driveshaft; align the marks made during dismantling on the tripod and the tulip. Fit the inner CV joint gaiter and its large clamp, securing the clamp as described in the previous paragraph (photos).

17 Refit the dynamic vibration damper, having ensured that it is positioned correctly. Fit and secure its clamp as described in paragraph 15.

18 Ensure that the gaiters are correctly positioned on the shaft grooves, and that they are not stretched or contracted when the driveshaft is at the specified standard length, then fit and secure the gaiter small clamps as described in paragraph 15.

5 Driveshaft overhaul – general information

The only repairs possible are the renewal of the CV joint rubber gaiters and the renewal of the inner CV joint components as a matched set (Section 4). Wear or damage to the outer CV joints or the driveshaft splines can only be rectified by renewing the driveshaft assembly.

4.5 Removing tripod circlip

4.6 Making alignment marks on driveshaft and tripod

4.9 Dynamic vibration damper on right-hand (longer) driveshaft. Note the markings (arrowed) made to ensure correct positioning on refitting

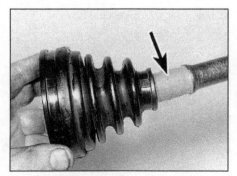

4.12 Sliding new inner CV joint gaiter onto driveshaft. Note tape wrapped around the driveshaft splines (arrowed) to protect gaiter

4.16A Packing inner CV joint tulip with grease

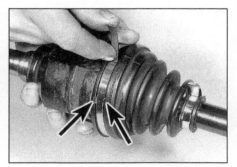

4.16B Fit clamp by bending its tongue back, then secure tongue with retaining tags (arrowed)

Chapter 9 Braking system

Contents

Degrees of difficulty

Easy, suitable for novice with little experience	**Fairly easy,** suitable for beginner with some experience	**Fairly difficult,** suitable for competent DIY mechanic	**Difficult,** suitable for experienced DIY mechanic	**Very difficult,** suitable for expert DIY or professional

Specifications

System type	....	Hydraulically-operated diagonally-split dual circuit, vacuum servo-assisted, discs front, (pressure-regulated) discs or drums at rear. Handbrake cable-operated on rear brakes.

Front brakes

Type	Disc (solid or ventilated), single-piston sliding caliper

Disc thickness:
  Solid:
    New .... 12.0 mm
    Minimum .... 11.0 mm
  Ventilated:
    New .... 18.0 mm
    Minimum .... 16.0 mm
Disc maximum run-out .... 0.15 mm
Brake pad friction material minimum thickness .... 1.0 mm

Rear brakes

Type:
  GTi 16 model .... Disc, single-piston sliding caliper
  All other models .... Self-adjusting single leading shoe drum
Drum rear brakes:
  Drum inside diameter:
    New .... 200.0 mm
    Maximum .... 201.0 mm
  Brake shoe friction material minimum thickness .... 1.0 mm
  Brake shoe-to-brake shoe handbrake lever clearance .... 0 to 0.35 mm
  Brake shoe handbrake lever shim thicknesses .... Various, between 0.2 and 0.9 mm
  Drum-to-shoe clearance .... 0.6 mm
Disc rear brakes:
  Disc thickness:
    New .... 9.0 mm
    Minimum .... 8.0 mm
  Disc maximum run-out .... 0.15 mm
  Brake pad friction material minimum thickness .... 1.0 mm

Brake pedal

Pedal height – from asphalt sheet	135 to 145 mm
Pedal free play	3 to 6 mm
Pedal reserve distance – @ 50 kg pressure:	
Drum rear brakes	At least 55 mm
Disc rear brakes	At least 60 mm

Torque wrench settings

	Nm	lbf ft
Piston stopper bolt to master cylinder	10	7
Vacuum servo unit:		
Master cylinder to servo unit nuts	13	10
Mounting nuts to bulkhead	13	10
Clevis locknut	25	18
Check valve (threaded end to union)	56	42
Brake pedal setting nut	37	27
Front brake caliper:		
To torque plate	25	18
Torque plate to hub carrier	88	65
Flexible hose union bolts	30	22
Hydraulic pipe unions	15	11
Bleed nipples	8.3	6
Wheel cylinder mounting bolts	10	7
Rear brake caliper:		
To torque plate	20	15
Torque plate to hub carrier	47	35
Cable support bracket	47	35
Handbrake lever to body	13	10
Handbrake lever adjuster locknut	5.4	4
Load-sensing proportioning valve:		
To mounting bracket	13	10
Mounting bracket to body	25	18
Adjusting bolt to rear suspension arm	25	18
Roadwheel nuts	103	76

1 General information

The braking system is of dual-circuit diagonally-split design, with each circuit controlling one front wheel and its diagonally-opposite rear wheel.

All models, except Estates, are fitted with a pressure-reducing valve which automatically limits the hydraulic pressure available at the rear wheels to reduce the risk of premature rear wheel lock-up. Estate models are fitted with a load-sensing proportioning valve (LSPV) which performs a similar task, but also takes into account the vehicle loading.

The front brakes employ single-piston sliding calipers, with solid discs fitted to models with 1.3 litre engines and ventilated discs to those with 1.6 litre engines. The rear brakes are self-adjusting drums on all models except the GTi 16, which has solid disc brakes.

All models are fitted with a vacuum-operated servo unit.

The handbrake system is cable-operated and acts on the rear brakes.

2 Front brake pads – renewal

Warning: Disc brake pads must be renewed on both front wheels at the same time – never renew the pads on only one wheel as uneven braking may result. Also, the dust created by wear of the pads may contain asbestos, which is a health hazard. Never blow it out with compressed air and don't inhale any of it. An approved filtering mask should be worn when working on the brakes. DO NOT use petroleum based solvents to clean brake parts. Use brake cleaner or methylated spirit only.

1 The brake pads are fitted with pad wear indicator plates. These emit a squeaking noise when the brake pad friction material wears down to 2.5 mm and they rub against the brake disc.

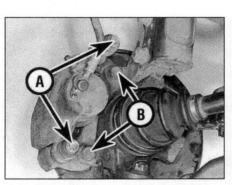

2.4 Caliper-to-torque plate bolts (A), torque plate-to-hub carrier bolts (B)

2.8 Fitting brake pad support plate to caliper torque plate

2 The thickness of the remaining friction material can be checked through inspection holes in the calipers (Chapter 1), but if any doubt exists about the condition of the friction material, the pads should be removed and checked.

3 To inspect or remove the brake pads, raise the front of the vehicle and support securely using axle stands. Remove the first roadwheel, then secure the brake disc in position using the roadwheel nuts.

4 Remove the two bolts securing the brake caliper assembly to its torque plate then lift away the caliper (photo). There is no need to disconnect the brake hose but, to prevent it from straining, suspend the caliper assembly using a length of wire.

5 Withdraw the brake pad retaining springs, the pads, their anti-squeal shims, the pad wear indicator plates and the four pad support plates, having noted their fitment.

6 Wipe away accumulated dust using a damp cloth, taking care not to inhale any of it.

7 Examine the brake pads for friction material (lining) thickness and uneven wear. If the slit in any pad (which indicates that there is 1 mm of friction material remaining) is no longer visible, the friction material has worn excessively and **all** the front brake pads must be renewed. If uneven wear has occurred, **all** four front brake pads again must be renewed, but ensure that the caliper slides freely on the torque plate (Section 3) and check the brake disc run-out (Section 4) to locate the cause.

8 Install new pad support plates to the torque plate (photo).

9 Being careful not to get oil or grease on the brake pad friction material, fit the new pad wear indicator plate(s) to the brake pad(s). Ensure that the arrow on each pad wear indicator plate points in the direction of disc rotation.

10 Fit the anti-squeal shim(s) to the rear of each brake pad, then install the brake pads on their pad support plates in the caliper torque plate (photo).

11 Refit the brake pad retaining springs, then sparingly apply a smear of copper brake grease to the brake pad-to-caliper contact faces (photo).

12 Remove a small amount of hydraulic fluid

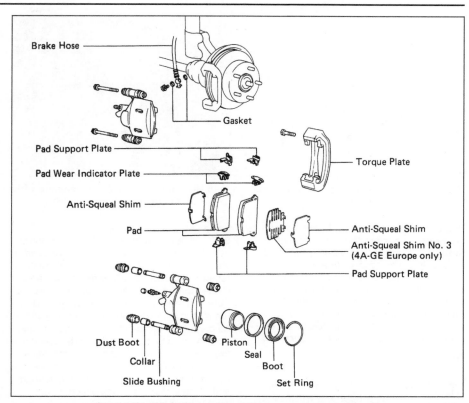

Fig. 9.1 Exploded view of front brake components (Sec 2)

from the master cylinder fluid reservoir, to allow the caliper piston to be pressed in without causing fluid spillage. An old (clean) battery hydrometer is ideal for this purpose.

13 Press in the caliper piston (using a hammer handle or similar) and refit the caliper to the torque plate; ensure that the dust boot does not become trapped.

14 Refit the bolts securing the caliper to its torque plate, and tighten them to their specified torque wrench setting.

15 Remove the roadwheel nuts used to secure the brake disc, then refit the front roadwheel and lower the vehicle to the ground. Fully tighten the roadwheel nuts to the specified torque wrench setting with the vehicle resting on its wheels.

16 Repeat the full procedure on the opposite brake assembly.

17 Depress the brake pedal a few times to ensure that the pads are positioned against the disc, then check that the fluid level is correct in the master cylinder reservoir (Chapter 1).

18 Dispose of the contaminated damp cloth safely.

3 Front brake caliper – removal, overhaul and refitting

Warning: Dust created by the braking system may contain asbestos, which is a health hazard. Never blow it out with compressed air and don't inhale any of it. An approved filtering mask should be worn when working on the brakes. DO NOT use petroleum based solvents to clean brake parts. Use brake cleaner or methylated spirit only.

Warning: Hydraulic fluid is poisonous; wash off immediately and thoroughly in case of skin contact and seek immediate medical advice if any fluid is swallowed or gets into the eyes. Certain types of hydraulic fluid are inflammable and may ignite when allowed to come into contact with hot components; when servicing any hydraulic system it is safest to assume

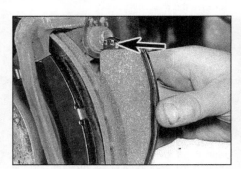

2.10 Fitting inboard brake pad to caliper torque plate. Note pad wear indicator plate (arrowed)

2.11 Lubricate contact faces as described, using specified grease

Fig. 9.2 Coat parts arrowed with specified grease (Sec 3)

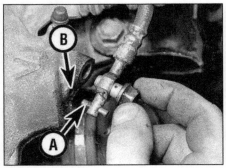

3.16 Hose union peg (A) must engage with front brake caliper hole (B)

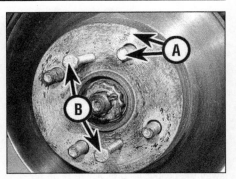

4.6 Alignment marks made to aid refitting (A), bolts inserted to draw disc off hub (B)

that the fluid is inflammable and to take precautions against the risk of fire as though it is petrol that is being handled. Finally, it is hygroscopic (it absorbs moisture from the air) – old fluid may be contaminated and unfit for further use. When topping-up or renewing the fluid, always use a good quality fluid of the specified type and ensure that it comes from a freshly-opened sealed container.

Removal

Hydraulic fluid is an effective paint stripper and will attack plastics; if any is spilt, it should be washed off immediately using copious quantities of fresh water.

1 Slacken the relevant roadwheel nuts, then raise the front of the vehicle and support it securely using axle stands. Remove the roadwheel and temporarily secure the brake disc in position using the roadwheel nuts.
2 Disconnect the brake hose from the caliper by removing its union bolt. Use a suitable container to catch escaping hydraulic fluid; placing two rubber discs on either side of the union and holding them with a pair of self-locking pliers assists in preventing excessive fluid loss.
3 Remove the two bolts securing the caliper assembly to its torque plate, then lift away the caliper assembly.

Overhaul

4 Place the caliper assembly on a clean, flat work surface and clean it thoroughly before dismantling it.
5 Remove the slide bushings, the dust-excluding boots and the collars from the caliper sliders/securing bolt locations, having noted their fitment.
6 Remove the set ring and the piston dust-excluding boot.
7 Apply air pressure (from a foot-operated tyre pump) to the fluid entry hole on the caliper assembly, to eject the piston.
8 Remove the piston seal, taking care not to

damage the cylinder bore.
9 Examine the surfaces of the piston and the cylinder bore. If they are scored, corroded or show evidence of metal-to-metal contact, renew the complete caliper as an assembly. If these components are in good condition, obtain a repair kit which contains all the renewable items. Component cleaning should be performed using only fresh hydraulic fluid.
10 On reassembly, coat the parts arrowed in Fig. 9.2 with lithium soap base glycol grease.
11 Fit a **new** piston seal to its groove in the cylinder bore, by manipulating it with the fingers only, then insert the piston.
12 Fit the **new** piston dust-excluding boot and the set ring.
13 Fit the collars and the dust-excluding boots to the caliper sliders/securing bolt locations, and ensure that the boots are correctly seated in their grooves on the caliper.
14 Install the slide bushings into the dust-excluding boots, and ensure that the boots are secured firmly to the grooves on each bushing.

Refitting

15 Locate the caliper assembly on the torque plate (having applied a smear of copper brake grease to its brake pad contact points), then refit the securing bolts and tighten them to the specified torque wrench setting. Take care not to allow oil or grease to contaminate the brake friction surfaces.
16 Refit the brake hose to the caliper, using new gaskets and tightening the union bolt to the specified torque wrench setting; ensure that the hose union peg engages its hole in the caliper (photo).
17 Bleed the hydraulic system (Section 16) and wash off any spilt fluid, then check that there is no sign of fluid leakage.
18 Remove the roadwheel nuts used to secure the brake disc, then refit the roadwheel. Lower the vehicle, then fully tighten the roadwheel nuts to the specified torque wrench setting with the vehicle resting on the ground.
19 Repeat the full procedure on the opposite brake assembly.

4 Front brake disc – inspection, removal and refitting

Note: *Before starting work, refer to the warning at the beginning of Section 3 concerning the dangers of asbestos dust.*

Inspection

1 Whenever the brake pads are being checked or changed, inspect the brake discs for wear, scoring and cracking. In cases of scoring it may be possible to have a disc refinished, provided the thickness is not reduced below the minimum specified, otherwise the disc must be renewed (a **new** disc is always the preferred option). Measure the disc thickness using a pair of vernier calipers and check that the disc is within the specified limit, if not, the disc will have to be replaced.
2 If a brake disc is thought to be distorted, check that the hub bearing axial play does not exceed the maximum specified (Chapter 10), then check the disc using a dial gauge with the stylus positioned 10 mm from the disc outer edge; alternatively, use feeler blades between the disc and a fixed point. Rotate the disc slowly during checking.

Removal

3 To remove a brake disc, slacken the relevant roadwheel nuts then raise the vehicle and support it securely using axle stands. Remove the roadwheel.
4 Unbolt the caliper assembly and suspend it securely, using a length of wire to avoid straining the brake hose. Remove the brake pads and associated components.
5 Unbolt the torque plate from the hub carrier.
6 Make relative alignment marks on the hub and brake disc (and remove the roadwheel nuts temporarily holding the brake disc in position if applicable), then pull the disc from the hub. If the disc is seized onto its hub mounting flange, draw it off by screwing two suitable bolts through the additional holes provided on the disc centre, then gently tap around the disc centre using a soft-faced hammer while evenly tightening the bolts (photo).

5.4 Remove lower caliper-to-torque plate bolt to allow rear caliper to be pivoted upwards for access to brake pads

5.9 Refitting brake pad to rear caliper torque plate – note pad wear indicator (arrowed)

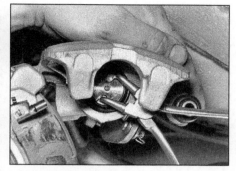

5.10 Using pliers to retract rear brake caliper piston

Refitting

7 Refitting is the reverse of the removal procedure, noting the following points.

(a) *Ensure that any protective coating is removed from a new disc.*

(b) *Clean carefully the contact surfaces of the hub and the brake disc using a wire brush.*

(c) *Ensure that the disc faces are kept free from oil or grease.*

(d) *Ensure that the alignment marks that were made on removal line up (alignment marks are not relevant if a new disc is being fitted).*

(e) *Tighten all disturbed nuts and bolts to their specified torque wrench settings.*

(f) *On completion, depress the brake pedal a few times until the pads are forced back into contact with the disc and normal pedal feel is restored.*

5 Rear brake pads – renewal

Note: *Before starting work, refer to the warning at the beginning of Section 2.*

1 The rear brake pads incorporate pad wear indicator plates which emit a squeaking noise during driving if the brake pads are worn.

2 The thickness of the remaining friction material can be checked through inspection holes in the calipers (Chapter 1), but if any doubt exists about the condition of the friction material, the pads should be removed and checked.

3 To inspect or remove the brake pads, raise the rear of the vehicle and support securely using axle stands. Remove the first roadwheel, then secure the brake disc in position using the roadwheel nuts.

4 Remove the lower bolt securing the caliper assembly to the torque plate (photo). Swivel the caliper assembly upwards for access to the brake pads and suspend it in this position using a length of wire. Do **not** disconnect the brake hose, or the handbrake cable.

5 Remove the brake pads and their anti-squeal shims, the pad guide plates and the

anti-rattle springs. Note the orientation and location of the components as they are removed.

6 Wipe away accumulated dust using a damp cloth, taking care not to inhale any of it.

7 Examine the brake pads for friction material (lining) thickness and uneven wear. Renewal of **all** the pads will be necessary if any are worn to the specified minimum thickness or less. If uneven wear has occurred, **all** four rear brake pads again must be renewed, but ensure that the caliper slides freely on the torque plate (Section 6) and check the brake disc run-out (Section 4) to locate the cause.

8 Install new pad guide plates and anti-rattle springs to the torque plate.

9 Fit the anti-squeal shim to the rear of each brake pad, then install the brake pads to the torque plate; note that the pad wear indicators must be on the topmost side of the fitted pads (photo). Be careful not to get oil or grease on the brake pad friction material.

10 Using a suitable pair of pliers, slowly turn the caliper piston clockwise whilst pushing it in until it locks (photo). Ensure that there is sufficient room in the master cylinder fluid reservoir for the expelled fluid; if necessary, remove some fluid from the reservoir using an old (clean) battery hydrometer.

11 Sparingly apply a smear of copper brake grease to the brake pad-to-caliper contact faces, then fit the pad protrusion into the piston stopper groove and refit the caliper assembly; ensure that the dust boot is not trapped. Refit the lower caliper-to-torque plate securing bolt and tighten it to the specified torque wrench setting.

12 Remove the roadwheel nuts used to secure the brake disc, then refit the rear roadwheel and lower the vehicle to the ground. Fully tighten the roadwheel nuts to the specified torque wrench setting with the vehicle resting on its wheels and remove the chocks.

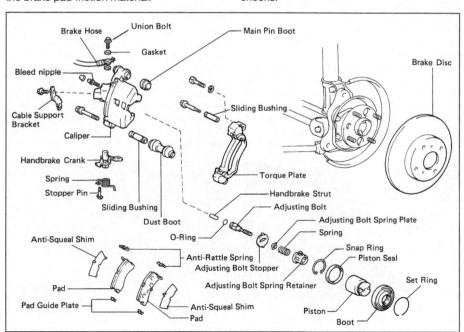

Fig. 9.3 Exploded view of rear disc brake components (Sec 5)

13 Repeat the full procedure on the opposite brake assembly.

14 Check that the fluid level is correct in the master cylinder reservoir (Chapter 1), then depress the brake pedal several times to position the brake pads and automatically adjust the handbrake mechanism at the rear calipers. Re-check the fluid level and top up as necessary.

15 Dispose of the contaminated damp cloth safely.

6 Rear brake caliper – removal, overhaul and refitting

Note: *Before starting work, refer to the warning at the beginning of Section 3 concerning the dangers of asbestos dust and hydraulic fluid.*

Note: *The use of Toyota special service tool 09756-00010 (or a suitable home-made alternative) is essential for safety during the performance of the overhaul operation. The tool, a compressor for the caliper piston spring, also prevents damage to the piston bore. If this tool is not available, or a suitable alternative cannot be fabricated, you are advised to entrust the overhaul operation to your Toyota dealer. Note that certain new components will be required during overhaul; check the parts availability before commencing.*

Removal

1 Slacken the relevant roadwheel nuts then, with the front roadwheels chocked, raise the rear of the vehicle and support it securely using axle stands. Remove the roadwheel and temporarily secure the brake disc in position using the roadwheel nuts.

2 Disconnect the brake hose from the caliper by removing its union bolt; note the two gaskets. Use a suitable container to catch escaping hydraulic fluid; placing two rubber discs on either side of the union and holding them with a pair of self-locking pliers assists in preventing excessive fluid loss.

3 Remove the lower caliper securing bolt, then pivot the caliper assembly upwards.

4 Disconnect the handbrake inner cable from

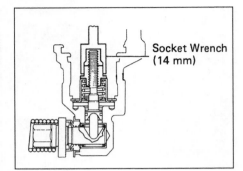

Fig. 9.4 Compressing the coil spring on the adjuster (Sec 6)

its crank on the caliper assembly, then remove the clip securing the outer cable to the caliper and withdraw the cable (photos).

5 Slide the caliper assembly off the main pin and remove it (photo).

Overhaul

6 Clean away all external dirt, then remove the sliding bushing and the boot.

7 Remove the main pin boot.

8 Extract the piston boot set ring, then withdraw the piston dust-excluding boot.

9 Using a suitable tool, unscrew the piston (by turning it anti-clockwise) and remove it from its bore. Extract the piston seal, taking care not to damage the cylinder bore.

10 Examine the surfaces of the piston and the cylinder bore. If they are scored, corroded or show evidence of metal-to-metal contact, renew the complete caliper as an assembly. If these components are in good condition, obtain a repair kit which contains all the renewable items. Component cleaning should be performed using only fresh hydraulic fluid.

11 Normally this will be the extent of the overhaul required, in which case reassembly can commence (paragraph 27 onwards). If, however, the handbrake mechanism is worn, corroded or otherwise damaged, overhaul it as follows.

12 Compress the coil spring on the adjuster, using the special tool (09756-00010) (or a home-made alternative) and a suitable socket, so that the snap ring can be removed. Do not over-compress the spring or the spring

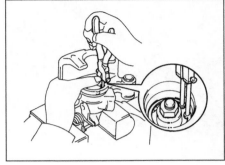

Fig. 9.5 Removing the snap ring – inset shows special tool (or home-made alternative) engaged to compress the coil spring (Sec 6)

retainer may be damaged; also ensure that the coil spring does not fly out as it could cause injury or damage.

13 Remove the snap ring.

14 Slowly withdraw as an assembly the spring retainer, spring, spring plate and adjusting bolt stopper together with the adjusting bolt. Take care to avoid damage to the components during removal, including the O-ring. Remove slowly the spring compressor, taking care not to allow the coil spring to fly out, then dismantle the assembly (note the orientation and order of the components as they are removed).

15 Remove the handbrake strut and the cable support bracket.

16 Remove the spring and the handbrake crank.

17 Unless the handbrake crank boot is to be renewed, it should not be removed. If removal is required, tapping lightly on the metal portion of the boot will free it. Remove the stopper pin.

18 Commence reassembly by tapping the stopper pin into position until the main body of the pin projects 25 mm.

19 Apply lithium soap base glycol grease to the components arrowed in Fig. 9.6.

20 Using a 24 mm socket, tap the handbrake crank boot into position on the caliper.

21 Install the handbrake crank; match the crank boot with the groove of the crank seal.

22 Install the cable support bracket flush

6.4A Disconnecting handbrake inner cable from rear caliper crank

6.4B Removing clip securing handbrake outer cable to rear caliper

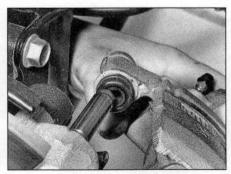

6.5 Sliding rear caliper off main pin

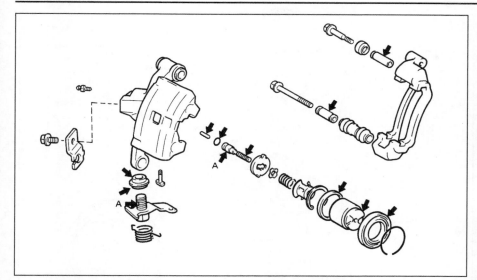

Fig. 9.6 Apply specified grease to areas arrowed and pack grease into areas marked 'A' (Sec 6)

6.30 Align piston with caliper lug as shown

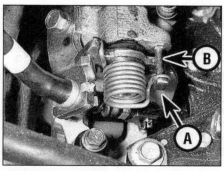

6.39 If correctly adjusted, handbrake crank (A) should contact stopper pin (B) when handbrake is released

against the caliper assembly. Check that there is a clearance of 0.6 mm between the handbrake crank and the cable support bracket.

23 Refit the handbrake crank spring.

24 Fit the handbrake strut, making sure that the needle rollers do not catch on the sides of the cylinder hole.

25 Install a new O-ring to the adjusting bolt, then reassemble the adjusting bolt stopper, spring plate, spring and spring retainer to it; ensure that the inscribed surface of the adjusting bolt stopper faces upwards and that the notches of the spring retainer align with those of the stopper. Compress the spring ready for refitting, using the special tool (or its home-made alternative).

26 Fit the compressed adjusting bolt assembly into the caliper assembly, then fit the snap ring with its opening towards the bleed nipple. Remove the spring compressing tool, and check that the adjusting bolt does not move when pulled upwards.

27 Turn the handbrake crank by hand and check that the adjusting bolt moves smoothly.

28 Install the **new** piston seal to its groove in the cylinder bore (by manipulating it with the fingers only).

29 Slowly screw the piston, in a clockwise direction, as far as possible into its bore, using a suitable forked tool.

30 Align the centre of the piston stopper groove with the positioning lug on the caliper assembly (photo).

31 Fit the piston dust-excluding boot and the set ring.

32 Install the main pin boot.

33 Install the boot and the sliding bushing.

Refitting

34 With the brake pads installed (Section 5), install the caliper assembly to the main pin; ensure that the boot end is fitted to the groove

of the main pin. Be careful not to allow oil or grease to contaminate the brake friction surfaces.

35 Reconnect the handbrake cable.

36 Sparingly apply a smear of copper brake grease to the caliper assembly brake pad contact points, then fit the pad protrusion into the piston stopper groove and refit the caliper assembly; ensure that the boot is not trapped. Refit the lower caliper-to-torque plate securing bolt and tighten it to the specified torque wrench setting.

37 Reconnect the brake hose, using new gaskets and tightening the union bolt to the specified torque wrench setting; ensure that the hose union peg engages the caliper slot.

38 Top up the master cylinder fluid reservoir with fresh fluid of the specified type, then bleed the relevant hydraulic circuit (Section 16). Wash off any spilt fluid and check that no leakage is evident.

39 Apply the footbrake and handbrake several times. Check that when released, the handbrake crank makes contact with its stopper pin ensuring correct adjustment (photo). Also check the adjustment at the other rear caliper assembly.

40 Check that the handbrake is correctly adjusted (Section 19).

41 Remove the roadwheel nuts used to secure the brake disc, then refit the rear roadwheel and lower the vehicle to the ground. Fully tighten the roadwheel nuts to the specified torque wrench setting with the vehicle resting on its wheels and remove the chocks.

42 Repeat the full procedure on the opposite brake assembly.

7 Rear brake disc – inspection, removal and refitting

Refer to Section 4.

8 Rear brake drum – removal, inspection and refitting

Note: *Before starting work, refer to the warning at the beginning of Section 3 concerning the dangers of asbestos dust.*

Removal

1 Slacken the relevant roadwheel nuts then, with the front roadwheels chocked, raise the rear of the vehicle and support it securely using axle stands. Remove the rear roadwheel.

2 With the handbrake fully released, withdraw the brake drum from the hub. If it is stuck, insert a screwdriver through the inspection hole in the backplate and hold the automatic adjusting lever away from the adjuster wheel: at the same time, reduce the adjustment of the mechanism by turning the adjuster wheel using another screwdriver inserted through the same backplate hole. If tapped holes are provided in the drum, suitably-sized bolts may be screwed in and tightened evenly to jack the drum off the hub (photo).

Inspection

3 Examine the interior (friction) surface of the brake drum for signs of wear, scoring and cracking. Measure the drum inside diameter using a pair of vernier calipers and check that the drum is within the specified limit, if light scoring or wear has occurred, it may be

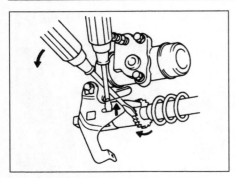

Fig. 9.7 Releasing brake adjuster (Sec 8)

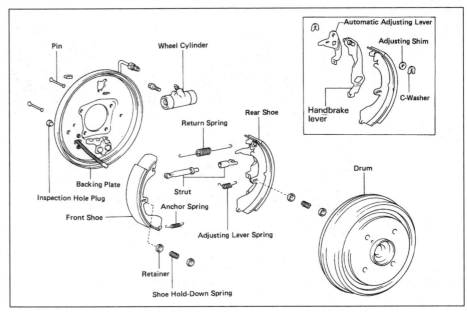

Fig. 9.8 Exploded view of rear drum brake components (Sec 8)

possible to have the damage machined out, provided the drum's inside diameter is not enlarged to more than the specified maximum; due to the nature of this task, consult your Toyota dealer or a reputable engineering company who can undertake the operation for you. In all other cases, the drum must be renewed.

4 Check the contact of the brake shoes with the drum friction surface – this will require the removal of the existing brake shoes (Section 9) if they are to be retained. If the contact is not satisfactory, renew the shoes and/or machine or renew the drum, as necessary.

Refitting

5 Ensure that no oil or grease is allowed to contaminate the brake drum or the brake shoes during refitting.

6 Reduce the length of the strut by turning the adjuster wheel, then refit the brake drum.

7 Operate the handbrake lever inside the vehicle several times, until a clicking sound can no longer be heard from the rear brake assembly, then fully release the handbrake.

8 Remove the brake drum and check that the drum-to-shoe clearance is as specified. Measure the drum inside diameter, then the outside diameter of the brake shoe friction material; the clearance is the difference between the two diameters. If the clearance is not as specified, check the operation of the handbrake system and rectify any faults as necessary.

9 With the correct drum-to-shoe clearance

obtained, refit the brake drum and the roadwheel.

10 Repeat the full procedure on the opposite brake.

11 Lower the vehicle to the ground and tighten the roadwheel nuts to the specified torque wrench setting, then remove the front roadwheel chocks.

9 Rear brake shoes – renewal

Warning: Drum brake shoes must be renewed on both rear wheels at the same time – never renew the shoes on only one wheel as uneven braking may result. Also, the dust created by wear of the shoes may contain asbestos, which is a health hazard. Never blow it out with compressed air and don't inhale any of it. An approved filtering mask should be worn when working on the brakes. DO NOT use petroleum based

solvents to clean brake parts. Use brake cleaner or methylated spirit only.

1 The thickness of the remaining brake shoe friction material can be checked through inspection holes in the backplates (Chapter 1), but if any doubt exists about the condition of the friction material, the brake drums should be removed to permit a thorough check.

2 Remove the first brake drum (Section 8) and wipe away accumulated dust using a clean damp cloth.

3 Disconnect the shoe upper return spring (photo).

4 To release the leading (forward) brake shoe, use a pair of pliers to depress the hold-down spring retainer and turn it through 90°, then release the pressure and withdraw the retainer, spring and pin.

5 Disconnect the anchor spring from the base of the leading shoe, and remove the leading shoe. Remove the anchor spring.

6 Release the trailing (rear) brake shoe from its hold-down spring as described in paragraph 4 (photo).

8.2 Using bolts to extract rear brake drum

9.3 Disconnecting brake shoe upper return spring (arrowed)

9.6 Releasing brake shoe hold-down spring

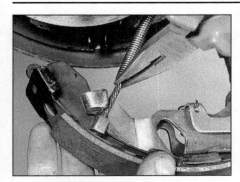

9.8 Releasing handbrake cable from trailing shoe lever

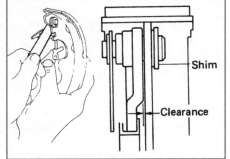

Fig. 9.9 Checking shoe-to-handbrake lever clearance (Sec 9)

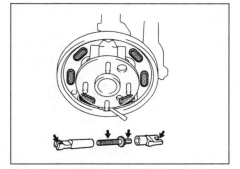

Fig. 9.10 Lubricate shaded areas on backplate and arrowed locations on strut as directed (Sec 9)

7 Release the handbrake cable from its retaining clips on the backplate.

8 Use a pair of pliers to release the handbrake cable from the lever on the trailing shoe, then remove the trailing shoe and strut (photo).

9 Unhook and remove the adjusting lever spring from the trailing shoe.

10 Remove the strut together with the return spring.

11 Prise out the C-washer, then remove the shim followed by the handbrake and automatic adjusting lever assembly, from the trailing shoe.

12 Having obtained new brake shoes, fit the handbrake and automatic adjusting lever assembly to the new trailing shoe using the original shim and a new C-washer. Check that the shoe-to-handbrake lever clearance is within the specified tolerances and adjust as necessary using a different shim (see Specifications). Note that each time the C-washer is removed a **new** one must be fitted.

13 Clean the automatic adjuster wheel threads and apply a light smear of high melting-point grease.

14 Further apply a light smear of high melting-point grease to the areas shown in Fig. 9.10.

15 Take great care not to contaminate the brake shoe friction material with oil or grease on reassembly.

16 Fit the strut to the trailing shoe. Set the strut and return spring in place and install the automatic adjusting lever spring.

17 Connect the handbrake cable to its lever on the trailing shoe. Fit the shoe to the wheel cylinder and backplate anchor block, ensuring that the handbrake cable locates correctly on the backplate.

18 Refit the trailing shoe hold-down spring, pin and retainer to secure the shoe.

19 Connect the anchor spring between the shoe lower ends then fit the leading shoe to the wheel cylinder and the backplate anchor block, with the strut correctly located. Refit the shoe hold-down spring, pin and retainer and reconnect the shoe upper return spring.

20 Check the operation of the automatic adjuster mechanism by moving back and forth the trailing shoe handbrake lever; the adjuster wheel should turn.

21 Refit the brake drum (Section 8), then repeat the full procedure on the opposite brake assembly.

22 Refit the rear roadwheels and lower the vehicle to the ground, then tighten the road-wheel nuts to the specified torque wrench setting. Remove the front roadwheel chocks.

10 Rear wheel cylinder – removal, overhaul and refitting

Note: *Before starting work, refer to the warnings at the beginning of Section 3 concerning the dangers of asbestos dust and hydraulic fluid.*

Removal

1 Remove the relevant brake drum (Section 8), and the brake shoes (Section 9), then disconnect the hydraulic union from the rear of the wheel cylinder. Collect spillage in a suitable container and plug or clamp the pipe to prevent excessive fluid loss.

2 Unbolt the wheel cylinder from the backplate and remove it (photo).

Overhaul

Note: *Before attempting to overhaul the unit, check the price and availability of individual components and the price of a new or reconditioned unit, as overhaul may not be viable on economic grounds alone. Also, read through the procedure and check that the special tools and facilities required are available.*

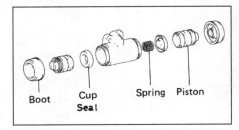

Fig. 9.11 Exploded view of wheel cylinder components (Sec 10)

Boot   Cup **Seal**   Spring   Piston

3 Remove the wheel cylinder from the vehicle and clean it thoroughly.

4 Remove the boots. Tap the end of the cylinder on a block of wood or apply air from a tyre pump to eject the pistons, then remove the spring. Note the orientation of the pistons.

5 Examine the surfaces of the pistons and their cylinder bores. If corrosion or scoring is evident, the wheel cylinder must be renewed as a complete unit. If these components are in good condition, obtain a repair kit which contains all the renewable items.

6 Remove the old seals from the pistons, having noted which way around the seal lips face, then clean the pistons using fresh hydraulic fluid.

7 Apply lithium soap base glycol grease to the new seals and the pistons, then manipulate the seals into position on their pistons using fingers only. Ensure that the seal lips are facing the correct way.

8 Fit the spring and slide the pistons into their respective bores, then securely locate the new boots.

Refitting

9 Refit the wheel cylinder to the backplate, tightening the mounting bolts to the specified torque wrench setting.

10 Remove the temporary plug or clamp from the hydraulic pipe and reconnect it to the wheel cylinder. Tighten the hydraulic union to the specified torque wrench setting.

10.2 Unbolting wheel cylinder from backplate – note clamp used to prevent excessive hydraulic fluid loss

11 Refit the brake shoes (Section 9) and the brake drum (Section 8).

12 Refit the roadwheel and lower the vehicle. Fully tighten the roadwheel nuts to the specified torque wrench setting with the vehicle resting on the ground, then remove the front roadwheel chocks.

13 Bleed the relevant brake hydraulic circuit (Section 16), wash off any spilt fluid and ensure that no leaks are evident.

11 Rear brake backplate/disc shield – removal and refitting

Note: *Before starting work, refer to the warning at the beginning of Section 3 concerning the dangers of asbestos dust.*

Removal

Drum rear brakes

1 Remove the relevant brake drum (Section 8), brake shoes (Section 9) and wheel cylinder (Section 10), then unbolt the rear stub axle (Chapter 10).

2 Remove the two bolts securing the handbrake cable to the backplate, then withdraw the handbrake cable.

3 Remove the backplate.

Disc rear brakes

4 Remove the brake disc (Section 7). Note that there is no need to disconnect the caliper; suspend it out of the working area using a length of wire.

5 Unbolt the rear stub axle (Chapter 10), then remove the disc shield.

Refitting

6 Refitting is the reverse of the removal procedure, noting the following points.

(a) *Refer to the relevant Sections of this Chapter and of Chapter 10 for specific information.*

(b) *Fit a new stub axle O-ring.*

(c) *Tighten all fastenings to their specified torque wrench settings (where given).*

(d) *On vehicles with drum rear brakes only, bleed any air from the relevant hydraulic circuit (Section 16).*

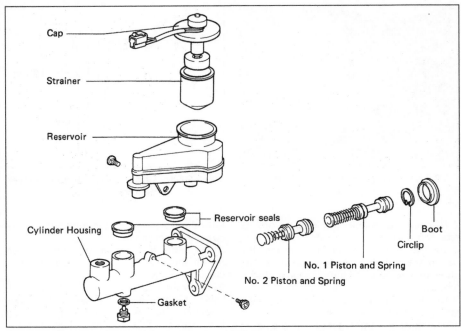

Fig. 9.12 Exploded view of brake master cylinder assembly (Sec 12)

12 Brake master cylinder – removal, overhaul and refitting

Note: *Check the availability of parts before removing or overhauling the brake master cylinder, as a new gasket and seal will be required.*

Note: *Before starting work, refer to the note at the beginning of Section 3 concerning the dangers of hydraulic fluid.*

Removal

1 Remove the air filter housing (Chapter 4) or the suspension strut brace (Chapter 10) for increased working clearance, according to model.

2 Disconnect the vacuum hose from the vacuum servo unit (photo).

3 Disconnect the brake fluid level warning switch multi-plug (located close to the fluid reservoir) (photo).

4 Remove the reservoir cap and syphon out the hydraulic fluid (**not** by mouth – an old but clean hydrometer is ideal).

5 Disconnect the hydraulic pipes from the master cylinder.

6 Remove the nuts securing the master cylinder to the vacuum servo unit, noting the 3-way union bracket arrangement on the left-hand side, then withdraw the master cylinder and its gasket.

7 Remove the boot from the end of the master cylinder.

Overhaul

8 Remove the retaining screw, then withdraw the reservoir from the master cylinder assembly.

9 Gently grip the flange of the master cylinder in a soft-jawed vice, then remove the two reservoir seals.

10 Push the pistons into the cylinder using a

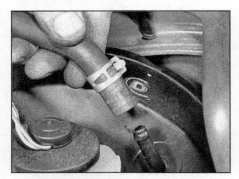

12.2 Disconnecting vacuum servo unit vacuum hose

12.3 Disconnecting brake fluid level warning switch multi-plug

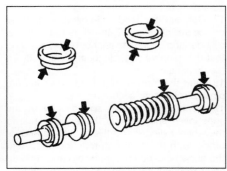

Fig. 9.13 Apply specified grease where indicated (Sec 12)

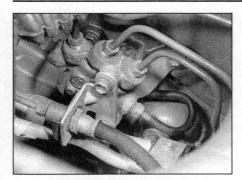

13.1 Pressure-reducing valve

screwdriver, then remove the piston stopper bolt and its gasket.

11 With the pistons still depressed, extract the circlip.

12 Tap the end of the cylinder body on a block of hardwood to eject the pistons and springs; do not allow the pistons to tilt as they are removed, or the cylinder bore may be scored. Note the location and orientation of the pistons as they are removed.

13 Examine the surfaces of the pistons and the cylinder bores. If they are scored or corroded, or show signs of metal-to-metal rubbing, the complete master cylinder must be renewed. Where these components are in good condition, obtain a repair kit which contains all the necessary renewable items.

14 Remove and discard the piston seals, having noted which way their lips face, then clean the pistons using fresh hydraulic fluid and manipulate new seals into position (using fingers only). Ensure that the seal lips face the correct way.

15 Apply lithium soap base glycol grease to the rubber components indicated in Fig. 9.13.

16 Being careful not to damage the seal lips, insert the pistons and springs into the cylinder bore. Depress the pistons and refit the circlip.

17 With the pistons fully depressed, refit the piston stopper bolt and its **new** gasket. Tighten the stopper bolt to its specified torque wrench setting.

18 Fit the two reservoir seals.

19 Push the fluid reservoir into position in its seals, then install its retaining screw. Note that the screw does not rigidly secure the reservoir, so do **not** overtighten the screw in an attempt to eliminate the gap between the screw head and reservoir body.

Refitting

20 Clean out the groove on the master cylinder mounting flange, then refit the boot to the master cylinder. Ensure that the 'UP' mark on the boot aligns with the groove.

21 Using a **new** gasket, refit the master cylinder to the vacuum servo unit and tighten the nuts to the specified torque wrench setting. Ensure that the 3-way union bracket freed during removal is correctly located.

22 Partially fill the fluid reservoir with fresh

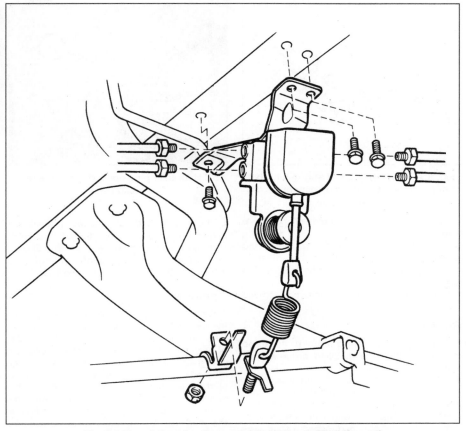

Fig. 9.14 Load-Sensing Proportioning Valve (LSPV) (Sec 14)

hydraulic fluid of the specified type, then bleed the master cylinder (Section 16). After bleeding, reconnect the hydraulic pipes to the master cylinder and tighten to the specified torque wrench setting.

23 Reconnect the brake fluid warning switch multi-plug, then top up the fluid reservoir and bleed each individual brake caliper/wheel cylinder (as applicable), in four separate operations (Section 16).

24 Reconnect the vacuum hose.

25 Refit the air filter housing (Chapter 4), or the suspension strut brace (Chapter 10), as applicable.

13 Pressure-reducing valve (except Estate) – general

Note: *Before starting work, refer to the note at the beginning of Section 3 concerning the dangers of hydraulic fluid.*

1 The valve is mounted on the engine compartment rear bulkhead and prevents the rear wheels from locking up during heavy brake applications; it works by reducing the hydraulic pressure available at the rear brakes in proportion to that available at the front brakes (photo).

2 Any fault can be rectified only by the renewal of the valve complete.

14 Load-sensing proportioning valve (Estate) – removal and refitting

Note: *Due to the specialised equipment required to check and accurately adjust the brake fluid pressure after refitting (or reconnecting) the valve, you are advised to entrust this task to your Toyota dealer or a suitably equipped specialist. The following procedure is given for circumstances where the task must be undertaken, but it is vitally important that the brake fluid pressure is checked and adjusted as necessary by your dealer (or other suitably equipped specialist) upon completion.*

⚠️ **Warning: If the fluid pressure is not checked and accurately adjusted, braking system performance may be severely impaired.**

Note: *Before starting work, refer to the note at the beginning of Section 3 concerning the dangers of hydraulic fluid.*

Removal

1 Chock the front wheels, then raise the rear of the vehicle and support it securely using axle stands.

2 Disconnect the hydraulic pipes from the

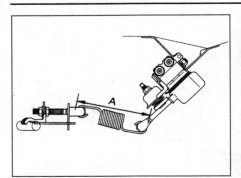

Fig. 9.15 Measuring LSPV spring length – reference points shown by dimension 'A' (Sec 14)

valve and plug their ends to prevent excessive fluid loss.

3 Accurately measure and note the spring length (Fig.9.15), then release the adjusting bolt and disconnect it from the suspension arm.

4 Undo the three mounting bolts and remove the valve.

Refitting

5 Install the valve and tighten its three mounting bolts to the specified torque wrench setting.

6 Install the adjusting bolt to the suspension arm and temporarily tighten the locknut arrangement. Measure the spring length, then re-adjust to obtain the original (noted) length. If this cannot be obtained, adjust it to its set-up length of 124.4 mm.

7 Remove the temporary plugs from the brake hydraulic pipes, then reconnect the pipes to the valve body and tighten to their specified torque wrench setting.

8 Refill the master cylinder fluid reservoir, then bleed the system (Section 16). Wash off any spilt fluid and check all disturbed unions to ensure that no fluid leakage is evident.

9 Lower the vehicle to the ground and remove the roadwheel chocks.

10 Have the brake fluid pressure checked, and adjusted if necessary, by your Toyota dealer or other suitably-equipped specialist (see the note and warning at the beginning of this Section).

15 Hydraulic pipes and hoses – inspection, removal and refitting

Note: *Before starting work, refer to the note at the beginning of Section 3 concerning the dangers of hydraulic fluid.*

Inspection

1 The hydraulic pipes, hoses, hose connections and pipe unions should be regularly examined.

2 First check for signs of leakage at the pipe unions, then examine the flexible hoses for signs of cracking, chafing and fraying.

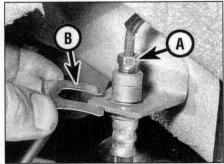

15.6 Hydraulic pipe union (A), flexible hose clip (B)

3 The metal hydraulic pipes should be examined carefully for signs of dents, corrosion or other damage. Corrosion should be scraped off; if the depth of pitting is significant, the pipes must be renewed.

Removal

4 Before disturbing any part of the system, the loss of hydraulic fluid can be minimised by removing the reservoir cap, stretching a piece of polythene film over the top of the reservoir and then refitting the reservoir cap. Other methods include the use of proprietary hose clamps, or suitable plugs. If a pipe is to be disconnected from the master cylinder, the reservoir should be emptied by syphoning out the fluid (**not** by mouth – an old but clean hydrometer is ideal).

5 To remove a section of pipe (after removing any shields where necessary), unscrew the unions at each end of the pipe and release it from any retaining clips and guides. Where the unions are exposed to the full force of the weather, they can sometimes be quite tight: if an open-ended spanner is used, burring of the flats is not uncommon and for this reason it is preferable to use a split ring spanner which will engage all the flats.

6 To remove a flexible hose, first clean the ends of the hose and the surrounding area then unscrew the unions from the hose ends where applicable, disconnect the hose from the caliper assembly (noting that new gaskets will be required on refitting). Remove the clip(s) securing the hose to its support bracket(s), and withdraw the hose (photo).

7 Brake pipes with flared ends and unions in place may be obtained from accessory shops, motor factors or Toyota dealers. They may be obtained individually or in sets, as available, requiring bending to fit using the defective pipe as a guide. Alternatively, brake pipes can be made up using a proprietary kit, follow the kit manufacturer's instructions. Whichever method is used, ensure that the pipes do not become kinked.

Refitting

8 Refitting is the reverse of the removal procedure, noting the following points.

(a) *Where possible, tighten all disturbed fasteners and unions to their specified torque wrench settings.*

(b) *Use new gaskets and ensure that the hose union peg engages with the caliper hole or slot, as applicable.*

(c) *Make sure that the brake pipes and hoses are securely supported in their clips and ensure that the hoses are not kinked, check that the hoses are clear of suspension and steering components and will remain clear during the movement of these components.*

(d) *Refit any shields where applicable.*

(e) *Whichever method was used to minimise hydraulic fluid loss, ensure that it is removed at the appropriate stage of the operation.*

(f) *Upon completion, bleed the brake hydraulic system (Section 16).*

16 Hydraulic system – bleeding

Note: *Before starting work, refer to the note at the beginning of Section 3 concerning the dangers of hydraulic fluid.*

1 If the master cylinder, pressure-reducing valve or load-sensing proportioning valve has been disconnected, then the complete system (both circuits) must be bled. If a component of only one circuit has been disturbed, it will only be necessary to bleed that particular circuit.

2 If the master cylinder has been disconnected or its fluid reservoir has been allowed to empty, first bleed the master cylinder before proceeding to the rest of the circuit.

3 Bleed one rear brake and its diagonally opposite front brake; this constitutes one circuit. Repeat this sequence on the remaining circuit if the complete system is to be bled.

4 **Do not** forget to keep the fluid reservoir topped up (with fresh fluid of the specified type) during any bleeding operation. If the level is allowed to drop too far, air may be drawn into the system necessitating bleeding of the entire system including the master cylinder.

5 Before commencing operations, ensure that all system hoses and pipes are in good condition and that all unions are tight and free from leaks.

Master cylinder bleeding

6 The master cylinder must be bled if it has been disconnected or if the fluid reservoir has been emptied.

7 Take adequate precautions to ensure that hydraulic fluid is not ejected with force from the master cylinder (which could cause damage or injury) during the following procedure.

8 Disconnect the hydraulic pipes from the master cylinder, place a container under it to catch the fluid that will be ejected and use

plenty of clean rag to prevent fluid spraying on to the surrounding components, then engage the aid of an assistant. Ensure that the fluid reservoir is topped-up with the specified type of fluid.

9 Have your assistant **slowly** depress the brake pedal and hold it down, then cover the master cylinder fluid outlets with your fingers and instruct the assistant slowly to release the brake pedal so that fluid is drawn forcibly down from the reservoir, Repeat as necessary.

10 Once the master cylinder passages are primed so that fluid is ejected at each downward stroke of the pedal, carry on **slowly** pumping the pedal until all the air has been ejected from the master cylinder; maintain the fluid level in the reservoir. When all the air has been expelled, reconnect the hydraulic pipes to the master cylinder (with the brake pedal held on a downward stroke) and tighten their unions to the specified torque wrench setting.

11 Top up the fluid level to the reservoir MAX mark, then bleed both hydraulic circuits using any of the following procedures.

Bleeding – two-man method

12 Gather together a clean glass jar and a length of rubber or plastic tubing (preferably clear) which will be a tight fit on the bleed nipples.

13 Engage the aid of an assistant.

14 Push one end of the tubing over the first bleed nipple and immerse the other end in the glass jar which should contain enough hydraulic fluid to cover the end of the tubing.

15 Open the bleed nipple approximately half a turn and have your assistant slowly depress the brake pedal fully. At the end of the pedal downstroke, tighten the bleed nipple (to obviate the possibility of any expelled air or fluid being drawn back into the system) then instruct your assistant to release the brake pedal slowly.

16 Repeat the operation until clean hydraulic fluid, free from any air bubbles, can be seen flowing through to the jar.

17 At the end of the bleeding procedure, tighten the bleed nipple (at the end of a pedal

16.22 Using a one-way valve kit to bleed air from brake hydraulic system at front brake caliper bleed nipple

downstroke) and remove the tubing. Tighten the bleed nipple to its specified torque wrench setting if possible; **do not** overtighten them.

18 Repeat the operation on the remaining circuit bleed nipple.

19 The other circuit can be bled using the same procedure, as necessary until the pedal feels firm again.

Bleeding – using a one-way valve kit

20 There are a number of one-way bleeding kits available from motor accessory shops. It is recommended that one of these kits is used wherever possible, as they eliminate the need for an assistant and greatly simplify the bleeding procedure by reducing the possibility of air being drawn back into the system.

21 To use a kit, always follow the manufacturers' instructions. A general guideline to usage is given below.

22 Connect the tubing to the first bleed nipple and open the bleed nipple approximately half a turn (photo). Place the equipment where it can be seen from the driver's seat.

23 Depress the brake pedal slowly and fully, then slowly release it, repeating until the expelled fluid is clear of air bubbles. The one-way valve will prevent expelled air or fluid from returning at the end of each brake pedal downstroke. Ensure that the fluid level in the master cylinder reservoir is kept well topped-up at all times.

24 At the end of the procedure, tighten the bleed nipple and remove the tubing. Repeat as necessary on the remaining bleed nipples in the circuit until all air is removed.

Bleeding – using a pressure-bleeding kit

25 These kits are available from motor accessory shops and are usually operated by air pressure from the spare tyre (remember to re-inflate it after use). Manufacturer's instructions should be followed; a general guide is given below.

26 By connecting a pressurised container to the master cylinder fluid reservoir, bleeding is then carried out by simply opening each bleed nipple in turn and allowing the fluid to run out through the tubing, rather like turning on a tap, until no air is visible in the expelled fluid. Tighten each bleed nipple to the specified torque wrench setting after bleeding.

27 Pressure-bleeding is particularly effective when bleeding 'difficult' systems or when bleeding the complete system at the time of routine fluid renewal.

All methods

28 When bleeding is complete, check the level in the fluid reservoir and top up to the MAX mark as necessary, using fresh fluid of the specified type.

29 Check the feel of the brake pedal. If it feels at all spongy, air must still be present in the system and further bleeding will be

required. Failure of the system to bleed properly (after a reasonable period of the bleeding operation) may be due to worn master cylinder seals.

30 Discard hydraulic fluid which has been expelled; it is almost certainly contaminated with moisture, air and dirt making it unsuitable for further use.

17 Vacuum servo unit – removal and refitting

Note: *A special service tool is required to set up a new vacuum servo unit on installation. If this tool is not available, you are advised to entrust the task to your Toyota dealer or other suitably equipped specialist. Also note that new gaskets will be required during refitting.*

Note: *Before starting work, refer to the note at the beginning of Section 3 concerning the dangers of hydraulic fluid.*

Removal

1 Remove the brake master cylinder (Section 12).

2 Undo the bolt securing the power steering pipe bracket (if applicable), located on the vehicle body underneath the brake master cylinder. The bracket has to be moved as the servo unit is withdrawn.

3 Unfasten and move aside the clutch master cylinder, there is no need to disconnect its

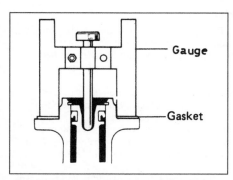

Fig. 9.16 Checking new vacuum servo unit pushrod clearance – gauge on master cylinder (Sec 17)

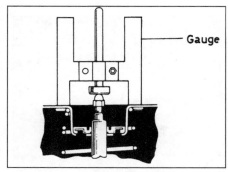

Fig. 9.17 Checking new vacuum servo unit pushrod clearance – gauge on vacuum servo unit (Sec 17)

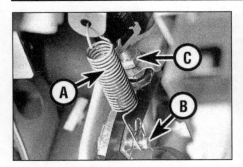

17.4 Brake pedal return spring (A), clevis pin and securing clip (B), stop-lamp switch (C)

17.5A Undo nuts (arrowed) securing vacuum servo unit to bulkhead . . .

17.5B . . . withdrawing servo unit and gasket

hydraulic pipe, but ensure that the pipe is not kinked (Chapter 6). On GTi 16 models note that it is likely that the clutch master cylinder cannot be moved until the vacuum servo unit is partially withdrawn.

4 Disconnect the servo unit pushrod from the brake pedal by disconnecting the return spring and removing the clevis pin and its securing clip (photo).

5 Undo the four nuts that secure the vacuum servo unit to the bulkhead (inside the vehicle) then, working in the engine compartment, carefully withdraw the servo unit and its gasket (photos).

6 Do **not** attempt to dismantle the vacuum servo unit, if it is defective it must be renewed.

Refitting

7 Refitting is the reverse of the removal procedure, noting the following points.

(a) Refer to the relevant Sections of this Chapter and of Chapter 6 for specific details.

(b) Where possible, tighten all disturbed fasteners and unions to their specified torque wrench settings.

(c) Renew all seals and gaskets disturbed.

(d) If a new vacuum servo unit is being fitted, the pushrod clearance must be checked using a special gauge. Place the gauge on the master cylinder (with the flange gasket in position), then adjust the pin until it just makes contact with the primary piston. Transfer the gauge to the vacuum servo

unit, the pin should just touch the end of the servo pushrod. If adjustment is necessary, grip the servo pushrod and turn the domed nut until the setting is correct.

(e) Bleed the complete brake hydraulic system (Section 16) after the brake master cylinder has been installed.

18 Vacuum servo unit check valve – removal and refitting

Removal

1 The check valve is located in the vacuum hose between the vacuum servo unit and the inlet manifold. Refer to Chapter 1 for details of the valve checking procedure.

2 To remove the check valve, first disconnect it from the vacuum hose (photo). It is connected either by two push-fit joints (secured by clips) or by one push-fit joint and one threaded union.

3 For valves with a threaded end, simply unscrew the valve from its union and remove it. On valves with two push-fit joints, release the mounting bracket bolt and remove the valve; note the orientation of the valve before removal to ensure correct subsequent refitting.

Refitting

4 Refitting is a reversal of the removal procedure. If the valve is of the type with a

threaded end, tighten it to the specified torque wrench setting; if it is the other type, ensure that it is fitted the right way round.

19 Handbrake – adjustment

1 The handbrake should be fully applied when the handbrake lever is heard to 'click' between four and seven times (drum rear brakes), or between five and eight times (disc rear brakes).

2 If the handbrake lever travel is incorrect it must be adjusted, but first of all establish that the rear brakes are correctly adjusted (Section 6 or 8, as applicable).

3 With the rear brakes correctly adjusted, remove the centre console rear section from inside the vehicle (Chapter 11).

4 Release the handbrake lever adjuster locknut and turn the adjuster nut until the setting is correct (photo).

5 Chock the front wheels, raise the rear of the vehicle and support it on axle stands. With the rear wheels off the ground, and the handbrake lever fully released, spin both rear wheels by hand and check that the brakes do not bind.

6 Once adjustment is correct, retighten the adjuster locknut to its specified torque wrench setting.

7 Lower the vehicle to the ground, then tighten the rear roadwheel nuts to the specified torque wrench setting. Remove the front roadwheel chocks.

8 Refit the centre console rear section (Chapter 11).

20 Handbrake cables – renewal

Primary cable

1 Remove the centre console rear section (Chapter 11).

2 Chock the front roadwheels then, with the handbrake lever fully released, disconnect the primary cable from the handbrake lever.

3 Raise the vehicle and support it securely using axle stands.

4 Working underneath the vehicle, draw the

18.2 Disconnecting vacuum hose from vacuum servo unit check valve

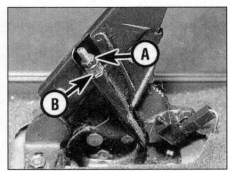

19.4 Handbrake lever adjuster locknut (A), adjuster nut (B)

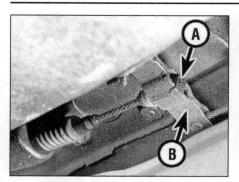

20.5 Handbrake primary cable end fixing (A), equaliser yoke (B)

20.8A Handbrake secondary cable forward securing clip (arrowed) . . .

20.8B . . . centre securing clip (arrowed) . . .

20.8C . . . and rear securing clip (arrowed)

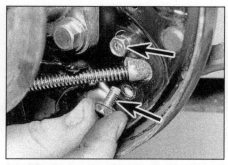

20.9 Remove bolts (arrowed) to release handbrake cable from rear (drum) brake backplate

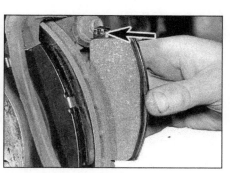

20.10 Disconnecting handbrake secondary cable from rear (disc) brake caliper

primary cable and its rubber protector out from the handbrake underfloor housing.

5 Push the primary cable into the equaliser yoke sufficiently to disengage the primary cable end fixing, then turn the end fixing through 90° to allow the primary cable to be withdrawn (photo).

6 Refitting is the reverse of the removal procedure, noting the following points.

(a) Ensure that the primary cable rubber protector locates correctly to the handbrake underfloor housing.

(b) Adjust the handbrake (Section 19).

Secondary cable

7 Disconnect the primary cable, as described above.

8 Disconnect the required secondary cable from the equaliser yoke then, working along the cable towards the rear of the vehicle, release the cable securing clips (photos).

9 If drum rear brakes are fitted, remove the brake drum and dismantle the brake shoes until the handbrake secondary cable can be disconnected from its lever on the trailing shoe (Sections 8 and 9). Once disconnected, unbolt the cable from the rear of the backplate and withdraw it (photo).

10 If disc rear brakes are fitted, release the caliper-to-torque plate securing bolt so that the caliper can be pivoted upwards, then disconnect the handbrake secondary cable from its crank on the caliper assembly (Section 6). Release the cable retaining clip and withdraw the cable (photo).

11 Refitting is the reverse of the removal procedure, noting the following points.

(a) Ensure that the cable(s) are correctly routed and located in the clips and guides.

(b) If drum rear brakes are fitted, tighten the cable securing bolts on the rear of the backplate(s) to the specified torque wrench setting.

(c) If disc rear brakes are fitted, tighten the caliper-to-torque plate securing bolt to the specified torque wrench setting.

(d) When both secondary cables are refitted, reconnect the primary cable and adjust the handbrake (Section 19).

21 Handbrake lever – removal and refitting

Removal

1 Remove the centre console rear section (Chapter 11).

2 Chock the front roadwheels then, with the handbrake lever fully released, disconnect the primary cable from the handbrake lever.

3 Disconnect the warning switch connection from the handbrake lever assembly (photo).

4 Raise the vehicle and support it securely using axle stands.

5 Working underneath the vehicle, draw the primary cable and its rubber protector out from the handbrake underfloor housing.

6 Undo the four bolts securing the handbrake lever to the vehicle floorpan (on the inside of the vehicle), then withdraw the assembly.

Note the fitment of the underfloor housing and the cable grommet.

Refitting

7 Refitting is the reverse of the removal procedure, noting the following points.

(a) Tighten all disturbed fastenings to their specified torque wrench settings.

(b) Reconnect the primary cable and adjust the handbrake (Section 19).

22 Brake pedal – removal, refitting and adjustment

Removal

1 Disconnect the battery negative terminal. Working inside the vehicle, remove the facia lower finish panel from the driver's footwell (Chapter 11).

21.3 Handbrake 'ON' warning switch connection (A), switch securing screw (B)

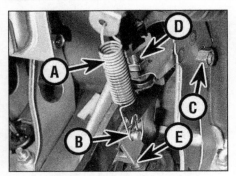

22.4A Brake pedal and associated components

A Pedal return spring
B Clevis pin and securing clip
C Pedal pivot bolt nut
D Stop-lamp switch
E Clevis and locknut

2 Unhook the return spring from the upper end of the pedal arm.
3 Pull out the spring clip and the clevis pin to disconnect the pushrod from the pedal arm.
4 Unscrew the nut from the pedal pivot bolt and remove the washer, remove the bolt, then withdraw the pedal arm. The pivot cross-shaft and bushes can be withdrawn as required (photos).

Refitting

5 Refitting is the reverse of the removal procedure, noting the following points.
(a) Tighten the disturbed fasteners, to their specified torque wrench settings (where given).
(b) Apply a smear of general-purpose grease to the pivot cross-shaft.
(c) Check the pedal height setting as described below.

Adjustment

Pedal height

6 Disconnect the battery negative terminal. Working inside the vehicle, remove the facia lower finish panel from the driver's footwell (Chapter 11).
7 Peel back the carpet and measure the pedal height; Fig. 9.18. Note that the measurement should be taken to the asphalt sheet; if it is not within specification, first slacken the stop-lamp switch locknut and unscrew the switch. Release the pushrod clevis locknut and turn the pushrod until the pedal height is correct, then retighten the clevis locknut.
8 Once the pedal height is correct, check the free play as described below.

Pedal free play

9 To check the pedal free play, first destroy the vacuum in the servo by depressing the brake pedal several times. Depress the brake pedal with the fingers until firm resistance can be felt; measure the distance through which the pedal travels from the fully-released position to the point where the resistance

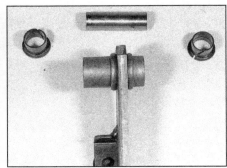

22.4B Brake pedal pivot cross-shaft and bushes

starts and compare the measurement obtained with that specified.
10 If adjustment is required slacken the pushrod clevis locknut and turn the pushrod until the free play is correct, then start the engine to confirm that free play exists in the activated system; recheck the pedal height on completion and repeat the procedure if necessary. Tighten the clevis locknut.
11 Check the stop-lamp switch setting (Section 23), then reconnect the facia lower finish panel components and refit the panel (Chapter 11). Reconnect the battery negative terminal.

Pedal reserve distance check

12 With the engine running and the handbrake fully released, apply the specified pressure to the brake pedal and maintain it while an assistant measures the distance from the top of the brake pedal rubber to the asphalt sheet (under the carpet). Under the specified pedal pressure, the distance should be at least that specified; if the measured distance is less there must be a fault in the system.
13 Check first that the system is free from fluid leaks and bleed the complete system (Section 16) to ensure that no air is present, then check for damaged or faulty components. Check particularly that the calipers are free to slide on their torque plates and that the rear (drum) brake self-adjusting mechanism is in good condition (where applicable).

23 Stop-lamp switch – adjustment, removal and refitting

Adjustment

1 The stop-lamp switch operates the stop-lamps at the rear of the vehicle in response to direct pressure on the brake pedal. It should be set so that the lamps light whenever the brake pedal is depressed, as soon as the pedal free play is taken up.
2 Access to the switch is much improved if the facia lower finish panel is first removed from the driver's footwell (Chapter 11).

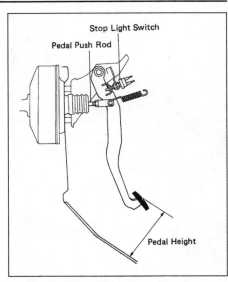

Fig. 9.18 Measuring brake pedal height (Sec 22)

3 Slacken the two nuts securing the switch and reposition the switch until the lamps light at the correct moment (see photo 22.4A); either have an assistant check the stop-lamps for you or disconnect the switch wires and use a multimeter to check when the switch contacts close, allowing current to flow. Tighten securely the two nuts, then switch on the ignition and check the operation of the stop-lamps.
4 Reconnect the facia lower finish panel components, and refit the panel (Chapter 11).

Removal

5 To remove the switch, disconnect its wires and unscrew the adjuster locknut.

Refitting

6 Refitting is the reverse of the removal procedure; adjust the switch setting.

24 Braking system warning lamps – general

1 The vehicle is fitted with a handbrake 'ON' warning switch and a low brake fluid level warning switch (incorporated into the master cylinder fluid reservoir cap). An appropriate warning light is mounted in the instrument panel.
2 Upon turning the ignition on, certain warning lights should illuminate as a bulb function check.
3 If the brake warning light on the instrument panel remains on, check that the handbrake is fully released. If the light fails to extinguish, check the brake fluid level and top up if necessary (note that any sudden drop in brake fluid level must be investigated immediately).
4 Refer to Chapter 12 for details of removal and refitting of applicable switches and of bulb renewal.

Chapter 10 Suspension and steering

Contents

Degrees of difficulty

| Easy, suitable for novice with little experience | | Fairly easy, suitable for beginner with some experience | | Fairly difficult, suitable for competent DIY mechanic | | Difficult, suitable for experienced DIY mechanic | | Very difficult, suitable for expert DIY or professional | |

Specifications

Front suspension

Type	Independent, with MacPherson struts and coil springs, anti-roll bar on some models
Hub bearing maximum axial play	0.05 mm
Chassis ground clearance – see Fig. 10.22:	
GTi 16 model	178 mm
All other models	186 mm

Rear suspension

Type	Independent, with MacPherson struts and coil springs, transverse arms and radius rods, anti-roll bar on some models
Hub bearing maximum axial play	0.05 mm
Chassis ground clearance see – Fig. 10.23:	
GTi 16 model	236 mm
All other models	242 mm

Steering

Type	Manual or power-assisted rack and pinion
Steering wheel maximum free play – at rim	30 mm

Roadwheels

Type	Pressed steel or aluminium alloy
Size:	
GTi 16 model	5.5J x 14
All other models	5J x 13
Rim maximum lateral run-out	1.0 mm

Tyres

Type	Tubeless, steel-braced radial

Size:

GTi 16 model	185/60 R 14 82H
All other models	155 SR 13,155 R 13 78S,155/80 R 13 78S,165 SR 13,165 R 13 82S, 165/80 R 13 82S,175/70 SR 13,175/70 R 13 82S, 175/70 HR 13, or 17550 R 13 82H according to model

Pressures – cold:	**Front**	**Rear**
155 SR 13,155 R 13 78S, 155/80 R 13 78S	1.9 bar (27 lbf/in²)	2.3 bar (33 lbf/in²)
165 SR 13,165 R 13 82S, 165/80 R 13 82S	1.8 bar (26 lbf/in²)	1.9 bar (27 lbf/in²)
175/70 SR13,175/70 R13 82S,175/70 HR13,175 /70 R13 82H, 185/60 R 14 82 H	1.8 bar (26 lbf/in²)	2.1 bar (30 lbf/in²)

Note: *Pressures apply only to original equipment tyres at speeds of up to 100 mph and may vary if any other make or type is fitted; check with the tyre manufacturer or supplier for correct pressures if necessary. For optional pressures at reduced loads and/or higher speeds, consult the vehicle's handbook or your Toyota dealer.*

Wheel alignment and steering angles

	Front	**Rear**
Camber angle:		
GTi 16 model	0° 5' negative ± 45'	0° 41' negative ± 45'
All other models	0° 10' negative ± 45'	0° 35' negative ± 45'
Maximum camber variation between sides	0° 30'	0° 30'
Castor angle	1° 20' positive ± 45'	
Maximum castor variation between sides	0° 30'	
Steering axis inclination/SAI – also known as kingpin inclination/KPI:		
GTi 16 model	12° 50' ± 45'	
All other models	12° 40' ± 45'	
Maximum SAI variation between sides	0° 30'	
Toe setting:		
Front	1.0 ± 1.0 mm toe-in	
Rear	4.0 ± 1.0 mm toe-in	
Maximum track rod length variation between sides	1.5 mm	
Maximum variation between sides of rear suspension rear transverse arm effective length – see Fig.10.25	3.0 mm	

Front wheel turning angles:	**Inside roadwheel**	**Outside roadwheel**
Toe-out in turns	21° 30'	20° 0'
Full lock – 1.3 models with non-assisted steering	38° 0'	33° 0'
Full lock – GTi 16 model with power-assisted steering	37° 0'	32° 0'
Full lock – all other models	37° 30'	32° 30'

Torque wrench settings

	Nm	**lbf ft**
Front suspension		
Suspension strut:		
Top mounting nuts	39	29
Central spring retaining nut	47	35
Strut-to-hub carrier nuts	263	194
Hub carrier-to-lower arm balljoint	127	94
Balljoint-to-suspension lower arm	142	105
Suspension lower arm:		
Front bolt-to-suspension crossmember	235	173
Bushing nut	137	101
Rear mounting bracket-to-body:		
Large bolts either side of bushing	127	94
Rearmost bolt	50	37
Small bolt and nut	19	14
Suspension crossmember-to-body:		
Front outboard bolts	206	152
Rear outboard bolts	127	94
Central bolts	61	45
Anti-roll bar-to-suspension lower arm:		
GTi 16 model	35	26
All other models	18	13
Rear suspension		
Suspension strut:		
Top mounting nuts	39	29
Central spring retaining nut	49	36
Strut-to-hub carrier	142	105
Stub axle-to-hub carrier bolts	80	59

Torque wrench settings

	Nm	lbf ft
Rear suspension (continued)		
Hub nut	123	91
Transverse arm pivot bolts and nuts	118	87
Radius rod pivot bolts and nuts	118	87
Anti-roll bar:		
Link mounting bolts and nuts	35	26
Mounting brackets-to-body	19	14
Steering		
Steering wheel nut	34	25
Steering column bulkhead hole cover	4.9	4
Steering column mounting nuts and bolts	25	18
Steering gear mounting nuts and bolts	59	44
Intermediate shaft universal joint clamp bolts	35	26
Rake-adjustable steering column components:		
Steering support bolts	19	14
Pawl locknut	7.8	6
Tilt lever retainer-to-lever lockbolt nuts	7.8	6
Tilt lever retainer nuts-to-steering support	10	7
Compression spring bolts	7.8	6
Track rod inner balljoints-to-steering rack	83	61
Track rod end-to-track rod locknut	56	41
Track rod end-to-hub carrier steering arm	49	36
Power-assisted steering components:		
Steering gear turn pressure tube unions	13	9
Steering gear fluid feed and return pipe unions	20	14
Steering pump fluid feed pipe union:		
GTi 16 model	47	35
All other models	44	32
Steering pump pulley nut:		
GTi 16 model	38	28
All other models	43	32
Steering pump mounting bolts:		
1.3 models	59	44
1.6 models	39	29
Steering pump adjusting bracket bolts – 1.6 GL Executive model	39	29
Steering pump bracket fasteners – GTi 16 model	39	29
Steering pump idler pulley bolts – GTi 16 model	39	29
Roadwheels		
Roadwheel nuts	103	76

1 General information

The suspension is fully independent, using MacPherson struts with coil springs.

At the front the roadwheel hub bearings are pressed into the hub carrier assemblies which are clamped to the bottom of each strut and are located, via a balljoint, by the suspension lower arms. The lower arms pivot on rubber bushings and are secured to the underbody by the crossmember. Some models are fitted with an anti-roll bar; GTi 16 models are also fitted with a brace across the strut top mountings.

At the rear, the roadwheel hub bearings are contained within the stub axle assemblies that are bolted to the hub carriers. The hub carriers are clamped to the bottom of each strut, each being located laterally by the two transverse arms pivoted from the crossmember; fore-and-aft location of each hub carrier is provided by a radius rod. Some models are fitted with an anti-roll bar.

The steering is by rack and pinion, with a universally jointed intermediate steering shaft. Some models have a non-assisted steering system and fixed steering column while others are fitted with power-assisted steering and a rake-adjustable column.

2 Front suspension anti-roll bar
– removal and refitting

Note: *A new exhaust gasket will be required during refitting. Except on GTi 16 models, new nuts will be required when reconnecting the anti-roll bar links.*

Removal

1 Slacken the front roadwheel nuts, raise the front of the vehicle and support it securely on axle stands. Remove the roadwheels.
2 Except on GTi 16 models, remove the nuts securing the anti-roll bar connecting links to the suspension lower arms and disconnect the links; note the mountings and discard the nuts.
3 On GTi 16 models, remove the nuts and disconnect the links from the anti-roll bar (photo). Use a suitably-sized Allen key to hold the balljoints, if necessary, to prevent them rotating.

2.3 Front anti-roll bar link nuts (arrowed) – GTi 16

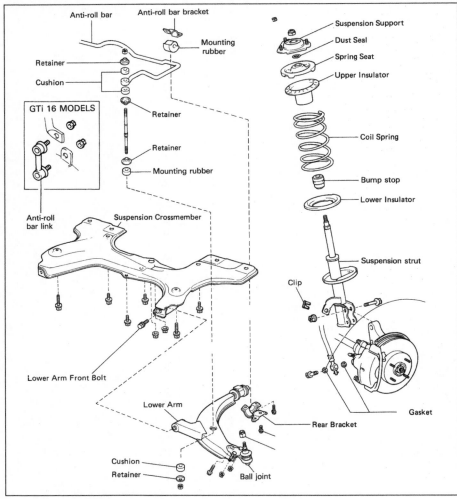

Fig. 10.1 Exploded view of front suspension components (Sec 1)

8 On GTi 16 models, check that the anti-roll bar link balljoints rotate freely and without harshness or sloppiness. Renew the links if necessary.

9 Examine all anti-roll bar mounting components. If any are worn or perished, renew them.

Refitting

10 Fit the mounting rubbers to the anti-roll bar so that the marks made on removal align. The arrow marking on the rubbers must be underneath and pointing towards the front of the vehicle.

11 Refitting is the reverse of the removal procedure, noting the following points.

(a) *New nuts must be used when reconnecting the anti-roll bar links, except on GTi 16 models.*

(b) *A new gasket must be used when reconnecting the exhaust system.*

(c) *Tighten all disturbed fastenings to their specified torque wrench settings (where given).*

(d) *Do not fully tighten the suspension lower arm rear mounting bracket fasteners until the vehicle is resting on its roadwheels and its front end has been bounced up and down a few times to settle the suspension components.*

(e) *On completion, check the front roadwheel alignment (Section 33).*

3 Front hub carrier – removal and refitting

Removal

1 Slacken the relevant roadwheel nuts, raise the front of the vehicle and support it securely on axle stands. Remove the roadwheel.

2 Remove the driveshaft retaining nut and its washer (Chapter 8, Section 2) (photo).

3 Remove the brake caliper complete with torque plate and suspend it clear of the working area (Chapter 9).

4 Using a dial gauge, check the hub bearing axial play. If it exceeds the maximum specified, the bearing must be renewed (Section 4).

4 Disconnect the exhaust pipe at the joint just behind the suspension crossmember; release the exhaust system mountings, as required, to allow the anti-roll bar to be withdrawn and support the exhaust system to avoid straining its mountings.

5 Mark the relative position of the anti-roll bar to its mounting rubbers using quick-drying paint.

6 Unbolt the suspension lower arm rear mounting brackets; unhinge and remove the anti-roll bar brackets, then remove the anti-roll bar with its mounting rubbers (photos).

7 Remove the anti-roll bar mounting rubbers, noting their orientation.

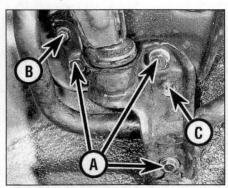

2.6A Front suspension lower arm rear mounting bracket – GTi 16

A *Bracket bolts*   B *Bracket nut*
C *Anti-roll bar bracket-to-lower arm bracket bolt*

2.6B Removing front suspension lower arm rear bracket, unhinging anti-roll bar bracket (arrowed)

3.2 Removing driveshaft nut cap

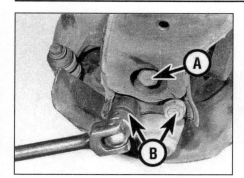

3.6 Balljoint-to-suspension lower arm bolt (A) and nuts (B)

5 Disconnect the track rod end from the hub carrier steering arm (Section 21, paragraphs 1 to 4).

6 Remove the bolt and two nuts securing the balljoint to the suspension lower arm, then separate the two (photo).

7 Remove the bolts and nuts securing the hub carrier to the suspension strut.

8 Withdraw the hub carrier and hub as an assembly, tapping if necessary with a soft-faced hammer on the driveshaft end .

Refitting

9 Refitting is the reverse of the removal procedure, noting the following points.

(a) Refer to the relevant Sections of this Chapter and of Chapters 8 and 9 for specific details of refitting the driveshaft nut and brake caliper.

(b) Tighten all disturbed fastenings to their specified torque wrench settings (where given).

(c) Loosely connect the balljoint to the suspension lower arm before securing the hub carrier to the suspension strut.

(d) On completion, check the front roadwheel alignment (Section 33).

4 Front hub bearings – renewal

Note: *In response to complaints of a knocking noise from the front hub bearing when driving at low speed over rough surfaces, a modified hub carrier and hub bearing became available (for fitting as a set). Consult your dealer for further details.*

Note: *Obtain a bearing renewal kit which contains all the relevant renewable components.*

1 Remove the hub carrier from the vehicle (Section 3). Clamp the assembly in a vice fitted with jaw protectors.

2 Using a screwdriver, prise out the dust deflector from the hub carrier inboard side.

3 Remove the suspension lower arm balljoint (Section 5).

4 Prise out the inner oil seal.

5 Extract the bearing circlip.

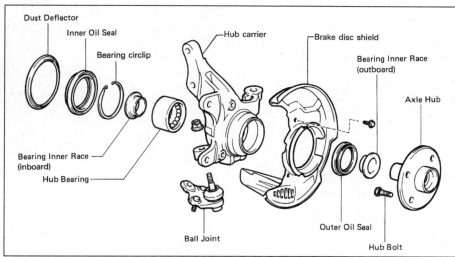

Fig. 10.2 Exploded view of front hub carrier components (Sec 4)

6 Remove the three bolts securing the brake disc shield.

7 Press the hub out of the hub carrier. Remove the brake disc shield.

8 Remove the bearing inner race from the hub carrier inboard side.

9 Draw the outboard bearing inner race from the hub.

10 Prise the outer oil seal out of the hub carrier.

11 To remove the hub bearing, first refit the removed outboard bearing inner race to the bearing. Drive the bearing squarely out from the hub carrier, towards the inboard side.

12 Ensuring that pressure is applied only to the bearing outer race, press the new bearing, as an assembly, squarely into the hub carrier from the inboard side.

13 Squarely drive the new outer oil seal into the hub carrier, with the lip of the seal facing outwards. Take care not to damage the oil seal lip, and apply a smear of grease to it once it is installed.

14 Apply liquid sealant to the brake disc shield mating surface, then refit it to the hub carrier.

15 Applying pressure only to the bearing inner race, press the hub into the hub carrier; use Toyota special tool SST 09310 – 35010 if available.

16 Fit a new bearing circlip.

17 Squarely drive the new inner oil seal into the hub carrier. Take care not to damage the oil seal lip, and apply some grease to the lip once the seal is installed.

18 Press a new dust deflector into the hub carrier, taking care not to distort it as it is installed (Fig. 10.4).

19 Refit the balljoint (Section 5).

20 Refit the hub carrier (Section 3).

5 Front suspension lower arm balljoint – removal and refitting

Note: *The balljoint securing nut (and split pin) must be renewed whenever they are disturbed.*

Removal

1 Remove the hub carrier from the vehicle (Section 3), then unscrew the nut securing the

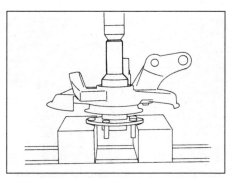

Fig. 10.3 Pressing the hub into the hub carrier (Sec 4)

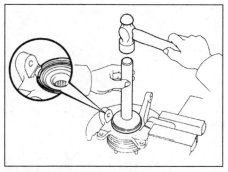

Fig. 10.4 Fitting a new dust deflector. Inset shows the cutout aligned to allow fitting of the lower arm balljoint (Sec 4)

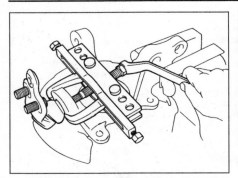

Fig. 10.5 Releasing the lower arm balljoint taper using a puller (Sec 5)

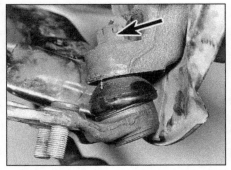

5.1 Nut and split pin (arrowed) securing balljoint to hub carrier

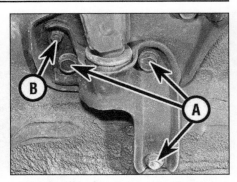

6.4 Front suspension lower arm rear mounting bracket – except GTi 16 – bolts (A) and nut (B)

balljoint to the hub carrier. Some models may have a split pin securing the nut; this must be extracted before unscrewing the nut (photo).
2 Using a suitable tool, press the balljoint out of the hub carrier.

Refitting

3 Refit the balljoint to the hub carrier as far as its taper will allow.
4 Draw the balljoint taper fully into the hub carrier by temporarily refitting the old securing nut and tightening it to a torque wrench setting of 20 Nm. Undo and discard the old nut.
5 Fit a new balljoint securing nut, tighten it to the specified torque wrench setting, then fit a new split pin (where applicable).
6 Refit the hub carrier (Section 3).

6 Front suspension lower arm – removal and refitting

Note: *On automatic transmission-equipped vehicles, the procedure given here applies only to the right-hand front suspension lower arm; the left-hand arm can be removed only after the suspension crossmember assembly has been removed from the vehicle (Section 7).*

Removal

1 Slacken the relevant roadwheel nuts, raise the front of the vehicle and support it securely on axle stands. Remove the roadwheel.

2 Disconnect (where fitted) the anti-roll bar link from the front suspension lower arm. Use quick-drying paint to mark the relative position of the anti-roll bar to its mounting rubber (Section 2).
3 Remove the bolt and two nuts securing the suspension lower arm to the balljoint, then separate the two.
4 Unbolt the suspension lower arm rear mounting bracket; unhinge and remove (where fitted) the anti-roll bar bracket (photo).
5 Support the suspension lower arm and remove the bolt securing the front of the arm to the crossmember; remove the arm (photo).

Refitting

6 Refitting is the reverse of the removal procedure, noting the following points.
(a) *Refit the anti-roll bar (where fitted) as described in Section 2*
(b) *Tighten all disturbed fastenings to their specified torque wrench settings (where given).*
(c) *Do not fully tighten the suspension lower arm rear mounting bracket fastenings until the vehicle is resting on its roadwheels and its front end has been bounced up and down a few times to settle the suspension components.*
(d) *On completion, check the front roadwheel alignment (Section 33).*

7 Front suspension crossmember assembly – removal and refitting

Removal

1 Slacken the roadwheel nuts, raise the front of the vehicle and support it securely on axle stands. Remove the roadwheels.
2 Disconnect (where fitted) the anti-roll bar link from the front suspension lower arms. Use quick-drying paint to mark the relative position of the anti-roll bar to its mounting rubbers (Section 2).
3 Disconnect both suspension lower arms from their balljoints.
4 Unbolt the suspension lower arm rear mounting brackets; unhinge and remove (where fitted) the anti-roll bar brackets and move the anti-roll bar towards the rear of the vehicle.
5 Support the engine/transmission crossmember as necessary, then undo the two engine rear mounting-to-suspension crossmember nuts. With an assistant supporting the suspension crossmember assembly, remove the remaining crossmember bolts and withdraw the crossmember (photos).
6 Remove the suspension lower arms from the crossmember assembly (if required) (Section 6).

6.5 Removing bolt securing front of suspension lower arm to crossmember

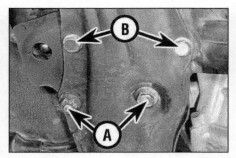

7.5A Engine rear mounting-to-suspension crossmember nuts (A), suspension crossmember-to-engine/ transmission crossmember bolts (B)

7.5B Removing one of suspension crossmember outboard bolts

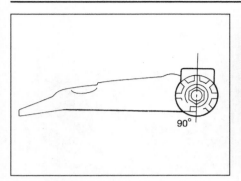

Fig. 10.6 Fit the new bushing to the lower arm so that the bushing centre-line is at 90° to the arm base (Sec 8)

9.3A Front suspension strut brace mountings at strut top mountings (arrowed) . . .

9.3B . . . and at bulkhead (arrowed) (GTi 16)

Refitting

7 Refitting is the reverse of the removal procedure, noting the following points.
(a) Refit the anti-roll bar (where fitted) as described in Section 2.
(b) Tighten all disturbed fastenings to their specified torque wrench settings (where given).
(c) Do not fully tighten the suspension lower arm rear mounting bracket fasteners until the vehicle is resting on its roadwheels and its front end has been bounced up and down a few times to settle the suspension components.
(d) On completion, check the front roadwheel alignment (Section 33).

8 Front suspension lower arm bushing – renewal

1 With the suspension lower arm removed from the vehicle (Section 6), clamp it in a vice fitted with jaw protectors.
2 Undo the bushing nut, then remove the retainer and the bushing.
3 Install a new bushing and the retainer as shown in Fig. 10.6, then fit the bushing nut and tighten it to its specified torque wrench setting. Refit the suspension lower arm (Section 6).

9 Front suspension strut brace (GTi 16) – removal and refitting

Removal

1 With the bonnet raised, disconnect the wiring support clip from the strut brace left-hand side.
2 Unbolt the ignition coil support bracket and move the ignition coil out of the working area.
3 Undo the four suspension strut top mounting nuts and the two bolts securing the strut brace to the bulkhead, then remove it (photos).

Refitting

4 Refitting is a reversal of the removal procedure; tighten all disturbed fasteners to their specified torque wrench settings (where given).

10 Front suspension strut – removal and refitting

Removal

1 Slacken the relevant roadwheel nuts then raise and support the front of the vehicle

securely on axle stands. Remove the roadwheel.
2 Disconnect the flexible hose from the brake caliper (Chapter 9).
3 Remove the clip securing the flexible hose to its support bracket on the suspension strut, then pass the hose through the bracket (photo).
4 Remove the bolts and nuts securing the hub carrier to the suspension strut, then separate the two; support the hub carrier assembly (photo).
5 Unscrew the suspension strut top mounting nuts, then remove the strut (photo).

Refitting

6 Refitting is the reverse of the removal procedure, noting the following points.
(a) Refer to Chapter 9 for details of refitting the flexible hose.
(b) Tighten all disturbed fasteners to their specified torque wrench settings (where given).
(c) Bleed any air from the brake hydraulic circuit(s) disturbed (Chapter 9).
(d) On completion check the front roadwheel alignment (Section 33).

10.3 Passing brake flexible hose through front suspension strut bracket

10.4 Separating hub carrier from suspension strut

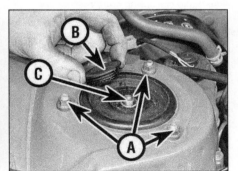

10.5 Suspension strut top mounting nuts (A), central dust-excluding cap (B) central spring retaining nut (C)

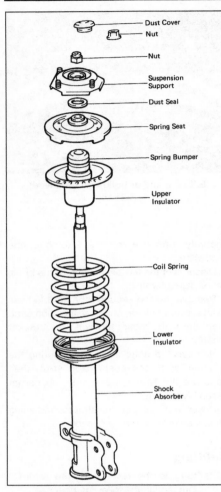

Dust Cover
Nut
Nut
Suspension Support
Dust Seal
Spring Seat
Spring Bumper
Upper Insulator
Coil Spring
Lower Insulator
Shock Absorber

Fig. 10.7 Exploded view of front suspension strut components (Sec 11)

11 Front suspension strut – overhaul

⚠️ **Warning: Before attempting to dismantle the front suspension strut a suitable tool to hold the coil spring in compression must be obtained. Adjustable coil spring compressors are**

11.9B Fitting suspension support

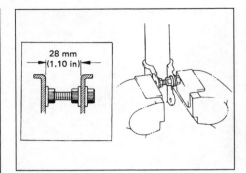

28 mm (1.10 in)

Fig. 10.8 Clamping a suspension strut in a vice to avoid distortion (Sec 11)

readily available and are recommended for this operation. Any attempt to dismantle the strut without such a tool is likely to result in damage or personal injury.
Note: *A NEW central spring retaining nut will be required on reassembly.*

1 Remove the strut from the vehicle (Section 10). Mount the strut in a vice as shown in Fig. 10.8, so that the strut is securely held without risk of distortion.

2 Fit spring compressors to each side of the spring and tighten them evenly to compress the spring until there is no pressure on the suspension support.

3 Remove the central dust-excluding cap from the suspension support, then clamp the spring upper seat so that it cannot rotate and unscrew the central spring retaining nut.

4 Remove the suspension support, the dust seal, the spring upper seat and the upper insulator, followed by the spring itself, the bump stop and the lower insulator.

5 If the compressed spring is to be transferred to a new strut, there is no need to release the coil spring from compression. If a new spring is to be fitted, release the compressors slowly and evenly until the spring is fully relaxed. Transfer the compressors to the new spring and compress it.

6 Before discarding a defective suspension strut, first loosen the ring nut at the top of the strut, by two or three turns, to allow the gas to escape.

11.10 Clamp spring upper seat as shown while central spring retaining nut is tightened

11.9A Fitting dust seal – note 'OUT' marking (arrowed) on spring upper seat

7 Refit the lower insulator, the bump stop and the spring.

8 Fit the upper insulator and the spring upper seat; note that the 'OUT' marking on the spring upper seat must face towards the outside edge of the vehicle when the strut is refitted.

9 Fit the dust seal to the spring upper seat, followed by the suspension support (photos).

10 Clamp the spring upper seat, fit a new central spring retaining nut and tighten it to its specified torque wrench setting (photo). Pack the suspension support bearing with grease, then fit the dust-excluding cap.

11 Carefully release the spring tension, ensuring that the spring locates correctly in the upper and lower seats, then remove the compressors.

12 Refit the suspension strut to the vehicle (Section 10).

12 Rear suspension anti-roll bar – removal and refitting

Removal

1 Slacken the rear roadwheel nuts, raise the rear of the vehicle and support it securely on axle stands. Remove the roadwheels.

2 Disconnect the anti-roll bar links, first from the suspension struts, then from the anti-roll bar itself; use an Allen key to prevent the link balljoints from rotating (photo).

12.2 Disconnecting anti-roll bar link from suspension strut

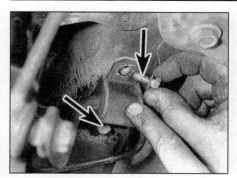

12.3A Removing anti-roll bar bracket bolts (arrowed)

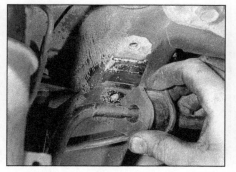

12.3B Removing anti-roll bar mounting rubber

13.3A Unbolting stub axle

3 Unbolt the anti-roll bar brackets and remove the mounting rubbers (photos).
4 Remove the fuel tank right-hand support strap rear bolt, to provide clearance for the anti-roll bar to be withdrawn. If required, the tank's left-hand support strap rear bolt may also be removed; securely support the fuel tank.
5 Manoeuvre the anti-roll bar out from the left-hand side of the vehicle.

Refitting

6 Refitting is the reverse of the removal procedure; tighten all disturbed fasteners to their specified torque wrench settings (where given).

13 Rear stub axle assembly – removal and refitting

Note: *A new O-ring will be required on refitting.*

Removal

1 Working as described in the relevant Sections of Chapter 9, remove the brake drum or (as applicable) the caliper assembly and brake disc. Note that there is no need to disconnect the hydraulic hose or handbrake cable; secure the braking system components clear of the working area, ensuring that the hose and cable are not kinked or distorted.
2 Using a dial gauge, check the hub bearing

axial play. If it exceeds the maximum specified, the bearing must be renewed (Section 14).
3 Using a suitably-sized socket inserted through the hub access holes, unscrew the stub axle securing bolts; remove the assembly and its O-ring (photos).

Refitting

4 Refitting is the reverse of the removal procedure, noting the following points.
(a) Refer to the relevant Sections of Chapter 9 for specific details of refitting the brake drum/disc.
(b) Fit a new stub axle O-ring.
(c) Tighten all fastenings to their specified torque wrench settings (where given).

14 Rear hub bearings – renewal

Note: *Obtain a bearing renewal kit which contains all the required renewable components as a matched set. Note that a new hub nut will be required.*

1 Remove the stub axle from the vehicle (Section 13).
2 Relieve the hub nut staking using an electric drill or a hammer and punch, then unscrew and discard the nut.
3 Press the hub out of the hub bearing housing.
4 Remove the inboard bearing inner race.

13.3B Removing stub axle O-ring

5 Draw the outboard bearing inner race off the hub.
6 Prise out the oil seal from the hub bearing housing.
7 Temporarily refit the outboard bearing inner race to the outboard side of the hub bearing. Support the hub bearing housing on blocks of wood, then press the bearing out squarely towards the inboard side.
8 Grease the bearing then press it, as an assembly, squarely into the hub bearing housing from the inboard side. Apply pressure to the outer race only.
9 Install a new oil seal.
10 Press the hub into the hub bearing housing. Take care to properly support the bearing inner races during this operation; use Toyota special tool SST 09608 – 30012 (09608 – 04030) if available (Fig. 10.10).

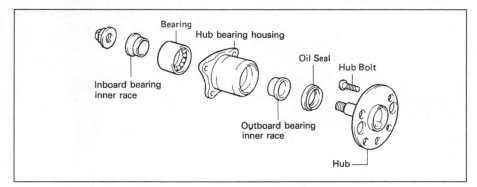

Fig. 10.9 Exploded view of rear stub axle assembly (Sec 14)

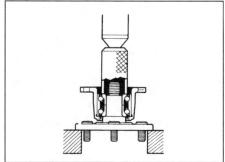

Fig. 10.10 Pressing hub into hub bearing housing using Toyota special tool (Sec 14)

14.12 Stake new hub nut as shown (arrowed)

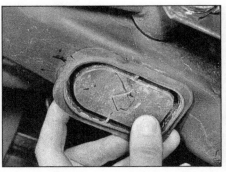

15.2 Removing plastic cover from rear suspension crossmember

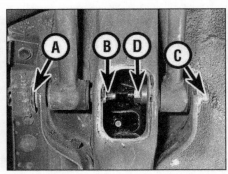

15.3A Rear suspension front transverse arm inboard pivot bolt (A) and nut (B), rear transverse arm inboard pivot bolt (C) and nut (D)

11 Install a new hub nut, tightening it to the specified torque wrench setting.

12 Using a hammer and punch, stake the nut collar into the stub axle groove (photo).

13 Refit the stub axle to the vehicle (Section 13).

15 Rear suspension transverse arms – removal and refitting

Removal

Front arm

1 Raise the rear of the vehicle and support it securely on axle stands. Remove the roadwheel only if the extra working space is required.

2 Remove the relevant plastic cover from the crossmember (photo).

3 Unscrew the nuts securing the inboard and outboard pivot bolts, noting the bolt collar and any plate or washer fitments under the nuts (photos). Tap out the bolts and withdraw the arm.

Rear arm

4 The procedure for removal is as described above but, before dismantling, use quick-drying paint or similar to make matchmarks on the toe-adjusting cam and suspension crossmember (photo). The toe-adjusting cam must also be withdrawn so that the arm inboard end can be removed from the crossmember.

Refitting

5 Refitting of both front and rear arms is the reverse of the removal procedure, noting the following points.

(a) Ensure that the nut, plate and washer fitments (where applicable) locate correctly.

(b) When refitting the rear arms, the matchmarks must align that were made on dismantling.

(c) Tighten all disturbed fastenings to their specified torque wrench settings.

(d) Do not fully tighten the pivot bolt nuts until the vehicle is resting on its roadwheels and its rear end has been bounced up and down a few times to settle the suspension components.

(e) On completion, check the rear roadwheel alignment (Section 33).

16 Rear suspension radius rod – removal and refitting

Removal

1 Raise the rear of the vehicle and support it securely on axle stands. Remove the roadwheel only if the extra working space is required.

2 Unscrew the front and rear pivot bolts, noting the nut plates (see photo 15.3B). Withdraw the rod.

Refitting

3 Refitting is the reverse of the removal procedure, noting the following points.

(a) Ensure that the nut plates locate correctly.

(b) Tighten all disturbed fastenings to their specified torque wrench settings.

(c) Do not fully tighten the pivot bolt nuts until the vehicle is resting on its roadwheels and its rear end has been bounced up and down a few times to settle the suspension components.

(d) On completion, check the rear roadwheel alignment (Section 33).

17 Rear hub carrier – removal and refitting

Removal

1 Remove the stub axle (Section 13).

2 Working as described in the relevant Sections of Chapter 9, remove the brake backplate or (as applicable) the brake disc shield.

3 Disconnect the rear suspension radius rod and transverse arms from the hub carrier (Sections 15 and 16).

4 Unscrew the nuts and bolts securing the hub carrier to the suspension strut and remove the hub carrier (photo).

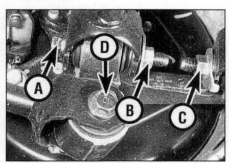

15.3B Rear suspension front transverse arm outboard pivot bolt (A) and nut (B), rear transverse arm outboard pivot bolt nut (C) and radius rod rear pivot bolt (D)

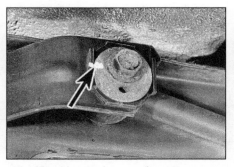

15.4 Matchmarks (arrowed) made on toe-adjusting cam and suspension crossmember before removing rear suspension rear transverse arm

17.4 Hub carrier-to-rear suspension strut nuts (arrowed)

Refitting

5 Refitting is the reverse of the removal procedure, noting the following points.

(a) Refer to the relevant Sections of this Chapter and of Chapter 9 for details of refitting suspension components and the brake backplate or disc shield.

(b) Tighten all disturbed fastenings to their specified torque wrench settings (where given).

(c) Bleed any air from the brake hydraulic circuit(s) disturbed (Chapter 9).

(d) On completion, check the rear roadwheel alignment (Section 33).

18 Rear suspension crossmember – general

1 The crossmember is fixed to the vehicle underside to locate the rear suspension transverse arm inboard ends accurately on the body.

2 It is recommended that this component should not be disturbed; should the crossmember need to be removed or renewed entrust the task to your Toyota dealer who can ensure the accurate alignment of the rear suspension components.

19 Rear suspension strut – removal and refitting

Removal

1 Working in the luggage compartment, as described in the relevant Sections of Chapter 11, remove the parcel shelf and trim as necessary to reach the suspension strut top mounting nuts (photo).

2 Slacken the relevant roadwheel nuts, raise the rear of the vehicle and support it securely on axle stands. Remove the roadwheel.

3 On models fitted with drum rear brakes, disconnect the hydraulic pipe at the suspension strut bracket, then remove the flexible hose securing clip and release the hose and pipe from the strut bracket (Chapter 9). Insert plugs to avoid dirt ingress and prevent excessive fluid loss.

4 Where fitted, disconnect the anti-roll bar link from the suspension strut, then slacken the anti-roll bar mounting bolts so that the bar can be swung down clear of the strut (Section 12).

5 Slacken the suspension transverse arm inboard and outboard pivot bolts (Section 15).

6 Slacken the suspension radius rod front and rear pivot bolts (Section 16).

7 Unscrew the nuts and bolts securing the hub carrier to the suspension strut and separate the two components (see photo 17.4), taking care not to stretch or distort the handbrake cable or, if applicable, the flexible hose.

8 Returning to the luggage compartment, unscrew the suspension strut top mounting nuts; have an assistant available to remove the strut.

19.1 Trim removed to expose rear suspension strut top mounting nuts (arrowed)

Refitting

9 Refitting is the reverse of the removal procedure, noting the following points.

(a) Refer to the relevant Sections of this Chapter for refitting suspension components and to Chapters 9 and 11 for details of refitting brakes and trim.

(b) Tighten all disturbed fasteners to their specified torque wrench settings (where given).

(c) Do not fully tighten the radius rod and transverse arm pivot bolt nuts until the vehicle is resting on its roadwheels and its rear end has been bounced up and down a few times to settle the suspension components.

(d) Bleed any air from the brake hydraulic circuit(s) disturbed (Chapter 9).

(e) On completion, check the rear roadwheel alignment (Section 33).

20 Rear suspension strut – overhaul

All procedures are the same as those described in Section 11 of this Chapter, noting the following points.

(a) Remove and refit the strut as described in Section 19.

(b) The central spring retaining nut may not be covered by a dust - excluding cap on all models; also, the dust seal is replaced by a collar underneath the nut.

(c) If a rear suspension strut is to be discarded always release first the gas

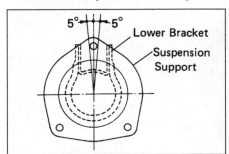

Fig. 10.12 Align suspension support with hub carrier locating bracket, as shown (Sec 20)

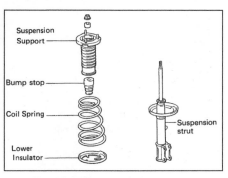

Fig. 10.11 Exploded view of rear suspension strut components (Sec 20)

pressure by drilling a 2 to 3 mm hole in the strut 10 mm up from the hub carrier bracket; observe all normal safety precautions whilst drilling, to prevent possible injury from flying metal chips.

(d) On reassembly, align the suspension support with the hub carrier locating bracket as shown in Fig. 10.12.

21 Steering gear rubber gaiter – renewal

Note: *The track rod end split pin and large (inboard) gaiter clip must be renewed whenever they are disturbed. A crowfoot adaptor will be required to tighten the track rod end-to-track rod locknut to its specified torque wrench setting.*

1 With the roadwheels in the straight-ahead position, slacken the relevant roadwheel nuts, raise the front of the vehicle and support it securely on axle stands. Remove the roadwheel.

2 Use a wire brush to scrub clean the exposed track rod threads, then use a straight edge and a scriber or similar to mark the relationship of the track rod end to the track rod.

3 Holding the track rod end, unscrew its locknut by one quarter of a turn,

4 Extract the split pin, then unscrew the nut securing the track rod end to the hub carrier steering arm until it is flush with the end of its thread. Using, if necessary, a universal balljoint separator tool, separate the track rod end from the hub carrier steering arm (photo).

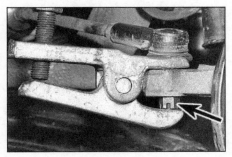

21.4 Using balljoint separator to separate track rod end from hub carrier steering arm – note nut (arrowed) protecting threads

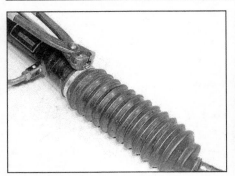

21.8 Fastening steering gear gaiter inboard clip

21.10 Fitting new split pin to secure track rod end nut

5 Counting the **exact** number of turns necessary to do so, unscrew the track rod end from the track rod. Mark the position of the locknut on the track rod and count the number of turns required to unscrew it so that it can be returned to exactly its original position on reassembly.
6 Release the gaiter clips and remove the gaiter.
7 Wipe away any dirt and old lubricant, then liberally apply molybdenum disulphide grease to the rack teeth, bush and track rod inner balljoint.
8 Fit the new gaiter and its new inboard clip to the steering gear, ensuring that they are correctly located, then fasten the clip to secure the gaiter (photo). Refit the small (outboard) gaiter clip, but do not fasten it yet.
9 Apply a light smear of grease to the track rod threads, then screw the track rod end locknut, followed by the track rod end, on to the track rod; each by the exact number of turns noted on removal. This should, of course, return the track rod end to within a quarter-turn of the locknut, with the alignment marks lined up that were made (if applicable) on removal.
10 Degrease the tapers of the track rod end stud and of the hub carrier steering arm, then press the track rod end firmly into the steering arm while the nut is refitted and tightened to its specified torque wrench setting. Insert a new split pin to secure the nut (photo).

11 If the vehicle is to be driven to have the wheel alignment checked, fasten the small (outboard) gaiter clip, then hold the track rod end and securely tighten the locknut; if applying the specified torque wrench setting use a crowfoot adapter and calculate the applied torque according to the adapter used. Otherwise, refer to Section 33.
12 Refit the roadwheel, then lower the vehicle to the ground. Fully tighten the roadwheel nuts to the specified torque wrench setting.
13 Bounce the front of the vehicle up and down a few times to settle the suspension components. Check the front roadwheel alignment (Section 33).
14 Ensure that the gaiter and small (outboard) clip locate in the track rod groove and that the gaiter is not twisted, then fasten the clip to secure the gaiter.

22 Track rod end – removal and refitting

Removal

1 Work as described in paragraphs 1 to 5 of Section 21.

Refitting

2 Work as described in paragraphs 9 to 14 of Section 21.

23 Steering wheel – removal and refitting

Removal

1 Disconnect the battery negative terminal.
2 Remove the facia lower finish panel from the driver's footwell and the steering column shrouds (Chapter 11).
3 Undo the screws securing the horn pad to the steering wheel, located on the reverse side of the steering wheel, then remove the horn pad, disconnecting the horn wiring (photo).
4 With the roadwheels in the straight-ahead position, unscrew the steering wheel nut (photo).
5 Mark the relative alignment of the steering wheel to the steering column shaft, then pull the steering wheel from the shaft. If it is tight, use a suitable puller; threaded holes are provided in the steering wheel hub for this purpose.

Refitting

6 Refitting is a reversal of the removal procedure, ensuring that the alignment marks made during removal line up (with the steering wheel centralised and the roadwheels in the straight-ahead position); tighten the steering wheel nut to the specified torque wrench setting.

24 Steering lock/ignition switch lock barrel – removal and refitting

Removal

1 Disconnect the battery negative terminal.
2 Remove the facia lower finish panel from the driver's footwell and the steering column shrouds (Chapter 11).
3 Insert the ignition key into the lock and turn it to the 'ACC' position.
4 Depress the lock barrel securing plunger, using a punch or similar inserted through the access hole in the lock housing, while pulling the key to withdraw the lock barrel (photo).

23.3 Disconnect horn wiring (arrowed) as horn pad is withdrawn

23.4 Undoing steering wheel nut

24.4 Depressing steering lock/ignition switch barrel plunger (arrowed) to release lock

Refitting

5 Refitting is a reversal of the removal procedure; ensure that the barrel is correctly aligned so that its shaft engages in the loom plate, and ensure that the plunger positively secures it.

25 Steering column – removal and refitting

Removal

1 Remove the steering wheel (Section 23).
2 Unclip the large multi-plug connector from the steering column, then disconnect the multi-function switch and ignition switch loom plate multiplugs (photo).
3 Remove the screws securing the multi-function switch, then remove the switch (photo).
4 Mark the relative position of the steering column shaft to the intermediate shaft upper universal joint, then remove the universal joint clamp bolt and washer (photo).
5 Undo the two bolts and two nuts securing the steering column tube (photo). Lower the column tube and release the column shaft from the intermediate shaft upper universal joint; if necessary, slightly open the joint jaws, using a screwdriver or similar. Remove the steering column assembly.

Refitting

6 Refitting is the reverse of the removal procedure, noting the following points.
(a) Tighten all disturbed fasteners to their specified torque wrench settings (where given).
(b) Ensure that the steering column shaft and intermediate shaft upper universal joint alignment marks made on removal, line up.

26 Intermediate shaft – removal and refitting

Note: *On vehicles with power-assisted steering, a crowfoot adaptor will be required to tighten the fluid pipe unions; the union O-rings must be renewed whenever they are disturbed.*

Removal

1 Disconnect the battery negative terminal.
2 Remove the facia lower finish panel from the driver's footwell (Chapter 11).
3 Mark the relative position of the steering column shaft to the intermediate shaft upper universal joint, then remove the joint clamp bolt and washer. Slightly open the joint jaws, using a screwdriver or similar.
4 Raise the front of the vehicle and support it securely on axle stands.
5 On vehicles with power-assisted steering, disconnect the fluid feed and return pipes from the steering gear. Insert plugs to avoid dirt ingress and prevent excessive fluid loss.

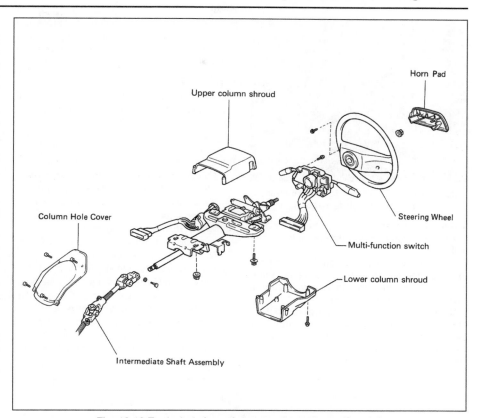

Fig. 10.13 Exploded view of the steering column (Sec 25)

25.2 Multi-plug connector clipped to steering column

25.3 Removing multi-function switch screws

25.4 Intermediate shaft upper universal joint clamp bolt (arrowed)

25.5 Steering column tube bolts (A), nuts (B) and ignition switch loom plate (C)

26.7 Intermediate shaft lower universal joint clamp bolt (arrowed)

6 Remove the steering column hole cover from the engine compartment side of the bulkhead.

7 Remove the clamp bolt and washer from the intermediate shaft lower universal joint, then slightly open the joint jaws using a screwdriver or similar (photo).

8 Carefully lever the lower universal joint up the steering gear pinion shaft until the relationship of the joint to the shaft can be marked, then separate the joint from the pinion shaft.

9 Working inside the vehicle, separate the intermediate shaft upper universal joint from the steering column shaft, then remove the intermediate shaft (noting its orientation).

Refitting

10 Refitting is the reverse of the removal procedure, noting the following points.

(a) Tighten all disturbed fastenings to their specified torque wrench settings (where given).

(b) Ensure that the alignment marks line up that were made on removal between the steering column shaft, the steering gear pinion shaft and the intermediate shaft universal joints.

(c) Check that the steering wheel is centralised when the roadwheels are in the straight-ahead position.

(d) If power-assisted steering is fitted, renew the sealing O-rings when refitting the fluid feed and return pipes. A crowfoot adaptor will be required to tighten the pipe unions to their specified torque wrench setting; calculate the torque according to the adaptor used. On completion, bleed the system (Section 32).

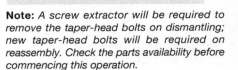

27 Steering column (non-adjustable) – dismantling and reassembly

Note: *A screw extractor will be required to remove the taper-head bolts on dismantling; new taper-head bolts will be required on reassembly. Check the parts availability before commencing this operation.*

Dismantling

1 Remove the steering column from the vehicle (Section 25) and clamp it, by one of the column tube brackets, in a vice fitted with jaw protectors. Ensure that the column tube itself is not distorted.

2 Using a centre-punch, mark the taper-head bolts securing the steering lock housing to the column.

3 Drill into the taper-head bolts and remove them with a screw extractor. Separate the steering lock housing and its clamp from the steering column.

4 Remove the upper circlip and withdraw the steering column shaft from the column tube.

5 Remove the circlip from the steering column shaft.

6 Using a screwdriver, remove the bushing from the base of the steering column tube.

7 Examine the bearing at the steering column tube upper end; if it is worn or damaged. the tube must be renewed.

8 Ensure that the steering lock mechanism operates properly. Remove the lock barrel (Section 24) and the ignition switch loom plate (Chapter 12) if the lock housing is to be renewed; transfer the lock and loom plate to the new housing, referring to the relevant text if necessary.

Reassembly

9 Fit a new bushing to the steering column tube, aligning the tube holes with the bushing projections.

10 Fit the circlip to the lower groove on the steering column shaft, then refit the shaft to the steering column tube. Fit the upper circlip.

11 Fit the steering lock housing and its clamp, using new taper-head bolts.

12 Tighten the taper-head bolts until their heads shear off.

13 Refit the steering column to the vehicle (Section 25).

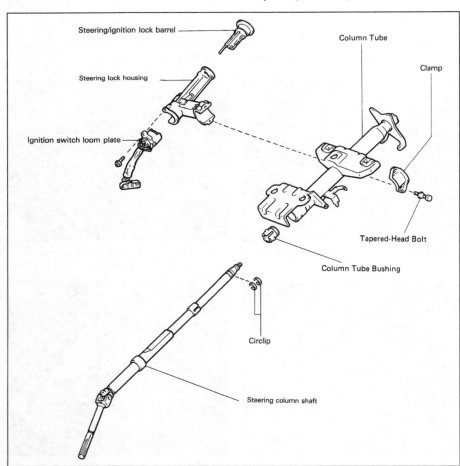

Fig. 10.14 Exploded view of non-adjustable steering column (Sec 27)

Steering/ignition lock barrel

Steering lock housing

Ignition switch loom plate

Column Tube

Clamp

Tapered-Head Bolt

Column Tube Bushing

Circlip

Steering column shaft

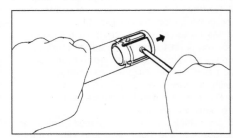

Fig. 10.15 Removing bushing at base of steering column tube (Sec 27)

28 Steering column (rake-adjustable) – dismantling and reassembly

Note: *A screw extractor and slide hammer will be required on dismantling, and NEW taper-head bolts, steering bolts and tilt pawl collars will be required on reassembly. Check the parts availability before commencing this operation.*

Dismantling

1 Remove the steering column from the vehicle (Section 25) and clamp it by one of the column tube brackets in a vice fitted with jaw protectors. Ensure that the column tube itself is not distorted.

2 Using a centre-punch, mark the taper-head bolts securing the steering lock housing to the column.

3 Drill into the taper-head bolts and remove them with a screw extractor. Separate the steering lock housing and its clamp from the steering column.

4 Disconnect and remove the two tension springs.

5 Remove the two compression spring securing bolts and the springs and bushes; take care to prevent the springs from flying out and causing injury or damage during removal.

6 Remove the two tilt lever retainers, noting the washer fitment.

7 Remove the two tilt pawls, noting the washer fitment, then remove the collars from the pawls.

8 Remove the two pawl stoppers.

9 Remove the tilt lever, tilt sub-lever and the lever lockbolt, noting the washer fitment.

10 Noting which bolt came from which side, remove the steering bolts. First obtain a nut and bolt of the same thread as the steering bolt; attach the bolt head to a slide hammer (fabricating a bracket if necessary), then attach the bolt threaded end to the steering bolt using the nut to secure them (Fig. 10.17) and pull out the steering bolt.

11 Remove the steering column lower tube, followed by the stopper on the base of the steering column shaft.

12 Remove the circlip from the top of the upper steering column tube; withdraw the steering column shaft from the tube and remove the spring, thrust collar and bearing, noting their order of fitting.

13 Remove the circlip from its location near the joint on the small (upper) section of the steering column shaft.

14 Remove the wiring harness clamp.

15 Unbolt the steering support from the lower steering column tube.

16 Remove the circlip at the base of the lower steering column tube, then withdraw the steering column shaft collar.

17 Using a screwdriver, remove the bushing from the base of the lower steering column tube.

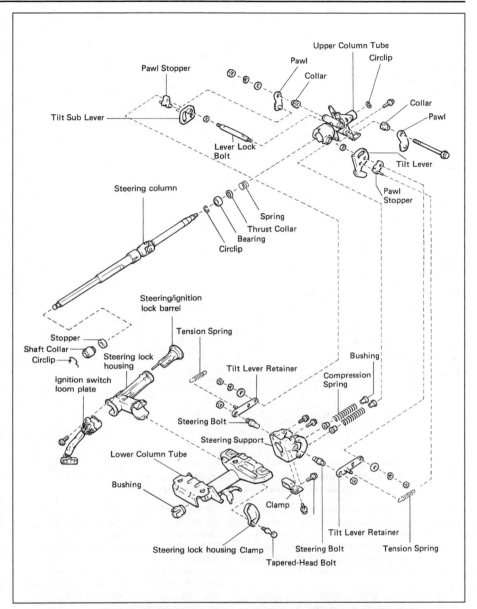

Fig. 10.16 Exploded view of rake-adjustable steering column (Sec 28)

18 Ensure that the steering lock mechanism operates properly. Remove the lock barrel (Section 24) and the ignition switch loom plate (Chapter 12) if the lock housing is to be renewed; transfer the lock barrel and loom plate to the new housing, referring to the relevant text, if necessary.

Reassembly

19 Refitting is the reverse of the removal procedure, noting the following points.

(a) *Coat the parts arrowed in Fig. 10.18 with molybdenum disulphide grease.*

(b) *Tighten all disturbed fasteners to their specified torque wrench settings (where given).*

(c) *Fit a new bushing to the base of the*

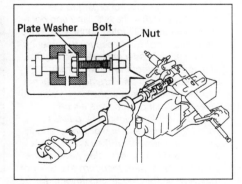

Fig. 10.17 Removing a steering bolt (rake-adjustable steering column) (Sec 28)

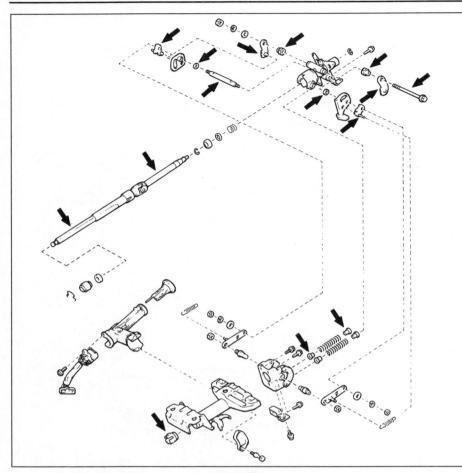

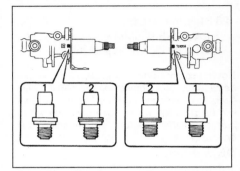

Fig. 10.19 Selection of steering bolts (rake-adjustable steering column) (Sec 28)

Each side's bolts are different and may be a plain or a grooved bolt according to the steering column tube markings
1 *Where this mark appears, select plain bolt*
2 *Where this mark appears, select grooved bolt*

29 Steering gear – removal and refitting

Note: *New track rod end split pins will be required on refitting. On power - assisted steering equipped vehicles, new fluid pipe union O-rings will be required; a crowfoot adaptor will be required to tighten the fluid pipe unions.*

Removal

1 Slacken the relevant roadwheel nuts, raise the front of the vehicle and support it securely on axle stands. Remove the roadwheels.
2 Disconnect the track rod ends from the hub carrier steering arms (Section 21, paragraphs 1 to 4).
3 Unbolt the harmonic damper from the suspension crossmember (photo).
4 It may be necessary to disconnect the transmission control cables and/or to remove the rear engine mounting (Chapters 7 or 1).
5 On power-assisted steering equipped vehicles, disconnect the fluid feed and return pipes from the steering gear and remove their O-rings; insert plugs to avoid dirt ingress and prevent excessive fluid loss.

Fig. 10.18 Coat components arrowed with specified grease on reassembly (rake-adjustable steering column) (Sec 28)

steering column lower tube, aligning the tube holes with the bushing projections.
(d) *Before refitting the lower steering column tube, fit the stopper and the collar to the base of the steering column shaft, refit the circlip to the base of the lower steering column tube.*
(e) *Select new steering bolts according to the markings on the upper steering column tube (Fig. 10.19); note that both left-hand and right-hand steering bolts are available as one of two types according to the markings, and that the left-hand and right-hand bolts are NOT interchangeable. Drive the steering bolts in to secure the steering column tubes, use a hammer and a block of wood to protect the threads from compression and be extremely careful not to attempt to fit them in the wrong side.*
(f) *Select NEW tilt pawl collars which eliminate all play (take the tilt pawls to your Toyota dealer when ordering) and fit them to the pawls. Fit the two tilt pawls and engage the tilt lever side pawl on the centre of its ratchet, then turn the collar of that pawl so that the tilt sub-lever side pawl engages centrally on its ratchet (ensuring that the teeth mesh) before*

tightening the pawl locknut.
(g) *Fit the steering lock housing and its clamp, using new taper-head bolts; tighten the taper-head bolts until their heads shear off.*
(h) *On completion, check that there is no steering column shaft axial play and that the rake-adjusting mechanism operates and locks correctly.*
(I) *Refit the steering column to the vehicle (Section 25).*

29.3 Removing harmonic damper from suspension crossmember

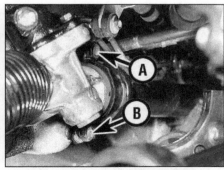

29.8 Steering gear mounting bracket nut (A) and bolt (B)

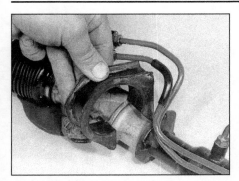

29.11 Removing a steering gear mounting rubber

6 Remove the steering column hole cover from the engine compartment side of the bulkhead.

7 Remove the clamp bolt and washer from the intermediate shaft lower universal joint, then slightly open the joint jaws using a screwdriver or similar.

8 Undo the nut and bolt securing each steering gear mounting bracket (photo). Remove the brackets and support the steering gear.

9 Carefully lever the universal joint up the steering gear pinion shaft until the relationship of the joint to the shaft can be marked, then separate the joint from the pinion shaft.

10 Withdraw the steering gear towards the right-hand side of the vehicle.

11 Remove the steering gear mounting rubbers, noting their fitted positions (photo).

12 The steering gear turn pressure tubes may be removed if required, noting the O-ring at each end of each tube.

Refitting

13 Refitting is the reverse of the removal procedure, noting the following points.

(a) *Tighten all disturbed fasteners to their specified torque wrench settings (where given).*

(b) *Ensure that the alignment marks line up that were made on removal between the steering column shaft, the steering gear pinion shaft and the intermediate shaft universal joints.*

(c) *Check that the steering wheel is centralised when the roadwheels are in the straight-ahead position.*

(d) *If power-assisted steering is fitted, renew the sealing O-rings when refitting the turn pressure tubes (if removed) and the fluid feed and return pipes. A crowfoot adaptor will be required to tighten the tube and pipe unions to their specified torque wrench setting; calculate the torque according to the adaptor used. On completion, bleed the system (Section 32).*

(e) *Reconnect the transmission control cables and/or refit the rear engine mounting, as applicable (Chapters 7 and/or 1).*

Fig. 10.20 Clamping a steering gear in a vice to avoid damage (Sec 30)

(f) *Reconnect the track rod ends to the hub carrier steering arms (Section 21, paragraphs 9 and 10).*

(g) *If any components have been disturbed, check the front roadwheel alignment (Section 33).*

30 Track rod –
removal and refitting

Note: *The claw washer must be renewed on refitting, check the availability of this component before starting work. A crowfoot adaptor will be required to tighten the track rod inner balljoint.*

Removal

1 Remove the steering gear f rom the vehicle (Section 29) and clamp it in a vice fitted with jaw protectors as shown in Fig. 10.20; do **not** clamp directly on the rack housing or irreparable damage may be caused.

2 Remove the steering gear rubber gaiter (Section 21).

3 Using a hammer and a chisel or punch, unstake the claw washer securing the track rod inner balljoint. Take great care to avoid hitting the steering rack.

4 Unscrew the track rod inner balljoint and remove the track rod and claw washer. If both track rods are removed, they must be labelled for refitting to their original sides of the steering rack.

Refitting

5 Fit a new claw washer, aligning its tags with the cut-outs on the end of the steering rack, then screw the track rod inner balljoint into the rack. Use a crowfoot adaptor to tighten the balljoint to its specified torque wrench setting; calculate the torque according to the adaptor used.

6 Stake the claw washer to secure the track rod inner balljoint, take great care to avoid hitting the steering rack.

7 Refit the steering gear rubber gaiter (Section 21, paragraphs 7 to 9).

8 Refit the steering gear to the vehicle (Section 29).

31 Power-assisted steering
pump – removal and refitting

Note: *A suitable crowfoot adaptor will be required to tighten the fluid pipe union to its specified torque on refitting. All pipe union seals and gaskets disturbed on removal must be renewed.*

Removal

1 Disconnect the battery negative terminal.

2 On 1.3 models, remove the air filter trunking; on 1.6 GL Executive models remove the air filter housing and trunking (Chapter 4).

3 On all models, remove the windscreen/tailgate washer reservoir and (where fitted) the right-hand side engine undershield (Chapters 12 and 11).

4 Remove the pump drivebelt; on some models, this will require the removal first of the alternator drivebelt (Chapter 1).

5 Except on GTi 16 models, disconnect the fluid feed pipe and return hose from the

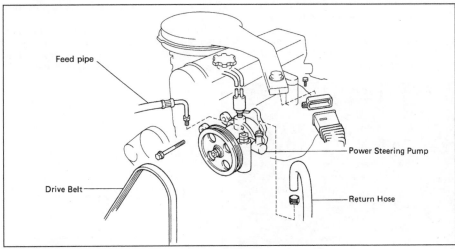

Feed pipe

Drive Belt

Power Steering Pump

Return Hose

Fig. 10.21 Typical view of power-assisted steering pump mountings – 1.3 models shown (Sec 31)

31.6 Fluid pipe support bracket (arrowed) – 1.6 models (typical)

31.8 Removing pump pulley – GTi 16 shown

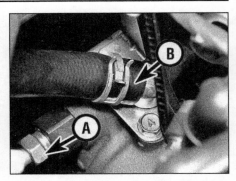

31.9 Pump feed pipe union (A) and return hose connection (B) – GTi 16

pump, noting the gaskets or seals fitted. Insert plugs to prevent excessive fluid loss and prevent dirt ingress.

6 On all 1.6 models, unbolt the fluid pipe support bracket from the base of the right-hand suspension turret (photo).

7 Disconnect (where fitted) the small-bore hoses from the pump air control valve.

8 Remove the pump pulley nut noting any washers fitted, then remove the pulley (photo). It may be necessary to support the engine using an engine support bar or a hoist, then to disconnect the engine mounting(s) and to move the engine slightly (taking great care not to strain any wiring, hoses, pipes and linkages, or to damagage components) to allow the pulley to be withdrawn.

9 On GTi 16 models, the fluid feed pipe and return hose should be disconnected from the pump and plugged at this stage, noting the gaskets or seals fitted (photo).

10 Unbolt the pump, removing the adjuster bolt and adjuster bracket as necessary (photo).

Refitting

11 Refitting is the reverse of the removal procedure, noting the following points.
(a) *Tighten all disturbed fasteners to their specified torque wrench settings (where given).*
(b) *Refer to the relevant Sections of this Chapter and of Chapters 1, 4, 11 and 12 for specific details.*

31.10 Pump mounting bolts (arrowed) – GTi 16

(c) *Fit a new gasket or seal to the fluid feed pipe union (if applicable).*
(d) *Use a crowfoot adaptor to tighten the fluid feed pipe union to its specified torque; calculate the torque according to the adaptor used*
(e) *Refit and tension the drivebelt(s) (Chapter 7).*
(f) *On completion, bleed the system (Section 32).*

32 Power-assisted steering system – fluid renewal and bleeding

Fluid renewal

1 Raise the front of the vehicle and support it securely on axle stands.

2 Disconnect the fluid return hose from the reservoir and allow the fluid to drain into a suitable container.

3 Start the engine and allow it to idle; turn the steering wheel from lock to lock while the fluid drains.

4 Stop the engine, then plug the fluid return hose connection on the reservoir. Fill the reservoir with fresh fluid of the specified type. Engage the aid of an assistant to start and stop the engine as required.

5 Start the engine and run it at 1000 rpm. After one or two seconds fluid should begin to discharge from the return hose; instruct an assistant to stop the engine immediately.

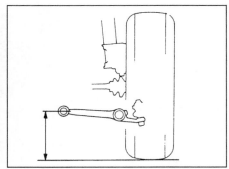

Fig. 10.22 Chassis ground clearance measuring point – front (Sec 33)

6 Top up the fluid reservoir and repeat the procedure given in paragraph 5 (keeping the fluid reservoir topped up) until there is no air in the fluid being discharged.

7 Remove the temporarily-fitted plug and reconnect the fluid return hose to the reservoir; work as quickly as possible to minimise fluid loss and prevent the need to repeat the procedure.

8 Bleed the system as follows.

Bleeding

9 If any part of the power-assisted steering system is disturbed, all traces of air must be bled from the system as follows.

10 Remove the reservoir filler cap and top up the fluid level to the maximum mark (Chapter 1).

11 Start the engine and run it at no more than 1000 rpm while slowly moving the steering several times from lock to lock to purge any air from the system into the reservoir.

12 With the engine still running, measure the reservoir fluid level and check that the fluid is not foaming or cloudy. Stop the engine and check that the fluid level does not rise more than 5.0 mm above that measured while the engine was running. If a problem is found disconnect the fluid return hose from the reservoir and plug the reservoir connection, then proceed from paragraph 4 of this Section onwards.

33 Wheel alignment and steering angles – general information

Front roadwheels

1 Accurate front roadwheel alignment is essential to provide positive steering and to prevent excessive tyre wear. Before considering the steering/suspension geometry, check that the tyres are correctly inflated, that the front roadwheels are not buckled, that the hub bearing axial play is within its specified limits (using a dial gauge), that the front and rear chassis ground clearance is as specified, and that the steering linkage and suspension components are in

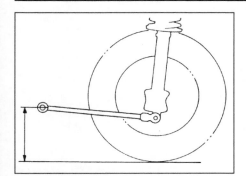

Fig. 10.23 Chassis ground clearance measuring point – rear (Sec 33)

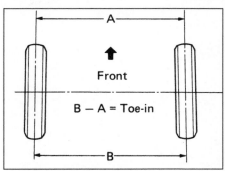

Fig. 10.24 Roadwheel toe setting measurement reference points (Sec 33)

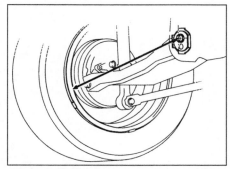

Fig. 10.25 Measuring effective length of rear suspension rear transverse arms. Inset shows cam used to adjust arm length/toe setting (Sec 33)

good order, without slackness or wear in their joints.

2 Wheel alignment consists of four factors:

Camber is the angle at which the front roadwheels are set from the vertical when viewed from the front of the car. 'Positive camber' is the amount (in degrees) that the roadwheels are tilted outward at the top from the vertical.

Castor is the angle between the steering axis and a vertical line when viewed from each side of the car. 'Positive castor' is when the steering axis is inclined rearward at the top.

Steering axis inclination is the angle (when viewed from the front of the car) between the vertical and an imaginary line drawn through the suspension strut upper mounting and the suspension lower arm balljoint.

Toe setting is the amount by which the distance between the front of the tyre tread centres differs from the distance measured between the rear of the tyre tread centres (measured at hub height).

3 With the exception of the toe setting all other steering angles are set during manufacture and no adjustment is possible. It can therefore be assumed that, unless the car has suffered accident damage, all the preset steering angles should be correct; if there is any doubt about their accuracy it will be necessary to enlist the aid of a Toyota dealer who has the equipment to identify any such problems.

4 Two methods are available to the home mechanic for checking the toe setting. The Toyota-approved method is to use a gauge to measure the distance between the front and rear tyre tread centres (at hub height). The other method is to use a scuff plate in which each front wheel is rolled across a movable

plate which records any deviation, or scuff, of the tyre from the straight-ahead position as it moves across the plate. Relatively inexpensive equipment of both types is available from accessory outlets, to enable these checks and subsequent adjustments to be carried out at home. When carrying out the checks, ensure that the equipment manufacturers' instructions are followed correctly; before measuring the toe setting, bounce the vehicle up and down a few times to settle the suspension components.

5 If after checking the toe setting it is found that adjustment is necessary, proceed as follows.

6 Turn the steering wheel to full left lock and record the number of exposed threads on the right-hand track rod. Now turn the steering to the opposite lock and record the corresponding number of threads on the left-hand side. If the same number of threads are visible on both track rods, adjustment can be made equally on both sides. If there are more threads visible on one side than the other it will be necessary to compensate for this during adjustment.

7 To alter the toe setting, first slacken the track rod-to-track rod end locknuts and release the small (outboard) steering gear gaiter clips (Section 21). Turn each track rod by a quarter of turn at a time, using self-locking pliers, to achieve the specified setting; recheck the setting each time the track rods are turned. *After adjustment there must be the same number of threads visible at the end of each track rod; this is extremely important.*

8 When adjustment is complete, tighten the locknuts and retighten the gaiter clips (Section 21, paragraphs 11 and 14).

Rear roadwheels

9 Refer first to paragraphs 1, 2 and 3 above for full information.

10 Only the toe setting can be altered; adjustment is made by rotating the cam at the inboard end of each rear transverse arm. Rotating a cam will alter the toe setting by approximately 2 mm with each graduation.

11 The method of checking the rear roadwheel toe setting is as described in paragraph 4 above; if adjustment is necessary, proceed as follows.

12 Measure the effective length of each rear transverse arm – ie the distance between each roadwheel rim and the corner of its respective cam bracket (Fig. 10.25); if both lengths are the same, proceed to paragraph 14.

13 If the lengths differ by more than the specified value the arms must be lengthened or shortened by the amount of toe setting error found. If the setting is tending towards toe-out, rotate its cam (see below) to lengthen the shorter-side suspension arm; if the setting is excessively toe-in, shorten the longer-side suspension arm. With the side-to side error within tolerances, recheck the toe setting.

14 Adjust the toe setting by slackening the transverse arm inboard pivot bolt nuts and by turning both cams to alter the affective length of both transverse arms by an equal amount. Tighten the arm pivot bolts to their specified torque wrench settings and recheck the toe setting.

15 When the toe setting is correct, recheck the distances measured in paragraph 11; repeat the procedure if necessary.

Notes

Chapter 11 Bodywork and fittings

Contents

Degrees of difficulty

Easy, suitable for novice with little experience	Fairly easy, suitable for beginner with some experience	Fairly difficult, suitable for competent DIY mechanic	Difficult, suitable for experienced DIY mechanic	Very difficult, suitable for expert DIY or professional

Specifications

Torque wrench settings	Nm	lbf ft
Front seat mounting bolts	37	27
Rear seat back side hinge-to-seat back	18	13
Rear seat lock striker-to-body – Estate	18	13
Rear seat cushion-to-body – Estate	18	13
Seat belt component mountings:		
Front retractor upper bolt	5.4	4
Rear retractor upper bolt – Liftback	7.8	5.8
Front clasp slide-bar engaging bracket-to-front seat	19	14
All other mounting bolts	43	32

1 General information

The bodyshell is made of pressed-steel sections in three-door Hatchback, four-door Saloon, five-door Liftback and five-door Estate configurations.

To minimise corrosion, pre-treated steel sheet is used extensively in bodyshell construction, the bodyshell is completely dipped in a solution of anti-corrosion chemicals and an anti-stone chipping protective coating is applied.

2 Maintenance – bodywork and underframe

The general condition of a vehicle's bodywork is the one thing that significantly affects its value. Maintenance is easy, but needs to be regular. Neglect, particularly after minor damage, can lead quickly to further deterioration and costly repair bills. It is important also to keep watch on those parts of the vehicle not immediately visible, for instance the underside, inside all the wheel arches, and the lower part of the engine compartment.

The basic maintenance routine for the bodywork is washing - preferably with a lot of water, from a hose. This will remove all the loose solids which may have stuck to the vehicle. It is important to flush these off in such a way as to prevent grit from scratching the finish. The wheel arches and underframe need washing in the same way, to remove any accumulated mud, which will retain moisture and tend to encourage rust. Paradoxically enough, the best time to clean the underframe and wheel arches is in wet weather, when the mud is thoroughly wet and soft. In very wet weather, the underframe is usually cleaned of large accumulations automatically, and this is a good time for inspection.

Periodically, except on vehicles with a wax-based underbody protective coating, it is a good idea to have the whole of the underframe of the vehicle steam-cleaned, engine compartment included, so that a thorough inspection can be carried out to see what minor repairs and renovations are necessary. Steam-cleaning is available at many garages, and is necessary for the removal of the accumulation of oily grime, which sometimes is allowed to become thick in certain areas. If steam-cleaning facilities are not available, there are some excellent grease solvents available which can be brush-applied; the dirt can then be simply hosed off. Note that these methods should not be used on vehicles with wax-based underbody protective coating, or the coating will be removed. Such vehicles should be inspected annually, preferably just prior to Winter, when the underbody should be washed down, and any damage to the wax coating repaired. Ideally, a completely fresh coat should be applied. It would also be worth considering the use of such wax-based protection for injection into door panels, sills, box sections, etc, as an additional safeguard against rust damage, where such protection is not provided by the vehicle manufacturer.

After washing paintwork, wipe off with a chamois leather to give an unspotted clear finish. A coat of clear protective wax polish will give added protection against chemical pollutants in the air. If the paintwork sheen has dulled or oxidised, use a cleaner/polisher combination to restore the brilliance of the shine. This requires a little effort, but such dulling is usually caused because regular washing has been neglected. Care needs to be taken with metallic paintwork, as special non-abrasive cleaner/polisher is required to avoid damage to the finish. Always check that the door and ventilator opening drain holes and pipes are completely clear, so that water can be drained out. Brightwork should be treated in the same way as paintwork. Windscreens and windows can be kept clear of the smeary film which often appears, by the use of proprietary glass cleaner. Never use any form of wax or other body or chromium polish on glass.

3 Maintenance – upholstery and carpets

Mats and carpets should be brushed or vacuum-cleaned regularly, to keep them free of grit. If they are badly stained, remove them from the vehicle for scrubbing or sponging, and make quite sure they are dry before refitting. Seats and interior trim panels can be kept clean by wiping with a damp cloth. If they do become stained (which can be more apparent on light-coloured upholstery), use a little liquid detergent and a soft nail brush to scour the grime out of the grain of the material. Do not forget to keep the headlining clean in the same way as the upholstery. When using liquid cleaners inside the vehicle, do not over-wet the surfaces being cleaned. Excessive damp could get into the seams and padded interior, causing stains, offensive odours or even rot.

> **HAYNES HINT** *If the inside of the vehicle gets wet accidentally, it is worthwhile taking some trouble to dry it out properly, particularly where carpets are involved. Do not leave oil or electric heaters inside the vehicle for this purpose.*

4 Minor body damage – repair

Note: *For more detailed information about bodywork repair, Haynes Publishing produce a book by Lindsay Porter called "The Car Bodywork Repair Manual". This incorporates information on such aspects as rust treatment, painting and glass-fibre repairs, as well as details on more ambitious repairs involving welding and panel beating.*

Repairs of minor scratches in bodywork

If the scratch is very superficial, and does not penetrate to the metal of the bodywork, repair is very simple. Lightly rub the area of the scratch with a paintwork renovator, or a very fine cutting paste, to remove loose paint from the scratch, and to clear the surrounding bodywork of wax polish. Rinse the area with clean water.

Apply touch-up paint to the scratch using a fine paint brush; continue to apply fine layers of paint until the surface of the paint in the scratch is level with the surrounding paintwork. Allow the new paint at least two weeks to harden, then blend it into the surrounding paintwork by rubbing the scratch area with a paintwork renovator or a very fine cutting paste. Finally, apply wax polish.

Where the scratch has penetrated right through to the metal of the bodywork, causing the metal to rust, a different repair technique is required. Remove any loose rust from the bottom of the scratch with a penknife, then apply rust-inhibiting paint to prevent the formation of rust in the future. Using a rubber or nylon applicator, fill the scratch with bodystopper paste. If required, this paste can be mixed with cellulose thinners to provide a very thin paste which is ideal for filling narrow scratches. Before the stopper-paste in the scratch hardens, wrap a piece of smooth cotton rag around the top of a finger. Dip the finger in cellulose thinners, and quickly sweep it across the surface of the stopper-paste in the scratch; this will ensure that the surface of the stopper-paste is slightly hollowed. The scratch can now be painted over as described earlier in this Section.

Repairs of dents in bodywork

When deep denting of the vehicle's bodywork has taken place, the first task is to pull the dent out, until the affected bodywork almost attains its original shape. There is little point in trying to restore the original shape completely, as the metal in the damaged area will have stretched on impact, and cannot be reshaped fully to its original contour. It is better to bring the level of the dent up to a point which is about 3 mm below the level of the surrounding bodywork. In cases where the dent is very shallow anyway, it is not worth trying to pull it out at all. If the underside of the dent is accessible, it can be hammered out

gently from behind, using a mallet with a wooden or plastic head. Whilst doing this, hold a suitable block of wood firmly against the outside of the panel, to absorb the impact from the hammer blows and thus prevent a large area of the bodywork from being "belled-out".

Should the dent be in a section of the bodywork which has a double skin, or some other factor making it inaccessible from behind, a different technique is called for. Drill several small holes through the metal inside the area - particularly in the deeper section. Then screw long self-tapping screws into the holes, just sufficiently for them to gain a good purchase in the metal. Now the dent can be pulled out by pulling on the protruding heads of the screws with a pair of pliers.

The next stage of the repair is the removal of the paint from the damaged area, and from an inch or so of the surrounding "sound" bodywork. This is accomplished most easily by using a wire brush or abrasive pad on a power drill, although it can be done just as effectively by hand, using sheets of abrasive paper. To complete the preparation for filling, score the surface of the bare metal with a screwdriver or the tang of a file, or alternatively, drill small holes in the affected area. This will provide a really good "key" for the filler paste.

To complete the repair, see the Section on filling and respraying.

Repairs of rust holes or gashes in bodywork

Remove all paint from the affected area, and from an inch or so of the surrounding "sound" bodywork, using an abrasive pad or a wire brush on a power drill. If these are not available, a few sheets of abrasive paper will do the job most effectively. With the paint removed, you will be able to judge the severity of the corrosion, and therefore decide whether to renew the whole panel (if this is possible) or to repair the affected area. New body panels are not as expensive as most people think, and it is often quicker and more satisfactory to fit a new panel than to attempt to repair large areas of corrosion.

Remove all fittings from the affected area, except those which will act as a guide to the original shape of the damaged bodywork (eg headlight shells etc). Then, using tin snips or a hacksaw blade, remove all loose metal and any other metal badly affected by corrosion. Hammer the edges of the hole inwards, in order to create a slight depression for the filler paste.

Wire-brush the affected area to remove the powdery rust from the surface of the remaining metal. Paint the affected area with rust-inhibiting paint, if the back of the rusted area is accessible, treat this also.

Before filling can take place, it will be necessary to block the hole in some way. This can be achieved by the use of aluminium or plastic mesh, or aluminium tape.

Aluminium or plastic mesh, or glass-fibre matting, is probably the best material to use for a large hole. Cut a piece to the approximate size and shape of the hole to be filled, then position it in the hole so that its edges are below the level of the surrounding bodywork. It can be retained in position by several blobs of filler paste around its periphery.

Aluminium tape should be used for small or very narrow holes. Pull a piece off the roll, trim it to the approximate size and shape required, then pull off the backing paper (if used) and stick the tape over the hole; it can be overlapped if the thickness of one piece is insufficient. Burnish down the edges of the tape with the handle of a screwdriver or similar, to ensure that the tape is securely attached to the metal underneath.

Bodywork repairs - filling and respraying

Before using this Section, see the Sections on dent, deep scratch, rust holes and gash repairs.

Many types of bodyfiller are available, but generally speaking, those proprietary kits which contain a tin of filler paste and a tube of resin hardener are best for this type of repair. A wide, flexible plastic or nylon applicator will be found invaluable for imparting a smooth and well-contoured finish to the surface of the filler.

Mix up a little filler on a clean piece of card or board - measure the hardener carefully (follow the maker's instructions on the pack), otherwise the filler will set too rapidly or too slowly. Using the applicator, apply the filler paste to the prepared area; draw the applicator across the surface of the filler to achieve the correct contour and to level the surface. As soon as a contour that approximates to the correct one is achieved, stop working the paste - if you carry on too long, the paste will become sticky and begin to "pick-up" on the applicator. Continue to add thin layers of filler paste at 20-minute intervals, until the level of the filler is just proud of the surrounding bodywork.

Once the filler has hardened, the excess can be removed using a metal plane or file. From then on, progressively-finer grades of abrasive paper should be used, starting with a 40-grade production paper, and finishing with a 400-grade wet-and-dry paper. Always wrap the abrasive paper around a flat rubber, cork, or wooden block - otherwise the surface of the filler will not be completely flat. During the smoothing of the filler surface, the wet-and-dry paper should be periodically rinsed in water. This will ensure that a very smooth finish is imparted to the filler at the final stage.

At this stage, the "dent" should be surrounded by a ring of bare metal, which in turn should be encircled by the finely "feathered" edge of the good paintwork. Rinse the repair area with clean water, until all of the dust produced by the rubbing-down operation has gone.

Spray the whole area with a light coat of primer - this will show up any imperfections in the surface of the filler. Repair these imperfections with fresh filler paste or bodystopper, and once more smooth the surface with abrasive paper. Repeat this spray-and-repair procedure until you are satisfied that the surface of the filler, and the feathered edge of the paintwork, are perfect. Clean the repair area with clean water, and allow to dry fully.

The repair area is now ready for final spraying. Paint spraying must be carried out

 HAYNES HiNT *If bodystopper is used, it can be mixed with cellulose thinners, to form a really thin paste which is ideal for filling small holes.*

in a warm, dry, windless and dust-free atmosphere. This condition can be created artificially if you have access to a large indoor working area, but if you are forced to work in the open, you will have to pick your day very carefully. If you are working indoors, dousing the floor in the work area with water will help to settle the dust which would otherwise be in the atmosphere. If the repair area is confined to one body panel, mask off the surrounding panels; this will help to minimise the effects of a slight mis-match in paint colours. Bodywork fittings (eg chrome strips, door handles etc) will also need to be masked off. Use genuine masking tape, and several thicknesses of newspaper, for the masking operations.

Before commencing to spray, agitate the aerosol can thoroughly, then spray a test area (an old tin, or similar) until the technique is mastered. Cover the repair area with a thick coat of primer; the thickness should be built up using several thin layers of paint, rather than one thick one. Using 400-grade wet-and-dry paper, rub down the surface of the primer until it is really smooth. While doing this, the work area should be thoroughly doused with water, and the wet-and-dry paper periodically rinsed in water. Allow to dry before spraying on more paint.

Spray on the top coat, again building up the thickness by using several thin layers of paint. Start spraying at one edge of the repair area, and then, using a side-to-side motion, work until the whole repair area and about 2 inches of the surrounding original paintwork is covered. Remove all masking material 10 to 15 minutes after spraying on the final coat of paint.

Allow the new paint at least two weeks to harden, then, using a paintwork renovator, or a very fine cutting paste, blend the edges of the paint into the existing paintwork. Finally, apply wax polish.

Plastic components

With the use of more and more plastic body components by the vehicle manufacturers (eg bumpers. spoilers, and in some cases major body panels), rectification of more serious damage to such items has become a matter of either entrusting repair work to a specialist

in this field, or renewing complete components. Repair of such damage by the DIY owner is not really feasible, owing to the cost of the equipment and materials required for effecting such repairs. The basic technique involves making a groove along the line of the crack in the plastic, using a rotary burr in a power drill. The damaged part is then welded back together, using a hot-air gun to heat up and fuse a plastic filler rod into the groove. Any excess plastic is then removed, and the area rubbed down to a smooth finish. It is important that a filler rod of the correct plastic is used, as body components can be made of a variety of different types (eg polycarbonate, ABS, polypropylene).

Damage of a less serious nature (abrasions, minor cracks etc) can be repaired by the DIY owner using a two-part epoxy filler repair material. Once mixed in equal proportions, this is used in similar fashion to the bodywork filler used on metal panels. The filler is usually cured in twenty to thirty minutes, ready for sanding and painting.

If the owner is renewing a complete component himself, or if he has repaired it with epoxy filler, he will be left with the problem of finding a suitable paint for finishing which is compatible with the type of plastic used. At one time, the use of a universal paint was not possible, owing to the complex range of plastics encountered in body component applications. Standard paints, generally speaking, will not bond to plastic or rubber satisfactorily. However, it is now possible to obtain a plastic body parts finishing kit which consists of a pre-primer treatment, a primer and coloured top coat. Full instructions are normally supplied with a kit, but basically, the method of use is to first apply the pre-primer to the component concerned, and allow it to dry for up to 30 minutes. Then the primer is applied, and left to dry for about an hour before finally applying the special-coloured top coat. The result is a correctly-coloured component, where the paint will flex with the plastic or rubber, a property that standard paint does not normally possess.

5 Major body damage – repair

Where serious damage has occurred, or large areas need renewal due to neglect, it means that complete new panels will need welding in; this is best left to professionals. If the damage is due to impact, it will also be necessary to check completely the alignment of the bodyshell; this can only be carried out accurately by a Toyota dealer using special jigs. If the body is left misaligned, it is primarily dangerous as the car will not handle properly and secondly, uneven stresses will be imposed on the steering, suspension and possibly transmission, causing abnormal wear or complete failure, particularly to items such as the tyres.

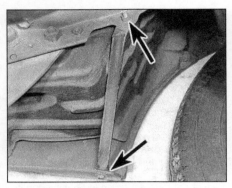

6.1 Bumper bracing strut bolts (arrowed)

6.2 Undoing front bumper upper rear edge bolt

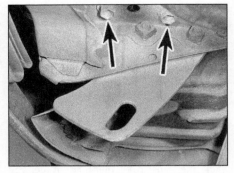

6.3 Front bumper bolts (arrowed) – right-hand side

6 Bumpers – removal and refitting

Removal

Front

1 Undo the bumper bracing strut bolts, then remove the strut on both sides of the vehicle (photo).
2 Remove the bolt securing each bumper upper rear edge to the front wings (photo).
3 Remove the two bolts securing each side of the bumper and withdraw the bumper, disconnecting the indicator multi-plugs (photo).

Rear

4 On all models except Estates, remove the three bolts securing each rear mudflap and remove them; note that each rearmost mudflap securing bolt also retains the bracing strut to the lower forward edge of the bumper (photo).
5 Remove the bolt securing each upper forward edge of the bumper to the rear wings.
6 On Estate models, remove the screw securing each lower forward edge of the bumper, then release the clips securing each upper forward edge.
7 On all models, unbolt the rear towing eye (photo).

8 Where the number plate illumination lamp is mounted on the bumper, disconnect its multi-plug (in the luggage compartment) and release its wiring from any securing clips.
9 Remove the nuts and/or bolts securing the main bumper mounting brackets and detach the bumper from the vehicle, withdrawing (if applicable) the number plate illumination lamp wiring and multi-plug (photo).

Refitting

10 Refitting is the reverse of the removal procedure.

7 Radiator grille – removal and refitting

Removal

1 With the bonnet raised, undo the single retaining screw (photo).
2 Release the clips securing each end of the grille, then remove the grille (photo).

Refitting

3 Position the grille in its aperture, then press each end in to engage the securing clips (having ensured that the clip plates are fitted to the tags on the headlamps) before refitting the retaining screw.

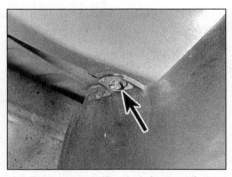

6.4 Rearmost mudflap bolt (arrowed) also secures bumper bracing strut

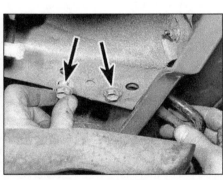

6.7 Removing rear towing eye (bolts arrowed)

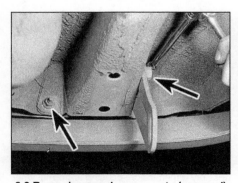

6.9 Removing rear bumper nuts (arrowed)

7.1 Undoing radiator grille retaining screw

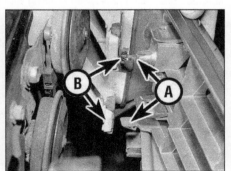

7.2 Radiator grille clips (A) and clip plates (B)

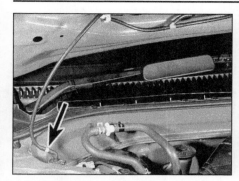

8.2 Disconnect windscreen washer jet hose at point arrowed

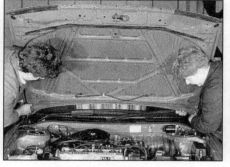

8.4 Removing the bonnet

9.3A Undoing bonnet release handle securing screws

8 Bonnet – removal, refitting and adjustment

Removal

1 Raise the bonnet and support it securely on its stay.

2 Disconnect the windscreen washer jet hose from the distribution valve (photo).

3 Use a marker pen to mark around the bonnet hinge positions as an aid to correct refitting.

4 With the aid of an assistant, support the bonnet and remove the bolts securing it to its hinges – note the position of the centring bolt, with round shoulders, fitted accurately on production to align the bonnet with its surrounding panels. Remove the bonnet (photo).

Refitting

5 Refitting is the reverse of the removal procedure, noting the following points.

(a) Apply a suitable rust-inhibitor to the exposed hinge locations.

(b) Align the hinges with the marks made on removal.

(c) Gently close the bonnet and ensure that it sits flush with its surrounding panels and that there is an equal gap between the bonnet and each front wing; the bonnet should close smoothly and positively, with no excessive force being applied. If this is not the case, adjustment is required; see below. Adjustment of the bonnet lock is covered in Section 10.

Adjustment

6 If lateral adjustment is required, first identify the centring bolt (refer to paragraph 4) and substitute a conventional bolt and washer. Adjustment can now be made by slackening the hinge-to-bonnet bolts until the bonnet can be moved on the hinges; tighten the bolts once the desired position is achieved.

7 Vertical adjustment of the bonnet rear end is achieved by altering the number of packing washers under the body side of the hinges.

8 Vertical adjustment of the bonnet front end is achieved by altering the height of the bonnet closure bump stops on the front panel.

9 After any adjustment has been made it may be necessary to adjust the bonnet lock which is described in Section 10.

9 Bonnet release cable – removal and refitting

Removal

1 Disconnect the battery negative terminal.

2 Disconnect the cable from the bonnet lock (Section 10).

3 Remove its securing screws and slide out the bonnet release handle from the facia lower finish panel, then remove the facia lower finish panel (Section 24) (photos).

4 Disconnect the cable from the release handle, then withdraw the cable, noting its routing and any grommets fitted.

Refitting

5 Refitting is the reverse of the removal procedure.

10 Bonnet lock – removal and refitting

Removal

1 Remove the radiator grille (Section 7).

2 Unbolt the lock from the front panel, disconnect the cable and remove the lock (photos).

Refitting

3 Refitting is a reversal of the removal procedure; before refitting the grille, gently close the bonnet to check that the lock retains the bonnet in the correct position; if required, slacken the lock securing bolts and move the lock as necessary until the setting is correct.

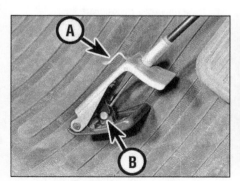

9.3B Bonnet release handle locating lug (A), cable end nipple (B)

10.2A Bonnet lock bolts (arrowed)

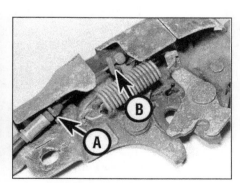

10.2B Bonnet release cable outer abutment (A), inner cable fixing (B), at lock

11.4A Removing retaining screw from recessed door-pull trim

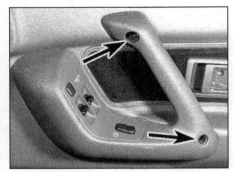

11.4B Combined door-pull/switch panel securing screw locations (arrowed)

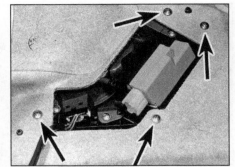

11.7 Combined door-pull/switch panel-to-inner trim panel securing screws (arrowed) – from panel reverse side

11 Door inner trim panels – removal and refitting

Removal

1 Disconnect the battery negative terminal if the vehicle is equipped with electric windows and/or central locking.

2 On vehicles without electric windows, remove the circlip securing the window regulator handle, then remove the handle and its plate.

3 Remove the interior door handle (Section 13).

4 Undo the screw and withdraw the recessed door-pull trim from the moulded 'armrest'

projection (if applicable). If a separate armrest or door-pull is fitted, this will be secured by two screws (Fig. 11.1). If a combined door-pull/switch panel is fitted, remove the two screws from its rear end but do not attempt to separate the assembly from the panel (photos).

5 On front doors only, remove the mirror mounting location trim (Section 15). Remove the single screw (where fitted) that is hidden behind a covering cap at the front upper edge of the panel.

6 The panel is secured by clips; while full panels have clips securing their front, rear and bottom edges, with the top edge fitting into the base of the window aperture, 'semi-trim' panels are secured by clips along all edges. Release the clips (using a suitable flat-bladed screwdriver with tape wrapped around its blade) and remove the panel, disconnecting any wiring.

7 Where a combined door-pull/switch panel assembly is fitted, undo the remaining screws from the reverse side of the panel to separate it from the panel if required (photo). Where switches and switch panels are to be removed, refer to Chapter 12.

Refitting

8 Refitting is the reverse of the removal procedure.

12 Door window glass and regulator – removal and refitting

Removal

Front

1 Remove the relevant door inner trim panel (Section 11).

2 Where applicable, disconnect the electric window relay and unbolt it.

3 Peel back and remove the protective plastic cover from the inside of the door, removing the armrest/door-pull reinforcement bracket and any plastic trim fixings as necessary (photo).

4 Remove the relevant exterior mirror

Door Belt Moulding
Glass Run
Door Glass
Outside Handle with Lock Cylinder
Armrest or Pull Handle (B type)
(C type)
(D type)
Inside Locking Knob
Inside Locking Link
Striker
Door Lock
Rear Lower Frame
(Equalizer Arm)
Glass Channel
Rear View Mirror
Cover
(3-door Hatchback) Front Lower Frame
Opening Control Link
Window Regulator
Door Check
Door Hinge
(Ex. 3-door Hatchback) Front Lower Frame
Armrest (A type)
Armrest Base
Service Hole Cover
Door Trim
Snap Ring
Door Inside Handle
Screw Cap
Plate
Regulator Handle

Fig. 11.1 Door interior trim panel and associated components – inset shows other armrest or door-pull types (Sec 11)

12.3 Armrest/door-pull reinforcement bracket securing screws (arrowed)

12.4 Removing front door belt moulding

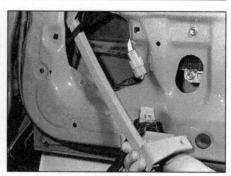

12.5 Removing door glass front guide channel

(Section 15), then release the door belt moulding securing clips and remove the moulding; take care not to kink or bend it (photo).

5 Removing the retaining screws (where fitted), withdraw the weatherstrip from the door and unbolt the front and rear guide channels (photo).

6 Disconnect, as necessary, the lock/handle linkages running towards the front of the door.

7 With the window glass lowered, reach through the holes in the lower part of the door to unbolt each end of the glass from the

regulator assembly, then lift out the window glass (photos).

8 On vehicles fitted with electric windows, disconnect the motor multiplug.

9 Unbolt the regulator assembly and withdraw it (photo).

Rear

10 Remove the relevant door inner trim panel (Section 11).

11 Peel back and remove the protective plastic cover from the inside of the door, removing the armrest/door-pull reinforcement bracket and any plastic trim fixings as necessary.

12 Removing the retaining screws (where fitted), withdraw the weatherstrip from the door.

13 Remove the securing screws and

withdraw the guide channel/division bar. Note that on models fitted with a blanking trim the top screw is located on the trim's upper forward edge and the bottom screw is located on the door's rear edge; on models fitted with a quarterlight, the top screw is hidden beneath the door seal, the centre screw is removed from the inner door panel and the bottom screw is removed from the door's rear edge (photos).

14 Release the door belt moulding securing clips and remove the moulding; take care not to kink or bend it.

15 On models fitted with a blanking trim, remove the securing screws from beneath the door seal and withdraw the blanking trim (photo).

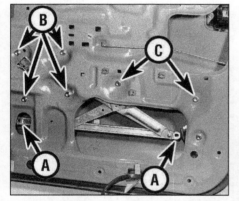

12.7A Window glass-to-regulator assembly bolts (A), regulator assembly mounting bolts (B), regulator equaliser arm mounting bolts (C)

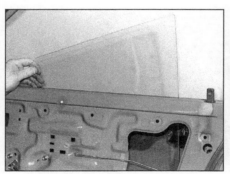

12.7B Removing front door glass

12.9 Withdrawing front door electric window regulator assembly

12.13A Removing guide channel/division bar top screw . . .

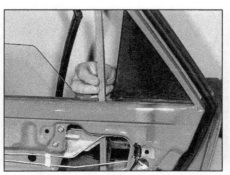

12.13B . . . to release bar – model with blanking trim shown

12.15 Blanking trim screws (arrowed)

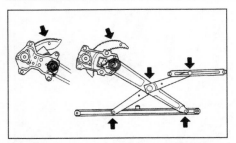

Fig. 11.2 Coat front window regulator components as shown with multi-purpose grease (Sec 12)

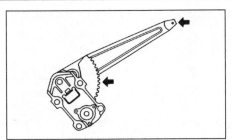

Fig. 11.3 Coat rear window regulator components as shown with multi-purpose grease (Sec 12)

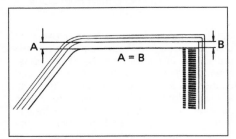

Fig. 11.4 Ensure window glass top surface is parallel to top of door frame (Sec 12)

16 On models fitted with a quarterlight, pull forwards and remove the quarterlight and its weatherstrip.

17 Disconnect the regulator arm from the forward edge of the window glass channel, then lift out the window glass (photos).

18 On vehicles fitted with electric windows, disconnect the motor multiplug.

19 Unbolt the regulator assembly and withdraw it.

Refitting

20 Refitting is the reverse of the removal procedure, noting the following points.

(a) *On refitting the regulator assembly, coat the regulator components with multi-purpose grease as shown in Fig. 11.2 or 11.3 (as appropriate); do NOT apply grease to the regulator spring.*

(b) *Ensure that the window glass top edge is parallel with the top of the door frame; if adjustment is required slacken the regulator equaliser arm mounting bolts and move the equaliser arm up or down in its bolt slots until the setting is correct,*

then re-tighten the bolts.

(c) *Check that the window glass moves smoothly up and down, with no trace of juddering (which would indicate component misalignment).*

(d) *A suitable sealant will be required to re-attach the protective plastic cover.*

13 Door lock, lock barrel and door handles – removal and refitting

Removal

Door lock

1 Remove the relevant door inner trim panel (Section 11).

2 Peel back the protective plastic cover on the inside of the door.

3 Remove the window glass and, on front doors, the guide channel covering the lock assembly (Section 12) (photo).

4 On vehicles fitted with central locking, disconnect the motor multiplug(s).

5 Disconnect all operating links and remove those that will impede lock removal; remove (where applicable) the lock 'pop-up' button by unclipping the linkage and unbolting the button (photo).

6 Undo the three screws securing the lock and, on vehicles fitted with central locking, the bolt securing the solenoid bracket, then remove the lock (photos).

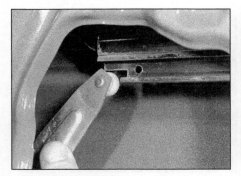

12.17A Disconnecting regulator arm from rear door window glass channel . . .

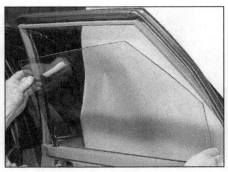

12.17B . . . to remove window glass

13.3 Window glass guide channel must be removed to reach front door lock

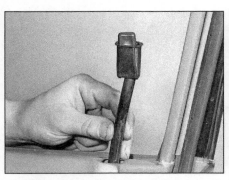

13.5 Withdrawing front door lock 'pop-up' button

13.6A Removing door lock securing screws . . .

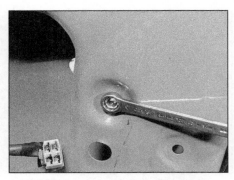

13.6B . . . remove (where fitted) bolt securing solenoid bracket . . .

13.6C . . . to withdraw door lock assembly (vehicle shown fitted with central locking)

13.8 Removing circlip (arrowed) securing lock barrel to exterior door handle

13.9A Undo screw securing interior handle . . .

Lock barrel

7 Remove the relevant exterior handle as described below.
8 Remove the circlip, depress the securing lugs and withdraw the lock barrel (photo).

Interior handle

9 Undo the single securing screw and slide the interior handle out of the inner trim panel; unclip and disengage the operating link from the back of the handle as it is withdrawn (photos).

Exterior handle

10 Remove the relevant door inner trim panel (Section 11).
11 Peel back the protective plastic cover on the inside of the door.
12 If the extra working space is required, remove the window glass (Section 12) and the lock (paragraphs 3 to 6 above).
13 Disconnect the operating link(s) from the exterior handle, unbolt the handle and remove it (photos).

Refitting

Door lock

14 Refitting is the reverse of the removal procedure, noting the following points.
(a) Apply multi-purpose grease to the lock sliding surfaces as shown in Fig. 11.5.
(b) Ensure that the operating link clips engage positively.

(c) Check the alignment of the door with its striker and adjust the striker position if necessary (Section14).
(d) A suitable sealant will be required to re-attach the protective plastic cover.

Lock barrel

15 Refitting is the reverse of the removal procedure.

Interior handle

16 Refitting is the reverse of the removal procedure; ensure that the operating link clip engages positively.

Exterior handle

17 Refitting is the reverse of the removal procedure, noting the following points.

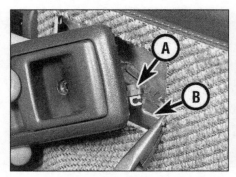

13.9B . . . and disconnect clip (A) from operating link (B)

(a) Refer, if necessary, to Section 12 and to the relevant paragraphs of this Section if the window glass or door lock are to be refitted.
(b) Ensure that the operating link clips engage positively.
(c) A suitable sealant will be required to re-attach the protective plastic cover.

14 Door – removal, refitting and adjustment

Removal

1 Disconnect the battery negative terminal.
2 Remove the relevant door inner trim panel

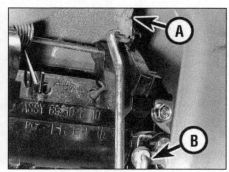

13.13A Exterior handle operating link clip (A), lock barrel operating link clip (B)

13.13B Unbolting exterior handle

13.13C Withdrawing front door exterior handle

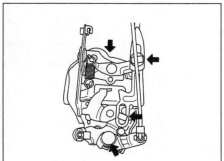

Fig. 11.5 Apply multi-purpose grease to lock sliding surfaces as shown (Sec 13)

14.3 Roll-pin (arrowed) securing door check arm to body bracket

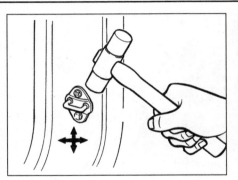

Fig. 11.6 Adjusting the door lock striker (Sec 14)

15.1 Removing a mirror glass

(Section 11). Disconnect, and draw out the wiring to the electrical components inside the door; also ensure that earth lead wiring is disconnected.

3 Drive out the roll pin securing the door check arm to its body bracket (photo).

4 Use a marker pen to mark around the door hinge positions as an aid to correct refitting.

5 With the aid of an assistant to support the door, remove the bolts and detach the door.

Refitting

6 Refitting is the reverse of the removal procedure, noting the following points.

(a) *Align the hinges with the marks made on removal and lightly tighten the hinge bolts, then gently close the door and check that it fits correctly in its aperture, with equal gaps at all points between it and the surrounding bodywork; if adjustment is required see below. Securely tighten the bolts.*

(b) *When the door fits correctly in its aperture, check that it fits flush with the surrounding bodywork; if adjustment is required, move the striker (see below).*

Adjustment

7 To adjust the doors in a forwards, rearwards and/or vertical direction slacken the hinge-to-body bolts; to adjust them in a left, right and/or vertical direction slacken the

hinge-to-door bolts. Securely tighten the bolts when the fit is correct.

8 The striker alignment should be checked after either the door or the lock has been disturbed. To adjust a striker, slacken its screws, re-position it and securely tighten the screws.

15 Exterior mirrors – removal and refitting

Removal

Mirror glass only

1 Tilt the mirror glass so that its bottom edge protrudes from the housing. Insert a flat-bladed screwdriver into the cut-out in the reverse side of the mirror glass clip-plate, then carefully prise out the mirror glass to unclip it from the swivel plate (photo).

Mirror assembly

2 Disconnect the battery negative terminal if an electrically-adjustable mirror is being removed.

3 If a manual remote-control mirror is being removed, undo the operating lever securing screw, then disconnect the lever.

4 Release the clip at the top of the mirror mounting location trim, then raise the trim to disengage its locating tags before removing it (photo).

5 If an electrically-adjustable mirror is being removed, remove the relevant door inner trim panel (Section 11) and peel back the protective plastic cover on the inside of the door until the mirror multi-plug can be disconnected (photo).

6 Undo the mounting screws and remove the mirror assembly; where an electrically-adjustable mirror is being removed, ensure that its wiring and multi-plug are not trapped as the assembly is withdrawn.

Refitting

Mirror glass only

7 Align the clips with the swivel plate then carefully push home the mirror glass until the clips engage (photo).

Mirror assembly

8 Refitting is the reverse of the removal procedure; note that suitable sealant will be required to re-attach the protective plastic cover.

16 Boot lid (Saloon) – removal, refitting and adjustment

Removal

1 Disconnect the battery negative terminal.

2 Open the boot and disconnect all relevant wiring.

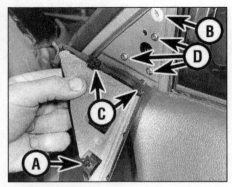

15.4 Release clip (A) from door (B), release trim from tags (C) to reach mirror mounting screws (D)

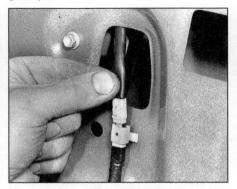

15.5 Disconnecting electrically-adjustable mirror multi-plug

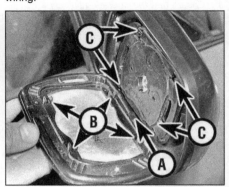

15.7 Cut-out for mirror glass removal (A), mirror glass clips (B), and swivel plate clips (C)

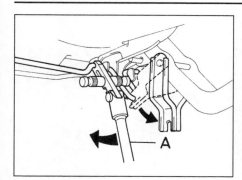

Fig. 11.7 Using removal tool (A) to disengage boot lid torsion bar from hinge connection (Sec 17)

18.2A Remove tailgate lock bolts (arrowed) . . .

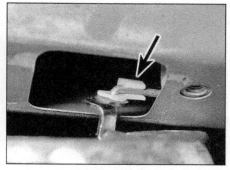

18.2B . . . and withdraw lock until operating rod(s) can be disconnected (clip arrowed)

3 Use a marker pen to mark around the boot hinge positions as an aid to correct refitting.

4 With the aid of an assistant, undo the bolts securing the boot lid to its hinges, then remove the boot lid; note the spacer/washer fitment. Do **not** attempt to remove the hinges until the torsion bars have been removed (Section 17).

Refitting

5 Refitting is the reverse of the removal procedure, noting the following points.

(a) Apply a suitable rust-inhibitor to the exposed hinge locations.

(b) Align the hinges with the marks made on removal.

(c) Gently close the boot and ensure that it sits flush with the surrounding panels and that there is an equal gap between the boot lid and each rear wing, the lid should close smoothly and positively, with no excessive force being applied. If this is not the case, adjustment is required; see below. Adjustment of the lock striker is covered in Section 18.

Adjustment

6 If lateral adjustment is required, slacken the hinge-to-boot lid bolts until the lid can be moved on its hinges once it is lowered; tighten the bolts once the desired position is achieved.

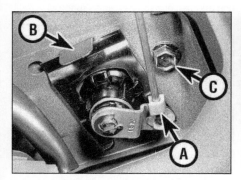

18.5 Tailgate lock barrel operating rod clip (A), lock barrel clip (B), lock barrel exterior surround bolt (C) – Hatchback

7 Vertical adjustment of the boot lid front end is achieved by altering the number of spacers/washers between the lid and its hinges.

8 After any adjustment has been made it may be necessary to adjust the lock striker (Section 18).

17 Boot lid torsion bar (Saloon) – removal and refitting

Note: A Toyota special tool is recommended for carrying out the following procedure, as the torsion bars may whip out and cause injury or damage if attempts are made to remove them without it, if this tool is not available, or an alternative cannot be fabricated from a long bar with a cranked, padded end, the task is best entrusted to your Toyota dealer.

Removal

1 Engage the tool on the first torsion bar as shown in Fig. 11.7.

2 Push down on the tool to disengage the torsion bar from its hinge connection, then swivel away the hinge connection.

3 Slowly and carefully lift the tool (whilst maintaining pressure on the torsion bar), to disengage the torsion bar from its hinge-end support bracket.

4 Slowly release the pressure and remove the tool.

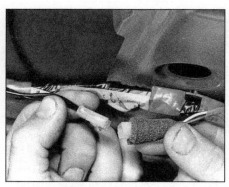

18.8 Disconnecting number plate lamp wiring – Estate

5 Disengage the torsion bar from its centre support and its anchor-end bracket, then remove it.

6 Repeat the procedure for the other torsion bar, as required.

Refitting

7 Refitting is the reverse of the removal procedure.

18 Boot lid/tailgate lock, lock barrel and handle – removal and refitting

Removal

Lock

1 Remove, where applicable, the tailgate interior trim panel (Section 24) and disconnect the lock courtesy lamp multi-plug.

2 Disconnect the lock operating rod(s), then unbolt the lock; on some vehicles, it may be necessary to partially withdraw the lock to allow sufficient access for the rod(s) to be disconnected (photos).

Lock barrel – except Estate

3 Remove, where applicable, the tailgate interior trim panel (Section 24).

4 Disconnect the lock barrel operating rod.

5 Remove, where fitted, the lock barrel exterior surround or the tailgate exterior trim panel, which are secured from the inside of the tailgate. Withdraw the clip and remove the lock barrel (photo).

Lock barrel – Estate

6 Remove the tailgate interior trim panel (Section 24).

7 Disconnect the operating rods from the handle and the lock barrel.

8 Disconnect the number plate illumination lamp wiring multi-plug (photo).

9 Undo, from the inside of the tailgate, the four nuts which secure the trim bar and withdraw the trim bar until the lock mountings can be reached (photo).

10 Undo the screws securing the lock barrel

18.9 Removing trim bar from tailgate –
Estate

18.10 Lock barrel guide screws (arrowed)
on reverse of trim bar – Estate

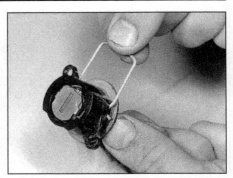

18.11 Removing Clip securing lock barrel
in guide – Estate

guide to the trim bar, then remove the lock barrel and guide (photo).

11 Remove the securing clip and withdraw the lock barrel (photo).

Handle – Estate

12 Remove the trim bar (paragraphs 6 to 9 above) until the handle mountings can be reached. If extra working space is required, prise the number plate illumination lamp wiring grommet from the tailgate and withdraw the lamp wiring; if the multi-plug will not pass through the tailgate hole release the wires from the multi-plug.

13 Undo the screws securing the handle to the trim bar, then remove the handle (photo). The handle grommet may be withdrawn from the tailgate if required.

Refitting

Lock

14 Refitting is the reverse of the removal procedure, noting the following points (photos).

(a) *Ensure that the operating rod clips engage positively.*

(b) *Check the alignment of the lock with its striker and adjust the striker position if necessary; the striker alignment should be checked after either the boot lid/tailgate or the lock has been disturbed. To adjust the striker, first remove the trim panel covering it (where fitted) (Section 24), then slacken the striker screws and move the striker until the fit is correct; securely tighten the screws and refit the trim.*

Lock barrel – except Estate

15 Refitting is the reverse of the removal procedure.

Lock barrel – Estate

16 Refitting is the reverse of the removal procedure, ensure that the number plate wiring grommet seats correctly as the trim bar is refitted.

Handle – Estate

17 Refitting is the reverse of the removal procedure; ensure that the handle grommet and the number plate wiring grommet seat correctly as the trim bar is refitted.

19 Boot lid/tailgate and fuel filler flap internal release mechanism – removal and refitting

Removal

1 The mechanism is cable-operated, with levers mounted on the floor next to the driver's seat and release catches on the boot lid/tailgate (except Estates) and the fuel filler flap.

2 To remove the lever unit, peel up the carpet, unscrew the mounting bolt and release the unit's locating tag. Withdraw the unit and disconnect the cables (photos).

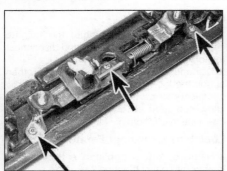

18.13 Tailgate exterior handle screws
(arrowed) on reverse of trim bar – Estate

18.14A Remove interior trim covering
tailgate lock striker . . .

18.14B . . . to reach lock striker/tailgate
remote release mechanism screws
(arrowed) – Liftback

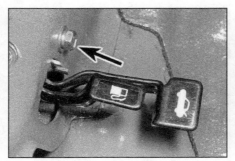

19.2A Undo bolt (arrowed) securing boot
lid/tailgate and fuel filler flap internal
release lever assembly . . .

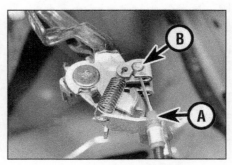

19.2B . . . then disconnect cable end
nipple (B) from lever and cable outer (A)
from lever bracket

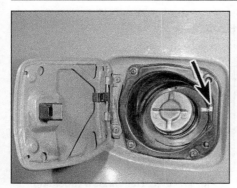

19.4A Unscrew fuel filler flap release catch retaining nut (arrowed) . . .

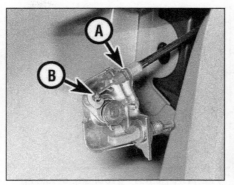

19.4B . . . then disconnect cable end nipple (B) from catch lever and cable outer (A) from catch bracket

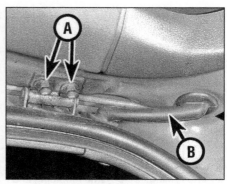

20.2 Tailgate hinge bolts (A), wiring grommet/protector (B)

3 The cables are routed through the inside of the vehicle, with the fuel filler flap cable crossing to the opposite side. Remove the rear seat and trim components and peel back the carpet as necessary to reach the cables if they are to be renewed.

4 To remove the fuel filler flap release catch, open the flap and unscrew the retaining nut, then remove the relevant interior trim (Section 24) and withdraw the catch into the luggage compartment. Disconnect the cable and remove the catch (photos).

5 To remove the boot lid/tailgate release catch open the boot lid/tailgate and remove, where fitted, the trim panel covering the lock striker (see photos 18.14A, 18.14B, and Section 24). Unscrew the striker screws, withdraw the striker/catch assembly and disconnect the cable.

Refitting

6 Refitting is the reverse of the removal procedure, referring to the relevant Sections of this Chapter.

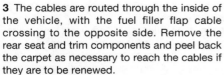

20 Tailgate – removal, refitting and adjustment

Removal

1 Disconnect the battery negative terminal.

2 Use a marker pen to mark around the tailgate hinge positions as an aid to correct refitting (photo).

3 Withdraw the central grommet/protector from the top of the tailgate, then disconnect the hose from the tailgate washer jet.

4 Remove the tailgate interior trim panel (Section 24), then disconnect the tailgate wiring and attach drawstrings to the multi-plugs; withdraw the remaining grommet/protector from the top of the tailgate and remove the wiring, leaving the drawstrings in place in the tailgate.

5 With an assistant supporting the tailgate, disconnect the support struts (Section 21).

6 With the aid of an assistant, unbolt the tailgate from its hinges and remove it.

Refitting

7 Refitting is the reverse of the removal procedure, noting the following points.

(a) Apply a suitable rust-inhibitor to the exposed hinge locations.

(b) Align the hinges with the marks made on removal.

(c) Gently close the tailgate and ensure that it sits flush with the surrounding panels and that there is an equal gap between it and each rear wing; the tailgate should close smoothly and positively, with no excessive force being applied. If this is not the case, adjustment is required; see below. Adjustment of the lock striker is covered in Section 18.

(d) Use the drawstrings to pull the wiring back down inside the tailgate.

Adjustment

8 If adjustment is required, slacken the hinge-

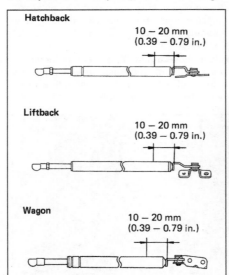

Fig. 11.8 Location for drilling hole in defective tailgate support strut (Sec 21)

to-tailgate bolts until the tailgate can be moved on its hinges once it is lowered; tighten the bolts once the desired position is achieved.

9 After any adjustment has been made it may be necessary to adjust the lock striker (Section 18).

21 Tailgate support strut – removal and refitting

Removal

1 Raise the tailgate and support it securely using a length of wood.

2 Prise the strut's cup end off its mounting ball, unbolt the other end of the strut, then remove the strut (photo).

3 Do not attempt to dismantle a defective strut, as it contains highly pressurised gas. Before discarding a defective strut, drill a 2 to 3 mm diameter hole at the position shown in Fig. 11.8 to allow the gas to escape, observe all normal safety precautions whilst drilling, to avoid possible injury from flying metal chips.

Refitting

4 Refitting is the reverse of the removal procedure; press the strut's cup end firmly over the ball, ensuring that it engages fully.

21.2 Prising tailgate support strut cup end off mounting ball

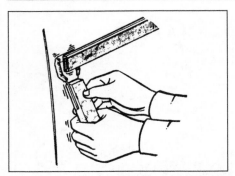

Fig. 11.9 Prising up bodyside moulding end (Sec 23)

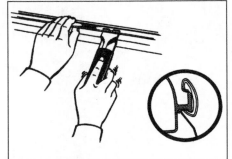

Fig. 11.10 Removing roof drip moulding using a hooked tool (Sec 23)

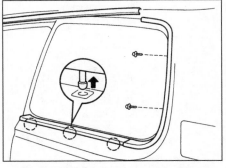

Fig, 11.11 Quarter window moulding retention – Hatchback (Sec 23)

22 Windscreen, rear window/ tailgate glass and rear quarter window glass – general information

1 Because the windscreen and rear window/tailgate glass are bonded in place with specific adhesives and special cleaning solutions and primers must be used for installation, it is therefore recommended that this work is entrusted to a Toyota dealer or windscreen replacement specialist.

2 The rear quarter window glass on Hatchback models is secured at its forward edge by nuts (concealed behind interior trim)

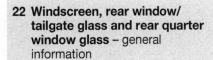

23.2A Rear spoiler mountings – GTi 16 – one of two screws underneath spoiler lip on outside . . .

and at its rear edge by a catch. To remove it, first remove the moulding shown in Fig. 11.11 for access to the securing nuts. Refitting is a reversal of the removal procedure.

23 Body exterior fittings – general information

1 The following text is intended as a guide only, illustrating typical methods used to remove and refit exterior trim components.

2 The rear spoiler on GTi 16 models is secured on the outside by screws concealed beneath the spoiler lip, and on the inside by screws concealed beneath plastic plugs on the tailgate (photos).

3 Liftback models have their rear spoilers secured by concealed fastenings, accessible after removing the relevant interior trim panels (Section 24).

4 Each side-skirt on GTi 16 models consists of two sections; the front section (four bolts) must be removed before the rear section is unbolted (photos).

5 Bodyside mouldings should not be re-used once removed; note that a suitable primer and adhesive must be used when fitting new mouldings (consult your Toyota dealer for availability).

6 To remove a moulding (having marked its location using masking tape), prise up approximately 30 mm of each end, then pull it away while cutting the adhesive with a knife;

to prevent damage to paintwork, wrap tape around the blades of all tools used. Remove all traces of old adhesive from the body using a suitable solvent.

7 On fitting a new moulding, use a hot-air gun or similar (not a blowlamp or other naked-flame appliance) to heat both the body and the new moulding. Heat the body to between 30 and 50°C (so that it is at a minimum of 20°C when the moulding is installed) and the moulding to between 30 and 60°C. Coat the hollowed ends of the moulding with the primer and allow it to dry for at least 30 seconds, then apply the adhesive on top of the primer; do not touch the primer or adhesive after application and note that the moulding must be installed within 7 minutes of applying the adhesive. Lift the backing sheet from the reverse side of the moulding then offer up the moulding with its ends 2 mm away from the edge of any opening panel; press the moulding into position without using excessive pressure. Any adhesive overflow can be removed with a plastic spatula and the body cleaned using a dry rag. Do not wash the vehicle for 24 hours after installing a moulding.

8 The trim covering the windscreen wiper linkage is secured by screws; the windscreen side mouldings (paragraph 10) may overlap its edges. The windscreen wiper arms must be removed (Chapter 12), before the trim can be removed.

9 Front and rear door belt mouldings are

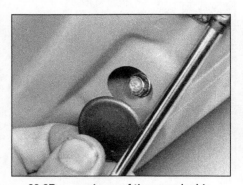

23.2B . . . and one of those on inside, covered by plastic plug

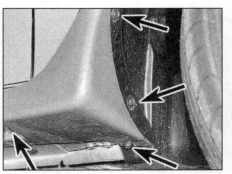

23.4A Side-skirt – GTi 16 – remove forward section bolts (arrowed) . . .

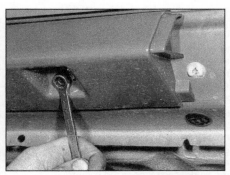

23.4B . . . before unbolting rear section

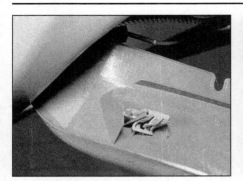

24.2 Typical interior trim panel hidden clip – tailgate shown

24.5A Removing steering lock/ignition switch lock barrel trim

24.5B Removing facia lower finish panel from driver's footwell

secured by clips; do not bend or kink the mouldings as they are removed or refitted.

10 Certain window-surround mouldings (notably those around the windscreen and rear window/tailgate glass) are not re-usable, the method of removal destroying the moulding itself; the removal and refitting of these are best entrusted to your Toyota dealer. Most side window and ventilation mouldings are secured by clips, nuts and/or bolts while some mouldings simply clip over a flange (Figs. 11.10 and 11.11); where possible, obtain access to the rear of the moulding, before attempting removal, to determine the method of fixing. If clips have to be released apply tape to the blade of the tool used, to help protect the vehicle paintwork from scratches.

11 Mudflaps and wheel arch liners are secured by screws or bolts.

24 Interior trim panels – general information

1 Most interior trim panels are secured by clips and/or screws; before attempting to remove a panel always inspect it closely to ensure that all fasteners are located and to decide on the correct approach for removal. Remember that if the panel is being removed for access to another component, it may only be necessary to lift one end of the panel.

2 A wide variety of clip types are used; hidden clips may be prised free, but some visible clips will require a different method eg the visible clips on Estate tailgate trim panels require their centres to be depressed before withdrawal (photo).

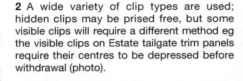

> **HAYNES HiNT** *When prising free a panel secured by hidden clips, wrap tape around the blade of the tool used to protect the paintwork.*

3 It may be necessary to remove components, such as seats, handles, etc, before a given panel can be removed; refer to the relevant Section of this Chapter for details; if electrical components have to be disconnected or removed, refer to Chapter 12.

4 The following procedures are given as examples, illustrating typical methods used.

5 To remove the steering column shrouds, remove the bonnet release handle from the facia lower finish panel (Section 9), then prise up and remove the steering lock/ignition switch lock barrel trim. Remove the four screws and withdraw the driver's footwell facia lower finish panel; disconnect the instrument panel dimmer control and speaker as the panel is withdrawn (photos).

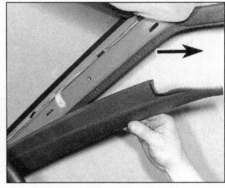

24.7 Remove 'A' pillar trim by pulling in direction of arrow

6 The shrouds can be removed by undoing the screws on their underside.

7 The 'A' (windscreen) pillar trims are each secured by two clips. To remove; first release the clips by pulling out the trim upper end, then withdraw the trim upwards to disengage its lower edge (photo).

8 To remove the B pillar trim on 4- and 5-door models, remove their retaining screws and lift both door sill scuff plates to release the base of the trim lower section. Release the lower section from its flange and remove it. The trim upper section can be removed similarly once the seat belt upper anchor bolt has been removed (photos).

24.8A Remove door sill scuff plate screws and lift plates . . .

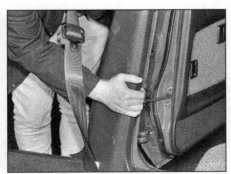

24.8B . . . then remove 'B' pillar trim lower section and seat belt . . .

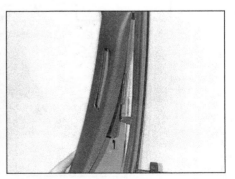

24.8C . . . to release trim upper section – Liftback

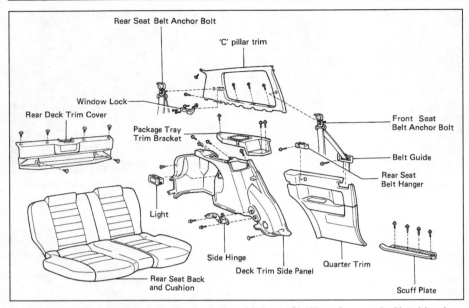

Fig. 11.12 Remove components shown to withdraw 'C' pillar trim panel – Hatchback (Sec 24)

9 For details of typical C pillar trim fastenings and removal procedure, see Fig. 11.12.

25 Seats – removal and refitting

Removal

Front

1 Slide the seat as far back as possible, then unbolt the seat runner forward ends.
2 Slide the seat as far forward as possible,

then remove the covers from the seat runner rear ends (photo).
3 Unbolt the seat runner rear ends from the floor, then move the seat and runner assembly forwards to disengage the seat belt clasp slide bar before removing the seat (photo).

Rear

4 The seat base is secured at its forward edge by bolts or by clips and, if it is of the forward-tilting type, will have a pull-up latch at its rear which must be released (photos). Where clips are fitted, move the levers on the clips to release the forward edge.

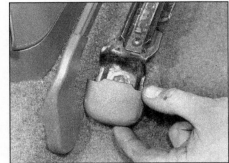

25.2 Removing cover from front seat runner rear end to expose seat mounting bolt

25.3 Disengage seat belt clasp slide bar (arrowed) to remove front seat

25.4A Rear seat base hinge bolt – forward-tilting base

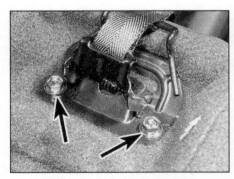

25.4B Pull-up latch-to-body bolts (arrowed) – forward-tilting seat base

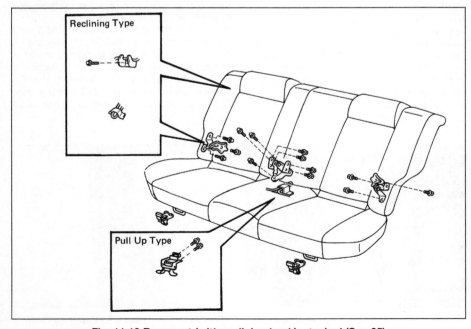

Fig. 11.13 Rear seat (with reclining back) – typical (Sec 25)

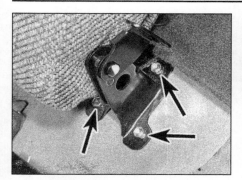

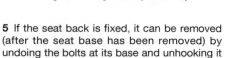

25.6 Split fold-down rear seat back centre hinge-to-body bolts (arrowed)

26.3 Unbolting front seat belt upper anchor

26.6A Removing front seat belt retractor unit/seat belt end anchor bracket bolt – except Hatchback

5 If the seat back is fixed, it can be removed (after the seat base has been removed) by undoing the bolts at its base and unhooking it from its upper mountings.

6 If the seat back is of the fold-down type the section(s) can be removed, after disengaging the upper mounting(s), by undoing the seat back-to-hinge securing bolts (photo). For vehicles with reclining rear seat backs, see Fig. 11.13.

Refitting

7 Refitting is the reverse of the removal procedure; ensure that all fasteners are securely tightened, to the specified torque wrench settings (where given).

26 Seat belts –
removal and refitting

> ⚠ **Warning: If the vehicle has been involved in an accident in which structural damage was sustained, all seat belt components MUST be renewed.**

Removal
Front

1 If the clasp is to be removed, remove the relevant front seat (Section 25); if the belt only

is to be removed, slide the seat as far forward as possible.

2 Remove the trim from the base of the 'B' pillar (Section 24) to reach the retractor unit.

3 Prise up the clip covering the belt upper anchor bolt, then remove the bolt; note the sequence of any plates, spacers and washers fitted (photo).

4 On Hatchback models, slide the belt guide out of the main trim panel (if not already done), then unbolt the anchor slide-bar and slip off the belt; note the sequence of any plates, spacers and washers fitted when removing the bolts and clamp the belt to prevent it retracting fully.

5 On all other models, prise up the clip covering the retractor unit lower/ belt end anchor bracket bolt.

6 On all models, unbolt the retractor unit; clamp the belt (except Hatchbacks) to prevent it retracting fully and note the sequence of any plates, spacers and washers fitted. Peel back the carpet (as applicable) and remove the belt assembly (photos).

7 On all models except Hatchbacks, once the 'B' pillar upper trim has been removed, the belt height adjustment slider can be unbolted if required: note the sequence of washers, etc, fitted (photo).

8 To remove the belt clasp, remove the relevant front seat (Section 25), then remove

the plastic trim covering the mounting of the clasp to the slide bar engaging bracket.

Rear

9 Remove the rear seat components (Section 25) as necessary to reach the seat belt end anchor bracket(s) and the lap-belt and clasp mountings. The retractor units are located behind the luggage compartment interior trim panels; refer to Section 24 for details of panel removal and refitting.

10 When unbolting a lap-belt and/or clasp, note the sequence of any plates, spacers and washers fitted.

11 To remove a belt first prise up the clip covering the upper anchor bolt then remove the bolt; note the sequence of any plates, spacers and washers fitted. Where belt guides are fitted, unclip them from the trim panels or remove the securing screws (as applicable). Unbolt the belt end anchor bracket; note the sequence of any plates, spacers and washers fitted and clamp the belt to prevent it retracting fully. Unbolt the retractor unit, noting the sequence of any plates, spacers and washers; if necessary, feed the belt through the trim aperture(s) before removing it (photo).

Refitting

12 Refitting is the reverse of the removal procedure, noting the following points.

26.6B Withdrawing front seat belt retractor unit – Liftback shown

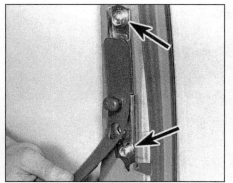

26.7 Remove 'B' pillar trim upper section and unscrew bolts (arrowed) to release front seat belt height adjustment slider

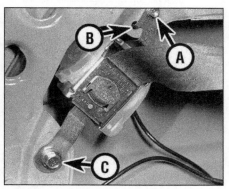

26.11 Liftback rear seat belt retractor unit bolts (A), locating tag (B) – luggage compartment interior trim panel removed

Fig. 11.14 Seat belts – Hatchback (Sec 26)

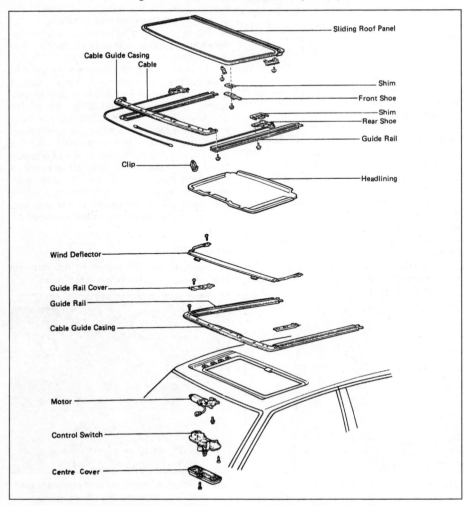

Fig. 11.15 Exploded view of sunroof components (Sec 27)

(a) Ensure that the original sequence is maintained of any plates, spacers and washers.

(b) When refitting rear seat belts, ensure that the lap belt and clasp sections cross over as shown in Fig. 11.14

(c) Tighten securely all disturbed fasteners, to their specified torque wrench settings (where given).

27 Sunroof – general information and adjustment

General information

General

1 The electrically-operated sunroof is controlled by a switch mounted in the switch/map light assembly next to the interior rear-view mirror, and is operated by a motor mounted behind the headlining above the switch.

2 In the event of electrical failure the sunroof can be closed manually, as follows. Remove the single screw and unhook the sunroof switch/map light cover at its rear edge. Then insert a large, flat-bladed screwdriver (included in the vehicle tool kit) through the access hole in the switch mounting plate to remove the large screw visible; take care not to lose the washer and spacer(s) when the screw is removed, as the sunroof cannot operate electrically without them (once the electrical fault has been traced and rectified). Close the sunroof as far as possible by hand, then insert the screwdriver into the hole (vacated by the removal of the large screw) and turn it fully to close the sunroof.

Sunroof switch – removal and refitting

3 Refer to Chapter 12, Section 12.

Sunroof motor – removal and refitting

4 Remove the sunroof switch; see Chapter 12, Section 12.

5 Remove all remaining components mounted on the headlining (Section 24).

6 With the front end of the headlining free, disconnect the motor multi-plug then, with the headlining carefully eased down, unbolt the motor and withdraw it.

7 Refitting is the reverse of the removal procedure.

Sunroof panel – removal and refitting

8 Open the sunroof halfway then loosen the clips on the front of the headlining panel (using a screwdriver with some tape on its tip). Slide the headlining panel rearwards to reach the sunroof panel front and rear shoe bolts; remove the front and rear shoe bolts from each side of the panel, noting the shims fitted, then remove the panel.

9 Refitting is the reverse of the removal procedure; adjust the panel, if necessary, as described below.

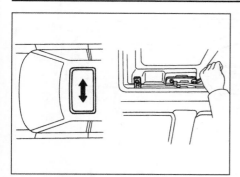

Fig. 11.16 Adjusting sunroof panel side-to-side alignment at rear shoes (Sec 27)

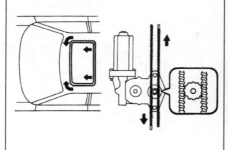

Fig. 11.17 Adjusting sunroof panel side clearances – clearance difference approximately 2 mm (Sec 27)

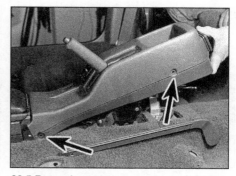

28.5 Removing centre console rear section – screw locations arrowed

Adjustment

10 The sunroof panel may be adjusted to correct differences in level between it and the roof, in side-to-side and forwards/rearwards alignment and differences in clearance from side-to-side. After any adjustments have been made, note that the sliding headlining panel must be fully refitted before rechecking the sunroof panel adjustment.

11 To check the sunroof panel height relative to the surrounding roof, measure at the centre of each side of the sunroof panel; all four measurements obtained should be ideally be 0 mm (ie a flush fit), with an upper limit of +1 mm and a lower limit of –2 mm. If any measurement obtained is outside these limits, open the sunroof panel halfway then release the clips securing the front of its headlining panel; slide the headlining panel rearwards until the shoe bolts can be undone, and alter the shim thicknesses as required (if the sunroof panel front edge sits proud of the roof when it is closed, even without a shim fitted, check the front shoe-to-stopper contact with the sunroof closed).

12 To adjust the panel alignment in its aperture, slide the headlining panel rearwards as described in paragraphs 8 or 11 above, then loosen the relevant shoe bolts and move the panel. Adjust in a forwards/rearwards direction by moving the front shoes (checking the front shoe-to-stopper contact once the

roof is closed) and in a side-to-side direction by moving the rear shoes.

13 If the sunroof panel appears to be twisted in its aperture, with different clearances on either side, the error can be corrected using one of two methods, depending on the amount of variation. If the difference is approximately 2 mm, remove the sunroof motor and move the relevant operating cable by one 'notch' to adjust the clearance; refit the sunroof motor on completion and recheck the clearance. If the difference is approximately 1 mm, adjustment is achieved by loosening the shoe bolts and moving the panel to its correct position. Check the front shoe-to-stopper contact once the roof is closed.

28 Centre console – removal and refitting

Removal

1 The centre console is of two-piece construction; the rear section must be removed first.

2 Disconnect the battery negative terminal.

3 Remove the front seats (Section 25).

4 Remove (where fitted) the mirror switch (Chapter 12).

5 Remove the securing screws (two at the rear and two at the front) and withdraw the console rear section (photo).

6 On models with a manual gearbox unscrew the gear lever knob, then raise the gear lever gaiter and remove it (photo). On models with automatic transmission, remove the shift knob and release the selector cover before disconnecting the selector cover illumination bulbholder.

7 Unclip the footwell trim panels from in front of the console (photo).

8 Remove the two screws from the front of the console front section and withdraw it (photo).

Refitting

9 Refitting is the reverse of the removal procedure.

29 Facia – removal and refitting

Removal

Note: *On dismantling, label all multi-plugs, cables, etc, to aid refitting. Note that a number of different types of screw are used to secure the various components; they must be refitted in their original locations.*

1 Remove both front seats (Section 25).

2 Remove the centre console (Section 28).

3 Remove the 'A' pillar trims (Section 24).

4 Remove the instrument panel (Chapter 12).

5 Remove (as applicable) the radio/cassette

28.6 Raising manual gearbox gear lever gaiter

28.7 Unclipping footwell trim panel

28.8 Removing centre console front section – screw location arrowed

29.5 Removing screws (arrowed) to withdraw stowage bin – where fitted

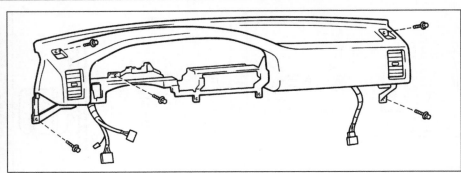

Fig. 11.18 Facia mounting bolt and multi-plug locations – left-hand drive shown (Sec 29)

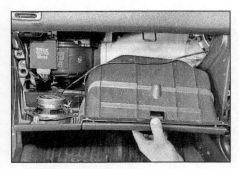

29.6 Removing facia lower finish panel/ glovebox assembly from passenger footwell

player (Chapter 12) or the stowage bin (photo).

6 Remove the facia lower finish panel/glovebox assembly from the passenger footwell, disconnecting the speaker as the assembly is withdrawn (photo).

7 Remove the heater control panel (Chapter 3).

8 Remove the screws securing the remaining centre stack trim and remove it.

9 Using a flat-bladed screwdriver, prise up the rear end of each demister vent grille and remove them.

10 Remove the facia mounting bolts and disconnect the wiring multi-plugs, check that

it is free to be removed and withdraw the facia, pulling it at an upwards angle to disengage the demister bar clips.

11 The components mounted on the facia reverse side can now be removed, if required.

Refitting

12 Refitting is the reverse of the removal procedure, noting the following points.

(a) Ensure that the wiring is correctly routed.
(b) Ensure that all components are retained with their original screw types.
(c) Adjust the heater control cables as described in Chapter 3.

Chapter 12 Electrical system

Contents

Degrees of difficulty

| **Easy,** suitable for novice with little experience | | **Fairly easy,** suitable for beginner with some experience | | **Fairly difficult,** suitable for competent DIY mechanic | | **Difficult,** suitable for experienced DIY mechanic | | **Very difficult,** suitable for expert DIY or professional | |

Specifications

System type	12 volt, negative earth

Battery

Type	Lead-acid
Capacity	Dependent on model
Minimum	14.0 mm

Starter motor

Type	Planetary, reduction or conventional pre-engaged	
Rating	0.8 or 1.0 kW	
Commutator diameter:	**Standard**	**Minimum**
Planetary and conventional type	28 mm	27 mm
Reduction type	30 mm	29 mm
Commutator insulation undercut	0.6 mm	0.2 mm
Commutator maximum run-out:		
Conventional type	0.4 mm	
Planetary and reduction type	0.05 mm	
Brush length:	**Standard**	**Minimum**
Conventional type	16.0 mm	10.0 mm
Planetary type	14.0 mm	9.0 mm
Reduction type	13.5 mm	8.5 mm
Armature endfloat/thrust clearance – conventional type	0.05 to 0.6 mm	
Brush spring load:	**Standard**	**Minimum**
Reduction type – 1.3 models	12 to 21 N	–
Reduction type – 1.6 models	18 to 24 N	12 N
Planetary type	16 N	9 N
Conventional type – 1.3 models	9.8 to 16 N	–
Conventional type – 1.6 models	14 to 16 N	10 N

Alternator

Rated output	40 A, 45 A, 60 A or 70 A
Regulated voltage – @ 2000 rpm (engine speed):	
40 A, 45 A	1 3.5 to 15.1 volts
60 A 70 A	13.9 to 15.1 volts
Drivebelt deflection	Refer to Chapter 1
Brush exposed length:	
Standard , ...	10.5 mm
Minimum	4.5 mm
Slip ring diameter:	
Standard	14.2 to 14.4 mm

Bulbs

	Wattage
Headlamp:	
Standard	45/40
H4	60/55
Front sidelamp	5
Direction indicator	21
Front direction indicator side repeater	5
Stop/tail lamps	21/5
Rear foglamp	21
Reversing lamp	21
Number plate lamp:	
Saloon	10
All other models	5
Courtesy lamps	10
Luggage compartment lamp:	
Saloon	3.8
All other models	3.8

Fuse number and code

Fuse number and code	Rating (amps)	Circuits protected
1 SEAT HTR	20	Seat heater
2 ECU-IG	15	Fuel injection system, air conditioning cooling system
3 STOP	15	Stop-lamps, anti-lock brake system
4 RADIO	7.5	Radio/cassette player, electric mirrors
5 ECU-B	10	Rear foglamp, anti-lock brake system
6 ENGINE	7.5	Charging system, engine glow system
7 WIPER	20	Windscreen/tailgate wipers and washers, headlamp cleaner
8 CIG	15	Cigar lighter, digital clock display
9 IGN	10	Charging system, discharge warning lamp, emission control system, electric underbonnet cooling fans, fuel injection system, engine glow system
10 TAIL	15	Tail lamps, parking lamps, sidelamps, number plate lamps, rear foglamp, instrument panel lamps
11 TAIL (RH)	10	Right-hand tail lamp, right-hand parking lamp, number plate lamps, instrument panel lamps
12 TAIL (LH)	10	Left-hand tail lamp. left-hand parking lamp
13 GAUGE	7.5	Gauges and meters (instruments), warning lamps and buzzers (except the 'discharge' warning lamp and 'door-open' warning lamps), 'econodrive' monitor, reversing lamps, air conditioning system, rear window demister, electric windows, central locking
14 TURN	10	Direction indicator lamps
15 SUNROOF	30	Sunroof
16 A/C	7.5	Air conditioning cooling system
17 HEAD (RH)	10	Right-hand headlamp
18 HEAD (LH)	10	Left-hand headlamp
19 HEAD (LH-UPR)	10	Left-hand headlamp (main beam)
20 HEAD (RH-UPR)	10	Right-hand headlamp (main beam)
21 HEAD (LH-LWR)	10	Left-hand headlamp(dip beam)
22 HEAD (RH-LWR)	10	Right-hand headlamp (dip beam)
23 HAZ-HORN	15	Emergency (hazard) flashers

Fuse number and code (continued)

	Rating (amps)	Circuits protected
24 EFI	15	Fuel injection system
25 EFI	15	Fuel injection system
26 CMH	30	Emission control system
27 RTR	30	Retractable headlamp system
28 DOME	10	Interior courtesy and luggage compartment lamps, clock, 'door-open' warning lamp
29 FAN-I/UP	7.5	Engine glow system. automatic choke
30 CHARGE	7.5	Charging system, discharge warning lamp, automatic choke
31 Spare	7.5	–
32 Spare	15	–
33 DEFOG	30	Rear window demister
34 DEFOG-I/UP	–	Rear window demister, engine glow system, automatic choke
35 CDS	30	Air conditioning system

Note: *Not all items listed are fitted to all models – see Fig. 12.15.*

Circuit breaker number

	Rating (amps)	Circuits protected
36	30	Electrically-operated windows, central locking
37	30	Rear window demister
38	30	Air conditioning system

Note: *Not all items listed are fitted to all models – see Fig. 12.15.*

Torque wrench settings

	Nm	lbf ft
Starter motor:		
Manual gearbox	39	29
Automatic transmission	46	34
Reversing lamp switch	40	30

1 General information and precautions

⚠ **Warning: Before carrying out any work on the electrical system, read through the precautions given in Safety First! at the beginning of this Manual.**

The electrical system is of the 12 volt negative earth type and consists of a battery, alternator, starter motor and related electrical components, accessories and wiring.

It is necessary to take extra care when working on the electrical system to avoid damage to semi-conductor devices (diodes and transistors) and to avoid the risk of personal injury. In addition to the precautions given in *Safety first!* observe the following when working on the system.

Always disconnect the battery negative terminal before carrying out removal or dismantling work which involves the vehicle electrical system.

Always remove rings, watches, etc, before working on the electrical system. Even with the battery disconnected, capacitive discharge could occur if a component live terminal is earthed through a metal object, which could cause a shock or a nasty burn.

Do not reverse the battery connections. Components such as the alternator or any other having semi-conductor circuitry could be irreparably damaged.

If the engine is being started using jump leads and a slave battery, connect the positive terminals of both batteries with one of the jump leads. Connect one end of the remaining jump lead to the slave battery negative terminal and the other end to a good earth on the vehicle to be started – not the discharged battery's negative terminal.

Never disconnect the battery terminals, or the alternator wiring, when the engine is running.

The battery leads and the alternator wiring must be disconnected before carrying out any electric-arc welding on the car.

Never use an ohmmeter of the type incorporating a hand-cranked generator for circuit- or continuity-testing.

When using a battery charger, always ensure that the battery is connected in accordance with the manufacturer's instructions.

2 Electrical fault-finding – general information

1 A typical electrical circuit consists of an electrical component, any switches, relays, motors, fuses, fusible links or circuit breakers related to that component and the wiring and connectors that link the component to both the battery and the chassis. To help you pinpoint an electrical circuit problem, wiring diagrams are included at the end of this Manual.

2 Before tackling any troublesome electrical circuit, first study the appropriate wiring diagrams to get a complete understanding of what components are included in that individual circuit. Trouble spots, for instance, can be narrowed down by noting if other components related to the circuit are operating properly. If several components or circuits fail at one time, then the problem is probably in a fuse or earth connection, as several circuits are often routed through the same connections.

3 Electrical problems usually stem from simple causes, such as loose or corroded connections, a blown fuse, a melted fusible link or a faulty relay. Visually inspect the condition of all fuses, wires (where possible) and connections in a problem circuit before testing the components. Use the diagrams to note which terminal connections will need to be checked in order to pinpoint the trouble spot.

4 The basic tools needed for electrical fault-finding include a circuit tester or voltmeter (a 12-volt bulb with a set of test leads can also be used), a continuity tester, a battery and set of test leads and a jumper wire, preferably with a circuit breaker incorporated, which can be used to bypass electrical components. Before attempting to locate a problem with test instruments, use the wiring diagram to decide where to make the connections.

Voltage checks

5 Voltage checks should be performed if a circuit is not functioning properly. Connect one lead of a circuit tester to either the negative battery terminal or a known good earth. Connect the other lead to a connector in the circuit being tested, preferably nearest to the battery or fuse. If the tester bulb lights, voltage is present: this means that the part of the circuit between the connector and the battery is problem free. Continue checking the rest of the circuit in the same fashion. When you reach a point at which no voltage is present, the problem lies between that point and the last test point with voltage. Most problems can be traced to a loose connection. **Note:** *Bear in mind that some circuits are only live when the ignition switch is switched to a particular position.*

Finding a short circuit

6 One method of finding a short circuit is to remove the fuse and connect a test lamp or voltmeter to the fuse terminals with all the relevant electrical components switched off. There should be no voltage present in the circuit. Move the wiring from side to side while watching the test lamp. If the bulb lights, there is a short to earth somewhere in that area, probably where the insulation has rubbed through. The same test can be performed on each component in the circuit, even a switch.

Earth check

7 Perform an earth test to check whether a component is properly earthed. Disconnect the battery and connect one lead of a self-powered test lamp, known as a continuity tester, to a known good earth point. Connect the other lead to the wire or earth connection being tested. If the bulb lights, the earth is sound.

Continuity check

8 A continuity check is necessary to determine if there are any breaks in a circuit. With the circuit off (ie no power in the circuit), a self-powered continuity tester can be used to check the circuit. Connect the test leads to both ends of the circuit (or to the positive end and a good earth); if the test lamp lights, the circuit is passing current properly. If the lamp does not light, there is a break somewhere in the circuit. The same procedure can be used to test a switch, by connecting the continuity tester to the switch terminals. With the switch turned on, the test lamp should light.

Finding an open circuit

9 When checking for possible open circuits, it is often difficult to locate them by sight because oxidation or terminal misalignment are hidden by the connectors. Merely moving a connector on a sensor or in the wiring harness may correct the open circuit condition. Remember this when an open circuit is indicated when fault-finding in a circuit. Intermittent problems may also be caused by oxidized or loose connections.

General

10 Electrical fault-finding is simple if you keep in mind that all electrical circuits are basically electricity flowing from the battery, through the wires, switches, relays, fuses and fusible links to each electrical component (bulb, motor, etc) and to earth, from which it is

passed back to the battery. Any electrical problem is an interruption in the flow of electricity from the battery.

3 Battery – testing and charging

Note: *On GTi 16 models, any diagnostic codes stored in the ECU will be erased when the battery leads are disconnected (Chapters 4 and 5). On all models, if the radio/cassette player has a security code, temporarily de-activate the code and re-activate it when the battery is reconnected; refer to the instructions and code supplied with the unit.*

1 Where a conventional battery is fitted, the electrolyte level of each cell should be checked and, if necessary, topped up with distilled or de-ionized water at the intervals given in Chapter 1. On some batteries the case is translucent and incorporates minimum and maximum level marks. The check should be made more often if the car is operated in high ambient temperature conditions.

2 Where a low-maintenance battery is fitted, it is not usually possible to check the electrolyte level.

3 Before suspecting the battery's electrical condition, always check the condition of the terminals, leads, connections and battery case as described in Chapter 1.

4 If topping up the battery becomes excessive and the battery case is not fractured, the battery is being over-charged and the voltage regulator will have to be checked.

5 If the car covers a very small annual mileage, it is worthwhile checking the specific gravity of the electrolyte every three months to determine the state of charge of the battery. Use a hydrometer to make the check; compare the results with the following table.

	Normal climates	Tropics
Discharged	1.060	1.030
Half charged	1.160	1.130
Fully charged	1.260	1.230

6 If the battery condition is suspect, first check the specific gravity of electrolyte in each cell. A variation of 0.040 or more between any cells indicates loss of electrolyte or deterioration of the internal plates.

7 A further test can be made by connecting a voltmeter across the battery terminals and operating the starter motor with the HT lead from the ignition coil earthed and the headlamps, heated rear window and heater blower motor switched on. If the voltmeter reading remains above 9.6 volts, the battery condition is satisfactory. If the voltmeter reading drops below 9.6 volts and the battery has already been charged, it is faulty.

8 In winter when heavy demand is placed on the battery (starting from cold and using more electrical equipment), it is a good idea to have the battery fully charged from an external source occasionally at a rate of 10% of the capacity (ie 6.6 amps for a 66 Ah battery); note that when performing a quick charge (6 amps or above, up to a maximum of 15 amps), the battery cell filler/vent caps must be removed.

9 Both battery terminal leads **must** be disconnected before connecting the charger leads (disconnect the negative lead first}. Continue to charge the battery until no further rise in specific gravity is noted over a four-hour period.

10 Alternatively, a trickle charger, charging at a rate of 1.5 amps can safely be used overnight.

4 Battery – removal and refitting

Note: *On GTi 16 models, any diagnostic codes stored in the ECU will be erased when the battery leads are disconnected (Chapters 4 and 5). On all models, if the radio/cassette player has a security code, temporarily de-activate the code and re-activate it when the battery is reconnected, refer to the instructions and code supplied with the unit.*

Removal

1 Disconnect the leads from the battery terminals, removing the earth (negative) first (photo).

2 Unfasten the battery securing clamp (photo). Lift out the battery, keeping it upright. The plastic tray beneath the battery has locating lugs on its base.

4.1 Disconnecting the battery earth (negative) terminal

4.2 Undoing the battery clamp

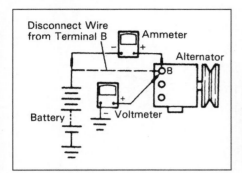

Fig. 12.1 Alternator test circuit (Sec 5)

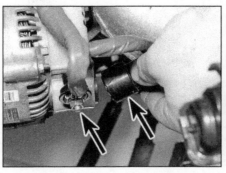

6.5 Disconnecting alternator electrical leads (arrowed)

6.6 Alternator pivot bolt (arrowed)

Refitting

3 Refitting is a reversal of the removal procedure; always connect the positive lead first, ensure that the battery is located securely and smear petroleum jelly over the battery terminals.

5 Charging system – testing

1 If the ignition warning lamp fails to illuminate when the ignition is switched on, first check the wiring connections at the rear of the alternator for security. If satisfactory, check that the warning lamp bulb has not blown and is secure in its holder. If the lamp still fails to illuminate check the continuity of the warning lamp feed wire from the alternator to the bulbholder. If all is satisfactory, the alternator is at fault and should be renewed or taken to an automobile electrician for testing and repair.

2 If the ignition warning lamp illuminates when the engine is running, ensure that the drivebelt is correctly tensioned (Chapter 1), and that the connections on the rear of the alternator are secure. Next check the alternator brushes and slip rings (Section 7). If the fault still persists, the alternator should be renewed or taken to an automobile electrician for testing and repair.

3 If the alternator output is suspect even though the warning lamp functions correctly, the regulated voltage may be checked as follows.

4 Connect up the circuit shown in Fig. 12.1 then start the engine.

5 Increase the engine speed to 2000 rpm, then check the ammeter and voltmeter readings. The ammeter reading should be less than 10 amps, whilst that on the voltmeter should be in the range specified.

6 Switch on the headlamps (main beam) and the heater blower motor (full power) then, with the engine speed again at 2000 rpm, check that the ammeter is recording 30 amps or above (this may be lower with a fully-charged battery). The voltmeter reading should be at the lower end of the specified range.

7 If the voltage is not as stated, the fault may

be due to a defective regulator or diode, a severed phase winding, or worn brushes, springs or slip rings. The brushes, slip rings and regulator may be attended to (Section 7), but if the fault still persists the alternator should be renewed or taken to an automobile electrician for testing and repair.

6 Alternator – removal and refitting

Removal

1 Disconnect the battery negative terminal.

2 If the extra working space is required, remove the air filter trunking/housing (Chapter 4).

3 Raise the front of the vehicle and support it securely on axle stands, then remove the engine compartment right-hand undershield for access from underneath.

4 Remove the alternator drivebelt as described in Chapter 1.

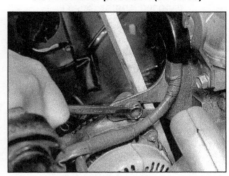

6.7 Adjusting alternator drivebelt

5 Disconnect the alternator electrical leads (photo).

6 Undo and remove the alternator pivot and adjusting clamp bolts, then remove the alternator from the vehicle (photo).

Refitting

7 Refitting is a reversal of the removal procedure; tension the drivebelt as described in Chapter 1 (photo).

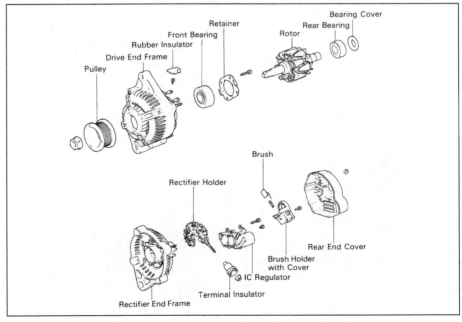

Fig. 12.2 Exploded view of the alternator (Sec 7)

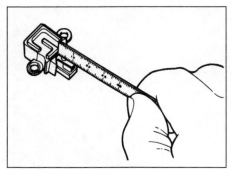

Fig. 12.3 Measuring alternator brush exposed lengths (Sec 7)

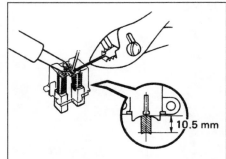

Fig. 12.4 Soldering new brush wire to the brush holder (Sec 7)

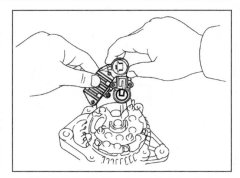

Fig. 12.5 Installing brush holder and voltage regulator (Sec 7)

7 Alternator brushes and regulator – renewal

Note: *If the brushes or regulator are to be renewed, note the VIN and any visible alternator markings to ensure that the alternator is correctly identified (from the several possible alternatives used) and the correct replacement parts are ordered from a Toyota dealer.*

1 Remove the alternator from the vehicle (Section 6) and thoroughly clean its exterior surfaces.

2 Remove the nut and terminal insulator (photo).

3 Remove the securing nuts, bolts or screws and withdraw the alternator end cover (photo).

4 Remove the two securing screws and withdraw the brush holder (photos).

5 Remove its securing screws and withdraw the regulator (photo).

6 Remove the brush holder cover to measure the brush exposed lengths; if either length is less than, or approaching, the specified minimum, both brushes must be renewed.

7 To renew the brushes, first remove the brush holder cover, then unsolder the brush wires and separate the worn brushes and springs from the holder. Pass the wire of each new brush through its spring, then refit each assembly and solder the wires to the outside

of the holder. Check that the brushes move smoothly in the holder and that their exposed lengths are as specified before cutting off any excess wire and refitting the cover.

8 Examine the slip rings to ensure that they are not rough or scored.

9 Install the brush holder and the regulator together from directly above the slip rings (see Fig. 12.5), ensuring that the brush holder cover does not slip to one side as it is being installed; ensure that there is a gap of at least 1 mm between the brush holder and the terminal connector (see Fig. 12.6). Tighten the brush holder and regulator securing screws.

10 The remainder of reassembly is a reversal of the dismantling procedure.

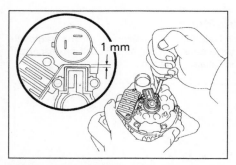

Fig. 12.6 Ensure that there is at least 1 mm between brush holder and electrical terminal connector (Sec 7)

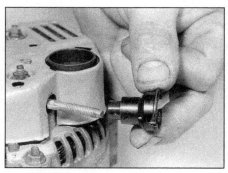

7.2 Removing alternator terminal insulator

7.3 Undo nuts (arrowed) to remove alternator end cover

7.4A Remove brush holder securing screws (arrowed) . . .

7.4B . . . to withdraw brush holder

7.5 Remove securing screws (locations arrowed) to release voltage regulator

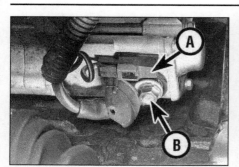

9.4 Starter motor solenoid feed connection (A) and main terminal (B) – seen from underneath

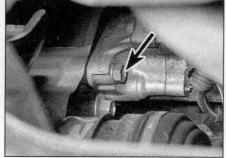

9.5 Starter motor lower securing bolt (arrowed)

9.6A Undoing starter motor upper securing bolt (arrowed)

8 Starting system – testing

1 If the starter motor fails to operate, first check the condition of the battery by switching on the headlamps. If they glow brightly then gradually dim after a few seconds, the battery is discharged.

2 If the battery is satisfactory, check the starter motor main terminal connections (on the solenoid), the solenoid feed connection (the small wire leading to the solenoid), and the engine earth cable connections for security.

3 If the starter motor still fails to turn, use a voltmeter (or 12 volt test lamp and leads) to ensure that there is battery voltage at the starter motor main terminal (the terminal to which the cable from the battery is connected).

4 With the ignition switched on and the ignition key in the 'start' position, check that voltage is reaching the solenoid feed terminal, and also the starter main terminal (the terminal to which the cable from the starter motor itself is connected).

5 If there is no voltage reaching the solenoid feed connection there is a wiring or ignition switch fault. If voltage is available, but the starter does not operate, then the starter or solenoid is likely to be at fault.

9.6B Removing starter motor

9 Starter motor – removal and refitting

Removal

1 Disconnect the battery negative terminal.
2 If the extra working space is required, remove the air filter trunking/housing (Chapter 4).
3 Raise the front of the vehicle and support it securely on axle stands.
4 Working underneath the vehicle, disconnect the small solenoid feed wire and the starter motor main lead, adjacent to it on the solenoid, which is secured by a nut and washer (photo).
5 Remove the starter motor lower securing bolt (photo).
6 Working from above, remove the starter motor upper securing bolt then withdraw the starter motor (photos). If clearance is too tight to allow removal from above, on certain models, removal is possible from underneath.

Refitting

7 Refitting is a reversal of the removal procedure; ensure that the securing bolts are fully tightened and that the electrical connections are secure.

10 Starter motor – brush renewal

Note: *On planetary-type starter motors, O-rings are fitted to either end of the field frame; if disturbed, these O-rings must be renewed. If the brushes are to be renewed, note the VIN and any visible starter motor markings to ensure that the motor is correctly identified (from the several possible alternatives used) and the correct replacement parts are ordered from a Toyota dealer.*

1 Remove the starter motor from the vehicle (Section 9) and thoroughly clean its exterior surfaces.
2 Where fitted, remove the motor's protective cover.

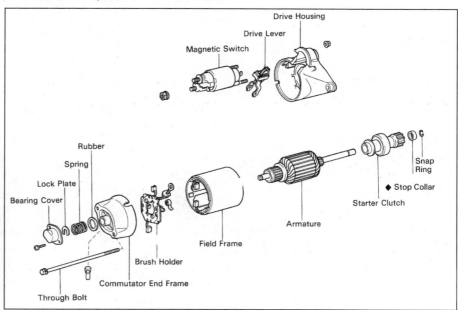

Fig. 12.7 Exploded view of conventional-type starter motor (Sec 10)

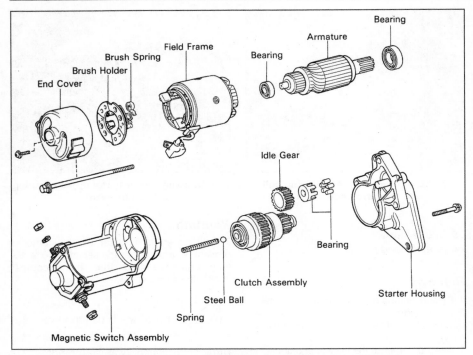

Fig. 12.8 Exploded view of reduction-type starter motor (Sec 10)

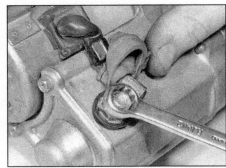

10.3 Disconnecting starter motor-to-solenoid lead . . .

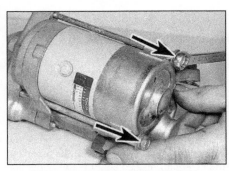

10.5 . . . unscrewing through-bolts (arrowed) to release field frame and armature . . .

3 Undo the terminal nut and disconnect the lead from the motor to the solenoid (photo).
4 On planetary- and conventional-type motors, undo the solenoid nuts and partially withdraw it to allow the plunger to be unhooked from the drive lever. Remove the solenoid.
5 On planetary- and reduction-type motors, undo the two through-bolts and withdraw the field frame and armature (photo).
6 On conventional-type motors, undo the bearing cover securing screws and withdraw the cover. Measure the armature thrust clearance (using feeler gauges between the lock plate and end frame); if the measurement obtained is outside the specified value, the motor must be renewed. Remove the lock plate, spring and rubber, then remove the two through-bolts and pull off the commutator end frame to expose the brush holder.
7 On planetary- and reduction-type motors, undo the two screws securing the commutator end frame (photo). Hold down the lead whilst withdrawing the commutator end frame; note that on planetary-type motors, the commutator end frame must be withdrawn at an angle to avoid interference between the water outlet hose and the brush holder and that the O-ring must be renewed.
8 Use a spring balance to measure the brush spring load, taking the reading the instant that the spring separates from the brush; if the results obtained differ from those specified, the springs must be renewed.

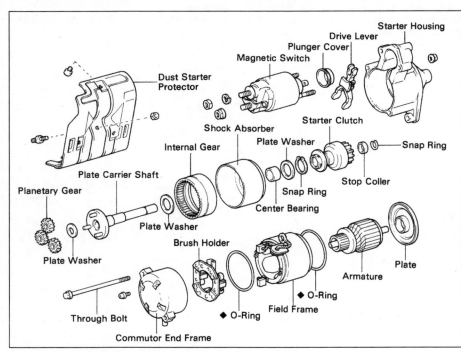

Fig. 12.9 Exploded view of planetary-type starter motor (Sec 10)

10.7 . . . undo screws and remove commutator end frame to reach brush holder . . .

10.9 . . . and release springs to allow brushes to be withdrawn – reduction-type motor shown

9 Using a screwdriver or similar, prise up the brush springs and withdraw the brushes from their guides in the brush holder (photo).
10 Remove the brush holder, then measure the length of all brushes; if any are less than, or approaching, the specified minimum all must be renewed.
11 To renew the brushes, cut their leads and solder on the new brushes (replacing the brush holder, where applicable, and ensuring a good soldered joint); do not allow the solder to run down the leads or allow excessive heat to transfer along the leads to the field coils. To prevent heat transfer when soldering, use pliers to grip the leads, thus acting as a heat sink. Dress the brushes using a fine emery cloth.
12 Check that there is no continuity between the brush holder positive and negative guides; if continuity occurs, the brush holder must be renewed.
13 Measure the diameter of the commutator and examine its surface. If the surface is dirty or burnt, it may be cleaned using 400 grade sandpaper then wiped with a solvent-moistened cloth; in extreme cases it may be necessary to skim the commutator using a lathe, but the commutator diameter must not be reduced beyond the specified minimum. Any skimming should be followed by surface-polishing using 400 grade sandpaper and wiping with a solvent-moistened cloth, then a check that the commutator insulation undercut is not below the specified minimum.

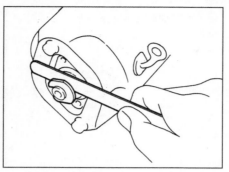

Fig. 12.10 Checking armature endfloat/thrust clearance – conventional-type starter motor (Sec 10)

Use a hacksaw blade if necessary to deepen the insulation undercut, but check that the edges are smooth afterwards.
14 Reassembly is a reversal of the removal procedure; note that new commutator end frame O-rings will be required, where applicable.

11 Fuses, fusible links, circuit breakers and relays – general information

Note: *Before renewing a fuse or a relay, ensure that the ignition is switched off; before investigating a wiring fault, the battery negative terminal should be disconnected.*
1 With the exception of the electric window relay (mounted in the driver's door on most models) and the tailgate wiper relay (mounted in the tailgate), the main fuses, circuit breakers and relays are contained either in the engine compartment fuse and relay boxes, behind the front footwell kick panels or behind the facia lower finish panels.
2 Specific details of fuse ratings and circuits protected are given on the lids of the fuse and relay boxes; further general information is given in the Specifications Section of this Chapter and in Fig. 12.15. A tool is provided for fuse extraction in the larger of the two engine compartment fuse and relay boxes.
3 To remove a fuse, first switch off the circuit concerned (or the ignition), then fit the tool

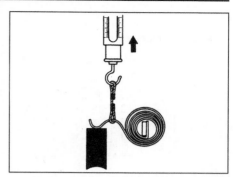

Fig. 12.11 Measuring starter motor brush lengths (Sec 10)

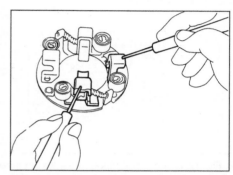

Fig. 12.12 Checking brush holder positive and negative guides for continuity (Sec 10)

and pull the fuse out of its terminals. Slide the fuse sideways from the tool. The wire within the fuse is clearly visible; if the fuse is blown it will be broken or melted.
4 Always renew a fuse with one of an identical rating; never use a fuse with a different rating from the original or substitute anything else. The fuse rating is stamped on top of the fuse; note that the fuses are also colour-coded for easy recognition (photo).
5 If a new fuse blows immediately, find the cause before renewing it again, a short to earth as a result of faulty insulation is most likely. Where a fuse protects more than one circuit, try to isolate the defect by switching on each circuit in turn (if possible) until the fuse blows again.
6 If any of the spare fuses are used, always

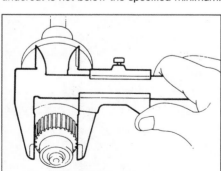

Fig. 12.13 Measuring commutator diameter (Sec 10)

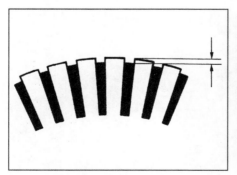

Fig. 12.14 Measuring depth of commutator insulation undercut (Sec 10)

11.4 Fuses on fuse block behind driver's footwell kick panel – typical

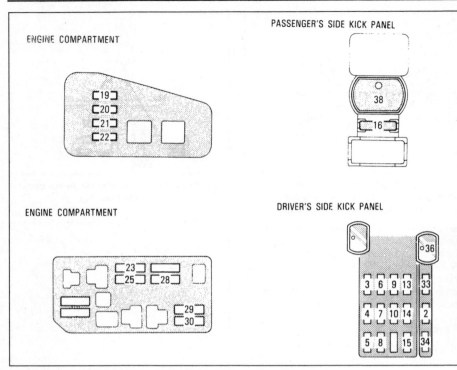

Fig. 12.15 A general guide to the layout fuses and circuit breakers, and their particular locations (Sec 11)

11.7 Main fusible links (arrowed) in box adjacent to battery positive terminal

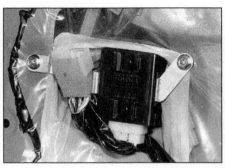

11.10A Electric window relay mounted behind driver's door inner trim panel

replace them immediately so that a spare of each rating is available.

7 Main fusible links are fitted in the box adjacent to the battery positive terminal: on some models further links may be found in the fuse and relay boxes (photo). The links are designed to melt in the event of a serious wiring fault, thus protecting the main wiring loom from damage; in the event of a link melting, the fault must be traced and rectified before the link is renewed. When renewing a fusible link, use **only** a genuine Toyota replacement part.

8 If a circuit breaker trips due to a fault in a particular circuit, first switch off the affected circuit and disconnect the battery negative terminal. Insert a thin needle or similar into the small hole in the circuit breaker until a 'click' is heard; the affected circuit should now operate

normally. If the circuit breaker trips again when its circuit is tested, switch off and trace and rectify the electrical fault (the circuit breaker itself can be tested only by substitution).

9 If a circuit or system controlled by a relay develops a fault and the relay is suspect, operate the system; if the relay is functioning it should be possible to hear it click as it is energized. If this is the case the fault lies with the components or wiring of the system. If the relay is not being energized, then either the relay is not receiving a main supply or a switching voltage, or the relay itself is faulty. Testing is by the substitution of a known good unit but be careful; while some relays are identical in appearance and in operation, others look similar but perform different functions.

10 To renew a relay, disconnect the battery negative terminal, then unfasten the relay mountings; where a relay is fitted into one of the fuse and relay boxes, simply pull it out of the socket and press in the new relay (photos). Reconnect the battery on completion.

12 Switches – removal and refitting

Note: *Always disconnect the battery negative terminal before removing any switch.*

Removal

Ignition switch

1 Refer to Chapter 10, Section 24.
2 To remove the ignition switch loom plate, remove the facia lower finish panel from the

11.10B Tailgate wiper relay mounted behind tailgate inner trim panel

12.2A Disconnect multi-plug (arrowed) . . .

12.2B . . . and remove securing screw(s) to withdraw ignition switch loom plate

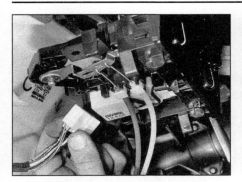

12.5 Disconnecting heater blower/fan motor switch multi-plug

12.6 Removing switch from centre stack finish panel

12.7 Hazard warning lamp switch securing screws (arrowed) on reverse of instrument finish panel

driver's footwell (Chapter 11). Disconnect the multi-plug, then remove the screw(s) securing the ignition switch loom plate to the steering lock/ignition switch housing; slide the loom plate off the end of the lock shaft (photos).

Horn switch (pad)

3 Refer to Chapter 10, Section 23.

Steering column multi-function switch

4 Refer to Chapter 10, Section 25.

Heater blower/fan motor switch

5 Remove the heater control panel (Chapter 3, Section 8) and disconnect the switch wires (photo). Unclip the switch from the panel.

Facia-mounted switches

6 The switches on the centre stack finish panel (either side of the steering wheel) may be removed by carefully prising them up, using a suitable flat-bladed screwdriver; disconnect their multi-plugs as they are withdrawn (photo).

7 To remove the hazard warning lamp switch, remove the instrument finish panel (Section 17, paragraphs 2 to 4), then undo the two screws securing the switch to the panel's reverse side and remove it (photo).

Electric window and central locking switches

8 Remove the relevant door inner trim panel with reference to Chapter 11.

9 Where a combined door-pull/switch panel is

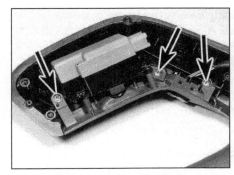

12.9 Switch panel securing screws (arrowed) on reverse of combined door-pull/switch panel

fitted, undo the remaining securing screws from the reverse side of the trim panel. The switch panel can be removed from the door-pull/armrest by removing its screws; the switches can then be removed from the switch panel by removing their securing screws or unclipping them, as applicable (photo).

10 Where switches are fitted flush on a door inner trim panel, they can be removed by bending up the metal retaining tags from the reverse side of the trim panel (photo).

Electrically-adjustable exterior mirror switch

11 Prise the switch carefully out of the centre console and withdraw it, disconnecting its multi-plug (photo).

12.10 Switch metal retaining tags (arrowed) on reverse of door inner trim panel

Courtesy lamp switches

12 Lift the rubber protector to expose the switch securing screw; remove the securing screw then disconnect the wiring as the switch is withdrawn from the door pillar (photo). The roof-mounted switches are an integral part of their respective lamp units.

Sunroof switch

13 Remove the switch/map light assembly cover securing screw then unhook the cover at its rear edge. Undo the screw securing the switch mounting plate and withdraw the mounting plate, disconnecting the multiplug (photo). The switch components are secured by screws to the mounting plate.

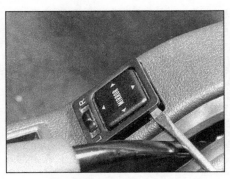

12.11 Removing electrically-adjustable exterior mirror switch from centre console

12.12 Removing courtesy lamp switch from door pillar

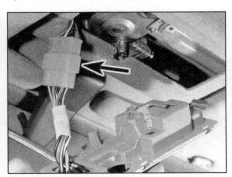

12.13 Removing sunroof switch/map light mounting plate – multi-plug arrowed

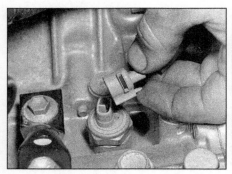

12.16 Disconnecting reversing lamp switch

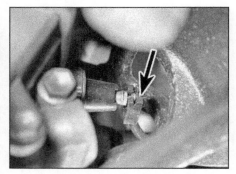

12.18 Oil pressure warning lamp/gauge switch connection (arrowed) – GTi 16 shown

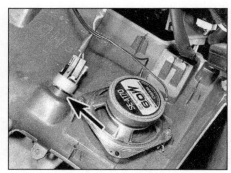

12.21 Instrument panel dimmer control connections (arrowed) on reverse of drivers footwell facia lower finish panel

Stop-lamp switch

14 Refer to Chapter 9, Section 23.

Handbrake 'ON' warning switch

15 Remove the centre console rear section (Chapter 11), disconnect the switch wiring and remove its securing screw, then remove the switch from the handbrake lever assembly front end.

Reversing lamp switch

16 Disconnect the switch multi-plug, then unscrew the switch from the transmission (photo).

Neutral start switch

17 Refer to Chapter 7, Section 13.

Oil pressure warning lamp/gauge switch

18 Disconnect the switch wire, then unscrew the switch from the front-facing side of the engine, behind the alternator (photo). Work quickly to minimise the loss of oil and temporarily plug the cylinder block aperture while the switch is removed.

Radiator cooling fan thermostatic switch

19 Refer to Chapter 3, Section 5.

Low brake fluid level warning switch

20 The low brake fluid level warning switch is integral with the brake fluid reservoir cap (Chapter 9).

Instrument panel dimmer control

21 Remove the facia lower finish panel from the driver's footwell (Chapter 11) and disconnect the dimmer control wiring (photo). Pull off the control knob to expose the unit's securing collar, unscrew the collar and withdraw the control.

Refitting

22 Refitting is the reverse of the removal procedure, noting the following points.
(a) Facia and electrically-adjustable exterior mirror switches ensure that the switches locate positively as they are pushed home.
(b) Reversing lamp and oil pressure switches – if an O-ring was fitted this must be renewed. If sealant was noted on the component's threads on removal this must be cleaned off and a suitable sealant applied on refitting. Tighten the switch securely.

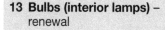

13 Bulbs (interior lamps) – renewal

General

1 Whenever a bulb is renewed, note the following points.
(a) Remember that if the lamp has just been in use the bulb may be extremely hot.

(b) Disconnect the battery negative lead before starting work.
(c) All bayonet-fitting bulbs are removed by pressing the bulb into its holder, twisting anti-clockwise and withdrawing; reverse to refit. Where a twin-filament bulb is fitted (eg the stop/tail lamp bulbs), the locating pins are offset so that the bulb can be fitted only one way correctly.
(d) Always check the bulb contacts and holder, ensuring that there is clean metal-to-metal contact between the bulb and its live contact(s) and earth. Clean off any corrosion or dirt before fitting a new bulb.
(e) Wherever bayonet-fitting bulbs are used ensure that the live contact(s) bear firmly against the bulb contact.
(f) Always ensure that the new bulb is of the correct rating and that it is completely clean before fitting it, this applies particularly to headlamp bulbs (Section 14).

Courtesy lamps

2 To renew the sunroof switch/map lamp assembly bulb, remove the lamp cover securing screw and unhook the cover at its rear edge; the bulb is a bayonet fitting (photo).
3 To renew a bulb in the courtesy lamp fitted centrally to the headlining, unclip the lens then pull the bulb from its holder (photo).
4 Refitting is the reverse of the removal procedure.

Luggage compartment lamp

5 On Estate models, remove the two screws and withdraw the lamp lens, then pull the bulb from its holder.
6 On Saloon models, twist and remove the lamp lens, then pull the push-fit bulb from its holder.
7 On all other models, if no lens securing screws are visible, prise up the lamp lens using a suitable flat-bladed screwdriver; if lens securing screws are visible, remove them and withdraw the lens. Pull the bulb from its holder.
8 Refitting is the reverse of the removal procedure.

13.2 Removing sunroof switch/map light cover

13.3 Removing centrally-mounted courtesy lamp lens

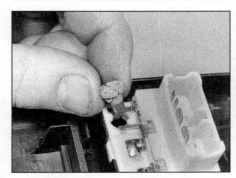

13.10 Removing bulbholder/bulb unit from a switch

13.11 Withdrawing bulbholder from heater control panel

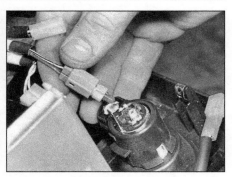

13.12 Withdrawing bulbholder from cigar lighter

Instrument panel warning lamps and illumination

9 Remove the panel (Section 17) and renew the bulbs (Section 18); reverse to refit.

Switch illumination

10 Remove the switch (Section 12). Where the bulb can be renewed separately from the switch, twist and withdraw the bulbholder; the bulb and bulbholder are a single unit (photo). Refitting is the reverse of the removal procedure.

Heater control panel illumination

11 Remove the heater control panel (Chapter 3, Section 8) and withdraw the bulbholder (photo). Check with a Toyota dealer whether bulb and bulbholder are available separately or not. Refitting is the reverse of the removal procedure.

Cigar lighter illumination

12 Remove the cigar lighter (Section 19) and withdraw the bulbholder (photo). Refitting is the reverse of the removal procedure.

Ashtray illumination

13 Prise up and remove the steering lock/ignition switch lock barrel trim, then remove the centre stack finish panel (Section 17, paragraphs 2 and 3). The bulbholder may be disconnected from the ashtray cover shroud to allow the bulb to be withdrawn

(photo). Refitting is the reverse of the removal procedure.

Automatic transmission selector illumination

14 Remove the securing screws and raise the selector cover until the bulbholder can be reached (it may be necessary to remove the shift knob), then withdraw the bulbholder and remove the bulb. Refitting is the reverse of the removal procedure.

---

14 Bulbs (exterior lamps) – renewal

General

1 Refer to Section 13, paragraph 1.

Headlamp

2 Working in the engine compartment, disconnect the multi-plug and remove the rubber cap from the back of the headlamp (if necessary remove the air filter housing or the coolant expansion tank – see Chapter 4 or 3), then release the bulb securing clip and withdraw the bulb (photos).
3 When handling the new bulb, use a tissue or clean cloth to avoid touching the glass with the fingers; moisture and grease from the skin can cause blackening and rapid failure of this type of bulb.

13.13 Withdrawing bulbholder from ashtray cover shroud

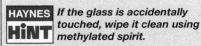

HAYNES HiNT *If the glass is accidentally touched, wipe it clean using methylated spirit.*

4 Refitting is the reverse of the removal procedure; ensure that the new bulb's locating tabs align with the reflector slots and that the rubber cap is refitted with the 'TOP' mark facing upwards.

Sidelamp

5 Raise the bonnet and undo the sidelamp retaining screws, then withdraw the sidelamp, manoeuvring it as necessary. Press the bulbholder into the lamp, twist anti-clockwise and withdraw it (photos).
6 Refitting is the reverse of the removal procedure.

14.2A Disconnecting headlamp multi-plug

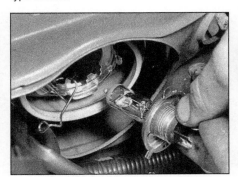

14.2B Withdrawing headlamp bulb

14.5A Undo mounting bracket-to-headlamp screw . . .

14.5B . . . and lower rear edge securing screw . . .

14.5C . . . so that sidelamp can be removed as shown . . .

14.5D . . . and bulbholder can be removed from sidelamp

14.7 Front direction indicator lens securing screws (arrowed)

Front direction indicator

7 Remove the two screws and withdraw the lens (photo). The bulb is a bayonet fitting. Installation is a reversal of the removal procedure, ensuring that any gasket fitted is correctly seated.

Front direction indicator side repeater

8 Using a thin flat-bladed screwdriver inserted between the lamp's rear edge and the body (with cloth or similar protecting the paintwork), release the lamp retaining lug and withdraw the lamp. Press the bulbholder into the lamp, twist anti-clockwise and withdraw it; the bulb is a push-fit in the holder (photos).
9 Refitting is the reverse of the removal

procedure; push the lamp into the body until the lug engages, ensuring that any gasket fitted is correctly seated.

Rear lamp cluster

10 Where the rear lamp clusters are secured by screws and locating pegs, open the tailgate and remove the visible screw(s). Withdraw the cluster, disengaging the locating pegs at the outer end, then press the bulbholder into the cluster, twist anti-clockwise and withdraw it; the bulb is a bayonet fitting (photos).
11 On all other models, unclip (if fitted) the cover from the luggage compartment interior trim panel, then depress the securing lugs and withdraw the bulbholder from the cluster; the bulbs are a bayonet fitting (photos).

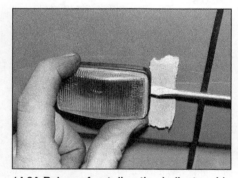

14.8A Release front direction indicator side repeater lamp from body . . .

14.8B . . . and remove bulbholder – lamp retaining lug arrowed

14.10A Undoing rear lamp cluster securing screws (arrowed) . . .

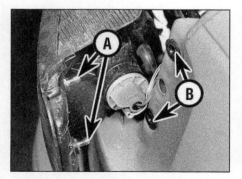

14.10B . . . to release pegs (A) from body locations (B) – Hatchback shown

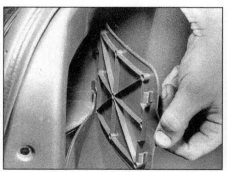

14.11A Unclip cover from luggage compartment interior trim panel . . .

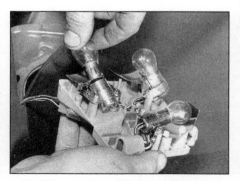

14.11B . . . then unclip rear lamp cluster bulbholder – Liftback shown

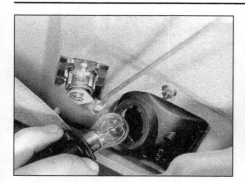

14.15 Withdrawing rear foglamp bulbholder – Liftback shown

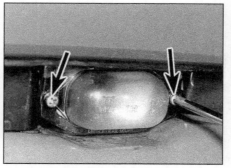

14.17 Number plate lamp lens screws (arrowed) – Estate

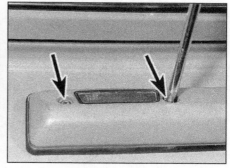

14.19A Remove securing screws (two arrowed) . . .

12 Refitting is the reverse of the removal procedure; ensure that any gasket fitted is correctly seated.

Rear foglamp

13 Where the foglamp is in the rear lamp cluster, refer to paragraphs 10 to 12.
14 Where the foglamp is secured by two visible screws to the tailgate, remove the screws and withdraw the lens; the bulb is a bayonet fitting.
15 Where the foglamp has no securing screws visible on the tailgate exterior, remove the tailgate interior trim panel (Chapter 11, Section 24). Twist the bulbholder anticlockwise and withdraw it; the bulb is a bayonet fitting (photo).
16 Refitting is the reverse of the removal procedure; ensure that any gasket fitted is correctly seated.

Number plate lamps

17 On Estate models, undo the lens securing screws from beneath the tailgate trim bar, remove the lens and withdraw the push-fit bulb (photo).
18 On Saloon models open the boot and remove the relevant interior trim panel to reach the rear of the lamp; press the bulbholder into the lamp, twist anti-clockwise and withdraw it.

19 On all other models, undo the screws securing the lens/housing and remove it from the rear bumper; the bulbs are a push-fit (photos).
20 Refitting is the reverse of the removal procedure; ensure that the lens/housing or (as applicable) any gasket fitted is correctly seated.

15 Exterior lamp units –
removal and refitting

Note: *Always disconnect the battery negative terminal before disturbing any lamp unit.*

Removal

Headlamp

1 Working in the engine compartment, disconnect the multi-plug from the back of the headlamp (if necessary remove the air filter housing or the coolant expansion tank – see Chapter 4 or 3).
2 Remove the radiator grille (Chapter 11).
3 Remove the sidelamp (Section 14, paragraph 5).
4 Undo the three nuts and the single bolt securing the headlamp unit and withdraw it, removing if required the lower headlamp trim/locating panel by unscrewing the panel retaining screws (photos).

14.19B . . . and withdraw bulb from number plate lamp lens/housing – Liftback shown

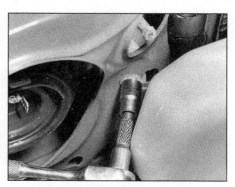

15.4A Removing headlamp inboard nut . . .

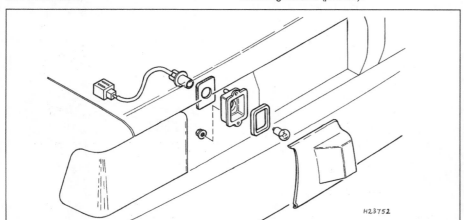

Fig. 12.16 Exploded view of number plate lamp – Saloon models (Sec 15)

15.4B . . . two outboard nuts (arrowed) (sidelamp removed for clarity) . . .

15.4C . . . and securing bolt (location arrowed) to remove headlamp unit

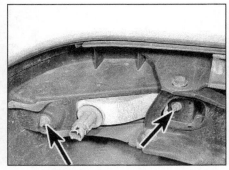

15.6 Front direction indicator lamp retaining nuts (arrowed)

15.9A Prise out grille from exterior of rear lamp cluster . . .

Sidelamp

5 Refer to Section 14, paragraph 5.

Front direction indicator

6 Remove the front bumper with reference to Chapter 11. Unscrew the retaining nuts and withdraw the lamp, removing the lamp lens first if necessary (Section 14) (photo).

Front direction indicator side repeater

7 Refer to Section 14, paragraph 8.

Rear lamp cluster

8 Where the rear lamp clusters are secured by screws and locating pegs, refer to Section 14, paragraph 10.
9 On all other models, remove the cluster bulbholder with reference to Section 14, paragraph 11. Undo the cluster retaining nuts; on Liftback models, prise out the grille on the exterior of the cluster and remove the additional securing screw (photos). Withdraw the cluster.

Rear foglamp

10 Remove the tailgate interior trim panel (Chapter 11, Section 24), then disconnect the foglamp multi-plug.
11 Working inside the tailgate, unscrew the lamp securing screws or nuts and withdraw the lamp: also remove (where necessary) the tailgate exterior trim panel retaining nuts and remove the panel to release the lamp.

Number plate lamps

12 On Estate models, remove the tailgate trim bar (Chapter 11, Section 18), then remove the retaining screws and withdraw the lamp unit, disconnecting the wiring.
13 On Saloon models, remove the bulbholder from the rear of the lamp; refer to Section 14, paragraph 18 and Fig. 12.16. Unscrew the lamp retaining nuts from inside the boot lid and withdraw the lamp, noting any gasket fitted.
14 On all other models, remove the relevant luggage compartment interior trim panel to disconnect the lamp multi-plug and to release the sealing grommet so that the lamp wiring can be released; remove the lens/housing from the bumper (Section 14, paragraph 19).

Refitting

15 Refitting is the reverse of the removal procedure, noting the following points.
(a) *Check and if necessary adjust the headlamp alignment (Section 16).*
(b) *Ensure that any gasket fitted is correctly seated.*

16 Headlamp beam alignment – general information

1 It is advisable to have the headlamp beam alignment checked and if necessary adjusted

by a Toyota dealer using optical beam setting equipment. Correct alignment of the headlamp beams is most important, not only to ensure good vision for the driver but also to protect other drivers from being dazzled.
2 If emergency adjustments have to be made, the headlamp aim should be checked and if necessary corrected by your Toyota dealer (or other suitably-equipped specialist) at the earliest possible opportunity.
3 Provision is made for separate vertical and horizontal adjustment of the headlamps by means of adjusting bolts accessible from the engine compartment; these are shown, for reference only, in Fig. 12.17.

17 Instrument panel – removal and refitting

Removal

1 Remove the steering wheel as described in Chapter 10.
2 Remove the facia switches from the centre stack finish panel (Section 12).
3 Remove the two centre stack finish panel securing screws, then pull the panel outwards to release its clips; disconnect the cigar lighter and ashtray illumination bulb wiring as the panel is removed.
4 Remove the instrument finish panel

15.9B . . . to remove additional rear lamp cluster securing screw – Liftback

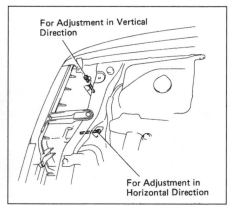

Fig. 12.17 Headlamp beam adjusting bolt locations (Sec 16)

For Adjustment in Vertical Direction

For Adjustment in Horizontal Direction

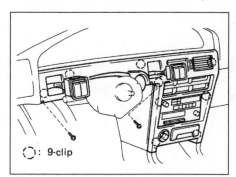

Fig. 12.18 Centre stack finish panel fasteners (left-hand drive shown) (Sec 17)

9-clip

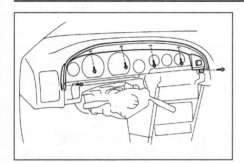

Fig. 12.19 Instrument finish panel screw locations (left-hand drive shown) – GTi 16 model (Sec 17)

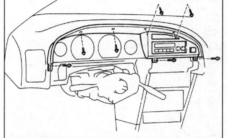

Fig. 12.20 Instrument finish panel screw locations (left-hand drive shown) – all other models (Sec 17)

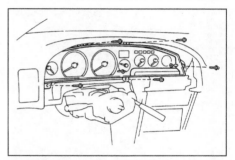

Fig. 12.21 Instrument panel screw locations (left-hand drive shown) – GTi 16 model (Sec 17)

securing screws and withdraw the panel, disconnecting the multi-plug(s) (photo).

5 Disconnect the speedometer cable in the engine compartment (Section 22).

6 Undo the instrument panel securing screws and remove the panel, disconnecting the speedometer cable and the multi-plugs (photos).

Refitting

7 Refitting is the reverse of the removal procedure.

18 Instrument panel components – removal and refitting

General

1 Remove the panel as described in Section 17.

Removal

Warning and illumination bulbs

2 Twist and withdraw the bulbholder, then withdraw the bulb (photo).

Printed circuit

3 Remove all bulbholders, then unscrew the printed circuit securing screws and release any clips; note that, where applicable, the printed circuit will have to be freed from its instrument terminal pins, and it may be necessary to separate the panel as the screws

holding the printed circuit also secure the instruments in the panel. Note the number of different types of screw fitted.

Instruments

4 Separate the panel sections as necessary, taking care not to lose or damage any graphic strips. The instruments are secured to the panel by screws; note the number of different types of screw fitted, and the washers.

Refitting

5 Refitting is the reverse of the removal procedure, noting the following points.

(a) *Printed circuit – ensure that the printed circuit is correctly located on its lugs and that the screws are refitted to their original locations, with their washers (where applicable).*

(b) *Instruments – ensure that the graphic strips are located correctly and that the screws are refitted to their original locations, with their washers (where applicable).*

19 Cigar lighter – removal and refitting

Removal

1 Disconnect the battery negative terminal.

2 Prise up and remove the steering lock/ignition switch lock barrel trim.

3 Remove the centre stack finish panel (Section 17, paragraphs 2 and 3).

4 Release the cigar lighter from the reverse side of the centre stack finish panel.

Refitting

5 Refitting is the reverse of the removal procedure.

20 Clock – removal and refitting

Removal

1 On GTi 16 models, the clock is part of the instrument panel; refer to Sections 17 and 18.

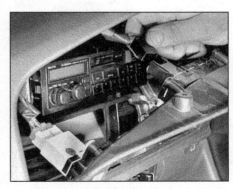

17.4 Disconnecting multi-plugs as instrument finish panel is withdrawn

17.6A Disconnecting speedometer cable from instrument panel

17.6B Disconnecting multi-plugs from instrument panel

18.2 Withdrawing a bulbholder from instrument panel

21.3 Horn securing bolt (arrowed)

The following procedure applies to all other models.

2 Disconnect the battery negative terminal.
3 Prise up and remove the steering lock/ignition switch lock barrel trim.
4 Remove the centre stack and instrument finish panels (Section 17, paragraphs 2 to 4).
5 Undo its securing screws, then remove the clock.

Refitting

6 Refitting is the reverse of the removal procedure.

23.5A Disconnecting windscreen wiper motor multi-plug

22.1 Disconnecting speedometer drive cable in engine compartment – two-piece cable shown

21 Horn – removal and refitting

Removal

1 Disconnect the battery negative terminal.
2 Remove the radiator grille as described in Chapter 11.
3 Unbolt the horn assembly and disconnect the multi-plug(s), then remove the horn(s) (photo).

Refitting

4 Refitting is a reversal of the removal procedure.

22 Speedometer drive cable – removal and refitting

Removal

1 Disconnect the cable from the transmission by unscrewing the cable end collar. On certain models a two-piece cable is fitted, which allows the cable to be disconnected further up its length (photo).
2 Remove the instrument panel (Section 17) until the cable upper end can be disconnected.
3 Release the bulkhead grommet and withdraw the cable.

Refitting

4 Refitting is a reversal of the removal procedure; ensure that the bulkhead grommet seats properly and that the cable is routed correctly, clear of any hot or moving components and with no twists, kinks, or sharp bends.

23 Windscreen/tailgate wiper motor and linkage – removal and refitting

Removal

Windscreen wiper motor and linkage

1 Disconnect the battery negative terminal.
2 Use strips of masking tape to mark the parked positions of the wiper blades on the windscreen.
3 Remove the trims covering the wiper arm nuts and unscrew the nuts, noting any washers fitted, then remove the wiper arms.
4 Remove the trim covering the wiper linkage (Chapter 11, Section 23).
5 Disconnect the wiper motor multi-plug, then undo the securing bolts (noting the earth lead location) and withdraw the motor until the connection can be reached between the motor crank and the linkage. Prise the motor crank ball from the linkage cup and withdraw the motor (photos).
6 To remove the linkage, unbolt it from the body and disconnect the ball and cup joints as necessary to withdraw the assembly through the body apertures; note the location and fitted order of any washers, spacers and seals (photo).

Tailgate wiper motor

7 Disconnect the battery negative terminal.
8 Use a strip of masking tape to mark the parked position of the wiper blade on the tailgate glass.
9 Lift up its cover and unscrew the wiper arm nut, noting any washers fitted, then remove the wiper arm (photo).

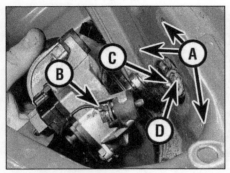

23.5B Remove securing bolts (A), noting earth lead (B), withdraw windscreen wiper motor and release ball (C) from cup (D)

23.6 Windscreen wiper linkage securing bolts (arrowed)

23.9 Undoing tailgate glass wiper arm nut

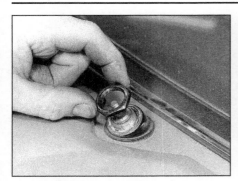

23.10 Removing tailgate wiper motor spindle securing nut

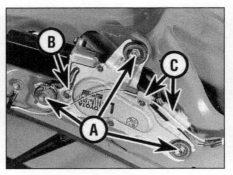

23.13 Remove tailgate wiper motor mounting bolts (A), noting earth lead (B) and release wiring from clips (C) – Liftback shown

24.2A Unbolting washer system reservoir

10 Unscrew the motor spindle securing nut (photo).

11 Remove the tailgate interior trim panel (Chapter 11, Section 24).

12 Unclip and disconnect the wiper motor wiring.

13 Unbolt and withdraw the wiper motor, noting the earth lead under one of the upper bolts and the fitted order of the washers and insulator bushes (photo).

Refitting

14 Refitting is the reverse of the removal procedure, noting the following points.

(a) Windscreen – ensure that the linkage ball and cup joints engage fully.

(b) Ensure that the earth lead is correctly refitted.

(c) Ensure that all washers, spacers, seals and insulator bushes (as applicable) are refitted in their original order.

(d) Refit the wiper arm(s) in their parked positions, then remove the tape.

24 Windscreen/tailgate washer system components – removal and refitting

General

1 The system comprises a fluid reservoir with an electric pump attached, an electrically-operated distribution valve (directing the fluid to the front or rear of the vehicle) and the jets, as well as the connecting hoses and the switches. Routine system checks are covered in Chapter 1. Whenever any of the electrical components is to be disconnected, the battery negative terminal should be disconnected first.

Removal

Reservoir

2 Unbolt the reservoir and release its base from the mounting; the pump can then be separated from the drained reservoir (see below), or can be removed with the reservoir (photos).

Pump

3 Remove and drain the reservoir, disconnect the pump wiring and hose, then pull the pump out of the reservoir grommet.

Distribution valve

4 Unbolt the valve from the front right-hand suspension turret disconnect its wiring and hoses and remove it (photo).

Hose

5 To remove a section of hose disconnect both ends, release it from any guides and withdraw it; where applicable, release any grommets or hose protectors fitted where the hose passes through a panel.

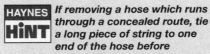

HAYNES HINT *If removing a hose which runs through a concealed route, tie a long piece of string to one end of the hose before removing it. When the end of the hose appears, untie the string.*

Jets

6 Disconnect the hose from the jet and release the jet from the reverse side of its mounting panel. Access to the tailgate glass jet is provided by a blanking grommet in the top centre of the tailgate inside panel; on GTi 16 models, also remove the rear spoiler (Chapter 11, Section 23) to reach the jet.

Refitting

7 Refitting is the reverse of the removal procedure, noting the following points.

(a) Pump/reservoir – renew the sealing grommet if there is any doubt about its condition.

(b) Hose – if refitting a length of hose which runs through a concealed route, use the string fitted on removal to draw the hose into place.

(c) Jets – ensure the jets locate securely into their panels.

(d) Do not forget to top up the reservoir with fluid.

25 Radio/cassette player – removal and refitting

Removal

1 Disconnect the battery negative terminal. If the radio/cassette player has a security code, temporarily de-activate the code and reactivate it when the battery is reconnected; refer to the instructions and code supplied with the unit.

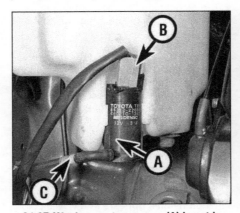

24.2B Washer system pump (A) is set in base of reservoir – note pump wiring (B) and hose (C)

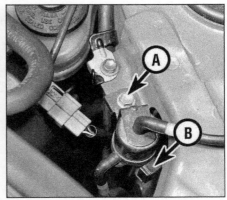

24.4 Washer system distribution valve bolted (A) to front right-hand suspension turret – note wiring (B)

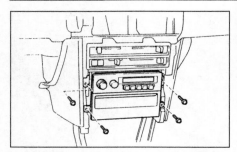

Fig. 12.22 Radio/cassette player screw locations – GTi 16 model (Sec 25)

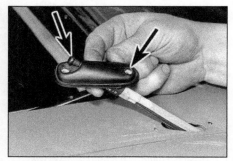

27.2 Radio aerial base mountings (arrowed) – typical – Liftback shown

2 Prise up and remove the steering lock/ignition switch lock barrel trim.
3 On GTi 16 models, remove the centre stack finish panel (Section 17, paragraphs 2 and 3). Remove the screws securing the radio/cassette player and withdraw it, disconnecting its aerial lead and multi-plug(s).
4 On all other models remove the centre stack and instrument panel finish panels (Section 17, paragraphs 2 to 4). Remove the screws securing the radio/cassette player and withdraw it, disconnecting its aerial lead and multi-plug(s) (photos).

Refitting

5 Refitting is the reverse of the removal procedure.

26 Speakers –
removal and refitting

Removal

1 To remove a front speaker, remove the facia lower finish panel from the footwell (Chapter 11, Sections 24 and 29), disconnect the speaker wiring and unscrew the retaining screws. Withdraw the speaker.
2 To remove a rear speaker, withdraw the interior trim panels (Chapter 11, Section 24) as necessary to reach the speaker connections and mountings; the procedure is then as described above.

Refitting

3 Refitting is the reverse of the removal procedure.

25.4A Removing radio/cassette player – typical – remove securing screws . . .

27 Radio aerial –
removal and refitting

Removal

1 Remove the radio/cassette player (Section 25) until the aerial lead can be disconnected from the back of the unit; tie a long drawstring to the end of the lead.
2 Remove the aerial base securing screws and withdraw the aerial, unclipping the lead from any guides and releasing any ties as necessary (photo). When the end of the lead appears, untie the drawstring.

Refitting

3 Refitting is the reverse of the removal procedure; use the drawstring to pull the lead back through the bodywork and ensure that the lead is secured by the clips or ties provided.

28 Wiring diagrams

1 The wiring diagrams have appropriate illustrations above each particular circuit as well as written descriptions, to aid the tracing of individual circuit components.
2 The diagrams follow on from one page to the next; a single diagram may be split into easily-managed sections and appear on several pages.
3 On each diagram, the feed wiring is shown at the top and the earth points at the bottom; each is allocated a letter (in either upper or lower case characters) which can be traced backwards. A description of each earth point location appears at the bottom of each diagram, whilst the feed wiring follows from one diagram to the next.
4 Note that many of the diagrams contain references to equipment and models not available in the UK; these should be ignored.
5 The wire colour-coding is given below. Where a hyphen appears in a wire's colour code the first letter(s) indicates the wire's main colour while the letter after the hyphen indicates the stripe colour.

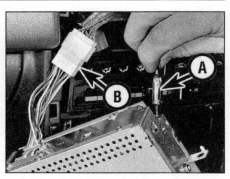

25.4B . . . and disconnect aerial lead (A) and multi-plug (B)

Code	Wire colour
B	Black
BR	Brown
G	Green
GR	Grey
L	Light blue
LG	Light green
O	Orange
2	Red
4	White
5	Yellow
1	Pink
3	Violet

6 A list of the abbreviations used in the wiring diagrams is given below, with their meanings. Some will not be applicable to the models covered in this Manual.

Abbreviation	Meaning
A.B.S.	Anti-lock brake system
A/C	Air conditioner
A/P	Air purifier
A/T	Automatic transmission
CB	Circuit breaker
C/P	Coupe type
ECT	Electronic controlled transmission
EDIC	Electrical diesel injection control
EFI	Electronic fuel injection
EUR	Europe
FF	Front engine front drive
FL	Fusible link
FR	Front engine rear drive
GEN	General
IG	Ignition
LH	Left-hand
LHD	Left-hand drive vehicles
LWR	Lower
O/D	Over drive
PKB	Parking brake (handbrake)
PPS	Progressive power steering
RH	Right-hand
RHD	Right-hand drive vehicles
SC	Spark control
S/D	Sedan (4-door saloon) type
SNV	Switch
TEMP	Temperature
TP	Throttle positioner
TWC	Three way catalyst
UPR	Upper
VSV	Vacuum switching valve
W/G	Wagon (5-door Estate) type

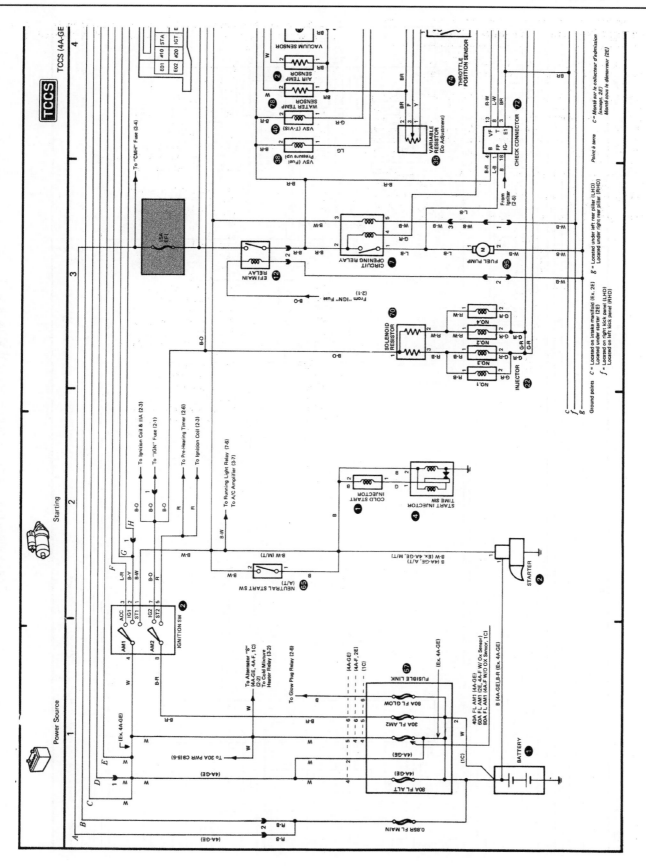

Typical wiring diagram for all models - 1987 to 1989

Typical wiring diagram for all models - 1987 to 1989 (continued)

Typical wiring diagram for all models - 1987 to 1989 (continued)

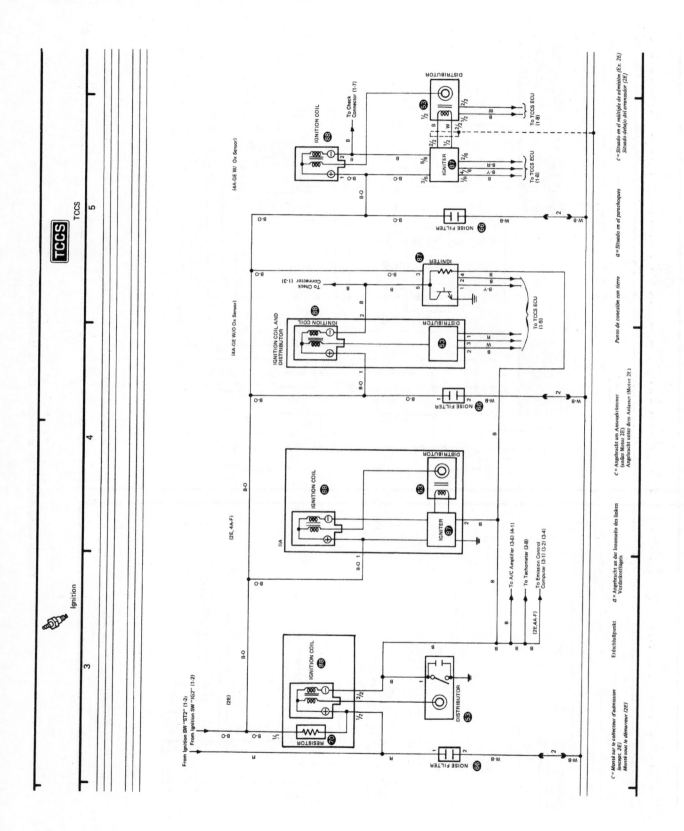

Typical wiring diagram for all models – 1987 to 1989 (continued)

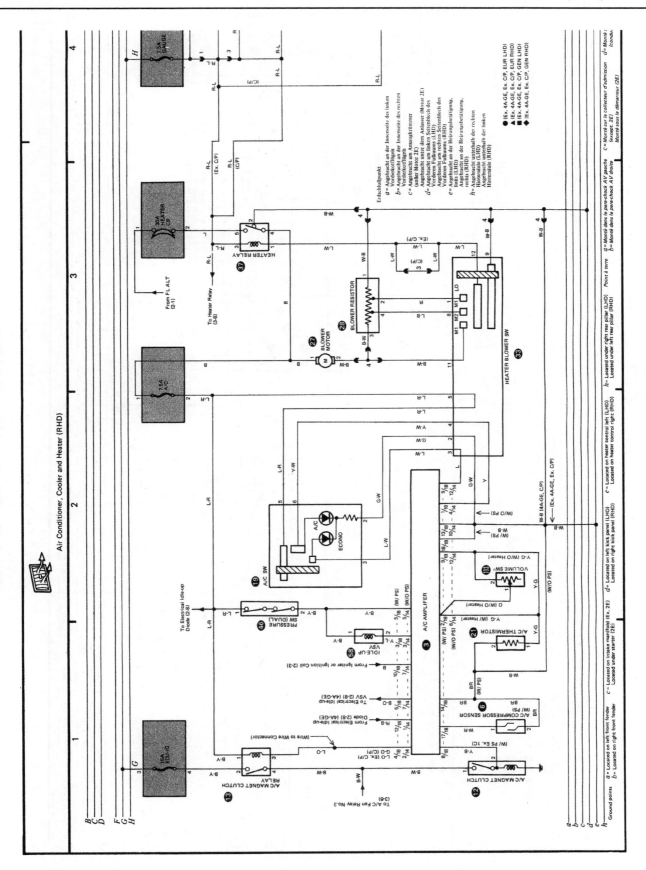

Typical wiring diagram for all models - 1987 to 1989 (continued)

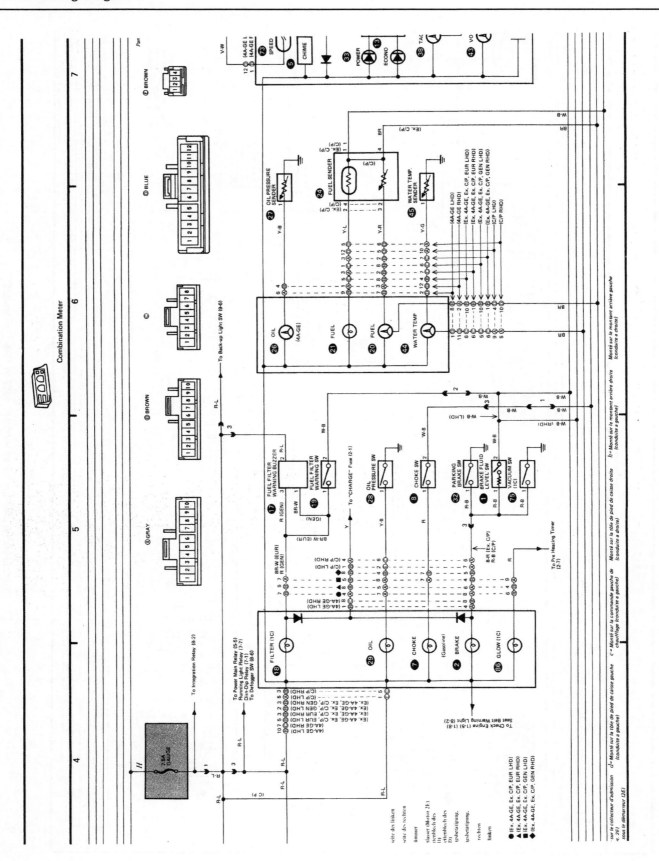

Typical wiring diagram for all models – 1987 to 1989 (continued)

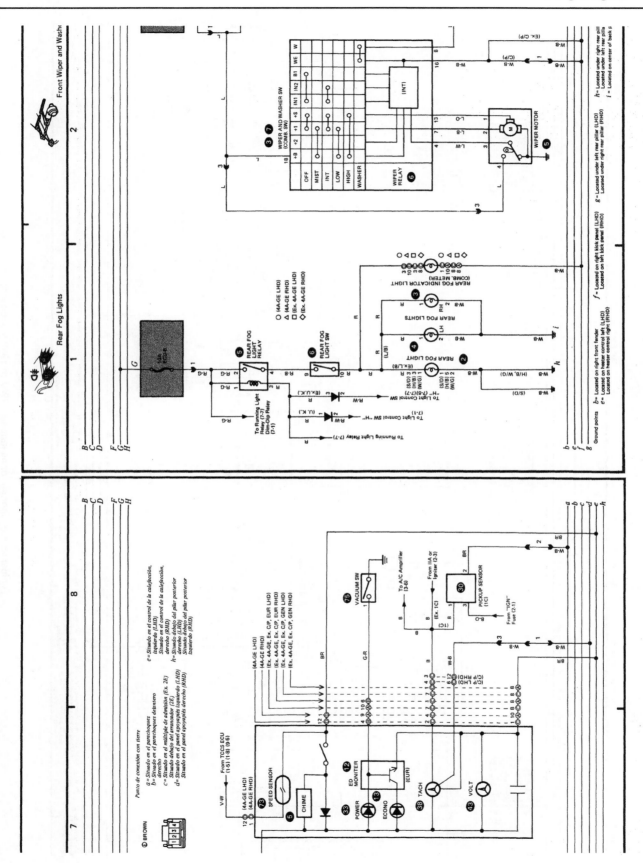

Typical wiring diagram for all models - 1987 to 1989 (continued)

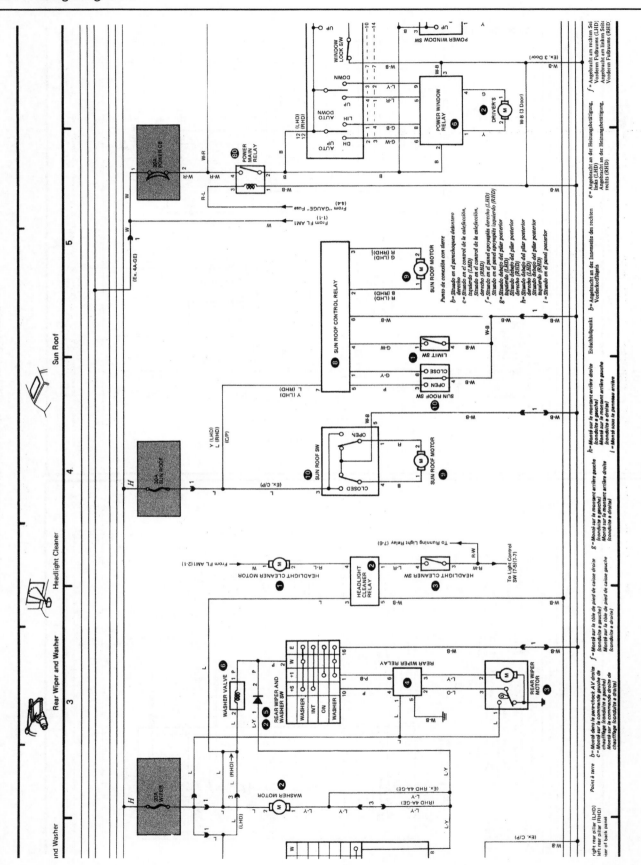

Typical wiring diagram for all models - 1987 to 1989 (continued)

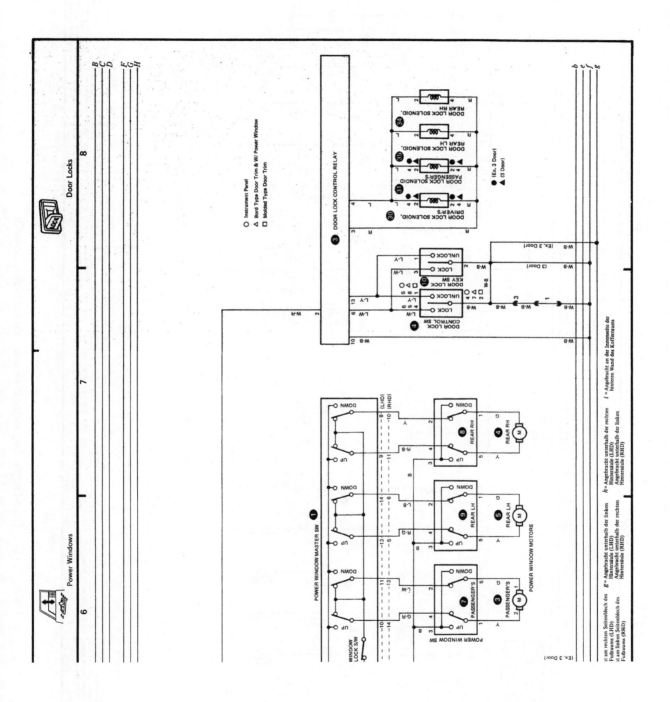

Typical wiring diagram for all models - 1987 to 1989 (continued)

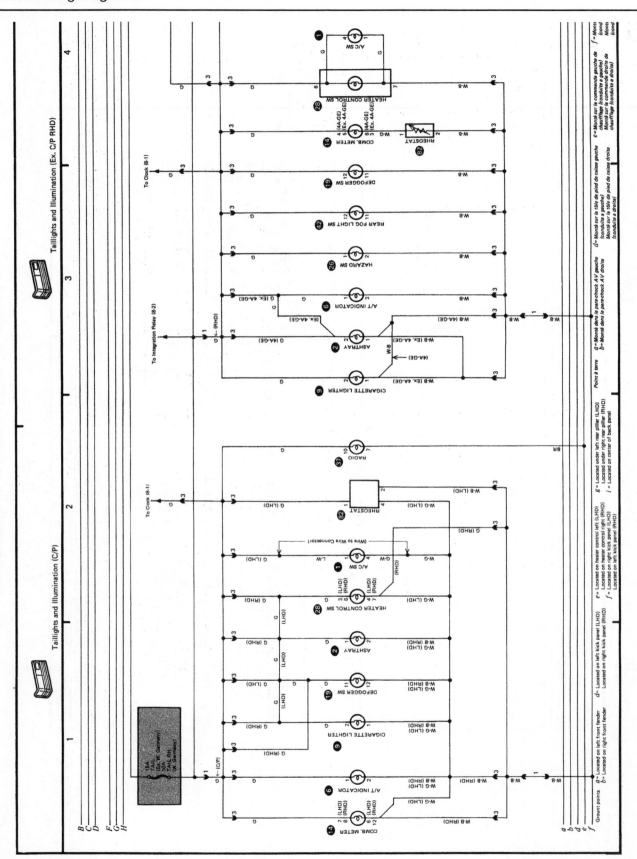

Typical wiring diagram for all models – 1987 to 1989 (continued)

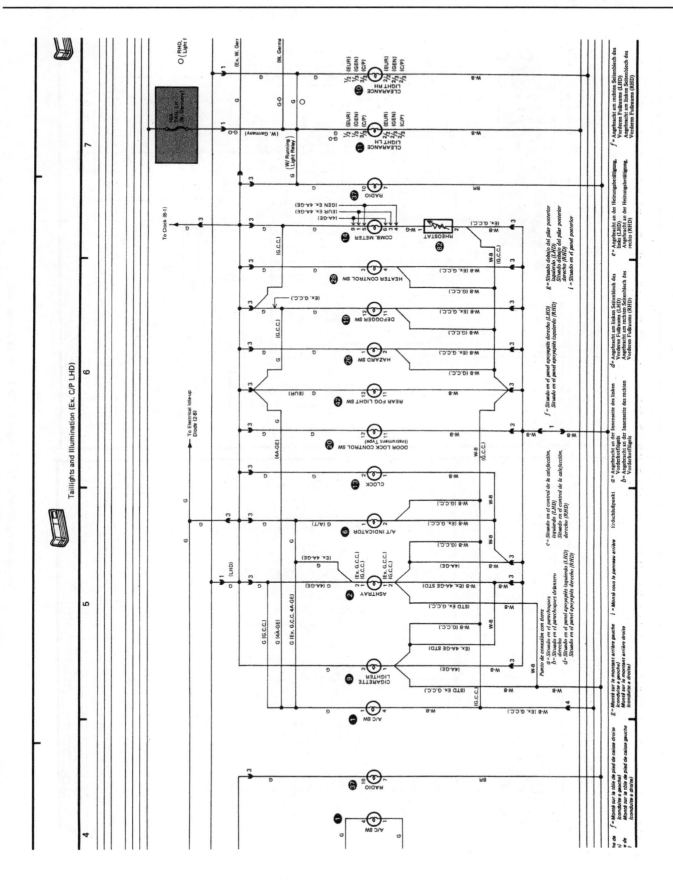

Typical wiring diagram for all models – 1987 to 1989 (continued)

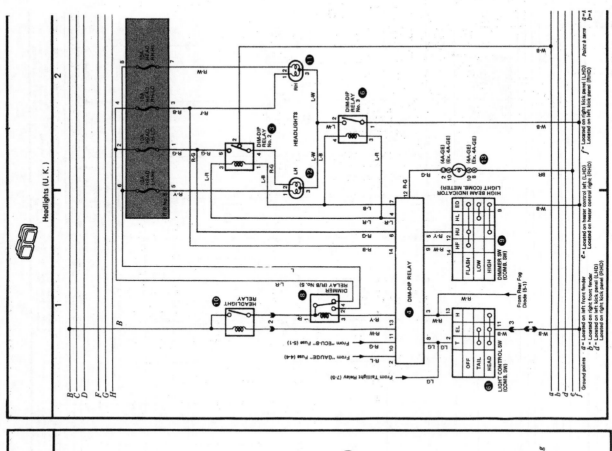

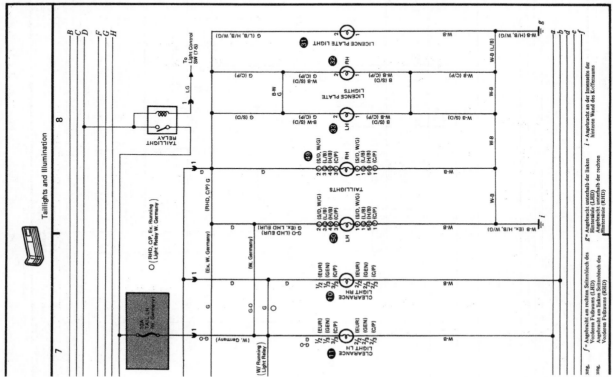

Typical wiring diagram for all models – 1987 to 1989 (continued)

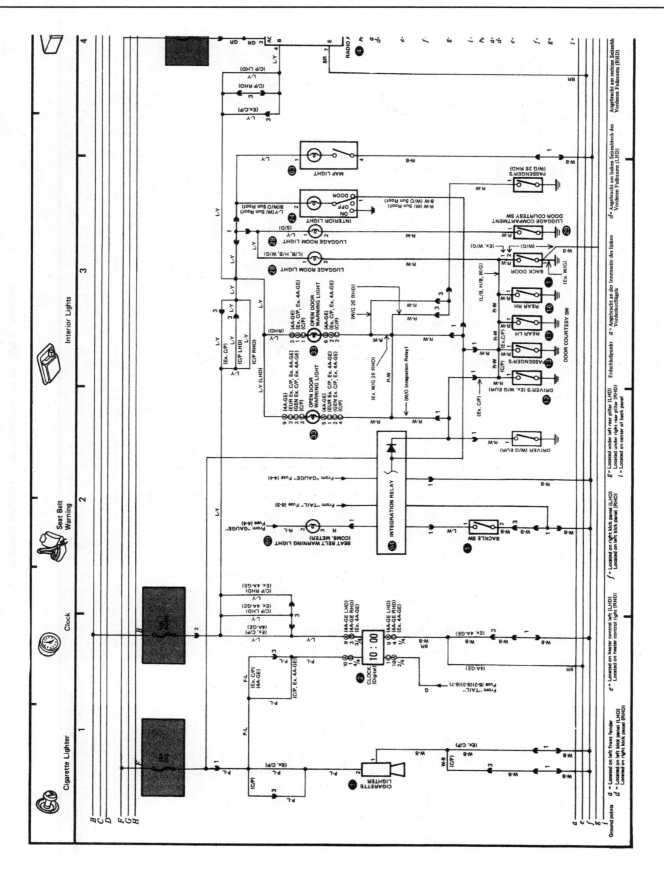

Typical wiring diagram for all models - 1987 to 1989 (continued)

Radio and Tape Player 4

Remote Control Mirrors 5

Rear Window Defogger (LHD) 6

Rear Window Defogger (RHD) 7

Typical wiring diagram for all models - 1987 to 1989 (continued)

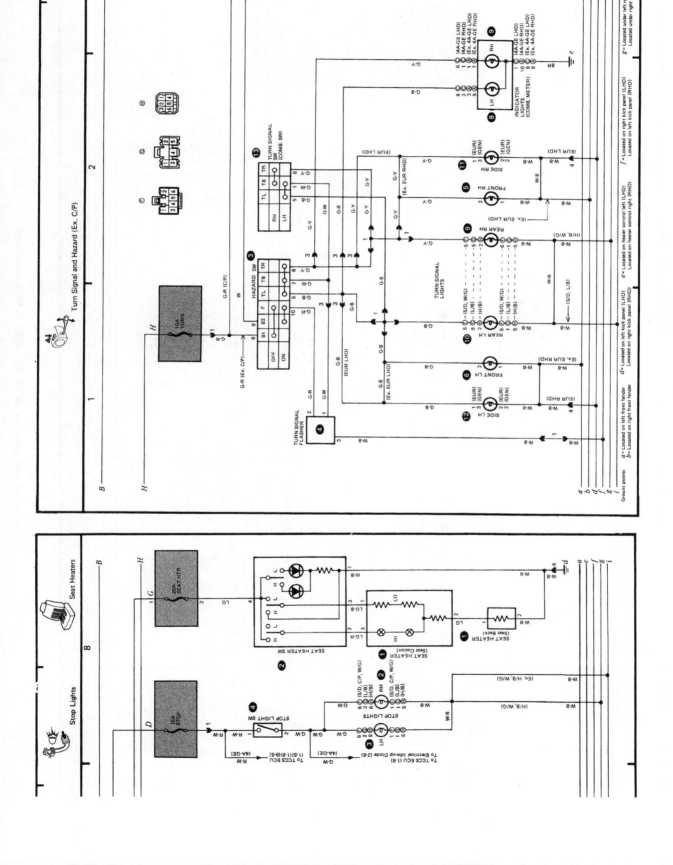

Typical wiring diagram for all models - 1987 to 1989 (continued)

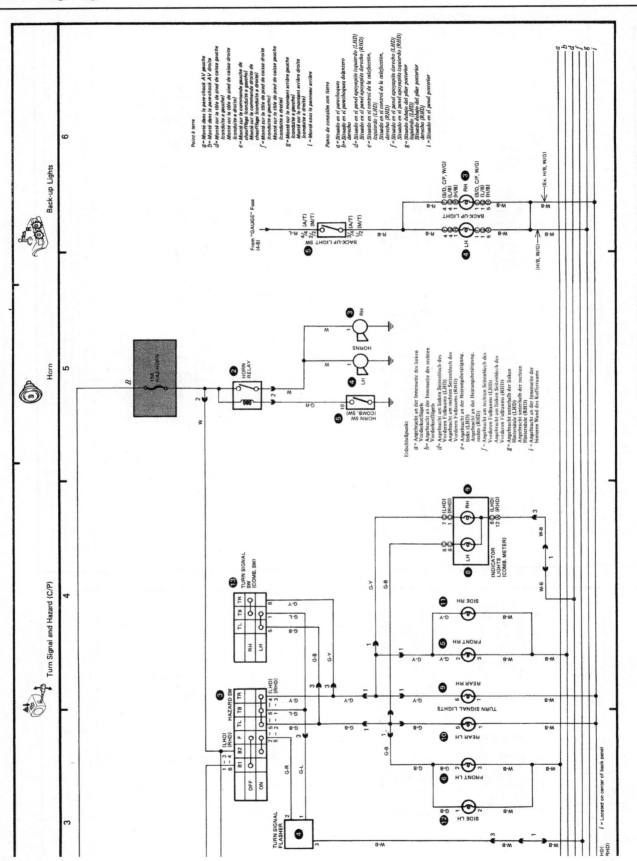

Typical wiring diagram for all models - 1987 to 1989 (continued)

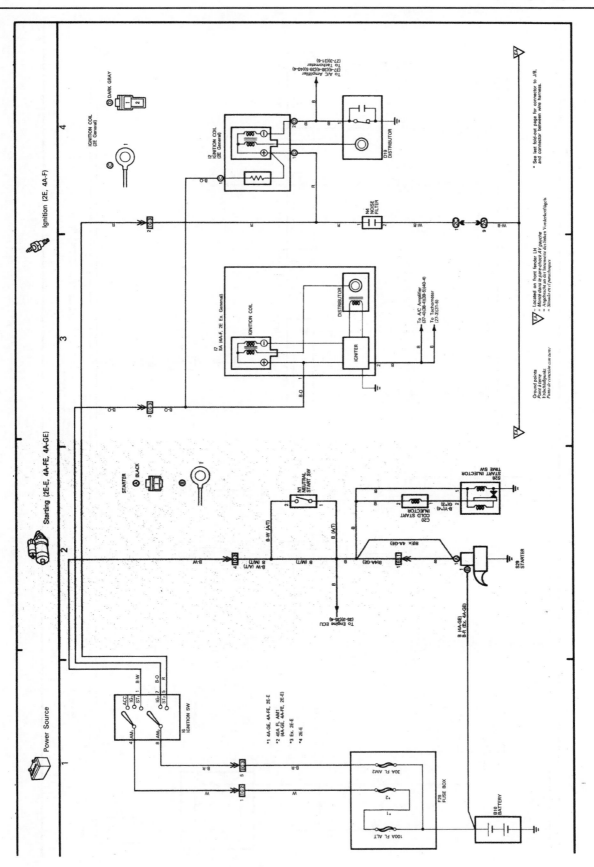

Typical wiring diagram for all models - 1990 on

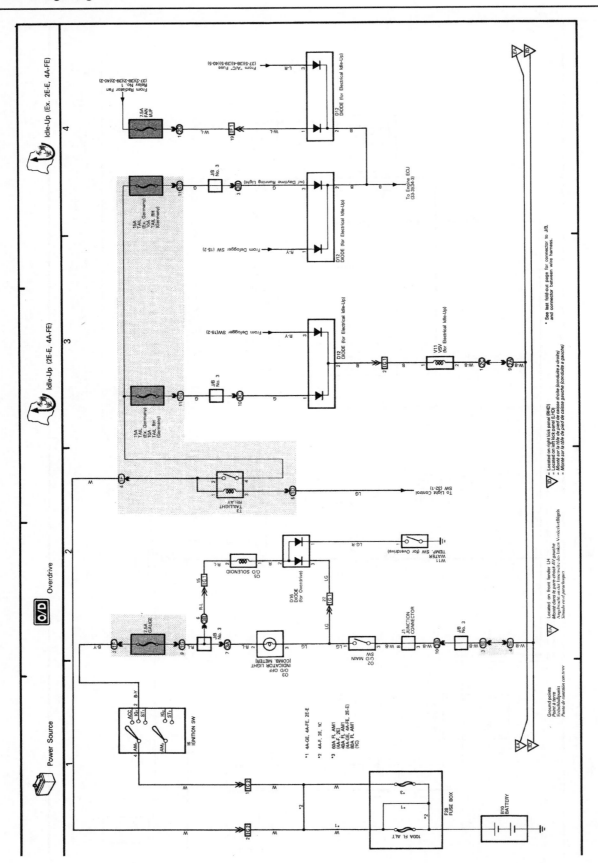

Typical wiring diagram for all models - 1990 on (continued)

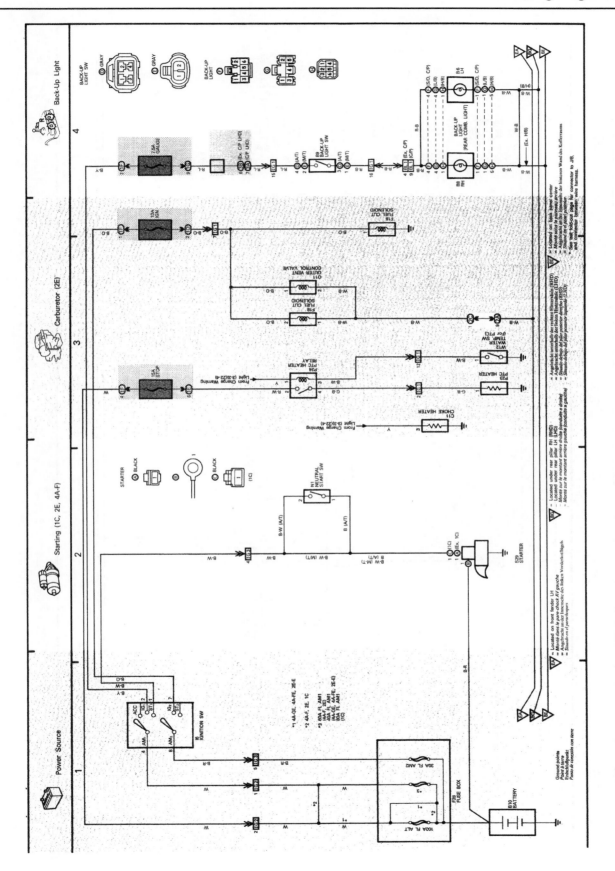

Typical wiring diagram for all models - 1990 on (continued)

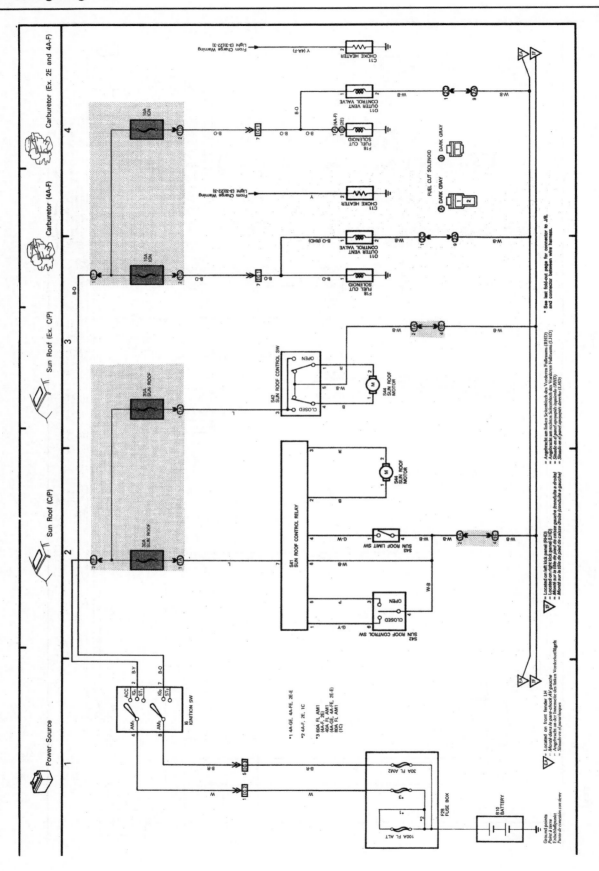

Typical wiring diagram for all models - 1990 on (continued)

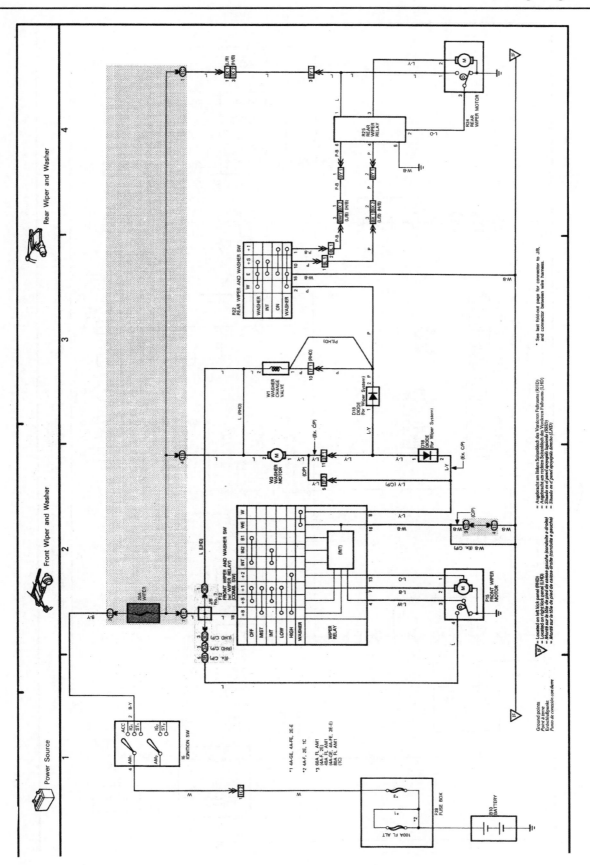

Typical wiring diagram for all models - 1990 on (continued)

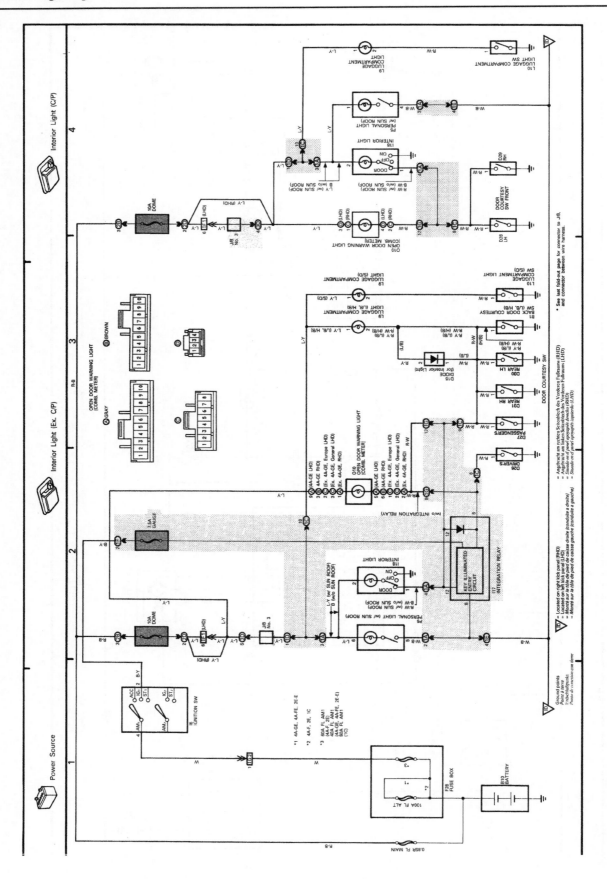

Typical wiring diagram for all models - 1990 on (continued)

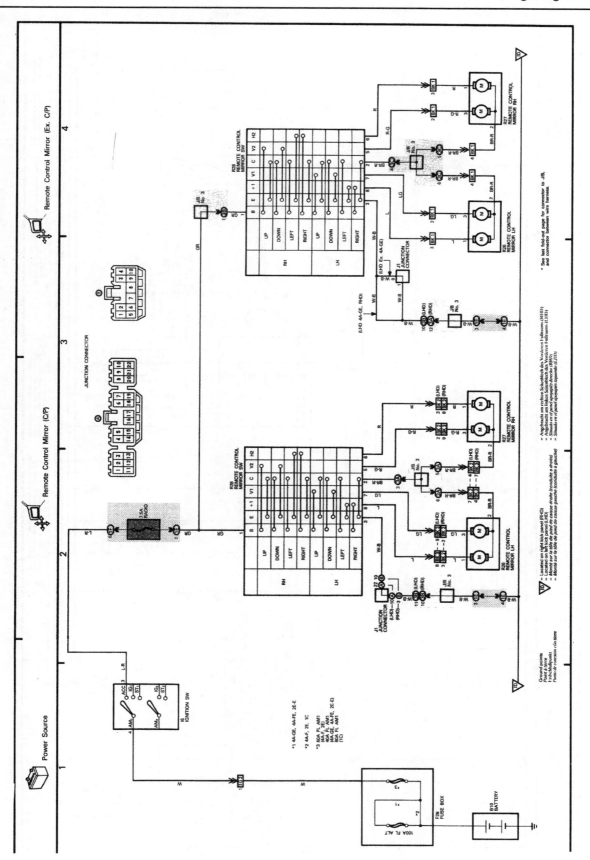

Typical wiring diagram for all models - 1990 on (continued)

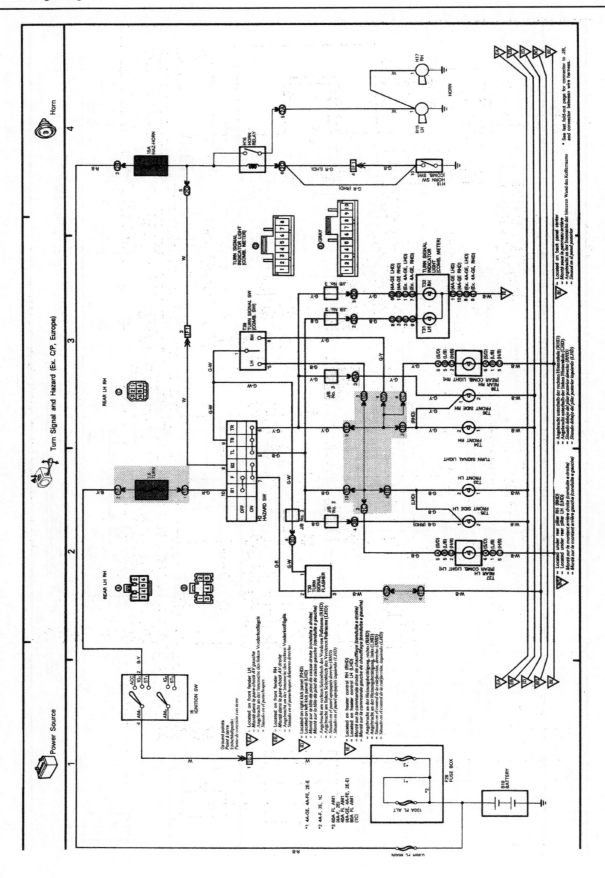

Typical wiring diagram for all models - 1990 on (continued)

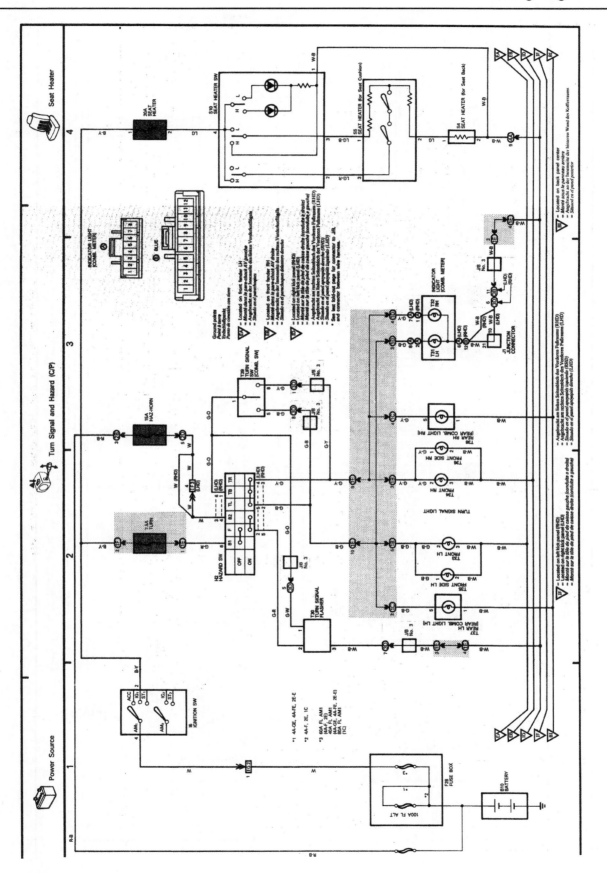

Typical wiring diagram for all models - 1990 on (continued)

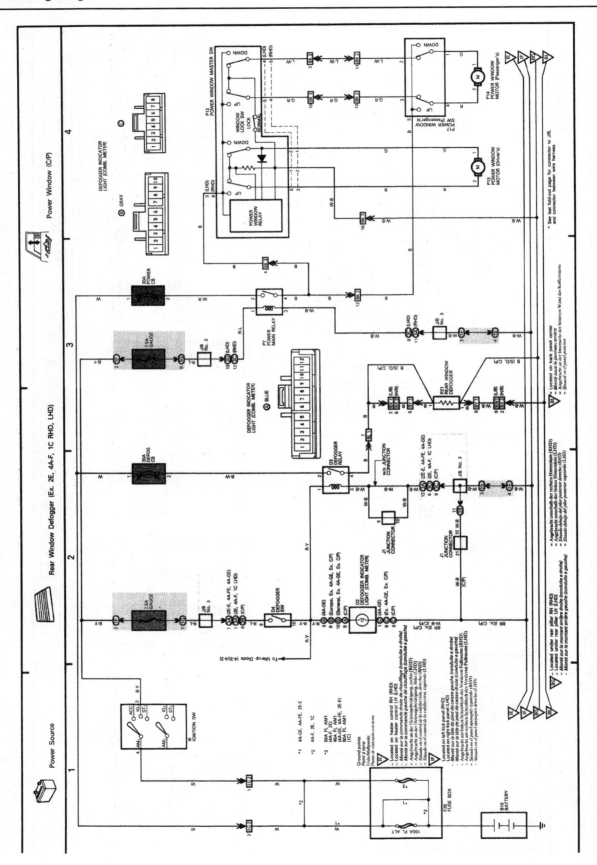

Typical wiring diagram for all models - 1990 on (continued)

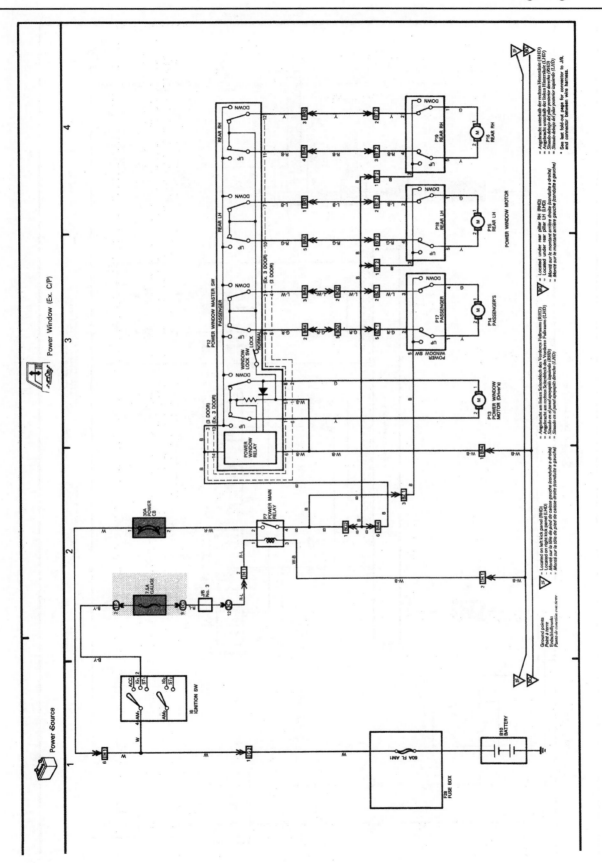

Typical **wiring diagram** for all models - 1990 on (continued)

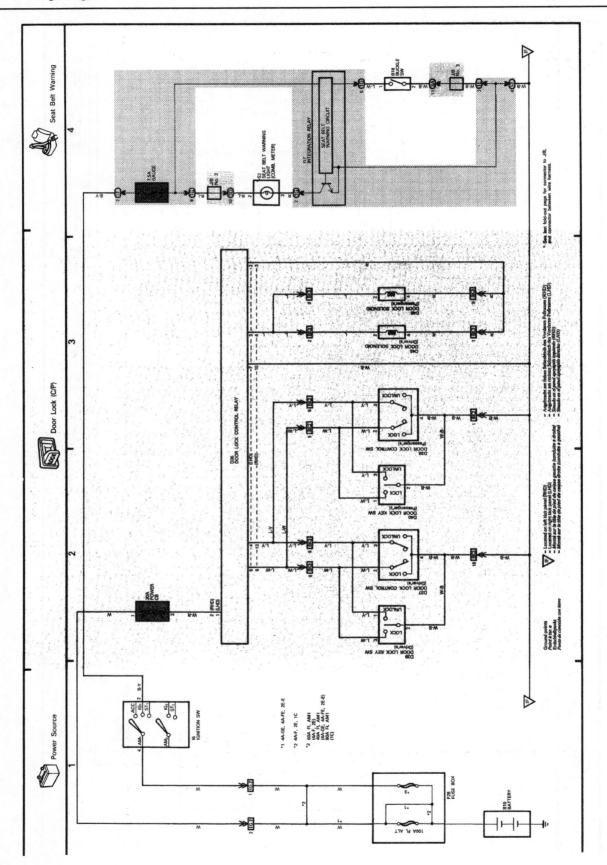

Typical wiring diagram for all models - 1990 on (continued)

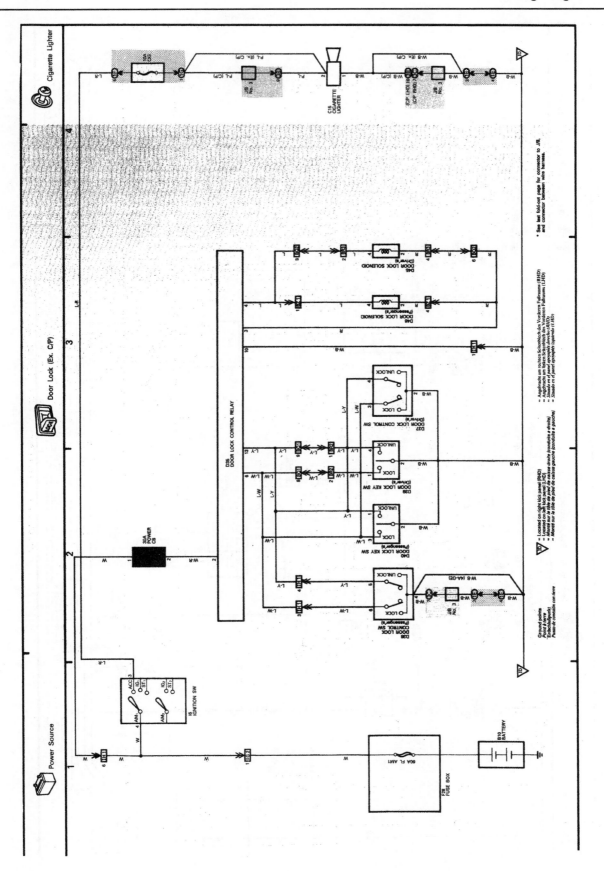

Typical wiring diagram for all models - 1990 on (continued)

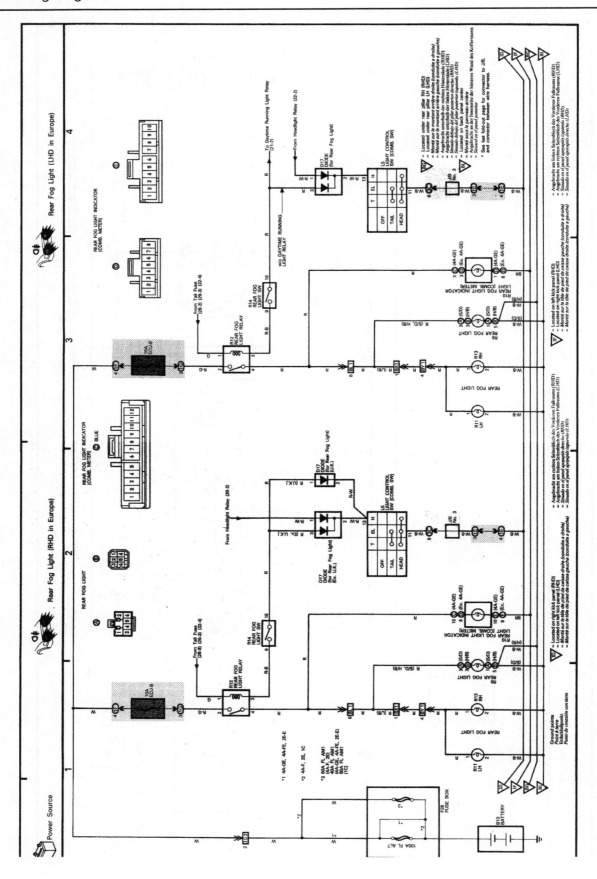

Typical wiring diagram for all models - 1990 on (continued)

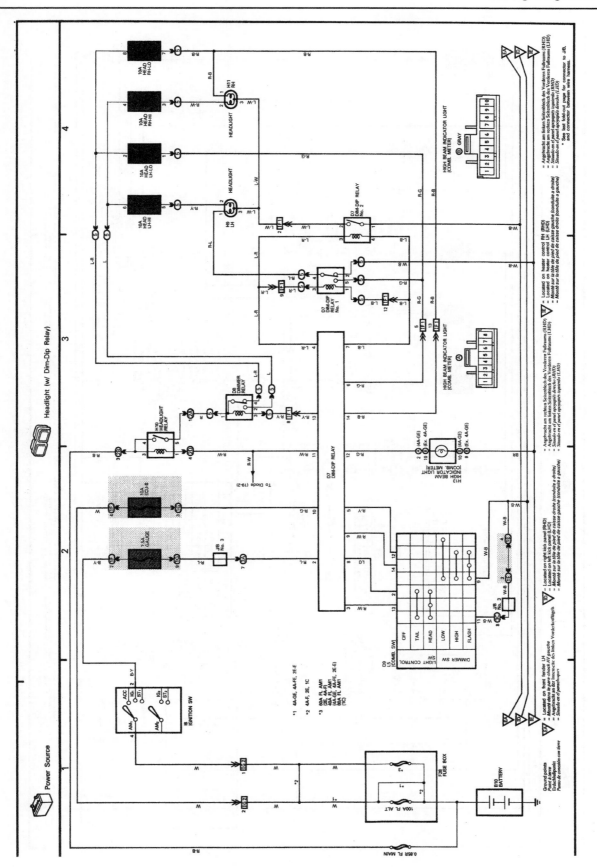

Typical wiring diagram for all models - 1990 on (continued)

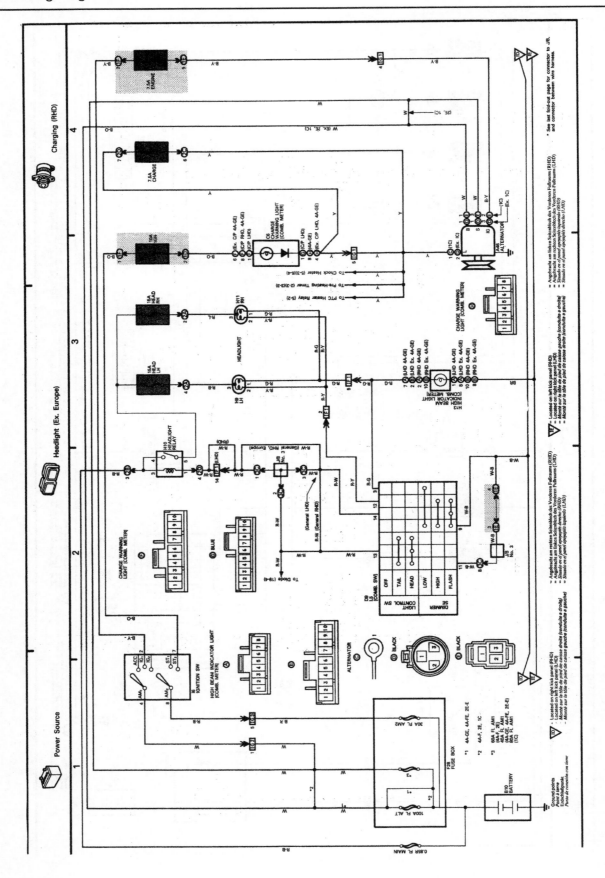

Typical wiring diagram for all models – 1990 on (continued)

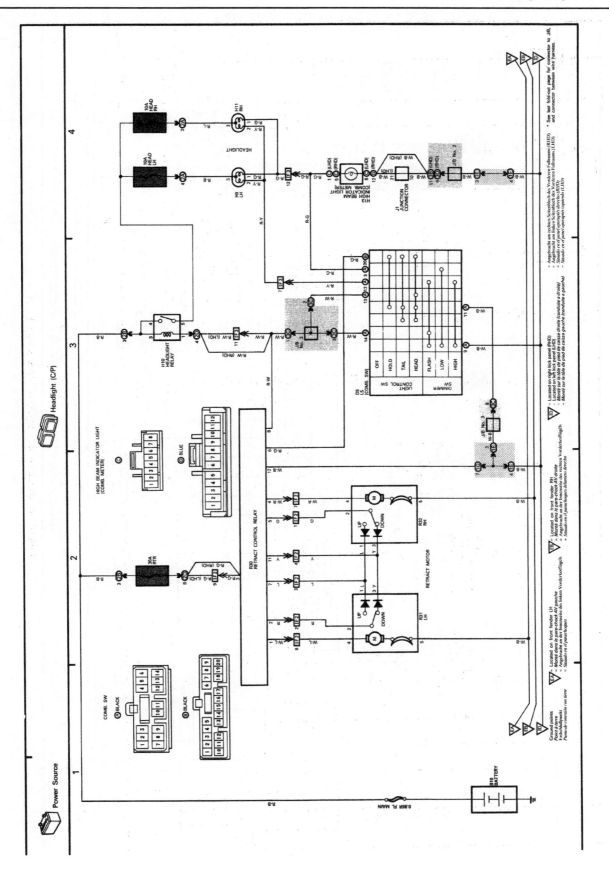

Typical wiring diagram for all models - 1990 on (continued)

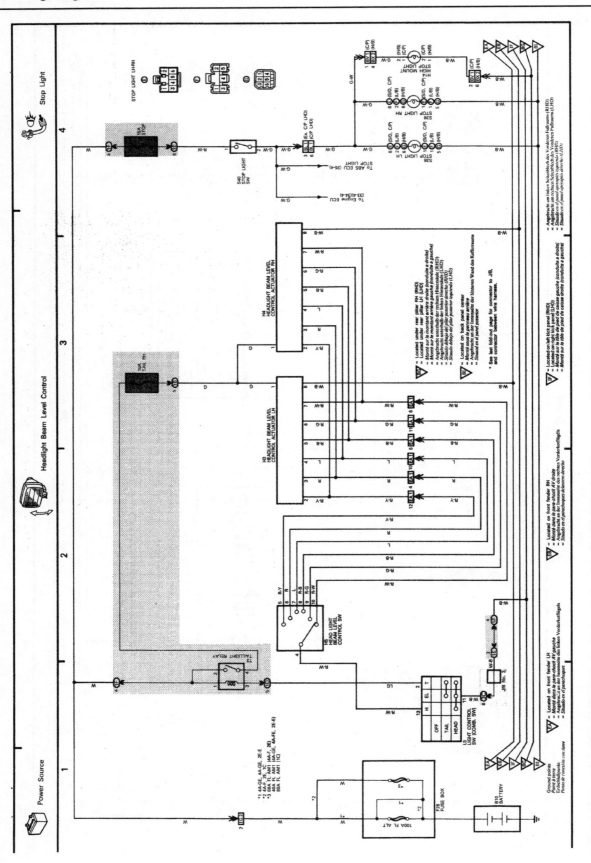

Typical wiring diagram for all models - 1990 on (continued)

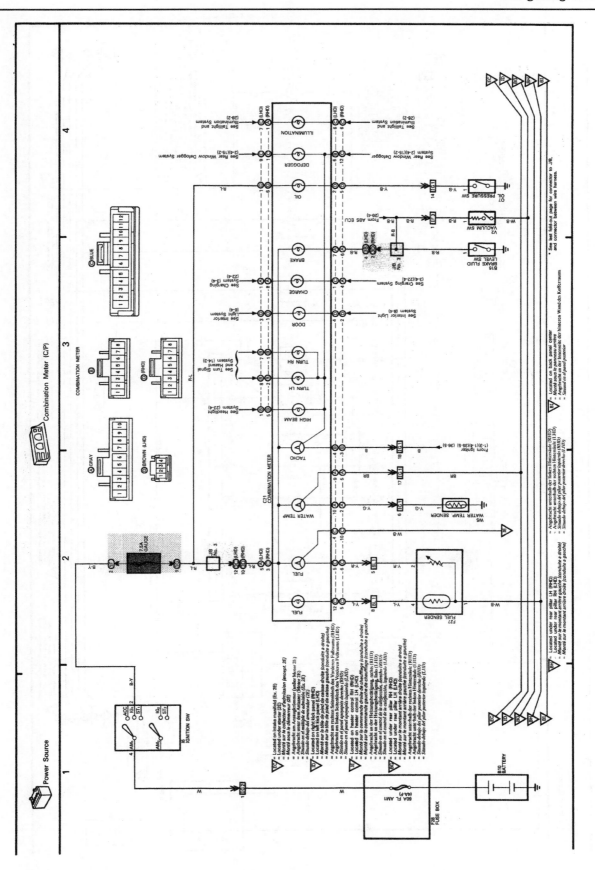

Typical wiring diagram for all models - 1990 on (continued)

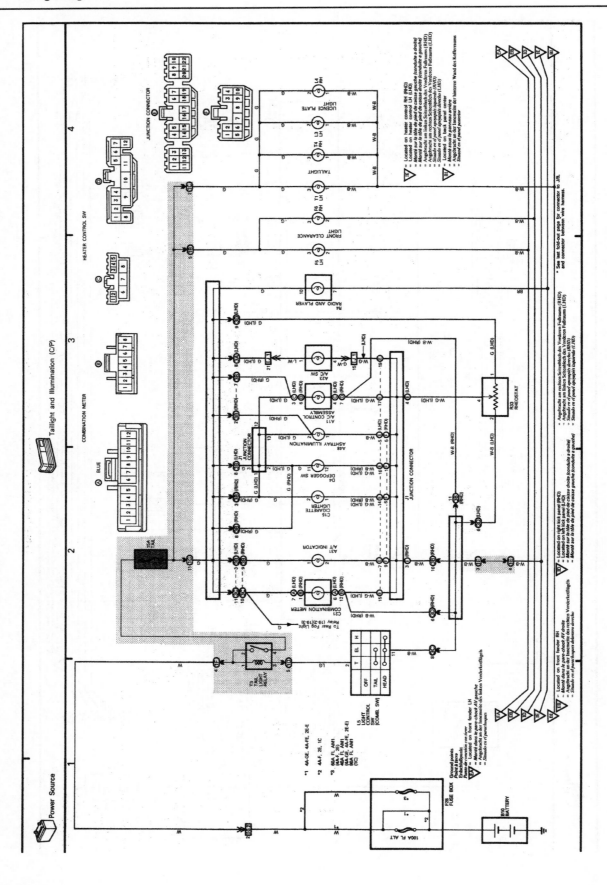

Taillight and Illumination (C/P)

Power Source

Typical wiring diagram for all models – 1990 on (continued)

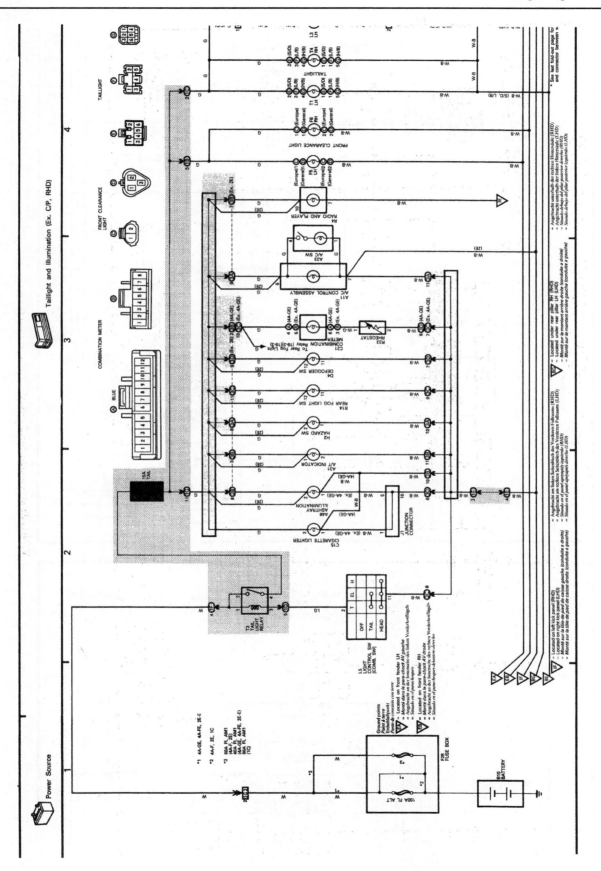

Typical wiring diagram for all models - 1990 on (continued)

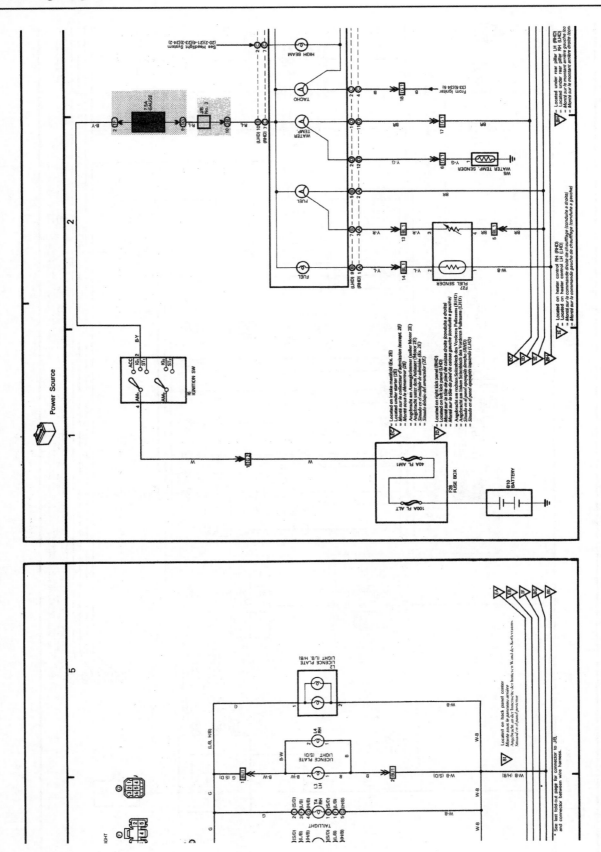

Typical wiring diagram for all models – 1990 on (continued)

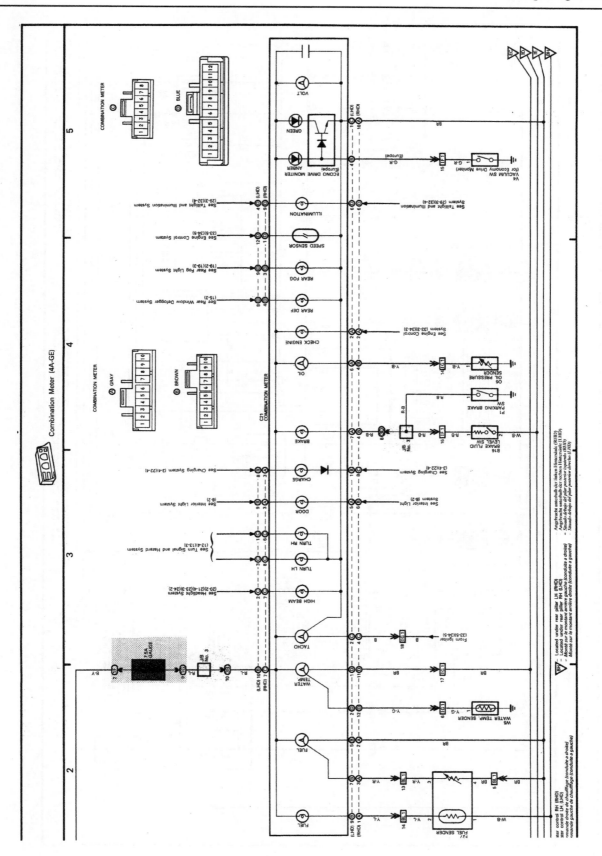

Typical wiring diagram for all models - 1990 on (continued)

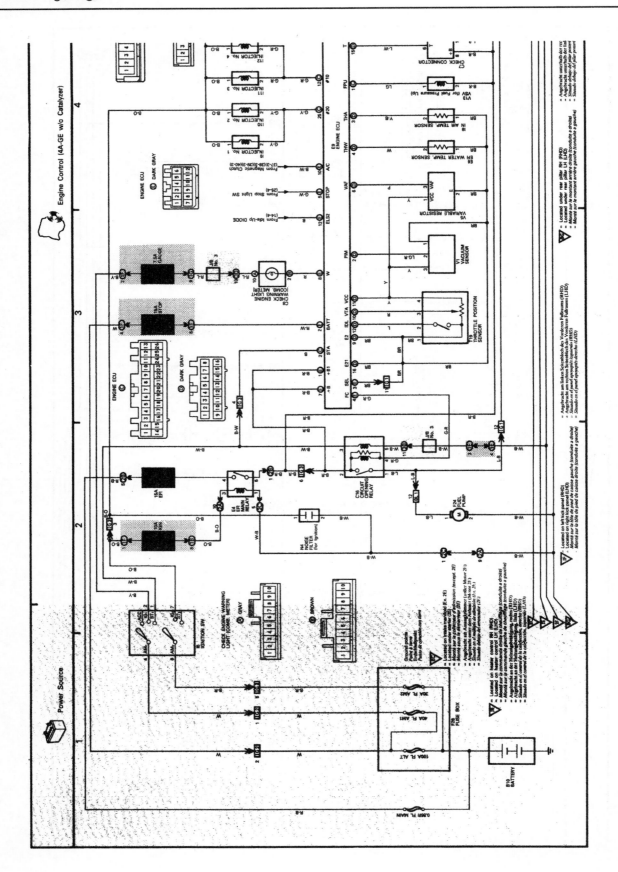

Typical wiring diagram for all models - 1990 on (continued)

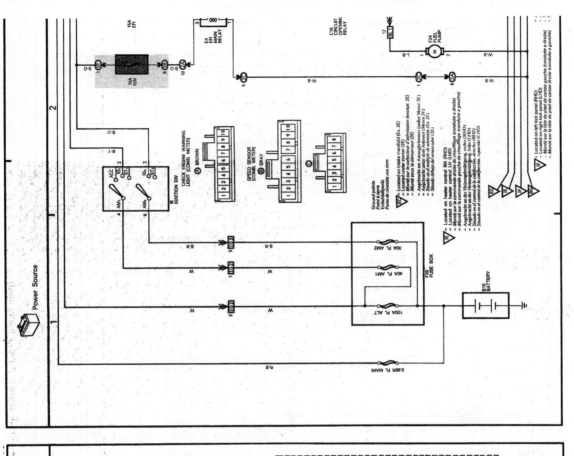

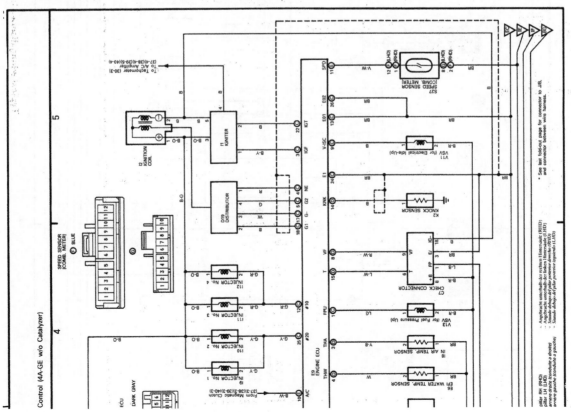

Typical wiring diagram for all models - 1990 on (continued)

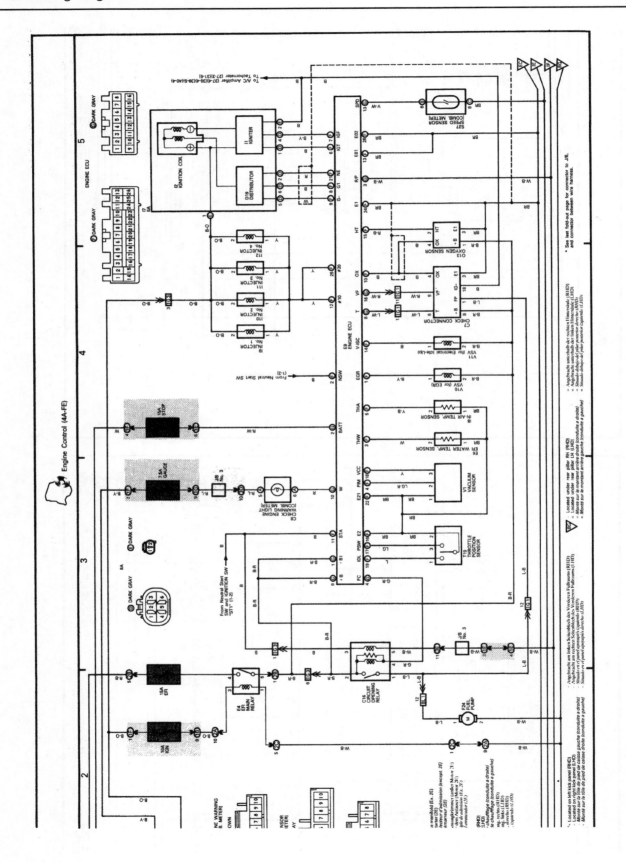

Typical wiring diagram for all models - 1990 on (continued)

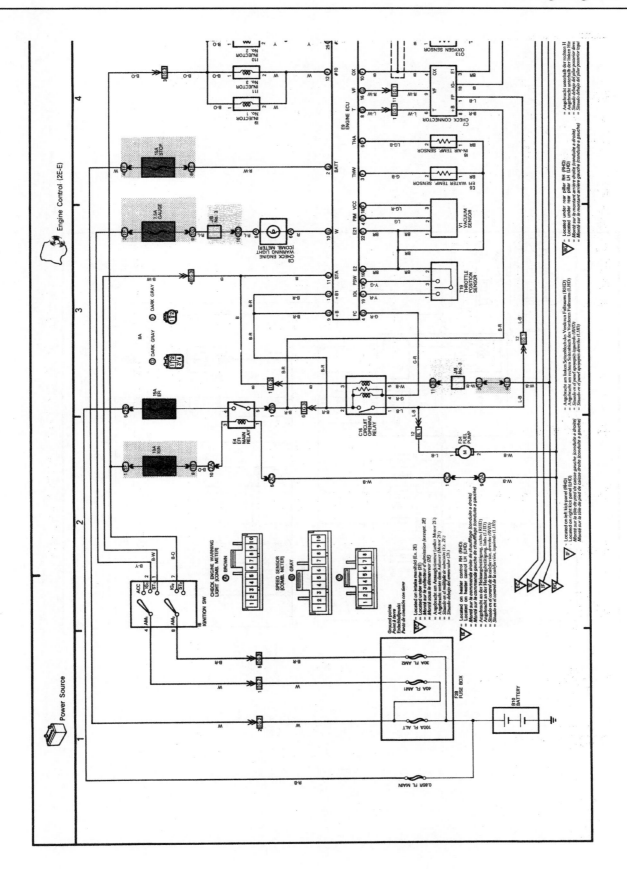

Typical wiring diagram for all models - 1990 on (continued)

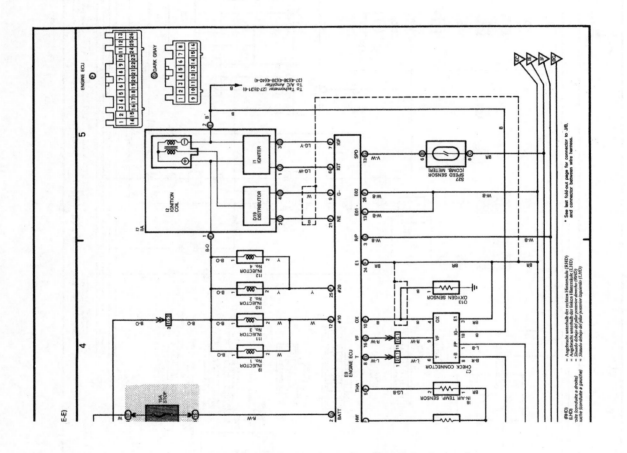

Typical wiring diagram for all models - 1990 on (continued)

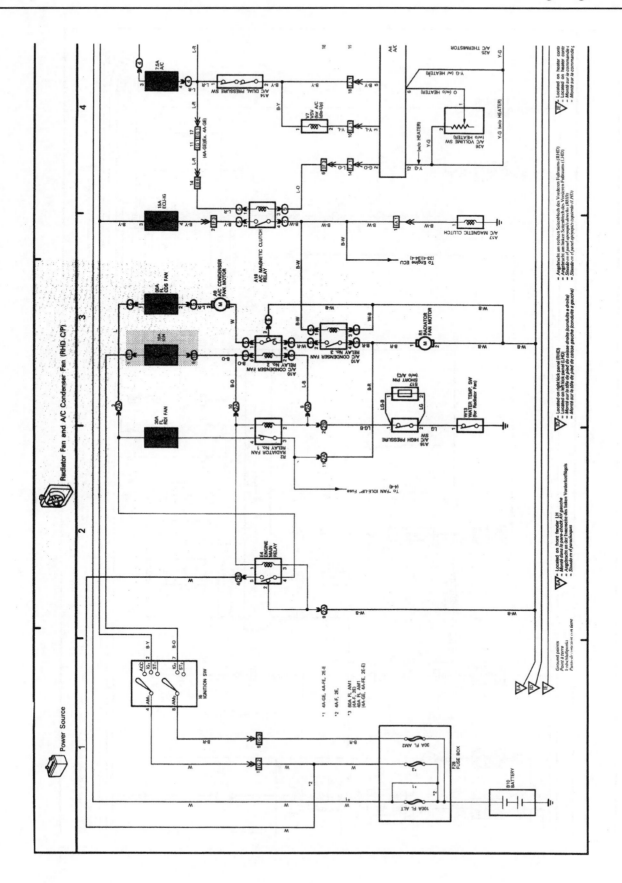

Typical wiring diagram for all models - 1990 on (continued)

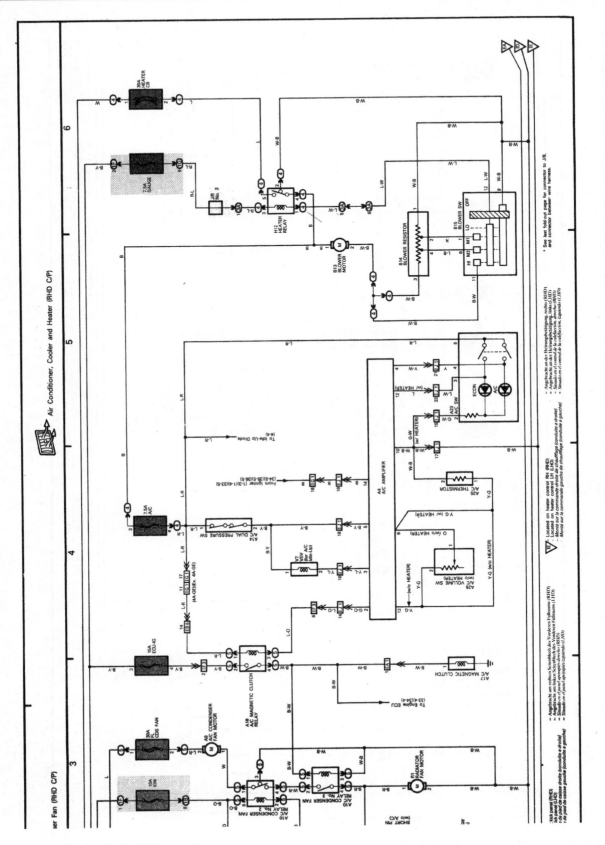

Air Conditioner, Cooler and Heater (RHD C/P)

Typical wiring diagram for all models - 1990 on (continued)

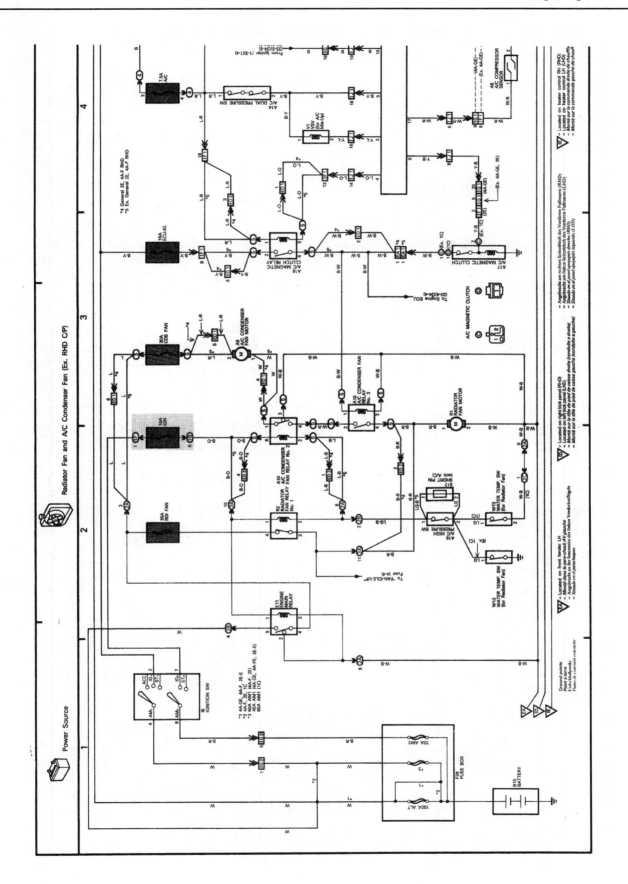

Typical wiring diagram for all models - 1990 on (continued)

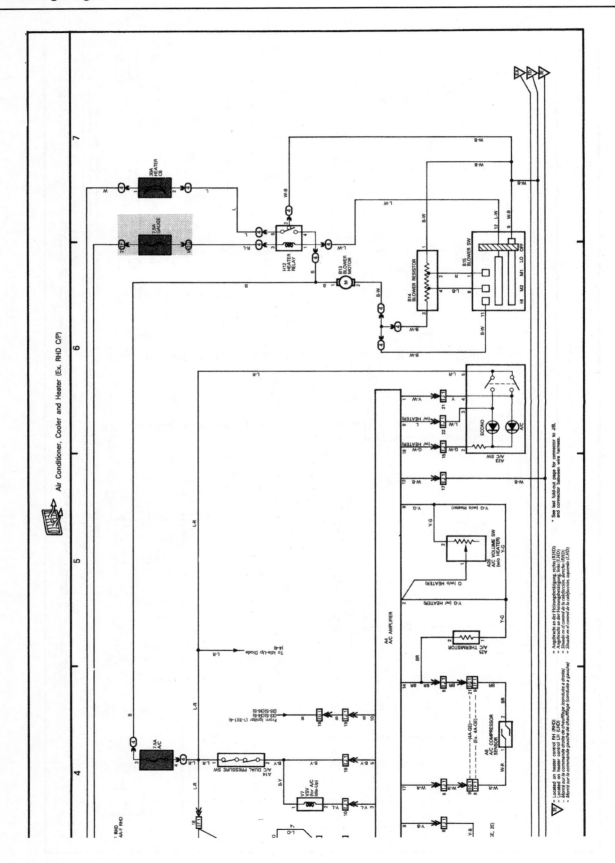

Typical wiring diagram for all models - 1990 on (continued)

This is a guide to getting your vehicle through the Certificate of Roadworthiness test. Obviously it will not be possible to examine the vehicle to the same standard as the professional COR tester. However, working through the following checks will enable you to identify any problem areas before submitting the vehicle for the test.

Where a testable component is in borderline condition, the tester has discretion in deciding whether to pass or fail it. The basis of such discretion is whether the tester would be happy for a close relative or friend to use the vehicle with the component in that condition. If the vehicle presented is clean and evidently well cared for, the tester may be more inclined to pass a borderline component than if the vehicle is scruffy and apparently neglected.

It has only been possible to summarise the test requirements here, based on the regulations in force at the time of printing. Test standards are becoming increasingly stringent, although there are some exemptions for older vehicles.

An assistant will be needed to help carry out some of these checks.

The checks have been sub-divided into four categories, as follows:

1 Checks carried out **FROM THE DRIVER'S SEAT**

2 Checks carried out **WITH THE VEHICLE ON THE GROUND**

3 Checks carried out **WITH THE VEHICLE RAISED AND THE WHEELS FREE TO TURN**

4 Checks carried out on **YOUR VEHICLE'S EXHAUST EMISSION SYSTEM**

1 Checks carried out **FROM THE DRIVER'S SEAT**

Handbrake

☐ Test the operation of the handbrake. Excessive travel (too many clicks) indicates incorrect brake or cable adjustment.
☐ Check that the handbrake cannot be released by tapping the lever sideways. Check the security of the lever mountings.

Footbrake

☐ Depress the brake pedal and check that it does not creep down to the floor, indicating a master cylinder fault. Release the pedal, wait a few seconds, then depress it again. If the pedal travels nearly to the floor before firm resistance is felt, brake adjustment or repair is necessary. If the pedal feels spongy, there is air in the hydraulic system which must be removed by bleeding.

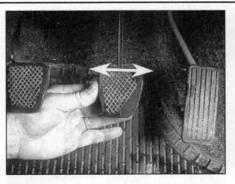

☐ Check that the brake pedal is secure and in good condition. Check also for signs of fluid leaks on the pedal, floor or carpets, which would indicate failed seals in the brake master cylinder.
☐ Check the servo unit (when applicable) by operating the brake pedal several times, then keeping the pedal depressed and starting the engine. As the engine starts, the pedal will move down slightly. If not, the vacuum hose or the servo itself may be faulty.

Steering wheel and column

☐ Examine the steering wheel for fractures or looseness of the hub, spokes or rim.
☐ Try to move the steering wheel from side to side and then up and down. Check that the steering wheel is not loose on the column, indicating wear or a loose retaining nut. Continue moving the steering wheel as before, but also turn it slightly from left to right.
☐ Check that the steering wheel is not loose on the column, and that there is no abnormal

movement of the steering wheel, indicating wear in the column support bearings or couplings.

Windscreen and mirrors

☐ The windscreen must be free of cracks or other significant damage within the driver's field of view. (Small stone chips are acceptable.) Rear view mirrors must be secure, intact, and capable of being adjusted.

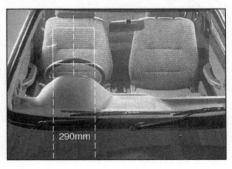

290mm

Seat belts and seats

Note: *The following checks are applicable to all seat belts, front and rear.*

☐ Examine the webbing of all the belts (including rear belts if fitted) for cuts, serious fraying or deterioration. Fasten and unfasten each belt to check the buckles. If applicable, check the retracting mechanism. Check the security of all seat belt mountings accessible from inside the vehicle.

☐ The front seats themselves must be securely attached and the backrests must lock in the upright position.

Doors

☐ Both front doors must be able to be opened and closed from outside and inside, and must latch securely when closed.

2 Checks carried out WITH THE VEHICLE ON THE GROUND

Vehicle identification

☐ Number plates must be in good condition, secure and legible, with letters and numbers correctly spaced.

☐ The VIN plate and/or homologation plate must be legible.

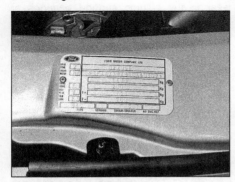

Electrical equipment

☐ Switch on the ignition and check the operation of the horn.

☐ Check the windscreen washers and wipers, examining the wiper blades; renew damaged or perished blades. Also check the operation of the stop-lights.

☐ Check the operation of the sidelights and number plate lights. The lenses and reflectors must be secure, clean and undamaged.

☐ Check the operation and alignment of the headlights. The headlight reflectors must not be tarnished and the lenses must be undamaged.

☐ Switch on the ignition and check the operation of the direction indicators (including the instrument panel tell-tale) and the hazard warning lights. Operation of the sidelights and stop-lights must not affect the indicators - if it does, the cause is usually a bad earth at the rear light cluster.

☐ Check the operation of the rear foglight(s), including the warning light on the instrument panel or in the switch.

Footbrake

☐ Examine the master cylinder, brake pipes and servo unit for leaks, loose mountings, corrosion or other damage.

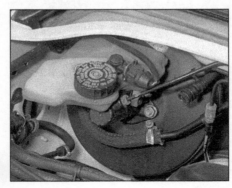

☐ The fluid reservoir must be secure and the fluid level must be between the upper (**A**) and lower (**B**) markings.

☐ Inspect both front brake flexible hoses for cracks or deterioration of the rubber. Turn the steering from lock to lock, and ensure that the hoses do not contact the wheel, tyre, or any part of the steering or suspension mechanism. With the brake pedal firmly depressed, check the hoses for bulges or leaks under pressure.

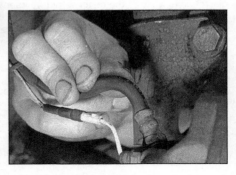

Steering and suspension

☐ Have your assistant turn the steering wheel from side to side slightly, up to the point where the steering gear just begins to transmit this movement to the roadwheels. Check for excessive free play between the steering wheel and the steering gear, indicating wear or insecurity of the steering column joints, the column-to-steering gear coupling, or the steering gear itself.

☐ Have your assistant turn the steering wheel more vigorously in each direction, so that the roadwheels just begin to turn. As this is done, examine all the steering joints, linkages, fittings and attachments. Renew any component that shows signs of wear or damage. On vehicles with power steering, check the security and condition of the steering pump, drivebelt and hoses.

☐ Check that the vehicle is standing level, and at approximately the correct ride height.

Shock absorbers

☐ Depress each corner of the vehicle in turn, then release it. The vehicle should rise and then settle in its normal position. If the vehicle continues to rise and fall, the shock absorber is defective. A shock absorber which has seized will also cause the vehicle to fail.

Exhaust system

☐ Start the engine. With your assistant holding a rag over the tailpipe, check the entire system for leaks. Repair or renew leaking sections.

3 Checks carried out
WITH THE VEHICLE RAISED AND THE WHEELS FREE TO TURN

Jack up the front and rear of the vehicle, and securely support it on axle stands. Position the stands clear of the suspension assemblies. Ensure that the wheels are clear of the ground and that the steering can be turned from lock to lock.

Engine and transmission

☐ Examine the engine for oil leaks, especially from faulty gaskets and oil seals, or a badly-seated oil filter. Also check the drain plug is secure.
☐ Examine the transmission for leaks, and check the drain and filler plugs are secure (if applicable).

Steering mechanism

☐ Have your assistant turn the steering from lock to lock. Check that the steering turns smoothly, and that no part of the steering mechanism, including a wheel or tyre, fouls any brake hose or pipe or any part of the body structure.
☐ Examine the steering rack rubber gaiters for damage or insecurity of the retaining clips. If power steering is fitted, check for signs of damage or leakage of the fluid hoses, pipes or connections. Also check for excessive stiffness or binding of the steering, a missing split pin or locking device, or severe corrosion of the body structure near any steering component attachment point.

Front and rear suspension and wheel bearings

☐ Starting at the front right-hand side, grasp the roadwheel at the 3 o'clock and 9 o'clock positions and shake it vigorously. Check for free play or insecurity at the wheel bearings, suspension balljoints, or suspension mountings, pivots and attachments.
☐ Now grasp the wheel at the 12 o'clock and 6 o'clock positions and repeat the previous inspection. Spin the wheel, and check for roughness or tightness of the front wheel bearing.

☐ If excess free play is suspected at a component pivot point, this can be confirmed by using a large screwdriver or similar tool and levering between the mounting and the component attachment. This will confirm whether the wear is in the pivot bush, its retaining bolt, or in the mounting itself (the bolt holes can often become elongated).

☐ Carry out all the above checks at the other front wheel, and then at both rear wheels.

Springs and shock absorbers

☐ Examine the suspension struts (when applicable) for serious fluid leakage, corrosion, or damage to the casing. Also check the security of the mounting points.
☐ If coil springs are fitted, check that the spring ends locate in their seats, and that the spring is not corroded, cracked or broken.
☐ If leaf springs are fitted, check that all leaves are intact, that the axle is securely attached to each spring, and that there is no deterioration of the spring eye mountings, bushes, and shackles.

☐ The same general checks apply to vehicles fitted with other suspension types, such as torsion bars, hydraulic displacer units, etc. Ensure that all mountings and attachments are secure, that there are no signs of excessive wear, corrosion or damage, and (on hydraulic types) that there are no fluid leaks or damaged pipes.
☐ Inspect the shock absorbers for signs of serious fluid leakage. Check for wear of the mounting bushes or attachments, or damage to the body of the unit.

Driveshafts (fwd vehicles only)

☐ Rotate each front wheel in turn and inspect the gaiters at both ends for splits or damage, and leaking lubricant. Also check that each driveshaft is straight and undamaged.

Rear axle (rwd vehicles only)

☐ Inspect the assembly for lubricant leaks.
☐ Check the drain and filler plugs are secure (if applicable).

Braking system

☐ If possible without dismantling, check brake pad wear and disc condition. Ensure that the friction lining material has not worn excessively, (A) and that the discs are not fractured, pitted, scored or badly worn (B).

☐ Examine all the rigid brake pipes underneath the vehicle, and the flexible hose(s) at the rear. Look for corrosion, chafing or insecurity of the pipes, and for signs of bulging under pressure, chafing, splits or deterioration of the flexible hoses.
☐ Look for signs of fluid leaks at the brake calipers or on the brake backplates. Repair or renew leaking components.
☐ Slowly spin each wheel, while your assistant depresses and releases the footbrake. Ensure that each brake is operating and does not bind when the pedal is released.

☐ Examine the handbrake mechanism, checking for frayed or broken cables, excessive corrosion, or wear or insecurity of the linkage. Check that the mechanism works on each relevant wheel, and releases fully, without binding.

☐ It is not possible to test brake efficiency without special equipment, but a road test can be carried out to check that the vehicle pulls up in a straight line.

Fuel and exhaust systems

☐ Inspect the fuel tank (including the filler cap), fuel pipes, hoses and unions. All components must be secure and free from leaks.

☐ Examine the exhaust system over its entire length, checking for any damaged, broken or missing mountings, security of the retaining clamps and rust or corrosion.

Wheels and tyres

☐ Examine the sidewalls and tread area of each tyre in turn. Check for cuts, tears, lumps, bulges, separation of the tread, and exposure of the ply or cord due to wear or damage. Check that the tyre bead is correctly seated on the wheel rim, that the valve is sound and

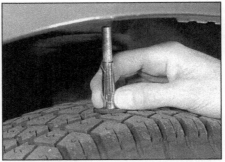

properly seated, and that the wheel is not distorted or damaged.

☐ Check that the tyres are of the correct size for the vehicle, that they are of the same size and type on each axle, and that the pressures are correct.

☐ Check the tyre tread depth. The legal minimum at the time of writing is 1.6 mm over at least three-quarters of the tread width. Abnormal tread wear may indicate incorrect front wheel alignment.

Body corrosion

☐ Check the condition of the entire vehicle structure for signs of corrosion in load-bearing areas. (These include chassis box sections, side sills, cross-members, pillars, and all suspension, steering, braking system and seat belt mountings and anchorages.) Any corrosion which has seriously reduced the thickness of a load-bearing area is likely to cause the vehicle to fail. In this case professional repairs are likely to be needed.

☐ Damage or corrosion which causes sharp or otherwise dangerous edges to be exposed will also cause the vehicle to fail.

4 Checks carried out on YOUR VEHICLE'S EXHAUST EMISSION SYSTEM

Exhaust emission checks - petrol models

☐ Have the engine at normal operating temperature, and make sure that it is in good tune (ignition system in good order, air filter element clean, etc).

☐ Before any measurements are carried out, raise the engine speed to around 2500 rpm, and hold it at this speed for 20 seconds.

Allow the engine speed to return to idle, and watch for smoke emissions from the exhaust tailpipe. If the idle speed is obviously much too high, or if dense blue or clearly-visible black smoke comes from the tailpipe for more than 5 seconds, the vehicle may fail. As a rule of thumb, blue smoke signifies oil being burnt (engine wear) while black smoke signifies unburnt fuel (dirty air cleaner element, or other carburettor or fuel system fault).

☐ An exhaust gas analyser capable of measuring carbon monoxide (CO) and hydrocarbons (HC) will be used by the garage performing the test. This is not a piece of equipment likely to be owned by the DIY mechanic. If it is wished to check emission levels before the test, a local garage may agree to do so for a small fee.

☐ The CO and HC emission levels permitted for test purposes will vary according to the legislation in force and also according to the age of the vehicle.

CO emissions (mixture)

☐ If the CO level cannot be reduced far enough to pass the test (and the fuel and ignition systems are otherwise in good condition) then the carburettor is badly worn, or there is some problem in the fuel injection system. On carburettors with an automatic choke, the choke may be at fault.

HC emissions

☐ Excessive HC emissions can be caused by oil being burnt, but they are more likely to be due to unburnt fuel. Possible reasons include:
(a) *Spark plugs in poor condition or incorrectly gapped.*
(b) *Ignition timing incorrect.*
(c) *Valve clearances incorrect.*
(d) *Engine compression low.*

Exhaust emission checks - Diesel models

☐ The only emission test applicable to Diesel engines is the measuring of exhaust smoke density. The test involves accelerating the engine several times to its maximum unloaded speed. Note: It is of the utmost importance that the engine timing belt is in good condition before the test is carried out.

☐ Excessive smoke can be caused by a dirty air cleaner element. Otherwise, professional advice may be needed to find the cause.

Length (distance)

Inches (in)	x 25.4	= Millimetres (mm)	x 0.0394 =	Inches (in)
Feet (ft)	x 0.305	= Metres (m)	x 3.281 =	Feet (ft)
Miles	x 1.609	= Kilometres (km)	x 0.621 =	Miles

Volume (capacity)

Cubic inches (cu in; in³)	x 16.387	= Cubic centimetres (cc; cm³)	x 0.061 =	Cubic inches (cu in; in³)
Imperial pints (Imp pt)	x 0.568	= Litres (l)	x 1.76 =	Imperial pints (Imp pt)
Imperial quarts (Imp qt)	x 1.137	= Litres (l)	x 0.88 =	Imperial quarts (Imp qt)
Imperial quarts (Imp qt)	x 1.201	= US quarts (US qt)	x 0.833 =	Imperial quarts (Imp qt)
US quarts (US qt)	x 0.946	= Litres (l)	x 1.057 =	US quarts (US qt)
Imperial gallons (Imp gal)	x 4.546	= Litres (l)	x 0.22 =	Imperial gallons (Imp gal)
Imperial gallons (Imp gal)	x 1.201	= US gallons (US gal)	x 0.833 =	Imperial gallons (Imp gal)
US gallons (US gal)	x 3.785	= Litres (l)	x 0.264 =	US gallons (US gal)

Mass (weight)

Ounces (oz)	x 28.35	= Grams (g)	x 0.035 =	Ounces (oz)
Pounds (lb)	x 0.454	= Kilograms (kg)	x 2.205 =	Pounds (lb)

Force

Ounces-force (ozf; oz)	x 0.278	= Newtons (N)	x 3.6 =	Ounces-force (ozf; oz)
Pounds-force (lbf; lb)	x 4.448	= Newtons (N)	x 0.225 =	Pounds-force (lbf; lb)
Newtons (N)	x 0.1	= Kilograms-force (kgf; kg)	x 9.81 =	Newtons (N)

Pressure

Pounds-force per square inch (psi; lbf/in²; lb/in²)	x 0.070	= Kilograms-force per square centimetre (kgf/cm²; kg/cm²)	x 14.223 =	Pounds-force per square inch (psi; lbf/in²; lb/in²)
Pounds-force per square inch (psi; lbf/in²; lb/in²)	x 0.068	= Atmospheres (atm)	x 14.696 =	Pounds-force per square inch (psi; lbf/in²; lb/in²)
Pounds-force per square inch (psi; lbf/in²; lb/in²)	x 0.069	= Bars	x 14.5 =	Pounds-force per square inch (psi; lbf/in²; lb/in²)
Pounds-force per square inch (psi; lbf/in²; lb/in²)	x 6.895	= Kilopascals (kPa)	x 0.145 =	Pounds-force per square inch (psi; lbf/in²; lb/in²)
Kilopascals (kPa)	x 0.01	= Kilograms-force per square centimetre (kgf/cm²; kg/cm²)	x 98.1 =	Kilopascals (kPa)
Millibar (mbar)	x 100	= Pascals (Pa)	x 0.01 =	Millibar (mbar)
Millibar (mbar)	x 0.0145	= Pounds-force per square inch (psi; lbf/in²; lb/in²)	x 68.947 =	Millibar (mbar)
Millibar (mbar)	x 0.75	= Millimetres of mercury (mmHg)	x 1.333 =	Millibar (mbar)
Millibar (mbar)	x 0.401	= Inches of water (inH₂O)	x 2.491 =	Millibar (mbar)
Millimetres of mercury (mmHg)	x 0.535	= Inches of water (inH₂O)	x 1.868 =	Millimetres of mercury (mmHg)
Inches of water (inH₂O)	x 0.036	= Pounds-force per square inch (psi; lbf/in²; lb/in²)	x 27.68 =	Inches of water (inH₂O)

Torque (moment of force)

Pounds-force inches (lbf in; lb in)	x 1.152	= Kilograms-force centimetre (kgf cm; kg cm)	x 0.868 =	Pounds-force inches (lbf in; lb in)
Pounds-force inches (lbf in; lb in)	x 0.113	= Newton metres (Nm)	x 8.85 =	Pounds-force inches (lbf in; lb in)
Pounds-force inches (lbf in; lb in)	x 0.083	= Pounds-force feet (lbf ft; lb ft)	x 12 =	Pounds-force inches (lbf in; lb in)
Pounds-force feet (lbf ft; lb ft)	x 0.138	= Kilograms-force metres (kgf m; kg m)	x 7.233 =	Pounds-force feet (lbf ft; lb ft)
Pounds-force feet (lbf ft; lb ft)	x 1.356	= Newton metres (Nm)	x 0.738 =	Pounds-force feet (lbf ft; lb ft)
Newton metres (Nm)	x 0.102	= Kilograms-force metres (kgf m; kg m)	x 9.804 =	Newton metres (Nm)

Power

Horsepower (hp)	x 745.7	= Watts (W)	x 0.0013 =	Horsepower (hp)

Velocity (speed)

Miles per hour (miles/hr; mph)	x 1.609	= Kilometres per hour (km/hr; kph)	x 0.621 =	Miles per hour (miles/hr; mph)

Fuel consumption*

Miles per gallon, Imperial (mpg)	x 0.354	= Kilometres per litre (km/l)	x 2.825 =	Miles per gallon, Imperial (mpg)
Miles per gallon, US (mpg)	x 0.425	= Kilometres per litre (km/l)	x 2.352 =	Miles per gallon, US (mpg)

Temperature

Degrees Fahrenheit = (°C x 1.8) + 32   Degrees Celsius (Degrees Centigrade; °C) = (°F - 32) x 0.56

It is common practice to convert from miles per gallon (mpg) to litres/100 kilometres (l/100km), where mpg x l/100 km = 282

Tools and Working Facilities

Introduction

A selection of good tools is a fundamental requirement for anyone contemplating the maintenance and repair of a motor vehicle. For the owner who does not possess any, their purchase will prove a considerable expense, offsetting some of the savings made by doing-it-yourself. However, provided that the tools purchased meet the relevant national safety standards and are of good quality, they will last for many years and prove an extremely worthwhile investment.

To help the average owner to decide which tools are needed to carry out the various tasks detailed in this manual, we have compiled three lists of tools under the following headings: *Maintenance and minor repair, Repair and overhaul,* and *Special.* Newcomers to practical mechanics should start off with the *Maintenance and minor repair* tool kit, and confine themselves to the simpler jobs around the vehicle. Then, as confidence and experience grow, more difficult tasks can be undertaken, with extra tools being purchased as, and when, they are needed. In this way, a *Maintenance and minor repair* tool kit can be built up into a *Repair and overhaul* tool kit over a considerable period of time, without any major cash outlays. The experienced do-it-yourselfer will have a tool kit good enough for most repair and overhaul procedures, and will add tools from the *Special* category when it is felt that the expense is justified by the amount of use to which these tools will be put.

Maintenance and minor repair tool kit

The tools given in this list should be considered as a minimum requirement if routine maintenance, servicing and minor repair operations are to be undertaken. We recommend the purchase of combination spanners (ring one end, open-ended the other); although more expensive than open-ended ones, they do give the advantages of both types of spanner.

- ☐ *Combination spanners:*
  Metric - 8 to 19 mm inclusive
- ☐ *Adjustable spanner - 35 mm jaw (approx.)*
- ☐ *Spark plug spanner (with rubber insert) - petrol models*
- ☐ *Spark plug gap adjustment tool - petrol models*
- ☐ *Set of feeler gauges*
- ☐ *Brake bleed nipple spanner*
- ☐ *Screwdrivers:*
  Flat blade - 100 mm long x 6 mm dia
  Cross blade - 100 mm long x 6 mm dia
  Torx - various sizes (not all vehicles)
- ☐ *Combination pliers*
- ☐ *Hacksaw (junior)*
- ☐ *Tyre pump*
- ☐ *Tyre pressure gauge*
- ☐ *Oil can*
- ☐ *Oil filter removal tool*
- ☐ *Fine emery cloth*
- ☐ *Wire brush (small)*
- ☐ *Funnel (medium size)*
- ☐ *Sump drain plug key (not all vehicles)*

Repair and overhaul tool kit

These tools are virtually essential for anyone undertaking any major repairs to a motor vehicle, and are additional to those given in the *Maintenance and minor repair* list. Included in this list is a comprehensive set of sockets. Although these are expensive, they will be found invaluable as they are so versatile - particularly if various drives are included in the set. We recommend the half-inch square-drive type, as this can be used with most proprietary torque wrenches.

The tools in this list will sometimes need to be supplemented by tools from the *Special* list:

- ☐ *Sockets (or box spanners) to cover range in previous list (including Torx sockets)*
- ☐ *Reversible ratchet drive (for use with sockets)*
- ☐ *Extension piece, 250 mm (for use with sockets)*
- ☐ *Universal joint (for use with sockets)*
- ☐ *Flexible handle or sliding T "breaker bar" (for use with sockets)*
- ☐ *Torque wrench (for use with sockets)*
- ☐ *Self-locking grips*
- ☐ *Ball pein hammer*
- ☐ *Soft-faced mallet (plastic or rubber)*
- ☐ *Screwdrivers:*
  Flat blade - long & sturdy, short (chubby), and narrow (electrician's) types
  Cross blade – long & sturdy, and short (chubby) types
- ☐ *Pliers:*
  Long-nosed
  Side cutters (electrician's)
  Circlip (internal and external)
- ☐ *Cold chisel - 25 mm*
- ☐ *Scriber*
- ☐ *Scraper*
- ☐ *Centre-punch*
- ☐ *Pin punch*
- ☐ *Hacksaw*
- ☐ *Brake hose clamp*
- ☐ *Brake/clutch bleeding kit*
- ☐ *Selection of twist drills*
- ☐ *Steel rule/straight-edge*
- ☐ *Allen keys (inc. splined/Torx type)*
- ☐ *Selection of files*
- ☐ *Wire brush*
- ☐ *Axle stands*
- ☐ *Jack (strong trolley or hydraulic type)*
- ☐ *Light with extension lead*
- ☐ *Universal electrical multi-meter*

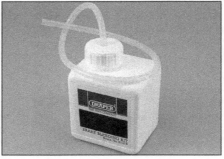

Sockets and reversible ratchet drive

Brake bleeding kit

Torx key, socket and bit

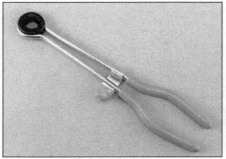

Hose clamp

Angular-tightening gauge

Special tools

The tools in this list are those which are not used regularly, are expensive to buy, or which need to be used in accordance with their manufacturers' instructions. Unless relatively difficult mechanical jobs are undertaken frequently, it will not be economic to buy many of these tools. Where this is the case, you could consider clubbing together with friends (or joining a motorists' club) to make a joint purchase, or borrowing the tools against a deposit from a local garage or tool hire specialist. It is worth noting that many of the larger DIY superstores now carry a large range of special tools for hire at modest rates.

The following list contains only those tools and instruments freely available to the public, and not those special tools produced by the vehicle manufacturer specifically for its dealer network. You will find occasional references to these manufacturers' special tools in the text of this manual. Generally, an alternative method of doing the job without the vehicle manufacturers' special tool is given. However, sometimes there is no alternative to using them. Where this is the case and the relevant tool cannot be bought or borrowed, you will have to entrust the work to a dealer.

- ☐ Angular-tightening gauge
- ☐ Valve spring compressor
- ☐ Valve grinding tool
- ☐ Piston ring compressor
- ☐ Piston ring removal/installation tool
- ☐ Cylinder bore hone
- ☐ Balljoint separator
- ☐ Coil spring compressors (where applicable)
- ☐ Two/three-legged hub and bearing puller
- ☐ Impact screwdriver
- ☐ Micrometer and/or vernier calipers
- ☐ Dial gauge
- ☐ Stroboscopic timing light
- ☐ Dwell angle meter/tachometer
- ☐ Fault code reader
- ☐ Cylinder compression gauge
- ☐ Hand-operated vacuum pump and gauge
- ☐ Clutch plate alignment set
- ☐ Brake shoe steady spring cup removal tool
- ☐ Bush and bearing removal/installation set
- ☐ Stud extractors
- ☐ Tap and die set
- ☐ Lifting tackle
- ☐ Trolley jack

Buying tools

Reputable motor accessory shops and superstores often offer excellent quality tools at discount prices, so it pays to shop around.

Remember, you don't have to buy the most expensive items on the shelf, but it is always advisable to steer clear of the very cheap tools. Beware of 'bargains' offered on market stalls or at car boot sales. There are plenty of good tools around at reasonable prices, but always aim to purchase items which meet the relevant national safety standards. If in doubt, ask the proprietor or manager of the shop for advice before making a purchase.

Care and maintenance of tools

Having purchased a reasonable tool kit, it is necessary to keep the tools in a clean and serviceable condition. After use, always wipe off any dirt, grease and metal particles using a clean, dry cloth, before putting the tools away. Never leave them lying around after they have been used. A simple tool rack on the garage or workshop wall for items such as screwdrivers and pliers is a good idea. Store all normal spanners and sockets in a metal box. Any measuring instruments, gauges, meters, etc, must be carefully stored where they cannot be damaged or become rusty.

Take a little care when tools are used. Hammer heads inevitably become marked, and screwdrivers lose the keen edge on their blades from time to time. A little timely attention with emery cloth or a file will soon restore items like this to a good finish.

Working facilities

Not to be forgotten when discussing tools is the workshop itself. If anything more than routine maintenance is to be carried out, a suitable working area becomes essential.

It is appreciated that many an owner-mechanic is forced by circumstances to remove an engine or similar item without the benefit of a garage or workshop. Having done this, any repairs should always be done under the cover of a roof.

Wherever possible, any dismantling should be done on a clean, flat workbench or table at a suitable working height.

Any workbench needs a vice; one with a jaw opening of 100 mm is suitable for most jobs. As mentioned previously, some clean dry storage space is also required for tools, as well as for any lubricants, cleaning fluids, touch-up paints etc, which become necessary.

Another item which may be required, and which has a much more general usage, is an electric drill with a chuck capacity of at least 8 mm. This, together with a good range of twist drills, is virtually essential for fitting accessories.

Last, but not least, always keep a supply of old newspapers and clean, lint-free rags available, and try to keep any working area as clean as possible.

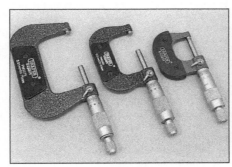

Micrometers

Dial test indicator ("dial gauge")

Strap wrench

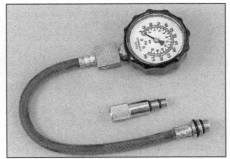

Compression tester

Fault code reader

Whenever servicing, repair or overhaul work is carried out on the car or its components, observe the following procedures and instructions. This will assist in carrying out the operation efficiently and to a professional standard of workmanship.

Joint mating faces and gaskets

When separating components at their mating faces, never insert screwdrivers or similar implements into the joint between the faces in order to prise them apart. This can cause severe damage which results in oil leaks, coolant leaks, etc upon reassembly. Separation is usually achieved by tapping along the joint with a soft-faced hammer in order to break the seal. However, note that this method may not be suitable where dowels are used for component location.

Where a gasket is used between the mating faces of two components, a new one must be fitted on reassembly; fit it dry unless otherwise stated in the repair procedure. Make sure that the mating faces are clean and dry, with all traces of old gasket removed. When cleaning a joint face, use a tool which is unlikely to score or damage the face, and remove any burrs or nicks with an oilstone or fine file.

Make sure that tapped holes are cleaned with a pipe cleaner, and keep them free of jointing compound, if this is being used, unless specifically instructed otherwise.

Ensure that all orifices, channels or pipes are clear, and blow through them, preferably using compressed air.

Oil seals

Oil seals can be removed by levering them out with a wide flat-bladed screwdriver or similar implement. Alternatively, a number of self-tapping screws may be screwed into the seal, and these used as a purchase for pliers or some similar device in order to pull the seal free.

Whenever an oil seal is removed from its working location, either individually or as part of an assembly, it should be renewed.

The very fine sealing lip of the seal is easily damaged, and will not seal if the surface it contacts is not completely clean and free from scratches, nicks or grooves. If the original sealing surface of the component cannot be restored, and the manufacturer has not made provision for slight relocation of the seal relative to the sealing surface, the component should be renewed.

Protect the lips of the seal from any surface which may damage them in the course of fitting. Use tape or a conical sleeve where possible. Lubricate the seal lips with oil before fitting and, on dual-lipped seals, fill the space between the lips with grease.

Unless otherwise stated, oil seals must be fitted with their sealing lips toward the lubricant to be sealed.

Use a tubular drift or block of wood of the appropriate size to install the seal and, if the seal housing is shouldered, drive the seal down to the shoulder. If the seal housing is unshouldered, the seal should be fitted with its face flush with the housing top face (unless otherwise instructed).

Screw threads and fastenings

Seized nuts, bolts and screws are quite a common occurrence where corrosion has set in, and the use of penetrating oil or releasing fluid will often overcome this problem if the offending item is soaked for a while before attempting to release it. The use of an impact driver may also provide a means of releasing such stubborn fastening devices, when used in conjunction with the appropriate screwdriver bit or socket. If none of these methods works, it may be necessary to resort to the careful application of heat, or the use of a hacksaw or nut splitter device.

Studs are usually removed by locking two nuts together on the threaded part, and then using a spanner on the lower nut to unscrew the stud. Studs or bolts which have broken off below the surface of the component in which they are mounted can sometimes be removed using a stud extractor. Always ensure that a blind tapped hole is completely free from oil, grease, water or other fluid before installing the bolt or stud. Failure to do this could cause the housing to crack due to the hydraulic action of the bolt or stud as it is screwed in.

When tightening a castellated nut to accept a split pin, tighten the nut to the specified torque, where applicable, and then tighten further to the next split pin hole. Never slacken the nut to align the split pin hole, unless stated in the repair procedure.

When checking or retightening a nut or bolt to a specified torque setting, slacken the nut or bolt by a quarter of a turn, and then retighten to the specified setting. However, this should not be attempted where angular tightening has been used.

For some screw fastenings, notably cylinder head bolts or nuts, torque wrench settings are no longer specified for the latter stages of tightening, "angle-tightening" being called up instead. Typically, a fairly low torque wrench setting will be applied to the bolts/nuts in the correct sequence, followed by one or more stages of tightening through specified angles.

Locknuts, locktabs and washers

Any fastening which will rotate against a component or housing during tightening should always have a washer between it and the relevant component or housing.

Spring or split washers should always be renewed when they are used to lock a critical component such as a big-end bearing retaining bolt or nut. Locktabs which are folded over to retain a nut or bolt should always be renewed.

Self-locking nuts can be re-used in non-critical areas, providing resistance can be felt when the locking portion passes over the bolt or stud thread. However, it should be noted that self-locking stiffnuts tend to lose their effectiveness after long periods of use, and should then be renewed as a matter of course.

Split pins must always be replaced with new ones of the correct size for the hole.

When thread-locking compound is found on the threads of a fastener which is to be re-used, it should be cleaned off with a wire brush and solvent, and fresh compound applied on reassembly.

Special tools

Some repair procedures in this manual entail the use of special tools such as a press, two or three-legged pullers, spring compressors, etc. Wherever possible, suitable readily-available alternatives to the manufacturer's special tools are described, and are shown in use. In some instances, where no alternative is possible, it has been necessary to resort to the use of a manufacturer's tool, and this has been done for reasons of safety as well as the efficient completion of the repair operation. Unless you are highly-skilled and have a thorough understanding of the procedures described, never attempt to bypass the use of any special tool when the procedure described specifies its use. Not only is there a very great risk of personal injury, but expensive damage could be caused to the components involved.

Environmental considerations

When disposing of used engine oil, brake fluid, antifreeze, etc, give due consideration to any detrimental environmental effects. Do not, for instance, pour any of the above liquids down drains into the general sewage system, or onto the ground to soak away. Many local council refuse tips provide a facility for waste oil disposal, as do some garages. If none of these facilities are available, consult your local Environmental Health Department, or the National Rivers Authority, for further advice.

With the universal tightening-up of legislation regarding the emission of environmentally-harmful substances from motor vehicles, most vehicles have tamperproof devices fitted to the main adjustment points of the fuel system. These devices are primarily designed to prevent unqualified persons from adjusting the fuel/air mixture, with the chance of a consequent increase in toxic emissions. If such devices are found during servicing or overhaul, they should, wherever possible, be renewed or refitted in accordance with the manufacturer's requirements or current legislation.

OIL CARE
FOLLOW THE CODE
OIL BANK LINE
0800 66 33 66
www.oilbankline.org.uk

Note: It is antisocial and illegal to dump oil down the drain. To find the location of your local oil recycling bank, call this number free.

Engine   1

Engine fails to rotate when attempting to start
Engine rotates but will not start
Engine difficult to start when cold
Engine difficult to start when hot
Starter motor noisy or excessively rough in engagement
Engine starts but stops immediately
Engine idles erratically
Engine misfires at idle speed
Engine misfires throughout the driving speed range
Engine hesitates on acceleration
Engine stalls
Engine lacks power
Engine backfires
Oil pressure warning light illuminated with engine running
Engine runs-on after switching off
Engine noises

Cooling system   2

Overheating
Overcooling
External coolant leakage
Internal coolant leakage
Corrosion

Fuel and exhaust system   3

Excessive fuel consumption
Fuel leakage and/or fuel odour
Excessive noise or fumes from exhaust system

Clutch   4

Pedal travels to floor – no pressure or very little resistance
Clutch fails to disengage (unable to select gears)
Clutch slips (engine speed increases with no increase in vehicle speed)
Judder as clutch is engaged
Noise when depressing or releasing clutch pedal

Manual gearbox   5

Noisy in neutral with engine running
Noisy in one particular gear
Difficulty engaging gears
Jumps out of gear
Vibration
Lubricant leaks

Automatic transmission   6

Fluid leakage
Transmission fluid brown or has burned smell
General gear selection problems
Transmission will not downshift (kickdown) with accelerator fully depressed
Engine will not start in any gear, or starts in gears other than Park or Neutral
Transmission slips, shifts roughly, is noisy or has no drive in forward or reverse gears

Driveshafts   7

Clicking or knocking noise on turns (at slow speed on full lock)
Vibration when accelerating or decelerating

Braking system   8

Vehicle pulls to one side under braking
Noise (grinding or high-pitched squeal) when brakes applied
Excessive brake pedal travel
Brake pedal feels spongy when depressed
Excessive brake pedal effort required to stop vehicle
Judder felt through brake pedal or steering wheel when braking
Brakes binding
Rear wheels locking under normal braking

Suspension and steering systems   9

Vehicle pulls to one side
Wheel wobble and vibration
Excessive pitching and/or rolling around corners or during braking
Wandering or general instability
Excessively stiff steering
Excessive play in steering
Lack of power assistance
Tyre wear excessive

Electrical system   10

Battery will not hold a charge for more than a few days
Ignition warning light remains illuminated with engine running
Ignition warning light fails to come on
Lights inoperative
Instrument readings inaccurate or erratic
Horn inoperative or unsatisfactory in operation
Windscreen/tailgate wipers inoperative or unsatisfactory in operation
Windscreen/tailgate washers inoperative or unsatisfactory in operation
Electric windows inoperative or unsatisfactory in operation
Central locking system inoperative or unsatisfactory in operation

The vehicle owner who does his or her own maintenance according to the recommended service schedules should not have to use this section of the Manual very often. Modern component reliability is such that, provided those items subject to wear or deterioration are inspected or renewed at the specified intervals, sudden failure is comparatively rare. Faults do not usually just happen as a result of sudden failure, but develop over a period of time. Major mechanical failures in particular are usually preceded by characteristic symptoms over hundreds or even thousands of miles. Those components which do occasionally fail without warning are often small and easily carried in the vehicle.

With any fault finding, the first step is to decide where to begin investigations. Sometimes this is obvious, but on other occasions a little detective work will be necessary, The owner who makes half a dozen haphazard adjustments or replacements may be successful in curing a fault (or its symptoms), but will be none the wiser if the fault recurs and ultimately may have spent more time and money than was necessary. A calm and logical approach will be found to be more satisfactory in the long run. Always take into account any warning signs or abnormalities that may have been noticed in the period preceding the fault – power loss, high or low gauge readings, unusual smells, etc – and remember that failure of components such as fuses or spark plugs may only be pointers to some underlying fault.

The pages which follow provide an easy reference guide to the more common problems which may occur during the operation of the vehicle. These problems and their possible causes are grouped under headings denoting various components or systems, such as Engine, Cooling system, etc. The Chapter and/or Section which deals with the problem is also shown in brackets. Whatever the fault, certain basic principles apply. These are as follows:

Verify the fault. This is simply a matter of being sure that you know what the symptoms are before starting work. This is particularly important if you are investigating a fault for someone else who may not have described it very accurately.

Don't overlook the obvious. For example, if the vehicle won't start, is there petrol in the tank? (Don't take anyone else's word on this particular point, and don't trust the fuel gauge either!) If an electrical fault is indicated, look for loose or broken wires before digging out the test gear.

Cure the disease, not the symptom. Substituting a flat battery with a fully charged one will get you off the hard shoulder, but if the underlying cause is not attended to, the new battery will go the same way. Similarly, changing oil-fouled spark plugs for a new set will get you moving again, but remember that the reason for the fouling (if it wasn't simply an incorrect grade of plug) will have to be established and corrected.

Don't take anything for granted. Particularly, don't forget that a 'new' component may itself be defective (especially if it's been rattling around in the boot for months), and don't leave components out of a fault diagnosis sequence just because they are new or recently fitted. When you do finally diagnose a difficult fault, you'll probably realise that all the evidence was there from the start.

1 Engine

Engine fails to rotate when attempting to start

- ☐ Battery terminal connections loose or corroded (Chapter 12).
- ☐ Battery discharged or faulty (Chapter 12).
- ☐ Broken, loose or disconnected wiring in starting circuit (Chapter 12).
- ☐ Defective starter solenoid or switch (Chapter 12).
- ☐ Defective starter motor (Chapter 12).
- ☐ Starter pinion or flywheel ring gear teeth loose or broken (Chapters 2 and 12).
- ☐ Engine earth strap broken or disconnected (Chapter 12).
- ☐ Automatic transmission not in Park/Neutral position or neutral start switch faulty (Chapter 7).

Engine rotates but will not start

- ☐ Fuel tank empty.
- ☐ Battery discharged (engine rotates slowly) (Chapter 12).
- ☐ Battery terminal connections loose or corroded (Chapter 12).
- ☐ Ignition components damp or damaged (Chapters 1 and 5).
- ☐ Broken, loose or disconnected wiring in the ignition circuit (Chapters 1 and 5).
- ☐ Worn, faulty or incorrectly gapped spark plugs (Chapter 1).
- ☐ Choke mechanism sticking or faulty – carburettor models (Chapter 4).
- ☐ Major mechanical failure (eg camshaft drive) (Chapter 2).

Engine difficult to start when cold

- ☐ Battery discharged (Chapter 12).
- ☐ Battery terminal connections loose or corroded (Chapter 12).
- ☐ Worn, faulty or incorrectly gapped spark plugs (Chapter 1).
- ☐ Choke mechanism sticking or faulty – carburettor models (Chapter 4).
- ☐ Other ignition system fault (Chapters 1 and 5).
- ☐ Low cylinder compressions (Chapter 2).

Engine difficult to start when hot

- ☐ Air filter element dirty or clogged (Chapter 1).
- ☐ Choke mechanism sticking or faulty – carburettor models (Chapter 4).
- ☐ Carburettor float chamber flooding (Chapter 4).
- ☐ Low cylinder compressions (Chapter 2).

Starter motor noisy or excessively rough in engagement

- ☐ Starter pinion or flywheel ring gear teeth loose or broken (Chapters 2 and 12).
- ☐ Starter motor mounting bolts loose or missing (Chapter 12).
- ☐ Starter motor internal components worn or damaged (Chapter 12).

Engine starts but stops immediately

- ☐ Insufficient fuel reaching carburettor/injectors (Chapter 4).
- ☐ Loose or faulty electrical connections in the ignition circuit (Chapters 1 and 5).
- ☐ Vacuum leak at the carburettor/throttle housing or inlet manifold (Chapter 4).
- ☐ Blocked carburettor jet(s) or internal passages carburettor models (Chapter 4).
- ☐ Blocked injector – fuel-injected models (Chapter 4).

Engine idles erratically

- ☐ Incorrectly adjusted idle speed and/or mixture settings (Chapter 1).
- ☐ Air filter element clogged (Chapter 1).
- ☐ Vacuum leak at the carburettor/throttle housing, inlet manifold or associated hoses (Chapter 4).
- ☐ Worn, faulty or incorrectly gapped spark plugs (Chapter 1).
- ☐ Incorrectly adjusted valve clearances (Chapter 1).
- ☐ Uneven or low cylinder compressions (Chapter 2).
- ☐ Camshaft lobes worn (Chapter 2).
- ☐ Timing belt incorrectly tensioned (Chapter 2).

Engine hesitates on acceleration

- ☐ Worn, faulty or incorrectly gapped spark plugs (Chapter 1).
- ☐ Carburettor accelerator pump faulty (Chapter 4).
- ☐ Blocked carburettor jets or internal passages – carburettor models (Chapter 4).
- ☐ Blocked injector – fuel-injected models (Chapter 4).
- ☐ Vacuum leak at the carburettor/throttle housing, inlet manifold or associated hoses (Chapter 4).
- ☐ Carburettor worn or incorrectly adjusted (Chapters 1 and 4).

Engine misfires at idle speed

- [ ] Worn, faulty or incorrectly gapped spark plugs (Chapter 1).
- [ ] Faulty spark plug HT leads (Chapter 1).
- [ ] Incorrectly adjusted idle mixture settings (Chapter 1).
- [ ] Incorrect ignition timing (Chapter 1).
- [ ] Vacuum leak at the carburettor/throttle housing, inlet manifold or associated hoses (Chapter 4).
- [ ] Distributor cap cracked or tracking internally (Chapter 1).
- [ ] Incorrectly adjusted valve clearances (Chapter 1).
- [ ] Uneven or low cylinder compressions (Chapter 2).
- [ ] Disconnected, leaking or perished crankcase ventilation hoses (Chapters 1 and 4).

Engine misfires throughout the driving speed range

- [ ] Blocked carburettor jet(s) or internal passages – carburettor models (Chapter 4).
- [ ] Blocked injector – fuel-injected models (Chapter 4).
- [ ] Carburettor worn or incorrectly adjusted (Chapters 1 and 4).
- [ ] Fuel filter choked (Chapter 1).
- [ ] Fuel pump faulty or delivery pressure low (Chapter 4).
- [ ] Fuel tank vent blocked or fuel pipes restricted (Chapter 4).
- [ ] Vacuum leak at the carburettor/throttle housing, inlet manifold or associated hoses (Chapter 4).
- [ ] Worn, faulty or incorrectly gapped spark plugs (Chapter 1).
- [ ] Faulty spark plug HT leads (Chapter 1).
- [ ] Distributor cap cracked or tracking internally (Chapter 1).
- [ ] Faulty ignition coil (Chapter 5).
- [ ] Uneven or low cylinder compressions (Chapter 2).

Engine stalls

- [ ] Incorrectly adjusted idle speed and/or mixture settings (Chapter 1).
- [ ] Blocked carburettor jet(s) or internal passages – carburettor models (Chapter 4).
- [ ] Blocked injector – fuel-injected models (Chapter 4).
- [ ] Vacuum leak at the carburettor/throttle housing, inlet manifold or associated hoses (Chapter 4).
- [ ] Fuel filter choked (Chapter 1).
- [ ] Fuel pump faulty or delivery pressure low (Chapter 4).
- [ ] Fuel tank vent blocked or fuel pipes restricted (Chapter 4).

Engine lacks power

- [ ] Incorrect ignition timing (Chapter 1).
- [ ] Carburettor worn or incorrectly adjusted (Chapter 1).
- [ ] Timing belt incorrectly fitted or tensioned (Chapter 2).
- [ ] Fuel filter choked (Chapter 1).
- [ ] Fuel pump faulty or delivery pressure low (Chapter 4).
- [ ] Uneven or low cylinder compressions (Chapter 2).
- [ ] Worn, faulty or incorrectly gapped spark plugs (Chapter 1).
- [ ] Vacuum leak at the carburettor/throttle housing, inlet manifold or associated hoses (Chapter 4).
- [ ] Brakes binding (Chapters 1 and 9).
- [ ] Clutch slipping (Chapter 6).
- [ ] Automatic transmission fluid level incorrect (Chapter 1).

Engine backfires

- [ ] Ignition timing incorrect (Chapter 1).
- [ ] Timing belt incorrectly fitted or tensioned (Chapter 2).
- [ ] Carburettor worn or incorrectly adjusted (Chapter 1).
- [ ] Vacuum leak at the carburettor/throttle housing, inlet manifold or associated hoses (Chapter 4).

Oil pressure warning light illuminated with engine running

- [ ] Low oil level or incorrect grade (Chapter 1).
- [ ] Faulty oil pressure transmitter (sender) unit (Chapter 2).
- [ ] Worn engine bearings and/or oil pump (Chapter 2).
- [ ] High engine operating temperature (Chapter 3).
- [ ] Oil pressure relief valve defective (Chapter 2).
- [ ] Oil pick-up strainer clogged (Chapter 2).

Engine runs-on after switching off

- [ ] Idle speed excessively high (Chapter 1).
- [ ] Faulty fuel cut-off solenoid – carburettor models (Chapter 4).
- [ ] Excessive carbon build-up in engine (Chapter 2).
- [ ] High engine operating temperature (Chapter 3).

Engine noises

Pre-ignition (pinking) or knocking during acceleration or under load

- [ ] Ignition timing incorrect (Chapter 1).
- [ ] Incorrect grade of fuel (Chapter 4).
- [ ] Vacuum leak at the carburettor/throttle housing, inlet manifold or associated hoses (Chapter 4).
- [ ] Excessive carbon build-up in engine (Chapter 2).
- [ ] Worn or damaged distributor or other ignition system component (Chapter 5).
- [ ] Carburettor worn or incorrectly adjusted (Chapter 1).

Whistling or wheezing noises

- [ ] Leaking inlet manifold or carburettor/throttle housing gasket (Chapter 4).
- [ ] Leaking exhaust manifold gasket or pipe to manifold joint (Chapter 1).
- [ ] Leaking vacuum hose (Chapters 4, 5 and 9).
- [ ] Blowing cylinder head gasket (Chapter 2).

Tapping or rattling noises

- [ ] Incorrect valve clearances (Chapter 1).
- [ ] Worn valve gear or camshaft (Chapter 2).
- [ ] Ancillary component fault (water pump, alternator, etc) (Chapters 3 and 12).

Knocking or thumping noises

- [ ] Worn big-end bearings (regular heavy knocking, perhaps less under load) (Chapter 2).
- [ ] Worn main bearings (rumbling and knocking, perhaps worsening under load) (Chapter 2).
- [ ] Piston slap (most noticeable when cold) (Chapter 2).
- [ ] Ancillary component fault (alternator, water pump, etc) (Chapters 3 and 12).

2 Cooling system

Overheating

- [ ] Insufficient coolant in system (Chapter 3).
- [ ] Thermostat faulty (Chapter 3).
- [ ] Radiator core blocked or grille restricted (Chapter 3).
- [ ] Electric cooling fan or thermoswitch faulty (Chapter 3).
- [ ] Pressure cap faulty (Chapter 3).
- [ ] Water pump drivebelt worn, or incorrectly adjusted (Chapter 1).
- [ ] Ignition timing incorrect (Chapter 1).
- [ ] Inaccurate temperature gauge sender unit (Chapter 3).
- [ ] Air lock in cooling system (Chapter 1).

Overcooling

- [ ] Thermostat faulty (Chapter 3).
- [ ] Inaccurate temperature gauge sender unit (Chapter 3).

External coolant leakage

- [ ] Deteriorated or damaged hoses or hose clips (Chapter 1).
- [ ] Radiator core or heater matrix leaking (Chapter 3).
- [ ] Pressure cap faulty (Chapter 3).
- [ ] Water pump seal leaking (Chapter 3).
- [ ] Boiling due to overheating (Chapter 3).
- [ ] Core plug leaking (Chapter 2).

Internal coolant leakage

☐ Leaking cylinder head gasket (Chapter 2).
☐ Cracked cylinder head or cylinder bore (Chapter 2).

Corrosion

☐ Infrequent draining and flushing (Chapter 1).
☐ Incorrect antifreeze mixture or inappropriate type (Chapter 1).

3 Fuel and exhaust system

Excessive fuel consumption

☐ Air filter element dirty or clogged (Chapter 1).
☐ Carburettor worn or incorrectly adjusted (Chapter 4).
☐ Choke mechanism sticking – carburettor models (Chapter 4).
☐ Ignition timing incorrect (Chapter 1).
☐ Tyres underinflated (Chapter 1).

Fuel leakage and/or fuel odour

☐ Damaged or corroded fuel tank, pipes or connections (Chapter 1).
☐ Carburettor float chamber flooding (Chapter 4).

Excessive noise or fumes from exhaust system

☐ Leaking exhaust system or manifold joints (Chapter 1).
☐ Leaking, corroded or damaged silencers or pipe (Chapter 1).
☐ Broken mountings causing body or suspension contact (Chapter 1).

4 Clutch

Pedal travels to floor – no pressure or very little resistance

☐ Clutch reservoir fluid level low (Chapter 1).
☐ Air in the clutch hydraulic system (Chapter 6).
☐ Broken clutch release bearing or fork (Chapter 6).
☐ Broken diaphragm spring in clutch pressure plate (Chapter 6).

Clutch fails to disengage (unable to select gears)

☐ Air in the clutch hydraulic system (Chapter 6).
☐ Clutch disc sticking on gearbox input shaft splines (Chapter 6).
☐ Clutch disc sticking to flywheel or pressure plate (Chapter 6).
☐ Faulty pressure plate assembly (Chapter 6).
☐ Gearbox input shaft seized in crankshaft spigot bearing (Chapter 2).
☐ Clutch release mechanism worn or incorrectly assembled (Chapter 6).

Clutch slips (engine speed increases with no increase in vehicle speed)

☐ Clutch reservoir fluid level too high (Chapter 1).
☐ Clutch disc linings excessively worn (Chapter 6).
☐ Clutch disc linings contaminated with oil or grease (Chapter 6).
☐ Faulty pressure plate or weak diaphragm spring (Chapter 6).

Judder as clutch is engaged

☐ Clutch disc linings contaminated with oil or grease (Chapter 6).
☐ Clutch disc linings excessively worn (Chapter 6).
☐ Clutch master cylinder piston sticking (Chapter 6).
☐ Faulty or distorted pressure plate or diaphragm spring (Chapter 6).
☐ Worn or loose engine or gearbox mountings (Chapter 2).
☐ Clutch disc hub or gearbox input shaft splines worn (Chapter 6).

Noise when depressing or releasing clutch pedal

☐ Worn clutch release bearing (Chapter 6).
☐ Worn or dry clutch pedal bushes (Chapter 6).
☐ Faulty pressure plate assembly (Chapter 6).
☐ Pressure plate diaphragm spring broken (Chapter 6).
☐ Broken clutch disc cushioning springs (Chapter 6).

5 Manual gearbox

Noisy in neutral with engine running

☐ Input shaft bearings worn (noise apparent with clutch pedal released but not when depressed) (Chapter 7).*
☐ Clutch release bearing worn (noise apparent with clutch pedal depressed, possibly less when released) (Chapter 6).

Noisy in one particular gear

☐ Worn, damaged or chipped gear teeth (Chapter 7).*

Difficulty engaging gears

☐ Clutch fault (Chapter 6).
☐ Worn or damaged gear selector cables (Chapter 7).
☐ Worn synchroniser units (Chapter 7).*

Vibration

☐ Lack of oil (Chapter 1).
☐ Worn bearings (Chapter 7).*

Jumps out of gear

☐ Worn or damaged gear selector cables (Chapter 7).
☐ Worn synchroniser units (Chapter 7).*
☐ Worn selector forks (Chapter 7).*

Lubricant leaks

☐ Leaking differential output oil seal (Chapter 7).
☐ Leaking housing joint (Chapter 7).*
☐ Leaking input shaft oil seal (Chapter 7).*

* Although the corrective action necessary to remedy the symptoms described is beyond the scope of the home mechanic, the above information should be helpful in isolating the cause of the condition so that the owner can communicate clearly with a professional mechanic.

6 Automatic transmission

Note: *Due to the complexity of the automatic transmission, it is difficult for the home mechanic to properly diagnose and service this unit. For problems other than the following, the vehicle should be taken to a dealer service department or automatic transmission specialist.*

Fluid leakage

☐ Automatic transmission fluid is usually deep red in colour. Fluid leaks should not be confused with engine oil which can easily be blown onto the transmission by air flow.

☐ To determine the source of a leak, first remove all built-up dirt and grime from the transmission housing and surrounding areas using a degreasing agent or by steam cleaning. Drive the vehicle at low speed so air flow will not blow the leak far from its source. Raise and support the vehicle and determine where the leak is coming from. The following are common areas of leakage.

(a) Sump (Chapters 1 and 7).
(b) Dipstick tube (Chapters 1 and 7).
(c) Transmission to oil cooler fluid pipes/unions (Chapter 7).

Transmission fluid brown or has burned smell

☐ Transmission fluid level low or fluid in need of renewal (Chapter 1).

Transmission will not downshift (kickdown) with accelerator fully depressed

☐ Low transmission fluid level (Chapter 1).
☐ Incorrect selector mechanism adjustment (Chapter 7, Part B).
☐ Kickdown cable not correctly adjusted (Chapter 7, Part B).

General gear selection problems

☐ Chapter 7, Part B, deals with checking and adjusting the selector cable/linkage on automatic transmissions. The following are common problems which may be caused by a poorly adjusted linkage.

(a) Engine starting in gears other than Park or Neutral.
(b) Indicator on gear selector lever pointing to a gear other than the one actually being used.
(c) Vehicle moves when in Park or Neutral.
(d) Poor gear shift quality or erratic gear changes.

☐ Refer to Chapter 7, Part B for the selector cable/linkage adjustment procedure.

Engine will not start in any gear, or starts in gears other than Park or Neutral

☐ Incorrect neutral start switch adjustment (Chapter 7, Part B).
☐ Incorrect selector cable/mechanism adjustment (Chapter 7, Part B).

Transmission slips, shifts roughly, is noisy or has no drive in forward or reverse gears

☐ There are many probable causes for the above problems, but the home mechanic should be concerned with only one possibility – fluid level. Before taking the vehicle to a dealer or transmission specialist, check the fluid level and condition of the fluid as described in Chapter 1. Correct the fluid level as necessary or change the fluid and filter if needed. If the problem persists, professional help will be necessary.

7 Driveshafts

Clicking or knocking noise on turns (at slow speed on full lock)

☐ Lack of constant velocity joint lubricant (Chapter 8).
☐ Worn outer constant velocity joint (Chapter 8).

Vibration when accelerating or decelerating

☐ Worn inner constant velocity joint (Chapter 8).
☐ Bent or distorted driveshaft (Chapter 8).

8 Braking system

Note: *Before assuming that a brake problem exists, make sure that the tyres are in good condition and correctly inflated, the front wheel alignment is correct and the vehicle is not loaded with weight in an unequal manner.*

Vehicle pulls to one side under braking

☐ Worn, defective, damaged or contaminated front or rear brake pads/shoes on one side (Chapter 1).
☐ Seized or partially seized front or rear brake caliper/wheel cylinder piston (Chapter 9).
☐ A mixture of brake pad/shoe lining materials fitted between sides (Chapter 1).
☐ Brake caliper mounting bolts loose (Chapter 9).
☐ Rear brake backplate mounting bolts loose (where applicable) (Chapter 9).
☐ Worn or damaged steering or suspension components (Chapter 10).

Noise (grinding or high-pitched squeal) when brakes applied

☐ Brake pad or shoe friction lining material worn down to metal backing (Chapter 1).
☐ Excessive corrosion of brake disc or drum. (May be apparent after the vehicle has been standing for some time (Chapter 1).
☐ Foreign object (stone chipping, etc) trapped between brake disc and splash shield (Chapter 1).

Excessive brake pedal travel

☐ Inoperative rear brake self-adjust mechanism (Chapter 1).
☐ Faulty master cylinder (Chapter 9).
☐ Air in hydraulic system (Chapter 9).
☐ Faulty vacuum servo unit (Chapters 1 and 9).

Brake pedal feels spongy when depressed

- ☐ Air in hydraulic system (Chapter 9).
- ☐ Deteriorated flexible rubber brake hoses (Chapter 9).
- ☐ Master cylinder mounting nuts loose (Chapter 9).
- ☐ Faulty master cylinder (Chapter 9).

Excessive brake pedal effort required to stop vehicle

- ☐ Faulty vacuum servo unit (Chapters 1 and 9).
- ☐ Disconnected, damaged or insecure brake servo vacuum hose (Chapter 9).
- ☐ Primary or secondary hydraulic circuit failure (Chapter 9).
- ☐ Seized brake caliper or wheel cylinder piston(s) (Chapter 9).
- ☐ Brake pads or brake shoes incorrectly fitted (Chapter 1).
- ☐ Incorrect grade of brake pads or brake shoes fitted (Chapter 1).
- ☐ Brake pads or brake shoe linings contaminated (Chapter 1).

Judder felt through brake pedal or steering wheel when braking

- ☐ Excessive run-out or distortion of brake discs or rear drums (as applicable) (Chapter 9).
- ☐ Brake pad or brake shoe linings worn (Chapter 1).
- ☐ Brake caliper or rear brake backplate mounting bolts loose (Chapter 9).
- ☐ Wear in suspension or steering components or mountings (Chapter 10).

Brakes binding

- ☐ Seized brake caliper or wheel cylinder piston(s) (Chapter 9).
- ☐ Incorrectly adjusted handbrake mechanism or linkage (Chapter 1).
- ☐ Faulty master cylinder (Chapter 9).

Rear wheels locking under normal braking

- ☐ Rear brake shoe/pad linings contaminated (Chapter 1).
- ☐ Faulty brake pressure regulator (Chapter 9).

9 Suspension and steering systems

Note: *Before diagnosing suspension or steering faults, be sure that the trouble is not due to incorrect tyre pressures, mixtures of tyre types or binding brakes.*

Vehicle pulls to one side

- ☐ Defective tyre (Chapter 1).
- ☐ Excessive wear in suspension or steering components (Chapter 10).
- ☐ Incorrect front wheel alignment (Chapter 10).
- ☐ Accident damage to steering or suspension components (Chapter 10).

Wheel wobble and vibration

- ☐ Front roadwheels out of balance (vibration felt mainly through the steering wheel) (Chapter 1).
- ☐ Rear roadwheels out of balance (vibration felt throughout the vehicle) (Chapter 1).
- ☐ Roadwheels damaged or distorted (Chapter 1).
- ☐ Faulty or damaged tyre (Chapter 1).
- ☐ Worn steering or suspension joints, bushes or components (Chapter 10).
- ☐ Wheel bolts loose (Chapter 1).

Excessive pitching and/or rolling around corners or during braking

- ☐ Defective shock absorbers (Chapter 10).
- ☐ Broken or weak coil spring and/or suspension component (Chapter 10).
- ☐ Worn or damaged anti-roll bar or mountings (Chapter 10).

Wandering or general instability

- ☐ Incorrect front wheel alignment (Chapter 10).
- ☐ Worn steering or suspension joints, bushes or components (Chapter 10).
- ☐ Roadwheels out of balance (Chapter 1).
- ☐ Faulty or damaged tyre (Chapter 1).
- ☐ Wheel bolts loose (Chapter 1).
- ☐ Defective shock absorbers (Chapter 10).

Excessively stiff steering

- ☐ Lack of steering gear lubricant (Chapter 10).
- ☐ Seized track rod end balljoint or suspension balljoint (Chapter 10).
- ☐ Broken or incorrectly adjusted power steering pump drivebelt (Chapter 1).

- ☐ Incorrect front wheel alignment (Chapter 10).
- ☐ Steering rack or column bent or damaged (Chapter 10).

Excessive play in steering

- ☐ Worn steering column universal joint(s) or intermediate coupling (Chapter 10).
- ☐ Worn steering track rod end balljoints (Chapter 10).
- ☐ Worn rack and pinion steering gear (Chapter 10).
- ☐ Worn steering or suspension joints, bushes or components (Chapter 10).

Lack of power assistance

- ☐ Broken or incorrectly adjusted power steering pump drivebelt (Chapter 1).
- ☐ Incorrect power steering fluid level (Chapter 1).
- ☐ Restriction in power steering fluid hoses (Chapter 10).
- ☐ Faulty power steering pump (Chapter 10).
- ☐ Faulty rack and pinion steering gear (Chapter 10).

Tyre wear excessive

Tyres worn on inside or outside edges

- ☐ Tyres underinflated (wear on both edges) (Chapter 1).
- ☐ Incorrect camber or castor angles (wear on one edge only) (Chapter 10).
- ☐ Worn steering or suspension joints, bushes or components (Chapter 10).
- ☐ Excessively hard cornering.
- ☐ Accident damage.

Tyre treads exhibit feathered edges

- ☐ Incorrect toe setting (Chapter 10).

Tyres worn in centre of tread

- ☐ Tyres overinflated (Chapter 1).

Tyres worn on inside and outside edges

- ☐ Tyres underinflated (Chapter 1).

Tyres worn unevenly

- ☐ Tyres out of balance (Chapter 1).
- ☐ Excessive wheel or tyre run-out (Chapter 1).
- ☐ Worn shock absorbers (Chapter 10).
- ☐ Faulty tyre (Chapter 1).

10 Electrical system

Note: *For problems associated with the starting system, refer to the faults listed under 'Engine' earlier in this Section.*

Battery will not hold charge for more than a few days

- [ ] Battery defective internally (Chapter 12).
- [ ] Battery electrolyte level low (Chapter 1).
- [ ] Battery terminal connections loose or corroded (Chapter 12).
- [ ] Alternator drivebelt worn or incorrectly adjusted (Chapter 1).
- [ ] Alternator not charging at correct output (Chapter 12).
- [ ] Alternator or voltage regulator faulty (Chapter 12).
- [ ] Short-circuit causing continual battery drain (Chapter 12).

Ignition warning light remains illuminated

- [ ] Alternator drivebelt broken, worn, or incorrectly adjusted (Chapter 1).
- [ ] Alternator brushes worn, sticking, or dirty (Chapter 12).
- [ ] Alternator brush springs weak or broken (Chapter 12).
- [ ] Internal fault in alternator or voltage regulator (Chapter 12).
- [ ] Broken, disconnected, or loose wiring in charging circuit (Chapter 12).

Ignition warning light fails to come on

- [ ] Warning light bulb blown (Chapter 12).
- [ ] Broken, disconnected, or loose wiring in warning light circuit (Chapter 12).
- [ ] Alternator faulty (Chapter 12).

Lights inoperative

- [ ] Bulb blown (Chapter 12).
- [ ] Corrosion of bulb or bulbholder contacts (Chapter 12).
- [ ] Blown fuse (Chapter 12).
- [ ] Faulty relay (Chapter 12).
- [ ] Broken, loose, or disconnected wiring (Chapter 12).
- [ ] Faulty switch (Chapter 12).

Instrument readings inaccurate or erratic

Instrument readings increase with engine speed

- [ ] Faulty voltage regulator (Chapter 12).

Fuel or temperature gauge give no reading

- [ ] Faulty gauge sender unit (Chapters 3 or 4).
- [ ] Wiring open-circuit (Chapter 12).
- [ ] Faulty gauge (Chapter 12).

Fuel or temperature gauges give continuous maximum reading

- [ ] Faulty gauge sender unit (Chapters 3 or 4).
- [ ] Wiring short-circuit (Chapter 12).
- [ ] Faulty gauge (Chapter 12).

Horn inoperative or unsatisfactory in operation

Horn operates all the time

- [ ] Horn push either earthed or stuck down (Chapter 12).
- [ ] Horn cable to horn push earthed (Chapter 12).

Horn fails to operate

- [ ] Blown fuse (Chapter 12).
- [ ] Cable or cable connections loose, broken or disconnected (Chapter 12).
- [ ] Faulty horn (Chapter 12).

Horn emits Intermittent or unsatisfactory sound

- [ ] Cable connections loose (Chapter 12).
- [ ] Horn mountings loose (Chapter 12).
- [ ] Faulty horn (Chapter 12).

Wipers inoperative or unsatisfactory in operation

Wipers fail to operate or operate very slowly

- [ ] Wiper blades stuck to screen or linkage seized or binding (Chapter 12).
- [ ] Blown fuse (Chapter 12).
- [ ] Cable or cable connections loose, broken or disconnected (Chapter 12).
- [ ] Faulty relay (Chapter 12).
- [ ] Faulty wiper motor (Chapter 12).

Wipers sweep too large or too small an area of the glass

- [ ] Wiper arms incorrectly positioned on spindles (Chapter 1).
- [ ] Excessive wear of wiper linkage (Chapter 1).
- [ ] Wiper motor or linkage mountings loose or insecure (Chapter 12).

Wiper blades fail to clean the glass effectively

- [ ] Wiper blade rubbers worn or perished (Chapter 1).
- [ ] Wiper arm tension springs broken or arm pivots seized (Chapter 1).
- [ ] Insufficient washer additive to remove road film (Chapter 1).

Washers inoperative or unsatisfactory in operation

One or more washer jets inoperative

- [ ] Blocked washer jet (Chapter 1).
- [ ] Disconnected, kinked or restricted fluid hose (Chapter 1).
- [ ] Insufficient fluid in washer reservoir (Chapter 1).

Washer pump fails to operate

- [ ] Broken or disconnected wiring or connections (Chapter 12).
- [ ] Blown fuse (Chapter 12).
- [ ] Faulty washer switch (Chapter 12).
- [ ] Faulty washer pump (Chapter 12).

Washer pump runs before fluid is emitted from jets

- [ ] Faulty one-way valve in fluid supply hose (Chapter 12).

Electric windows unsatisfactory in operation

Window glass will only move in one direction

- [ ] Faulty switch (Chapter 12).

Window glass slow to move

- [ ] Incorrectly adjusted door glass guide channels (Chapter 12).
- [ ] Regulator seized or damaged, or in need of lubrication (Chapter 12).
- [ ] Door internal components or trim fouling regulator (Chapter 12).
- [ ] Faulty motor (Chapter 12).

Window glass fails to move

- [ ] Incorrectly adjusted door glass guide channels (Chapter 12).
- [ ] Blown fuse (Chapter 12).
- [ ] Faulty relay (Chapter 12).
- [ ] Broken or disconnected wiring or connections (Chapter 12).
- [ ] Faulty motor (Chapter 12).

Central locking system unsatisfactory in operation

Complete system failure

- [ ] Blown fuse (Chapter 12).
- [ ] Faulty relay (Chapter 12).
- [ ] Broken or disconnected wiring or connections (Chapter 12).

Latch locks but will not unlock, or *vice-versa*

- [ ] Faulty master switch (Chapter 12).
- [ ] Broken or disconnected latch operating rods or levers (Chapter 12).
- [ ] Faulty relay (Chapter 12).

One solenoid/motor fails to operate

- [ ] Broken or disconnected wiring or connections (Chapter 12).
- [ ] Faulty solenoid/motor (Chapter 12).
- [ ] Broken, binding or disconnected operating rods or levers (Chapter 12).
- [ ] Fault in door latch (Chapter 12).

Buying spare parts

Spare parts are available from many sources; for example, Toyota garages, other garages and accessory shops, and motor factors. Our advice regarding spare part sources is as follows.

Officially appointed Toyota garages – This is the best source for parts which are peculiar to your car, and are not generally available (eg complete cylinder heads, badges, interior trim, etc). It is also the only place at which you should buy parts if the vehicle is still under warranty. To be sure of obtaining the correct parts, it will be necessary to give the storeman your car's vehicle identification number, and if possible, take the old parts along for positive identification. Many parts are available under a factory exchange scheme – any parts returned should always be clean. It obviously makes good sense to go straight to the specialists on your car for this type of part, as they are best equipped to supply you.

Other garages and accessory shops – These are often very good places to buy materials and components needed for the maintenance of your car (eg oil filters, spark plugs, bulbs, drivebelts, oils and greases, touch-up paint, filler paste, etc). They also sell general accessories, usually have convenient opening hours, charge lower prices and can often be found not far from home.

Motor factors – Good factors will stock all the more important components which wear out comparatively quickly (eg exhaust systems, brake pads, seals and hydraulic parts, clutch components, bearing shells, pistons, valves, etc). Motor factors will often provide new or reconditioned components on a part exchange basis – this can save a considerable amount of money.

Vehicle identification numbers

Modifications are a continuing and unpublicised process in vehicle manufacture, quite apart from major model changes. Spare parts manuals and lists are compiled upon a numerical basis, the individual vehicle identification numbers being essential to correct identification of the component concerned.

When ordering spare parts, always give as much information as possible. Quote the car model, year of manufacture, body and engine numbers as appropriate.

The *vehicle identification plate* is located on bulkhead at the rear of the engine compartment.

The *manufacturer's identification plate* is also located on the bulkhead at the rear of the engine compartment, and gives the vehicle build code specifications as well as carrying a duplication of the vehicle identification number.

The *engine number* is located on the forward facing side of the engine block, at the flywheel end, for all engine types.

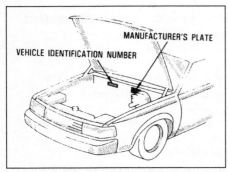

Location of the vehicle identification number (VIN), and the manufacturer's identification plate

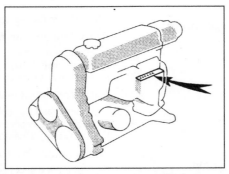

Engine number location for 2E engines

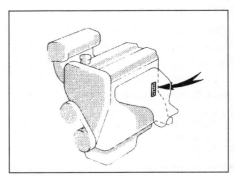

Engine number location for 4A-F and 4A-GE engines

A

ABS (Anti-lock brake system) A system, usually electronically controlled, that senses incipient wheel lockup during braking and relieves hydraulic pressure at wheels that are about to skid.

Air bag An inflatable bag hidden in the steering wheel (driver's side) or the dash or glovebox (passenger side). In a head-on collision, the bags inflate, preventing the driver and front passenger from being thrown forward into the steering wheel or windscreen.

Air cleaner A metal or plastic housing, containing a filter element, which removes dust and dirt from the air being drawn into the engine.

Air filter element The actual filter in an air cleaner system, usually manufactured from pleated paper and requiring renewal at regular intervals.

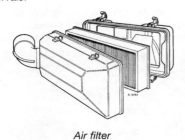

Air filter

Allen key A hexagonal wrench which fits into a recessed hexagonal hole.

Alligator clip A long-nosed spring-loaded metal clip with meshing teeth. Used to make temporary electrical connections.

Alternator A component in the electrical system which converts mechanical energy from a drivebelt into electrical energy to charge the battery and to operate the starting system, ignition system and electrical accessories.

Ampere (amp) A unit of measurement for the flow of electric current. One amp is the amount of current produced by one volt acting through a resistance of one ohm.

Anaerobic sealer A substance used to prevent bolts and screws from loosening. Anaerobic means that it does not require oxygen for activation. The Loctite brand is widely used.

Antifreeze A substance (usually ethylene glycol) mixed with water, and added to a vehicle's cooling system, to prevent freezing of the coolant in winter. Antifreeze also contains chemicals to inhibit corrosion and the formation of rust and other deposits that would tend to clog the radiator and coolant passages and reduce cooling efficiency.

Anti-seize compound A coating that reduces the risk of seizing on fasteners that are subjected to high temperatures, such as exhaust manifold bolts and nuts.

Asbestos A natural fibrous mineral with great heat resistance, commonly used in the composition of brake friction materials.

Asbestos is a health hazard and the dust created by brake systems should never be inhaled or ingested.

Axle A shaft on which a wheel revolves, or which revolves with a wheel. Also, a solid beam that connects the two wheels at one end of the vehicle. An axle which also transmits power to the wheels is known as a live axle.

Axleshaft A single rotating shaft, on either side of the differential, which delivers power from the final drive assembly to the drive wheels. Also called a driveshaft or a halfshaft.

B

Ball bearing An anti-friction bearing consisting of a hardened inner and outer race with hardened steel balls between two races.

Bearing The curved surface on a shaft or in a bore, or the part assembled into either, that permits relative motion between them with minimum wear and friction.

Bearing

Big-end bearing The bearing in the end of the connecting rod that's attached to the crankshaft.

Bleed nipple A valve on a brake wheel cylinder, caliper or other hydraulic component that is opened to purge the hydraulic system of air. Also called a bleed screw.

Brake bleeding Procedure for removing air from lines of a hydraulic brake system.

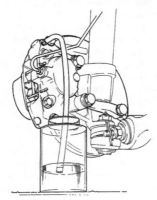

Brake bleeding

Brake disc The component of a disc brake that rotates with the wheels.

Brake drum The component of a drum brake that rotates with the wheels.

Brake linings The friction material which contacts the brake disc or drum to retard the vehicle's speed. The linings are bonded or riveted to the brake pads or shoes.

Brake pads The replaceable friction pads that pinch the brake disc when the brakes are applied. Brake pads consist of a friction material bonded or riveted to a rigid backing plate.

Brake shoe The crescent-shaped carrier to which the brake linings are mounted and which forces the lining against the rotating drum during braking.

Braking systems For more information on braking systems, consult the *Haynes Automotive Brake Manual*.

Breaker bar A long socket wrench handle providing greater leverage.

Bulkhead The insulated partition between the engine and the passenger compartment.

C

Caliper The non-rotating part of a disc-brake assembly that straddles the disc and carries the brake pads. The caliper also contains the hydraulic components that cause the pads to pinch the disc when the brakes are applied. A caliper is also a measuring tool that can be set to measure inside or outside dimensions of an object.

Camshaft A rotating shaft on which a series of cam lobes operate the valve mechanisms. The camshaft may be driven by gears, by sprockets and chain or by sprockets and a belt.

Canister A container in an evaporative emission control system; contains activated charcoal granules to trap vapours from the fuel system.

Canister

Carburettor A device which mixes fuel with air in the proper proportions to provide a desired power output from a spark ignition internal combustion engine.

Castellated Resembling the parapets along the top of a castle wall. For example, a castellated balljoint stud nut.

Castor In wheel alignment, the backward or forward tilt of the steering axis. Castor is positive when the steering axis is inclined rearward at the top.

Catalytic converter A silencer-like device in the exhaust system which converts certain pollutants in the exhaust gases into less harmful substances.

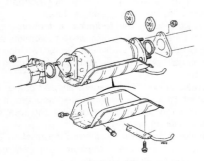

Catalytic converter

Circlip A ring-shaped clip used to prevent endwise movement of cylindrical parts and shafts. An internal circlip is installed in a groove in a housing; an external circlip fits into a groove on the outside of a cylindrical piece such as a shaft.

Clearance The amount of space between two parts. For example, between a piston and a cylinder, between a bearing and a journal, etc.

Coil spring A spiral of elastic steel found in various sizes throughout a vehicle, for example as a springing medium in the suspension and in the valve train.

Compression Reduction in volume, and increase in pressure and temperature, of a gas, caused by squeezing it into a smaller space.

Compression ratio The relationship between cylinder volume when the piston is at top dead centre and cylinder volume when the piston is at bottom dead centre.

Constant velocity (CV) joint A type of universal joint that cancels out vibrations caused by driving power being transmitted through an angle.

Core plug A disc or cup-shaped metal device inserted in a hole in a casting through which core was removed when the casting was formed. Also known as a freeze plug or expansion plug.

Crankcase The lower part of the engine block in which the crankshaft rotates.

Crankshaft The main rotating member, or shaft, running the length of the crankcase, with offset "throws" to which the connecting rods are attached.

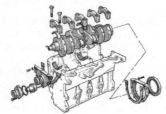

Crankshaft assembly

Crocodile clip See Alligator clip

D

Diagnostic code Code numbers obtained by accessing the diagnostic mode of an engine management computer. This code can be used to determine the area in the system where a malfunction may be located.

Disc brake A brake design incorporating a rotating disc onto which brake pads are squeezed. The resulting friction converts the energy of a moving vehicle into heat.

Double-overhead cam (DOHC) An engine that uses two overhead camshafts, usually one for the intake valves and one for the exhaust valves.

Drivebelt(s) The belt(s) used to drive accessories such as the alternator, water pump, power steering pump, air conditioning compressor, etc. off the crankshaft pulley.

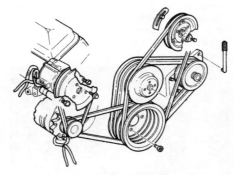

Accessory drivebelts

Driveshaft Any shaft used to transmit motion. Commonly used when referring to the axleshafts on a front wheel drive vehicle.

Drum brake A type of brake using a drum-shaped metal cylinder attached to the inner surface of the wheel. When the brake pedal is pressed, curved brake shoes with friction linings press against the inside of the drum to slow or stop the vehicle.

E

EGR valve A valve used to introduce exhaust gases into the intake air stream.

Electronic control unit (ECU) A computer which controls (for instance) ignition and fuel injection systems, or an anti-lock braking system. For more information refer to the *Haynes Automotive Electrical and Electronic Systems Manual*.

Electronic Fuel Injection (EFI) A computer controlled fuel system that distributes fuel through an injector located in each intake port of the engine.

Emergency brake A braking system, independent of the main hydraulic system, that can be used to slow or stop the vehicle if the primary brakes fail, or to hold the vehicle stationary even though the brake pedal isn't depressed. It usually consists of a hand lever that actuates either front or rear brakes mechanically through a series of cables and linkages. Also known as a handbrake or parking brake.

Endfloat The amount of lengthwise movement between two parts. As applied to a crankshaft, the distance that the crankshaft can move forward and back in the cylinder block.

Engine management system (EMS) A computer controlled system which manages the fuel injection and the ignition systems in an integrated fashion.

Exhaust manifold A part with several passages through which exhaust gases leave the engine combustion chambers and enter the exhaust pipe.

F

Fan clutch A viscous (fluid) drive coupling device which permits variable engine fan speeds in relation to engine speeds.

Feeler blade A thin strip or blade of hardened steel, ground to an exact thickness, used to check or measure clearances between parts.

Feeler blade

Firing order The order in which the engine cylinders fire, or deliver their power strokes, beginning with the number one cylinder.

Flywheel A heavy spinning wheel in which energy is absorbed and stored by means of momentum. On cars, the flywheel is attached to the crankshaft to smooth out firing impulses.

Free play The amount of travel before any action takes place. The "looseness" in a linkage, or an assembly of parts, between the initial application of force and actual movement. For example, the distance the brake pedal moves before the pistons in the master cylinder are actuated.

Fuse An electrical device which protects a circuit against accidental overload. The typical fuse contains a soft piece of metal which is calibrated to melt at a predetermined current flow (expressed as amps) and break the circuit.

Fusible link A circuit protection device consisting of a conductor surrounded by heat-resistant insulation. The conductor is smaller than the wire it protects, so it acts as the weakest link in the circuit. Unlike a blown fuse, a failed fusible link must frequently be cut from the wire for replacement.

G

Gap The distance the spark must travel in jumping from the centre electrode to the side electrode in a spark plug. Also refers to the spacing between the points in a contact breaker assembly in a conventional points-type ignition, or to the distance between the reluctor or rotor and the pickup coil in an electronic ignition.

Adjusting spark plug gap

Gasket Any thin, soft material - usually cork, cardboard, asbestos or soft metal - installed between two metal surfaces to ensure a good seal. For instance, the cylinder head gasket seals the joint between the block and the cylinder head.

Gasket

Gauge An instrument panel display used to monitor engine conditions. A gauge with a movable pointer on a dial or a fixed scale is an analogue gauge. A gauge with a numerical readout is called a digital gauge.

H

Halfshaft A rotating shaft that transmits power from the final drive unit to a drive wheel, usually when referring to a live rear axle.

Harmonic balancer A device designed to reduce torsion or twisting vibration in the crankshaft. May be incorporated in the crankshaft pulley. Also known as a vibration damper.

Hone An abrasive tool for correcting small irregularities or differences in diameter in an engine cylinder, brake cylinder, etc.

Hydraulic tappet A tappet that utilises hydraulic pressure from the engine's lubrication system to maintain zero clearance (constant contact with both camshaft and valve stem). Automatically adjusts to variation in valve stem length. Hydraulic tappets also reduce valve noise.

I

Ignition timing The moment at which the spark plug fires, usually expressed in the number of crankshaft degrees before the piston reaches the top of its stroke.

Inlet manifold A tube or housing with passages through which flows the air-fuel mixture (carburettor vehicles and vehicles with throttle body injection) or air only (port fuel-injected vehicles) to the port openings in the cylinder head.

J

Jump start Starting the engine of a vehicle with a discharged or weak battery by attaching jump leads from the weak battery to a charged or helper battery.

L

Load Sensing Proportioning Valve (LSPV) A brake hydraulic system control valve that works like a proportioning valve, but also takes into consideration the amount of weight carried by the rear axle.

Locknut A nut used to lock an adjustment nut, or other threaded component, in place. For example, a locknut is employed to keep the adjusting nut on the rocker arm in position.

Lockwasher A form of washer designed to prevent an attaching nut from working loose.

M

MacPherson strut A type of front suspension system devised by Earle MacPherson at Ford of England. In its original form, a simple lateral link with the anti-roll bar creates the lower control arm. A long strut - an integral coil spring and shock absorber - is mounted between the body and the steering knuckle. Many modern so-called MacPherson strut systems use a conventional lower A-arm and don't rely on the anti-roll bar for location.

Multimeter An electrical test instrument with the capability to measure voltage, current and resistance.

N

NOx Oxides of Nitrogen. A common toxic pollutant emitted by petrol and diesel engines at higher temperatures.

O

Ohm The unit of electrical resistance. One volt applied to a resistance of one ohm will produce a current of one amp.

Ohmmeter An instrument for measuring electrical resistance.

O-ring A type of sealing ring made of a special rubber-like material; in use, the O-ring is compressed into a groove to provide the sealing action.

Overhead cam (ohc) engine An engine with the camshaft(s) located on top of the cylinder head(s).

Overhead valve (ohv) engine An engine with the valves located in the cylinder head, but with the camshaft located in the engine block.

Oxygen sensor A device installed in the engine exhaust manifold, which senses the oxygen content in the exhaust and converts this information into an electric current. Also called a Lambda sensor.

P

Phillips screw A type of screw head having a cross instead of a slot for a corresponding type of screwdriver.

Plastigage A thin strip of plastic thread, available in different sizes, used for measuring clearances. For example, a strip of Plastigage is laid across a bearing journal. The parts are assembled and dismantled; the width of the crushed strip indicates the clearance between journal and bearing.

Plastigage

Propeller shaft The long hollow tube with universal joints at both ends that carries power from the transmission to the differential on front-engined rear wheel drive vehicles.

Proportioning valve A hydraulic control valve which limits the amount of pressure to the rear brakes during panic stops to prevent wheel lock-up.

R

Rack-and-pinion steering A steering system with a pinion gear on the end of the steering shaft that mates with a rack (think of a geared wheel opened up and laid flat). When the steering wheel is turned, the pinion turns, moving the rack to the left or right. This movement is transmitted through the track rods to the steering arms at the wheels.

Radiator A liquid-to-air heat transfer device designed to reduce the temperature of the coolant in an internal combustion engine cooling system.

Refrigerant Any substance used as a heat transfer agent in an air-conditioning system. R-12 has been the principle refrigerant for many years; recently, however, manufacturers have begun using R-134a, a non-CFC substance that is considered less harmful to the ozone in the upper atmosphere.

Rocker arm A lever arm that rocks on a shaft or pivots on a stud. In an overhead valve engine, the rocker arm converts the upward movement of the pushrod into a downward movement to open a valve.

Rotor In a distributor, the rotating device inside the cap that connects the centre electrode and the outer terminals as it turns, distributing the high voltage from the coil secondary winding to the proper spark plug. Also, that part of an alternator which rotates inside the stator. Also, the rotating assembly of a turbocharger, including the compressor wheel, shaft and turbine wheel.

Runout The amount of wobble (in-and-out movement) of a gear or wheel as it's rotated. The amount a shaft rotates "out-of-true." The out-of-round condition of a rotating part.

S

Sealant A liquid or paste used to prevent leakage at a joint. Sometimes used in conjunction with a gasket.

Sealed beam lamp An older headlight design which integrates the reflector, lens and filaments into a hermetically-sealed one-piece unit. When a filament burns out or the lens cracks, the entire unit is simply replaced.

Serpentine drivebelt A single, long, wide accessory drivebelt that's used on some newer vehicles to drive all the accessories, instead of a series of smaller, shorter belts. Serpentine drivebelts are usually tensioned by an automatic tensioner.

Serpentine drivebelt

Shim Thin spacer, commonly used to adjust the clearance or relative positions between two parts. For example, shims inserted into or under bucket tappets control valve clearances. Clearance is adjusted by changing the thickness of the shim.

Slide hammer A special puller that screws into or hooks onto a component such as a shaft or bearing; a heavy sliding handle on the shaft bottoms against the end of the shaft to knock the component free.

Sprocket A tooth or projection on the periphery of a wheel, shaped to engage with a chain or drivebelt. Commonly used to refer to the sprocket wheel itself.

Starter inhibitor switch On vehicles with an automatic transmission, a switch that prevents starting if the vehicle is not in Neutral or Park.

Strut See MacPherson strut.

T

Tappet A cylindrical component which transmits motion from the cam to the valve stem, either directly or via a pushrod and rocker arm. Also called a cam follower.

Thermostat A heat-controlled valve that regulates the flow of coolant between the cylinder block and the radiator, so maintaining optimum engine operating temperature. A thermostat is also used in some air cleaners in which the temperature is regulated.

Thrust bearing The bearing in the clutch assembly that is moved in to the release levers by clutch pedal action to disengage the clutch. Also referred to as a release bearing.

Timing belt A toothed belt which drives the camshaft. Serious engine damage may result if it breaks in service.

Timing chain A chain which drives the camshaft.

Toe-in The amount the front wheels are closer together at the front than at the rear. On rear wheel drive vehicles, a slight amount of toe-in is usually specified to keep the front wheels running parallel on the road by offsetting other forces that tend to spread the wheels apart.

Toe-out The amount the front wheels are closer together at the rear than at the front. On front wheel drive vehicles, a slight amount of toe-out is usually specified.

Tools For full information on choosing and using tools, refer to the *Haynes Automotive Tools Manual*.

Tracer A stripe of a second colour applied to a wire insulator to distinguish that wire from another one with the same colour insulator.

Tune-up A process of accurate and careful adjustments and parts replacement to obtain the best possible engine performance.

Turbocharger A centrifugal device, driven by exhaust gases, that pressurises the intake air. Normally used to increase the power output from a given engine displacement, but can also be used primarily to reduce exhaust emissions (as on VW's "Umwelt" Diesel engine).

U

Universal joint or U-joint A double-pivoted connection for transmitting power from a driving to a driven shaft through an angle. A U-joint consists of two Y-shaped yokes and a cross-shaped member called the spider.

V

Valve A device through which the flow of liquid, gas, vacuum, or loose material in bulk may be started, stopped, or regulated by a movable part that opens, shuts, or partially obstructs one or more ports or passageways. A valve is also the movable part of such a device.

Valve clearance The clearance between the valve tip (the end of the valve stem) and the rocker arm or tappet. The valve clearance is measured when the valve is closed.

Vernier caliper A precision measuring instrument that measures inside and outside dimensions. Not quite as accurate as a micrometer, but more convenient.

Viscosity The thickness of a liquid or its resistance to flow.

Volt A unit for expressing electrical "pressure" in a circuit. One volt that will produce a current of one ampere through a resistance of one ohm.

W

Welding Various processes used to join metal items by heating the areas to be joined to a molten state and fusing them together. For more information refer to the *Haynes Automotive Welding Manual*.

Wiring diagram A drawing portraying the components and wires in a vehicle's electrical system, using standardised symbols. For more information refer to the *Haynes Automotive Electrical and Electronic Systems Manual*.

Note: *References throughout this index relate to Chapter•page number*

Preserving Our Motoring Heritage

< The Model J Duesenberg Derham Tourster. Only eight of these magnificent cars were ever built – this is the only example to be found outside the United States of America

Almost every car you've ever loved, loathed or desired is gathered under one roof at the Haynes Motor Museum. Over 300 immaculately presented cars and motorbikes represent every aspect of our motoring heritage, from elegant reminders of bygone days, such as the superb Model J Duesenberg to curiosities like the bug-eyed BMW Isetta. There are also many old friends and flames. Perhaps you remember the 1959 Ford Popular that you did your courting in? The magnificent 'Red Collection' is a spectacle of classic sports cars including AC, Alfa Romeo, Austin Healey, Ferrari, Lamborghini, Maserati, MG, Riley, Porsche and Triumph.

A Perfect Day Out

Each and every vehicle at the Haynes Motor Museum has played its part in the history and culture of Motoring. Today, they make a wonderful spectacle and a great day out for all the family. Bring the kids, bring Mum and Dad, but above all bring your camera to capture those golden memories for ever. You will also find an impressive array of motoring memorabilia, a comfortable 70 seat video cinema and one of the most extensive transport book shops in Britain. The Pit Stop Cafe serves everything from a cup of tea to wholesome, home-made meals or, if you prefer, you can enjoy the large picnic area nestled in the beautiful rural surroundings of Somerset.

John Haynes O.B.E., Founder and Chairman of the museum at the wheel of a Haynes Light 12.

< Graham Hill's Lola Cosworth Formula 1 car next to a 1934 Riley Sports.

The Museum is situated on the A359 Yeovil to Frome road at Sparkford, just off the A303 in Somerset. It is about 40 miles south of Bristol, and 25 minutes drive from the M5 intersection at Taunton.
Open 9.30am - 5.30pm (10.00am - 4.00pm Winter) 7 days a week, *except Christmas Day, Boxing Day and New Years Day*
Special rates available for schools, coach parties and outings Charitable Trust No. 292048